G000057210

ENGLISH PLACE-NAME SOCIETY. VOLUME LIX/LX
FOR 1981–2 & 1982–3

GENERAL EDITOR
K. CAMERON

THE PLACE-NAMES OF DORSET

PART III

ENGLISH PLACE-NAME SOCIETY

The English Place-Name Society was founded in 1923 to carry out the survey of English place-names and to issue annual volumes to members who subscribe to the work of the Society. The Society has issued the following volumes:

Communications concerning the Society and membership should be addressed to: THE HON. DIRECTOR, English Place-Name Society, School of English Studies, The University, Nottingham NG7 2RD.

ENGLISH PLACE-NAME SOCIETY. VOLUME LIX/LX

THE PLACE-NAMES OF DORSET

By

A. D. MILLS

PART III

THE HUNDREDS OF REDLANE,
SIXPENNY HANDLEY, STURMINSTER NEWTON,
WHITEWAY, BUCKLAND NEWTON,
BROWNSALL, SHERBORNE

ENGLISH PLACE-NAME SOCIETY

1989

Published by the English Place-Name Society

© English Place-Name Society 1989

ISBN: 0 904889 13 0

Typeset at Oxford University Computing Service
by TeipSet, 24 Tan-y-Cae, Aberystwyth

Printed in Great Britain at the
University Press, Cambridge

The collection from unpublished documents of material for all the
Dorset volumes has been greatly assisted by generous grants
received from the British Academy.

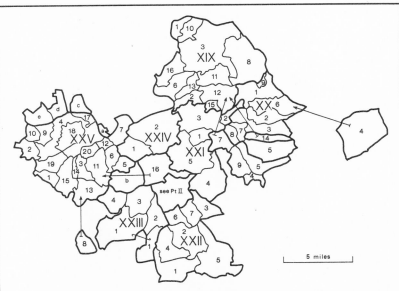

North Dorset: Hundreds and Parishes

XIX Redlane
1 Bourton
2 Fifehead Magdalen
3 Gillingham
4 Hanford
5 Iwerne Courtney
6 Kington Magna
7 Manston
8 Motcombe
9 Child Okeford
10 Silton
11 East Stour
12 Stour Provost
13 West Stour
14 Sutton Waldron
15 Todber
16 Buckhorn Weston

XX Sixpenny Handley
1 Cann
2 Compton Abbas
3 Fontmell Magna
4 Sixpenny Handley
5 Iwerne Minster
6 Melbury Abbas
7 East Orchard
8 West Orchard
9 Shaftesbury

XXI Sturminster Newton
1 Hinton St Mary
2 Margaret Marsh
3 Marnhull
4 Okeford Fitzpaine
5 Sturminster Newton

XXII Whiteway
1 Cheselbourne
2 Hilton
3 Ibberton
4 Melcombe Horsey
5 Milton Abbas
6 Stoke Wake
7 Woolland

XXIII Buckland Newton
1 Buckland Newton
2 Mappowder
3 Pulham
4 Wootton Glanville

XXIV Brownsall
1 Stourton Caundle
2 Stalbridge

XXV Sherborne
1 Beer Hackett
2 Bradford Abbas
3 Long Burton
4 Castleton
5 Bishop's Caundle
6 Caundle Marsh
7 Purse Caundle
8 Up Cerne
9 Nether Compton
10 Over Compton
11 Folke
12 Haydon
13 Holnest
14 Leweston
15 Lillington
16 Lydlinch
17 Oborne
18 Sherborne
19 Thornford
20 North Wootton

Formerly in Somerset
a Goathill
b Holwell
c Poyntington
d Sandford Orcas
e Trent

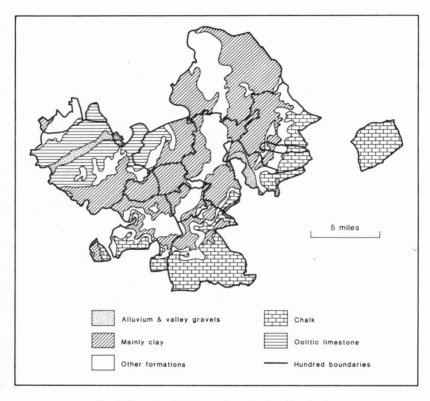

Alluvium & valley gravels

Chalk

Mainly clay

Oolitic limestone

Other formations

Hundred boundaries

5 miles

North Dorset : Geology, also showing Hundreds

CONTENTS

XIX. REDLANE HUNDRED
and GILLINGHAM LIBERTY

Redlane hundred consists of the pars. of Fifehead M., Kington M., Silton, E and W Stour, Todber and B. Weston (all formerly part of the GeldR hundred of *Gelingeham*), and of Hanford, Iwerne C., Manston, Ch. Okeford and Sutton W. (all formerly making up the GeldR hundred of *Ferendone*), *v.* Eyton 123f, Anderson 137–40, VCHDo **3** 140–1, 145–6. Stour P., now a separate liberty, was formerly also in the GeldR hundred of *Gelingeham*, but was included in Redlane hundred in 1327 *SR*, 1332 *SR*. Thorton in Marnhull par., in *Gelingeham* hundred in GeldR, is a tithing in Redlane hundred in 1327 *SR*, 1664 HTax, 1795 Boswell. Gillingham liberty consists of only part of the original GeldR hundred of *Gelingeham*, namely the pars. of Bourton, Motcombe and Gillingham itself (as in 1664 HTax, 1795 Boswell).

REDLANE HUNDRED

(*Hund' de*) *La Redelane* 1252, 1270 (1371) Pat, 1280 *Ass*, 1285 FA, 1288 *Ass* (*Gillingham et-*), 1446 Fine, *La Rede Lane* 1270 Pat, *Redelane et Gilyngham* 1280, *Gillingham et Redelane, la Redelone* 1288 *Ass, Redelane* 1303 FA, Pat *et freq* to 1448 ib, *Redlane* 1325 Inq aqd, 1542 LP, *Rede lane* 1539 ib, *Red Lane* 1664 HTax.

Ridelawe (for *-lane*) 1252 Fees, *la Ridelan* 1265 Misc, *Rydelan(e)* 1303 FA, 1326 Orig *et freq* to 1444 *MinAcct, Ridelane* 1325 Pat *et freq* to 1428 FA (*-et Gillyngham*), *la Rydelane* 1332 SR

Redendale (sic) 1270 Pat

La Radelawe (for *-lane*) 1273 Cl

Reedlane 1451 FF

Named from Red Lane ('the red lane', *v.* **rēad, lane**) in Todber par. *infra*. This place would be roughly central when the new hundred was formed in the 13th cent. by the amalgamation of *Ferendone* hundred with part of *Gelingeham* hundred (i.e. the 'out-hundred'). For further speculation as to why this name was chosen for the new hundred, *v.* N.H. Field, DoNHAS *Newsletter* **18** (December 1981), 6–9. In

1664 HTax, *Redlane* was also the name of a tithing in Sturminster Newton hundred.

FERENDONE HUNDRED (lost), *Ferendone hundret* c.1086 GeldR, *Ferdon'* 1178 P, *Ferndone* 1178 ChancR, *Ferendon'* 1212, 1219 Fees, named from Farrington in Iwerne C. par. *infra*.

GILLINGHAM HUNDRED and LIBERTY, *Gelingeham hundret* c.1086 GeldR, *hundr' de Gellingeham* 1130, *Gillingeham-hundredum* 1178, *intrinseco hundredo de Gillingeham . . . de forinseco ejusdem hundredi* 1188 P, *Hundredum de Gillingeham* 1212 Fees, 1262 Pat, 1265 Misc, 1303 FA, (*Hund' de*) *Gillingham* 1244 *Ass*, 1252 Ch *et freq* to 1300 *GillCt, Hund' de Geling-, Gylingham* 1244 Ass, *Gyllyngham* 1280 QW, *Hund' de Redelane et Gilyngham* 1280 *Ass*, *hondredum de Gillingeham et La Redelane* 1285 FA, *Hund' de Gillingham et* (*de la*) *Redelane* 1288 *Ass*, (*Hund' de*) *Guillyngham* 1303 FA, *Gillyngham* 1397 WRO, *Hund' de Ridelane et Gillyngham* 1428 FA, *the Quenez . . . libertie and free warren adioyning to hyr graces Forest of Gyllyngham* 1535 *Ct*, *Liberty of Gillingham* 1592 VCHDo (**2** 146), 1664 HTax. Named from Gillingham *infra* which was the *caput* of the hundred and to which manor it was appurtenant (Anderson 136–7). The original meeting-place of the GeldR hundred may have been Motcombe par. *q.v. infra*.

STOUR PROVOST LIBERTY, *liberty of Stowre Preaux* 1592 VCHDo (**2** 146), *Liberty of Stowre Provost* 1664 HTax, *v.* Stour Provost par. *infra*.

Bourton

Bourton is in Gillingham liberty, *v.* note under Redlane hundred *supra*.

BOURTON (ST 768303) ['bɔːtən], *Bureton(')* 1212 Fees, 1244 *Ass*, 1310 Ipm, *Burton(')* 1244 *Ass*, 1258 *For*, 1268, 1280 *Ass*, 1310 Ipm, 1332 SR (p), *Burthon* 1258 *For*, *Borton(')* 1268 *Ass*, 1275 RH (p), 1280, 1288 *Ass*, 1317 *GillCt*, *Boriton(e)* 1285 FA (p), 1292 *GillCt*, *Boryton'* 1288 *Ass*, *Buryton'* 1288 *ib* (p), *Bourton* 1774 Hutch[1], 'fortified farmstead' or 'farmstead near a fortified place', *v.* **burh-tūn**, cf. East & West Burton 1 176.

CHAFFEYMOOR FM, GRANGE, HILL & HO (ST 762302), John *atte Chauye* 1327 *SR*, *Ester Chavy* 1438 *GillCt, close called Chavie, peece of Morish grounde in Chavye Common* 1609 *LRMB, Lt & Long Chaffey* 1839 *TA*, perhaps from **ceaf** 'chaff' (an extended sense 'rubbish, fallen twigs' is suggested for Cheveley C 125), and **īeg** 'land partly surrounded by water, dry ground in a marsh, well-watered land'; the name may have originally referred to the land between two streams which rise near here, *v.* **atte** 'at the', **ēasterra** 'more easterly'.

SANDWAY (ST 774306), Thomas *Attesandwey*, Richard *Atte Sandweye* 1292 *GillCt*, Robert- 1327 *SR*, John- 1332 SR, William *atte Sandwey(e)* 1343 *For, Sandway, Sandy Cl* 1839 *TA*, '(at) the sandy way', *v.* **atte**, **sand**, **weg**; perhaps originally with reference to the road from Bourton to Zeals (W); a Sand Pit is marked (6″) beside this road.

ADCROFT HO. BLACKWATER FM. BOURTON BRIDGE, 1811 OS. WEST BOURTON, 1811 ib. BRICKYARD LANE, named from Brick, Pipe & Tile Works (6″), cf. *Brick and Tile Yd* 1839 *TA*. BRIDGE FM, near Bourton Bridge *supra*. BULBS FM. BULLPITS, 1839 *TA, Bulls' Pits* 1837 *ib* (Silton), *grove called Bullpitts* 1609 *LRMB*, *v.* **bula, pytt**, cf. Pulpit Wood Bk 164. CLAY LANE, *Clay Lane Ho* 1839 *TA*, cf. *Clay Md* 1837 *ib* (Silton), Old Clay Pit (6″). DOVEHAYES FM. FACTORY HILL & POND, named from Bourton Foundry (6″), cf. Hutch[3] 3 625 and the f.n. Yarn Barton *infra*. FILCHERTON, *Flushington Ho* 1839 *TA*, cf. the nearby field *Fulshington Deptly* 1839 *ib, v.* f.ns. *infra*; this name would appear to be a late (and perhaps purely analogical) formation in -*ton* (*v.* **tūn**), since it is no doubt to be associated with *meadow called Vilkers* 1609 *LRMB* and with the family of John *le Fylkere* 1327 *SR* (Silton); the house is called *Shorthedge* 1811 OS, cf. the f.n. *Shorthedge* 1839 *TA*. FLAMBERT'S FM. FORGE LANE, *Forage-* 1811 ib, named from Smithy (6″), *v.* **forge**. FORTY POND, cf. *grounde called Fortie als. Bovys* 1609 *LRMB, Gt & Lt Forty* 1837 *TA* (Silton), *Gt & Lt Varty* 1839 *TA, v.* **forð-īeg**

'island in marshland'; *Bovys* is a surname, *v.* Reaney *s.n.*
Bovis. GROVEHOUSE FM, cf. *campo dicto le Groue* 1317 *GillCt,*
The Grove, Groves Closes 1609 *LRMB, Grove and Coppice,*
Groves Md 1839 *TA, v.* **grāf(a)** 'grove, copse'. HIGH CROSS
(lost), 1811 OS, cf. Robert *de Cruce de Burton* 1258 *For.*
HIGHFIELD HO. HIGH ST., *High Street (Md)* 1839 *TA.*
KING'S GREEN CTG, 1839 *ib,* cf. Mathew *Kinge* 1609 *LRMB,*
King's Mead in Gillingham par. *infra.* KITE'S NEST (LANE).
LONG LANE, 1811 OS, along the county bdy and giving name
to *Longlane myll* 1575 Saxton, *Long Lane mill* 1870 Hutch[3],
cf. Walter *de la Lane de Burton* 1258 *For, v.* **lane.** MANOR
FM. MARVIN'S FM, cf. Thomas *Marvine* 1609 *LRMB*
(Motcombe). MIDNEY LANE, named from *Myddenhull'* 1438,
Mydnell', Middehell' 1501 *GillCt, Midnill* 1609 *LRMB, Gt
& Lt Midney, Midneys* 1839 *TA,* 'the middle hill', from
midd (wk.obl. *middan),* **hyll.** MILL LANE, cf. *Rob' Atte
Mull'* . . . *in molend' de Boriton'* 1292, *Mullanende* 1415
GillCt, Longlane myll 1575 Saxton (*v.* Long Lane *supra*), *one
water corne mill* 1609 *LRMB, Mill* [Bridge] 1791 Boswell,
The Mill Acre 1837 *TA* (Silton), *Mill Md* 1839 *ib, v.* **atte,**
myln, lane, ende[1]. MOUNT PLEASANT, -*Ctg* 1839 *ib,* cf. 1
38–9. PRIMROSE FM. QUEEN OAK, *Queene Oake Close* 1609
LRMB, Queen Oak Ho 1839 *TA, v.* **cwēn, āc,** no doubt
named from one of the Queens of England who at different
dates possessed the manor of Gillingham, *v.* Hutch[3] 3 616,
cf. Thorngrove in Gillingham par. *infra;* there is another
Queen's Oak named in the 16th cent. bounds of Gillingham
Forest, *v.* Motcombe f.ns. *infra.* ST GEORGE'S CHURCH, cf.
Chapel Cl and Yd 1839 *TA.* TAN LANE, possibly to be
associated with *Tannehous* 1475, 1501, *Tanhous* 1475 *GillCt,*
an early instance of **tanhouse** 'a building in which tanning is
carried on'. TINKER'S LANE.

FIELD-NAMES

The undated forms in (*a*) are 1839 *TA* 91 (Gillingham), except for those
marked † which are 1837 *ib* 189 (Silton). The undated forms in (*b*) are
1609 *LRMB.* Spellings dated 1307, 1438, 1441 are *GillCt,* 1310 Ipm, 1609
LRMB, 1664 HTax.

(a) Ash Md (cf. Thomas *de Fraxino* 1307); Beacons and Reeves Ho; Gt & Lt Beakly (probably *Bacliffe* 1609, second el. perhaps **clif** 'bank'); Beer Ho and Gdn; †Bench Lds; †Bleach Yd (cf. Yarn Barton *infra*); Bottom Md; Bourton Cl; Brachers Orchd; Mitchells Breach ((*close called*) *Breache* 1609, *v.* **bræc**[2]); Brixeys Md; (Gt & Lt) Broad Md, Ryalls Broad Md (*Broade Meade* 1609, *v.* **brād, mǣd**); †Butts' Cl; Calves Cl; Childs Ho; †Clapham Cl; Clift Coppice, Woolcots Clift (*v.* **clif** 'bank', cf. *Southcleeves infra; Woolcot* is a surname); Cobridge, Cubberidge; Cold Md; Common Pce; Cooks Hays (probably to be identified with *Crookes haies* 1609, from the surname *Crook* and **(ge)hæg**); †Coppice; Coppice Grd & Md; Dead Croft (*Deade Crofte* 1609, *v.* **dēad** 'dead, i.e. infertile', **croft**); †Deep Leys Pce, (Cucklington & Fulshington) Deptly (*Deplaye* 1609, *v.* **dēop** 'deep', **lēah** 'wood, glade', giving name to Depley Copse & Fm (6″) in Cucklington So near the county bdy, cf. Filcherton *supra*); †Dick(l)ey Pce, Dickly; Doctors Orchd; Dorslys (*Dorsley* 1609); Dowfitts (cf. John *Duffett* 1664 (Gillingham)); Dry Cl; Eastments Ho (cf. Christopher *Eastmond* 1664); Elms; Farthings Grd (cf. Joan *Farthinge* 1609); Field Cl; Foots Arable & Md; Garden's; Gasson(')s (*meadowe called Gaston* 1609, *v.* **gærs-tūn** 'paddock'); †Goors' Pce; Great Fd & Mdw; Hay-House; Head Acre; Higher Grd & Md; †Hill Cl; Hilly Cl; Hobbs Mdw & Orchd (*close called Hobbs* 1609, from **hobb(e)** 'tussock', or the surname *Hobb*); Holly Holmes (two forms of the same word, *v.* **holegn** 'holly'); Home Md (-*Meade* 1609) & Plat (*v.* **mǣd, plat**[2]); House Cl or Home Cl; †House Grd; Jumicks; Jupe(')s Cl & Coppice (cf. Ralph *Juper*, Giles *Jupp* 1664); Kingsbury (this field lies on the county bdy); Kitty Md; Long Cl & Grd; Longlands; Lower Fd & Md(w); Ludlands; Gt & Lt Lynch (*v.* **hlinc**); †The Mead (cf. *The Meade Close* 1609, *v.* **mǣd**); Middle Grd; †Moot Hill Pce (perhaps from **(ge)mōt** 'meeting, assembly'; on the county bdy); Mullens Cl Upper Grd, Mullens Middle Fd and Plant.; New Cl; Oak Tree Grd; Oat Cl; Old Down (*le Oldedoune* 1441, cf. *close arr' called Downe* 1609, *v.* **eald, dūn**); Old Ho and Gdn; Lr, Lt & Old Orchard, Orchard Gdn, †The Orchard, †Upr Orchard; Paddock Orchd (cf. *Longe Parrocke* 1609, *v.* **pearroc**); Pitmans Ho and Gdn; Pound Yate (*v.* **pund, geat**); Property; Quar Cl, †Quarry Cl (*v.* **quarre**); Red Lion Inn; Roses Orchd; Slades; Snatch Md; Soagars; (†)Spring Md; Spring Orchd; Square Cl; Staffords; Stower [Bridge] 1791 Boswell (over R.Stour); (Grays) Strop (a variant of **strap**, cf. Thomas *Graye* 1609 (Motcombe)); Long Tags (probably ModE **tag** 'tail-piece', cf. **tægl**); Teoffee Mdw & Plat (perhaps ModE **toffee** in allusion to tough or sticky ground, *v.* **plat**[2]); (Lt) Three Wells; Tiphooks; Tithing Plat (cf. *The Tythinge Close* 1609, *v.* **tēoðung, plat**[2]); Turnip Fd; Two Furlongs; Gt & Lt Underhills (*close called Under hill* 1609, *v.* **under, hyll**); Gt & Lt Voscombs; Water Md(w); (Gt) Whethams (*close called Wedd(h)ams* 1609); Yarn Barton, Hr & Lr Yarnbarton (*v.* **gearn** 'yarn', no doubt with reference to the former flax and sack-making industry in Bourton, *v.* Hutch[3] **3** 625, cf. Factory Hill & Pond, Bleach Yd *supra*).

(b) *Birche Meade* (v. **birce**); *pasture called Burges* (the surname *Burges(s)*); *Burton feilde* (v. par. name *supra*); *Wester Coppehey* 1438, *Cope haies* 1609 (v. **westerra, (ge)hæg**, first el. perhaps **copp** 'top of a hill'); *close called Doll Pitts* (v. **pytt**; first el. probably **dāl** 'dole, share', for the spelling cf. *Petty dolles* 1626 Gl 4 118); *Edge Closse* (v. **ecg, clos(e)**); *Fernehill* (v. **fearn, hyll**); *close called Funocke* (second el. perhaps **āc** 'oak-tree'); *Greene haies* (v. **grēne[1], (ge)hæg**); *close called Hame, -Hams* (v. **hamm**); *Horse Poole Close* (v. **hors, pōl[1]**); *closse . . . called Ivescripple* (no doubt analogous with, though probably not to be identified with, *yuyescrepel* 1247 (1270) For (wrongly transcribed *Thuyescrepel* in Hutch[3] 3 663), a point in the bounds of the manor of Gillingham, probably somewhere near the present Whistley Coppice in Gillingham par. *infra*; the second el. is **crypel** 'a burrow', cf. PN W 422, PN Gl 4 116, but since the first el. is probably **īfig** 'ivy', the sense of the name may be 'place where ivy creeps, place overgrown with ivy'; if however the two names do indeed refer to the same place, a surname may be possible as first el., cf. James *Ivye* 1664); *close called Land Sheare* (v. **land-sc(e)aru**); *Midnam* (perhaps 'middle enclosure', from **midd** and **hamm**, cf. Midney Lane *supra*); *Northefeilde* (v. **norð**); *Odeslade* 1310 (v.**slæd** 'valley', first el. possibly the OE pers.n. *Oda*, cf. the f.n. *Slades supra* and Slait Barn in Silton par. *infra*); *Pennie Meade* (v. **pening** 'a penny', hence 'meadow paying a penny rent'); *Southcleeves* (from a pl. form of **clif** 'bank', cf. Clift Coppice *supra*); *arr' called Thorowaye* (from OE **þurh**, ME *thurgh* 'through', and **weg** 'road', cf. **thurghfare**).

Fifehead Magdalen

The source for early spellings of names in this par. abbreviated AcctStAug is *Some Manorial Accounts of St Augustine's Abbey, Bristol* (Bristol Record Society), ed. Arthur Sabin, 1960.

FIFEHEAD MAGDALEN (ST 784216)

Fifhide 1086 DB (f.80), *Fifhidam* (acc.) 1135–54 (1318), 1153–4 (1318) Ch, *Fyf(h)ide* 1285 ib, 1288 *Ass*, *Fifhyde* 1285 FA, *Fifide* 1291 Tax, 1428 FA, *Vifhide* 1316 FA, 1332 SR, *Fyshude* (for *Fyf-*) 1327 *SR*, *Fyf(e)hed(e) juxta Henstrigge, -rygge* 1473, 1481 Drew
Lifiden (sic, for *Fif-*) 1158 France
Fifhide Abbatis 1268 *Ass*, *Fiffide-* 1280 *ib*, *Fyfide-* 1288 *ib*, *Fyffyde Sancti Augustini* 1364 *For*
Fifyde Maudaleyne 1388 Drew, *Vifide Maudeleyne* 1393 Pat, *Fyffeh(u)yd(e) Maud(e)lyn* 1460 Cl, Fine, IpmR, *Fighfeld Magdalyn* 1535 VE, *Fifehead Magdelen* 1664 HTax

'(Estate of) five hides', from **fīf** and **hīd**, a common p.n., cf. Fifehead Neville par. **2** 95; *Henstrigge, -rygge* is the adjacent par. of Henstridge So. This manor was assessed at five hides in DB (VCHDo **3** 88), and was granted in the 12th cent. to the abbey of St Augustine, Bristol (Hutch[3] **4** 56, VCHDo **3** 57), hence the affixes in 1268 and 1288. The later affix is from the dedication of the church, *v.* St Mary Magdalene's Church *infra*. According to Hutch[3] **4** 56, Fifehead Magdalen was called alternatively (but with no indication as to date) *'Fifehide Abbas,* vulgo *Marnhull infra Fifehide,* from its vicinity to Marnhull'. For the development *Fighfeld* in 1535, cf. Fifield O 351, W 207.

TRILL BRIDGE (ST 790206), 1791 Boswell, 1811 OS, *Tryllebrigge* 1492, *-bryge* 1525 AcctStAug, cf. *Trelmyll* 1492 ib, *Trill Field* 1686 *DRO, -Bar* 1826 Gre, and the f.ns. *(Poor) Trill, Trill Mdw* 1839 *TA* in this par. as well as f.ns. in Stour P. and Marnhull pars. both *infra, v.* **brycg, myln.** This name is probably to be associated with the surnames of Robert *de Trul* 1268 *Ass,* Walter *de Tril* 1316 *AD* (Marnhull), William *Tril* 1327 *SR* (this par.), Walter *Trul* 1327 *ib, -de Tryl* 1332 SR (Marnhull), 1335 *For, -de Tril* 1338 *ib.* Trill Bridge itself is on R. Stour, but *Tril/Trul* may originally have been the name of the small stream (now unnamed) which rises E of Stour P., forming the Marnhull–Stour P. par. bdy (cf. *lacum inter Marnehull et Stower* 1570 *KCC*) and joining R. Stour just below Trill Bridge. The same stream-name, which may be from OE ***tyrl** 'that which turns or rolls along', is common in the SW and occurs elsewhere in Do, *v.* Trill Fm in Beer Hackett par. *infra,* Darknoll Brook in RNs. *infra,* cf. Ekwall RN 409, 418.

CALE BRIDGE, 1811 OS, *Cale or Caule* [Bridge] 1791 Boswell, cf. *Gt, Middle & Outer Caile Fd* 1839 *TA,* named from R. Cale; an earlier bridge here was *pontem de Stapelbrigge* 1270 *For* (in the bounds of Blackmoor Forest), from Stalbridge par. *infra.* COKING LANE, cf. *Coken* 1839 *ib,* leading to Coking Fm in W Stour par. *infra.* CROKERFORD (lost), 1541 AcctStAug, 1543, 1649 Hutch[3], 1774 Hutch[1], *Cokerford* (sic) 1492 AcctStAug, perhaps 'potters' ford', from **croccere** and

ford, cf. Crockleford Ess 326; according to Hutch[3] 4 58, 'this name is not now known (1870)'. FIFEHEAD HILL. FIFEHEAD HO, 1811 OS. FIFEHEAD MILL, 1811 ib, *Brown's Mill* 1765 Tayl, cf. *Mill Cl* 1839 *TA*; there were two mills in Fifehead M. in 1086 DB (VCHDo 3 88), cf. also *Cokerelmull, -myll* 1492 AcctStAug (cf. John *Cokerel* 1332 SR, *v.* **myln**) and *Trelmyll* 1492 AcctStAug (*v.* Trill Bridge *supra*). FIFEHEAD WD, cf. *The Wood* 1839 *TA*. FROGHOLE WITHY BED, *Froghole* (*Withy bed*) 1839 *ib*, *v.* **frogga, hol**[1], **wīðig**. GREAT MOOR, 1839 *ib*, cf. *Inner Moor* 1839 *ib*, *v.* **mōr**. HIGHER FM. LOWER FM. MANOR FM, *The Manor Farm House* 1839 *ib*. ST MARY MAGDALENE'S CHURCH, cf. 'church of *Lifiden*' (for *Fif-*) 1158 France, 'church of *Fyfhid*' Eliz ChancP. THE VILLA.

FIELD-NAMES

The undated forms are 1839 *TA* 83. Spellings dated 1327 are *SR*, 1332 SR, 1492, 1525 AcctStAug, 16 *Glyn*, 1664 HTax.

(*a*) Back Orchd; Bankside Cl or Dunfords; Barley Hams (*v.* **hamm**); Broad Cl; Browns Md (cf. Robert- 1525, William *Browne* 1664); Buck Yd; Burgess Cl; Burn Brake (probably for -*Bake*, *v.* **burnbake**); Butchers Cl or Croft; Clay Stile (*v.* **stigel**); Comelake Md; Coppice Grd; Cox's Trill (cf. Thomas *Cox* 1664, *v.* Trill Bridge *supra*); Crabtree Cl; Crews Home Cl; Culverhays (*v.* **culfre, (ge)hæg**); Dry Md; 40 Acres; 4 Acres; Galpines Middle & Wheat Fd; Hill Gaston (*v.* **gærs-tūn**); Goose Marsh; Gore Acre Ho (*le Gores* 1525, *v.* **gāra**); Green Cl; The Grove (*v.* **grāf(a)**); Ham Mdw, Lt & Upr Ham (*v.* **hamm**); Hannams Home Cl (or Leg), Hannams New & Well Cl (*v.* **leg**); Hilly Cl; Home Cl & Grd; Island Orchd; Gt & Lt Lambs Grd; (South of) Larkhill; Lashmoor (Leaze) (cf. Latchmore Pond in Motcombe par. *infra*, *v.* **lǣs**); Little Coppice & Fd; Long Md; Lower Fd; The Manor Pound; (Gt & Lt, Upr & Lr) Middle Fd (cf. *campo de Fifhed*' 16); Gt & Lt Narlong; New Cl (Mead); North Fd; Old Lane; Orchard(s); Ozier Grd (*v.* **osier**); Paddock; Inner & Outer Park; Parratts Great Cl or Slades Grd, Parratts New & Poor Cl; Pennyworth (probably in allusion to a penny rent, *v.* **pening**); Pit Cl (cf. Adam *atte Putte* 1327, 1332, *v.* **atte, pytt**); Lr & Middle Pleam, (Cowhill or) Upr Pleam, Pleam Orchd; Puxey Cl (perhaps a stream-name analogous with Pucksey Brook, *v.* RNs. *infra*); Rackhay (*v.* **rakke, (ge)hæg**); Shebus Cl or Shelves; Solvers Fd & Md; South Hay (Orchd) (*v.* **(ge)hæg**); Splatts (a form of **splott**); Square Cl; Stalbridge Mdw (from Stalbridge par. *infra*); Hr & Lr Stern or Stert (*v.* **steort**); Swans Nest; Swyer (*v.* **swēora, swīra** 'neck of land'); Thorn Cl; Tobys Cl; Toogoods Middle & Upr Fd; Webbs Marsh; Lr Well Cl; Small Withy Bed, Withy Hams (*v.* **wīðig, hamm**); Woodcroft; Wooliss; Young Orchd.

(b) *atten Asshe* (p) 1327 ('at the ash-tree', *v.* **atten, æsc**); *As(s)hel(l)-worthes* (a cottage) 1492 (probably a surname); *Ianyns* (a cottage) 1492 (a surname); *le Nethercourt, le Ouercourt* 1492 (*v.* **neoðerra** 'lower', **uferra** 'higher', **court** 'manor'); *Restes* v.l. *Roses* (a cottage) 1492 (a surname); *Sampsons* (a cottage) 1492 (a surname); *le Tray* (perhaps ME *tray* 'shallow open vessel' in some figurative sense); *Wullans Lane* 1525.

Gillingham

Gillingham is in Gillingham liberty, *v.* note under Redlane hundred *supra.*

GILLINGHAM (ST 808265) ['gilinəm]
?*Gillingaham* 993 (l10) *Cott* (S 876), (*wið*) *Gillinga hám* 11 ASC (D), (*wið*) *Gillinga* 12 ib (E) both s.a. 1016, *Gillingaham* e12 FW, 12 SD
Gelingeham 1086 DB (6 x), Exon, 1209 LibR, *Ingelingeham, Gelingham* 1086 DB, *Gellingeham* 1130 P, 1155 PR, 1168 P, 1196 ChancR, 1212 Fees, *Gellingham* 1258 *For, Egeling-, -yngham* 1280 *Ass*
Gilling' 1135–54 (1317) Ch
Gyllingeham, Ghillingeham 1152–8 MontC, *Gillingeham* 1156 RBE, 1161, 1194–9 P, John RBE, 1201–6 P, 1208 ChancR, 1209 FF *et freq* to 1310 Ipm, *Gilling'ham* 1201 P, ChancR, 1210 P, *Gilinge-* 1209 LibR, *Gillenge-* 1229 Cl, *Gylling(g)e-* 1236, 1263 ib, *Gillynge-* 1310 Ipm, *Gyllyngeham* e15 LHyda
Gildingeham 1156 PR, *Geldingeham* 1157 ib, 1159 P, *Goldingeham* 1160 ib
Gillingham 1198 P, 1200 ib, FineR, 1201 Cur, P, 1204 LibR, ClR, P, 1205–9 ib *et passim* with variant spellings *Gil-, Gyl-, Gyll-, -yng-*; *Gyllynghame* c.1300 DCMDeed
Killingham 1199 P, 1265 Cl
Guillingh' 1262 Cl

Probably 'homestead or village of Gylla's people', *v.* **-ingas** (gen.pl. *-inga*), **hām**, as suggested by Karlström 50, Ekwall DEPN and PN *-ing* 127, cf. Fägersten 5, Gilscott D 85. A pers.n. **Gylla* is not recorded but Ekwall supposes it may be a hypocoristic form of a pers.n. **Gyðla* postulated for Givendale YW 154. Gillingham K (now pronounced with initial [dʒ] and Gillingham Nf are probably of identical origin, *v.* Ekwall DEPN, cf. KPN 303–4, PN K 128–9. In the second of the two forms from ASC the omission of *-ham* is simply an error, whilst the 12th cent. form *Gilling'* is no doubt an abbreviated form of *Gillingham.* The early spellings in *Gel(l)*- are due to AN substitution of *e* for *i, v.* Zachrisson IPN 113, Feilitzen 50, and the form *Egeling-, -yngham* apparently has prosthetic *e.* In the DB form *Ingelingeham* the preposition *in* has been wrongly attached to the name, and the 12th cent. forms from the Pipe rolls with *-ld-* are probably also errors. The bounds of the manor of Gillingham are given in 1247 (1270) *For* (E 32/11/m. 4v), reproduced in Hutch³ **3** 663. Gillingham was divided into two tithings, called *Gillingham Major or the Town Tithing* and *Gillingham Minor or the Free Tithing* in 1869 Hutch³; the former is *Gillingham Towne Tithing* 1664 HTax, *Gillingham Major* 1795 Boswell, the latter is *Fretethyng', Middelton' Frethething'* 1288 *Ass, Liber(a) Decenna* 1327 *SR,* 1332 SR, *Free Tithing* 1664 HTax, *Gillingham Minor alias Free* 1795 Boswell, *v.* **frēo, tēoðung,** Milton on Stour *infra.*

STREET-NAMES: Cᴇᴍᴇᴛᴇʀʏ Rᴅ, named from Cemetery (6″) cf. William *de Cimiterio* 1295 *GillCt*; Hᴀʀᴅɪɴɢs Lᴀɴᴇ, *Hardinges-* 1609 *LRMB*, cf. 'land of John *Hardyng'* 1313 Cl, John *Hardyng'* 1332 SR (Silton), *Hardyngeshull(')* 1374 *For*, 1441 *GillCt, v.* **lane, hyll**; Kɪɴɢscᴏᴜʀᴛ Rᴅ, named from King's Court Palace in Motcombe par. *infra*; Lᴏᴅʙᴏᴜʀɴ, for this st.n. *v.* Lodbourn Fm *infra;* Tᴏᴍᴋɪɴs Lᴀɴᴇ; Wʏᴋᴇ Sᴛ., *Wykestrete* 1501 *GillCt*, cf. *Weeke Streate Meade* 1609 *LRMB, Wyke Street Pdk* 1839 *TA, Wykeweyeslane* 1411 *GillCt*, leading to Wyke Marsh *infra, v.* **strǣt, weg, lane.** A lost st.n. is *Churchestrete* 1535 *Ct* (*v.* St Mary the Virgin Church *infra*). Buildings include *GildeAule* 1441 *GillCt, the Guildhall* 1609 *LRMB* (*v.* **gild-hall**, cf. Richard *atte yeldhouse* 1356 *GillCt*, probably with reference to the same place, *v.* **atte, gild, hūs**); *howse called the Crowne* 1609 *LRMB; Phoenix* (Inn) and *Red Lion* (Inn) 1824 Pigot; *The Free School* 1869 Hutch³; cf. also John *atte Inne*, William *atte Nywe Inne* 1411 *GillCt, v.* **atte, nīwe, inn.**

Bᴀʀɴᴀʙʏ Bʀɪᴅɢᴇ (lost, ST 807265), 1568, 1869 Hutch³, *Barnabesbrigg, -brugg* 1300 ib, *-brugge* 1381 *GillCt, Barnabyes-, Barnabeesbryg'* 1438 *ib*, cf. *Joh' Barnabe de Gillingham* 1270 *For, Joh' Barnebay . . . in molend' quod dicitur Barnebay* 1292 *GillCt*, Simon *Barnabe* 1372 FF, 1374

For, Barnabesmull' 1381 *GillCt, claus' apud Barnabyes* 1475
ib, Johannis Butte de Barnabe 1535 *Ct* (cf. another juror in
the same document called *Johannis Butte de Pesemershe, v.*
Peacemarsh *infra*), 2 *mills called Barnabies Mills* 1609
LRMB, v. **brycg, myln**. This bridge is mentioned in the
bounds of the forest of Gillingham (1300, 1568 Hutch[3] **3**
620, 621, 656), and is perhaps to be identified with *Pontem de
petra* ('stone bridge') in the forest bounds of Hy3 (14) Cerne,
cf. foll. It is apparently called *Town Bridge* in 1791 Boswell.

BAY (ST 812270), BAY BRIDGE & FM. The bridge is *Porridge
Bay* [Bridge] 1791 Boswell, *Pough'fordebrig'* 1415,
Powgh'rygge-, Pokeryge brygge 1501 *GillCt, v.* Bowridge
Hill *infra*; *Bay* no doubt represents ModE **bay**[2] 'an
embankment to form a dam' as in Bay Bridge W 303. Other
early names for this bridge, also given in the bounds of the
forest of Gillingham, are *Lodburn Bridge, which of old time
was called the Bridge of Merford* 1568 ib (**3** 621) (*v.*
Lodbourn Fm *infra*), and (probably) *Kingesbrigge* Hy 3 (14)
Cerne (*v.* **cyning, brycg**, cf. King's Mead *infra*).

BOWRIDGE HILL (FM) (ST 814275), *Poghrigge* 1292 *GillCt,
-rygge* 1438 *ib, Pogherygge* 1306 *ib* (p), *-rigge* 1333 *For* (p),
Pougherig' 1411 *GillCt, Porridge Hill, Mannors als. Boridge*
1609 *LRMB, Porredge Hill* 1650 *ParlSurv, Boughridge Hill*
1811 OS, *Bowridge Hill Md* 1839 *TA*, probably 'ridge
shaped like a pouch or bag', *v.* **pohha, hrycg**, and the f.n.
Manors *infra*, cf. Poughley Brk 290 and the references there
to other p.ns. which may contain the el. **pohha**. This place
gave name to *Powgh'rygge-, Pokeryge brygge* 1501 *GillCt,
Porridge Bay* [Bridge] 1791 Boswell, *v.* Bay Bridge *supra*; the
same bridge is apparently earlier called *Pough'fordebrig'* 1415
GillCt, from the same first el. with **ford**.

BUGLEY (BRIDGE & FM) (ST 785246)
 Bogeley(e) 1275 RH, 1310 Ipm, 1311 Cl all (p), *-lee* 1295,
  1306 *GillCt* both (p), *-leygh'* 1306 *ib* (p), *-leigh* 1313 Cl
  (p), *-legh* 1313 ib (p), 1362 *For* (p), *-le* 1374 *ib* (p), 1381
  GillCt, Boggeley 1280 *Ass* (p), *Bogley* 1811 OS
 Bugeley 1300 *GillCt* (p), *-legh* 1311 Cl (p), *Buggeleye* 1312

Fine (p), 1356 *GillCt, -le(e)* 1316 Inq aqd, 1317 FF both (p), *Buglegh* 1312, 1313 Cl both (p), *Bugleystret* 1501 *GillCt, Bugleigh, -ley (Streete), Buglie Meade* 1609 *LRMB, Bugley or Bogley* 1795 Boswell, *Bugly (Grd), Under Bugly, Long & Short Bugl(e)y* 1839 *TA Bouglee* 1327 *SR* (p), *Bougeleyeslane* 1415 *GillCt*

Probably 'Bucge's clearing or wood', from the OE fem. pers.n. *Bucge* and **lēah**, although it is possible that the first el. is ME **bugge** 'a boggart, a hobgoblin', cf. Bugley W 158 which is apparently analogous, *v.* **lane, strǣt**. It should perhaps be noted that the earliest form of the p.n. in independent use (i.e. not used as a surname) is 1356 *GillCt*.

ECCLIFFE (ST 799253), *Molend' de Egcliue, Eg(g)cliue* (p) 1292 *GillCt, molend' de Ecclyue* 1300 *ib, molendinum de Hoggecleve* 1338–40 Glast, *Egglive* 1364 Hutch[3], *Ecklyue-, Ekclyuemull'* 1411 *GillCt, Ekclyuesmull', Ekclyf Mull'* 1415 *ib, Ecliffe, Eckley furlonge, Ecklie Mill* 1609 *LRMB, Ekelly Mill* [Bridge] 1791 Boswell, *Accliff Mill* 1811 OS, *Eccliff Mill (Md)* 1839 *TA*. This place is on R. Stour and the second el. is **clif** 'bank'; there is still a mill here (marked 6″), *v.* **myln**. The first el. is probably the OE pers.n. *Ecga*, for which *v.* Acton Gl 2 228, Eagle Hundred Brk 289. Fägersten 6 (followed by Smith EPN 1 14) derives the name from OE *æt þǣm clife* '(place) at the bank', citing the surnames of John *Attecliue, -clyue* 1244 *Ass*, Walter *atte Clyue* 1332 SR; but although these surnames may well refer to the 'cliff' at this place (cf. also Walter *de Clyve* 1258 *For*, Adam *Attecliue* 1292 *GillCt*), the early forms now cited for Eccliffe clearly show that the first el. of this p.n. cannot be ME *atte* < OE *æt þǣm*.

FOREST FM (ST 828299), FOREST SIDE (ST 814295), *Forest-side* 1811 OS, cf. *Forest Md & Lds* 1839 *TA*, named from *foresta (regis) de Gilling(e)ham* 1222 Pat, 1231, 1234, 1236, 1238 Cl *et passim*, 'Queen Philippa's forest of *Gyllyngham*' 1337 ib, 'forest and park of *Gillyngham*' 1402 Pat, 'the king's forest of *Gyllyngham* and his park within the latter' 1461 ib, *Gyllingham Forest'* 1519 *Ct, the parke Forrest*

Eliz *For*, cf. also *Boscum de Gilling(e)ham* Hy3 (14) Cerne, 1228 Cl *et freq, bosco de Gillingham extra parcum* 1234 Cl, *forinseco bosco extra parcum de Gillingeham* 1238 ib, and *v*. Park Fm *infra*. The bounds of the forest of Gillingham are given in Hy3 (14) Cerne (also Hutch[3] **3** 662–3), in 1300, 1364, 1568 Hutch[3] **3** 620–1, 656–7, and in 1338–40 Glast, cf. also 1624 (p1816) *DCMMap* and the discussion of the bounds by C.D. Drew in Roscoe 34–5. It was disafforested c.1627 (Hutch[3] **3** 651); at this date there were four 'walks' in the forest, *Woods-end-walk* (*v*. Woodsend Fm in Motcombe par. *infra*), *Clear-walk* or *Middle-walk* (*v*. Donedge Lodge Fm in Motcombe par. *infra*), *Laund-walk* (*v*. Lawn Bridge & Fm *infra*), and *the Bailiff's-walk* (*v*. f.ns. *infra*).

GUTCH POOL FM (ST 839285), GUTCH POOL HOLE, *the water called Gowge Pole, of old called Horeappledore* 1568 Hutch[3], *Gutch Poole House* 1650 *ParlSurv, Gouge-pool* 1811 OS. The 1568 form is from the bounds of the forest of Gillingham, earlier names for this point being *la Hore Apeldure* Hy3 (14) Cerne, *la Horeapeldere* 1247 (1270) *For, Horeappledore, Horeapeldes* (sic) 1300 Hutch[3], *Hor Appildor'* 1338–40 Glast, 'the grey (boundary) apple-tree', *v*. **hār**[2], **apuldor**. Gutch Pool Hole is in R. Lodden where it crosses the county bdy to form the par. bdy between Gillingham and Motcombe; the farm is by R. Lodden ⅓ mile SW. The unexplained Gutch Pool Ho W192 (*Gowge Pole* 1567) and Gutch Common ib 210 (*Gutches* 1635, *Goch* 1773) are no doubt identical in origin. They may contain eModE *gouge* 'chisel or spade with concave blade', 'to hollow or scoop out', with some such sense as 'pool formed by digging or scooping out'. But if the names are old, the first el. is perhaps a derivative in **-ic** of OE ***gotu***, ***gote*** 'water-course, channel, stream', cf. **gyte** 'pouring forth, flood', some spellings perhaps having been influenced by eModE *gouge*.

HAM CMN (ST 819258), HR & LR HAM FM, *Hamme* 1152–8 MontC, 1333 *For* (p), 1374 *ib* (*-iuxta Mageston'*), *in la Hamme* 1270 ib (p), 1295, 1307 *GillCt* both (p), *la Hamme* 1295 *ib, Hammes* 1362 *For, le Hamme* 1438 *GillCt, Hampe* (*iuxta Gillingham*) 1461 IpmR, 1570 *Prideaux, Ham* 1575

Saxton, 1869 Hutch[3], *Ham common* 1627 ib, *Hamlease* 1664
HTax, *Ham* (*Cross & Hills*), *Ham Mead* (*Cmn*) 1839 *TA, v.*
hamm 'enclosure, river-meadow', **lǣs** 'pasture', Madjeston
infra; situated by R. Lodden.

HUNTINGFORD (ST 810300)
    Huntingeford Hy 3 (14) Cerne (2 ×), *Huntingford* 1300
        Hutch[3] (*pontem de-*), 1568 ib (*-Bridge*), 1609 *LRMB*
        (*-Howse*), 1811 OS, *Huntyngford*(') 1333 *For* (p), 1438
        GillCt, *Hontyngford*(*e*) 1381 *ib*
    Hunteneford 1258 *For* (p), 1268 *Ass* (p), 1270 *For* (p), 1306
        GillCt, *Huntenford* 1338 *For*
    Huntreford 1258 *For* (p)
    Hunteford' 1292 *GillCt*
    Huntleford 1364 Hutch[3], (*-Lane*) 1609 *LRMB, Huntil-*
        fordbrig' 1415 *GillCt*, *Huntelford*' 1438 *ib, Huntil*(*l*)-
        ford(*e*) (*Bridge*) 1609 *LRMB*

'The hunters' ford, the ford used by people going
hunting', from OE **hunta** (gen.pl. *huntena*) and **ford**, with
brycg, cf. Huntingford Gl 2 257. In *Hunting*(*e*)*ford*, etc, the
-ing- is probably analogical, but influence from OE
hunting 'hunting' is possible. The isolated 13th cent. form
Huntreford may show dissimilation of *n-n* to *n-r* or contain
OE **huntere** 'hunter'. The forms *Huntleford*, etc, presumably show dissimilation of *n-n* to *n-l*. The ford (marked 6″) is
where a road crosses Shreen Water near the county bdy, and
is mentioned in the bounds of the royal forest of Gillingham,
in the perambulation of Hy 3 (14) Cerne making the starting
and finishing point of the bounds, so that the association
with hunting is clear. It is even possible that Huntingford is
to be identified with the small DB manor of *Gelingeham* held
TRW by Edward *venator* ('the huntsman'), *v.* VCHDo 3
113.

LANGHAM (ST 773258), HR & LR LANGHAM FM, *Langeham*
1156, 1157 PR, 1173 RBE, 1246 Ipm, 1303 FA, 1309 Inq
aqd, 1310 FF (*-juxta Gyllyngham*), 1375 Pat, *Langham* 1159,
1194–1197 P, 1251–2 Fees, 1609 *LRMB et passim*, *Lanham*
1197–1208 P, *Lagenham* (sic) 1274 Hutch[3], 1315 Pat,

Langenham 1280 *Ass,* 1301 *GillCt,* 1303 FA, 1316 FF, 1346, 1428, 1431 FA, 1475 *GillCt,* 1494 Ipm, *Langnam* 1501 *GillCt, Langham (Fm)* 1811 OS, 'the long enclosure or river-meadow', *v.* **lang**[1], **hamm**; a stream rises here. There is mention of a chapel at Langham in 1494 Ipm.

LODBOURN (FM) (ST 807273), *Lurteborne* 1438 *GillCt, Lodburn Bridge, which of old time was called the Bridge of Merford* 1568 Hutch[3], *Lodborne* 1609 *LRMB, Lotburn* 1628 Hutch[3] , *Ladborn Green* 1811 OS, 'the dirty stream', from **lort(e)** and **burna**, cf. Ekwall RN 259 and an identical name in Winfrith N. par. **1** 184. It was perhaps originally the name of (this stretch of) Shreen Water, by which stream the farm lies. *Lodburn Bridge* is now Bay Bridge *supra*; the 1568 identification with *the Bridge of Merford* is wrong, *v.* Colesbrook *infra*.

MADJESTON (ST 808251), MADJESTON BRIDGE & FM
  Malg'eston 1205, 1206 ClR
  Magerston 1256 FF, 1275 RH (p), 1303 FA, 1315, 1337 Ipm, 1338 Cl, 1346 FA, 1420 Cl, 1428 FA, *Magirstone* 1278 Misc, 1285 FA, *Magereston* 1303 FA, 1402 Cl, *Mageriston* 1337 Ipm, *Mageryston* 1429 Cl, *Maggerston* 1420 IpmR
  Maugereston 1266 FF, *Maugerston* 1268 *Ass,* 1299 Ipm, *Mangirston* (for *Mau-*) 1272 ib
  Maggeston 1342 *For, Mageston* 1343 *ib,* 1360 Ipm, 1361 Fine, 1371 FF, 1412, 1431 FA, 1486 Ipm, 1811 OS, *Magstone* 1569 KCC, *Magestone* 1774 Hutch[1], *Magiston Green* [Bridge] 1791 Boswell
  Margerston 1381 Cl
  Madgeston 1609 *LRMB, Madjeston* 1839 *TA*

'Madalgar's or Malger's manor', from the OG pers.n. *Madalgar, Malger* (OFr *Maugier*) and **tūn**, probably a post-Conquest p.n. like Pierston *infra*, cf. IPN 131. For the pers.n., which occurs as *Malger* in DB (twice in Do entries), *v.* Forssner 184, Tengvik 190, Reaney *s.n. Mauger*, and cf. Maugersbury Gl **1** 222 which may contain an OE adaptation *Mæþelgār of this pers.n.

MILTON ON STOUR (ST 802287), MILTON FM & LODGE
  Miltetone, Mideltone 1086 DB
  Mid(d)elton(e) Hy 3 Ipm, 1235–6, 1242–3 Fees, 1244 *Ass*
    (p), 1268, 1280 *ib* (*domo de-*), 1285 FA *et freq* to 1431
    FA
  Milton(') 1275 Cl, 1288 *Ass*, 1318 FF (*-juxta Gillyngham*)
    et passim, '*Milton* up(on) *Stoure*' 1397, 1413 Fine *et*
    passim, '*-by Selton*' 1399 Pat, *Mylton* 1316 FA, *-super*
    Stowre 1512 *Pars*
  Mildinton 1287 Cl   *Multon super Stoure* 1397 IpmR

'Middle farm', *v*. **middel**, **tūn**, perhaps so called from its
position midway between Gillingham and Silton par. *infra*.
There were mills at both of the DB manors in 1086 (VCHDo
3 92, 109).

NEWBURY HO (ST 812262), *Nywebury* 1295, 1306, 1415
GillCt, *Niw(e)bury* 1300, 1438 *ib*, *Newebury* 1441 *ib*,
Newber(r)ie 1609 *LRMB*, 1626 *Poll*, *-borough* 1617 *ib*,
-bery 1668 *ib*, *Newberry Ho* 1839 *TA*, 'new manor house',
from **nīwe** and ME *bury* (from dat.sg. *byrig* of OE **burh**).

PARK FM (ST 822256), 1811 OS, named from *parcus* (*regis*)
de Gilling(e)ham Hy3 (14) Cerne, 1228 Cl, 1232 Pat *et passim*,
ad clausturam Parci de Gyllingham 1288 *Ass*, *Gyllingham park*
1504 Pat, *the quenes parke of Gyllyngham, the parke at the*
copes 1535 *Ct*, *the Parke of Gillingham* 1700 *Weld*[1], cf. *bosco*
de Gillingham extra parcum 1234 Cl, *Gt, Home & West Park*,
Park Md 1839 *TA*, *v*. **park**. On this medieval deer park,
within the forest of Gillingham, *v*. Cantor & Wilson **5** 223–7,
cf. Forest Fm *supra* and the f.n. *Gt Pale Md infra*.

PIERSTON FM (ST 795284)
  Poerston(e) 1247 (1270) *For* (*bosci de-*), 1268 *Ass*, 1278
    Hutch[3], 1285 FA, 1288 *Ass, Poereston* 1257 FF
  Peterstone 1278 Misc, *Petreston* 1316 FA
  Preston' 1280, 1288 *Ass, Preston or Pierson* 1795 Boswell,
    Preston or Peeston 1869 Hutch[3]
  Power(e)ston 1303 FA, 1305 Abbr, 1333 FF, 1428 FA
  Powkerston 1346 FA

Poureston 1396 IpmR, 1397 Cl ('-by *Gylyngham*'), 1415
  IpmR, Fine
Pyryston 1431 FA
Pur(e)ston 1481 IpmR, 1502 Ipm
Perston 1629 *Ct, Pearston Cmn* 1839 *TA, Pierston* 1869
  Hutch[3]

'Poer's manor', a post-Conquest name in **tūn** like Forston
and Herrison 1 340 (*v.* IPN 131). Adam *Poer* held land in
Gillingham in 1258 *For* (10, m. 7r), and Aleyn *le Poer* is
mentioned in connection with this place in 1268 *Ass* (202, m.
11d); the surname is probably from OFr *Pohier* 'a Picard', *v.*
Reaney *s.n. Poor.* The forms *Peters-, Petreston(e)* suggest
early confusion of the first part of the name with the
common pers.n. and surname *Piers* (of which *Peter*, from Lat
Petrus, was the learned form). The *Preston* forms show
metathesis of *r* as well as association with the common p.n.
type from **prēost** 'priest' and **tūn**.

SANDLEY (1″, apparently misnamed or renamed STANLEY
1902 6″) (ST 773248), SANDLEY LODGE (6″), (*Gillingham*)
Sandley 1609 *LRMB, Gt & Lt Sandley, Sandly Coppice*
1839 *TA*, probably to be identified with *Sandhull(e)* 1292
GillCt et freq to 1428 FA all (p), *Sanhulle* 1327 *SR* (p),
Sandehull 1329 FF (p), 1353 Pat (p), *Sandhill* 1330 Orig (p),
Sandhullebrigg' 1415, *Saundell' yate* 1501 *GillCt*, 'sandy hill',
from **sand** and **hyll**, with **brycg, geat**. For the development
of *-hill* to *-ley* (note the transitional form in *-ell'* showing
weak stress in a medial position), cf. Fowley W 273, EPN 1
275.

STOCK FM, HILL (ST 786267), LANE, LODGE & WATER , cf.
Stokkefeld' 1441, *Stokford'* 1501 *GillCt, Stockfeild* 1609
LRMB, Stock (waye) 1626, 1629 *Poll, the Stock Close* 1686
SxAS, (Gt, Hr & Lt) Stock, Wyke Stock, Stock Cl 1839 *TA*,
either from **stocc** 'tree-stump' or **stoc** 'secondary settlement'
(note especially the form *Wyke Stock* with reference to Wyke
infra), with **feld, ford, weg, clos(e)**.

THORNGROVE (ST 794257), *Thorn grave* 1275 Roscoe,
Thorngraue, -grave 1292 *GillCt*, 1313 Cl, *-groue, -grove*

1301 *GillCt*, 1313 Cl, *Thornegraue* 1415 *GillCt*, *-grove* 1609 *LRMB*, *the Quenes ferme of Gyllyngham* Eliz For, *Queene Farme als.* *Thorne Grove*, *Thorn(i)e grove furlonge* 1609 *LRMB*, *Thorngrove*, *or Queen's* 1795 Boswell, *(Under) Thorngrove* 1839 *TA*, *Thorngrove or the Queen's Manor* 1869 Hutch[3], 'thorn-tree copse', from **þorn** and **grāf(a)**, with **furlang**, cf. Robert *Atthe thorne* 1295, Maud *Atte Thorne* 1317 *GillCt, v.* **atte** 'at the'. In 1774, according to Hutch[1] 2 229, Thorngrove was 'still called Queen's Farm, where was supposed to have been anciently a house for her reception', cf. *the Quenes Commons* Eliz For, the f.n. Lains Mead *infra*, Forest Fm and Park Fm *supra*, Queen Oak in Bourton par. *supra*.

WYKE FM, HALL & HO, WYKE MARSH (ST 799265), *Wyke* 1244 *Ass* (p), 1278 Misc, 1285 FA (p), 1288 *Ass* (p), 1292 *GillCt* (p), 1317 *ib et passim*, *Wykelake* 1441 *ib*, *Weeke* Eliz ChancP, 1609 *LRMB*, (*-Lake*, *-Meade*), 1648 *SxAS* (*ferme of-*), *Wykemarsh* 1774 Hutch[1], *Wyke Ho & Marsh* 1811 OS, *Wyke(')s Marsh Grd & Inclosure* 1839 *TA, v.* **wīc** 'dwelling, farm, dairy-farm', **lacu** 'stream', **mǣd** 'meadow', **mersc** 'marsh'.

WYNDLAM FM (ST 789297)
 Windelham 1086 DB, Exon, 1285 FA, *Wyndelham* 1268 *Ass* (p), 1276 FF, 1285 FA, 1304 FF, 1306 Abbr, 1481 IpmR
 Winesham 1242–3 Fees, *Wyndessam* 1244 *Ass* (p)
 Wyndelesham, *Wydelesham* 1244 *Ass* both (p)
 Wyndham 1278 Misc
 Wyldenham 1333 FF
 Windland Fm 1841 *TAMap*

This place is near R. Stour and the name may mean 'river-meadow with a windlass', from **windels** and **hamm**, cf. Broadwindsor par. *infra*, Windsor Brk 26–7. It is, however, possible that the first el. of Wyndlam is an OE pers.n. *Windel*, cf. Windlesham Sr 152, *wyndelescumb* BCS 721 (D).

BAINLY BOTTOM (*Baily-* 1811 OS), FM & HO, 3 *closes called Binley* 1609 *LRMB, Gt Bainly, Bainly Grd* 1839 *TA*, 'clearing where beans are grown', from **bēan** and **lēah**, with **botm**, cf. Beanley Nb (DEPN); for the development of the first el., cf. Beynhurst Brk 59. BENJAFIELD's FM, *Bengeruylesgrove* 1313 Cl, *Bengerville* 1568 Hutch[3], 1811 OS, *Bengfeldes* 1583 *SPDom, Benjafield* 1641 Hutch[3], *Benjey Hills* 1839 *TA*, a manorial name, cf. John (*de*) *Bengervill* 1300 Hutch[3], 1373 *For*, Agnes- 1327 *SR*, John *Bengervile* 1374 *For*, *v.* **grāf(a)** 'grove, copse'. BLEET FM (1774 Hutch[1], 1869 Hutch[3], *Bleet* 1811 OS) & LANE, probably SCy dial. *bleat* 'cold, bleak' (from the OE adj. **blēat** 'wretched, miserable'), cf. Bleatham Sx 101, but earlier spellings are needed; there is a Hunger Hill Fm 1 mile E in E Stour par. *infra*. BLOOMER'S FM, cf. *Bloomers Lane & Md* 1839 *TA*. THE CHANTRY, cf. 'the chantry of St Katharine in the parish church of *Gillyngham*' 1399 Pat, *claus' iuxta Cantariam* 1501 *GillCt*, *close called Chauntrie, meadowe called Chantrue* (sic) 1609 *LRMB*, *Chantry* [Bridge] 1791 Boswell, *Chantry* (*Md*) 1839 *TA, v.* **chantry**; on the chantry of St Catherine in Gillingham, dissolved c.1541, *v.* Hutch[3] **3** 642. COLD HARBOUR, (*Gt & Lt*) *Cold Harbour* 1839 *TA*, 'cold shelter', *v.* **cald**, **here-beorg**; just W of Gillingham by the road to Wincanton So. There is evidence for an extensive RB settlement near here (RCHM **4** 35–6). COLESBROOK, [-Bridge] 1791 Boswell, probably a late name, but cf. Alexander *Cole* 1332 SR, *v.* **brōc**; a bridge here over Shreen Water is named in the bounds of the forest of Gillingham as *pontem de Mereford* 1300 Hutch[3] (Shreen Water was earlier *aquam de Mere, Merewater* because it rises at Mere W, *v.* **ford**, RNs. *infra*). COMMON MD (LANE), *Common Mead* 1811 OS, 1869 Hutch[3] (*Cumber Mead, or as it is commonly called now-*); the earlier name is *Comermede* 1300 *GillCt, common mead . . . called Comb Mead* (sic) 1588 Hutch[3], *Cumbermeade* 1609 *LRMB, Comber Mead* 1629 Hutch[3], *v.* **mǣd**, first el. possibly the OE pers.n. *Cumbra*, cf. Cumberwell W 117, Cumberwood Gl **3** 149. COMPTON STUD, perhaps to be associated with *Comptonesplace* 1415 *GillCt*, from the surname *Compton* (probably from one of the Do places with this name) and **place** 'residence'. THE CROFT, cf. Robert *de* (*la*) *Crofte* 1300

GillCt, close called (the) Crofte 1609 *LRMB, Craft Md* 1839
TA, v. **croft** 'small enclosed field'. CROSS LANE, *Crosselane*
1475 *GillCt*, probably **cross** adj. in the sense 'lying across';
on 1811 OS this lane links two other lanes running parallel to
each other. CULVERS FM & LANE, cf. Roger *atte Coluerhouse*
1327 *SR, Culver Cl & Md* 1839 *TA, v.* **culfre-hūs**
'dove-cot', **culfre** 'dove'. DAIRY HO. EASTERLY COPSE, *close
called Easterleas* 1609 *LRMB, Easter Leaze* 1839 *TA, v.*
ēasterra 'more easterly', **lǣs** 'pasture', the current form *-ly*
probably arising from a misunderstanding of *-leaze* as a pl.
or possessive form of *-lea*; it is near the E par. bdy. THE
ELMS, cf. *Elms Grd* 1839 *TA*. FIELD LANE. FIR TREE INN.
FOLLY FM (1811 OS) & LANE, *v.* **folie, folly**. FURZE HO, cf.
Furze Knaps 1839 *TA, v.* **fyrs, cnæpp**. GILLINGHAM BRIDGE
(lost), 1869 Hutch[3], called *Wyke Street* [Bridge] 1791
Boswell and probably on the site of *Stourebrugg', -brigge*
1356 *GillCt*, 'bridge over R. Stour', *v.* **brycg**, RNs. *infra*, cf.
Ralph *de Ponte de Gillingham* 1288 *Ass, Barnaby Bridge
supra*. GREAT HO. GREEN LANE. HARRY LODGE'S LANE.
HAYHOUSE FM. THE KENDALLS, *Gt & Hither Kendle, Wykes
Keandall* 1839 *TA*, probably to be associated with *molend' de
Kynhull'* 1280 *Ass* and possibly with *Kernellforde* 1609
LRMB, second el. **hyll** 'hill', first el. **cyne-** 'royal' or ME
kyn(e) 'cows', with **ford**, cf. John *Wyke* 1374 *For,* Wyke Fm
supra; the place is situated between R. Stour and Shreen
Water. KINE BUSH LANE, *Cane Bush* 1839 *TA*, probably
cane 'cane, reed', the modern form having been altered to
dial. **kine** 'cattle'. KING'S MEAD (lost, ST 780250), 1869
Hutch[3], *Kyngmede* 1415 *GillCt, Kinge Meade* 1609 *LRMB,
Kingsmead* 1811 OS, *King Md* 1839 *TA*, cf. *(la) Kyngesmere*
1295, 1317 *GillCt*, no doubt part of the royal demesne, *v.*
cyning, mǣd, mere[1] 'pool', cf. King's Court Palace in
Motcombe par. *infra*. KNAPP HO, *Knap Ho & Orchd* 1839
ib, v. **cnæpp** 'hillock'. LANCH LANE, running N to form the
par. and county bdy, probably to be associated with *the
Landshiere otherwise the Lordes Landshiere* 1654 *EgCh,
Lancher Cl, Landshard Corner* 1839 *TA, v.* **land-sc(e)aru**
'boundary', cf. *le Lanschore* 1301 *GillCt* which is from the
related and synonymous **land-scoru**. LANGHAM LANE &
PLANTS., cf. *viam . . . apud Langenham* 1301 *GillCt*,

Langhams Ash 1839 *TA*, named from Langham *supra*. LAWN
BRIDGE (1811 OS, *Lane-* 1791 Boswell) & FM (1774
Hutch[1]), named from *le launde Walke* 1519 *Ct*, *le Lane
Walke* 1612 *Eg*, *Launda or Morgan's Lodge, Launda Walk*
1625 Hutch[3], *Laund-walk and lodge there* 1627 ib, *the Lawnes*
1647 SC, *the Lawne (Walke), The Great-, The Litle Lawne*
1650 *ParlSurv, Lawn (Md)* 1839 *TA, v.* **launde** 'a forest
glade', **walk** 'a division of a forest', cf. Forest Fm *supra*.
LITTLE MARSH, 1811 OS, *Litlemersshe* 1501 *GillCt, v.* **lȳtel,
mersc**. LODDEN BRIDGE (FM), *Lydenebrigge* 1441, *Ledynbrug,
Ledenbrugge* 1475, *Ledyn brygge* 1501 all *GillCt, Laden*
[Bridge] 1774 Hutch[1], *Litton* [Bridge] 1791 Boswell, *Ledden
Bridge* 1811 OS, 'bridge over R. Lodden', *v.* **brycg**, RNs.
infra; Lydenham 1268 *Ass* (p) (*v.* **hamm** 'river-meadow') and
furlonge called Lydden 1609 *LRMB* also take their name from
this river. LONGBURY (a tumulus, *Long Barrow* 1811 OS),
LONGBURY HILL LANE, *Langborowe hill* 1609 *LRMB,
Langburie hill* 1626 *Poll, Langberry Hill, Longberry, (Lt)
Lon(g)berry Hill* 1839 *TA*, cf. *Langeborghsfurlang'* 1415
GillCt, v. **lang[1], beorg** 'mound, tumulus', RCHM 4 36
(where the barrow is referred to as Longbury or Slaughter
Barrow, cf. Slaughter Gate *infra*). LONGELM FM . LONGMOOR
FM, *Longmoor* 1811 OS, cf. *Longmore Meade* 1650 *ParlSurv,
Long Moor Md* 1839 *TA, v.* **lang[1], mōr** 'marshy ground',
mǣd. LOX LANE (COVERT & FM), *Lockslane* 1599 Hutch[3],
Lockes Lane Paddocke 1651 *EgCh, Lox Lane (Grd)* 1839 *TA*,
cf. Roger *Lok* 1327 *SR, meadowe in Lockes* 1609 *LRMB*; Lox
Lane Fm is named *Shearstock* 1811 OS, perhaps an error, cf.
Shearstock Fm & Ho *infra*. LYDFORD'S LANE. MALTHOUSE
FM, cf. *one maulte mill* 1609 *LRMB, Malthouse Gdn &
Orchd* 1829 *TA*. MAPPLEDORE HILL, *Mapeldore(s)hull(e)*
1411, *Map(er)dorehull'* 1438 *GillCt, Mapledore-, Mapowder
Hill* 1609 *LRMB, Mapperton Hill (Cmn & Inclosure)* 1839
TA, 'maple-tree hill', from **mapuldor, hyll**; the *TA* form
Mapperton may be an error but may represent a genuine
alternative from **mapuldor** and **tūn** 'farm, estate', cf. also
Mapeldorham 1244 *Ass* (p), *v.* **hamm** 'enclosure'. MARTINS
LANE, cf. *Martynschapell'* 1438, *via Regia in venella in parte
borial' de Martyns Elme* 1475 *GillCt, Martins Md* 1839 *TA*,
v. **chapel(e), elm**, cf. John *Martyn* c.1450 *AddRoll*, Richard

Marten 1664 HTax. MOOR LANE, cf. Richard *Attemoure, -de la More* 1292 *GillCt*, Walter *atte Moure* 1327 *SR*, Roger *atte More* 1397 *WRO, meadowe called the Moore* 1609 *LRMB, (Hr & Middle) Moor* 1839 *TA, v.* **mōr** 'marshy ground', **atte** 'at the'. MUDDOCK'S COPSE, *Muddockes* 1609 *LRMB, Muddicks Coppice, Gt. Muddicks* 1839 *TA*, probably a surname. NATIONS (RD), *Gt Nations, Nations Orchd & Plat* 1839 *TA*, probably a surname, *v.* **plat**². NORTHMOOR FM, *North Moor* 1839 *ib, v.* **mōr**. PEACEMARSH (FM, TERRACE & VILLA), *Pesemershe* 1535 *Ct, Peasemarsh* 1628 Hutch³, *Peace Marsh* 1811 OS, 'marshy land where peas are grown', *v.* **pise, peosu, mersc**, cf. *Lt Pea Grd* 1839 *TA*, Peasmarsh Sx 531. PLOT PLANT. POUND LANE, cf. *Pound Cl, Pound Shave* 1839 *TA, v.* **pund, sc(e)aga** 'a small wood', and cf. Osbert *de Pondfald'* 1292, *-de Puntfald'* 1306 *GillCt*, Peter *de Ponfald* 1327 *SR, Pounefold'* 1411 *GillCt*, from **pund-fald** 'pound, pinfold'. PRIMROSE CTGS. PURNS MILLS, *Burns Mill* 1811 OS, *Perns (Mill)* 1839 *TA*, cf. John *Perne*, Richard *Pearne* 1664 HTax. REDMOOR FM, *Redmoor* 1811 OS, *-Inclosure* 1839 *TA, v.* **rēad** 'red' or **hrēod** 'reed', **mōr**. RIDGE HILL FM, cf. *cottage called Rudgeley* 1609 *LRMB, v.* **hrycg, hyll, lēah**. RIDLEY PIT, *Redelegh* 1313 Cl, *Rydelegh'* 1317 *GillCt*, *Ridley furlonge, Redley-, Rudley Meade* 1609 *LRMB, Rudlie Meade* 1626, *Rydleyslade* 1629 *Poll, Ridly Pit Fd* 1839 *TA*, 'red or reedy clearing', *v.* **rēad** (wk.obl. *rēadan*) or **hrēod, lēah, furlang, mǣd, slæd, pytt**, cf. Redmoor Fm *supra*; several quarries are marked (6″) in the vicinity. RING GROVE, *(Bottom, Gt & Poor) Ringrove, Ringrove Plat* 1839 *TA, v.* **grāf(a), plat**², first el. uncertain. ROLLS BRIDGE FM, *Roolsbridge Md* 1839 *TA*, probably to be associated with *Rolfys* 1501 *GillCt*, from the surname *Rolf*; it might be noted that the tenant-in-chief of one of the manors of *Geling(e)ham* in 1086 DB was Turstin fitz *Rolf* ' (VCHDo **3** 90), the origin of the pers.n. being ON *Hrolfr*. ROPE FM, *v.* **rāp**. ROSE CTG. ST MARY THE VIRGIN CHURCH, cf. *æcclesiam de Gelingeham* 1086 DB, 'church of St Mary, *Gillingham'* 1330 Pat, Richard *atte Churche* 1356 *GillCt, Churchestrete* 1535 *Ct, the Churche Howse, Churche Meade, the Church Yeard* 1609 *LRMB, v.* **cirice, atte**, cf. foll. ST SIMON & ST JUDE CHURCH (Milton on Stour), built 1860, but the 'ancient free Chapel' at Milton

(Hutch[3] 3 627) may be that referred to as 'the (old) chapel of *Gilling(e)ham*' 1241, 1244, 1249 Lib; for other references to medieval chapels in Gillingham, *v.* Langham and Martins Lane *supra*, King's Court Palace in Motcombe par. *infra*. SATCHEL'S DOUBLE, cf. *Sachells Wells* 1839 *TA*; *Double* refers to two adjacent plantations. SHEARSTOCK FM & HO, *Sherestokys* 1501 *GillCt*, *3 closes called Sherstockes, ten' called Sheestockes* 1609 *LRMB*, probably a surname; Shearstock Fm is *Knap Fm* 1811 OS, *v.* **cnæpp**, cf. Lox Lane Fm *supra*. SLAIT BARN, cf. (*Gt, Hr, Lr, Lt & Middle*) *Slait* 1839 *TA, v.* **slæget** ' a sheep pasture'. SLAUGHTER GATE (site of), 1774 Hutch[1], (*pasture by*) *Slaunders Yate* 1609 *LRMB, Claundersgate* (sic) 1624, *Slanders Gate* 1642 Hutch[3], cf. *Slanders Leigh* 1686 *SxAS, -Leaze* 1839 *TA, v.* **geat** 'gate', **læs** 'pasture', *Sla(u)nder* being presumably a surname; the modern form is the result of the popular association of this place (near Longbury *supra*) with the slaughter of the Danes at the battle of Penselwood So in 1016, *v.* Hutch[3] 3 615 where it is also pointed out that 'it is still [1869] often called Slandersgate'. SLAUGHTERGATE FM, 1811 OS, named from prec. SLODBROOK FM & LANE, named from Slod Brook, *v.* RNs. *infra*. SPICKETT'S BRIDGE, CTG & FM, *Spekett's* [Bridge] 1791 Boswell, presumably a surname. SPRINGFIELD, cf. (*Gt & Lt*) *Spring Cl, Spring Grd* 1839 *TA, v.* **spring** 'well-spring' or 'young wood'. STANDPITTS LANE, *la Stonputtes* 1415 *GillCt, Stanpits* 1839 *TA*, 'stone pits', *v.* **stān**, **pytt**; quarries are marked nearby (6″). STANLEY (1902 6″), apparently an error for Sandley *supra*. STARBOURN HILL CMN (lost), 1811 OS, on the Do-W county bdy, cf. the f.n. Star Mead PN W 484. TOWN MILLS, *Towne Mills* 1664 HTax; other references to mills here or elsewhere in Gillingham include Jacob *de molendino* 1327 *SR*, Alice *atte Mulle* 1332 SR, *one water corne mill, one fullinge mill, one maulte mill, Mill Crofte, Millcrosse furlonge, Mill Meade, Millwaye* 1609 *LRMB, Mill Head, Mill Md, Mill Silk Ho & Gdn* 1839 *TA, v.* **myln**, **atte**; on the manufacture of silk in Gillingham, *v.* Hutch[3] 3 615. VICARAGE, *Mansione vicarii ecclesie* 1411 *GillCt, the Vicearage Howse* 1609 *LRMB*. WATERLOO FM, in the SE corner of the par., no doubt a transferred name commemorating the battle. WAVERING LANE, possibly a modern rationalization (appropriate in describing the lane's somewhat meandering course) of *Wynelynglane(forlang)* (probably for *Wyuel-*) 1313 Cl, the first part of which is from OE **wifel** 'beetle', or an OE pers.n. *Wifel* (cf. also *Wyuelestenement* 1415 *GillCt*), and **-ing**[2], hence 'beetle infested place' or 'Wifel's place', cf. *Wifelinge* 949 (m10) BCS 880 (K, *v.* KPN 97, 283, EPN **1** 289). WESTBROOK FM & RD, *Westbrooke (feilde)* 1609 *LRMB*, named from West Brook, a small tributary of R. Stour, *v.* RNs. *infra.* WHEAT CLOSE, *Wheat Cl (Coppice)* 1839 *TA*. WHISTLEY COPPICE & FM, *Westley* 1811 OS, *Whistley Fm* 1869 Hutch[3], *v.* **west**, **lēah**. WHITE HILL CMN, *Whitehill Cmn* 1811 OS, named from White Hill W 181. WITHY SLADE COVERT, *furlonge called Wythers slade* 1609 *LRMB*, *Withey Slade* 1839 *TA*, *v.* **slæd** 'valley'; for the surname, associated in the modern forms with **wīðig** 'willow', *v.* Withies Fm in Motcombe par. *infra.* WOODHOUSE CROSS, *Woodhowse Crosse, Woodhowse feilde (before the Crosse)* 1609 *LRMB, Wood Ho Cross* 1811 OS, *Woodescross Grd* 1839 *TA*, 'house in the wood', or 'house made of wood', *v.* **wudu, hūs**, with **cros** 'a cross'. WOOLHOUSE FM, *domum q' vocatur le Wlhus, -qui dicitur Wldhus, de la Wldhuse* (p) all 1292 *GillCt*, cf. *Woolhouse Md* 1842 *TA* (W Stour), near Springfield *supra* and by R. Stour, first el. **wyll(a)** 'spring, stream', cf. the f.ns. Woolfield(s), Woollens *infra*, or **wull** 'wool', cf. *le Wollehouse* in Poole **2** 43.

FIELD-NAMES

The undated forms are 1839 *TA* 91; for those fields in Gillingham *TA* but now in Bourton, *v.* under Bourton par. *supra.* Spellings dated Hy 3 (14) are Cerne, 1234, 1236, 1240, 1252, 1253, 1289, 1313, 1369, 1402[1] Cl, 1244, 1268, 1280, 1288 *Ass*, 1247 (1270), 1258, 1270, 1333, 1335, 1338, 1343, 1362, 1368, 1373, 1374, Eliz *For*, 1275 RH, 1275[1] Roscoe, 1275[2], 1299, 1316, 1318, 1382, 1385, 1402[2], 1466 Pat, 1278 Misc, 1285 FA, 1300[2], 1403, 1431, 1525, 1526, 1568, 1591, 1599, 1618, 1625, 1627, 1629 Hutch[3], 1317[1] FF, 1327 *SR*, 1332 SR, 1338–40 Glast, 1366 *AD*, 1410 *Bodl*, c.1450 *AddRoll*, 1501[2], 1504 Ipm, 1512 *Pars*, 1519, 1535 *Ct*, 1541, 1552, 1557, 1570 *Prideaux*, 1586 *Comm*, 1609 *LRMB*, 1617, 1626, 1629[2], 1656, 1668 *Poll*, 1639 *EgCh*, 1650 *ParlSurv*, 1664 HTax, 1686 *SxAS*, 1687, 1700 *Weld*[1], 1774 Hutch[1], 1791 Boswell, 1884 *TA* alt.app., and the rest *GillCt*.

(a) Acre (Grd) (*parcell . . . called the Acre* 1609, *v.* **æcer**); Adam's Fd; Alford's Plat (cf. Thomas *Alford* 1664); Alfreds Cl; Gt & Lt Allotment, Allotment Fair Grd, (Gt) Allotment Lane; Gt & Lt Ames, Ames's Flg; Arable Grd & Pce; Aricks Dry Cl; (Hanging & Lt) Axtons; Balls Grd; (Hr & Lr) Ban(n)isters; Bantoms; Hr & Lr Barge (*v.* **barge** 'a barge', perhaps with reference to a ferry, *v.* PN Brk 538, 850); Barley Cl; Gt Barn Castle, Barn Cl & Grd (cf. *Barne Haies* 1609, *the close above the barne, -below the barne* 1686, *v.* **bere-ærn, castel(l), (ge)hæg**); Barnetts; Gt, Lt & Upr Barrow (cf. *Barweȝete* 1313, Nicholas *atte Barwe* 1415, *v.* **beorg** 'hill, tumulus', **geat** 'gate', **atte** 'at the'); Gt & Lt Barton Hill, Gt & Lt Bare Barton (*Barton Hill* 1609, named from 'the barton' 1299 *et freq* to 1466, *Bertona(m de Gyllingham*) 1316, 1366, 'the (farm of) *Berton*' 1318, 1382, *Bartone* 1373 (p), *v.* **bere-tūn, bær-tūn** 'corn farm, outlying grange', **hyll, bær**[1] 'bare, without vegetation'); Becks Cl & Pdk; Bells Grd; Bensfurlong (cf. *Bennetts Furlonge* 1609, from the pers.n. or surname *Benn(et)*); Billands (Rannetts); Billings (Md); Bishops (*Buysshopes* 1501, *close called-*, *pasture called Bu(i)shopps* 1609, cf. John-, Robert *Biss(c)hop* 1327, Robert *Buishopp* 1609); Blackdown (*v.* **blæc, dūn**); Blackfords (or Malsters Fd) (cf. Malthouse Fm *supra*); Blacklands; Gt & Lt Blind Md (*Blinde Mead* 1609, *v.* **blind, mǣd**, cf. foll.); Blindwell (*loco voc' Blyndewell* 1519, *v.* **blind** 'hidden by vegetation', **well(a)** 'spring, stream'); Blue Coat School Grd; Bottles Corner Orchd; Bottom Md (cf. Peter-1270, Adam *de la Botme* 1292, Geoffrey- 1298, John *atte Botme* 1332, *Butme* (a close) 1411, 1475, *v.* **botm** 'valley bottom', **atte**); (Lr & Yonder Bourton Cl (named from Bourton par. *supra*); Bowdens (cf. Richard *Bouedene* 1292, Thomas *Bowden* 1664); Bowers Md (cf. Christopher *Bower* 1664); Bowles's Orchd (cf. William *Bowles* 1609); Brambly (Flg) ((*la*) *Bremelhey(e)* 1275, 1292, 1306, *atte Bremelhey(e)* 1292, 1298, *-heygh'* 1306 all (p), 'bramble enclosure', *v.* **brēmel, brembel, (ge)hæg, atte**); Brickells Grd (cf. Brickells Cliff in Motcombe par. *infra*); Brickly (cf. *Brickmore* 1609, probably alluding to brickmaking, *v.* **brick, mōr**, cf. Brick & Tile Works (6″)); Broad Croft (*Broade Crofte* 1609); Broad Flg ((*la*) *Brodeforlang, -forlong* 1313, *v.* **brād, furlang**); Broadmaish [Bridge] 1791 (sic, probably for *-marsh*); Broad Md (*Broade Meade* 1609); Broadway Grd; Broddens (Md & Orchd) (cf. John *Brodden* 1664); Brooks Door; Browns Grd & Lane (*Brouneslane* 1362, *Brownes lane* 1700, cf. Edmund *Browne* 1609, *v.* **lane**); Bulket; Bulls Hill Orchd, Bulls Still (*one parrocke called Bulls* 1609, cf. *Boleslane* 1475, Margaret *Bulle* 1541); Burltons Grd (cf. Roger *Burleton* 1664); Burn Bake (*v.* **burnbake**); Bushes; Bush Grd; Butts (Fd & Grd), Butts 4 Acres (cf. *Butthaies* 1609, *v.* **butt**[2] or **butte, (ge)hæg**); Calves Cl (1609); Cards Acre & Lane, Card's Grd (cf. *Carr's-lane* (sic) 1627, John *Card* 1664); Carmins Orchd; Carpenters Md; Cherry Orchd; Chubbs Md; Churches Md; Clarks Altmt & Grd (*Clerkyslond'* 1501, *v.* **land**, cf. Robert *clericus* 1327, Thomas *Clarke* 1664); Clay Lds; Clements (Orchds) (cf. Alice- 1327, John *Clement* 1664); Clift (Md), Clifts (Croft) (cf. *messuage called Clyflowse or Clyfhows* 1504, *Cliffe Howse Crofte* 1609, *v.* **clif, hūs, croft**, cf. Eccliffe *supra*); Close; Clover Grd (cf. *the Clover Close* 1686, *v.* **clāfre**); Coaks Fd (cf. William *Cok* 1258); Coleshard (*v.* **sceard** 'cleft, gap', first el. possibly **col**[1] 'coal, charcoal', cf. *Coale haies* 1609, *v.* **(ge)hæg**); Colliers Cl & Md (cf. prec.); Colts Grd; Common (Inclosure) (*the common* Eliz); Coneygar(s) (*v.* **coninger** 'rabbit-warren', cf. 'the warren of the manor and lordship of *Gillyngham'* 1369); Little Content (probably a litotes for 'discontent', hence a derogatory name for poor ground); Cooks Hays 1884 (*v.* **(ge)hæg**); Coppice (Cl & Grd), Copse Md (cf. *the copes* 1535, *v.* **copis**); Coroner's Plot; Corn Fd & Grd (cf. *Corne Close* 1609); Courtnys Pce (cf. George *Courtney* 1664); Cowleaze; Cox's Md & Pce (cf. Laurence *Cockes* 1609, *Cox his house* 1664); Crab's Cl; Croadcotts 1774 (probably a surname); Crooked Md (-*Meade* 1609); Cupids; Cutsblade or Long Md (possibly to be associated with *quarries at Cutterbeds* 1627, perhaps an early instance of the mining term *cutter* 'a crack or fissure intersecting the bedding or lines of stratification' (from 1756 NED), with *bed* in the geological sense 'layer or stratum' (from 1616 ib)); Dam (*v.* **damm**); Dark Lake (probably an altered form of Dock Lake *infra*); Davidges (cf. Robert *Dauage* 1332 (W Stour)); Dock Lake (*Docklake* 1609, *v.* **docce** 'dock, water-lily', **lacu** 'stream'); Doctors Plat (*v.* **plat**[2]); Lt Doggrells Fd & Grd (cf. *Dogerelleshey(e)* 1501, *Doggrel's-lane* 1627, from a surname and **(ge)hæg** 'enclosure', **lane**); Doubts (*Doutescroft* 1438, *doutes* 1501, from the ME surname *Dout(e)* (common in 1332 SR) and **croft**); Doves or Ham Mead Cmn (*v.* Ham Cmn *supra*); (Lt) Dowding(s) (cf. Robert *Dowdinge* 1609, *Dowdings house* 1664); Dowfith 1884; Dry Cl (*Drye Close* 1609); Dry Lays (*v.* **lǣs**) & Grd; Ducox (*close called Durcockes* 1609); Dummicks; Durns Ho & Gdn; Hr, Lr & Middle Dun Willow (*v.* **dunn**); Eddicks Hill; 8 Acres (*the close contegning eight acres at Sticklands Hill* 1686, *v. infra*); 18 Acres; 11 Acres or Gt Ground; Ellis's Md (cf. Alice *Elys* 1327 (Silton), *E(y)lislond'* 1441, *Eyleslonde* 1475, John *Ellis* 1664, *v.* **land**); Elmers; Farthings Pdk (cf. Juliana *Ferthyng* 1327, *in domo Ricardi ferthyng'* 1374); Feoffee Grd; 15 Acres; First Fd; 5 Acres and Hill; Flax Grd (cf. *Flexham*, (two) *Flexheyes* 1313, *v.* **fleax, hamm, (ge)hæg**); 4 Acres (Common Md); 14 Acres; Freaks Coppice & Md; Hr & Lt Freary, Gt Freary Barton and Barn (*le Frary* 1313, from ME **frary** 'a brotherhood, a fraternity', cf. the Dominican friars mentioned at Gillingham in 1267 VCHDo 2 92); Hr & Lr French, Hr French Grd (cf. *the further-, the greate french close* 1686, *v.* **Frensche** 'French', although the allusion is not clear); Yonder French Grass (*v.* **french grass**); Frys; Furnbrook Grd (cf. Fernbrook Fm in Motcombe par. *infra*); (Gt & Lt) Furzy Grd (cf. *the two furze closes att Sticklands Hill* 1686, *v. infra*); Gallis's; Garlins; Gas Ho; Gassens (*le Gasten'* 1501, *v.* **gærs-tūn**); Gatehouse's Cl (cf. John *Gethous(s)e* 1535, Motcombe f.ns. *infra*); (Lt) Godwins Grd; Goors (cf. Hugh *de la gore* 1268, *v.* **gāra**); Grace Hays (*v.* **(ge)hæg**); Great Cl, Grd, Hays & Plat (*v.* **(ge)hæg, plat**[2]); Green Hays (*Grenehay(e)* 1475, 1557, *v.* **grēne**[1], **(ge)hæg**); Green Md (*Greene Meade* 1609); Greens Cl (cf. John *atte grene* 1292, Walter *Atte greyne* 1306, William *Greene* 1609); Grogers Md; Grove (Md), Lt Groves (*close called the Grove* 1609, *v.* **grāf(a)**); Haines (*clauso*

Ancelini Haym 1362, *Haymesclos, Haymestret* 1415, *East Hayne* 1431, *lytill Haymes* 1501, *Haymes's-lane* 1627, *East Haimes, East-, West Haymes* 1700, cf. Clement *Heym* 1258, *-Haym* 1270, William *Hayn, -Haym* 1317[1], Haines Fm in Motcombe par. *infra, v.* **clos(e), strǣt, lȳtel**); Halls (*tenement* . . . *sometymes Halles* 1609); Halves (cf. *Harves Acre* 1609); Ham(s) (*v.* **hamm**); Hancocks (*Hancockes* 1609); Hanging (Land & Lane) (*Hanggingge-* 1317, *la Hangynglond(e)* 1438, *v.* **hangende, land**); Hangings (Hill) (*v.* **hanging** 'steep slope'); Hannams Grd (cf. *Hammond(e) crafte* 1541, William *Hamond* 1333, Morgan *Hamond*, Thomas *Hamman* 1664, *v.* **croft**); Harrisons; Harvest (Slait) (*v.* **slæget**, cf. the form cited under Halves *supra*); Hatch Md (cf. Robert *de Hacche* 1300, *-atte Hacche* 1327, and John *de Haccheghyte* 1306, William *attehaccheyate* 1356, *v.* **hæcc** 'hatch, half-gate', **hæcc-geat** 'hatch-gate, wicket'; in 1391 Pat there is an order to make a *flodehache* (i.e. 'a floodgate, a sluice') between the forest of Gillingham and the park of Conrish W); Hays Bridge (cf. Robert *Hayes* 1664); Gt & Lt Hazel Hole (*Haselholt(e)* 1270, 1292, 1327 all (p), 1568 (*-pound*), 1609 (*West-*), *-houlte* 1292 (p), *Hasi(l)holts* 1687, 1700, 'hazel wood', *v.* **hæsel, holt**); (Lt) Heron, Herring (cf. Robert *de la Hurne* 1270, Richard *Atte Herne* 1306, *la Hurnycroft, Hurnelane* 1313, *Herne-, Hurnelane* 1438, *Hurnynglane* 1475, *Hearne Lane Bridge* 1609, *v.* **hyrne** 'angle, corner, projection of land', **atte, croft, lane**); Herridges Cl; Hibberts; Higher Close Orchd; Higher Fd & Grd; Hill (cf. Henry *de la Hylle* 1244, *v.* **hyll**, cf. foll.); Gt & Lt Hills (cf. Phillip *Hyll* 1535, *Thomas Hills Orchard Close* 1656, Hulls Grd *infra*); Hilly Grd; Hindon Lane (leading to Hindon W); Hinds Grd; Hinston Md; Home Fd, Flg, Grd & Marsh; Home Md (or Pdk); Lt Horse Grd, Horse House Grd, Horse Hills (cf. *Horshale* 1313, *v.* **hors, h(e)alh**); Part of Horsingtons (cf. *boscum de Horssington, qui est in com' Wiltes'* 1300[2], *Horsyngton* 1501[2], *Hors(s)yngton'* . . . *infra Gyllyngham* 1512, ground . . . *called Horsingtone, in the county of Wilts, which Horsingtone of old time was a wood, which is now wasted and destroyed* 1568, *Horsington in Gillingham* 1591; this place is mentioned in the bounds of the forest of Gillingham (Hutch[3] 3 620–1, 656) which here followed the county bdy, cf. Horsington Lane in Mere W 179 where the name is associated with Henry *de Horsington* (member for Mere in 1305) and is thought to be probably of manorial origin. It may however be an independent name of the same origin as Horsington So ('farm of the grooms' from **hors-þegn** and **tūn**) or as Horsington Li ('farm called after Horsa', from the OE pers.n. *Horsa* and **-ingtūn**)); Hounslow (perhaps analogous with Hounslow Mx 26, 'hound's tumulus', *v.* **hund, hlāw**, cf. *hundeshlæwe* Brk 686); House or Picked Cl (*v.* **pīcede** 'pointed'); Gt & Lt Howard; Gt & Lt Hulks (*le Hulk'* 1300, *Holk'* 1356, *v.* **hulc** 'a shed, a hut'); Hulls Grd (cf. Elias *de Hull(e)* 1285, 1292, 1295, cf. Hill(s) *supra*); Hundred Acres (Orchd) (cf. *Hundred Acres Meade* 1650, an ironical name for a small field); Hungry Hill (a derogatory name for poor ground, *v.* **hungrig**); Hunts; Hurdling Lane Grd; Inclosure; In Lands (*v.* **inland**); Inner Grd; Innox (*close called Inoakes* 1609, *v.* **inhoke**); Ipshill Cl; Hr & Yonder Jubilee (probably named to commemorate the fiftieth anniversary

of the accession of George 3 (reigned 1760-1820)); Jukes's Cl & Grd (cf.
John *Jukes* 1664); Kimbrys Md (possibly to be associated with *Kyngesbury*
1501, *v.* **cyning** 'king', **burh** (dat.sg. *byrig*) 'fortified place, manor', cf.
King's Court Palace in Motcombe par. *infra*); Kinging Croft; Kington
Grd and Coppice (*ten' voc' Kyngton'* (. . . *reddidit in manus domini Regis*)
1381, *Kyngtons*(*hayes*) 1501, probably named from their proximity to
Kington M. par. *infra, v.* **(ge)hæg**); Lains Md (cf. *Queenes Lane* 1609,
Queene Laines als *Queene Lines* als the *Laynes* 1654 *EgCh, v.* **leyne**);
Lands; Lane (cf. Edith *in le lane* 1327, *v.* **lane**); Lankeys (*langhey* 1501,
Longe Haies als. *Copie Hayes* 1609, *v.* **lang¹, copis, (ge)hæg**); Ledgey
Grd; Leg (*v.* **leg**); Leigh (*close called Ley* 1609, *v.* **lēah**); (Late James)
Lights (cf. Helen *Lighte* 1609); Lillys; Linches (cf. Richard *Attelinche*
1292, *v.* **atte, hlinc**); Little Cl; Little Fd (*Litelfeld'* in *Buggeleye* 1356,
paruum campum de Bogele 1381, *Little Feild* 1609, *v.* **lȳtel, feld**, cf. Bugley
supra); Little Gdn & Grd; Little Hays (*v.* **(ge)hæg**); Little Lds; Little Md
(*Litle Meade* 1650); Little Orchd & Plat (*v.* **plat²**); Loading Croft; Lodge
Farm Grd (*messuage called . . . Lodge* 1650); Long Cl & Croft; Longford
(*Langeforde* 1609, *v.* **lang¹, ford**); Long Grd (Md); Long Lds; Long Md
(*Longe Meade* 1609); Long Orchd; Lower Fd & Grd; The Lower Mdw;
Loxtons (*Lockstones* 1599, *Loxens* 1609, cf. Lox Lane *supra*); (Gt, Lt &
Yonder) Madjeston Fd (*Madgeston feilde* 1609), Madjeston Green (from
Madjeston *supra*); Malm Grd (*v.* **m(e)alm** 'sandy or chalky soil'); Gt
Manors, Manors Orchd (*Manners* (*Meade*), *Mannors* als. *Boridge* 1609,
Manners 1700, cf. Henry *de Maners* 1327, 1335, *v.* **mǣd**, Bowridge Hill
supra); Mans Md (cf. Thomas *le Man* 1327, 1332); Marl Leaze, Marlpit
(Grd) (cf. *Marlynglane* 1438, *v.* **marle, marling, lǣs, pytt, lane**);
Marsh's Md (cf. Richard *de Marisco* 1292, *-atte Mersche* 1307, *v.* **atte,
mersc**); Matthews Pdk (cf. *Matheas Strete* 1501, *William Mathewes house*
1664, Joan *Mathias* 1327, John *Mathew* 1535, *v.* **strǣt**); Lr May Grd;
Mead, Meadow Grd (cf. *Mead Close* 1609, *v.* **mǣd**); Meshams; Middle Fd
& Grd; Middle Md (*the Middle Meade* 1609); Millards, (Lt) Mil(l)wards
(K)nap (cf. John *Muleward* 1327, *v.* **cnæpp**); Milton Down, Fd &
Inclosure (named from Milton on Stour *supra*); Mitchells (Fd) (cf.
Nicholas *Michell* 1664); Mogers (cf. William *Moger* 1609); Mullens's (cf.
John *Mullens* 1609); Neath Way (probably '(land) beneath the way', *v.*
beneoðan, weg); New Cl & Md; Newmans Ho (cf. Roger *le Nieuman*
1327); Newtons Orchd; (Short) 9 Acres (*Nine Acres* 1609); (Long) North
Cl; North Orchd; Lr & Middle Notley (probably 'nut wood', from **hnutu**
and **lēah**);Nursery; Oak Cl (cf. Nicholas *atte Noke* 1441, 'at the oak-tree',
v. **atte(n), āc**); Old Hays (*the old Hayes* 1568, *Olde Hayes* 1609, *v.* **ald,
(ge)hæg**); Old Man's Md and Grd; (Hr, Lr, Old & Young) Orchard,
Orchard Grd, Inclosure & Md (cf. Peter *Attorchard* 1327, *Orchard Meade*
1609, *v.* **atte, orceard**); Orchards (possibly a surname, cf. prec.); Paddock
(Orchd); Gt Pale Md (from **pale** 'a fence', with reference to the former
deer park of Gillingham, *v.* Park Fm *supra*, Palemead Coppice in
Motcombe par. *infra*, cf. foll.); Pales Hill (*meadowe at Pales* 1609, from a
surname or the same el. as prec.); E & W Paradise (*v.* **paradis**); Parfitt-,

Parpit Row (perhaps corrupt spellings for *Harpit, v.* Harpitts Fm in
Kington M. par. *infra, v.* **rāw**); Parish Long Grd (cf. *Parishe Landes*
1609); Parkers (Long Grd) (cf. William *Parkere* 1327 (Silton)); Parsons,
Parson's Grove (*Personesgroue* 1411, *v.* **persone, grāf(a)**); Lt Pea Grd (cf.
Peacemarsh *supra*); (Three Corner Grd or) Peak (*v.* **pēac**); Gt & Lt
Penning (Coppice) (*parrocke of pasture called Pennynge* . . . [MS torn]
1609, *v.* **penning** 'pen, enclosure', cf. Pound Lane *supra*); Pennys Hay (cf.
Adam *Peny* 1327, *v.* **(ge)hæg**); Perches (Gdn & Orchd) (*close called
Purchase* 1609, perhaps ModE *purchase* 'that which is bought, etc', or the
surname *Purchase*); Phripps Grd; Pierce Hays (*Peirse haies als. Purley haies*
1609, cf. John *Peers* 1557, *v.* **(ge)hæg**; *Purley* may be analogous with
Purley Brk 215 or Purley Sr 54); Pimperne (Leaze) (this place on the
county bdy occurs in the bounds of the forest of Gillingham as *Pinperleghe*
Hy 3 (14) Cerne, *Pymper-, Pimperleygh* 1300 Hutch[3] 3 620, 656,
Pymperleygh hedge 1568 ib 3 621, also as *Pimperleigh* 1364 ib 3 657; it is
discussed in PN W 180 under PIMPERLEAZE RD (6") in Mere par., where it
is pointed out that the first part of the name may be analogous with
Pimperne par. 2 110, *v.* **lēah** 'wood, clearing'); Pinhorns Plat (*v.* **plat²**); Pit
Cl & Md; Pitmans (Md) (cf. Robert *Pitman* 1664); Pits Orchd; Plat(s), Plat
Orchd (*v.* **plat²**); Pool Md (*Poulmede* 1317², *Pullmead, Poole Meade* 1609,
v. **pōl, mǣd**); Poor Cl, Grd & Plat (*v.* **plat²**); Poplar Md; Priest('s)
(*Prestes* 1609, cf. *Prestersh', -hersche* 1317², *-erssh'* 1441, *Presteles* 1501,
Presthaies 1609, *v.* **prēost** 'priest', **ersc** 'ploughed field', **lǣs** 'pasture',
(ge)hæg 'enclosure', cf. Parsons *supra*); Quar (Cl & Slait) (*the Quarr Close*
1686, cf. *in quadam quarrera* 1288, *v.* **quarre, slæget** 'sheep pasture');
Ralph Ditch & Hays (cf. *Rawleslond'* 1501, John *Raul* 1327, Walter *Raules*
1332, *v.* **land, dīc, (ge)hæg**); Rames Hays (cf. John *Raymus* 1327, *v.*
(ge)hæg); (Gt, Hr & Lt) Ramslade (*Ramslade(s)* 1609, 1686, perhaps from
slæd 'valley' with **ramm** 'ram', **hramsa** 'wild garlic' or **hræfn** 'raven');
Ransoms; Raygrass, Ray Grass (perhaps **rye-grass**, or from **eegrass**
'aftermath', with initial *R-* due to metanalysis of preceding *Higher,
Lower,* etc, but cf. foll.); Ray Mdw (possibly to be associated with *parrocke
called Itteriye* 1609, which may represent ME *atter iye* '(place) at the
island', *v.* **atter, ī(e)g**, cf. Ray Brk 55, Rye Sx 536); (Fan) Read(') Grd (cf.
Reedes house, John *Reed* 1664; *Fan* is for *Fanny,* a pet-form of *Frances*);
(Hither & Yonder) Red Fd; Reeves; Ridgey Grd (perhaps to be associated
with *viam que vocatur Rigwey* 1300, *v.* **hrycg-weg**); Rings; Broad Robin
(*Grete Robyn* 1501, *one howse called Great Robins and one close meadow
called Great Robins* 1609, presumably the pers.n. or surname *Robin,* with
grēat 'great'); Rough Grd; Running Md (*Runninge Meade* 1609, *v.*
running 'pasturage, stream'); Rush Grd; Gt Rushy Grd, Rushy Md;
Ryalls (cf. Ryal's Plant. in Motcombe par. *infra*); Rye Cl; Lt Sands;
Sangers (Cl) (cf. John *Sanger* 1664); Scammels (cf. William *Scamel* 1258,
Thomas *Scammell* 1664); School Grd; Corn Scully, Scully Md (*Skullie*
1609, perhaps to be associated with *le Shull(e)* 1438; this may represent OE
sciell 'shell' and the form *Skullie* may represent an adjectival form, cf. the
f.ns. *Shill, Stonschulye* 1 230, Do dial. *skilly* 'scaly' (Barnes 100)); (Lt)

Seniors (cf. Thomas *Signior* 1609); 7 & 17 Acres; Sextons (*Sextons Meadowe* 1609); Sheeps Croft; Gt Sheeps Head; Sheppards Altmt (cf. Edward *Shepperd* 1535); Sherborne School Altmt & Grd; Sherrys; Short Croft; Simes (cf. William *Symes* 1664); 6 Acres; 6 Small Fds; Skydown; Slade (cf. *Slades* 1609, *v.* **slæd** 'valley', or a surname); (Hither) Smeath Down (cf. Smiths Md *infra*); Hr & Lr Smiths Grd; Smiths Md (*Smethemede* 1501, *Smythe-, Smithmeade* 1609, *v.* **mǣd**, first el. probably **smēðe**[1] 'smooth, level' as in Smeath Down *supra*, later taken to be the surname *Smith*, cf. prec.); Snatch Md 1884; Snooks Grd (Bottom) (cf. Christopher *Snooke* 1609); Sparrow Md, Sparrows (cf. John *Sparrow* 1664); Spear Acre Md and Coppice (*v.* **spear**); Square Cl & Grd; Steeven's Grd (cf. John *Stephens* 1664); Sticklands Hill (1686; *Stickland* may be a reduced form of *Stikelweyeslane* 1415, also called *Stikelwey* 1441, *Stykel-, Stekelway* 1475, '(lane at) the steep way', from **sticol, weg, lane**, cf. Winterborne Stickland par. 2 131; *Stykelinch* 1306 probably contains the same first el. with **hlinc** 'ridge'); Stile Stones (cf. Walter *atte Style* 1441, *v.* **atte, stigel**); Stipends Pdk; Stoney Plat (*v.* **plat**[2]); Stour Md (by R. Stour); Straw Grd; Strings (*v.* **string(s)**); Strop (a variant of **strap**); Stub Cl (*Stubb Close Meade* 1650, *v.* **stubb** 'tree-stump', cf. *Stubbs* 1609 which may however contain the surname *Stubb(s)*); Summer Grd & Md, (Lt) Summerleaze (cf. *Somer Haye* 1609, all denoting land used in summer, *v.* **sumor, lǣs, (ge)hæg**); Suttons Cl; Sweethams; Sweetmans Md; Swyers Md; Temples Altmt (cf. Richard *Temple* 1609); 10 Acres; 10 Pound Md (presumably an allusion to the price paid); (Short) 13 Acres; 30 Acres; Thistly Cl; Thistle Grd; 3 Acres; Three Corner Cl; Three Corner Grd (or Peak) (*v. supra*); Three Corner Plat (*v.* **plat**[2]); Tineland and Paddock; Tinneys; Tiphooks 1884; Tomlins (*Tomalins* 1609, the surname *Tomlin*); Toogoods Cl; Topps Md; Hr & Lr Trills (*Grete Tryllys, Litill Trilles* 1501, *Great-, Little Trills* 1609, cf. *Trilleheyes*, Richard *Trille* 1438, *v.* **grēat, lȳtel, (ge)hæg**; the surname is from Trill Fm in Beer Hackett par. *infra* or from one of the other places with this name, cf. Trill Bridge in Fifehead M. par. *supra*); Trim Trams (*furlonge called Trim tram* 1609, ModE **trim-tram** 'a personal ornament of little value' (from 1523 NED), 'a lich-gate, a kissing-gate' (from 1842 ib)); Turners; (Short) 12 Acres (*la Twelfacres* 1415, *v.* **twelf, æcer**); 20 Acres; 2 Acres; Upper Grd; Vanners Pdk (cf. John *Vanner* 1552); Gt Varty (*v.* **forð-īeg** 'island in marshland'); Gt Vern Goose (sic) (perhaps for *-Gores*, in which case the name is analogous with *Ferngore* in Motcombe par. *infra*); Gt & Lt Vining (*vivinge* (for *vininge*) 1247 (1270), John *de la Viningge, -yngge, -de la Vyninge, -atte Vinynge* 1292, Thomas *Atthe Vynygge* (sic) 1295, *-atte Vinigge* (sic) 1300, William *atte vynyng* 1343, 2 closes called *Broade Vinninge als. Broade Vynings* 1609, *v.* **fīning** 'place where wood is heaped, a clearing', **atte**, cf. Fyning Sx 39); Gt & Lt Wager (Md) (*Watgar('*) 1275 (p), 1275[1], *-ger* 1313, *la Whaggers* 1415, *Whagger* Eliz, *Wadger* 1609, 2 closes called the *Whaggers* 1650, *Wagger Meade acre* 1700, 'gore of land where wheat is grown', from **hwǣte** and **gāra**); Water Md (cf. *Watersladesmede* 1415, *-sladys-* 1501, Walter *Atte Watere* 1306, *Water Pitt* 1609, *v.* **wæter,**

slæd, mǣd, atte, pytt); (Hither) Way Grd; Well Grd (cf. John *Attewell'* 1292, Richard *atte Wille* 1415, *Well Close* 1609, *v.* **atte, well(a), wiell(a)** 'spring, stream', cf. Woolfield(s), Woollens *infra*); (Gt & Hr) West Batch (*West Batche* 1609, *v.* **batch**); West Md; Whitelys Pce; (Gt) Whites Grd, Whites (Md) (cf. Henry *White* 1609); Williams (cf. *close called Ricarde Williams* 1609, *Williams house* 1664); (Gt) Willis('s) (cf. Susan *Willis* 1664); (Hr & Lr) Willow Bed, Willow Bed (Coppice & Md) (cf. *Wythymoureshey* 1441, *Withiemore Hedge, withiebedd* 1609, *v.* **wīðig** 'willow', **mōr, hege** 'hedge' or **(ge)hæg** 'enclosure', **hecg, bedd**); Wimples; Winding Ld; (Gt & Lt) Witch (*v.* Witch Lane in E Stour par. *infra*); Hr, Lr & Middle Wood Bridge; Woodland Fd (*Woodlande* 1609, *Woodland als. Hillgroves Lodge* 1625, cf. John *de la Wodeland'* 1268, *v.* **wudu**, land; *Hillgrove* is probably a p.n., cf. *The Hilgrove* 1627, *v.* **hyll, grāf(a)**)); Woodwater Lane (from Woodwater Fm in Motcombe par. *infra*); Woolfield(s) ((*la*) *Wolfeld, Wolfeldforlang* 1313, *Wulfeld'* 1501, *Woole feild* 1609, *v.* **well(a), wyll(a)** 'spring, stream', **feld**, cf. Well Grd *supra* and foll.); Hr, Lr & Lt Woollens, Woollen(s) Lane, Clarks Grd or Lt Woollens Lane, Woollens Md (*close called Woolland* 1609, *Woollands gate* 1617, *Wollande, Wollandes gate* 1626, from **land** with **wōh** 'crooked' or the same first el. as prec.); Worthy (*v.* **worðig** 'enclosure'); Yarnbarton (*v.* **gearn, bere-tūn**); Yonder Fd; Zoands (probably to be associated with *Soneslane* 1475, *Soynnes* 1501, from the surname *Sone* and **lane**).

(b) Abell stone (*close at-*) 1609; *Allen's pit* 1627; *Auereyescot'* 1411 (the surname *Averay, v.* **cot**); *Axtel(l)* 1525, 1526; *Back Lane* 1609; *the Baleys Walke* Eliz, *a surrounding waste or common called the Bailiff's-walk* 1627 (with reference to the bailiff of the forest of Gillingham, cf. *baillivo de Gillingeham* 1234, 1240, *v.* **walk** 'division of a forest', Forest Fm & Side *supra*); *Barkers Hill* 1609; *Bealings house* 1664 (cf. Thomas *Bealing ib);* *Belbuglies* 1609 (perhaps 'Bell (a pet-form of Isobel) Bugly's (ground)', the surname from Bugley *supra*); *le Benche* 1317[2] (*v.* **benc**); *Berlond* 1441 (*v.* **bere** 'barley', **land**); *Bettescoumbe* 1410 (perhaps identical in origin with Bettiscombe par. *infra*); *Blakehey* 1411 (*v.* **blæc, (ge)hæg**); *Blyndelane* 1415 (*v.* **blind**); *West Bockhayes* 1700 (*v.* **(ge)hæg**); *Boreswill', Boreswilleshull'* 1411 (probably to be associated with John *de Borewoll'* 1307, perhaps 'spring or stream frequented by the boar', or 'Bārs spring or stream', from **bār**[2] or the OE pers.n. *Bār* and **will(a), wyll(a)**, with **hyll** 'hill'); *Boweputtes* 1438, *-pyttes* 1501 (*v.* **boga** 'bow, bend', **pytt**); *le Brech* 1317[2], *Breache* 1609 (*v.* **brǣc**); *Britfurlang'* 1411 (*v.* **furlang**); *Bright'nettesplace* 1415 (*v.* **place**); *Brittoneschambre* 1313 (*v.* **chambre**); *Broadclose* 1609; *Brooke Close* 1609; *Buddeslane* 1438 (the surname *Budd*); *Buglinche, Bulynche* 1609 (*v.* **hlinc**, for the first el. *v.* Bugley *supra*); *Burneheye* 1313 (*v.* **burna** 'spring, stream', **(ge)hæg**); *Burylane* 1415 (cf. *Ber(r)y Crofte* 1609, 1618; the first el. of both names may be ME *bury* (from dat.sg. *byrig* of OE **burh**) in the sense 'manor house'); *Claundoneslane, Clandownhyslane* 1441 (cf. 'close of John *de Claundon'* 1313, *messuag'* . . . *quondam Claundones* 1438; the surname may be from Clandon 1 377, Clandon Sr or Clandown So); *closes called Clayes als. Home Leaze* 1609 (the surname

Clay); *Cloyers* 1438 (cf. Roger *Cloyer'* 1332 (Fifehead N.)); *Cokerelles-parrok'* 1438 (the surname *Cockerell*, *v.* **pearroc**); *Cotehayes* 1639 (*v.* **cot, (ge)hæg**); *Coubere* 1289 (*v.* **cū** 'cow', **bǣr²** '(woodland) pasture' or **bearu** 'wood'); *Craneburn* 1275, *Cramborne Watter* 1535, *Cranbourne-lake* 1627 ('stream frequented by cranes', *v.* **cran, burna, wæter, lacu**, cf. Cranborne par. **2** 205 and foll.); *Craynsemore* 1609 (from **cran** and **mōr** 'marshy ground', cf. prec.); *Crepettes* 1501; *ten' voc' Cressebiens* c.1450 (cf. Robert *Cressebien ib*); *Crouchestenement'* 1381, *Crouchehey* 1411 (cf. John *de Cruce* (*de Wyke*) 1292, 1300, William *atte Crouche* 1317², Richard *atte Crouch(e)* 1327, 1335, John *Crouche* 1381, *v.* **atte** 'at the', **crūc³** 'a cross', **tenement, (ge)hæg**, Wyke *supra*, cf. *Cristenecros, Cristine Cros* 1411 which may be 'Christian cross' from **Cristen** and **cros**, and cf. Woodhouse Cross *supra*); *Crundelford'*, *Crowndelfforde* 1441 (*v.* **crundel** 'quarry', **ford**); *Cunvers bridge* 1609; *mes' voc' Devenyssh'*, -*Northdevenyssh'* 1475, *close called Denix* 1609 (cf. Francis *Devenish* 1664); *2 parrockes called Diggers* 1609 (probably a surname); *la Done* 1292, *la Doune* 1301, *le doune* 1501 (*v.* **dūn** 'hill, down'); *Douch Meade* 1609; *Dowerclos* 1438 (*v.* **dowere** 'dowry', **clos(e)**); *Droveyate* 1501 (*v.* **drāf, geat**); *Dunhurst(e)* 1373, 1402¹ (a prison), 1402² (a lodge) (in the forest of Gillingham, *v.* **dūn** 'hill, down', **hyrst** 'wood, wooded hill'); *Easter Close* 1609 (*v.* **ēasterra** 'more easterly'); *Eastham* 1609 (a close, *v.* **ēast, hamm**); *Eggynglane* 1438; *Eldehull'* 1306 (p) (the full form is Walter *Attare Eldehull'*, 'at the old (i.e. long cultivated) hill', *v.* **atter, eald, hyll**, cf. foll); *Eldelond'* 1381, *Oldlande* 1501, *O(u)lde Land(e)* 1609, *Oldlands* 1609, *Oldland Innocks* 1700 (probably 'arable land left unused', *v.* **eald, ald, land**, with **inhoke**, cf. also *Oldelondescrofte* 1411, *Oddeslaneslond'* (sic) 1415, *Oldelondeslane* 1475, which probably denote 'enclosure and lane at *Oldelond'* respectively, *v.* **croft, lane**); *messuage called the Elliotts* 1650; *Ermeleygh'* 1317², *Erneley or Garnleigh Grove* 1629 (perhaps to be compared with Armley YW **3** 210, Yarmley D 413, which may contain **earm** 'wretched, poor' or an OE pers.n. *Earma*, *v.* **lēah**); *Everetts house* 1664; *de la Fenne* 1268 (p) (*v.* **fenn**); *Fernie Close Meade, Farnerclosse* (sic) *pasture* 1609 (*v.* **fearnig**); *Filthamesplace* 1415, *Filthammesheyes* 1441, *Feltons Haye* 1609 (from the family of William *de Fyletham* 1327 who took his name from Feltham Fm in the adjacent par. of Silton *infra*, *v.* **place, (ge)hæg**); *de la Forde* 1288 (p) (*v.* **ford**); *la Fotlond* 1313 (*v.* **fōt, land**); *Foxe Holes* 1609 (*v.* **fox-hol**); *Fryweldesmed'* 1501 (*v.* **mǣd**, probably with a surname); *meadow called Furlonge* 1609 (*v.* **furlang**); *Gillingham feilde* 1609 (cf. Richard *in le Felde* 1356, *the Comon feild* 1700, *v.* **feld**); *Gillottes* 1441 (cf. 'land of *Gylot* Haym' 1313, and the f.n. Haines *supra*); *Godefreyelane* 1441, *Gotfreyeslane* 1475, *close called Godfries* 1609 (the surname *Godfrey*, *v.* **lane**); *Goldberry Hayes* 1668 (*v.* **(ge)hæg**); *Goredaker* 1313 ('plot with a gore', *v.* **gāra, -ede, æcer**); *Gountes* 1441 (probably a surname); *Gousmede* 1411, *Goose Meade* 1609 (*v.* **gōs, mǣd**); *Grangerhisbrigge, Graungeresbrigge* 1441 (from **gra(u)nger** 'one in charge of a grange', possibly as a surname, cf. *grangiam regis de Gillingham* 1252, *v.* **brycg**); *Greate Meade* 1609; *Gretesherde* 1475 (*v.* **grēat, sceard** 'gap'); *Gussicheshey* 1441 (a surname from one of the Do places called Gussage, *v.* **(ge)hæg**); *Halgewal* 1258 (p), *Halgh(e)well(e)* 1268, 1285, 1295 all (p), *Halewoll(e)* 1270, 1332 (p), *Halewell'* 1288, 1338 both (p), 1441, *Haliwell'* 1292 (p), *Hal(g)well(e)* 1300 (p), *Hallewelle* 1327 (p) ('holy well, spring or stream', *v.* **hālig, well(a), wyll(a)**, cf. Holwell· 1 240); *claus' voc' Hang'ere* 1411, *le Hanger* 1475 (*v.* **hangra** 'wood on a steep hillside'); *Harlinge Lane* 1609 (perhaps to be associated with 'land of John *Harlewyn'* 1313); *Harperes* 1441, *Harpers Hedge* 1609 (cf. Amice *Harpirs* 1327, *-Harpours* 1332 (W Stour)); *Hawkyns* 1535 (a surname); *le Hegge* 1313 (*v.* **hecg**); *in the Heigh'* 1415 (p) (*v.* **(ge)hæg**); *Helwayesford'* 1501; *Hen Meade* 1650 (*v.* **henn**); *boscus de Henton* 1253, 1258 ('high farm', from **hēah** (wk.obl. *hēan*) and **tūn**, cf. Hinton St M. par. *infra*; a wood within the forest of Gillingham); *Heuedforlange* 1301 (*v.* **hēafod, furlang**); *Hilcottes* 1609 (cf. Robert *Hullecote* 1368, perhaps from a local p.n. from **hyll** and **cot**); *furlonge called Hitche, 2 closes called Hitches* 1609 (*v.* **hiche** 'enclosure of hurdles for penning sheep'); *Hobson Meade* 1609 (the surname *Hobson*); *Hodyesmull'* 1411 (a surname with **myln**); *Holemers* 1275[1], 1300, *-merchs* (sic) 1295 (p) , *-mersch* 1317[2], *Holmers(s)he* 1501, 1609 ('hollow marsh', *v.* **hol[2], mersc**); *le Home close* 1570, *Home Close meade* 1609; *Hope Close* 1609 (*v.* **hop[1]**); *Hurlescruche* 1292, *Erles* 1609 (from **eorl** 'nobleman' or the surname derived from it, *v.* **crūc[3]** 'a cross', cf. *Crouchehey supra*); *Hustyngesmersshe* 1501 (*v.* **mersc**, first el. perhaps lOE *hūsting* 'council (held by the King)', but the precise sense is uncertain); *Keynesbrugge* 1381, *Kenesbrigg'* 1411, *Kenebrygge* 1475 (cf. *2 closes called Keynes* 1609, Hugh *Keyne* 1332 (Shaftesbury), *v.* **brycg**; *Mr Kirkes Farme* 1650; *Lake* 1275 (p), *de la lake* 1292, *atte Lake* 1292, 1332 all (p), *the Lake* 1686 (*v.* **lacu** 'stream', **atte**); *Lamp Close* 1609 (*v.* **lampe**); *Langedon'* 1295 (p), *-doune* 1438 (v. **lang[1], dūn**); *Langley Hill* 1609 (*v.* **lang[1], lēah**); *la Leghe* Hy 3 (14), *(la) Leygh* 1300[2] (mentioned in the bounds of Gillingham forest, and to be identified with Lyemarsh in Mere W 180, *v.* **lēah**, cf. Robert- 1292, Roger *in la Legh'* 1356, who probably also belong here); *Leuelyveshey* 1441 (cf. John *Leuelyf'* 1332 (Cattistock), *v.* **(ge)hæg**); *la Lupeghite* 1298 (*v.* **hlīep-geat**); *Mann'ishe hams* 1609 (*v.* **hamm**; this form may belong under the f.n. Manors *supra*); *landa regis de Martleg'* 1236, 'the glade of *Marleye'* 1275[2], 'the lawn of *Marleghe'* 1278, (lodge of) *Mardele* 1368, 1385, 1403, *Mardle* 1402[2] ('wood or clearing infested by martens', *v.* **mearð, lēah**, a common p.n., cf. Martley Wo 62, Marley YW 4 164; this place was in Gillingham forest); *Max's cottage* 1627; *Melkershaye* 1475 (cf. Alan *le Melkere* 1332 (B. Weston), *v.* **(ge)hæg**); *Middechave* 1501 (*v.* **midd, sc(e)aga**); *Mid(d)elforlang* 1313 (*v.* **middel, furlang**); *Milkcrofte (Furlonge)* 1609 (*v.* **milc, croft**, cf. *Melkershaye supra*); *Attaremire* 1317 (p) (*v.* **atter, mire**); *howse called Mogges* 1609, *Megges house* 1664; *Montiers house* 1664 (cf. John *Mountiard* 1362); *the Morrowe Masse Landes* 1586 (from **morrow-mass** 'the first mass of the day'); *Morrow Leaze* 1609 (*v.* **morgen** 'morning', **lǣs**); *Northebury* 1368 (*v.* **norð, burh** (dat.sg. *byrig*)); *in camp' boriali* 1415, *the North Filde* 1541, *(the) North(e)feild(e)* 1609; *North'leygh'* 1356 (*v.* **lēah**); *Otecroft(e)* 1438, 1475, *Odcrofte* 1501 (*v.* **āte, croft**); *Ouer-* 1438,

Overclose 1609 (*v.* **uferra** 'higher'); *Oxstounesmersh'* 1475 (*v.* **mersc** 'marsh'; the first el. is probably a surname from a p.n. Oxton (Ch, YW, etc.)); *Palp(h)itro(e) Hill* 1609, *Palpitroe* 1626, *Walpetroe* (sic) 1629 (the origin of this name is obscure); *tenement called the Parlore* 1609 (*v.* **parlour**); *Pinfrithe* 1609 (*v.* **fyrhð, (ge)fyrhðe** 'wood', first el. uncertain); *Pitchers* 1609 (a surname); *Players* 1501, 1609 (a surname); *Pleystret(e)* 1275, 1280, 1295, 1332 all (p), *Pleistret* 1300 (p) (from a p.n. *Pleystrete*, though not necessarily in this par., *v.* **plega, stræt**, 1 185, 231); *Pond Close* 1609; *la Purihegge, la Puryhegh, Pirihey* 1313 (cf. Isabel *Attepurye*, Richard *Attepurie* 1306, John *atte Purie* 1327, *v.* **pirige, pyrige** 'pear-tree', **hecg, hege** 'hedge', **atte**); *Ridelusesmull'* 1381, *Releishe Mill* 1609, *Red Linch Mills* 1664 (*v.* **myln**, named from John *Ridelysch'* 1381, John *Redelisch' de Prousmull'* 1411, John *Redelish' Molendinar'* 1415; *Prousmull'* may be another name for this mill, first el. the surname *Prouse*); *Riokesslade* 1519 (*v.* **slæd** 'valley', first el. probably a surname); *Rownde Meadowe* 1609 (*v.* **round**); *la Rydeforhurde* 1317[2] (*v.* **rēad** 'red', **forierð** 'projecting piece of ploughland'); *Sadelburn'* 1295, *-bern* 1431, *Saddlebornes* 1609 (*v.* **sadol, burna**); *Schireuesmoure* 1292 (*v.* **scīr-(ge)rēfa, mōr**); *Schutouere* 1295 (*v.* **scyte** '(steep) slope or hill', **ōfer**[1] 'bank' or **ofer**[2] 'slope'); *Selegyevessetle, Selyessetle* 1247 (1270) (*v.* **setl** 'seat', cf. Kingsettle Fm in Motcombe par. *infra*; the first el. may be an unrecorded OE fem. pers.n. *Selegifu*, with or without analogical inflection; this place is mentioned in the bounds of the manor of Gillingham where it bordered on Somerset); *Selehayes* 1501 (*v.* **(ge)hæg**, first el. perhaps **sele**[2], **siele** 'willow copse'); *Shagh'ey* 1411 (*v.* **sc(e)aga, (ge)hæg**); *Sharlond'* 1415 (*v.* **sc(e)aru, land**); *closse called Shedbriche* 1609 (perhaps a form of the derogatory term *shit-breech* (from 1648 NED) found also as a surname (Reaney OES 294)); *Sherlocks house* 1664; *Shopp Mead* 1609 (*v.* **sc(e)oppa**); *Shorthey* 1411 (*v.* **sc(e)ort, (ge)hæg**); *Shudells* 1627 (probably a surname); *Silford* 1275 (p), *Sylford'* 1295 (*v.* **ford**, first el. perhaps **syle**[1], **sylu** 'bog' or **sulh** (gen.sg. *sylh*) 'gully', cf. Silverton D 569 and DEPN); *Silleplace* 1501 (*v.* **place**, first el. probably the surname *Sille*); *Skimehayeslane* 1475 (for the first el. cf. Do dial *skim* vb 'to mow the bunches of rank grass in a summerleaze' (Barnes 100, first recorded in this sense c.1830 NED), also 'to plough land very lightly' (from 1799 ib), *v.* **(ge)hæg, lane**); *Smalelane* 1415 (*v.* **smæl**); *Smokaker* 1313 (*v.* **smoke, æcer**); *Soparslane* 1501 (the surname *Soper*); *Sotingestoke* Hy 3 (14), *la Shetinge-, la Shetenestoke* 1270 (p), *la Schetyngstokk'* 1295 (p), *Schetingstock* 1300 (p), *Schetyngstocke* 1317[2] (p), *Schotestok* 1333, *Shetyngstok(e)* 1362 (the second el. is perhaps **stocc** 'tree-trunk, stump' rather than **stoc** 'secondary settlement'; the first may be the ME verbal sb. **schoting** 'shooting, archery' (from OE *scēotan* 'to shoot' and **-ing**[1])); *the Sowth Filde* 1541, *(the) South(e) feild(e)* 1609 (*v.* **sūð**); *(la) Southlane* 1415, 1441, *Sowth'lane* 1475; *Sparkes haye* 1609 (*v.* **(ge)hæg**, with a surname); *le Stathe* 1441 (*v.* **stæð** 'river-bank'); *Stayrok* 1247 (1270) (a point in the bounds of the manor of Gillingham, possibly from **āc** 'oak-tree' and **stæger**[1] 'stair' or **stæger**[2] 'steep', here perhaps in the sense 'lofty'); *Steward Bushe* 1609; *Stodelane* 1438 (*v.* **stōd**); *atte Stone*

1301 (p) (v. **atte, stān**); *Stonemede* 1441 (v. **stān, mǣd**); *la Stoniestrete* 1247 (1270) (v. **stānig, strǣt**); *Stoninges Bridge* 1609 (possibly a surname, but perhaps an altered form of **stānen** 'made of stone'); *le Strete* 1570 (v. **strǣt**); *de la Sturte* 1268, *de la Sterte* 1285, 1288, *atte sterte* 1362 all (p) (v. **steort** 'tail of land', **atte**); (*la*) *Suthmede* 1313, *South*(*e*) *Meade* 1609 (v. **sūð, mǣd**); *Suthovre* 1275 (p), *-ouere* 1292 (p), *South'ouere* 1411, *-over* 1501 (v. **sūð, ōfer**[1] 'bank' or **ofer**[2] 'slope'); *Thornehill* 1609 (v. **þorn, hyll**); *Trayeshey* 1441 (v. **(ge)hæg**, probably with a surname); *Tuckers* 1609 (a surname); *Tudelane* 1381, *Tutlane Innokys* 1501 (the first el. may be the OE pers.n. *Tud*(*d*)*a*, v. **lane, inhoke**, cf. also *Tuttmead* 1609 which may contain the same first el.); *Turveshethe* 1247 (1270), *Turueseth*(*e*) 1292, 1295, *Toruesethe* 1292 (perhaps from **turf** and **hǣð**); *Vergersmulle* 1438 (a surname and **myln**); *Verne Hill* 1609 (v. **fearn**); *attevllehull'* 1307 (p) (v. **atte, hyll**; *-vlle-* may represent **wyll**(**a**) 'spring, stream', cf. the f.n. Woolfields *supra*); *Vteryshill'* 1501 (a surname and **hyll**); *Warder*(*e*)*s Ham* 1501, 1609 (a surname and **hamm**); *cottage called Wares* 1609 (a surname, or to be associated with *la Weres infra*); *Warrocks, Warrickes Acre* 1609 (a surname; *Weggeshey* 1501 (v. **(ge)hæg**, cf. John *Wegge* 1332 (Sherborne)); *la Weres* 1415, *le Weres* 1441 (cf. Robert *Atte Were* 1292, John *atte Were* 1327, v. **wer** 'a weir', **atte**); *Weryngesten't* 1411 (the surname *Werring*, **tenement**); *la Westham* 1313, *Westham* 1609 (v. **west, hamm**); *Whiplers* 1609 (a surname); *Wilkins* 1664 (cf. Henry *Wilkins* ib); *Wodeʒettesfeld, Wodyet*(*es*)*feld'* 1313, *Wodyetes–* 1317[2], *Wodeʒetesweye* 1381, *Wodeyatfeld'* 1501, *Woody*(*e*)*ates Feilde* 1609 ('(the field and way at) the gate in the wood', from **wudu, geat, feld, weg**, cf. W Woodyates par. 2 271); *Wodehewerescroft* 1415 ('wood-cutter's enclosure', v. **wodehewer, croft**, though *Wodehewer* could be a surname, v. Thuresson 74); *Wodemede* 1415 (v. **mǣd**); *Woodcroftes* 1609 (v. **croft**); *Woodhaies feild* 1609 (cf. John *de Wodehaye* 1300, v. **wudu, (ge)hæg**); *Wowacr*(*e*) 1411, 1475 (v. **wōh** 'crooked', **æcer**); *Wratts Hill* 1609 (probably a surname); *Wrydesplace* 1438 (the surname *Wride*); *Wykingesmore* 1247 (1270) (v. **mōr**, cf. Thomas *Wykyng'* 1332 (Cranborne)); *Wynbroke* 1292, *Wyndbrok*(*e*) 1295, 1306 (v. **brōc**, first el. probably **(ge)wind**[2] 'a winding stream'); *Atte yhete* 1317 (p) (v. **atte, geat**); *yuyescrepel* 1247 (1270) (v. the f.n. *Ivescripple* in Bourton par. *supra*).

Hanford

HANFORD (ST 850115)

Hanford(') 1086 DB, 1212 Fees, 1230 ChancR, 1285 FA, 1575 Saxton *et passim, Haunford*(') 1228 Cl, 1240 FF, 1288 *Ass*

Hamford(') 1197 FF, 1230 P, 1240, 1242 Ch, 1244 *Ass*, 1251–2 Fees, c.1270 *Seymer* (p), 1280 *Ass*, QW *et freq* to 1428 FA, *-forde* 1291 Tax, 1332 SR, *Hampford*(') 1241

Ch, 1242–3 Fees, 1275 RH, 1374 Pat
Enforde 1210–12 RBE
Han(n)eford 1280 *Ass*
Honforde 1399 Cl
Handford 1664 HTax

Probably 'ford at the stone', from **hān** and **ford**, as suggested by Ekwall DEPN: **hēah** (wk.obl. *hēan*) 'high, chief' is a less likely first el. in view of the absence of *Hen*-spellings (apart from the form *Enforde*), cf. Six. Handley par. *infra*. The site of the original ford was perhaps where the track called Holloway Lane in Shillingstone par. *supra* crosses R. Stour towards Hanford Ho and where a ford is still marked 6"; two of the fields near this ford are in fact called *Hanfords Ford* 1828 *TA* (Shillingstone). There were two mills at Hanford in 1086 DB (VCHDo 3 84), cf. also 'the mill of *Hamford*' 1242 Ch.

BOURNES BARN, GT BOURNES, *a field called by the neighbouring peasantry 'Great Bones'* 1869 Hutch[3] 1 309; a Roman villa site found here in 1860 included human remains, hence perhaps the name, *v*. RCHM 3 104. CLIFF COPPICE, along the bank of R. Stour, *v*. **clif** 'cliff, bank', cf. William *de La Phaleyse* c.1270 *Seymer*, from Fr *falaise* 'cliff'. FOX DITCH COPPICE. HAMBLEDON PLANT., from Hambledon Hill in Ch. Okeford par. *infra*. HANFORD CHAPEL, cf. 'the church . . . of *Hamford*' 1242 Ch. HANFORD HO. LEIGH WD, *Leawude* c.1270 *Seymer*, *v*. **lēah** 'wood', **wudu**. NUTCOMBE WD, probably a transferred name, from Richard '*Nutcomb* of *Nutcomb* co. Devon' who married the daughter of Robert Seymer, lord of the manor of Hanford, in 1692 (Hutch[3] 4 63); there are four places called Nutcombe mentioned in PN D. PARK COPPICE.

FIELD-NAMES

The forms are from c.1270 *Seymer*.

(b) *forurtha vocat' heued aker* (*v*. **forierð**, **hēafod**, **æcer**); *loco q' vocat' La Slayitte* (*v*. **slæget** 'sheep pasture').

Iwerne Courtney or Shroton

Part of Iwerne Minster par. was transferred to this par. in 1914.

IWERNE ['juːən] COURTNEY or SHROTON ['ʃrɔːtən] (ST 860125)
Werne 1086 DB, *Ywern(e)* 1212 Fees, 1292 Cl, *Iwern(e)*
1219 Fees, 1242 Cl
Iwerton' 1242 Cl
Yuern' Curtenay 1244 *Ass*, *Ywerne-* 1261 Ch, *Iwern
Curtenay* 1273 Ipm, *Ywernne-, Iuerne C(o)urten(e)y(e)*
1280 *Ass, Iwerne Curtenay* 1285 Pat, *-Cortenai* 1285 FA,
Werne Curteney, -Cortenay, Hywern' Curteney 1280 *Ass,
Iuerne- kurteney* 1288 *ib et passim* with variant spellings
Iwern(e)-, Ywern(e)-, Hywerne- (1315 Pat), *Iverne-* (1428
FA), *Yeverne-* (1462 Pat), *-Curt-, -Co(u)rteney(e), -enay*;
Iwarne Courteney als. Yewern Courteney 1474 Pat, *Iwerne
Courtenay or Cowrteney* 1501 Ipm
Schyreuetone 1337 *Rawl, Shereueton* 1374 FF, *Shereneton*
(for *Shereue-*) 1388, 1455 *ib, Iwern Courteney called
'Schereveton'* 1398 Pat, *Iwern(e) Courteney als. Shyrev-
ton, -Shereveton* 1403 *ib, Shreton* 1559 *Harl, Shrawton*
1575 Saxton, *Shro(w)ton* 1633, 1679 DorR, 1774
Hutch[1], 1870 Hutch[3], *Iwerne Courtnay als. Shroton*
1795 Boswell

Named from R. Iwerne, which also gives name to Iwerne
Minster par. *infra* and Steepleton Iwerne par. **2** 114, *v*. RNs.
infra; for the DB identification, *v*. VCHDo **3** 97, DBGazetteer 121. The manorial affix is from the Courtenays, Earls of
Devon, cf. Hawise *de Curtenei* 1212 Fees, Robert *de
Curtenay* 1242 Cl, John *de Curtenay* 1261 Ch, 1280 *Ass*, etc,
v. Hutch[3] **4** 85, 88. The isolated form *Iwerton'* contains **tūn**
'farm, estate'. The alternative name Shroton means 'sheriff's
farm or estate', from **scīr-(ge)rēfa** and **tūn**, and is thus
identical in origin with Shrewton W 236 and Shurton So
(DEPN); the manor of *Werne* belonged in 1086 DB to
Baldwin the sheriff (*vicecomes*), this being Baldwin of Exeter,
sheriff of Devon (VCHDo **3** 48, 97). The bounds of an
Anglo-Saxon estate of 2 hides in the W of the present par.
are given in 958 (15) *ShaftR* (S 656).

FARRINGTON (FM) (ST 841154) ['færiŋdən], *Ferendone* 1285 FA (p), *Farendon(e)* 1315 Cl (p), 1322 Fine (p), 1324 Inq aqd, 1327 Cl *et freq* to 1336 FF (p), *Feredona* n.d. (1372) *ChrP, Farindon* 1377 IpmR, *Faryngdon* 1412 FA, *Farrington* 1664 HTax, *Far(r)ingdon* 1774 Hutch[1], 1811 OS, 1870 Hutch[3], 'fern-covered hill', from **fearn** and **dūn**, cf. Faringdon Brk 365; the modern spelling in *-ton* is apparently recent, the only early instance being the single 17th cent. form. The place gave name to the GeldR hundred of *Ferendone*, an earlier name for (part of) Redlane hundred, *v. supra*.

RANSTON (ST 863122), *Iwerne* 1086 DB, *Iwerne Randelleston* 1257 *Ass, Randolveston(e)* 1274, 1277 Pat, 1277 Ch *et freq*, with variant spellings *-olues-*, *-alues-*, *-ulues-*, *-ulves-*, *-elves-*, *-alves-*, to 1488 Ipm, *Randelfeston(e)* 1273 Ipm, 1280 QW, *Radulueston', Randulfeston'* 1280 *Ass, Randolf(e)ston(e)* 1288 ib *et freq* to 1431 FA, *Randalfston(e)* 1348 Ipm, *Randel(e)sto(u)n* 1346, 1403 Pat, *Randolston* 1362 ib, 1428 FA, *Randolfeston als. Randeleston* 1399 IpmR, *Radulftone* 1547 Ct, *Ranston* 1795 Boswell, 'Randulf's manor', a post-Conquest name in **tūn** like Pierston in Gillingham par. *supra* (*v.* IPN 131). For the DB identification, *v.* Eyton 63, 137, VCHDo **3** 90, DBGazetteer 125. The *Randulf* in question has not been traced with certainty, but the place may perhaps have taken its name from *Randulf* Avenel, grandfather of Hawise de Courtenay, *v.* Hutch[3] **4** 85, cf. par. name *supra*, Fägersten 12 fn. 1.

ABBEY WD, *Abbey* 1838 *TA*, allusion uncertain. APPLIN'S FM. BESSELLS, 1838 *ib*. BOYNE'S LANE PLECK, *Boys Lane* 1829 *EnclA, Bays Lane Pleck & Down* 1838 *TA*, probably to be associated with *lands . . . called Boyes* 1573 Hutch[3] **1** 299, from the ME surname *Boye, v.* **plek** 'small plot of ground', cf. Boyne's Coppice **2** 115. BULL PIT (COPPICE), *Bull Pit* 1829 *EnclA, Bullspit* 1838 *TA*, perhaps a pit for bull-baiting, *v.* RCHM **3** 131. COOMBE BOTTOM & WD, *Combe* 1838 *ib*, *v.* **cumb** 'valley'. CORN MILL, cf. Mill Pond *infra*; there were two mills at Iwerne C. in 1086 DB (VCHDo **3** 97), besides one at Ranston (ib **3** 90). DITCHEY COPPICE, *Detchey* 1829

EnclA, Dichey 1838 *TA*, perhaps with reference to the small rectangular earthwork marked 6″, *v.* **dīc** 'ditch', **(ge)hæg** 'enclosure', RCHM 3 131. FAIR FD, *The Fair Grd, Horse Fair (Copse)* 1838 *ib*, cf. *a fair kept in the fields under Arnold's Hill on Holy-rood Day* 1555 Hutch[3], *Shreton Fayer* 1559 *Harl, v.* **feire**; an annual fair is still held here for horses, cattle and cheese (Kelly). FALLOW WD, *Fallows Lane & Wd* 1838 *TA*, from the surname *Fallow.* FROG LANE (BRIDGE), *Froglane* [bridge] 1791 Boswell, *Frog Lane Md* 1838 *TA, v.* **frogga.** FURZE DOWN, *(Gt) Furze Down* 1838 *ib, v.* **fyrs, dūn,** cf. Furzhill *infra.* FURZEY CLOSE WD, *Furzey Cl* 1838 *ib, v.* **fyrsig.** HR & LR FURZHILL, *-Furze Hill* 1838 *ib*, cf. Furze Down *supra.* GALLOWS CORNER, 1811 OS, on the par. bdy. HAPPY VALLEY. HELLUM FM, cf. the f.ns. *Hillum Fd, Marsh, Md & Orchd* 1841 *TA* (Iwerne M.). LADY MD, 1838 *TA*, by tradition belonging to 'The Free School' here according to Hutch[3] 4 102, and therefore perhaps named from Dame Elizabeth Freke, lady of the manor, who had a schoolhouse set up in 1705, cf. however the dedication of the church to St Mary. LODGE, *The-* 1838 *TA.* MILL POND, *-Mdw* 1838 *ib, v.* Corn Mill *supra.* MOUNT SLOE, perhaps from **slōh** 'slough, mire', but there are no early forms. NEW FIELD COPPICE & LANE, *New Fd* 1838 *TA.* PARK PLANT., *Hr-* 1838 *ib*, cf. 'a park, 20 acres' 1555 Hutch[3]. POND COPPICE, 1829 *EnclA*, cf. *Water or Pond Mdw* 1838 *TA.* RANSTON FM (cf. *Ranston Ho* 1838 *ib*), RANSTON HR BARN (*Ranston Barn* 1838 *ib*), RANSTON HILL, all named from Ranston *supra*, cf. *Ranston Copse* 1811 OS, *-Md* 1838 *TA.* RICKETT'S BED, 1838 *ib.* ROAD PLANT. ST JOHN THE BAPTIST'S CHURCH (at Farrington), cf. *Farringdon Chapel and Grd* 1838 *TA, v.* Hutch[1] 2 319. ST MARY'S CHURCH, cf. *ecclesie de Iwerne Curtenay* 1310 Salis, 'the church of *Iwern(e) Courteney als. Shyrev-, -Shereveton*' 1403 Pat. SHROTON BRAKE (cf. *The Brake* 1838 *TA, v.* **bræc**[1]), CTG, HO & LINES (1811 OS, cf. *Gt, Hr & Lt Lynes, Corn & Green Lynes* 1838 *TA*, probably from **leyne** 'layer, tract of arable land', but cf. Ralph *Lyon* 1327 SR, 1332 SR), all named from the alternative par. name *supra.* THE SHRUBBERY, *Shrubbery (Walks and Plant.)* 1838 *ib.* STROUD'S FM, cf. *Strouds Grd* 1838 *ib*, probably a surname from one of

the places with this name. TRAY TOWN, on the par. bdy,
from **troy town** 'a maze', cf. **1** 322. HR & LR WALKWAY,
1829 *EnclA, Hr & Lr Walking* 1838 *TA*, two plantations
surrounded by various tracks. WELL HO. HR & LR WELL
WD, *Hr & Lr Well* 1838 *ib, v.* **well(a)** 'spring, stream', cf.
also Robert *atte Welle* 1327 *SR*, although this form may refer
to the chalybeate spring (marked 6″) at Farrington, for which
v. Hutch[1] **2** 319. The 6″ name is possibly to be associated
with *on wung wylle* in the Anglo-Saxon bounds of Iwerne M.
par. *infra*. WILLIS'S SHROTON FM, *v.* par. name *supra*.

FIELD-NAMES

The undated forms are 1838 *TA* 115. Spellings dated 958 (15) are *ShaftR*
(S 656). Those dated 1227 are FF, 1327 *SR*, 1332 SR, n.d. (1372) *ChrP*,
1555 Hutch[3], 1559, 1560 *Harl*, 1618 *Map*, 1664 HTax, and 1829 *EnclA*.

(*a*) Alder Bed Md; Ashey Coppice 1829; Barn Fd, Hr Barn; Barton and
Close; (Upr) Breach (*v.* **bræc**); Brewhouse Cl; Brick Kiln Cmn; Lt
Brooks; Burrett(s); Chapel Hays (*v.* **(ge)hæg**, cf. site of Chapel marked 6″
at Ranston *supra*); Clavies; Hr & Lr Common (cf. *Ewern Common* 1555);
Common Md; Cow Grd; (Lr) Cowleaze (with Cribhouse); Hr Crewkhorn,
Crewkhorn Md (probably 'crooked horn', alluding to shape, cf. the ME
surname *Croukorn* 1332, from **crōc** and **horn**, cf. *Sherpehorn' infra*; the
spelling may have been influenced by Crewkerne So); Crews Fd;
Darnwood; Lt Down; Dry Grd; (Hr) Dry Leaze (cf. *West leaze* 1618,
probably in this par., *v.* **læs**); The (Lr) 18 Acres; Farringdon Lane & Mill
(named from Farrington *supra*); The Fish Ponds; Gt & Lt Flippins,
Flippins Barn & Md (cf. Richard *Flippen* 1664); Hr & Lr Floodings; Fold
(or Lambing) Yard (*v.* **fal(o)d**); (Old) French Grass (*v.* **french grass**);
Great Grd; Green Grd & Lane; Hanging Fd; Hatch Md (*v.* **hæc(c)**); Hill
Grd & Ho; Old Hollow Rd; the Home Cl 1829; Home Grd & Md, The
Home Orchd; Horse Grd; Humber Mdw (cf. the f.n. Humber in the
adjacent par. of Iwerne M. *infra*); Gt & Lt Kerleys Grd; Hr, Lr & Lt
Leg(g) (*v.* **leg**); Little Md (over the Brook); Long Cl & Md; Lower Md;
Marsh Cl (cf. *mariscum de Ywern' Curtenay* n.d. (1372)); Mead Path;
Merry Fd (*Mirifeld* 1227, *v.* **myrge**); Middle Fd & Md; Mote Md (*v.*
mote 'moat'); Neat Md (*v.* **nēat** 'cattle'); 9 Acres; Norridge; North Md
(*Northmedes, the Medes* 1560, *v.* **mǣd**); Oat Cmn & Coppice, Hr & Lr Oat
Fd; Old Nell Orchd; The Orchard; Gt, Old & Young Orchd; Paddock;
Piece; (New) Pitt Fd (*v.* **pytt**); The Pleck (*v.* **plek**); Plot; Gt & Lt
Ridgeway (*v.* **hrycg-weg**); Rogers Grd; Rough Grd; Sand Pitt; Seawell;
Sheep Sleight (*v.* **slæget**); Shelleys Grd; Shute (**scēot**[3] 'steep slope' or
scyte '(steep) slope or hill'); Stoney Ld; 10 Acres; Three Corner Clump;
Timber Yd; Toppers Grd (cf. John- 1327, Robert *Tappehar(e)* 1332,
James *Tapper* 1664); Hr & Lr Tuffins Fd; Water or Pond Mdw; Water

Mdws; Whiteacre; The White Heart (sic) Inn; Widhays Ash; Withey Bed.
(b) *Arnold(e)s Hill* 1555, 1559; *on cranemere, of cranemere* 958 (15) (cf.
on cranmere in Iwerne M. par. *infra*); *on ða dich, þanne swo be diche* 958
(15) (*v.* **dīc** 'ditch'); *on þe lang dich* 958 (15) (*v.* **lang**[1], **dīc**); *to late mere*
958 (15) (cf. *on lacmere* in Iwerne M. par. *infra*); *Sherpecrofte, -horn'* n.d.
(1372) (*v.* **croft, horn,** cf. Crewkhorn *supra*; the first el. is probably
scearp 'sharp, pointed', cf. the variant *Sherpe* for the surname *Sharpe* in
SR 100); *onlang sledes* 958 (15) (*v.* **slæd** 'valley'); *on ða smale þornes* 958
(15) (cf. *on ne smal þornes* in Iwerne M. par. *infra*); *on þene weie, andlang
weies* 958 (15) (*v.* **weg** 'way').

Kington Magna

KINGTON MAGNA (ST 768232)
    Chintone 1086 DB (2 ×)
    Kinton(') 1203 Cur, 1206 ClR, 1210 P, 1244 *Ass,* 1252 Ch,
        1280 *Ass* (*Magna-*), *Kynt(t)on* 1244 *Ass,* 1250, 1251 FF,
        1280 *Ass* (*Mochele-*), *Michelekenton'* 1280 *ib, Kyneton*
        1575 Saxton, *Keinton Magna* 1795 Boswell
    Kington(') 1242–3 Fees (*Magna-*), 1256, 1266 FF, 1268
        Ass (*Grant-*), 1272 Ipm, 1280 *Ass,* 1290 Ch (*Great-*), 1316
        FA, *Kyngton(e)* 1244 *Ass,* 1253, 1265, 1268 FF
        (*Magna-*), 1268 FF (*Grant-*) *et freq* with variant
        spellings *Kyngeton(')* 1288 *Ass,* 1428 FA, *Kyngthon* 1340
        NI, *Kyngton-Magna* 1367 AD, *Machil Kyngton,
        Machelkyngton* 1412 FA
    Kyngton' Plukenet, -Plugenet 1280 *Ass, Kington Ploket,
        Kingtonploket* 1408, 1429 IpmR, *Kyngton Ploket* 1409
        Cl
    Kyngeston' 1327 SR, *Kyneston' Magn'* 1528 Rent

'Royal manor', *v.* **cyne-** (later replaced by **cyning**
'king'), **tūn,** a common p.n.; the smaller of the two DB
manors was held TRE and TRW by a king's thegn (VCHDo
3 110). The manor was granted to Alan *Plugenet* in 1266 FF,
cf. Alan *Plukenet* 1280, *-de Plokenet* 1288 *Ass,* Sibyl
Plukenet 1325 Cl, *v.* Hutch[3] **4** 69. The suffix *Magna* (Lat
magna 'great'), alternating with **grant, grand** (OFr) and
micel, mycel (OE), distinguishes it from Little Kington in
W Stour par. *infra*.

Hʀ & Lʀ Nʏʟᴀɴᴅ (Fᴍ) (ST 739221, 748217) ['nailənd]
  Iland 1086 DB, 1205 RC, 1381 Pat, *Inlande* (sic) 1086 DB,
  Liland' 1212 Fees, *Lylande* 1236 FF, *Ylond*(') 1244 *Ass*,
  1418 Pat, *la Ilond(e)* 1380 *Weld*[1], 1420 Hutch[3], *Le
  Ylond, La Ilond* 1431 FA, *Ilond* 1477 IpmR
  Lay(e)lond(e) 1303, 1428 FA, *Lailond* 1346 ib
  Le Islond 1420 Hutch[3]
  Neylond als. *Ilond* 1554 SoDoNQ **6**
  Nylond (*Mo(o)re*) Eliz *LRMB*, *Nilonde* 1581, *Nyland* 1584
  Weld[1], *Niland or Iland, anciently a manor, now two farms
  called Upper and Lower Niland* 1774 Hutch[1]

'The island', i.e. 'the dry ground in a marsh', *v.* **īeg-land,
le, la**, with **mōr** 'marshy ground'. The initial *N-* in the
modern form is from metanalysis of ME **atten** 'at the', cf.
Nayland Sf (*Neiland* 1227 DEPN) which is identical in
origin. The DB form *Inlande* is probably an error, perhaps
showing confusion with **inland** 'land near a residence'. Hr
and Lr Nyland lie between R. Cale and Bow Brook, both
rivers being marked 'liable to floods' (6").

Bᴀᴄᴋ Lᴀɴᴇ, cf. Hugh *in le Lane* 1327 *SR*, *v.* **lane**. Bᴏᴡᴅᴇɴ
(Fᴍ), *Gt Bowden Grd, Strap Grd or Lt Bowden, Bowdens
Orchd* 1846 *TA*, probably to be associated with Walter
Bo(u)edon' 1327 *SR*, 1332 SR, 'above the hill', *v.* **bufan,
dūn**, cf. Bovingdon Bk 187; this is the highest part of the
par. (438'). Bʀᴇᴀᴄʜ Lᴀɴᴇ, cf. *Breach* (*or Crib Cl*) 1846 *TA,
v.* **brǣc** 'land broken up for cultivation', **cribbe**. Bʀᴏᴀᴅᴍᴇᴀᴅ
Lᴀɴᴇ, cf. William *atte Mede* 1332 SR, 1340 NI, *Kynpus
Brodemede* Eliz *LRMB*, (*Hr, Lr & Lt) Broad Md, Common
Md or Broad Md* 1846 *TA, v.* **atte, mǣd, brād**; *Kynpus* is
probably a surname, perhaps a form of that represented in
Kimber's Ho & Home Grd 1846 *ib*. Bʏᴇ Fᴍ, *Bay* 1811 OS,
cf. *Bye Md* 1846 *TA, v.* **byge**[1] 'a corner, an angle, a bend',
perhaps with reference to a right-angled turn in the par. bdy
here, or to the meandering Filley Brook. Cʜᴀᴘᴇʟ Hɪʟʟ,
apparently named from the Methodist chapel built 1851 on
the site of *Chapel* 1846 *TA*. Cᴏᴍᴍᴏɴ Lᴀɴᴇ (Fᴍ), *Common
Lane* 1846 *TA*. Cᴏᴜʀᴛʜᴏᴜsᴇ Sʜᴏᴏᴛ (local), a spring, *v.*
scyte; for a possible connection with a manorial court, *v.*
M.S. Ross, DᴏNHAS **107** 24. Cʀᴏᴡɴ Iɴɴ. Fɪᴇʟᴅ Lᴀɴᴇ, cf.

Field Cl 1846 *ib.* FIVE BRIDGES, 1811 OS, *Five-, Fyvebridge*
(*upon Cale ryvar* . . . *There be 5 principall arches, where of it
takethe name*) 1535–43 Leland, *ye fyue bridges* 1575 Saxton,
v. **brycg.** FOLLY FM, cf. *Folly Orchd* 1846 *TA, v.* **folie.**
HARPITTS FM & LANE, cf. *Harpis Coppice* 1846 *ib*, probably
to be associated with *Harpete* 1206 Hutch[3] (3 618), 'grey pit',
v. **hār², pytt**; Harpitts Lane is on the par. bdy. HOLY
TRINITY CHURCH, cf. *ecclesiam de Kington'* 1280 *Ass.* JUAN'S
LANE, cf. William *Jones* 1664 HTax. KINGTON HILL.
LAWRENCE FM, cf. *Laurences Orchd, Lawrence(s)* 1846 *TA.*
LOWER FM, 1870 Hutch[3]. MANOR FM (2 x). MOORMILL
WITHY BED, named from Moor Mill just across the county
bdy in So, cf. *Brodemore, Morefurlonge, Nyland Mo(o)re* Eliz
LRMB all in this part of the par., *v.* **brād, mōr** 'marshy
ground', **furlang**, Nyland *supra.* NEW TOWN. NYLAND LANE,
THORN COVERT & WITHY BED (*plott called Wythy bedd* Eliz
LRMB, v. **wīðig, bedd**), all named from Nyland *supra.*
PROSPECT CTG. ROADS LANE, cf. *Road Md, Hthr* & *Yonder
Roads* 1846 *TA, v.* **rād**, here no doubt denoting a firm track
through a marshy area. TANNER'S FM, *Tanners* 1811 OS.

FIELD-NAMES

The undated forms are 1846 *TA* 118. Spellings dated 1252 are Ch, 1280
Ass, 1305 Banco (Drew), 1327 *SR*, 1332 SR, 1340 NI, 1346 FA, 1501
GillCt, Eliz *LRMB*, 1664 HTax, 1791 Boswell and the rest DoNHAS **107**
(1985) 23–46 (M.S. Ross, 'Kington Magna: a parish survey').

(*a*) Anthonys Grd; Bacon Plat (*v.* **plat²**); Bainton; Barley Cl; Barn Grd
(and Orchd), Barn Yd; Barns End; Base Hill; Bayley Ley (*Ley* may be
ModE dial. *ley, lay* 'pasture land', *v.* **lǣge**); Bean Cl (*Beanefeild* 1661);
Bears (cf. John *Attebere* 1327, -*atte Ber'* 1332, Thomas *de la Bere* 1346, *v.*
atte, bǣr² or **bearu**); Benison (perhaps ModE *benison* 'blessing', a
complimentary name for good ground); Bindle (*Byndle* 1630); Hr &
Middle Bottom, (Yonder) Bottom Md (*v.* **botm**); (Gt & Lt) Bow (*Bowe
Close* Eliz, *Bow* [Bridge] 1791, probably **boga** in the sense 'river bend'; the
fields lie in a bend of Bow Brook, which probably takes its name from this
feature, cf. *atte Brouke infra, v.* RNs *infra*); Bowling Green; Briants (cf.
William *Brine* 1664); Gt Bringtons, Lt Bringtons Ley, Bringtons Md (cf.
Bayley Ley *supra*); Broad Cl (1634) & Ham (*v.* **hamm**); Gt & Lt Broad
Leaze (*v.* **lǣs**); Gt & Lt Burgamy, Burgamy Md (cf. Stephen *Bergaueny*
1332); Burn Bake (*v.* **burnbake**); Cammick Hay (*v.* **cammoc**
'rest-harrow', **(ge)hæg**); Causeway Cl (*v.* **cauce**); Charles Ham (*v.*
hamm); Chubbs Cl, Md & Orchd (cf. widow *Chubb* 1664); Clements;

Clover Cl; Coat (*v.* **cot** 'cottage, hut'); Common (Cl & Md) (cf. Broadmead Lane *supra*); Coneygar, Cuningar (*v.* **coninger** 'rabbit-warren'); Coppice Cl, Lt Copse Grd (*v.* **copis**); Corn Grd; Cox Ley (near to Lye *infra*); Crib Ho and Yd (*v.* **cribbe**); Crooked Ham (*v.* **hamm**); (Long) Cross (*v.* **cros** 'a cross' or **cross** 'lying across'); C(r)owling; Custins (Orchd); Davidge(s) (cf. William *Davidge* 1664 (B. Weston)); Dibbens Grd (cf. Thomas *Dibben* 1664); Dowsetts Cl; 8 Acres; Elderton's Barn, Home Grd & Orchd; Elky Md; Hr & Lr Eurick; 15 Acres; Filly Brook Md, Filly Brooks (named from Filley Brook, *v.* Filley Brook Fm in B. Weston par. *infra*); 5 & 4 Acres; Four Ways; French Grass (*v.* **french grass**); Frog Moor; Furzy Cl; Gammersay; Gauntless Fd; Gawful and Gareland (cf. Gore Ld *infra*); Gear Lawn; Dry Goose Ham, Goose Ham Md (*Gooseham* Eliz, *v.* **gōs, hamm**); Gore Ld (cf. *Gardland Way* (sic) 1630, *v.* **gāra**); Great Ham (*v.* **hamm**); Green Cl; Grib Md (perhaps a form of **cribbe**, cf. Crib Ho *supra*); Grove (*v.* **grāf(a)**); Ham (Pool) (*v.* **hamm**); Hanging Ld (or Higher Gdn) (*Hanginglond* 1305, *v.* **hangende**); Harlocks Md; Hartmore; Hatcher's Common Cl; Hill Cl (1658); Hilly Grd; Home Grd & Md (cf. *Whomeclose* Eliz); Hook (Mdw) (*close called Hook, Hook Meade* Eliz, *v.* **hōc** 'hook, angle, bend in a river', cf. foll.); Hookstead(s) (possibly from the same el. as prec. with **stede** 'place, site', though the compound is not noted by Sandred); Horse Lynchs (*v.* **hlinc**); Icely Moor (or Haywards Ham) (*E(a)stley Mo(o)re* Eliz, *v.* **ēast, lēah, mōr**; for the development *East-* to *Ice-*, cf. Icen Way 1 352, East or Ice Hill 1 369); Ice Water Md (possibly with the same development as prec. and therefore to be associated with *Estemeade* Eliz, *v.* **ēast, mǣd**); Innox (*v.* **inhoke**); Jacobs Bridge & Orchd; James's Cl; July Mdw 1885; Kents; Kings Corn (cf. *Kingscombe Bottom* 1630, *v.* **cumb**); Kings Way (cf. *Keyntway* 1630); Knightn(e)y (Md), Whittaker's Knightney (*mead called Knightney, Knightey* (sic) *Meade* Eliz, probably from **cniht** 'youth, servant, retainer' (with analogical ME gen.pl. *-ene, v.* **-ena**) and **ēg, īeg** 'island, dry ground in marsh'; the fields so called lie between Bow Brook and R. Cale); Lanes Orchd (cf. Hugh *in le lane* 1327, *v.* **lane**); Lannings Grd (cf. John *Laning* 1664); Leaners; Leg Grd; Let Moor; Limpins Hill; Little Fd, Grd, Md & Orchd; Little Ham (*Lytle Hamme* Eliz, *v.* **hamm**); Long Cl (Orchd); Long Grd & Md; Longland, Long Lds; Lye (probably **lēah** 'wood, clearing in a wood', cf. Cox Ley *supra*); Lynchy Cl (*v.* **linchet**); Marl Cl; Mead; Middle Flg & Grd; Mitchard Well; Mudley; Mullins's (Broad Md and Broad Hatch), (House called) Mullins's Stall (*v.* **hæc(c), stall**, cf. John *Mullens* 1664 (B. Weston)); New Cl (Md) (*New Close* Eliz); Gt & Lt New Yeat (*v.* **geat** 'gate'); 9 Acres; North Hill & Moor; Oat Cl; Orchard (Md); Oxen Leys (Md & Orchd) (*v.* **oxa, lǣs**); Paddock Orchd; Pay Stall; Perretts Orchd; Philips Cl; Pill Acre (*v.* **pyll**); Pipland; Plat(t) (*v.* **plat**²); Quar Cl (*v.* **quarre**); Rogers Bridge; Rose Hill; Round Tree (1630); (Furzy) Sandley (named from Sandley in Gillingham par. *supra*); 7 Acres; Shabbicks; 6 Acres; Slait (*v.* **slæget** 'sheep pasture'); Small Spiney (*v.* **spinney**); South Fd or Pce (*Southfeld* Eliz); Spring Cl; Stable Grd; Stall Grd & Md (*v.*

stall); Gt & Lt Stone Shell (perhaps a late survival of a name containing the el. **stān-scilig** 'stony (ground)', cf. ME f.ns. 1 113, 230, 328; the subsoil of these fields is 'an orange gravel, consisting of sand and broken flint with some pieces of Greensand chert' (ex.inf. Mrs M S Ross)); Strap (Orchd) (*v.* **strap**); Stubbs; Summer Grd, Summer Leaze or Home Grd; Tartyland Orchd; Thorns Cl; Thorny Bush Grd; Tree Grd; Turverland 1766; Underwood 1751; Vetch Cl (*v.* **vetch**); Wares Grd or Md (cf. Thomas *Ware* 1664); Water Barton; West Way; Willow Bed; Withebye (cf. *Withybull* (sic) c.1540, *v.* **wīðig**, Bye Fm *supra*); Withey Bed (cf. prec.); Wolbens; Wood Lds (cf. 'wood of *Kinton*' 1252); Hr & Lr Worthy (*v.* **worðig** 'enclosure'); Yelwell, Yelvil (Md & Orchd), Yillvill (the first el. may be **eald** 'old' with **feld** 'open country, unit of arable land'); Yonder Flg.

(*b*) *attenasche* (p) 1327 ('at the ash', *v.* **atte(n), æsc**); *Batty Acre* 1630; *atte Brouke* 1327, *-Broke* 1332, *-Broak* 1340 all (p) (*v.* **atte(n), brōc**, perhaps with reference to Bow Brook, *v.* RNs. *infra*); *Chauntes Land* 1664[2]; *Dayzhay* 1634 (*v.* **(ge)hæg**); *East Field Close* 1733; *Eastwater* 1661; *Edemeade* Eliz (*v.* **mǣd**, first el. uncertain); *Gaston Lane* 1630 (*v.* **gærs-tūn**); *Goaffeland* 1703; *Heycroft* 1280 (p), *-crofte* 1501 (*v.* **hēg** 'hay', **croft**); *Higgin's Clift* 1630 (*v.* **clif**); *Long Hobbs* 1685; *Kingshead mede* 1608; *Kinstow Close & Bottom* 1664[2]; *Lytle Close* Eliz; *Northclose* Eliz; *Northfeld* Eliz; *Ridgeway Close* 1661 (*v.* **hrycg-weg**); *Rodmede* c.1540, 1608 (*v.* **hrēod** 'reed'); *Stockmeadow* 1634 (*v.* **stocc**); *Traunsie Hamme* Eliz, *Traunsehame* 1608 (*v.* **hamm**, first part of the name uncertain); *Turnoverland Close* 1658; *Weston's Lane* 1630; *Wilrige* 1244 (*v.* **hrycg** 'ridge', first el. possibly **wiell(a)** 'spring, stream'); *close called Ynkepense* Eliz (no doubt a surname from Inkpẹn Brk 309); *Youle Acre* 1630.

Manston

Manston (ST 815154)

> *Manestone* 1086 DB, 1348 (15) *ShaftR, -tun'* 13 *Glyn* (p), *Salkeld* (p), 1269 Ch (p), *-ton(')* 1230, 1232 Cl, 1244 *Ass* all (p), 1259 Pap, 1268 *Ass* (p) *et freq* to 1340 NI, *Maneston' in Redelane* 1288 *Ass*
> *Manneston(')* 1196 ChancR (p), 1235–6, 1242–3 Fees, 1244 *Ass* (p) *et freq* to 1535–43 Leland (*-als. Manston*)
> *Manston(')* 1268 *Ass,* 1285 FA both (p), 1288 *Ass et passim, -stone* 1285 FA, 1332 SR, 1351 (c.1407) *Shaft*
> *Mainston* 1291 Tax (v.l)
> *Maunston* 1330 Ipm (p)

'Man(n)'s farm', from the OE pers.n. *Man(n)* and **tūn**, cf. Manston YW 4 115 which is probably identical in origin.

Redelane is Redlane hundred *supra*. It may be of interest to note that a Henry *le Man* is listed as a tax-payer in Manston in 1327 *SR* and 1332 SR, although his surname is probably to be derived from *man(n)* in the sense 'servant' rather than from *Man(n)*.

NORTHWOOD COPPICE & FM (ST 812168), *Northwode* 1332 SR (p), *North Wood Coppice, North Woode Meades* 1667 *Salkeld, Northwood Coppice, Lt North Wood Down, North Wood* (*Farm Ho*) 1839 *TA*, 'north wood', *v.* **norð, wudu**; at the northern end of the par. On 1811 OS, the farm is called *Cribs Fm*, but this name should perhaps have been attached to Crib Ho Fm c.½ mile N in Marnhull par. *infra*.

CONNEGAR FM, cf. *Gt, Middle & Outside Conygars* 1839 *TA*, *v.* **coninger** 'rabbit-warren'. CORN MILL (disused), MILL RACE, cf. *Grist Mill, Mill Md* 1839 *TA*; there were two mills at Manston in 1086 DB (VCHDo 3 95). MANOR FM. MANSTON BRIDGE (over Fontmell Brook), cf. Robert *atte bruge* 1327 *SR*, William *atte Brigge* 1332 SR, *v.* **atte, brycg**. MANSTON COPSE. MANSTON FM, formerly *Bushfield Fm* 1811 OS, cf. *Bush Feildes, messuage called Bush Feilds house* 1667 *Salkeld, v.* **busc**. HR MANSTON FM (*Higher Manston* 1811 OS). LR MANSTON FM. MANSTON HO. MIDDLE HO. PLOUGH INN. ST NICHOLAS'S CHURCH, cf. *ecclesia parochiali de Manston'* 1292 (c.1407), *capelli beati marie de Manstone* 1351 (c.1407) *Shaft*, 'the church of *Manston'* 1403 Pat.

FIELD-NAMES

The undated forms are 1839 *TA* 138. Spellings dated 1327 are *SR*, 1332 SR, 1340 NI, 1346 FA, 1661 Hutch[3], 1664 HTax, 1667, 1682 *Salkeld*, 1673 *SxAS*, 1791 Boswell.

(a) Apple Tree Grd; Lt Arcdon, Arcdon Hill; Barn Marsh; Bean Cl; Gt & Lt Beds; Gt Bowden, Lt Bawden; Broad Cl (Md); Broad Leaze; Buckyhays; Bush Md; Cash moor Md (cf. Cashmoor in Six. Handley par. *infra*); Cleve(s), Cleves Md(w) (probably a surname from the oblique form of **clif** 'cliff, bank'); Cliffords Md; Clover Md; Coels Mdw, Coles Cl (cf. Richard *Cole* 1664); Coppice; Corner Marsh; Corn Nether Leaze; Crib-House (*v.* **cribhouse**); Cross [Bridge] 1791; Dairyhouse Gdn & Orchd; Dry Md; Gt East Fd, East Fd (New) Md (*greate Eastfeild, Litell East Feild, Little East Feild Meade* 1667); 8 Acres; Elloway (Md); Hr & Lr

Ewelands (perhaps to be associated with *greate Elverlands* 1667, the second el. of which could be **furlang** or **land**); Forber (Mdw); The 4 Acres; Fox Holes (Mdw) (*seaven closes . . . called Foxholes* 1673, *v.* **fox-hol**); Froghole (*v.* **frogga, hol**[1]); Frys (Md) (cf. John *le Fre(e)* 1327, 1332, John *Fry* 1664); Goddens (cf. Thomas *Godwin* 1664); Grass Nether Leaze; Great Grd & Md; Grove Park (*v.* **grāf(a)**)); Gruffetts Grd; Hembrys; Holts Cl; Home Cl, Fd & Grd; Gt Hook Hight (*v.* **hōc**); Horse Marsh; Hosey's [Bridge] 1791; Hurds or Great Grd; Legs (Md); Lewis's Marsh; Little Coppice & Md; Long Md (Orchd); Maple Grd; Mapley (Mdw); Gt, Inner, Lt, Long & Middle Marsh (*the Midle Marsh* 1667), The Marsh, Marsh Cl & Mdw (*v.* **mersc**); Marven Md; Middle Flg; Mores Md; Nicholas's and North Wood (cf. Philip *Nicholas* 1664, *v.* Northwood *supra*); Gt North Down Cowleaze, Gt & Lt North Down Md; Little Nortons or Ham (*v.* **hamm**); (Old) Orchard; Parsons Marsh; Pit Grd; Poets Cl; Pond Cl (Orchd); Quar Grd (*v.* **quarre**); Further & Hr Ramson (*grounds called Ramsons* 1667, *the Outer and Inner Ramsons als. Ramsells* 1682, *v.* Ram's Hill in Marnhull par. *infra*); Ray Grass, Rye Grass; 7 Acres; Shortlands; South Fd (Md); Staverland Cl; Sterts (Summer Leaze), Gt Sturts (*ground called Sterts* 1667, cf. John *atte Sterte* 1340, *v.* **steort** 'tail of land', **atte** 'at the'); Stour Md (*Stower Meade* 1667, by R. Stour, *v.* **mǣd**); Swaines Grd; Swine Paddock; Thatchers Leaze (*Overthatcher's Lease* 1661); Three Cornered Md; War Cl; Ways Grd (Md); Westpher Grd, Ho & Md; Westwood (1682, *West Wood Coppice* 1667, cf. Northwood *supra*); Willow Bed; Withy Bed; Woodcock Paddock.

(*b*) Badds (Meade) 1667, 1682 (a surname with **mǣd**); *Comages Coppice* 1667 (a surname); *the High Woods* 1667; *the Newe House* 1667; *New Meade* 1667; *Thornton Lane* 1667 (leading to Thorton in Marnhull par. *infra*); *atte Wall* 1346 (p) (*v.* **atte, wall**); *atte Watere* 1340 (p) (*v.* **wæter**).

Motcombe

Motcombe is in Gillingham liberty, *v.* note under Redlane hundred *supra*. Part of this par. (Enmore Green) was transferred to the borough of Shaftesbury in 1933.

MOTCOMBE (ST 849253)

> *Motcumbe* Hy 3 (14) Cerne, 1244 *Ass* (p), 1280, 1288 *ib*, 1292 *GillCt*, 1310 Ipm, -*cumb'* 1268 *Ass*, -*combe* 1502 Ipm *et passim, Mottcombe* 1609 *LRMB*
>
> *Motecumb(e)* 1244 *Ass* (p), 1258 *For* (p), 1270 *ib*, -*combe* 1415 *GillCt*, 1417 Pat, 1455 Cl, 1650 *ParlSurv*
>
> *Mocumb'* 1268 *Ass, Moucomb* 1275 RH (p)
>
> *Mottecumbe* 1270 *For*, 1288 *Ass* (p), -*combe* 1372 Pat, 1497 Ipm
>
> *Modecombe* 1371 *For*, 1397 *WRO*

Medecombe (sic) 1371 *For*
Notcombe (sic) Eliz ChancP

'Valley where meetings are held', from **(ge)mōt** and
cumb, identical with Motcombe Sx 431, cf. Modbury
hundred and Modbury in Swyre par. both *infra*. This may
well have been the meeting-place of the GeldR hundred of
Gelingeham, v. under Redlane hundred *supra*.

COPPLERIDGE (ST 844266), E & W COPPLERIDGE FM,
Copidockridge, Copley Ridge, Copplie Ridge Pounde 1609
LRMB, Copulridge 1811 OS, *Copple Ridge (Ho)* 1838 *TA*,
'ridge at the pollarded oak-tree', from **(ge)coppod, āc,**
hrycg, with **pund**. The first part of the name is *le Coppedeoc*
1301 *GillCt, atte Coppedok(e)* 1327 *SR*, 1343 *For* both (p),
atte Coppedeok' 1356 *GillCt* (p), *Copped-oak* 1627 Hutch[3];
analogous is Copdock Sf (*Coppedoc* 1195), which Ekwall
DEPN derives from **coppede** 'having a top', a possible
though less likely first el. for both the Sf and the Do names.

COWRIDGE COPSE (ST 844280), *(fosse de) Kurhigge* Hy 3 (14)
Cerne, *Curugge* 1258 *For* (p), *Corrigge* 1270 *ib* (p), *Courigge*
1292 *GillCt* (p), 1333 *For* (p), *Co(u)rygge* 1300 *GillCt* (p),
1327 *SR* (p), *Cowridge* 1300, 1568 Hutch[3], 1650 *ParlSurv*
(*close called-*), (*Upr*) *Cowridge, Cowridge Altmt, Barn,*
Coppice & Md 1838 *TA*, 'ridge where cows are pastured', *v.*
cū, hrycg; the land rises here to 400'.

ENMORE GREEN (FM) (ST 858232), *Hendemer'* 1258 *For,*
Enedemer(e) 1275 RH (p), 1292 *GillCt*, 1338–40 Glast, 1411
GillCt, Enmer 1475 *ib, Enmore green(e)* 1527, 1663 Hutch[3]
('where is a poole of water, and diverse springs and wells'),
Enmer-, Elmer Greene 1609 *LRMB, Elmer-, Elmore-green*
1627 Hutch[3], *Elmore or Enmoor Green* 1774 Hutch[1], *Elmore*
Green 1811 OS, 'duck pool', *v.* **ened, mere[1]**, with **grēne[2]**,
identical with Enmore So (DEPN); the second el. has been
confused with **mōr** 'marshy ground', cf. Ashmore par. **2** 201.

FERNBROOK BRAKE, CTG & FM (ST 837241), *Fernbroc,*
Farnbroc' 1251 Cl, *Ferenbroken* 1275 RH (p), *Fernebrooke*

1657 *EgCh*, *Fern-brook* 1811 OS, named from Fern Brook, a tributary of R. Lodden, *v*. RNs. *infra*.

FERNGORE (lost, ST 859270), 1270 *For*, 1292 *GillCt*, 1327 *SR* all (p), 1811 OS, *Frengore* Hy 3 (14) Cerne, *Fernegore* 1300, 1568 Hutch³, *Ferengore* 1307 *GillCt* (p), *Wyrnegore* 1332 SR (p), *Vernegore* 1397 *WRO* (p), 1438 *GillCt*, *Estvernegors* 1475 *ib*, *2 closes called Fernie Gores* 1609 *LRMB*, *Fern Gore Ho* 1838 *TA*, 'point of land where ferns grow', *v*. **fearn**, **fearnig**, **gāra**; this place is mentioned in the bounds of the forest of Gillingham (*v*. Forest Fm & Side in Gillingham par. *supra*), the 'gore' having left a marked kink in the present county bdy (here coterminous with the old forest bdy).

KING'S COURT PALACE (site of, ST 818263), KING'S COURT BRIDGE & WD, *Hr & Lr* (*Outer*) *Kings' Court* 1838 *TA*, *Kings Court Plat* 1838 *ib* (Gillingham), *King's Court* 1869 Hutch³, probably to be identified with [land] *desuper la Palyce* 1317 *GillCt*, from **paleis** 'a palace' or (a less likely alternative) **palis**, **paleis** 'a fence of pales, a palisade'. Other references that possibly belong here include *domorum Regis-* 1201, 1207 P, *domus Regis apud/de Gilling(e)ham* 1204 ib, 1224 Pat, *castelli Regis de Gillingeham* 1206 P, 'king's houses and court of *Gillingham*' 1252 Pat, 'court' 1313 Cl, 'the old king's court' 1403 Hutch³. 'The Palace' was a royal hunting residence within the deer park of Gillingham, *v*. Park Fm in Gillingham par. *supra*, Hutch³ 3 618–9, Cantor & Wilson 5 224–5, RCHM 4 51–2. There were two chapels here in 1253 ib ('the King's chapel' and 'the Queen's chapel', cf. *capella Regis de Gillingham* 1258 Cl). One of the manors of *Gelingeham* belonged to the king in 1086 DB (VCHDo 3 65).

KINGSETTLE FM (ST 862257) & WD, *Kingessetle* Hy 3 (14) Cerne, 1247 (1270) *For*, *Kaingessetle* Hy 3 (14) Cerne, *Kyngesettl* 1268 *Ass* (p), *Kyng(g)essecle* (*juxta Scheftebyry*) 1275 RH (p), 1280 QW, *Kyngessete* (sic) 1280 ib, *King(es)-*, *Kynges(h)ech(e)* (sic) 1280 *Ass*, *Kingessettle* 1285 FA (p), *Kyng(g)esset(t)le* 1292 *GillCt* (p), 1327 *SR* (p), 1332 SR (p), 1335 *For* (p), 1338–40 Glast, 1340 NI (p), *Kynsettle* 1369 Pat (p), *Kynges(s)etle*, *Kyngsetell'*, *Kyngsetellane* 1441 *GillCt*, *Kyngessetyls lane* 1501 *ib*, *the hill called Kingsettel* 1568 Hutch[3], (*closes called*) (*Nether-*, *Over*) *Kingsettles* 1609 *LRMB*, *Kingseth* (sic) 1618 *Map*, *King Settle* 1620 Hutch[3], *Kingsettle Fm* 1811 OS, *Kingsettles Copse & Ho* 1838 *TA*, literally 'king's seat', from **cyning** and **setl**, perhaps as suggested by Fägersten 29 used as a hill-name to indicate a lofty situation, cf. the analogous Kingsettle (Hill) So (DEPN). The farm (at 450') and the wood (at 500–700') lie on the slope of a hill that reaches 800'. On the other hand, since the place lies within the old royal forest of Gillingham (*v.* Forest Fm & Side in Gillingham par. *supra*), there may well have been a royal lodge or the like here to which the name referred, cf. King's Court Palace *supra*. As noted by Fägersten 29, a tradition (cited in J. J. Reynolds, *The Ancient History of Shaftesbury*, p.7) that the place owes its name to Alfred's resting here on his way to the battle of Edington in 878, need not be taken too seriously.

NORTH HAYES FM (ST 861262), *le Northhey* 1317, *la North'mest North'hey* 1415, *Northayes* 1501 all *GillCt*, *Nort(he)haies* 1609 *LRMB*, 1657 *EgCh*, *Northay* 1811 OS, *North Hays* (*Ho*) 1838 *TA*, 'northern enclosure(s)', *v.* **norð**, **(ge)hæg**, **norðmest** 'northernmost'; the farm lies N of Kingsettle Fm *infra* and NE of Motcombe village.

WOLFRIDGE FM (ST 834277), *Wolfridge* 1811 OS, probably to be identified with *Welrigge* 1292, *-rygge* 1295 *GillCt*, *Wilrygge* 1327 *SR* (p), *Wolrig'* 1411 *GillCt*, *v.* **well(a)**, **will(a)**, **wyll(a)** 'spring, stream', **hrycg** 'ridge'; the farm is beside a stream, though the maps show no ridge-like feature here; it is possible, however, that the farm takes its name from the higher ground ½ mile E near North End *infra*, which lies between Cowridge and Coppleridge both *supra*.

WOODSEND FM (now MANOR FM (1″), ST 843246), *attewodesende* 1258 *For* (p), *Wodeshende* 1275 RH (p), (*la*) *Wodes(h)ende* 1280 *Ass*, 1292 *GillCt* (p), 1411 *ib*, *atte Wodeseynde*, *de fine Nemoris* 1300 *ib* (p), *Wudeseynde* 1301 *ib* (p), *atte Wodes(h)ende* 1307 *ib* (p), 1335 *For* (p), 1356 *GillCt* (p), *closes called Woodes Endes, Woodes End Pastures* 1609 *LRMB, le woods ende Walkes* 1612 *Eg, Woodend* 1625 Hutch[3], *Woods-end-walk* 1627 ib, *parcell of wast and wooddye ground called Woods end Walke and the tenement or lodge built thereon* 1650 *ParlSurv, Woodsend* 1811 OS, *Woods End Fm Ho* 1838 *TA*, 'the end of the wood', *v.* **wudu, ende**[1], **atte** 'at the', **walk** 'division of a forest'; this was one of the four 'walks' of the forest of Gillingham (*v.* Forest Fm & Side in Gillingham par. *supra*).

ALLOTMENT FM & PLANT., cf. *lands called the Allotments 1650 ParlSurv, Hthr & Yonder Allotment, Allotment Lane* 1838 *TA, v.* **allotment**. BITTLES GREEN (FM), *Biddles Green(e)* 1609 *LRMB*, 1627 Hutch[3], *Brittles Green* (sic) 1811 OS, *Bettles Green Ho* 1838 *TA*, cf. *ten't called Comptons Place als. Biddles Place* 1609 *LRMB, v.* **grēne**[2], **place**, cf. *Pet' fil' le Bedel de Corrigge* 1270 *For*, John *le Budel* 1327 *SR*, John *Budel* 1397 *WRO*, William *Biddell* 1609 *LRMB* (Bourton), *v.* Cowridge Copse *supra*; it is very unlikely that this name is to be associated with the OE bdy mark (*on*) *bytelesmor*, (*of*) *bitelesmore* as was suggested by Fägersten 28, *v. Bittlesmore* in Shaftesbury par. *infra*. BRICKELLS CLIFF, BRICKELLS POND FM, *Brickells, Brickells' Clift & Plot* 1838 *TA*, cf. *John Brickell's* [land] 1627 Hutch[3], *Brickles Paddock* 1799 ib, John *Brickle* 1664 HTax, *v.* **clif**; near to The Cliff *infra*. BRIDEWELL (LANE), *Bridewell* 1811 OS, probably **bridewell** 'a prison', perhaps used figuratively (and derogatorily) of a remote or infertile spot (the place is near the par. and county bdy). THE BUTTS, cf. *close called-, tenement called Butts* 1609 *LRMB*, perhaps **butt**[2] 'archery butt' or **butte** 'short strip at right angle to others, strip of land abutting on a boundary' (the place is on the old par. bdy), but cf. James *Butt* 1664 HTax. THE CLIFF, CLIFF CTG, cf. (*tenement called*) (*the*) *Cliffehowse* 1609 *LRMB, Clift Fd, Clift House Md* 1838 *TA, v.* **clif** 'steep bank', **hūs**; some of the 13th and 14th cent. pers.ns. (*Attecliue, de Clyve*, etc) cited under Eccliffe in Gillingham par. *supra* may well refer to this place. THE CORNER, CORNER FM, cf. John *atte Cornere* 1381 *GillCt, Corner Md* 1838 *TA, v.* **corner** 'a corner, a nook', **atte** 'at the'; there is a pronounced double bend in the lane here. COWHERD SHUTE FM, *Cowards Shoot* 1811 OS, cf. 'the close of John *Couhirde*' 1313 Cl, Roger *le Couhurde* 1327 *SR*, John *Cowarde* 1609 *LRMB*; *Shute* may represent **scēot**[3] or **scyte** both of which mean 'steep slope', topographically appropriate for this place. CULVERHOUSE FM, *atte Culuerhuse* 1301 *GillCt* (p), *atte Coluerhouse* 1327 *SR* (p), *Culverhouse* 1362 *For* (p), 1811 OS, *Colverhous* 1369 Pat (p), *tenement called Culver Howse* 1609 *LRMB, v.* **culfre-hūs** 'dove-cot', **atte** 'at the', cf. *Culverhay(s Md)* 1838 *TA* from **culfre** 'dove' and **(ge)hæg** 'enclosure'. DONEDGE LODGE FM, *Donnedge-lodge* 1627 Hutch[3], *Dunheade Lodge* 1637, *Don-head(e)s Lodge* 1638, 1642 *EgCh, Donhead Lodge* 1811 OS, (*-Fd*) 1838 *TA*, 'edge or end of the down', from **dūn, ecg, hēafod**, cf. Downhead So (DEPN), Donhead W 187; the form *Dimmedge* (sic) *or Great Lodge* 1625 Hutch[3] probably also belongs here. This lodge is associated with *Clear-walk or Middle-walk* in 1627 Hutch[3], also mentioned as *the clere walk* Eliz *For, le cleare walke* 1612 *Eg, Le Cleere or the Middle Walk* 1625 Hutch[3], *that wast and wooddy ground called Cleare Walke with the Lodge thereon* 1650 *ParlSurv*; this 'walk' of Gillingham forest is named from *lez clerys* 1519 *Ct, v.* **clere** 'forest glade', **walk** 'division of a forest', *v.* Forest Fm & Side in Gillingham par. *supra.* (LR) DUNCLIFFE FM, *Dunclift Fm Ho* 1838 *TA*, named from Duncliffe Hill in Stour P. par. *infra*; Lr Duncliffe Fm is *Blackstone* 1811 OS, *Blakeston* 1300, *Blackestone* 1568 Hutch[3], 'the black stone', *v.* **blæc, stān**, perhaps a reference to a bdy stone, since *Blakeston* (like *Dunclyve*) is mentioned in the bounds of the forest of Gillingham (*v.* Forest Fm & Side in Gillingham par. *supra*). EIGHT ACRE PLANT, *Eight Acres* 1838 *TA*. FISHY MEAD COPSE, *Fishey Md (Coppice)* 1838 *TA*; a small stream runs nearby, so perhaps 'enclosure where fish are caught', from **fisc** and **(ge)hæg**. FOREST FM, *Little Lodge* 1811 OS, *Little Lodge Ho* 1838 *TA*, cf. *Lodge Md* 1838 *ib*, within the old forest of Gillingham, for which *v.* Forest Fm & Side in Gillingham par. *supra.* FROG LANE (FM), *Frog Lane* 1838 *TA*, cf. *Froglondis* 1501 *GillCt, v.* **frogga, land, lane**, cf. also *Vroggemere* in f.ns. *infra.* THE GRANGE. GRANT'S COPSE. GUEST'S FM. HAINES FM, cf. *howse called Hames* 1609 *LRMB, Upr Haines, Haines Md* 1838 *TA*, the surname

Haine(s) or *Haim(es)*, cf. Gillingham f.ns. *supra*. HAWKER'S
HILL (PLANT.), *Hawkers' Hill* 1838 *TA*, cf. *Hawkers-bottom*
1627 Hutch[3], *Hawkers' Bottom* 1838 *TA*, by Latchmore
Pond *infra*, so probably 'hill and valley used by hawkers', *v.*
hafocere, hyll, botm, though the first el. is possibly a
surname; *Three Hawkers* 1609 *LRMB* is perhaps also to be
associated with this name. HUNT'S FM, *Huntes* 1501 *GillCt*,
Hants (sic) *or Humbers* 1838 *TA*, the surname *Hunt*, and cf.
Thomas *Humber* 1664 HTax. THE KENNELS. KNAP (KNAPP
1″) HILL, *v.* **cnæpp**. LADY'S COPSE, *Ladies-* 1838 *TA*.
LARKINGLASS FM, *Larkinglass* 1811 OS, 1838 *TA*, from
ModE *larking-glass* 'a machine with mirrors, used to attract
larks to the net' (1826 NED). LATCHMORE POND, *Lachemer(e)*
1356, 1475 *GillCt*, *Lasmore* 1577 *KCC*, *Latchmore-pond*,
-pool 1627 Hutch[3], *Latchmore (Meade)* 1660 *SxAS*,
Lashmore Pond 1811 OS, 'the swampy pool', *v.* **læc(c)** 'bog',
mere[1], a common p.n. (EPN **2** 10); for the development to
-more, cf. Enmore Green *supra*. LIMBRICK (lost, ST
863250), 1811 OS. LONG CROSS, 1811 OS, *close called Longe
Crosse* 1609 *LRMB*, *Longcrosse* 1660 *SxAS*, *v.* **lang**[1], **cross**
'cross-roads', the name aptly describing the junction of four
roads here. MANOR FM (1″), *v.* Woodsend Fm *supra*.
MOTCOMBE HO (PLANTS.), *Motcombe Ho* 1811 OS. MOT-
COMBE PARK, cf. *N & S Park, Upr W Park* 1838 *TA*.
NETTLEBED, *Nettle-bed* 1627 Hutch[3], *v.* **netel(e), bedd**. NEW
LANE (a farm), 1799 Hutch[3], *Newlane* [Bridge] 1791 Boswell,
perhaps to be associated with *Newlondis alias dict' Homeclose*
1501 *GillCt*, *close called Newlande* 1609 *LRMB*, *v.* **nīwe,
land**. NORTH END (FM), *North End* 1799 Hutch[3], *Northend*
1811 OS, *North End Ho and Homestead* 1838 *TA*, *v.* **norð,
ende**[1]; it is 1½ miles N of Motcombe village. THE NURSERY,
Nursery 1838 *TA*. OATES PLANT. PALEMEAD COPPICE, *Middle
Pale Md* 1838 *ib*, *v.* **pale** 'a fence'; with reference to the
former deer park of Gillingham, *v.* Park Fm in Gillingham
par. *supra*. PAYNE'S PLACE, 'a messuage with appurtenances
in *Motecombe* . . . late of William *Payn*' 1455 Cl, *Paynesplace*
1475 *GillCt*, 1627 Hutch[1], *Pains-Place* 1774 ib, *v.* **place**
'residence', cf. Richard *Payn* 1332 SR. PENSBURY CTGS, HO
& PLANT., *Pensbury Ho* 1799 Map, *-(Turnpike) Ho* 1838 *TA*,
-Gate 1845 *TAMap*. THE PLANTATION. POTTLE'S HILL

PLANT., *2 closes . . . called Pottlehills* 1609 *LRMB, Pottle Hill* (*Plant.*) 1838 *TA, v.* **hyll**, cf. William *Potel* 1327 *SR.* POUND, cf. Coppleridge *supra.* PUG'S HOLE, cf. *Pucksyde Meade, Puckmore* 1609 *LRMB, Puxey* [Bridge] 1791 Boswell, *Puxey Md* 1838 *TA, v.* **pūca** 'puck, goblin', **hol¹**, **sīde**, **mæd, mōr.** QUOITS COPSE, *Co(y)tesheyes* 1368 *For, Coyteshayes, -haies* 1501 *GillCt, Coytes* 1609 *LRMB, Quoits* 1838 *TA, v.* **(ge)hæg** 'enclosure', cf. William *le Coyt* 1292 *GillCt,* John *Coyt* 1327 *SR.* RED HOUSE FM. ROYAL OAK INN, *The Royal Oak Ho & Gdn* 1838 *TA.* RYAL'S PLANT., *Ryalls* 1609 *LRMB,* 1838 *TA,* probably to be associated with the family of Richard *de Ri-, Ryhull'* 1292 *GillCt,* John *de Ryhulle* 1327 *SR,* 1335 *For,* although the p.n. which gives rise to this surname may not have been in this par., *v.* **ryge** 'rye', **hyll** 'hill'. ST MARY'S CHURCH, cf. *terram . . . iuxta ecclesiam* 1292 *GillCt, Churcheclose, Churche Streete* 1609 *LRMB, Church Cl* 1838 *TA.* SHERBORNE CAUSEWAY, 1811 OS, *the causey that ledithe to Scheftesbyry* 1535–43 Leland, *Sherbourne causeway* 1568 Hutch³, *the Cawsey leadinge to Sherborne Common* 1609 *LRMB, Sherburne Cawsey* 1650 *ParlSurv, v.* **cauce** 'raised way across marshy ground', Shaftesbury par. and Sherborne par. both *infra.* SHORTS GREEN FM, cf. William *Shorte* 1609 *LRMB.* THANE'S FM, *Kinsworth* 1811 OS, perhaps 'king's enclosure' from **cyning** and **worð**; it is just S of Kingsettle Fm & Wd *supra.* TURNPIKE WD, by the Gillingham-Shaftesbury road. WELL HO, cf. *Wellmeade* 1609 *LRMB, v.* **well(a)**, **mæd.** WHITE HOUSE FM, *White Ho* 1811 OS. WITHIES FM, *Wethers* 1535 *Ct, ground . . . called Wythers* 1568 Hutch³, *close called Withers* 1609 *LRMB, Withers Fm* 1811 OS, cf. Richard *Wyther de Motecumbe* 1270 *For,* Roger *Wyther* 1327 *SR.* WOODWATER FM, *Woodwater* 1811 OS, *-Ho* 1838 *TA,* cf. *grounde lyeinge att or neere the River or water called Woodwater* 1638 *SxAS, v.* **wudu, wæter**; the farm lies by R. Lodden. WOOLCOTT'S FM. YEW TREE CTG.

FIELD-NAMES

The undated forms are 1838 *TA* 154. Spellings dated Hy 3 (14) are Cerne, 1244 *Ass,* 1247 (1270), 1258, 1270, 1333, 1338, 1342, 1343, 1362, 1371, 1373, 1374 *For,* 1275 RH, 1285 FA, 1300², 1364, 1473, 1568, 1599, 1624,

1718, 1799 Hutch[3], 1313, 1455 Cl, 1327 *SR*, 1332 SR, 1338–40 Glast, 1340 NI, 1397 *WRO*, 15 *Shaft*, 1535 *Ct*, 1609 *LRMB*, 1650 *ParlSurv*, 1657 *EgCh*, 1660 *SxAS*, 1664 HTax, 1791 Boswell, and the rest GillCt.

(*a*) Alder Bed Plot (cf. *Alregate* 1292, *-ghete* 1295, 1317, *-ghite* 1300, *-ghyte* 1306 all (p), *Alder Close* 1609, *v.* **alor** 'alder', **geat**); Late Aldridge's Ho; Amour Md (*Almour* 1371, *v.* **mōr** 'marshy ground', first el. perhaps **ǣl** 'eel'); Arable Fd & Ld; Asp Plain (cf. *Apsehey* 1411, *v.* **æspe** 'aspen-tree', **(ge)hæg**); Balls' Grd; Banisters; (Lt) Barn Cl (1799), (Lt) Barn Grd, Barn Md(w) & Plot (cf. *Barne haies, the Barne Meade* 1609, *v.* **bere-ærn, (ge)hæg, mǣd**); Barnes Pdk 1799; The Barracks Ho & Gdn; Bean Cl (*Beane Close* 1609) & Altmt (*v.* **bēan**); Beer Ho & Gdn; Bessant Grd; Betties; Black Hedge; Blackhouse Md and Corner (*Black Howse Meade* 1609, *v.* **blæc, hūs, mǣd**); Lr and Upr Bonds (cf. Edward *Bond* 1664); Bottom Grd & Md (*Bottome Meade* 1609); Boundens; Bounds' Plat (*v.* **plat**[2]); Bowers' (Md) (cf. Thomas *Bower* 1609); Bowling Ally (*one bowelinge allye* 1609); (Plantation or) Boyne, Gt & Lt Boyne, Lt Lodge Boyne, Shepherds' Boyne, Thorning Boyne (possibly a transferred name from R. Boyne in Ireland, and perhaps commemorative of the battle fought there in 1690, cf. Shepherds' Md *infra*; *Thorning* is probably from **þyrning** 'place growing with thorns'); Bramble Cl, Bramblecoomb (cf. *Brimble Combe* 1609, *v.* **brēmel, brǣmel, brembel, brǣmbel** 'bramble', **cumb**); The Old Brewery Ho and Gdn, Further & Hr Brewhouse Md; Brick Cl 1799; Bridge Piece Plant., Bridge Plat (*v.* **plat**[2]); Brigley; Broadfurlong (*Broade Furlonge* 1609); Broad Md (*Broade Meade* 1609); Brook Cl; Browns' Md (cf. Anthony *Browne* 1664); Burbages 1799; Burnbake (*v.* **burnbake**); Burts(' Hills) (cf. Edward *Berte* 1327 (Milton on Stour)); Bushey Cl; Bush Short Lds (*Bushie Shorte landes* 1609); Butlers' (Cl) (cf. John *Butler* 1609); Butter Print (1718, perhaps a pasture which produced good butter, or so named from some topographical resemblance to a *butter-print*); Calves Grd (cf. *Calfes Meadowe* 1609); Charity Ld; Clover Grd; Cold Fd (*Coale Feild* 1609, *v.* **col**[1] 'coal, charcoal', cf. *Cole Haies* 1609 which may contain the same first el. or a surname *Cole*, cf. Coles *infra*, *v.* **(ge)hæg**); Cold Harbour (*v.* **cald, here-beorg**; this field is near, but not beside, the road from Shaftesbury to Sherborne); Hr, Lr & Middle Coles (cf. Everard *Cole de Motecumbe* 1270); Collis's; Common Altmt; Coppice Cl & Fd; Copse (Cl & Grd); Corn Grd; Cow Cl; Cowslip (second el. possibly **slæp** 'slippery place'); Crooked Joan (a field of very irregular shape) ; Curstoons; Curtis's Cl; Dock and Lt Hilly Grd; Lt and Yonder Down; New Dry Cl, Dry Md (cf. *the Drie grounde, Drie Haies* 1609, *v.* **drȳge**); Dun Cl (Boyne) (perhaps to be associated with *Dunghaie Close* 1609, *v.* **dung, (ge)hæg**, cf. Boyne *supra*); Dunclift Cl (named from Duncliffe Hill in Stour P. par. *infra*); Dungeon Copse (*v.* **dungeon**); Dun Water (*Durnewatereshey* 1415, *tenement called Durnewaters* 1609, named from William *de la Durnewotr'* 1258, Richard *de la Durnewatere* 1292, Edith *de la Dernewatere*, Richard *Atthe Derne Watere* 1295, Michael *atte Durne Watere* 1327, William *atte Durnewatre* 1342, Richard *Durnewater* 1397, 1415, 'hidden stream', *v.* **dierne, dyrne, wæter**, with **atte** 'at the',

(ge)hæg 'enclosure'); East Coppice; East Hays (*E(a)sthaies* 1609, 1657, *v.*
(ge)hæg, cf. West Hays *infra*); Eaton Ctg; 18 & 11 Acres; 11 and 3 Acres;
Extons' Dry Cl; Fern Hills; 5 Acres; Folletts' Coppice, Hr & Yonder Fd;
Ford Fd; The Fountain Inn, Fountain Mdw; 4 Acres (*Fower-* 1609);
Allotment (Gt Fowles) (*Fowles Wood* 1568, *Vowles* (*Coppice*) 1609, the
surname *Fowle*); (Gt) French Md; Furzy Cl; Gappers; Garden Fd;
Gatehouse Cl (cf. Thomas *Gatehowse* 1609); Godwins Altmt; Great Altmt,
Gdn, Grd & Hays (*v.* **(ge)hæg**); Great Md (*the Great Meade, Greate
Meade als. Ludhaie* 1609, *v.* **mǣd**, **(ge)hæg**; *Lud-* may represent a
pers.n., cf. Reaney s.n. *Ludkin*); Great Plot; Inner & Outer Great Wood;
(Gt, Lt & Lr) Grove (*Grove* 1609, *v.* **grāf(a)**); Grove Md (*Groves Meade*
1609, held by John *Grove ib,* cf. *Mr Groues house* 1664); (The) Hanging,
Lr Hanging, Hanging Grd & Md (*v.* **hanging**); Haskells' Md, E & W Gt
Haskells; Haylock; Gt & Lt Hay Md, Hays Md; Higher Copse; (Gt & Lr)
Hill, The Hill (Top); Hill Clift (*v.* **clif**); Hill Cl ((*Over*) *Hill Clos(s)e* 1609,
v. **uferra**) & Pdk; Hill Fd Coppice; (Lt) Hilly Cl (*Hillyclose* 1660), (Lt)
Hilly Grd; Hobbs' Leaze (*v.* **lǣs**, cf. John *Hobbes* 1332, *domus Willelmi
Hobbes* 1374); Hr & Lr Home Bush (*Home* here may represent dial. *holm*
'holly', *v.* **holegn**); Home Cl (1609), Fd & Md (1609); Home Grd (and
Brake) (*v.* **bræc**[1]); Home Wood Pdk; The Hop Yd; Horse Cl & Grd;
Hundred Acres; Hurds' Grd (cf. John *le Hurde* 1327 (Milton on Stour));
Inner Grd; Jeffreys' Md (cf. William *Geffrai* 1332, *-Jefferyes* 1664);
Jones's Md (cf. Agnes *Jones* 1327); The Keepers' Ho; Keinton's 1799
(*Keinton, Little Kintons* 1609, probably identical with the f.n. Kington in
Gillingham par. *supra*); Kings' Cl (cf. John *Kinge* 1609); Lake House Md
(*closes called Lackhowse* 1609, *v.* **lacu** 'stream'); Lamberts' Ho; The Lane;
Leg (Md) (cf. *The Leg* 1799, *The Lagge, Lagg Meade* 1609, *v.* **lagge, leg**);
Leggs'; Lindsays (cf. John *Lyndesy* 1327 (Milton on Stour)); Linhays
(*Lynne haies* 1609, *v.* **(ge)hæg**, first el. probably **līn** 'flax', but cf. Do dial.
linhay 'lean-to-shed' (Barnes 79)); Little Altmt; Little Mead (Cl), Little
Mdw (*Little Meade* 1609); Little Pdk & Plat (*v.* **plat**[2]); N & S Little Wd;
Gt & Lt Lockyears'; Lodge Ho; Loinsley Grd; Long Cl (*Longe-* 1609),
Grd, Md (*Long(e) Mead(ow)e* 1609), Orchd & Strap (*v.* **strap**); Luxers (sic)
Lane [Bridge] 1791 (from Lox Lane in Gillingham par. *supra*); Main Cl;
The Malthouse; Man Md (*Mann Meade* 1609, probably **(ge)mǣne**
'common'); Maton Cl; Lr & Middle Mead, Meadow, Meadow Grd or
Baked Mead (cf. *Mottecombe mede* 1501, *The Meade* 1609, *v.* **mǣd**); Mead
Hays (*Croftam voc' Medehey . . . et una graua quondam vocat'
Medeheyesleigh'ton* 1411, *meadowe called Meadayes* 1609, *v.* **mǣd**,
(ge)hæg, **lēac-tūn** 'vegetable garden'); Meeting Ho; Messiters Plat (*v.*
plat[2]); Middle Grd; Middle Hedge (1609, *Middelheg* 1415, *-hegge* 1501,
-hege, Myddelhegges 1535, *v.* **hecg**); Middle Md 1799; Milestone Grd;
Milking Barton (*v.* **barton**); Motcombe Street [Bridge] 1791; Motyards
(Cl) (cf. John *Metyard* 1664); New Cl (Orchd) (*Newclose* 1609); Dry &
Wet Newmans' (*6 closes called Newnams* (sic) *and Hills* 1609, cf. Henry *le
Nywman* 1270, Roger *Newman* 1609); New Md & Orchd; New Yeate (*la
Nyweghete* 1317, *la Nywe3ateslane* 1415, *Newyate* 1475, 1609, *Nuyate* 1475,

Newyats bushes, -Lane 1568, 'new gate', *v.* **nīwe, geat, lane**); 9 Acres; (Lt) North Leaze (*v.* **lǣs**); Oat Cl & Leaze (*v.* **lǣs**); The Old Lane; (Old) Orchard, Orchard Altmt & Md; Gt & Lt Oxmoor; Packmoor (*Pokemour* 1371, *v.* **pūca** 'goblin', **mōr**); (Far) Paddock, Paddock Gdn; Paradise (and Strap) (*close . . . called Paradice* 1609, *v.* **paradis** (here ironical, *v.* B.K. 248) , **strap**); The Parish Pound; Park Gate 1799, The Park (identified with *Kingsettle Park* 1824 Map by J.D. Wilson, DoNHAS **98** 9, *v.* Kingsettle Fm *supra*); (Gt & Lt) Parsons' Hill (*Parsons Hill* 1650, cf. *Parsons Close* 1609); Pasture Grd; (N & S) Peaked Cl (*Peakat Close* 1609, *v.* **peked** 'pointed'); Peartree Md; Pentridge Md (probably named from Pentridge par. **2** 235); Perrys' (Lane) (cf. *la Purihegge* in Gillingham par. *supra*); Petteys (*Pettis Close* 1609, the surname *Pett(e)y*); (N & S) Picked Cl (*v.* **pīcede** 'pointed'); Pinkmore (*v.* **mōr**, first el. probably **pinca** 'finch, chaffinch'); Pipers' (*Pyperescroft, Pipereshegh* 1313, *-heyes* 1371, *Pypers* (*Haye*) 1609, cf. William (*le*) *Pipere* 1327, 1332, *v.* **croft, (ge)hæg**); Plat (*v.* **plat**[2]); Pond Fd (cf. *Ponde Close, -meade* 1609, *v.* **ponde**); Ponds' Hanging (1799 Map) & Ho (*v.* Hanging *supra*); Poor Grd; Pullens; Pump Cl; The Quarry (cf. *Quarr Meade* 1609, *v.* **quarre**); Queens' Grove (*Queen's-grove meadow, -wood* 1624, cf. *Queen's Oak* 1568 (on Gillingham Forest bdy), and *v.* Thorngrove in Gillingham par. *supra*); Ramsmoor (*Rammesmoreshull* 1362, *v.* **ramm, mōr, hyll**); Raygrass (*v.* **rye-grass**); Redwell 1799 (*Radewlle* Hy 3 (14), *-well* 1275 (p), 1300[2], 1473, *-woll* 1332 (p), *Redewell(e)* 1247 (1270), 1338–40, 1343 (p), 15, *Rathewelle* 1327 (p), *Redwell* 1364, *Rodwell* 1568, 'red spring or stream', *v.* **rēad** (wk. obl. *-an*), **well(a), wyll(a)**; the place is mentioned in the bounds of Gillingham forest and manor); Richards' Md; Ridge Cl (cf. *Rudgie Close* 1609, *close called the Small Ridge* 1650, *v.* **hrycg**); (The) Rough Grd; Roundhills (1609); Ruffity (probably **rūhet** 'rough ground'); Rushy Cl; Gt & Lt Russells' (cf. Alice *Russel* 1313); Sadbrook (*2 closes called Sudbrookes* 1609, possibly '(land) south of the brook', *v.* **sūðan, brōc**, cf. Southbrook Md *infra*); Sadlers' Cl; Sangers' (cf. Gillingham f.ns. *supra*); 7 Acres; Sharphays (*Sherpehayes* 1501, *v.* **scearp** 'pointed', **(ge)hæg**); Shepherds'-, Sheppards Md (cf. Joan *Sheppard* 1609); Shooters' Coppice; 6 & 16 Acres; Skydons; Hr & Lr Snells (cf. John *Snel* 1313, 1332); South Altmt; Southbrook Md (cf. Sadbrook *supra*); Spring Plat (*v.* **plat**[2]); Square Cl & Md; Gt & Lt Stable Cl; Stall Grd (*v.* **st(e)all**); Stickelewell Md (*Stickle Well Meade* 1609, *v.* **well(a)** 'spring, stream', first el. probably **sticol** 'steep', i.e. 'with steep banks'); Stoney Lds (*Stonie land* 1609); Store Ho; Strap (Md) (*v.* **strap**); Strings (*v.* **string(s)**); Sturton's Pdk 1799; (Home) Summer Grd, (Home) Summerleaze (*v.* **sumor, lǣs**); Temples Altmts (cf. Richard *Temple* 1609); 10 Acres (*tenacres* 1609); T Grd (so named from its shape); Thickett Md, Inner & Outer Thicketts (*v.* **þiccett**); Inner & Outer Thomas's Grd; Three Acres; Three Meads; Three Yards (*v.* **gerd, gierd**); Toll Gate Ho & Pdk; Tomkins's Orchd & Plant.; Turks; Turners Style; 12 Acres; 2 Acres (Altmt); Vanners (cf. Gillingham f.ns. *supra*); Verney Grd (*v.* **fearnig**); Vetch Grd (*v.* **vetch**); Wallnut Grd, Wallnut Tree Pdk; Water Md(s); (Lr & Outer) Way Grd;

West Coppice; West Hays ((*la*) ·*Westhey* 1415, 1501, *West Haies* 1609, *v.* **west, (ge)hæg**, cf. East Hays *supra*); West Pdk; Wheat Cl & Grd; General Whitelocks' (*ten*' *Whitloc* 1415, *vie voc*' *Whitelockes* 1501, *meadowe* . . . called *Whetlockes* 1609, cf. Edith *Whitlok* 1327 (Silton)); Whites' Grd (cf. *John Whites house* 1664, *White's Corner* [Bridge] 1791); Hr & Lr Whitmoore (*vill*' *de Wytemore* 1244, 1275 (p), 1292, *Witemore* 1298, *Whytemour(e)stret* 1415, *Whytemors* 1475, *v.* **hwīt** 'white', **mōr, strǣt**); Cloves (sic, perhaps for Clover) Willis's, Gt & Rushey Willis's (cf. Gillingham f.ns. *supra*); Willow Plat (*v.* **plat²**); Withey Bed; Wood; Woollands(' Copse) (*Woolandes* 1609, cf. Woollens in Gillingham par. *supra* and foll.); Wool Md (Plant.) (*Wol(le)mede* 1411, *v.* **wyll(a)** 'spring, stream', **mǣd**); Yeatmans'; Yonder Fd, Grd & Hills.

(*b*) *Abrahams bridge* 1609; *tenement called Bagman* 1609; *Batterstockes* 1609; *Beere Meade* 1609 (cf. Richard *de la Bere* 1285, 1333, *v.* **bearu** or **bǣr²**); *la Bitene* Hy 3 (14), *le Byttene* 1300, *Byten* 1364, (close called) *Bytterne* 1455 (in the bounds of Gillingham forest, *v.* **bytme, bytne** 'valley bottom'); *Blyndlane* 1609 (*v.* **blind**); *meadowe called Breache* 1609 (*v.* **brǣc**); Chipstreete 1609 (probably **cēap** 'trade, market'); *Cokemanneslond*' 1415 (*v. Koggesmannestune infra*); *Collins* 1609; *Cookes Meade* 1609; *Cottlehaies* 1657 (*v.* **(ge)hæg**); *Coxe Crofte* 1609; *Crabbes Cottages* 1609; *Nethere Crouchouse* 1371 (cf. *Joh*' *fil*' *Walteri atte Crouche de Motecoumbe* 1342, *v.* **crūc³** 'cross, **neoðerra, hūs**, atte); *Cutterbills* 1609; *Cuttermeade* 1609; *Drakes* 1441, *Drake Howse Close* 1609, (the surname *Drake*); *Gouldestenement*' 1411, *Gouldes* 1441, 1609; *Grauntgowbrigg*' 1373 (*v.* **brycg**, first el. possibly **grant, grand** 'great', middle el. uncertain); *Great Close* 1609; *Half Acre* 1609; 'a close called the *Hanger*' 1455 (*v.* **hangra**); *claus*' *vocat*' *Haselstaire* 1411, *Hasilsteyers* 1455, *Haselstayres* 1475 (*v.* **hæsel** 'a hazel', **stǣger¹** 'a stair'); *Hills* 1609 (a surname); *Holewal* 1270, *-wales* 1475, (*Nether*) *Hollwells* 1609, 1660 (*v.* **hol²** 'hollow', **walu** 'ridge', cf. Holwell par. *infra*); *via apud le Holewoye* (sic) 1441, *Hollwaies* 1609 (*v.* **hol²** 'hollow', **weg**); *Hoopers Haye* 1609 (*v.* **(ge)hæg**); *Howens* 1609; *Huckeshayes* 1568, *Huckes haies* 1609 (*v.* **(ge)hæg**); *Jackes Haies* 1609; *Jehaies* 1609; *Koggesmannestune, -tone* Hy 3 (14), *Tukemannestone* 1247 (1270) (sic, for *Cuke-*), *Cokemaneston* 1300², *Cokemanstone* 1568 ('Cokeman's estate', a late name in **tūn** no doubt to be associated with the ancestors of Richard *Cokeman* 1332 (Shaftesbury), cf. also *Cokemanneslond*' 1415, *v.* **land**; *Cokemaneston* was a point on the old bdy of Gillingham forest and manor near the present Motcombe-Shaftesbury bdy); *Lockes Lane* 1609; *Longe Hills* 1609; *Lutchehaies* 1609; *Lynchehey* (*close*) 1455, 1475, *Lynchaies* 1609 (*v.* **hlinc, (ge)hæg**); *Mouresplace* 1475, *Mores* 1501 (a surname *Mo(u)re, v.* **place**); *Muddlie Closse* 1609; *Nether Leas* 1609 (*v.* **lǣs**); *Northe lands als. Davidges Meade* 1609; *Olandes* 1609; *Osworthe Place* 1609; *Overleys* 1609 (*v.* **uferra, lǣs**, cf. *Nether Leas supra*); *Over Meade* 1609; *Palmers* 1609; *Peaked Mead* 1650 (*v.* **peked**); *Pershull*' 1441, *Great Persehill, Litelpersehill* 1455 (*v.* **hyll**, first el. probably the pers.n. *Piers*, cf. the f.n. Pierce Hays in Gillingham par. *supra*); *Pittie Meade* 1609; *Portesham* 1609 (*v.* **hamm**); *Preston* 1609 (probably from **prēost** and **tūn**);

Pyle Cross 1568 (*v.* **pīl** 'a stake'); *Raddweles, Radewelles*(*cros*) 1441 (a manorial name, from the family named from the f.n. Redwell *supra*, cf. 'land . . . late of William *Radewell*' 1455, *v.* **cros**); *Rie Close* 1609; *Sexhaies* 1609 (*v.* **(ge)hæg**, probably with **sex** 'six'); *Shaftesburie Hill* 1609 (from Shaftesbury par. *infra*); *Shephowse Meade* 1609 (*v.* **scēap-hūs**); *Slaye Acre* 1609 (*v.* **slege** 'sheep pasture'); *Sledges* 1660; *Sommers* 1609; *Soulescumbe* Hy 3 (14), *-combe* 1300², *Solescombe* 1364, *Sowlescombe* 1568 (*v.***cumb** 'valley', first el. possibly **sulh** 'gully'; in the bounds of Gillingham forest); *South Street* 1599; *Stylehaies* 1609 (*v.* **stigel, (ge)hæg**); *Teswell'* 1338–40 (in the bounds of Gillingham forest, possibly from **tǣse** 'useful' with **well(a)** 'spring, stream'); *Thorne Hayes* 1609; *the Thorny Close* 1650; *Three Horne Meade* 1609 (*v.* **horn**); *Till haies* 1609 (first el. probably a surname); *Top*(*e*)*hull* 1258, 1275 both (p), *Topenhull* 1292, 1332, 1343 all (p), *Tepenhil* 1338 (p), *Toppenell'* 1501, *Topnills* 1609 ('Toppa's hill', from an unrecorded OE pers.n. *Toppa* assumed by Ekwall for Topcliffe YN), and **hyll**); *Upper Howse Groundes* 1609; *Vallis* 1609; *Vrey haie* 1609 (*v.* **(ge)hæg**); *Vroggemere* Hy 3 (14), *Frogge*(*s*)*mere* 1275 (p), *Froggemere* 1292 (p), 1300², *Frogmere* 1340, *a certain pole or pitt . . . which anciently was called Frogmeare* 1568 ('frog pool', *v.* **frogga, mere¹**; in the bounds of Gillingham forest); *Wassalls* 1609; *Whettles* 1609; *Woodes* 1609; *Wearmewlle* Hy 3 (14), *Weremeswelle* 1270 (p), *Wermeswelle* 1300², *-woll'* 1307, *Wormswells* 1609 (*v.* **well(a), wyll(a)** 'spring, stream'; if the first form is reliable, the first el. is probably **wearm** 'warm' as in Warmwell par. 1 170, but *-s-* in the other forms suggests a pers.n., perhaps an OE pers.n. *Wearm* (from **wearm** 'warm', cf. Reaney s.n. *Warme*); in the bounds of Gillingham forest); (*Great*) *Younges* 1609 (a surname).

Child Okeford

Part of this par. was transferred to Okeford Fitzpaine in 1884.

CHILD OKEFORD (ST 835127)

> *Acford* 1086 DB (2 x), *-forda* Exon, *-ford*(*e*) 1155 MontC, c.1185 Templar, 1208 Cur, 1245 Cl, *Akford* 1244 Ipm, *Ocf*(*f*)*ord'* 1332 SR, n.d. (1372) ChrP
>
> *Chiltaneford* (sic) 1210–12 RBE, *Chiltacford* 1212 Fees
>
> *Childacford*(*e*) 1227 FF, 1280, 1288 *Ass*, 1291 Tax, *et freq* to 1346 FA, *-akford*(') 1242–3 Fees *et freq* to 1367 Pat, with variant spellings *Chyld-, -hac-*; *Chyld Acford* 1284 Ipm, *Childeacford* 1297 Pat, *Chyldacford als. Childocford* 1310 Ipm, *Child Hakforde* 1412 Cl, *Childe Acford* 1428 FA
>
> *Childocford*(*e*) 1236 FF *et freq* with variant spellings *Chyld-, -ok-* to 1501 Ipm, *Child*(*e*) *Okford* 1307 Ipm,

1365 Cl, *Child(e)ockef(f)ord(e)* 1396 IpmR, 1546 (16)
Bartelot, Childokford als. Childakford 1461 Pat, *Chyld-okford als. Chyldokyford* 1498 Ipm, *Childeokford* 1501
ib, *Childockford* 1653, *Childe Ockeford* 1659 *Seymer,
Child Ockford* 1870 Hutch[3]
Childe(h)okeford 1262 FF, 1397 Cl, 1415, 1429 Fine, 1431
FA, *Child(h)okeford(e)* 1281 FF, 1284 Ipm *et freq* to
1501 Ipm, *Child(e) Okeford* 1410 Fine, 1495 Ipm, *Child
Oakeford* 1664 HTax
Chillakeford', Chilacford (p) 1268 *Ass, Chil(l)okford* 1412
FA, *Chylockford* 16 Hen[2]
Chidekford (sic) 1280 *Ass, Chidocford* 1310 Fine
Chyldayford (sic) 1291 Tax, *Childeyford* (sic) 1428 FA
Child Okfeld (sic) 1306 Cl   *Cheldokford* (sic) 1399 Pat
Childekforde otherwise Childakforde 1423 Cl, *Childekeford*
1447 Pat
Chyldeokesford 1550 *PlR*
Chele Aukford 1575 Saxton

One of a group of three pars. which share the name
Okeford, 'oak-tree ford', from **āc** and **ford,** the others being
Okeford Fitzpaine *infra* and Shillingstone (*olim Okeford
Shilling*) **2** 238. The site of the original ford is now lost, but
it may have been where the road from Child Okeford crosses
R. Stour at what is now Hayward Bridge *infra.* The
distinguishing affix *Child* is probably from **cild** in the sense
'son of a royal or noble family', though the particular
reference is obscure. Fägersten 14 notes the possibility that
cild may have been used as a title by Earl Harold, who held
TRE one of the two DB manors of Child Okeford (VCHDo
3 66); this Harold was the son of Earl Godwin whose father
is stated to have been Wulfnoð *cild* in MS F of ASC
(Plummer **1** 138). However the absence of gen.sg. inflection
in the forms might then be unusual, cf. Childswickham Gl **2**
6 which has the sg. affix but with consistent -(*e*)*s*. An original
gen.pl. inflection (lOE *cilda*) might better explain the forms,
if it could be assumed that the affix is of lOE rather than
eME origin, with eME loss of ending in the triple compound
(*Childe-* 1262 FF, 1297 Pat are the only 13th cent. forms
with -*e*, as against the common forms without ending

throughout the 13th cent.); for gen.pl. *cilda* as affix, cf. Chilcompton So (DEPN), Chieflowman D 552. The meaning may then be 'the Okeford manor belonging to the young noblemen' or the like, cf. the common p.n. Chilton Brk 497, etc. On the other hand it is possible that the distinguishing affix *Child* is in origin a topographical term **celde**, WSax **cielde** 'a spring', cf. also Chilcombe par. *infra*. The two earliest 13th cent. spellings in *Chilt-* are no doubt due to AN influence, v. Feilitzen 97.

As Hutch³ 4 77 puts it, 'here were always two manors'. There were two in DB, each assessed at five hides. That held TRW by the king (VCHDo 3 66) is to be identified with *Ockford Superior* 1753 Hutch³, *Trenchard's-Manor, Ockford-Superior or Upper* 1774 Hutch¹, *Okeford Upper* 1795 Boswell, named from the family of John *Trenchard* 1485 Hutch³ 4 78. For the other DB manor, held TRW by the Count of Mortain (VCHDo 3 84), v. *Lower Okeford infra*.

FONTMELL PARVA (ST 828146), *Parva Funtemel(l)* 1250 Drew, 1360 FF, *Litel Fontemell* 1308 Banco (Drew), *Litil Funtymels* 1412 FA, *Lytel Fountemel* 1431 IpmR, *-fontemell* 1431 FA, *Little-Fontmel or Fontmel-Parva* 1774 Hutch¹, named from Fontmell Brook on which it stands, v. RNs *infra*; *little* (Lat *parva*) to distinguish it from Fontmell Magna par. which lies upstream 3 miles NE.

HAMBLEDON HILL (ST 848122), 1555 Hutch³, *Hameledun'* c.1270 Seymer, *Hambledon, Humbledown* 1560 Harl, *Hamildon hill* 1773 Bayly, *Hamildon or Hambledon-Hill* 1774 Hutch¹, *Hamilton Hill* 1811 OS, 'the scarred or mutilated hill', from **hamol, hamel** and **dūn**, no doubt with reference to the earthworks of the Neolithic causewayed enclosure and Iron Age hill-fort here. It is a common name, occurring in at least seven counties (EPN 2 231). The form (*on*) *hamelendune* (*north ecge*) cited under this name by Fägersten 15 is of course identical in origin but does not belong here; it describes part of Fontmell Down in Fontmell Magna par. *infra*.

HAYWARD BRIDGE (ST 824121) & LANE, *pontem de Hayford* 1268 *Ass,* 1270 *For,* 1280 *Ass,* QW, '*Hayford* Bridge' 1270

Hutch³, *pontem de Heyford* 1280 QW, *Haifordesbrigge* 1337 DorR, *Hayward ys Brygge* 1494 *Cecil, Eyford-* c.1540 Leland, *Heward Bridge, Hewood Bridge, -Bredge* 1584 Hen², *Hayford-* 1618 *Map, Heyford Bridge* 1620 Hutch³, *Hayward-Bridge* 1774 Hutch¹, *Ha(y)ward Bridge* 1870 Hutch³, 'hay ford', i.e. 'ford used at haymaking time', from **hēg** and **ford**, with **brycg**, cf. Heyford O 218. The road from Child Okeford to Shillingstone (Hayward Lane) crosses R. Stour here. The confusion of the name with ME *hayward* (< OE *hege-weard* 'hedge keeper') is first evident in the form from 1494. There is no support for the supposition in Hutch³ **4** 79 that the bridge was earlier called *Haydon Bridge*.

CHURCH FM, near St Nicholas's Church *infra*. COMMON DROVE. LR COMMON RD, cf. *Common* 1583 *SPDom, the higher Common and Lower Common* 1652 *DCMDeed, Hr & Lr Common* 1839 *TA*. DUCK ST., 1811 OS, *Duke St* 1826 Gre. FERNHAYES COPSE, *Fernhayes* 1702, *Ferny Lands* 1721, *Fernlong otherwise Ferney land* 1788 all *DCMDeed, v.* **fearn, (ge)hæg**. FONTMELL FM, named from Fontmell Parva *supra*, but earlier *Brickhouse* 1811 OS, cf. *Brick Cl* 1839 *TA*, and Brick Works (6″) one mile S. GOLD HILL (FM), *Gold Hill* (*Cmn*), *Goldhill Orchd* 1839 *TA, -Fm* 1870 Hutch³, probably 'hill where (marsh) marigolds grow', from **golde** and **hyll**, cf. Gold Hill Brk 330. GREENWAY LANE, *Greenway* (*Lane*) 1839 *TA*. HANFORD FM, *Handford Farm* 1767 *DCMDeed*, named from the neighbouring par. of Hanford, but earlier *Chistill* (*als Chistills*) 1648, 1722, *Chesil* 1725, *Chissel* 1788 all *DCMDeed, Chisel* 1811 OS, cf. also the f.n. *Chisell* 1839 *TA*, from **cisel** 'gravel'. LT HANFORD (1″), cf. prec. HAZEL COPSE. HILL BOTTOM PLANT., *Hill Bottom* 1839 *TA*, with reference to Porter's Hill *infra*. LONG LYNCH, (*Gt & Lt*) *Lynch* 1838 *ib, v.* **hlinc** 'ridge, bank'. MANOR FM & HO. MILLBROOK HO, [-Bridge] 1791 Boswell, near a small stream, cf. Edith *atte Brouke* 1327 *SR*, 'at the brook', *v.* **atte, brōc**, though this may refer to Fontmell Brook (*v.* RNs *infra*), cf. also foll. MILLWAY'S LANE, *Myllewaydrove* 1612 *SRO*, cf. *Great-, Little Millwaies* 1729 *DCMDeed*, (*Gt*) *Millway(s)* 1839 *TA, v.* **myln, weg, drāf**; there were three mills in the two manors of *Acford* in DB (VCHDo **3** 66, 84), and there is mention of a mill on R. Stour in n.d. (1372) *ChrP*, cf. also prec. and *Tucking Mill* 1839 *TA*. MONK'S YARD (local), cf. *Monks* 1736 *DCMDeed*, William *Monke* 1652 *ib*. NETMEAD LANE, *Nett Meade* 1652, *Neat Mead* 1725 *DCMDeed*, *Net Md* 1839 *TA*, first el. possibly **nēat** 'cattle'. NEWBURY COPSE. NICHOLAS'S COPSE, -*Coppice* 1839 *ib*, perhaps to be associated with St Nicholas's Church ¼ mile SW, but cf. Mrs *Nicholls* 1664 HTax. CHILD OKEFORD HO. OKEFORD COPPICE. LOWER OKEFORD (lost, ST 831132), 1811 OS, *Child Ockford Lower Farm* 1725 *DCMDeed*, *Ockford Inferior* 1753 Hutch³, *Mr Seymer's Manor or Ockford Inferior or Lower* 1774 Hutch¹, the DB manor held by the Count of Mortain (VCHDo **3** 84), cf. par. name *supra* and *v*. Hutch³ **4** 78–9. PIT ORCHARD. PORTER'S HILL (LANE), *Porters Hill* 1839 *TA*, cf. Mr *Porter* 1664 HTax (Iwerne C.). RECTORY, cf. *Lr Parsonage Grd* 1839 *ib*. RIDGEWAY LANE, *Ridgeway* 1788 *DCMDeed*, *Ridge Way, Hr & Lr Ridgeway, Ridgeway Orchd* 1839 *ib*, *v*. **hrycg-weg**. ST NICHOLAS'S CHURCH, cf. 'church of *Cheldokford*' 1399 Pat. SANDY LANE. SOUTHFIELD LANE, *Southfield* [Bridge] 1791 Boswell, (*Hr & Lr*) *Southfield* 1839 *TA,* south of the village. TERRACE COPPICE, *mess' called Tarryes* 1648 *DCMDeed*, from the surname *Tarry, Terry,* cf. Terrace Fm in Stour P. par. *infra*.

FIELD-NAMES

The undated forms are 1839 *TA* 60. Some fields in this par. in 1839 are now in Okeford F. par. *q.v. infra*. Spellings dated 1327 are *SR*, 1332 SR, 1340 NI, n.d. (1372) *ChrP*, 1612 *SRO*, 1653 *Seymer*, 1664 HTax, 1791 Boswell, 1870 Hutch³, and the rest *DCMDeed*.

(*a*) Acre and half; Alder Cl (Coppice), Alder Moore (*v*. **alor**); Arnolds Md (*Arnold's Corner* 1702, cf. Thomas *Arnold* 1664); Barley Cl; Beckhams; Birds Fd (cf. Thomas *Burt* 1664); Blackley (Md); Blackmoor; Black's [Bridge] 1791 (*Blackbridge* 1762); Blandfords Way; Brandiss [Bridge] 1791; Brandlep; Breach (Orchd) (*v*. **brǣc**); Brimsams Barn and Cl; Broad Cl; Hr & Lr Broodfield (sic); Bush Cl; Butts Ho & Md (1689, cf. Robert *Butt* 1664); Calves Grd; Castles; Chalwell (Orchd) (probably 'cold spring or stream' from **ceald** and **well(a)**, cf. Belchalwell in Okeford F. par. *infra*); Cleverhays; Coppice; Cosats Md; Cowleaze; Crate Ho and Orchd (*v*. **croft**); Crawls; Culverland (*v*. **culfre** 'dove'); Dodcrate; Downs; (Locks) 8 Acres; Fontmill Md (*v*. Fontmell Parva *supra*); Furze Cl;

Gardeners Coppice; Gate Md; Giddy Acre; Gore (v. **gāra**); Goss's Grd; Great Md; Haines Cl (cf. James *Hayne* 1653); (Lt) Ham (v. **hamm**); Harveys Acre (cf. John *Heruy* 1332 (Manston)); Haycroft, Hayhouse (cf. Hayward Bridge *supra*); Herringway (Orchd) (*Herrings Hay* 1729, a surname with **(ge)hæg**); Higher Md; Holly Wool (1797, perhaps WSax **wylla** 'spring, stream'); Holways (Coppice); Home Fd, Grd & Plot (*the Homeclose* 1648, *the Home Ground* 1729); Hop Gdn Orchd; Horse Md; House Grd; Jacobs Ladder (no doubt a complimentary name for a pleasant or productive field); Jubbers; Kennicksfield, Kinnick(s) Fd; Kimbers Acre (*Kimbers Tenement* in tenure of widow of John *Kimber* 1767); Knot; The Legg (v. **leg**); Legs Orchd; Long Cl (behind Town); Long Md or Stones Longmoor, Gt Long Md, Lt Long Moors (*Longmore* 1721); Louseland; Lower Md; Mansion Ho; Markston(e); Middle Fd & Md; New Cl; 9 Acres; Northfield (1654); Norton Hedge (probably 'north farm' from **norð** and **tūn**); Orchard; Paddock Orchd (*Parock* 1702); Parish Pound; Park (Fd); Parks Orchd; Peddle Md (*Piddle Furlong* 1788); Play Cl (1702); Pleasure Grd and Pond; Pleck (v. **plek**); Plots (*Plot's farm* 1870); Pond Cl; Poor Grd; Queen Bower; the Rack Plots 1762; Ratfurlong (-*forland* 1702); Running Acre (v. **running**); Scards Md (*Scard's Brook* [Bridge] 1791); Shorlocks Orchd; Shoulder of Mutton Orchd (so called from its shape); Slick beard (identical in origin to the f.n. Sleek Beard in the adjacent par. of Shillingstone 2 242, *sleek* being a variant of *slick* from **slicu** 'smooth'); Sluis's [Bridge] 1791; Soreland; Stable; Stitching (v. **sticcen**); Ston(e)y Lds & Md; Summer Grd; 3 Acres; Tilleys Md (cf. Robert-, Walter *Till(e)y* 1664); Towns Md, Gt Towns; Trenchard (for this surname v. par. name *supra*); Tuckers Hams (cf. John *le Toukere* 1327 and foll., v. **hamm**); Tucking Mill ([-Bridge] 1791); 12 Acres (1729); (Chalk pit) Twiland(s) (cf. the chalk pits marked 6″ N of Hambledon Hill); Verney Ld (cf. foll.); Vernhays (Coppice) (v. **fearn**, **(ge)hæg**); Watering pieces (v. **watering**); Watering Place; Whist Lane; Winshard ('gap fit for a wagon', v. **wægn**, **sceard**; this field lies beside Hayward Lane *supra*); Withy Bed; Woods Md; Yonder Fd.

(b) *Bandolls mead* 1612; *Chillpitt furlonge* 1648; *atte Crouke* (p) 1340 (v. **atte**, **crōc** 'bend'); *Derthehilla* n.d. (1372) (v. **hyll**, first el. possibly **drit** 'dirt'); *the Farmers ham* 1652 (v. **hamm**); *Goosehill or Gooseham* 1661 (v. **gōs**); *Higher Mead* 1725; *Lamphayes* 1702 (v. **lampe**, **(ge)hæg**); *Lot(te)meade* 1661, 1722 (v. **hlot**); *Marle Lane* 1612 (v. **marle**); *Rowham* 1648, 1722 (v. **rūh**, **hamm**); *Scotts* (*Meade*) 1648, 1661 (cf. Robert *Scott* 1652).

Silton

SILTON (ST 783294)

Seltone 1086 DB, 1285 FA, 1330 Ipm, -*ton*(') 1194 P, 1222 ClR, 1230 P (p), 1268, 1280 *Ass*, 1297 Cl, Pat, 1314 *AddCh*, 1318–25 Ipm, 1325, 1326 Fine, 1331 Cl, Pat *et*

freq to 1415 Fine ('-by *Gyllyngham*')
Selleton' 1230 ChancR (p), *Seleton'* 1280 *Ass*
Salton' 1268, 1280, 1288 *Ass*, 1291 Tax, 1303 FA, 1319,
   1330 Ipm, 1340 NI, 1346 Ipm, FA, 1428 ib
Cylton' 1327 *SR, Cil-, Cylton* 1519 *Ct*
Silton(') 1332 SR, 1402 Pat, 1431 IpmR, FA *et passim,*
   Sylton 1361 Pat, 1412, 1428 FA *et passim, Silton or Sylton*
   1497 Ipm

v. **tūn** 'farm, village'. The first el. is probably, as
suggested by Fägersten 15, **sealh** 'a sallow, a willow', the
development to *Sil-*, etc reflecting the raising of *e* to *i*.
Identical in origin is Salton YN 57. The relatively late
appearance of the *i/y* forms in the 14th century, and the
absence of *u* forms, tend to speak against the first el. being
the derivative **sele²**, **siele** 'a sallow grove, a willow copse',
thought probable by Ekwall DEPN, although there may well
have been some interchange of this el. with **sealh**.

FELTHAM FM (ST 774301), *Fyletham* 1327 *SR* (p) (2 ×),
Filtham 1332 SR (p), *Fyltam* 1541 *Prideaux* (p), *Feltham*
1811 OS, 'hay enclosure', from **fileðe** and **hamm**, identical
in origin with Feltham So (DEPN) and Fillham D 285, cf.
Studies² 171.

BAGMORE CTGS, FM & WD, *Gt Bagmore, Bagmore Wd* 1837
TA, v. **mōr**; for a possible first el., cf. *Baggeridge* 2 284.
CARD'S FM, cf. John *Card* 1664 HTax (Gillingham) and
Gillingham f.ns. *supra.* CHURCH RD, from St Nicholas's
Church *infra.* DUNN'S LANE. FANTLEY LANE, cf. *Fainthleys'*
Grd, Faintley's Orchd 1837 *TA.* FITZ FM. FURZE HILL CMN,
1837 ib, *Furzehill Cmn* 1811 OS, *v.* **fyrs.** GRIMSEY LANE.
LOWER CMN (lost, ST 790302), 1811 OS. MANOR FM. MILL
(unnamed), cf. *Bostesmill* 1372 FF, *Mill* [Bridge] 1791
Boswell, *Mill Md, Orchd & Pool* 1837 *TA, v.* **myln**; the
surname *Bost* is recorded once in 1332 SR though not in
connection with this par.; there were three mills in Silton in
1086 DB (VCHDo 3 92). THE ROOKERY, a house. ST
NICHOLAS'S CHURCH, cf. 'the church of *Salton'* 1315 Drew,
'the church of *Sylton'* 1361 Pat, *Church Cl, Church Stones*

1837 *TA*. Silton Lodge & Wd (1837 *ib*). Slait Barn, named from *Sheep Slait* 1837 *ib*, *v.* **slæget** 'sheep pasture'; the association of this name with the lost f.n. *Odeslade* in Bourton par. *supra*, suggested by Fägersten 16, is very unlikely. Stour Bridge, 1791 Boswell, cf. *Stour Hay(e)s'* (*Pce*) 1837 *TA*, named from R. Stour, *v.* **(ge)hæg**. Stroud Cmn, 1811 OS, cf. *Stroud Ho* 1826 Gre, *Stroud Md & Pce* 1837 *TA*, probably to be associated with Robert *de la Strode* 1288 *Ass* (Gillingham) and *tenementum Ade atte Strode* 1314 *AddCh*, *v.* **strōd** 'marshy ground overgrown with brushwood', **atte**. Waterloo Lane & Mill (*Mill* 1837 *TA*), no doubt a name commemorating the battle of 1815, cf. the f.n. Waterloo in W Stour par. *infra*. Weaver's Hole, perhaps to be associated with Robert- 1314 *AddCh*, John *atte Hole* 1372 FF, *v.* **atte** 'at the', **hol¹** 'hole, hollow'. Wyndham's Oak, *Judge Wyndham's Oak* 1870 Hutch³, so called from Sir Hugh *Windham* of Orchard Wyndham So, who bought the manor of Silton soon after 1660 (Hutch³ 4 106); he is listed as *Mr Serjeant Windham* in 1664 HTax.

FIELD-NAMES

The undated forms are 1837 *TA* 189. Some fields in Silton *TA* are now in Bourton par. *q.v. supra*. Spellings dated 1314 are *AddCh*, 1327 *SR*, 1332 *SR*, 1664 HTax, 1791 Boswell.

(*a*) Adder Croft; Akey Md; Barn Grd; Barrow Fd (*v.* **beorg**; this field lies alongside Grimsey Lane *supra*); Beast Cl; Benneys' or 100 Acres (a small field); Blacklands (Mdw); Bleach Yd (freq.); Browns' Pdk; Bulls' Legs (*v.* **leg**); Bunns' Cl and Brake (*v.* **bræc¹**, cf. Sedwell *Bunn* 1664); Burlton's [Bridge] 1791; Burton Fd (from Bourton par. *supra*); Bushes Pce; Bushey Grd; Butts' Md (cf. Robert *Butt* 1664); Bye Cl (*v.* **byge¹** 'a corner, an angle'; the par. bdy forms a right angle here); Clay Md (near Clay Lane 6″ which is partly in this par., partly in Bourton par. *q.v. supra*); Close (Md); Bourton Coney-geer, Long & Way Coney-geer (*v.* **coninger** 'rabbit-warren', Bourton par. *supra*); Coppice (Md); Lr Cowleaze, Upr Cowleys (*v.* **læs**); Cribb Cl, Cribb Ho Orchd (*v.* **crib(house)**); The Croft; Daws' Orchd; Deep Leys' (partly in Bourton par., cf. Bourton f.ns. *supra*); Drift-way Ho (*v.* **drift**); Eastwood Coppice Grd; Ennicks Coppice & Pce; Evins' Hays; Fern Cl; 5 Acres; Fords' Pine; Gt & Lt Forty, Forty Md (*v.* Forty Pond in Bourton par. *supra*); 4 Acres Pce; 14 Acres; (The) Furlong; Gully Md (*v.* **gully**); Lt & Upr Hallings; The Ham (*v.* **hamm**); Haverdales; Gt & Lt Hayland; Home Cl; Horse Park & Plat (*v.* **plat²**); House Md & Pdk; Kites' Nest; Land Cl; Lane; Linch Hayes (*v.* **hlinc**,

(ge)hæg); Little Breach (v. **bræc**); Little Croft & Md; Little (Wood) Pce; Long Cl (Coppice); The Mead, Lr & Upr Mead(ow); The Moor(es) (v. **mōr**); Mount Folly; New Cl and Skilling (v. **skilling** 'shed'), Gt & Lt New Cl; 9 Acre Pce; North Cl (Driftway) (v. **drift**); Oat Cl; (The) Orchard; Oxleys' (v. **oxa, læs**); The Park, Book Park, Horse Park, Old Park, Ridouts Park (v. **park**; *Book* may represent **bucc** 'a buck, a male deer'; Hutch[3] **4** 106 mentions 'the park of the old manor-house' E of the church); Penning's and Horse Plat (probably **penning** 'pen, enclosure'); Gt & Lt Pinneys'; The Pond; Quarr Grd, Quarry Cl (v. **quarre**, cf. Old Quarry 6"); Ridouts' Md & Park; Russells Pce; Ryelands; Gt Sandleys, Lt Sandhills (these adjacent fields bear different forms of the same name, cf. Sandley in Gillingham par. *supra*); 17 Acres Pce; Sheep Wash Pdk; Shephards' Pce (cf. William *bercarius* 1327); Silver Md & Well (v. **seolfor**); Slade Brook (v. **slæd**, cf. Slod Brook in RNs. *infra*); Spinney (Lane); Stand Grass; Steels' Md; High Still; Stocken [Bridge] 1791 (v. **stoccen** 'made of logs'); Stock Pce, Stocks (possibly to be associated with Adam *atte Stokke* 1327, Richard *de Stock'* 1332, v. **atte** 'at the', **stocc** 'tree-stump'); Summerleaze (Orchd); Lt & Long Taggs'; Taylors' Hayes; 10 Acres Pce; 30 Acres; 3 Acres; 3 Corners; 3 Gates; Throat (v. **þrote**, possibly with reference here to a narrow lane); 12 Acre(s) (Pce); 2 Acres; Water Md; West Fd; White Cross Pce; Withey Bed.

(b) *atte Clyve* 1327 (p) (v. **atte** 'at the', **clif** 'bank, cliff'); *atte ford'* 1314 (v. **ford**); *atte mere* 1327 (p) (v. **mere**[1] 'pool' or **(ge)mære** 'boundary').

East and West Stour

STOUR, EAST & WEST (ST 799228, 785229) [stauə]
  Sture 1086 DB (2 ×), 1304 Pat, ?*Stawere* 1201 Cur, *Stures* 1212 Fees, Hy 3 (14) Cerne, 1242 Ch, 1285 FA, 15 ShaftR, *Stur'* 1291 Tax, *Stoure* 1316 FA, *Stowers* 1576 HaRO
  Stur(e) Cosin 1244 *Ass* (p), 1285 FA, 1288 *Ass*, -*Cosyn* 1288 ib, 1314 FF, *Stures Cosin, -Cosyn* 1268 *Ass*, 1270 For (-*de feodo Andr' Wake*), *Estures Cusin* 1270 ib, *Stour(e) Cosin* 1300 Hutch[3]
  Stures Cusyn Westouere 1244 *Ass*, *Stoure Cosyn Estouer* 1299 Banco, *Stoure Cosyn Estovere et Westoure, Stoure Cusyn Estovere et Westovere* 15 ShaftR
  Sturewestouere 1268, 1288 *Ass*, *Sture Westouere, Stoureswestouer* 1288 *Ass*, *Westouere* 1288 ib, 1332 SR, *St(o)ur(e)westover(e)*, -*Westover(e)* 1290 Ch, 1327 SR, 1362 For, 1412 FA, 1473 Pat, c.1500 Eg, *Stourewestoure*

1362 *For*, *Sturee Westhovere* 15 *ShaftR*, *Westover* 1572
HaRO
Sturewake 1280 *Ass*, *Sture Wake* 1327 *SR*, *Stoure Wake*
1332 SR, 1346 Ipm, 1412 FA, *Stour(e)wake* 1347 Cl, 1362
For, 1501 Ipm, *Storewake* 1501 Ipm
Stoure Estouere 1371 FF, *Stour Estover(e)* 1375 Pat, c.1500
Eg, *Sture hestovere* 15 *ShaftR*, *Estover(e)* 1443, 1569
KCC, 1572 *HaRO*, *Stowerestouer* 1537 *AD*, *-Estover*
1570 *KCC*, 1572 *HaRO*
East Stower, *West Stower* 1664 HTax, 1811 OS

Named from their situation on R. Stour, *v.* RNs. *infra*.
The affixes *Estouere* and *Westouere* mean 'east bank' and
'west bank' respectively, *v.* ēast, **west**, ōfer[1], cf. Langport
So which has identical affixes *-Estover*, *-Westover* in 1472
Pat. The other affixes (*Cosin* and *Wake*) are manorial.
William *Cusin* is mentioned in connection with (E) Stour
in Hy 3 (14) Cerne (*Boscum Willelmi Cusin, scilicet de
Stures*), and Ralph *Wake* is associated with (E and W)
Stour in 1285 FA, 1290 Ch, 1304 Pat, also Andrew *Wake*
in 1270 *For*, cf. Stoke Wake par. *infra* for these same two
families. The form *Stowers* in 1576 *HaRO* denotes 'the
two places called *Stower*'; *-s* in the earlier spellings is no
doubt a similar use of the pl. form.

East Stour

BLACK VENN (ST 825236), *la Blakeuenne* Hy 3 (14) Cerne,
Blakefenne 1247 (1270) *For*, 1275 RH (p), 1338–40 Glast,
-fen 1577 *HaRO*, *Blacke Fenn* 1609 *LRMB*, 'dark-coloured fen', *v.* **blæc** (wk. obl. *blacan*), **fenn**; this place is
mentioned in the bounds of the forest of Gillingham. The
name is identical in origin with Blackven in Fontmell M.
par. *infra*.

BACK ST., cf. Front St. *infra*. BROWN'S LANE. BULLEN'S
FM, cf. *Bullens Grd & Md* 1842 *TA*, Peter *Bullien* 1572
HaRO, William *Bullen* 1664 HTax. CHRIST CHURCH, cf.
domum voc' le church howse 1572 *HaRO*. CHURCH FM, near
prec. CLAY HILL HO, 1842 *TA*. COLE STREET FM & LANE,
manor of Colstrete 1504 Ipm, *Colestrete* 1557 *Prideaux*,

Cole-street 1627 Hutch[3], *Coal Street* 1811 OS, *Colestreet Ho and Homestead* 1842 *TA*, *Cold Street Fm* 1842 *TAMap*, probably 'street along which charcoal is carried', *v.* col[1] 'coal, charcoal', **strǣt**. COMMON LANE, named from E Stour Cmn *infra*. COTT HO & LANE, *v.* **cot** 'cottage, hut'. COWSLIP FM. CROWN (P.H.). DOREY'S COPPICE. FERN HILL. FIR TREE CTG. FRONT ST., cf. Back St *supra*. FRY'S FM. HARTGILL FM, cf. *Hargills* 1842 *TA*. HAYHOUSE (lost, ST 808247), 1811 OS. HEAD LANE. HEAVLAND LANE, cf. *Heave, Heave Land (or Marks Plat)* 1842 *TA*, probably ModE dial. *heave* 'a heap, a hillock' (EDD), cf. I 312; the lane crosses a hill; for Marks Plat, *v.* f.ns. *infra*. HIGH BRIDGE MILL, HIGHBRIDGE WILLOW BED, named from High Bridge in W Stour par. *infra*, cf. *Mill Cl* 1842 *TA*. HIGH GROVE FM, *High Grove* 1811 OS. HUNGER HILL (COPPICE & FM), *Hungry Hill Farm Ho* 1842 *TA*, a derogatory name for poor ground, *v.* **hungor**, **hungrig**. KING'S ARMS (P.H.). KNAP CORNER, *v.* **cnæpp** 'hill-top, hillock'. LAMB'S HOUSE FM, *Lambs Ho* 1842 *TA*. LINTERN LANE, cf. *port voc' Linterne gate* 1577 HaRO, *Gt & Lt Linterns, Davis's Lintern* (cf. Tristram *Davys* 1664 HTax), *Linterns Corn Grd & Md* 1842 *TA*, perhaps from ME *lyn(n)et* 'flax, lint' (cf. Do dial. *linnet* 'lint, tinder', Barnes 79) and **ærn** 'building'. LOTMOOR HILL, 1842 *TA*, *Lotmoor* 1811 OS, cf. *Stowre More* 1501 GillCt, from **mōr** 'marshy ground' with **hlot** 'lot, share, allotment', *v.* par. name *supra*. MANOR FM. NEW HOUSE FM. NEW RD. PENNYMOOR PIT FM, *Penymoor Pit* 1811 OS, possibly an allusion to a penny rent, *v.* **pening**, **mōr**, **pytt**. QUARRY, cf. *le Quare de Estover . . . voc' the Lordes Quare* 1576 HaRO, *Quar Grd, Quarry Plat Gdn and Limekiln* 1842 *TA*, *v.* **quarre** 'quarry', **plat**[2]. E STOUR CMN, *Stower Estover Comen'* 1572 HaRO, *Eastower Comon* 1651 KCC, *Common* 1842 *TA*, *v.* **common**, par. name *supra*. WHITE HORSE (P.H.). WITCH LANE, *portam voc' Wyche gate, Wycheate* 1577 HaRO, *Gt & Lt Witch, Witch Grd* 1842 *TA*, *Witch* 1839 *ib* (Gillingham), probably from **wice** 'wych-elm' and **geat** 'gate'.

FIELD-NAMES

The undated forms are 1842 *TA* 206. Spellings dated 1327 are *SR*,
1332 SR, 1572, 1576, 1577 *HaRO*, 1595 Hutch[3], and 1651 *KCC*.

(*a*) Arable Fd; Ash Cl; (Gt & Lt) Ash Croft (*Ascroft(e) lane, -yate*
1572, *Austcrofts Yate* 1576, *v.* **æsc, croft, lane, geat**); (Lt) Axtons; Bean
Cl; Bond Md; Gt & Lt Bowers (cf. David *Bower* 1572); Brach, (Lt) Breach
(*le Breche* 1577, *v.* **bræc** 'land broken up for cultivation'); Broad Croft &
Leaze (*v.* **læs**); Broad Md (*Brodemeade Lane* 1577, *v.* **brād, mæd**); (Lt)
Brockways (cf. William *Brokeway* 1572); Bushy Leaze; Butchers Md;
Butlers Cl (cf. William *Butler* 1572); Butts Hr & Lr Common (*v.* **butte**, or
a surname); Calves Cl & Md; Carraway (so named from a crop of the
caraway plant, *v.* B. Kerr, DoNHAS **89** 254); Clarks Orchd; (Gt) Cle(a)ve,
Cleve Plant. (*v.* **clif** (dat.sg. *clife*) 'cliff, bank'; these fields lie along R.
Stour, cf. *molend' de Clive, -Clyue* 1288 *Ass* on the opposite bank of the
river in W Stour par. *infra*); Common Altmt; Two Common Closes;
Common 8, 7, 6 & 10 Acres; Common (Hill) Pce; 8, 5 & 10 Acre Common
Pce; (The) Hr & Lr Common Pce; Coppice Grd (cf. *Eastower Coppice*
1651); (Lt) Corn Grd; Court Md; Courtnys Md; Crab Tree; Culverhays
(*v.* **culfre**); Dry Grd & Plat (*v.* **plat**[2]); Duntl(e)y (Grd) (named from
Duncliffe Hill which is partly in this par., *v.* Motcombe par. *supra*); Elms
Md (cf. Green Plack *infra*); Ennicks; (Gt) Firth (*v.* **fyrhð** 'wood'); 5 & 4
Acres; French Md (possibly an allusion to **french grass**); Gibbs Md;
Gosborn (perhaps 'goose stream' from **gōs** and **burna**, but cf.
Goseborowhedge 1577); Great Fd; Green Plack (cf. *terr' voc' the plecke above
the great elme* 1577, *v.* **plek** 'small plot of ground'. cf. Elms Md *supra*);
Grove or Lt Bow Wd; Gully Md; Haines (cf. Thomas *Hayn* 1572);
Hanging Land Md (*v.* **hangende**); Hanners Md; Hilly Harpies,
Harpies-, Harpits Md (named from Harpitts Fm in Kington M. par.
supra, cf. also *Harper's* [Bridge] 1791 Boswell); Hassocks (*v.* **hassuc**
'clump of coarse grass'); Higher Grd and Common; Higher Orchd; Hilly
Grd; Home Grd & Md; Hopkins Cl, Pdk & Plat (*v.* **plat**[2]); Inner Grd;
Island; Ledge Moor; Leg Grd, Md & Orchd (*v.* **leg**); Little Grd; Long
Grd; Longlands; Lower (sic); Lower Grd & Md; Loxleys Md; Marks Plat
(*v.* **plat**[2]); Matchams (1577, a surname); Meadow (Grd); Merryfield (*v.*
myrge); Middle Hedge Md; Milking Yd; Miss Plat (*v.* **plat**[2]; *Miss* may
represent 'Mistress's'); Mounts; Mud Ho; Needle; New Cl & Ctg;
Newmans Batch (cf. Geoffrey *Newman als. Everard* 1595, *v.* **batch**
'hillock'); Newtons Orchd; 9 Acres; North Croft & Fd; Old Lane; Orchard
Grd; Pasture Grd; Pensile; Phil(l)ips'(s) (Pdk) Md; Pimperne (this seems
to be another instance of the name discussed under Pimperne par. **2** 110,
the field lies below a hill alongside a small unnamed tributary of R. Stour);
Pit Cl; (Dry & Lt) Plat (*v.* **plat**[2]); Pond Cl; Press; Davids Prize, Hr &
Yonder Prize (probably a complimentary name for a particularly good
field); Red Fd; Ridge Grd; (Gt) Rookhay (*v.* **hrōc, (ge)hæg**); Ruth Md; 7
Acres; (Gt) Short (Ld); Sims's Ho; 6 Acres; (Lt) Slait (*v.* **slæget** 'sheep
pasture'); Slodbrook Cmn (*Sladbroke* 1577, cf. Edward *atte Broke* 1332, *v.*

slæd 'valley', brōc 'stream', atte 'at the', cf. Slodbrook Fm in Gillingham par. *supra*); Spring Grd; Stacys Hanging (*v.* hanging 'steep slope'); Stall Grd; Stones (Orchd); Strap (*v.* strap); John Streets Ctg; Sulters; Summer Grd (Behind Stents); Summerleaze; Sweethams; (Middle & Yonder) Taylors (cf. Richard *Taillur* 1327); Thorny Hays (*v.* (ge)hæg); 3 Acres; 3 Corner Grd; 3 Yards (*v.* gerd 'measure of land'); 12 Acres; Wares Orchd; The Warren; Water Md; West Fd; West Hays Orchd (*v.* (ge)hæg); Willow Bed; Yonder Md.

(*b*) *Ferewood* 1577; *Haywards plote* (1577).

West Stour

COKING FM (ST 762215), *Cokeynecroft* 1315 Banco (Drew), *Coking* 1811 OS, *Lt Cokin*(*g*), *Cokin*(*g*) *Md & Strap* 1842 *TA*, *Cockan Fm* 1869 Hutch[3], cf. also *Coken* 1839 *TA* (Fifehead M.), probably from ME cokaygne 'imaginary land of abundance and bliss', no doubt used in a jocular or ironical sense, cf. 1 12 and Cockaynes Ess 325, *v.* croft, strap; the farm is in the extreme SW corner of the par., remote from the village, and in the flood plain of R. Cale.

LT KINGTON FM (ST 775232), *Chintone* 1086 DB, *Parva Kynton* 1238 FF, *Parva Kington'* 1242–3 Fees, *Parva Kyngton*(*e*) 1268, 1280 FF, 1285, 1303, 1346, 1428, 1431 FA, *Little Kyngton* 1272 Ipm, 1367 AD II, *-Kington* 1290 Ch, 1811 OS, Litil Kyngton 1412 FA, *Kyngton Parva* 1462 IpmR, *Keinton Little* 1795 Boswell, 'little' to distinguish this place from Kington Magna par. *supra, v.* Lat parva, OE lȳtel. *Ouerkyngton'* 1346 *UD* may also belong here, *v.* uferra 'upper'.

CHURCH FM, 1869 Hutch[3], named from St Mary's Church *infra*. HIGH BRIDGE, 1791 Boswell, *Highbridge* 1576 HaRO, cf. *Highbridge Md* 1842 *TA*, High Bridge Mill in E Stour par. *supra, v.* hēah, brycg. LABURNUM VILLA. THE LYNCH, *Linchill* 1811 OS, *Lynch Cl, Hill & Md* 1842 *TA, v.* hlinc 'ridge', hyll. MANOR FM, *the-* 1869 Hutch[3]. ST MARY'S CHURCH, cf. 'a chapel called The Hermit' (sic) 1586 Hutch[3] 3 636. SHIP (P.H.), *Ship Inn* 1811 OS, cf. *Ship Ham* 1842 *TA, v.* hamm 'river-meadow'. STOUR FM. STOUR HILL (FM), *Stower Hill* 1811 OS, *-Ho* 1842 *TA, -Fm* 1869 Hutch[3].

FIELD-NAMES

The undated forms are 1842 *TA* 207. Spellings dated 1288 are *Ass*, 1327 *SR*, 1332 SR, 1362 *For*, 1367 AD II, 1572, 1576, 1577 *HaRO*, 1664 HTax, and 1791 Boswell.

(*a*) Barns Moor Hill (cf. *John Barnes house* 1664 (Stour P.)); Beatons Coking (*v.* Coking Fm *supra*); Bennetts Md; (Lt) Botters Hills; Bramble Croft; Broad Croft; Burdens Cl (cf. Richard *Burden* 1664); Inner & Outer Butts, Butts Mdw (*v.* **butte**); Calerate (possibly for *-crate* from **croft**); Catty Orchd, Cotty Gdn (*Cote Hayes* 1572, *Cotehay* 1576, *v.* **cot** 'cottage', **(ge)hæg** 'enclosure'); Chesters Well (recently identified by M.S. Ross, DoNHAS **106** 118, as the site of a Roman settlement, so perhaps originally from **ceaster**); Chicklands; Coomb-Bottom Md, Coomb Hill (*v.* **cumb**); Coppice (Cl); Corn Fd; Crib Ho Grd (*v.* **cribhouse**); Culverhays (*v.* **culfre** 'dove', **(ge)hæg**); Down Pce and Downs (*v.* **dūn**); Duncans; Footlands; Four Ways; Furzy Cl; Garden Cl; Gore (or 3 Acres) (*v.* **gāra**); Gravel Pit Ham (*v.* **hamm**); Great Cl & Fd; Great Md or Nuns Md; Greens Ham (cf. William *Grene* 1572, *v.* **hamm**); Harpers, Gt & Hilly Harpis, Harpies-, Harpits Hill (all named from Harpitts Fm in Kington M. par. *supra*); Heron (probably **hyrne** 'angle, corner'); Higher Grd; Hill Cl Bottom; Gt & Lt Hillies (Md) (cf. *Hilless* [Bridge] 1791); Hilly Cl; Hiscocks Md & Orchd; Hole Md; Home Fd, Grd & Md; Inn Md; Kinsoms; Leg Md (*v.* **leg**); Little Md & Orchd; Long Croft Cmn; Long Flg (*Longeforlonge* 1367, *v.* **lang¹**, **furlang**); Longmans Hill (cf. *Langmansfelde hedge* 1576, the surname *Longman* with **feld**, **hecg**); Long Md (or Staceys Southey) (*v.* Southey *infra*); Lowerloo (*v.* Waterloo *infra*); Lower Md; Merry-field (*v.* **myrge**); Middle Ham (*v.* **hamm**); Middloo (*v.* Waterloo *infra*); Nappers Mdw; Nether Leaze (*v.* **lǣs**); New Cl; North Cl; Northfield Cl & Md; Old Hall Orchd; Old Wood Cmn; Orchard; Piethorn; Hr Pill or the S part of Southey, Lt Pill, Middle Pill or 2 Closes N of the Lake (*v.* **pyll** 'small stream', Southey *infra*); Popes Stile (cf. *hamstyle* 1576, *v.* **hamm**, **stigel**); Putons; Quar Cl (*v.* **quarre**); Gt & Lt Roomer, Roomer Corner; Rough Cl; St Vincent (probably commemorating the naval victory off Cape St Vincent in 1797); Sawpit Orchd; Shear Hays (*v.* **(ge)hæg**); Shelves (*v.* **sc(i)elf**); Gt & Lt Shorts; Southey; Stable Ham (*v.* **hamm**); Thorns Cl; Turnfurlong and Hound staff (perhaps **trun** 'round'; the meaning of *Hound staff* is not clear); Vanners (cf. Edward *Wanner* 1572); Virgins Ho; Waterloo (probably a name commemorating the battle of 1815 like Waterloo Lane in Silton par. *supra*. Wellingtons *infra*; Lowerloo and Middloo *supra*, the names of fields adjacent to this one, are presumably humorous adaptations of Waterloo); Lt Water Md or Home Md; Wellingtons (a field adjacent to Waterloo *supra*, and therefore no doubt commemorating the Duke of Wellington); Well Orchds (cf. Henry *de ffonte de Westouere* 1288); Winchells Md; Withey Bed, -Moor (*Whitheybedde style* 1577, cf. *moram in villa de Stourewestover'* 1362, *v.* **wīðig**, **bedd**, **stigel**, **mōr**); (Lt) Woods (cf. Robert *Bythe Wode* 1327,

-*Bithewode* 1332 (E Stour), *v.* **bī, wudu**); Woolhouse Md (cf. Woolhouse Fm in Gillingham par. *supra*).

(*b*) *molend' de Clive*, -*Clyue in villa de Sturewestouere* 1288 (*v.* **clif** (dat.sg. *clife*) 'cliff, bank', no doubt with reference to the bank of R. Stour on which the mill would be situated, cf. the f.n. Cle(a)ve in E Stour par. *supra* and cf. *Seuemelne infra* for another (and contemporary) mill here; there were three mills in *Sture* (E & W Stour) in 1086 DB, *v.* VCHDo 3 82); *in the hulle* 1327, *in thehyle* 1332 both (p) (the same person; in view of the preposition *in*, probably from **halh** (WSax dat.sg. *hēale*) 'nook', the spelling *hulle* showing confusion with **hyll** 'hill'); *Hythefeldes* 1576 (probably **hȳð** 'landing place on a river-bank'); *molend' de Seuemelne* (2 x), *Seuermelne* 1288 (the form *Shuvemelne* 1247 (1270), in the bounds of Gillingham forest probably also belongs here, *v.* **myln**; if the *Seue-* forms are to be trusted, the first el. may be **seofon** 'seven' in some undetermined sense, or ME *seue* from OE *sifa* 'sieve', perhaps with reference to some sort of hatch or grating).

Stour Provost

Stour Provost is a separate liberty, *v.* under Redlane hundred *supra*.

STOUR PROVOST (ST 794216)

Stur 1086 DB, *St(o)ure* 1324 Fine, 1330 Pat, 1412 FA

Stures Pratellorum 1243 Cl, *Estures de Pratellis* 1270 *For,* *Sture Pratell[is]* 1285 FA, *Sturepratele* 1288 *Ass,* *Sture P'tell'* 1291 Tax, *Stoure Pratell'* 1348 Pat

Stures Prewes 1268 *Ass, Sture Preauus* 1270 *For, Sturepreues* 1280 *Ass, Stur(e) Prewes* 1288 *ib,* 1297 Cl, Pat, 1327 *SR, Sturprewes* 1307 FF, *Stour(e) Prewes* 1311 Cl *et freq* to 1465 Pat with variant spellings *Stouere-, Stow(e)re-, Store-, -preus, -prewes, -Prewys, -Prewis, -Prowes; Stoure Preaux* 1337 Pat, *Stoure Prews* als. *Stoure Prewes* 1411 ib, *Stoure Uprewes* (sic) 1412 FA, *Stourepreaulx* 1420, 1448 Pat, *-priaulx* 1462 ib, *Stowre Preaux* 1538 KCC, 1575 PlR, *Stover-* 1538 KCC, *Stower Preaux(e)* 1575 *ib*

Stowr' Preves 1517 KCC, *Stowre prevys* 1533 PlR, *Stoure Provys* 1535 VE, *Stowr' Provost* 1549 PlR, *Stower Provouste* 1568 Hutch³, *-Proveste* 1575 KCC, *Stower Provost* als. *Stower Preaux* 1651 *ib*

Named from its situation on R. Stour, cf. E & W Stour pars. *supra*. The earlier affixes are from the possession of this manor during the 12th and 13th centuries by the abbey of St Leger, Préaux (*de Pratellis, de Preus,* etc); in fact it probably belonged to this abbey at the time of DB, the TRW tenant-in-chief being Roger de Beaumont whose father had founded the abbey (VCHDo **3** 37, 141). The later adaptation of the affix to *Provost* reflects the fact that the manor was given by Edward IV (1461–83) to (the Provost of) King's College, Cambridge (Hutch[3] **4** 513), who sold it in 1925.

DUNCLIFFE HILL (ST 826226), *capud de Dunclive* 1247 (1270) *For, -clyve* 1300 Hutch[3], *-cleve* 1338–40 Glast, *-clyf(e)* 1441 *GillCt,* l16 *KCC, -cliffe* 1568 Hutch[3] (*the top of-*), 1609 *LRMB* (*-Hill*), *-clyffe Hill* 1574 Hutch[3], *Donclyfe* 1364 ib, *-cloyf* 1364 *For, Duneclyffe* 1572 *HaRO, Dunkly or Duncliff hill* 1774 Hutch[1], *Doncliff* 1811 OS, *Dunclift Hill* 1838 *TA* (Motcombe); the form *Dunkweie* Hy 3 (14) Cerne also belongs here but is apparently corrupt, though it may be a contraction of *Dunklifweie, v.* **weg** 'road'. The second el. of Duncliffe is clearly **clif** 'steep slope of a hill-side, escarpment'. The first el. may well be **dūn** 'hill, down' (for the somewhat tautological compound, cf. Dundridge Bk 144, second el. **hrycg** 'ridge'), but the adj. **dunn** 'dun, dull brown, dark' gives better sense, and more appropriately describes Duncliffe Hill, a prominent feature which rises to 691' and which 'makes its dark presence felt in all this part of Dorset' (M. Pitt-Rivers, *Dorset,* 1968).

SHADE HOUSE FM (ST 805212), *Sharde-* 1570, *Sherdehowse* 1577 *KCC,* probably to be associated with Robert *atte Shirde* 1340 NI, *v.* **sceard** 'a cleft, a gap (as in a fence)', **hūs, atte,** cf. William *Sherde* 1457, *inclosure at Sherdes* l16 *KCC.*

TERRACE FM (ST 802224), cf. (*via regal' apud*) *Terry(e)s-, Terrieslane* 1420, 1489, 1517, (*portam apud*) *Tarries-, Tarryeslane* 1443, 1444, (*portam vocat'*) *Tyrryestherne, porta apud Tarryescrofte* 1439, *Tarres gate* 1575 all *KCC, Gt & Lt Tarrass, Tarrass Fd & Orchd* 1841 *TA,* all named from the family of William- 1327 *SR,* Robert *Terry* 1332 SR, *v.*

lane, þyrne 'thorn bush', **croft** 'small enclosed field', **geat** 'gate'. The farm is near the junction of Scotchey Lane (perhaps the earlier *Terryslane*) with the road from E Stour to Stour P.

WADMILL FM (ST 817198)

'wood of *Wabenhull*' 1300 Hutch[3], *prato de Wabemille* (probably for *Wabenulle*) 1339 *AddCh*, *Wabnell*', *-nel(l)* *Meade* 1570, *Wabney meede* 1575, *Wab(b)nell Meade* 1576, *-Coppice* 1651, *Wabnull Mead* l16 all *KCC*
Wavenhill 1421, *Wavelenesmede* 1425 *KCC*
Wapenellwode, *Whapenellmede* 1444, *Wapilmede* 1452, *Wapnell* 1465, *Wapenyll* 1489 all *KCC*
Wadmell (*Custom*) *Md*, *Wadmill Md* 1841 *TA*

The second el. is clearly **hyll** 'hill' with reference to the 200' hill spur on which the farm is situated. The first el. is probably a pers.n., although its form is uncertain. If the earliest spellings are to be trusted, they may point to a pers.n. **Waba*. This is not recorded from OE, but cf. the OE **Wafa* (or **Wāfa*) found as *Waua* in DB (Kt, v. Feilitzen 409) and suggested for the first el. of Wavendon Bk 39 and Wandon Hrt 24 (a cognate of OE **Wafa* would be the fem. pers.n. *Waba* 9th cent. given in *Libri confraternitatum Sancti Galli, Augiensis, Fabariensis*, ed. P. Piper, Berlin 1884, p.363, and OE **Wāfa* would be cognate with OE *Wǣba*, OG *Waibilo*, etc). The comparatively recent assimilation *-bn-* (*-vn-*, *-pn-*) > *-dm-* in the medial consonant cluster may be partly due to popular etymology; there was probably never a mill here (unless the palaeographical assumption about the form *Wabemille* 1339 is incorrect), although it is possible there was an early mill some ½ mile W in Todber, v. the *TA* f.n. Wood Mill in Todber par. *infra*.

ALL SAINTS' CHURCH (at Stour Row). ANGEL LANE, cf. *Angel Md* 1841 *TA*. BASKERVILLE'S FM. BUTTS LANE, cf. *Butts* 1841 *TA*, from **butt**[2] 'archery butt' or **butte** 'short strip at right angles to others'. CHEQUER (FM), *Checker Fm* 1811 OS, possibly from **cheker** 'ground of chequered appearance' but perhaps alternatively from ModE dial. **chequer** 'the wild service tree'. COLLEGE ARMS (P.H.), from King's College, Cambridge, *v.* par. name *supra.* DUNCLIFFE CTG, (HR) DUNCLIFFE FM, DUNCLIFF HALL FM (*Dunley Hall* 1811 OS), DUNCLIFFE WD (1841 *TA*, cf. *copicia domini vocat' Dunclifes* 1570, *Dunclife Copce* 1576, *Middle Duncliffe Coppice, Duncliffe Moore Coppice* 1651 all *KCC, v.* **copis**), all named from Duncliffe Hill *supra.* GILLET'S FM. GOOD'S FM, cf. William *Good* 1664 HTax. GREAT HOUSE FM. GREEN LANE. HAWKER'S FM & LANE, *Hawkers* 1577 *KCC, Hawkers Fm* 1811 OS, cf. Robert *Hawker* 1664 HTax. HILL FM, cf. Richard *attehulle* 1327 *SR*, William *atte Hill* 1340 NI, *v.* **atte** 'at the', **hyll.** HUNT'S FM, cf. Robert *le Hunte* 1327 *SR*, Thomas *Hunt* 1425 *KCC.* JOLLIFFE'S FM. KING'S FM, cf. *Mr Peter Kinges house* 1664 HTax. LYDE HILL FM, cf. *Light Hill Acre & Cmn* 1841 *TA*, perhaps to be associated with the lost f.n. *L(e)ightes infra*; there is probably no connection with the *TA* f.n. *Lyde infra*, since this field lies a mile NW of Lyde Hill Fm. MANOR FM. MILL LANE, *viam . . . usque molendinum domini* 1465 *KCC*, cf. Stour Provost Mill *infra.* NEW GATE, perhaps to be associated with *Estovers gate* 1575 *KCC, v.* **geat** and E Stour par. *supra.* PIGEON HOUSE FM, 1811 OS. RIVERSDALE FM, by R. Stour. RUDDOCK'S FM, cf. *Radickes gate* 1577 *KCC.* ST MICHAEL'S CHURCH, cf. 'church of *Stourprewes*' 1358 Pat; the abbey of St Leger of Préaux (*v.* par. name *supra*) did not establish a cell or priory here according to VCHDo **2** 48, but the following references should be noted: *domus . . . in Stures Prewes* 1268 *Ass*, 'priory of *Stoure Prewes*' 1392, 1405 Pat, 'the priory of *Prihaulx* or manor of *Stourepriaulx*' 1462 ib. SCOTCHEY HILL & LANE, *Scotchy Cmn, Corner & Pce* 1841 *TA*. STACYS FM (lost, ST 803215), 1811 OS, cf. Alice *Tacye* (sic) 1664 HTax. STOUR LANE, cf. *Stower Streete* 1651 *KCC.* STOUR PROVOST MILL, cf. *molend' aquatic', molend' fullonic'* 1457, *molendinum domini* 1465, *Myllaker* 1570, *Millmeade* 1575, *Ye Lordes Myll, Ye Myll Pond* l16 all *KCC, Mill Cl & Water* 1841 *TA, v.* **myln**; there was a mill at Stour Provost in 1086 DB (VCHDo **3** 89). STOUR ROW, a hamlet, no doubt **rāw** 'a row' in the sense 'a street lined with a row of houses'; it is possibly to be connected with (*cotag' iuxta*) *le Woderew(e)* 1421, 1477 *KCC*, from **wudu** 'a wood' and the cognate **rǣw** 'a row of houses (or trees)', cf. Woodrow 2 97, 102, PN Wo 239, PN W 129. SWEET'S FM. THOMAS'S FM (GATE 1"). TILE HOUSE FM, *Tiled Ho* 1811 OS, *v.* **tiled**. VANNER'S FM. WHITE POST. WOODVILLE (FM), *Woodvill* 1774 Hutch[1], -*ville* 1811 OS, probably a development of *Wodefeld* 1444 *KCC*, *v.* **wudu**, **feld**, cf. *bosco in Stures Pratellorum* 1243 Cl. YEATMAN'S FM, cf. Martin-, Richard *Yat(e)man* 1664 HTax. YEW TREE FM.

FIELD-NAMES

The undated forms are 1841 *TA* 208. Spellings dated 1258, 1270 are *For*, 1268, 1288, 1337 *Ass*, 1300, 1385, 1627 Hutch[3], 1327 *SR*, 1549 *PIR*, 1664 HTax, 1791 Boswell, and the rest *KCC*.

(*a*) Acre, Lr Acre Cl; All Lake; Ancley; Apple Tree Md; Lt Ash (cf. *Aysshefurlong'* 1443, *v.* **æsc**, **furlang**); Bake Ho (*the bakehouse, bakehouse-haie* 1575, *v.* **bæc-hūs**, **(ge)hæg**); Bakers Md; Barn Md (cf. *cotag' voc' lytle barne* 1570); Benoak (*Bynoke Copice* 1651; -*noke* may be '(place) at the oak', *v.* **atten**, **āc**); Blacklands; Bottom Fd; Bramble Cl (*Bremley Closes* 1573, cf. foll.); Gt Brambly, Brambly Corner, Grd & Leg (*Bremeleyhaye* 1489, *Bremelehey* 1490, 'bramble enclosure', from **brēmel** and **(ge)hæg**, cf. also *Bremellond'* 1425, *Bremlylond'* 1452, *Bremilande* 116; the forms *Bremeley-, Bremly-* suggest an adj. derivative, *v.* -**ig**[3]); Broad Cmn; Broad Hay (*v.* **(ge)hæg**); Broad Md; Burts Md; Bushy Cmn; (Lt) Butterwell(s) (*v.* **butere**, **well(a)**, cf. PNGl 4 108); Butts; Calves Pen (cf. *Calfes Cloose* 1569); Castle Md (cf. *super Castello* 1570, *Castle Cop(i)ce* 1575, 1651, *v.* **castel(l)**; the field is by Duncliffe Fm at ST 823219); Clarks ((*claus' apud*) *Clerkes* 1420, 1517, *Clerkeslond* 1453, cf. Richard *clericus* 1327, Philip *Clerk* 1420); Clover Cl & Grd; Coal Pit; (Gt, Hr, Lr, Lt, Middle & Upr) Common (cf. *Stower Comen* 1569, *Todbere comon als. Stoure' Preauxe comon* 1575, *v.* Todber par. *infra*); Common Cl (cf. *ye comon close belonging to the Farme, Joseph Dowdinges Comon Close, Ellen Grayes Comon Close, Richard Lillyes Comon Close* 1651); Coomb(es) Cl; Coppice Cl, Corner (1651), Grd & Md (cf. *in copic' domini* 1569); Corn Grd; (Inner, Outer & Yonder) Custom Md; Daisey Grd; Dewlands; Dippers; Drove Way; Dry Cl; Dunclift Md & Moor (*v.* Duncliffe Ctg *supra*); 8 Acre Md, 8 Acres; Elmoor (Cl); Encroachment; Farm Coppice & Fd; 5 Acres; 40 Acres; 4 Acre Md, 4 Acres; Further Grd; (Gt & Lt) Furzy (probably 'furze enclosure', from **fyrs** and **(ge)hæg**); Garden Plat, -Plot (*v.* **plat**[2], **plot**); Gore Pce (cf. Peter *atte Gore* 1404, *v.* **atte** 'at the', **gāra** 'point of land'); Great Grd, Md & Orchd; Great Hill; (The) Grove (*claus' voc' Grove, Grove Close* 1570, *v.* **grāf(a)**)); Hain(e)s Moor (*Haynesmoore Coppice* 1651, *v.* **mōr**, cf. William *Hayme* 1457); Halletts Md; Hanging Grd (*v.* **hangende**); Hangmans Cl; Hannafers; Lt & Long Harpers Md; (Lt) Hatch Md (*v.* **hæc(c)** 'hatch, gate', possibly in the sense 'sluice, floodgate', cf. *Will' Wayte* [the miller] . . . *emend' lez flodehacches pertinent' ten' suo* 1478; Hatch Md is the name of two separate fields, both near to streams); Long Hayward Rd (*v.* **hayward**); Hedge Row (cf. *Heggethorn'* 1421, *v.* **hecg, þorn**); Henvills (cf. Robert *Henfeild, the house of Wid' Hendfeilds* 1664); Higher Grd & Md; Hill Md; Hilly Md; Hillis (cf. *Mr Hills house* 1664); Lr Hiscocks; E & W Home Fd; Home Grd; Home Md (*Hommeade* 1575); Homestead (Yd); Hoopers (*terr' voc' Hoper(e)s* 1465, 1529, *Hoopers Severall* 1651, cf. John *Hooper* 1457, *v.* **severell** 'plot of privately owned land'); Jordans (*ten' voc' Jordanys* 1462, *Jurdans* 1529); Kick Acre, Lt Cake Acre (probably from the analogical sg. form *keck* of dial. **kex** 'hollow-stemmed umbelliferous plant', cf. Barnes 75, *s.v.* **kecks, kex**); Kimbers Grd; Land Cmn; Lane; (The) Leg (*v.* **leg**); Little Gdn, Grd & Plot; Little Md (*Lytleme(a)de* 1570); Locksleys; Long Cmn & Grd; Long Md (*Long(e)meade* 1570); Lotmoor Hill (*v.* **hlot**); Lower Grd, Md & Wd; Lyde (beside an unnamed tributary of R. Stour, possibly from **hlȳde** 'noisy stream'); Marl(pit) Grd, Marlpits; Marnhul(l) Path (*v.* Marnhull par. *infra*); Matthews Hill (cf. *Mathies* 1549); Mays Cl (cf. Thomas *May* 1664); The Mead (*Meade* 1571, *ye meadewe* l 16, cf. *cotag' ex opposito le Medeȝete* 1405, *v.* **mǣd, geat**); Middle Grd & Mead; Moggs Hill; Morgans Md (cf. Francis *Morgan* 1664); Moses Cmn; Mow Md; Gt Nancy, Nanc(e)y Gdn & Orchd, Nancy Yeat (Grd) (*v.* **geat**; *Nanc(e)y* is obscure); New [Bridge] 1791; New Cl; 9 Acres; 9 and 11 Acres; North Cl (*Northe-* 1570); (Lt) North Fd (*Northfilde* 1569); Nursery Md; (Young) Orchard (cf. *Orchard Close* 1571); Over Lake (*v.* **uferra, lacu**); Out Cl; Outer Grd; Ox Acre & Cl (cf. *Oxenlease* 1571, *v.* **oxa, lǣs**); Paddock; Pancake Cl (the name of three fields beside a stream; perhaps originally an allusion to shape or soil); Parish Grd; Peters; Pig's Hay (cf. Robert *Picke* 1664, *v.* **(ge)hæg**); Pit Grd (cf. *Pitclose* 1569, *Pytte Close, Pytmede* 1570, Pug Pit *infra, v.* **pytt**); Popple Street, Popples (*Paplestrete* 1575, *v.* **papol, popol** 'pebble'); Pug Pit ('pit haunted by a goblin', *v.* **pūca, pytt**, cf. John *de la Putte* 1288, Pit Grd *supra* and foll.); Puxey Acre (the first el. may be **pūca** 'goblin', with **(ge)hæg** or **ēa**, cf. prec. and the f.n. Puxy 1 203); Quarry Cl; Rack(e)y Cl; Red Lane; Reeve Plot (cf. *ten' voc' Reveholdes* 1570, *v.* **(ge)rēfa, hold**); Rooks (*Rokesclose* 1421, 1443, the surname *Rook*); Rough Coppice & Grd; Round Cl; Rushy Grd; Sand Pits (*Sandepittes* 1443, *v.* **sand, pytt**); Scots Cl; Gt, Lt & Middle Setty (*claus' voc' Sethay* 1420, *Sythay* 1425, *Cit(t)eheys* 1485, 1490, *Cities* 1569, *Cyties, Cyty(e)s* (*hedge*) 1570; this may be a compound of **(ge)set** 'stable, fold' or **sæt** 'trap' and **(ge)hæg** 'enclosure'; the same origin is perhaps possible for some of the places called City in PN W 68, 141, PN Brk 284, etc); 7 Acres; Sharlands Cl; Sheep(s) Sl(e)ight (*v.* **slæget** 'sheep pasture'); Shortlands; 6 Acres (*Syxakers* 1570); Smithy; Soldiers Grd; (Gt & Lt) Spring Cl; Square Grd; Stair Cl; Stake or Overlake, Stake Md, Stock Md (*v.* **staca** 'stake, post', apparently showing confusion with **stocc** 'stump', cf. Over Lake *supra*); Stone, Stone Grd, Stone Md and Quarry (cf. *semitam apud Stone in the/le feld* 1425, *v.* **stān, feld**); Strode (*v.* **strōd** 'marshy land overgrown with brushwood'); Stuble Cmn (*v.* **stubbil**);

Sturmys; Summer Fd, Grd & Leaze (*v.* **lǣs**); Swellings (*Swelyngeslane* 1439, *Swellentislane* 1485, *Swellettes lane* 1517, *Swellens bridge* 1570, cf. also *enclosure at Siolient* (sic) l16; perhaps a surname from a p.n. such as Sullens Wt 23 or Swelling Hill Ha (Gover's typescript 87)); Tennes Cmn; Terment; Thorny Coppice; 3 Acres, 3 Acre Hay (*v.* **(ge)hæg**); Todber Gate Pce, Todber Path (Md) (named from Todber par. *infra*); Toll Ho and Gdn; Top Grd; Topps Hill; Tree Grd; Trill (Heap & Md) (*Trill Meade* 1573, probably named from the stream that flows into R. Stour near Trill Bridge *q.v.* in Fifehead M. par. *supra*); Trims Home Grd & Long Grd; Tuckers Grd; 2 Acres, 2 Acre Md; Webbs (*ten' voc' Webbys* 1478, *the house of Mr Webb* 1664); Weir Plot; Well Md; Wheat Cl (*Whe(a)teclose* 1570, 1575, cf. *Wheateearshe* 1575, *v.* **hwǣte, ersc, ærsc** 'stubble field'); Whippers Plat (*v.* **plat**²); With(e)y Bed (Gdn); Wood Cl & Flg (cf. *Wodelese* 1439, *Woodcroftes* 1570, *v.* **wudu, lǣs, croft**); Woodlake [Bridge] 1791; Woods Coppice; Woolfreys; Yarn Barton; Young Orchard.

(*b*) *Aleynesplace* 1443 (cf. John *Aleyn* 1420); *terr' voc' Anket(t)ell(e)s* 1569, 1570 (cf. John *Anketill* 1457); *claus' voc' Awtman* 1420, *Awtmannesclose* 1421, *Awtemanclose* 1425 (a surname); *le Backsid* 1570 (*v.* **backside**); *prat' voc' Backwurthyes* 1570, *buckworthies* 1573, *Blackewurthies* 1575 (possibly a surname); *ten' voc' Bledons* 1485 (probably a surname); *claus' voc' Boys* 1492 (a surname); *le Breche* 1420, *le breache* 1575 (*v.* **brǣc**); *Bro(o)declose* 1570, 1576 (*v.* **brād**); *Brokeclose* 1570 (*v.* **brōc**); *Bryxies-* 1268, *Brixies-* 1300, *Brykeswode* 1478, *the way by Brixeys* 1627 (the surname *Brixey* from the OE pers.n. *Beorhtsige*, with **wudu**); *lez Burgheys* 1489, *le burrougheys* 1570 (*v.* **burg** 'a burrow'); *Burywode* 1444 (probably ME *bury* (from dat.sg. *byrig* of OE **burh**) in the sense 'manor house'); (*ten' voc'*) *Carpenters* 1405, 1529, *Carpynters* 1465 (the surname); (*terr' voc'*) *Carra(u)ntes* 1571, 1575 (cf. John *Carent* 1457, *v.* 1 57); *Catshave* 1443, *claus' voc' le Cotteshave* 1492, *Cottishave* 1570 (probably 'copse frequented by (wild) cats', *v.* **catt, sc(e)aga**); *Coltclose* 1571 (*v.* **colt**); *Cow Close* 1571; *Cox* 1570 (the surname *Cock*); *Crochehous* 1462 (*v.* foll.); *Crowchehyll* 1529, *Crechelles Meade* 1570 (first el. of this and prec. is probably **crūc**³ 'a cross', with **hyll, mǣd**); *in orient' campo* 1570; *le Overfernylond* 1420 (*v.* **uferra, fearnig, land**); *Foteacr'* 1443 (*v.* **fōt, æcer**); *ten' voc' Fygers* 1478 (a surname); *cotag' voc' Garrettes* 1570 (the surname *Garrett*); *grete close* 1575 (*v.* **grēat**); *atte Halle* (p) 1405 (*v.* **atte, h(e)all**); *claus' voc' Hertes* 1421, *Hortes Way* 1651 (the surname *Hart*); *terr' voc' Hilemannys* 1465, *Hylmans* 1529 (the surname *Hillman*); *terr' voc' Hobbes, -ys* 1529 (the surname *Hobb(s)*); *Innemede* 1465, *-Meade* 1570, *Inme(a)de* 1529, 1569 (*v.* **in** 'inner', **mǣd**); *terr' voc' Irynges* 1490 (a surname); *Jobbes Lane* 1577 (the surname *Job*); *Le Lagge* 1457 (*v.* **lagge** 'marsh', cf. *Py Meade infra*); *lame closes* (*v.* **lamb**); *la Leigh* 1421, *La Leygh'* 1443 (*v.* **lēah** 'wood, clearing in a wood', cf. foll.); *terris voc' Leis* 1569, *Lyghes* 1570 (cf. John *Lygh* 1457, *-Ligh* 1485; the forms *terr' voc' L(e)ightes* 1572, 1573 also apparently belong here, perhaps with excrescent *-t* due to influence from foll., cf. Lyde Hill Fm *supra*); *terris voc' Leyton* 1569, *Leigh-* 1572, *Leytons* 1573 (*v.* **lēac-tūn** 'herb garden', or a surname from this source);

lymboroghislane 1492 (cf. Robert *Lymborwe* 1404, John *Lymborugh'* 1443, Lymburgh's Fm in Marnhull par. *infra*); *Ye Longe Fore pitt* l16 (*v.* **fore**); *Ye Longe Furlong* l16; *the Lordes feild, ye Lordes Woodd* l16 (cf. *in bosco domini* 1420); *Lyppyeate* 1575 (*v.* **hlīep-geat** 'a leapgate'); *Madelymepitte-hill* 1576 (*v.* **līm-pytt, hyll**; *Made-* is presumably the p.p. of *make* with a sense 'produced (by burning limestone)', cf. *limemaker* 1573 NED and *made stone* 'stone rough hewn at the quarry' Barnes 80); *Midleclose* 1570; *atte More* 1385, *Attemore* 1444 both (p) (*v.* **atte, mōr**); *Netherclose* 1571; *Newe Copce* 1577 (*v.* **copis**); *Oues-* 1337, *Oveshey* 1465, (*ye old*) *Oveshey* l16 (*v.* **(ge)hæg**; the first el. is probably a ME surname *Ove* from the OE pers.n. *Ofa*); *a stoninge bridge usq'* Plowemans *Corner* 1577 (*v.* **stānen** 'made of stone', **corner**, the surname *Plowman*); *Poulehays* 1457 (probably the surname *Poul, Paul, v.* **(ge)hæg**); *Poundeclose* 1570 (*v.* **pund**); *le lagg prati vocat'* Py Meade 1571 (*v.* **pīe**[1] 'insect' or **pīe**[2] 'magpie', cf. *Le Lagge supra*); *ten' voc'* Pynt(*e*)ne(*y*)s 1529, 1570 (a surname); *Shopclose* 1570 (*v.* **sc(e)oppa** 'shed'); *Sladefurlong'* 1443 (*v.* **slæd, furlang**); *Southeclose* 1570; *in camp' australi* 1443, *Sowthe filde* 1569; *Sym'es* 1570 (cf. Robert *Symys* 1457); *Tifles* 1570, *Tiphills Coppice* 1651 (cf. Robert *Tifle* 1270); *metam* ('boundary') *voc' le Wale* 1425 (*v.* **walu** 'ridge of earth or stone'); *Warresplace* 1443, *Warrs* 1575 (the surname *Warr, v.* **place**); *Watermeade* 1569 (*v.* **wæter**); *Waterslippes, -ys* 1452, *Watershippys* 1457, 1492, *Watershipps* (*Comon Close*) 1570, 1651 (*v.* **wæter-scipe** 'water channel', perhaps as a surname from some other place so called; *-slippes, -ys* is probably an error but could represent **slip(p)e** 'narrow strip of land'); *le Westclose* 1571; *Westfilde* 1569; *Attewik* (p) 1258 (*v.* **atte, wīc** 'dwelling, dairy farm'); *Yelder close* 1570 (probably **elle(r)n**, ME *eldre* 'eldertree', with prosthetic *y-*); *Yenderclose* 1573 (ME *зender, зonder* 'yonder', cf. *Netherclose supra*).

Sutton Waldron

SUTTON WALDRON (ST 863157)

> (*at, of*) *suttune* 932 (15) *ShaftR* (S 419)
> *Sudtone* 1086 DB
> *Sutton(e)* 1212 Fees, 1220 Cur, 1235–6, 1242–3 Fees, 1262 Ipm *et passim* with affix *-Walerand* 1297 Cl, Pat, *-Walrond(e)* 1314 Ipm *et freq* to 1451 Pat, *-Walraund* 1318 Ipm, *-Walrand(e)* 1369, 1405 Cl, *-Walround* 1424 AD II, *-Warlonde* (sic) 1425 Cl, *-Wallerond* 1428 FA, *-Walron* 1545 Hutch[3], *-Waldron* 1664 HTax
> *Sotton(e)* 1285, 1303 FA, *Sotton' Walrond'* 1431 (15) *Wim*

'South farm', from **sūð** and **tūn**, 'south' perhaps in relation to Fontmell Magna par., cf. the note added to the bounds of the Anglo-Saxon estate of Fontmell Magna in 932 (15) *ShaftR* (S 419): *and at suttune ligð XXIIII akeres meade þat hirð in to funtmel*. The manorial affix is from *Waleran* (*venator* 'the huntsman') who held this manor ˙ as tenant-in-chief in 1086 DB (VCHDo 3 96) or from his descendants, cf. Walter *Walerand, -rant* who is mentioned in connection with this place in 1210–12 RBE, 1212 Fees, cf. Hutch³4 107, Eyton 65.

COMBE BOTTOM, *v.* **cumb**. MANOR FM. PEN COPSE, near foll. PEN HILL (356'), PENHILL COPSE, cf. *Penhill* 1701 *Glyn, Penhill* (*Cl*), *Pen Cl* 1845 *TA*, a Brit hill name from PrWelsh ***penn¹** 'hill', *v.* discussion under Sixpenny Handley hundred and Sixpenny Fm in Fontmell Magna par. both *infra*. ST BARTHOLOMEW'S CHURCH. SATAN'S SQUARE (local), an earthwork, called *The Devil's Trencher and Spoon* 1765–7 Map, *v.* RCHM 4 86. SPRING COPSE. SUTTON CLUMP. SUTTON HILL (FM & PLANT.), cf. *Sutton downe* 1618 *Map, Downlands* 1845 *TA, v.* **dūn**. SUTTON WALDRON HO. VALE FM. WEST FM.

FIELD-NAMES

The undated forms are 1845 *TA* 213. Spellings dated 1366 are Pat, 1444 *MinAcct*, 1583 *SPDom*, 1618, c.1776 *Map*, and 1915 *TA* alt.app.

(*a*) Brickfield 1915; Broad Cl; the Drove; the East Common (cf. *Common* 1583); East Fd c.1776; Font hill (probably named from the adjacent par. of Fontmell Magna); Ledge Fd c.1776; The Marsh (*le Mershe* 1444, *v.* **mersc**); (Lr) North Fd; Shelves (*v.* **sc(i)elf**); Whiteway.

(*b*) *Asshemede* 1444 (*v.* **æsc, mæd**); *Blaclond'* 1444 (*v.* **blæc, land**); *Burrowes* (a coppice) 1618 (probably a surname); *Busmereshale* 1444 (the surname *Busemer* found in 1332 SR, cf. Reaney s.n. *Bismire*, with **h(e)alh** 'nook', cf. *Sutton Hales infra*); *le Calfhey* 1444 (*v.* **c(e)alf, (ge)hæg**); *Grasslade* 1444 (*v.* **gærs, slæd**); *prat' voc' Holebroke* 1444 (cf. *to holebroke* 932 (15) *ShaftR* (S 419) 'to the hollow brook' in the bounds of Fontmell M., *v.* **hol², brōc**); *le Homeclose* 1444 (*v.* **home**); *Humbermede* 1444 (probably the pre-English r.n. **Humber**, with **mæd**); *Medecrofte* 1444 (*v.* **mæd, croft**); *Meere* 1618 (a coppice near the par. bdy, so probably **(ge)mǣre** 'boundary'); *Melkewell'* 1444 ('spring or stream with milky coloured water', *v.* **meoluc, well(a)**); *le Morwelese* 1444 (*v.* **morgen** 'morning', **lǣs** 'pasture'); *pontem apud le Oldmyll'* 1444 (*v.* **(e)ald, myln**; there is mention of a mill at Sutton Waldron in 1086 DB (VCHDo 3 96)); *le Orchard'* 1444 (*v.* **orceard**); *Stavelokmede* 1444 (*v.* **mæd**, probably with a surname); 'a place called *Sutton Hales* on the king's highway between *Blaneford* and *Shaftesbury*' 1366 (*Hales* may be a pl. of **h(e)alh** 'nook', cf. *Busmereshale supra*); *Sutton Peak* 1618 (a pointed coppice, so perhaps **pēac** in the sense 'point'); *Voxle* 1444 (*v.* **fox, lēah**, probably to be identified with *on foxlee* in the Anglo-Saxon bounds of Iwerne M. par. *infra*); *le Vyveacr*' 1444 (*v.* **fīf, æcer**); *pontem apud le Were* 1444 (*v.* **wer**, cf. Weir marked 6″ where par. bdy crosses Fontmell Brook); *Whetehyll*' 1444 (*v.* **hwǣte** 'wheat', **hyll**).

Todber

TODBER (ST 800201) ['tɔdbə]
  Todeberie 1086 DB, *-beria* Exon, *-bire* 1209 P, *-b*' 1212
    Cur, *-ber(e)* 1244 *Ass*, 1270 *For*, 1280 *Ass*, 1285 FA,
    1291 Tax, 1293 Ipm *et freq* to 1362 Cl, *-byr*' 1244 *Ass*,
    -berwe 1268 *ib*, *-bur* 1278 Banco, 1316 FA
  Toteberg(a) 1177–94 BrutC, ?1177–94 France, *-bera* 1194
    P, *-berge* 1212 Cur, *-bire* c.1217 Sarum, *-ber(e)* 1299
    BrutC *et freq* to 1495 *Sher* (p), *-byr*' 1244 *Ass*, *-berwe*
    1268 FF, *-bur* 1316 FA, *Toterberg*' (sic) 1212 Cur
  Totdeberia 1194 P, *-bere* 1268 *Ass*
  Toddebir 1228 FF, *-bur*' 1258 *For*, 1280 *Ass*, *-bere*
    1278–84 Ipm, 1288 *Ass*, 1297 Pat, *-bery* 1280 *Ass*
  Tudebur' 1258 *For*, *-bery* 1270 *ib*, *Tudboro* 1575 Saxton
  Todbur 1278 Banco, *-bury* 1411 Cl, *-bere* 1664 HTax
  Tuttebur 1303 FA   *Tottebere* 1327 SR
  Totbere 1306 Banco, 1479 IpmR, 1503 Ipm
  Tokebere (sic) 1331 Ipm
  Tedebere 1347 Cl   *Tidebere* 1371 *For*

Both first and second els. of this name are uncertain. The first el. is probably the pers.n. *Tota*, but **tōte** (gen.sg. *-an*) 'a lookout' cannot be ruled out. Some of the early spellings for the second el. suggest **beorg** 'hill, barrow', others point to **bearu** 'wood, grove' or **bǣr²** '(woodland) pasture', and a few show confusion with **burh** (dat.sg. *byrig*) 'fortification'. (On the problems of interpreting SW p.ns. in *-ber*, etc, *v.* PN D 107 s.n. Shebbear). An OE *tōtanbeorg* 'hill used as a look-out', although only one possible explanation of the name, would have analogies in names containing the el.

tōt-hyll (*v.* EPN s.v.), cf. also *on toten berg'* in the Anglo-Saxon bounds of Six. Handley par. *infra*; the land rises in the N of the par. to over 250 feet.

CHURCH LANE, named from CHURCH (6"), cf. 'the chapel of *Toteberga'* ?1177-94 France, *ecclesie de Tidebere* 1371 *For, Chapel Md* 1840 *TA*, Parsonage Fm *infra*. GANNETTS, *Gannets* 1811 OS, *Gannath, Gannatt Md* 1840 *TA*, probably a surname. HAYES COPPICE, 1840 *ib*, cf. *The Hays, Hays Corn Grd, Hay's Md* 1840 *ib*, all named from Hayes (Fm) in Marnhull par. *infra*. HUNT'S HILL, cf. *Hunts Cmn* 1840 *ib*, the surname *Hunt*. MANOR FM. NORTHFIELD HO, named from *campus Borialis* 1339 *AddCh, North field* 1840 *TA*. PARSONAGE FM, cf. *terra persone capelle de Totebere* 1339 *AddCh*. RED LANE, *Redelane* 1244 *Ass* (p), *Redlane* 1503 Ipm, 1774 Hutch[1] 2 328 ('. . . a very small hamlet, situated about half a mile S.W. from Todbere, remarkable for nothing but its giving a name to a hundred'), *Redling Ho, Red-, Ridling Cl* 1840 *TA*, *v.* **rēad, lane**, Redlane hundred *supra*. SHAVE LANE, cf. *Gt Shave, North Shave* (*Md*) 1840 *TA*, *v.* **sc(e)aga** 'a small wood', cf. the lost *Catshave* in the adjacent par. of Stour P. *supra*. TEMPLE'S CTGS, *Templars Fm* 1811 OS.

FIELD-NAMES

The undated forms are 1840 *TA* 227. The fields marked † are now in Marnhull par. *infra*. Spellings dated 1212 are Cur, 1258 *For*, 1300 (1362) Pat, 1327 *SR*, 1332 SR, 1339 *AddCh*, 1549, 1557 *PlR*, 1570, 1575 *KCC*, and 1664 HTax.

(*a*) Austes (possibly Anstes); Bad(d)s (Md(w)); Barn Cl; Broadland (*Brodelonde* 1339, *v.* **brād, land**); Broughton Crop; Calves Grd; Corn Grd; Crews Bottom (*v.* **botm**); Crow Mdw; Denhams; Dibbens; Five Yards (*v.* **gierd**); Frances Yarn; Gardens; Great Common (cf. *Todbere Comon als. Stoure' Preauxe Comon* 1575); Great Down; Great Md; Hatchers Gdn (cf. Thomas *Hatcher* 1664); Holloway Plot (*v.* **hol**[2], **weg**); Home Fd, Grd & Md; Kernell; Key Hay (perhaps 'enclosure that can be locked', *v.* **cǣg, (ge)hæg**); Kings Md (cf. Thomas *Kyng'* 1332, *terr' Joh' le Kyng* 1339); Lime Kiln; Lines (*v.* **leyne**); Little Fd & Md; Lower Mdw; Lower path; Middle Grd; Milking Barton; Moggs Hill; Mundays Cmn; Orchard; Paddock; (Gt & Lt) Pye Lane (*v.* **pīe**[1] 'insect' or **pīe**[2] 'magpie'); Quarry Cl & Md (quarries marked 6"); The Pound; 6 Acres; Todber

Green; †Todber Moor (*Todberemore* 1557, cf. *feno de Totdeberia* 1194 P, *v.*
mōr 'marshy ground'); Todber path; Lt Toms; 12 Acres; Wheat Cl; (Lt)
Woodland (cf. *boscus de Tudebur'* 1258); (Gt & Lt) Woodmill Md, (Gt)
Wood Mill (these fields alongside the stream (*Todbere Lake* 1570) forming
the E bdy of Todber par. seem to take their name from Wadmill Fm in
Stour P. par. *supra*, but the former mill at Todber may have been here, cf.
molendinum in Toterberg' (sic) 1212, 'the mill of *Totebere*' 1300 (1362), and
the mill at Todber in 1086 DB (VCHDo 3 92)).

(*b*) *apseg'ne* 1339 (*v.* **æspe** 'aspen-tree', second el. perhaps **grēne**[2]
'grassy spot' or, if the reading is -*g'ue*, **grāf(a)** 'grove'); *Canefordushay*
1339 (*v.* **(ge)hæg** 'enclosure', with a surname from Canford M. 2 2);
Grenes house 1664 (a surname); *Heuudhakur* 1339 (*v.* **hēafod, æcer**); *in the
Mersch* 1327, *in the Merssh'* 1332 (both (p), *v.* **mersc**); *Overleyghe* 1339 (*v.*
uferra, lēah); *Schortelonde* 1339 (*v.* **sc(e)ort, land**); *campus australis* 1339
('south field'); *Stoklonde* 1339 (first el. probably **stocc** 'tree stump');
Todbere Fylde 1549 (*v.* **feld**).

Buckhorn Weston

Buckhorn Weston (ST 757247)

> *Weston(e)* 1086 DB, 1210–12 RBE, 1212 Fees, 1220 Cur,
>   1235–6, 1242–3 Fees, 1249 FF *et freq* to 1428 FA,
>   *Westun'* 1248 *Weld*[2]
> *Boukeresweston* 1275 Banco, 1317 FF, 1345 Pat, 1387, 1403
>   Cl, *Bokeres Weston(e)* 1285 FA, 1288 *Ass*, *Bukeres
>   Weston* 1289 Orig, 1348 Ipm, Cl, 1361 ib, *Bouker(e)s
>   Weston* 1303, 1412 FA, 1414 Fine, *Bukeresweston* 1310
>   FF, 1360 Ipm
> *Bukereweston* 1286 Orig, *Bokereweston'* 1288 *Ass*, *Burkere-
>   weston* (sic) 1301 FF, *Buckerweston* 1550–3 BM I
> *Bakeres Weston'* 1288 *Ass*
> *Bokernesweston* 1344, *Boukernes Weston* 1398 IpmR,
>   *Buckerns Weston* 1543 *AD*
> *Bo(u)kerne Weston* 1346 FA, 1352 FF, 1428, 1431 FA,
>   *Bowkerneweston* 1428 ib, *Weston Bukkehorne* 1535 VE,
>   *Buckerswerton* (for -*weston*) als. *Buckhorne* 1647 DorR,
>   *Buchorne Weston* 1664 HTax
> *Weston Maundevyll* 1387 Pat, -*vyle* 1412 FA, -*vile* als.
>   *Boukers Weston* 1414 Fine, *Boukerswaston* als. *Weston
>   Maundevile* 1414 IpmR
> *Bokesweston* 1424 AD II

Bakeres Weston als. Weston Moygne 1486, *Bokerys Weston otherwise called Weston Moygn* 1494 Ipm

'West farm', *v.* **west, tūn**, perhaps referring to its situation in relation to Gillingham. The addition *Boukeres-*, etc, later *Buckhorn-*, has not been satisfactorily explained. Fägersten 4 offers no suggestion. Tengstrand MN 90 suggests that it contains OE *būc* 'belly, stomach; pitcher', a word not hitherto noted in p.ns. but here used as a hill-name to describe the 414' hill N of the village, either in a compound with **ærn** 'house' (with sporadic reduction of ME -*ern* to -*er*), or with interchangeable suffixes -*ere* and **-ern* (cf. discussion of Pimperne **2** 110–12). Ekwall DEPN (also *Selected Papers* 78), citing only two 13th cent. spellings in *Bokere(s)-*, suggests 'of the scribe(s)' from OE *bōcere* 'scribe'; this explanation is adopted by Smith EPN **1** 39. However, in view of the late appearance of -*ern*- (from 1344) and the interchange of *Bouk-, Bok-, Buk-* among the 13th cent. forms, neither explanation seems quite satisfactory. *Boukeres-*, etc should rather be associated with the ME occupational term *bouker* 'a buck-washer, a bleacher' (Fransson 109, in surnames from 1229), a derivative of ME *bouken* (< OE **būcian*) 'to steep in lye, to bleach' (surviving as ModE dial. *buck* OED vb.², cf. also ModE dial. *buck* OED sb.³, recorded as (E) Do dial. by Barnes 52: 'Buck (E.) A book or washing of clothes'). *Bouker* may then have been a byname of one of the early lords of the manor of Weston, or it may have reference to a specific feudal service (for another Do p.n. that may refer to a place where cloth was bleached, cf. Blashenwell **1** 8). The forms with -*es* (*Boukeres*, etc) may have originally represented a gen.sg. form, but these could be taken to be either sg. or pl. Thus the later appearance of -*n*- in forms from 1344 is probably to be explained as the analogical ME wk.gen.pl. ending -*ene* (*v.* **-ena**) common in Do in the 14th cent. (as in e.g. the forms for Fryer Mayne **1** 208, Winterborne Monkton **1** 266), with the addition of a further analogical -*s* to the already pl. form *Bouker(e)ne* in some spellings. The *Buc(k)horne* of 1647 and 1664 and modern *Buckhorn* are clearly a result of popular etymology based on this form (it may be of interest to note that the compound *buck-horn* 'the horn of a buck' is not on record before 1447–8 NED, except in surnames from 1271 MED, although a quite distinct ME word *buk-horn* (probably from MDu) 'cured fish' is on record from 1391 MED).

The other affixes, *Maundevyll* and *Moygne*, are of the common manorial type. Part of the manor was held by Robert *de Maundevill* of Geoffrey *de Maundevill* in 1268 FF, cf. also Robert *de Ma(u)ndevill(e)* 1310 ib, 1346 Hutch[3], John *de Mandeville* 1360 ib, and land here came to the *Moygne* family (which gave its name to Owermoigne 1 138) at the end of the 14th cent. through marriage, *v.* Hutch[3] 4 115–6.

ABBEY FORD BRIDGE, by ABBEY FORD (disused), *Abbisford* 1838 *TA*, on the par. and county bdy, no doubt an allusion to the former possession of the adjacent So par. of Abbas and Temple Combe by the Abbess of Shaftesbury, *v.* **ford**. CAGGYPOLE FM, *Caggeypole* 1811 OS, first el. dial. *caggy* 'decaying; tainted, etc', perhaps related to the vb. (also dial.) *cag* listed by Barnes 53 with the meaning 'to surfeit; cloy, clog', thus no doubt with reference to 'a stagnant pool, choked with (decayed) vegetation', *v.* **pōl**[1] 'pool, pond, pool in a river'; the farm lies close to Filley Brook ('the foul or dirty brook', *v.* RNs. *infra*), so the name may have referred to an ox-bow lake or the like; note the change in the course of the brook indicated by the present position of the par. bdy just S of the farm. COMMON FM, cf. *Hr & Lr Common*, (*Gt*) *Common Pce* 1838 *TA*. CONYGAR FM, *Conygar(s)* 1838 *ib*, *v.* **coninger** 'rabbit-warren'. COURT FM, *Cort Farm* 1647 DorR, *v.* **court**. DUNSTER, 1811 OS, perhaps analogous with Lt Dunster Fm in Marshwood par. *infra* or Dunster So (DEPN). FILLEY BROOK FM, *Filleybrook* 1811 OS, named from Filley Brook on which it stands, *v.* RNs. *infra*. GIGG LANE, *Gig Lane Grd* 1838 *TA*, ModE **gig** 'a light, two-wheeled, one-horse carriage' (from 1791 NED), cf. *gig-road* 1824 NED. HARDING'S FM. HARTMOOR (FM & HILL), *Hartmoor* 1811 OS, *v.* **heorot**, **mōr**, cf. an identical name in Pulham par. *infra*. HILL FM, cf. *Hill* 1838 *TA*, named from Weston Hill *infra*. HOPE FM, cf. *Hope Cl* 1838 *TA, v.* **hop**[1] 'small enclosed valley'. HURDICK (lost, ST 769253), 1811 OS, (*Lamberts*) *Hurditch, Lr Hurdick* 1838

TA, v. **heorde-wīc** 'a herd farm', cf. Thomas *Lambert* 1664 HTax. NEW BARN. NEWHOUSE FM. PELSHAM FM, *-farme* 1648 SC, *Pelsam* 1774 Hutch[1], *Pelsham* 1795 Boswell, *Pulsham* 1811 OS; the forms are too late for a safe etymology, but this may be from **hamm** 'enclosure' with the ME pers.n./surname *Pell*, or, if the name is older, with the OE pers.n. *Pēol* found in Pelsall St (DEPN). PICKFORD'S FM. PITT HOUSE FM. QUARR (FM), *Quarr* 1811 OS, *v.* **quarre** 'a quarry'. RECTORY, cf. *the Parsonage house* 1664 HTax, *Gt & Lt Parsonage, Parsonage (New) Cl & Hill, Parsonage Common Pce* 1838 *TA.* ST JOHN THE BAPTIST'S CHURCH, cf. 'church of *Weston(e)*' 1268 FF, *Church Yd* 1838 *TA.* SHAVE HILL, *Broad Shawe (wood), Long Shawe* 1647 DorR, *(Long) Shave, Shave Flg* 1838 *TA, v.* **sc(e)aga** 'a small wood, a copse'; for the development, cf. Shave Cross in Marshwood par. *infra.* SHEPHERD'S HILL. SHUTE'S LANE. SMALLSFORD LANE (lost), 1811 OS, *Small's Ford* [Bridge] 1791 Boswell, *Small Ford* 1838 *TA,* a name for part of what is now Shave Hill *supra.* STAPLETON ARMS INN, from the *Stapleton* family, lords of the manor since the 19th cent. (Hutch[3] **4** 116), although there was a William *de Stapleton* here in 1317 FF. TUNNEL HEAD (PLACE), named from railway tunnel. VESEY'S HOLE (HILL), *v.* **hol**[1] 'a hollow, a valley'. WADLIN (lost, ST 763246), 1811 OS, perhaps to be associated with *Wadman's Collycomb* 1838 *TA, v.* f.ns. *infra.* WESTON FD, HILL & HO.

FIELD-NAMES

The undated forms are 1838 *TA* 31. Spellings dated 1249, 1268, 1317 are FF, 1316, 1346 FA, 1327 *SR*, 1332 SR, 1340 NI, 15 *ShaftR*, 1646, 1648 SC, 1647 DorR, 1650, 1720 Hutch[3], and 1664 HTax.

(a) Bakers Cl (cf. *Mr Baker, minister* 1650); Barelain (form uncertain, but perhaps from **leyne, lain** 'tract of arable land'); Lt Barn Cl; Barren Cl; Bean Cl; Gt & Lt Berry Croft (*Bury Croft* 1647, *v.* **croft** 'enclosure' with ME *bury* (from dat.sg. *byrig* of OE **burh**) in the sense 'manor house'); Billinghams; Black Croft; Blackers and Shave Flg (*v.* Shave Hill *supra*); Bowstall Gdn; Brake Wd (*v.* **bræc**[1]); Breach (*v.* **bræc**); Broad Croft; Broad Leaze (*v.* **læs**); Broad Wall; Brockley Down (from **brōc** 'brook' or **brocc** 'badger' with **lēah** '(clearing in a) wood'); Brook Fd, Flg & Md (*v.* **brōc**); Browns (cf. William *Bron* 1327); Bushey Cl; Butchers Grd; Bye Mill (named from Bye Fm in Kington M. par. *supra*); Calves Cl (cf. *Calfe hay* 1647, *v.* **c(e)alf, (ge)hæg**); Cammic Hill (from **cammoc** 'cammock', listed by Barnes 53 as *cammick* 'the plant rest-harrow'); Clarks-, Clerks Cl (cf. Edmund *Clark* 1650); Clinch's Ho and Gdn; Collie Md, Gt & Lt Collycombe, Collycomb or Smallford (perhaps analogous with Colly Fm in Allington par. *infra, v.* **cumb** 'valley', *Smallsford Lane supra*); Coppice Grd; Cow Park (Cmn & Md); Crispins, Crispens Orchd; Cutlinch; Deep Md; Dirt Croft; Donners Md and Cmn; Drews; Eastmost & Westmost Durcroft (*v.* **croft**, perhaps with **dēor** 'animal'); Ell Grd (possibly **ellern, elle(n)** 'elder-tree'); Ennicks (*v.* **inhoke**); (Hr & Lr) Field, Field Acre; 15 Acres; Filly Brook (Md or Bridge Cl) (*v.* Filley Brook Fm *supra*); Fish Croft; 5 (and 6) Acres; Flat(t) Cl; Four Way Grd; Gt French, French Grd; Gillers Lain (*v.* **leyne, lain**); Godminster; Goldridge; Gommers Md; Great Cl & Md; Lt Greens, Green Cl (cf. Roger *Grene* 1664); East & West Grove, Small Grove and Leg (*v.* **grāf(a), leg**); Guthings (Md), Guttrings Md; Halves (*v.* **he(a)lf**); Harpiss Md, Harpits (cf. Harpitts Fm in Kington M. par. *supra*); Hill Top; Holly Wd; Home Grd; Late Hunts; Huson's Cmn; Land; East & West Leaze (*v.* **lǣs**); Light Horn; Lime Kiln; Linchey Cl; Little Cl; Little Elm (or 15 Acres); Little Fd, Flg & Md; Long Cl, Fd & Md (*Langemede* 15, *v.* **lang**[1], **mǣd**); Lower Grd; Lushens (cf. Philip *Lucyen* 1249, *-Lucien* 1317); Maidments (Orchd); Marsh Flg; (Inner & Lr) Mead; Middle Cl & Grd; Middle(s) Fd; Mill or Clerks Cl (cf. Bye Mill, Clarks Cl *supra); .* Moor(e) (*the Moore* 1647, *v.* **mōr**); New Cl; 9 Acres; Lr, New & Young Orchard (cf. William *de la Orchard* 1316, Thomas *atte Orchard* 1346, *v.* **orceard**, **atte**); (Lawn) Ox Cl (cf. *pasture called the Lawne* 1647, *v.* **launde**); Pease Dean(e) (*v.* **pise** 'pease', **denu** 'valley'); Plackars, Plackers (Md); Poor Grd (cf. *Poor Ho* 1811 OS); Rag Md (*v.* **ragge**); Rick Yd; Ridge(wa)y Cl (*v.* **hrycg-weg**); Ridley Cl; Hr & Lr Mount Rodber, Quarrymount Rodber; Rushey Cl; Sanderland (Fd); Gt & Lt Sands; Sandsons; She(e)rbicks; Sleights; Square Cl; Stall Md; Starve Land (no doubt a derogatory name for poor ground); Sticklinch (probably analogous with Sticklinch So which is 'steep ridge' from **sticol** and **hlinc**); Stone House Orchd; Strap (*v.* **strap**); Sudges; Tanswell Md; 10 Acres; 3 Acres; Three Corner'd Grd; Tithingmans Yd; Townsend Cl; Lt Trench (*v.* **trenche**); Eams's & Long 2 Acres; Vinings; Wadman's Collycomb (cf. *Wadlin,* Collycombe *supra*); Water Md (cf. John *atte Watere* 1327, *v.* **wæter, atte**); Wheat Cl; Wood Bars (*v.* **barre**); Hr & Lr Wood, Lt & Middle Wood, Wood Md; Woodlands Leg (*v.* **leg**); Worthy Hill (*v.* **worðig** 'enclosure'); Yonder Grd.

(b) *Bydeshale(s)gate* 15 (*v.* **geat**, first el. perhaps a surname); *Conet farme* 1648 (cf. Nicholas *Conett* 1646 (Dorchester)); *Eldeber* 1268 (*v.* **eald** 'old', with **bǣr**[2] 'woodland pasture' or **bearu** 'wood'); (John) *atte Hatheheyhach'* (p) 1327 (no doubt the same man as John *Hacchete* 1340, thus *Hathe-* is probably for *Hache-, v.* **hæc(c), hæcc-geat, (ge)hæg, atte**); *New-gate* 1720 (cf. John *atte Yate* 1332, *v.* **geat**); *the North Feild* 1647; *the South Feild* 1647; *la Stounlond* 15 (*v.* **stān, land**); *pasturam . . . appellatum vacherie* 15 (*v.* **vacherie** 'a dairy farm'); *atte Were* (p) 1332 (*v.* **wer**).

XX. SIXPENNY HANDLEY HUNDRED

This hundred is the result of the amalgamation, probably in the 13th cent., of the two GeldR hundreds of *Sexpene* (which contained Compton Abbas, Fontmell Magna, Iwerne Minster and Melbury Abbas), and *Hanglege* (which consisted only of Handley itself), both having once belonged to Shaftesbury Abbey, *v.* Anderson 140–1, VCHDo **3** 137, 139. East & West Orchard were originally tithings in Iwerne Minster and Fontmell Magna respectively. Shaftesbury, already a borough in DB, is included here for topographical convenience; in fact Cann, always closely associated with Shaftesbury and now comprising most of the rural parts of the borough, is included in this hundred by Hutch[1] and Boswell.

SIXPENNY HANDLEY HUNDRED

> *Sexpene hundret* c.1086 GeldR, (*hund' de*) *Sexpen'* 1212
> Fees, *Sexpenne* 1244, 1268 *Ass*, 1303, 1346 FA, c.1500
> Eg, *Sexepenne* 1244 *Ass*, 1316 FA, *Sexpen* 1303 FA, 15
> ShaftR, 1428 FA, 1535 VE
> *Hanglege hundret* c.1086 GeldR, (*hund' de*) *Hanlegh(e)*,
> *-leg'* 1244 *Ass*, *Henlegh* 1303, *-leigh* 1316 FA
> *Hundred' de Henleg' et de Sexpon* 1265 Misc, *hund' de*
> *Henley et Sexpenne, -de Sexpenn' et de Hanleg'* 1268 *Ass,*
> *hund' de Sexpenne et de Henleye* 1275 RH, *hund' de*
> *Sexpenne et Henlegh(e)* 1280 *Ass*, 1280 (1490) Pat *et freq*
> to 1332 SR with variant spellings *-Henleye, -Hen(ne)le*;
> *hundredum de Sexpen et Hanle* 1431 FA
> *Sixpenhanley hd* 1542 LP, *Seppenhanley hd* 1570 Ander-
> son, *Hundred of Sixpenny Handly* 1664 HTax

The hundred takes the two parts of its present name from Sixpenny (Fm) in Fontmell M. par. and from Handley par. for both of which *v. infra.*

ALCESTER LIBERTY, a small area SW of Shaftesbury, according to Hutch[3] **3** 54 containing 'the manors and farms of Anketell's Place, Blintesfield, Glydeford, le Gore and that of the Dean of Sarum'; for early forms and origin of the name, *v.* Alcester in Shaftesbury par. *infra* and foll., and cf. Anketil's Place, Blynfield Fm, Lydford Fm all in Cann par. *infra*, Gore in Marg. Marsh par. *infra.*

BLINCHISFELD HUNDRED (lost), a 12th cent. hundred, taking its name from Blynfield in Cann par. *infra q.v.* and possibly an earlier name for Alcester Liberty *supra.*

Cann

The present par. is a comparatively recent formation. In 1894 large parts of the Shaftesbury pars. of St James and Holy Trinity were transferred to Cann for civil purposes, and at the same date parts of Cann were included in the borough of Shaftesbury, further parts being transferred to the borough in 1920 and 1933.

CANN (ST 872215) [kæn], *Canna* Hy 1 (15) *ShaftR, Canne* 1202 P, 1244 *Ass,* 1323 Inq aqd, 1327 *SR* (p) *et freq* to 1564 *Glyn, Canme* (or *Camne*) (sic) 1268 *Ass,* Kanne 1288 *ib* (p), *Caune* (sic, for *Canne*) 1354, 1357 Cl, *Canne iuxta bertona Shafton* c.1500 *Eg, Can* 1575 Saxton, 1615 Map, 1655 *HBr, The Parish of St Rombald, or St Rowald, alias Cann* 1744 Hutch[1], *Can(n) St Rumbold(s)* 1795 Boswell, *Shaston St Rumbold alias Cann* 1840 *TA.* From OE **canne** 'a can, a cup', used topographically for 'a hollow, a deep valley' with reference to the situation of this place in a steeply sided valley; for an analogous simplex name, *v.* Canna D 481. The dedication of the church, now within the boundary of Shaftesbury borough, is to St Rumbold, *v.* further the section on Parishes and Churches in Shaftesbury *infra.* The form *bertona* refers to Barton Hill in Shaftesbury *infra.*

ANKETIL'S PLACE (site of) (ST 857222), 1774 Hutch[1], *mes' voc' Anketellesplace* 1453 *Midd, Anctill's Place* 1732 Coker, *Anketell's Place* 1869 Hutch[3], cf. *tenement' Willelmi Anketill* c.1407 *Shaft, Anketilleslane* 1441 *Wim, Anketyll' lane* 1494 *HarlCh,* named from a family mentioned in connection with Shaftesbury since the 13th cent., e.g. Roger *An(c)ketil* 1244 *Ass,* Ed 1 (c.1407) *Shaft,* William *Anketil* 1327 *SR, v.* **place,** **lane;** the mansion house was pulled down in the late 18th cent. (Hutch[3] **3** 61, RCHM(Do) **4** 9).

BLYNFIELD FM (ST 839219)
blinchesfelde (*þanen ealden herepaþe þæt schet to-*) 932 (15) *ShaftR* (S 419), *Blinchesfeld* c.1140 (1340) Ch, *-feld(e)*

13 *Glyn* (p), 1244 *Ass* (p), 1307 Anderson (p), 1327 *Glyn* (p), *Blinchis-* 1168 P, *Blinchesfeldhdr'* 1168 ChancR, *terra de Blinschesfelde que est in Sturminstr'* 13 GlastR, *Blynchesfeld(e)* 1315 Anderson (p), 1327 *SR* (p), 1341 Salis (p), 15 *ShaftR* (p), *Blyncheffeild'* (for *-esf-*) 1332 SR (p)

(*on*) *blinnesfeld* 958 (15) *ShaftR* (S 656), *Blynnesfylde* (*capella de-*) n.d. (1500) Hutch³, *Blynsfeld(e)* 1455 Cl, 1486 *KCC*

Blingesfelda (*terram . . . de-*) c.1140 *AddCh, -feld* 1154–8 (1340) Ch

Blinchildfeldhdr' 1169, 1170 P, *Blinkefeldhundredum* 1176 P, *Blinkisfeldhdr'* 1176 ChancR

Blinchefeld' 1244 *Ass* (p), 1275 Cl (p), *Blynchefeld* 1258 FF (p), 1323 (c.1407), 1332 (c.1407) *Shaft* both (p), c.1500 *Eg* (p)

Blyndefeld(') 1244 *Ass* (p), 1274 FF (p), *Blindefeud* 1244 *Ass* (p), *Blyndesfeld(')* 1332 SR (p), 1442 Ipm (p)

Bleinchesfeld 1268 *Ass* (p), *Blenchusfelde* 1339 *AddCh* (p)

Blyntesfeild 1283 *Cecil* (p), 1327 *SR* (p), *-feld(e)* 1340 NI (p), 1360 Ipm, 1404 *KCC* (p), 1474 *Wim, Blintisfeld'* 1332 SR (p), *Blintesfeld* 1362 Cl (p), *-field* 1811 OS, *Blintsfield* 1841 *TAMap*

Blynfelde 1550 Pat

The two earliest forms are from 15th cent. copies of 10th cent. Anglo-Saxon charters. 'The old highway that runs to *blinchesfelde'* occurs in the OE bounds of Fontmell M. par. *infra*, the 'highway' being probably the present Sturminster N.–Shaftesbury road at Kit Hill *infra* 1¼ miles S of the present Blynfield Fm. (*On*) *blinnesfeld* is from the OE bounds of Thorton in Marnhull, a small estate which seems to have extended NE beyond the present bounds of Marnhull to include much of the present par. of Margaret Marsh as well as the SE corner of Marnhull itself; (*on*) *blinnesfeld* is likely to have denoted part of the northernmost bdy of the 10th cent. estate, which very probably followed the modern bdy of Margaret Marsh where it passes ½ mile S of the present Blynfield Fm. Another point in the Fontmell M. bounds, and clearly to be connected with these forms, is *on blinches broc, of panne broke* (932 (15) *ShaftR* (S 419)), describing it seems the stream (a feeder of Key Brook) which forms the W bdy of Cann par. and which branches upstream just SW of Blynfield Fm.

Kökeritz 128 is probably correct in taking the first el. of these names to be an English r.n. **Blinch* (OE **blinc*) 'the glittering river', relating it to ModE *blink, blench* (OE *blencan*) and *blank. Blinches broc* would then be 'the stream called *Blinch*' (*v.* **brōc**), and Blynfield 'the tract of open land by the *Blinch* or through which the *Blinch* runs' (*v.* **feld**). Cf. Anderson 139 who, while citing the same related words, prefers to interpret the postulated term as possibly meaning 'glade, opening' on the grounds that 'river-names are usually feminine' (cf. however Ekwall RN lxxxi), and adds 'after all, its genitival form may point to the first el. being a pers.n.'.

There is probably no need, with Anderson 138, 'to reckon with two Blynfields, one, the original Blynfield, in Marnhull nr Sturminster Newton, the other, the present Blynfield Fm nr Shaftesbury, a manorial name derived from the *Blinchesfeld* family that flourished in the 13th and 14th centuries'. The boundary points in the two charters cited can in fact be reconciled as referring to the present Blynfield, though it is indeed likely (cf. Anderson *loc. cit.*) that in the 10th cent. the **feld** still denoted a fairly extensive tract of open land rather than a precise location.

It will be noted that in the series of six 12th cent. spellings from P and ChancR, Blynfield is designated a hundred (*h(un)dr(edum)*). The identification of these proposed by Fägersten, that they represent an alternative (and earlier) name for Alcester Liberty, is supported by the inclusion of *terram . . . de Blingesfelda* in the foundation charter (c.1140 *AddCh*) of Alcester Abbey (cf. also the grant of Blynfield manor to the Abbey in 1293 Sydenham 51), and by the later inclusion of Blynfield (as well as Gore in Marg. Marsh) within the bounds of the Liberty (*v.* under Sixpenny Handley hundred *supra*). Cf. Anderson 139, who suggests that *Blinchisfeld* hundred is probably an alternative (and earlier) name for Redlane hundred.

The 13th cent. form from GlastR referring to 'the piece of land of *Blinschesfelde* which is in *Sturminstr*' is to be explained with reference to the location of the 10th cent. form (*on*) *blinnesfeld* discussed above; the original **feld** clearly extended into that part of the Thorton estate which later became Margaret Marsh, and the latter was a tithing in Sturminster Newton hundred.

According to Drew, the probably corrupt form 'the church of *Blendfort*' 1101–18 (e17) France, identified with Blandford F. in the index to France and by Fägersten 50, belongs here. Cf. *capella sancti petri* here in c.1140 *AddCh*, *capella de Blynnesfylde* n.d. (1500) Hutch[3] **3** 88, and reference to a former chapel here in Hutch[1] **2** 35.

GILDENOCK (lost, about ST 871221), 1620 Hutch[3] (**3** 415), *la Gildenhoke*, (*la*) *Gulden(e)ok*(') 1280 *Ass*, *la Gyldeneok*, *la Gildeneok(e)* 1280 QW, *Goulder oke* 1618 *Map*, 'the golden oak-tree', *v.* **gylden**, **āc**; a point in the 'out-bounds' of Cranborne Chase (**2** 193), described as being situated between French Mill *infra* and St Rumbold's Church.

GUY'S MARSH (FM) (ST 844205), *Gyesmersch* 1401 ShaftMR, *-merssh* c.1407 *Shaft*, *Gyes Marshe* 1564 *Glyn*, *Marsh* 1811 OS, *Gays Marsh Grd* 1840 *TA*, *Gay's Marsh* 1841 *TAMap*, *Guy's Marsh Fm* 1869 Hutch[3], from **mersc** 'marsh' and the pers.n. or surname *Guy* (< OFr), though no person with this name has been noted in connection with the place. There seems to have been here a tract of marshy ground, originally no doubt simply *Marsh*, which gave name also to Marsh Cmn in Fontmell M. par. and to Margaret Marsh par. (both *infra*, 1 and 1½ miles SW of Guy's Marsh respectively), *v.* under Margaret Marsh for some earlier simplex forms that may (partly) belong here.

HOLM AND IVY FM (ST 856216), *la Holmene Theuele* 1341, *la Holmunthevel'* 1394, *Holm in the Bynele* 1401 all *Salis*, *Holemandivile* 1548 *Weld*[1], cf. *Holm and Ivy Mead, Home Bush* 1840 *TA*, 'the holly bush or thicket', from **holegn** (Do dial. *holm*) probably with an adjectival suffix **-en**[2], and **þȳfel**. The 1401 form, half rationalized (*-ene The-* > *-in the-*) and half garbled or corrupt (*Bynele* for *thyuele?*), already suggests that the compound was no longer understood; the 1548 and modern forms continue the process of rationalization and popular etymology, the modern form resulting from the conventional association of holly and ivy.

LITTLE DOWN (ST 868241), 1568, 1628 Hutch[3], 1840 *TA, viam super liteledoune* 1356 *GillCt, Liteldo(u)ne* 1362 *For et freq* to 1438 *GillCt, Lyteldoune* 1362 *For, lytyldowne* c.1500 *Eg, Little Downe* (*one windemill uppon-*) 1609 *LRMB, v.* **lȳtel** 'little', **dūn** 'hill, down'; the ground rises to 760' here, but reaches over 800' just to the N.

LYDFORD FM (ST 842203), *Glideford* 1280 *Ass* (p), 1333 (c.1407) *Shaft* (p), 1340 NI (p), 1442 Hutch[3], *Glidford* 1289 (c.1407) *Shaft* (p), *Glydeford(')* 1327 *SR* (p), 1332 SR (p), 1333 (c.1407) *Shaft* (p), 1389 *DCMDeed*, 1774 Hutch[1], 1795 Boswell, 1869 Hutch[3], *Glydfordemyll'* 1360 *AddCh, Lydford* 1502 Ipm, 1841 *TAMap, Glydford* 1811 OS, *Lidford* 1869 Hutch[3] , cf. *Further & Rushy Lydford, Lydfords* 1840 *TA*, 'ford frequented by the kite or other bird of prey', from **glida** and **ford**, with **myln**, cf. Glyde Path Hill I 351. The ford (and mill) may have been on the small stream just WSW of the farm or on R. Stirchel to the E. The unusual loss of initial *G-* is to be noted.

BISHOP'S FM, cf. *Bishop's Hanging & Md* 1840 *TA*, Roger *Bisshop* 1316 FF, *v.* **hanging** 'steep slope'. BOYNE FM, HOLLOW & VILLA, BOYNMEAD FM (1931 6", SPRINGFIELD CTG 1902 6"), cf. *Boyn Md* 1799 *Map, Boyne Head* 1840 *TA*; if the stream, a feeder of R. Stirchel, flowing in the valley called Boyne Hollow was called *Boyne* (NB also *Boyne Head*), this is perhaps a transferred commemorative name from the Irish river which gave name to the battle of the Boyne, 1690; however a somewhat similar cluster of *Boyn(e)-* names predating this battle (*Boynhyll* 1534) and therefore of different (though unexplained) origin, occurs in PN Brk 56; the first el. of both sets of names may of course be the OE pers.n. *Boia* (gen.sg. *-n*). BOZLEY FM, cf. *Boazely Md* 1840 *TA*. BRAEMOUNT. BREACH CMN (1841 *TAMap*) & CTG, *commun' pastur' vocat' la Brech'* 1385 *Salis, le Breech* 15 *Shaft, Brechemede* 1433 *Salis, le Breach* 1562 *Weld*[1], 1671

Waller, cf. *Breach Cl* 1840 *TA*, *v.* **bræc** 'land broken up for cultivation', **mǣd**. CANN CMN (1811 OS), FM & MILL (1811 OS). CANNFIELD FM, *Cann-Field-House* 1840 *TA*, named from *Cann Fd* 1840 *ib.* CHERRY ORCHARD FM & LANE, *Cherry Orchard* 1811 OS. CHURCH FM, near St James's Church, Shaftesbury. COLE'S LANE (FM), *Coles Lane* 1840 *TA*, cf. *tenement' Willelmi Cole* 14 (c.1407) *Shaft*; the farm is *Bilbecks* 1811 OS. EDWARDS FM, *Edwards's* 1869 Hutch³. FOOT'S HILL. FOUL HILL, *Fowel-* 1562 *Weld*¹, *Fowlehill* 1565 ib, 1668 *Waller*, *v.* **fugol** 'bird', **hyll**; the first el. is perhaps less likely to be a surname, but cf. *tenement'* . . . *quod Ricardus Fowell' iam tenet* 1473 *Sher*. This name has now been altered to Foyle Hill on recent street plans of Shaftesbury. FRENCH MILL (LANE), *molendinu' Fraunceis, de molendino Frauncisci, Frenssh myll* 1500 Hutch³, *molendin' Franceis* c.1500 *Eg*, *French-Mill* 1546 Hutch³, *French Mill* [Bridge] 1791 Boswell, *French-Mill-House, French Mill Fd* 1840 *TA*, no doubt so called from its possession by a Frenchman (or by someone with a surname *Franceis*), OFr *Franceis* 'French, Frenchman' and the Lat form *Franciscus* here both alternating with ME **Frensche**, cf. Henry *Fraunceys* Ed 2 (c.1407) *Shaft*, French's Fm **2** 265, and the analogous French Mill Wt 150. Sydenham 79 conjectures that the name may contain ME *fraunchise*, but the forms do not support this, cf. Little Francis **1** 268. FROGHOLE FM, *Froghole* 1841 *TAMap*, cf. *Froghole Md* 1840 *TA*, *v.* **frogga**, **hol**¹. GEAR'S MILL, 1841 *TAMap*, *Low Mill* 1811 OS, perhaps to be associated with *Danyelesmulle, v.* the f.n. Daniels *infra*. GOODS BARN (lost), 1811 OS, cf. John *le Gode* 1332 SR, Peter *Goude* 1388 *HarlCh*. GRANT'S FM. GREEN'S FM, cf. Christopher-, Mathew *Grene* 1664 HTax. HEATH FM, *Heath Farm House* 1840 *TA*, named *West Heath* 1811 OS to distinguish it from *East Heath* ib, now East Heath Fm in Donhead St Mary par. W, *v.* **hǣð**. HIGHER BARN. KIT HILL, 1841 *TAMap*, *Kits Hill* 1811 OS, the pers.n. or surname *Kit*, or **cȳta** 'kite'. LITTLE LONDON, 1841 *TAMap*, on the par. bdy remote from the village. MAMPITTS FM , *v.* **malm** 'sand, soft stone', **pytt**, cf. **1** 151. MAYO FM, cf. Thomas *Mayo* 1664 HTax. MILL POND (2 ×), 1840 *TA*, by Cann Mill and French Mill both *supra*. NEW LANE (FM).

PAYNTHOUSE FM, *Pint Ho* 1811 OS, *Paint-House* 1841 *TAMap*; this is probably ModE *penthouse* (from ME **pentis**) 'an outhouse or shed with sloping roof, an annex' (the variant spelling *paint-house* is recorded 1606 NED), cf. **1** 350. PONSONBY FM. REST HARROW, no doubt the plant name **restharrow**, cf. Cammic Hill in B. Weston par. *supra*. ROSE CTG. ST JAMES'S CMN, 1811 OS, in the large area of the modern par. of Cann formerly belonging to Shaftesbury St James. SPRINGFIELD CTG, *v.* Boynmead Fm *supra*. SPRAG(G)S MILL (lost), 1838 *TAMap*, 1840 *TA*, cf. Robert *Spraggy* 1295 (c.1407) *Shaft*, *Spragg's* [Bridge] 1791 Boswell, and the f.n. Spragg's Orchd in Melbury A. par. *infra*; just E of Cann Mill *supra*. THREE WAYS, where three roads meet. WEST-WOOD FM, *West(e)wode* 1280 QW, *West Wood* 1840 *TA, v.* **west, wudu**; it lies W of the village near the old par. bdy. WHITE'S FM, cf. John *Whyte* 1446 Hutch[3], *Whites* (f.n.) 1840 *TA*. WILKIN'S FM, cf. Robert *Wilkyns* 1427 *HarlCh*, *Wilkins Cl* 1840 *TA*. WINCOMBE LANE, 1845 *TAMap*, leading to Wincombe in Donhead St Mary par. (W). YEWTREE CTG.

FIELD-NAMES

The undated forms are 1840 *TA* 185 (*Shaston St James*), except for those marked † which are 1840 *TA* 186 (*Shaston St Rumbold alias Cann*), and those marked ‡ which are 1840 *TA* 184 (*Shaston Holy Trinity*). Spellings dated 1327 are *SR*, 1328, 1380 *Sher*, 1332 SR, 1340 NI, 1360[1] *AddCh*, 1360[2] Ipm, 1369 Cl, 15, 1446, 1472, 1474[2], 1509, 1574, c.1620, 1625, 1642, 1647, 1687, 1869 Hutch[3], 1410 *HarlCh*, 1432, 1441, 1453, 1474[1] *Wim*, 1450, 1564 *Glyn*, c.1500, 1782 *Eg*, 1548, 1560, 1562 *Weld*[1], 1578 Hutch[1], 1618 Map, 1650, 1655 *HBr*, 1664 HTax, 1670, 1685 *Waller*, 1673 *Whil*, 1740 SRO, 1841 *TAMap*, and the rest *Shaft* (c.1407). Many of the lost f.ns. listed under Shaftesbury par. may well have been within the area now comprising the par. of Cann.

(a) Abbotts Md (cf. Robert *Abbott* 1664); Acre; †Adams's Gdn (cf. John *Addams* 1664); Alcaster Gdn (from Alcester in Shaftesbury par. *infra*); ‡Andrews Cl; Angiers Cl; †Bagbarrow; †Barfoot's Fd; Barn Cl (*Barne-* 1650), Grd & Md; ‡Barn Cl; †Barn Grd; †Barters' Md; †Beacon Hills (*v.* **(ge)bēacon**); ‡Beast Lease; Belly's Grd; End of Lane or Bennett Md (cf. Joan *Benoyt* 1372 (c.1407), (house called) *Bennet's* c.1620); Birnbecks (probably from **burnbake**); Bottomfield; Bottom Md; †Bottom Md; Brake (*v.* **bræc**[1]); Brickyard Bldgs & Gdn; †Brinsombe (*v.* Brimscombe Fm in Shaftesbury par. *infra*); Broad Cl, Leaze & Moor; †Broad Cl; †Broadway;

†Brockway's Cmn (cf. John *Brocwey* (bailiff) 1441); (†)Broom Cl; †Bullbeggars'; Butter Print (probably a figurative name referring to shape or appearance); Calves Cl; †Canncombs (Hanging) (*v.* **hanging** 'steep slope'; *Canncomb* is probably 'valley at Cann', *v.* **cumb**); †Cann Grd; Carrot Cl; Chaffeys Md; Chalk(y) Grd; †Lt Churnhills; †Coleman's; Colsum; Common; †Common Cl & Pce; Coneygar Cl (*v.* **coninger** 'rabbit-warren'); Cooksland (cf. John *Cook* 1366 (c. 1407)); Coppice (Cl); †Copse Grd; †Copy Hill; †Corner Cl; Corn Grd; †Cowleaze, Cow Lease; †Cox's Cl (cf. John *Cocks* 1446, Thomas *Cox* 1664); Dallymoor; Hr & Lr Daniels (*Danielesfeld* 1369, *Daniels felde* c.1500, *Danyellislande* 1474[1], cf. *Danyel(e)smulle* 1328, 1380, *Danyell Mulle* 1441, *-Mylle* 1453, Adam *Danyel* 1395 (c.1407), 1472, *v.* **feld, land, myln**; the *TA* fields are near Gear's Mill *q.v. supra*); Davis's Md (cf. Mathew *Davys* 1664); †Deep Mdw; Droveway; Dry Grd & Md; Duckland; †Dynely; East Fd; †East and Middle Fd (*Midel Fieldes* 1740); Edmunds Hays (*v.* **(ge)hæg,** cf. William *Edmond* 1340); 8 Acres; ‡8 Acres (1740); †18 Acres; (†)11 Acres; Ellyhay; †Envy Cl; Farthingsland (*Farthinglands* 1548, *Farding lands* 1560, *Farthing Lands* 1670, probably from **fēorðung** 'fourth part', with reference either to a measure of land or to a rental of a farthing, *v.* **land**, but cf. Roger *Ferthing* 1327, *-Ferthyng* 1340); †Field Pce; Fields Moor; First Grd; Fishers Md (*Fysshersmede* 1474[1], cf. *de tribus croftis terre quas Walterus Vysshere tenet* 1397 (c.1407), *v.* **mǣd**); (†)5 Acres; ‡5 Acres (1740); Fors Thorn; (†)4 Acres; ‡4 Acres; ‡(Dowlands) 14 Acres; Franklans (cf. William *Franklin* 1687); Free Grd or New Gate; Frys (cf. Randal *le Frie* Ed I (c.1407), John *le Frye* 1332); Furzy Grd; ‡Ganny and House Md; †Gappers' Copse; †Garden by the Pound; Garden Fd & Grd; Gaston (*Broad-, Long garston* 1673, *v.* **gærs-tūn** 'grass enclosure'); ‡Gate Cl; †Gibbett Cl & Plant. (*v.* **gibbet**); Gore Md (named from Gore Fm in Marg. Marsh par. *infra*); Grammers Grd, Grandfers Grd (adjacent fields, named from colloquial or dialectal forms of *grandfather* and *grandmother, v.* Barnes 67); Great Grd & Md; Green Cl; Green Lane (-Fm 1841 *TAMap*); †Hanging; Hanging Cl; Harveys Md (cf. *tenement' Magisteri Walteri Hervy* 1310 (c.1407)); Hastings Md; Hatch Md; †Hawkers' Hill; †Lt Hawksdown (*v.* Hawksdean Fm in Shaftesbury par. *infra*); †Higher Fd & Grd; ‡Higher Grd; Outside & Middle Hill (cf. John *at Hull'* 1360[1], 'tenement called *the Hull'* 1474[2], *v.* **hyll**); Hilly Grd & Md; †Hilly Grd; Home Cl, Fd, Grd & Md; †Home Grd; Hoopers Md (cf. *mesuag' . . . quod Johannes Houpere tenet* 1397 (c.1407)); Hopes Paddock; Horny Grd; Horse Cl; House Grd; ‡House Paddock & Six Acres; Hundred Acres (an ironical name for a very small field); Huntswood (cf. John *le H(o)unte* 1327, 1332, Agnes *la hounte* 1327, *cotag' Alic' Hunte* 1377 (c.1407)); Ivy House Lane; ‡Jackass Grd; Jacksons; Jacobs; Kings Hill, †Hither & Yonder Kingshill (cf. Robert *(Le) Kyng(')* 1327, 1332); Knowle Hays (1647, possibly to be identified with *Cnoel* c.1500, *v.* **cnoll** 'hill-top, hillock'); †Lamberts' Barn and Yd; †Landsleys'; ‡Lane Side (Fd); †Lavy's Cl; Leek Hays; Leg; †The Limekiln, Limekiln Pce and Cmn; †Little Fd; Little Grd & Md; †The Lodge-House; Lodge Md; Loits (cf. *tenement' Petri (le) Loyt* Ed 2

(c.1407), 1327 (c.1407)); Long Cl & Grd; †Gt & Lt Longly; Long Md; †Lower Fd; Lower Grd & Md; †Meekleys' (Coppice); †Middle Close Gdn & Md; Middle Grd; Miles Md (cf. Thomas *Miles* 1664); Milking Barton; †Moore's Mds, Mower (cf. *Moor Mead* 1625, Adam *atte Moure* 1360², Adam *Att more* c.1500, *v.* **mōr, atte**); Mustards; †New Cl; (†)9 Acres; Oakhays; Orchard; †Oxencroft Md (partly in Shaftesbury *q.v. infra*); The Paddock, Lt Paddock; †Park; Park Md, Park Moor Lds (*Parkmore* 1578, *v.* **park, mōr**); Parkers Md (cf. William *Parker* 1664); Parsons Cl & Grd; †Pennys' Hanging, Hr Pennys'; Pickford Cl or Sexty Md (perhaps to be associated with *Sexkesterye Lane* 1568 Hutch³ 3 621, mentioned in the bounds of Gillingham forest, which is probably from ModE **sextry** 'sacristy, residence of a sacrist(an) or sexton'); Pig Brook; Pighays (*Pyggesheye* a1335 (c.1407), *-heygh'* 1474¹, *Pig-Hayes* 1642, *v.* **pigga, (ge)hæg**); Piles Hill (perhaps to be connected with *Pylemede* 1358 (c.1407), *claus' voc' Pile* 1548, *-Pyles* 1562, *-Pile als. the Cliffe* 1685, *v.* **pīl** 'a shaft, a stake', **mǣd**); Pit Grd; Plantation (freq); ‡Platt (*v.* **plat²**); Pond(s) Cl; Poor Grd; †Porters' Copse & Md (cf. *mes' nup' Henrici Porter* 1405 (c.1407)); †The Pound; Pound Md (cf. *pinfold p'och'i Sancti Jacobi Shaston* 1670); Puckmoor (*-more* 1869, from **pūca** 'goblin' and **mōr**, cf. the f.n. Packmoor in Motcombe par. *supra* and foll.); Puxy (perhaps 'goblin-haunted stream' from **pūca** and **ēa**, cf. Puxy 1 203; the field lies beside a stream and near to prec.); †The Quarry-Plat (*v.* **plat²**); †Rack Cl (Orchd) (*Rack Close Garden* 1782, *v.* **rakke**); †Ray Grass(*v.* **rye-grass**); †Rix Cl; †Roadway Pce; †Robins' Hanging (*v.* **hanging**); Roundhill; ‡Royal Oak Ho and Gdn; Ruddocks; Rushy Md; Rye Grd; Sand Hill; †7 Acres; Sexty Md (*v.* Pickford Cl *supra*); Shepherds-, Sheppards Leaze (cf. *Shepherd's Close* 1625, Edward *Sheperde* 1509); Silver Cl; (†)6 Acres; †Smithick Fd (perhaps 'building of the smiths', from **smið** (gen.pl. *-a*) and **wīc**, like Smethwick Ch, St); Snooks (cf. John *Snook* 1687); †The Snug Arms Ho and Ld; †Spring Cl & Ctg; Square Md; Stave Ld; †Stoney Pce; Summer Grd; Swans (cf. John *Swayn* 1410); †Swyer (*v.* **swīra** 'neck of land'); Targells Grd; †10 Acres; ‡10 Acres (*North-, South Ten Acres* 1740); (†)3 Acres; Three Corner Grd; †Tulks' Md (cf. Richard *de Tolk'* 1288 (Six. Handley Hd)); (†)2 Acres; Upper Grd; Vanners (cf. William *Vanner* 1574); Venns Hill; †Vincents' Md (cf. *tenement' Thome Vincent* Ed I (c.1407)); †Water Hays Orchd; Water Mdw; †West Brook (cf. William- 1244, John *Biwestebrok(e)* 1268, 'to the west of the brook', *v.* **bī, westan, brōc**); †West Leaze (Coppice); (†)Whitings (cf. John *Wytyng* 1401 (c.1407)); Whittles; †Winterbourne (*v.* **winter, burna**; the field lies beside a small stream); Withy Bed; †Wood Cl; (†)Yonder Grd; Yonder Md.

(b) *Croucheheyse* 1564, *Crouch Hayes* 1642 (*v.* **crūc³** 'cross', second el. **hæs** 'brushwood' or a pl. form of **(ge)hæg** 'enclosure'); *Favyford* 1618 (on R. Stirchel downstream from French Mill *supra, v.* **ford**, first el. uncertain); *Nytheclose* 15, *claus' voc' La Nythe* 1432, 1441 (*v.* **clos(e)**; probably to be associated with the lost f.ns. *prat' de Nithewode, prat' de la Nithe, -Nyth* 1450 in Fontmell M. par. *infra*, since all these fields may have been near to where the par. boundaries of Fontmell and Cann (formerly Shaftesbury) meet at about ST 842200; the compounded forms *Nytheclose, Nithewode* might lead one to suppose a first el. **beniðan** 'beneath', as in *Nythewey* 1 328 and several D names (PN D xxxvii, 658), thus '(land) beneath the close and wood', in which case the simplex forms *Nythe, Nith* would have to be taken to represent an elliptical, substantival use of the preposition denoting 'land beneath (the close or wood)'; however it may be preferable to suggest that the names contain OE *nīð*, ME *nithe, nythe* 'envy, malice, hatred, hostility', thus denoting disputed land (especially likely if these fields were in fact on a boundary) or land difficult to cultivate (cf. Envy Cl *supra*, and for other derogatory f.ns. formed from abstract terms, e.g. *Care Fd, Vexation, v.* Ch 5 397-8); *Ropkyns* 1564 (a surname).

Compton Abbas

COMPTON ABBAS (ST 870185) ['kɔmtən]
  (to) Cumtune, atte Cumtune 956 (14) *ShaftR* (S 630)
  Cuntone 1086 DB
  Cum(p)ton' 1268, 1280, 1288 *Ass*, 1342 Pat, *Cumpton Abbatis(se)* 1293 FF, 1428 FA, *Cumptona* 15 *ShaftR*
  Compton(e) 1280 *Ass*, 1291 Tax, 1327 *SR*, 1332 SR *et passim, Compton(')* *Abbatisse* 1340 NI, 1391 *Glyn*, *-Abbas* 1676 *Salkeld*
  Contuna 15 *ShaftR* (p)

'Farm in the valley', from **cumb** and **tūn**, one of five Do pars. with this name. This manor belonged to Shaftesbury Abbey from 956, hence the affix *Abbas*, a reduced form of Lat **abbatissa** (gen.sg. -(*a*)*e*) 'abbess'. The Anglo-Saxon bounds of the manor are given in S 630. The form *Cumtun* 871-7 (15) BCS 531 cited by Ekwall DEPN for this place, together with *Kuntune* 871-7 (15) BCS 532, probably do not belong here, but to Compton Bassett W 262 (VCHDo 2 73, Finberg No. 212). There was a mill here in 1086 DB (VCHDo 3 82).

HAWKCOMBE LANE (ST 859184), named from a group of fields, near the par. bdy, called *Hawcombe (Fd)* 1842 *TA* (this par.), *Hawkham Cl & Coppice* 1837 *ib* (Fontmell M.), which are to be identified with *on holencumb* 956 (14) *ShaftR* (S 630) in the Anglo-Saxon bounds of Compton A., coinciding with *to holencumbe, of þanne cumbe* 932 (15) *ib* (S

419) in the Fontmell M. bounds, *v.* **hol**[2] (wk.obl. *holan*) 'hollow, deep', **cumb** 'valley'.

TWYFORD (FM) (ST 855186), *Tweyford'* 1395 (e15) *MiltRoll, -vorde* 1395 *MiltC, Twyford(e)* 1564 *Glyn,* 1692 *Salkeld,* 1842 *TA, Twiford* 1575 Saxton, 1646 SC, 1774 Hutch[1], cf. *Twyfordes Marshe* 1564, *Twyfordes Common* 1576 both *Glyn, Twyford Cmn & Gate* 1842 *TA,* 'double ford', *v.* **twī-, ford**, a common p.n. found in several English counties; the road here crossed two streams, one called Twyford Brook, the other unnamed.

BAKER'S FM, probably to be associated with Thomas *Baker,* assigned a messuage in Twyford in 1842 DCMDeed, but cf. Hugh *Pistor* ('the baker') who held ½ hide in Compton A. in 15 *ShaftR* (Hutch[3] **3** 535). BERE KNAP, 1869 Hutch[3], *Bareknap* 1811 OS, *Beer Knap* 1842 *TA,* cf. *claus' voc' le Beare, cotag'* . . . *voc' Bearehayes* 1564 *Glyn, Gt & Lt Beer, Summer Beer, Beer Lane* 1842 *TA,* probably **bǣr**[2] '(wood-land) pasture', with **cnæpp** 'hillock', 'short sharp ascent', **(ge)hæg** 'enclosure', **sumor** (indicating use only in summer). BURDEN'S FM. COMPTON DOWN, *-Downe* 1618 *Map, le Downe* 1564 *Glyn, v.* **dūn** 'hill, down'. EAST & WEST COMPTON, *East(e)-, West(e) Compton* 1564 *Glyn,* 1664 HTax, 1842 *TA, Compton Abbas East, -West* 1795 Boswell, the two tithings into which the manor was divided. CROCKER'S FM, 1842 *TA, Cockers* (sic) 1692 *Salkeld, Crockers* 1811 OS. DRONES LANE, 1842 *TA.* ELBURY HILL, by Elbury Copse *q.v.* in Fontmell M. par. *infra.* GLYN FM, cf. Sir Richard Carr *Glyn,* to whom the manor was sold in 1809 Hutch[3] **3** 535. GOURD'S FM, cf. Roger *Gourd* 1664 HTax. GUMM'S FM, cf. *Gunnis Orchd* (sic) 1842 *TA.* JUBILEE COLUMN. MANOR FM, probably *the Farme house* 1664 HTax. PRYSTOCK FM, *Priestock or Prystock* 1864 DCMDeed, perhaps from **prēost** and **stoc**. RECTORY, cf. *the Parsonage house* 1664 HTax. ST MARY'S CHURCH (remains of). TUCKER'S FM, cf. John *Tucker* 1564 *Glyn* (Melbury A.). WELL HO. WHITEHALL, *White Hall* 1842 *TA,* cf. William *atte Halle* of Compton 1330 Cl, *v.* **heall, atte**. WILLIS FM , cf. Richard *Wylly* 1327 *SR.*

FIELD NAMES

The undated forms in (*a*) are 1842 *TA* 66, in (*b*) 956 (14) *ShaftR* (S 630). Some fields in Compton A. *TA* are now in Fontmell M. par. *q.v. infra*. Spellings dated 1327 are *SR*, 1332 SR, 1340 NI, 1395 *MiltC*, 1395 (e15) *MiltRoll*, 1564, 1576, 1698 *Glyn*, 1588 Hutch³, and 1692 *Salkeld*.

(*a*) Andrews Mdw (cf. Cristina *Andreu* 1327); Apple Tree Grd; Benalders (*claus' pastur' voc' Bynaller* 1564, perhaps '(place) within the alders', *v.* **binnan, alor**); Berrow Hay (*v.* **beorg, (ge)hæg**); Black Cl; Blaken Fd (*Blagdon* 1842 DCMDeed, *v.* **blæc, dūn**); Bolton Fd; Bradley (Orchd) (*v.* **brād, lēah**); Breach Md (*v.* **brēc**); Brimble Down (*v.* **brembel** 'bramble'); Brinslade; (Corn) Broad Fd; Broad Md; Brockley (Orchd) (*v.* **lēah**, first el. probably **brōc**, cf. Jacob *atte Bro(u)k(e)* 1327, 1332, 1340, 'at the brook', John *Byyandebrouke* 1327, William *Bynghandebrouk'* (sic) 1332, 'beyond the brook', *v.* **atte, begeondan**); Broom Cl; Bulls Wd (cf. Juliana *la Bole* 1327, John *le Bole* 1332, 1340); Clay Md; Close; Coles Orchd; Gt & Lt Common; Common Cl; Coppice, Copse Cl; Cow Grd; Crete (probably from **croft**); Culverland Fd (*v.*culfre 'dove'); Gt & Lt Down Hills; Dry Grd; Dungey; Forked-, Furked Bridge Fd (*v.* **forked**); Furrow Md (Orchd) (*v.* **furh**); Gapstitch (*v.* **gappe, sticce**¹); Garston (*v.* **gærs-tūn**); Great Coombe (Fd) (*v.* **cumb**); Great Grd; Greenhays (*v.* **(ge)hæg**); Green Wd (Leg) (*claus' voc' Grenewooddes* 1564, from **grene**¹, **wudu**, or a surname, with **leg**); Grove (*v.* **grāf(a)**); Half pence (*a messuage and three closes called Halfpence* 1692, cf. *Halfepence Lane* 1698, no doubt in allusion to a rent, *v.* **halfpenny**); Gt & Lt Half Yards (*v.* **gierd** 'measure of land'); Hanaple; Hanging (Md & Orchd) (*v.* **hanging, hangende**); Hare Cl; Haythorne; Hill Cl; Home Cl, Grd & Orchd; Howells (Orchd); Incombe (Fd); Kings Cl, Grove & Hill (cf. Richard (*le*) *Kyng* 1327, 1340); Knowles; Lawrence Md (cf. *toft' voc' Lawrence Place* 1564, Thomas *Laurence* (rector) 1588, *v.* **place**); Leg (*v.* **leg**); Litley; Little Grd; Marsh Cl (cf. *Compton Mersche* 1395, *-mersshe* 1395 (e15), *v.* **mersc**); Merefield; Milking Orchd; Moor Cl; Mutchell Wd (*v.* **micel, mycel** 'big'); New Cl; Norwood (Poor Altmt) (probably **norð** 'north', **wudu**); Nursery Orchd; Hr & Lr Orchard; Pales (*v.* **pale**); Park (Lane & Leg); Pear Tree Cl; Potatoe Gdn; The Pound; Puckhay (first el. probably **pūca** 'goblin', *v.* **(ge)hæg**); Purchless; Red Hills; Rickyard; Ride Lane Cl (*v.* **ride**); Rushy Cl; Ryalls (Orchd); Shere Md; Shines Hay; Short Lds; Soap ashes (cf. ModE *soap-ashes* 'ashes of certain kinds of wood used in forming a lye in soap-making' (also used as a manure)); Sops (cf. ModE *sop* 'soaked bread, etc' (thus perhaps alluding to soggy ground), 'tuft of wet green grass amongst hay', 'something of small value'); Southends; Starton Md; Stone Hills; Stroners Md; Strouds; Summer Grd; Swines Head; Swyer Fd (*v.* **swīra** 'neck of land'); 10 Acres; 3 Closes; Top Grd; 12 Acres; Twentown Fd; Tylers Orchd; Vincents Cl (cf. *pratum nuper in tenur' Thome Vyncent* 1564); Vowles Hay; Water Mdw; Waters Pdk; Wellard Fd; Hr & Lr West (cf. *Compton Westfilde* 1576); West Down; Whitens Acre (Leg) (*claus' voc' Whiteson' Aker, Whitynges* 1564,

Whiteings 1692, *v.* **æcer**, cf. Whitings Fm in Melbury A. par. *infra*); Whore (probably from **ōra**[1] 'bank'); Whoreswood (cf. Agnes *la Hore* 1327, John *(le) Hore* 1332, 1340); Wood Cl.

(*b*) *atte Asshe* 1332, *atte Naish* 1340 both (p) (cf. William *de fraxino* 1327, *v.* **atte(n)** 'at the', **æsc** 'ash-tree'); *tenement' voc' Balwyn'* 1564 (cf. William *Baldewyne* 1332 (Six. Handley)); *terr' quondam Boyles* 1564; *terr' voc' Carpenters* 1564; *Compton mede* 1576 (*v.* **mǣd**); *oð dollen beorge* (corresponding to *on dollen berch* in the Fontmell M. charter 932 (15) ShaftR (S 419), 'Dol(l)a's hill or tumulus', from the OE pers.n. *Dol(l)a* and **beorg**; the pers.n. *Dola* is once on record (Redin 75) and is adduced from Dolbeare and Dolbury D 464, 574); *on þat ealde ad* ('the old beacon', *v.* **eald**, **ād**, cf. *ðone ealdan ad* in 957 (12) BCS 987 (Staffordshire); perhaps to be located at or near the site of the later Melbury Beacon in Melbury A. par. *infra*); *on fern helle* ('fern hill' , *v.***fearn**, **hyll**); *at here weg* ('highway', *v.* **here-weg**); *on holenwylle, of hollenwelle* (corresponding to *to holenwelle, of þan welle* in the Fontmell M. charter 932 (15) ShaftR (S 419), 'hollow spring, or spring in a hollow', *v.* **hol**[2], **well(a)**, **wyll(a)**); *on þane imeren hole weg* ('hollow way on the boundary', *v.* **(ge)mǣre** (the form *imeren* is corrupt), **hol**[2], **weg**); *Hulle* n.d. (15) ShaftR (*v.* **hyll** 'hill', cf. Hill Fm in Iwerne M. par. *infra*; the existence of a place with this name in either Compton A. or the adjacent par. of Melbury A. is suggested by the context in which the form cited appears in ShaftR (f. 96b): *Hugo de Blynchesfeld . . . tenuit . . . ten' apud hulle . . .* [rubric] *in Mellebury et Compton*; probably to be associated with the same place are Richard *de Hulle* and Emma *atte Hulle* 1327 SR, 1332 SR (both taxed in a joint list for both pars.; Fägersten 24 without apparent justification associated the latter with Hill Fm in Fontmell M. par. *infra*)); *terr' voc' Hurlyns* 1564 (a surname); *on anne hus* ('a (certain) house', *v.* **hūs**); *on þa lake, adun one þat lake* (2 ×) ('the stream', *v.* **lacu**); *on lippen stagen* (probably 'Lippa's stake or boundary post', from an OE pers.n. *Lippa* and **staca** as suggested by Forsberg 139-40; for the pers.n. *v.* PN Sx 81, PN Ca 261, but cf. PN Brk 728); *on þat litlen lake* ('the little stream', *v.* **lȳtel**, **lacu**); *longethorne aker* 1576 (*v.* **lang**[1], **þorn**, **æcer**); *Sowdon'* 1576 (probably 'south hill', *v.* **sūð**, **dūn**); *on tor scylget, on torchil gat* (the first and final els. are **torr** 'rock, rocky peak' and **geat** 'gate, gap, pass'; the medial el., the spelling of which may be corrupt, is thought by Ekwall DEPN s.n. Skilgate So to be late OE **scyl** 'boundary' (cf. also EPN **2** 124–5), but it may possibly be **scielf**, **scylf** 'shelf, ledge' or even **sciell** 'shell' (which apparently occurs in some undetermined sense in later Do f.ns. like *Shill* **1** 230, *le Shull(e)* (s.n. Scully) in Gillingham par. *supra*); the point described is at the E extremity of the par., near the top of the prominent 810' hill N of Hatts Barn where the present E-W road crosses the line of a cross-dyke); *be wirtrume* (2 ×) (*v.* **wyrt-truma** 'root, root-stock', -*e* representing either dat.sg. -*an* or dat.pl. -*um*).

Fontmell Magna

FONTMELL MAGNA (ST 865170) ['fɔntməl]
   ffuntemel 871–877 (15) *ShaftR* (S 357(1)), (*in*) *Funtemel ib*
      (S 357(2)), *ffuntemel, Funtemel,* (*in to*) *funtmel* 932 (15)
      ShaftR (S 419)
   Fontemale 1086 DB
   Funtemel(l)(') 13 *Glyn,* 1201 Cur (p), 1244 *Ass* (p), 1280 *ib,*
      1280 (1490) Pat, 1290 (15) *ShaftR et freq* to 1406 Pat,
      -mele 1395 *MiltC, Funteymel, Funtenel, Futumel* (sic)
      1268 *Ass, Magnam Funtemell'* 1391 *Glyn, Funtmill* 1648
      SC, 1664 HTax (*East-, West-*), 1704 *Salkeld* (*Great-*),
      Funtmell Magna 1795 Boswell
   Fontemel(l)(') 1244 *Ass,* 1258 Pap, 1280 QW, 1288 *Ass,*
      1291 Tax *et freq* to 1402 Pat, *Fontenel* 1291 Tax,
      Fontimel 1303, 1346 FA, *Great-Fontmel* 1774 Hutch[1],
      Fontmell Magna 1795 Boswell
   Fountemel(l) 1280 QW, 1345 FF *et freq* to c.1560 *Glyn*
      (*Easte-, West-*), *Fountmell* 1415 Pat, 1535 VE, 1659
      Salkeld, Fountymell 1428 FA, *Fowntemell* c. 1500 *Eg*

Named from Fontmell Brook which rises near here, *v.*
RNs. *infra*; Lat **magna** 'great' to distinguish it from
Fontmell Parva in Ch. Okeford par. *supra. East* and *West*
F(o)unt(e)mell, -mill are the names of two tithings in c. 1560
Glyn, 1664 HTax. The Anglo-Saxon bounds of the manor
are given in S 419.

STREET-NAMES: CHURCH ST., *v.* St Andrew's Church *infra*; NORTH ST.;
PARSONAGE ST., leading to Rectory (6"); WEST ST. Buildings include *le
Common Backehouse* c. 1560, *-bakhowse* 1576 both *Glyn, v.* **bæc-hūs** 'a
bake house'.

BEDCHESTER (FM) (ST 853175) ['bedʒestə]
   Bedeshurst(e) Hy 1 (15) *ShaftR,* 1354, 1372, 1374 FF, 1392
      Pat, 1395 *MiltC,* 1431 FA, 1535 VE, c.1560 *Glyn,*
      Bedyshurst(') 1395 (e15) *MiltRoll,* 1541 Hutch[3]
   Bedehurst 1392 IpmR, 1412 FA
   Butesurste (p), *Butesursta* (2 ×) n.d. (15) *ShaftR*
   Bedcister 1575 Saxton, 1811 OS, *-cester* 1576 *Glyn,* 1711
      Salkeld, -ceister 1774 Hutch[1], 1869 Hutch[3], *-chester*
      1869 ib

Bedi-, *Bedyhurst als. Bedcister* 1659, 1692 *Salkeld*

The second el. is clearly **hyrst** 'copse or wooded hill', with late analogical modification to -*cester* (only recently -*chester*) due to shift or loss of *r* and weakening of stress in the final part of the name, as in Hogchester in Wootton F. par. *infra, v.* also Zachrisson ANInfl 81–2, Fägersten 23–4. The first el. is probably a pers.n., but its exact form is difficult to determine, perhaps **Bīedi, *Bēdi* as suggested by Ekwall DEPN, or *Bæde* as suggested by Fägersten 23 comparing Beeson (*Bedeston* l14) D 333 (cf. also *Bædes wel* BCS 125 Wo). The two forms in *Butes-* from *ShaftR* are probably erratic. Another form to be taken into account, though this too may be slightly corrupt, is (*up on*) *beteswirþe sled* in the Anglo-Saxon bounds of Fontmell M. (932 (15) *ShaftR* (S 419)); this describes a point less than ½ mile N of the present Bedchester and presumably contains the same pers.n. with **wyrð** 'enclosure' and **slæd** 'valley'.

BLACKVEN CMN & FM (ST 837193), *Blakkefennysmersche* 1395 *MiltC, Blackefennysmersshe* 1395 (e15) *MiltRoll, Blacafen* n.d. (15) *ShaftR, Blakevenne* 1450, *Blackfen(ne)* 1505, 1576, *Blacke Fennes* (*Marshe*) c. 1560, *Blackefen(n)(e)s marshe* 1576, *Black Venn Common* 1700 all *Glyn, Black Fenns, Blackfenn Cmn and Waste* 1837 *TA*, identical in origin with Black Venn in E Stour par. *supra, v.* **blæc** 'dark-coloured', **fenn** 'fen', **mersc** 'marsh'.

LONGCOMBE BOTTOM (ST 885177), 1702 *Glyn,* cf. (*to*) *langencumbes hauede* 932 (15) *ShaftR* (S 419), 'to the head or upper end of the long valley', *Longcombefeild* 1702 *Glyn, Longco(o)mb Cl & Fd* 1837 *TA, v.* **lang**[1], **cumb**, **hēafod**, cf. Littlecombe Bottom *infra.*

SIXPENNY FM (ST 844169), *Sexepenne* 1340 NI (p), *Sexpenne* n.d. (15) *ShaftR* (p), *mes' voc' Seppens* c. 1560 *Glyn,* to be associated with the bdy clause *on ðæs lutlen seaxpennes suð eke* 'upon the southern edge of the little **Seaxpenn*' in the Anglo-Saxon bounds of Fontmell M. (932 (15) *ShaftR* (S 419)), where **Seaxpenn* refers to Pen Hill (356') in Sutton W. par. *supra.* The second el. is PrWelsh **penn**[1] 'hill', cf.

Ekwall DEPN s.v. who notes the probability that the word was to some extent used by the Anglo-Saxons as an appellative. The first el. is almost certainly **Seaxe** 'Saxons' (in an uninflected form *Seax-*) as first supposed by Zachrisson RomK 49 and later by Anderson 141 (rather than **seax** 'sword, knife', or (figuratively) 'stone, rock', preferred by Fägersten 20, Kökeritz 122). There is an interesting parallel (though with inversion) in Pensax Wo, unexplained in PN Wo 67 but thought to be probably 'the hill of the Saxons' by Ekwall DEPN, *v.* also Jackson 226, 539. It is possible that Pen Hill, earlier **Seaxpenn*, marks an ancient Saxon bdy as supposed by Anderson 141; what is certain is that it gave name to the old GeldR hundred of *Sexpene*, its position near the centre of the hundred making it an appropriate meeting place, *v.* Sixpenny Handley hundred *supra*.

WOODBRIDGE (HO & MILL) (ST 847183), (*on*) *wde brigthe*, (*to*) *wde bricge*, (*to*) *wdebrige* 932 (15) *ShaftR* (S 419), (*od*) *wdebrige*, (*of*) *wudebricge* 963 (15) *ib* (S 710), *Woodbridge* 1618 *Map*, *Wood Bridge* 1842 *TA* (Compton A.), cf. *Wodebrygge-mede*, *Wodebrygg(e)wode* 1395 *MiltC*, 1395 (e15) *MiltRoll*, probably 'the wooden bridge' rather than 'the bridge in or by a wood' (although cf. the last form), *v.* **wudu, brycg, mǣd**, cf. the identical Woodbridge Sf (DEPN). The 10th cent. forms are from the Anglo-Saxon bounds of Fontmell M. and E Orchard. An E–W road crosses R. Stirchel here.

BALFOUR'S WD (1″). BINEGAR, possibly identical in origin with Binnegar 1 146, but perhaps a transferred name from that place or Binegar So. BLATCHFORD'S FM, perhaps a surname from Blatchford D 207, but possibly to be connected with *messuag' voc' Blatche* c. 1560 *Glyn*, which may be eModE *blatch* 'blacking' (NED, from a1500), 'black stuff or soot' (Barnes), with reference to dark soil, or the surname *Blac(c)h(e)* (< OE *Blæcca*) found in Do in 1327 *SR* and 1332 *SR* though not in this par. or Hd. THE BORDER, a long, narrow plantation, *v.* **border**. COW GROVE FM. CROFTS FM, cf. *Craftes (Mede)* 1576 *Glyn*, *Creates Cl* 1837 *TA*, from **croft** 'enclosure' or a surname, **mǣd**. CROSS HO, cf. *Cross*

Barn 1837 *TA*, near site of Cross (6"). THE DAIRY. ELBURY COPSE, *Ellbury* 1701 *Glyn*, on the par. bdy by Elbury Hill in Compton A. par. *supra*; the first part of this name is just possibly to be associated with *þurh þo aelres* 'through the alders' on the Anglo-Saxon bdy of Fontmell M. (932 (15) *ShaftR* (S 419)), *v.* **alor, elre** 'an alder'. FIRTHILL COPSE, -*Cl & Coppice* 1837 *TA, Furthill* 1702 *Glyn*, cf. *Furtellesmede* 1450 *ib*, from a surname with **mǣd**. FONTMELL DOWN, 1811 OS, cf. *Common Downs* 1837 *TA*, referred to in the bdy clause *on hamelendune north ecge* 'on the north edge of the scarred or flat-topped hill' in the Anglo-Saxon bounds of Fontmell M. (932 (15) *ShaftR* (S 419)), *v.* **hamol, hamel, dūn**, cf. Hambledon Hill in Ch. Okeford par. *supra* with which this form was wrongly identified by Fägersten 15 (followed by Tengstrand 213). FONTMELL HILL HO (1"), cf. *Fontmell Hill* 1701 *Glyn*, Hill Fm *infra*. FONTMELL WD, -*Woods* 1837 *TA*, referred to in the bdy clause *to wde* 'to the wood' in the Anglo-Saxon bounds of Fontmell M. (932 (15) *ShaftR* (S 419)), *v.* **wudu**. FORE TOP, a 700' high projecting ridge sloping away from an 810' hill one mile ENE, thus '(land) in front of the hill-top', or 'part of the hill-top that juts forward', *v.* **fore, topp**. GORE CLUMP, named from Gore (Fm) in Ashmore par. **2** 202. GREEN FM. GUPPLE'S COPSE (-*Coppice* 1837 *TA*) & Fm, cf. Maurice *Gopyl* 1327 *SR*, William *Gopyld'* 1332 SR; *Gogylysclos* (if this is for *Gopylys*-) 1395 (e15) *MiltRoll* belongs here, the surname probably having been confused with *Gogg* found in Goggs Md *infra*. LT & LR HARTGROVE FM, named from Hartgrove in E Orchard par. *infra*. HATCH COVERT, *v.* **hæc(c)**, possibly in the sense 'sluice' or 'grating' (weir marked 6"), cf. *Hatch Md* 1837 *TA*. HATCHERS. HIGHER MILL (lost, at ST 875170), 1811 OS, near Mill Pond 6", probably to be identified with *Estmille* 1450, *East Mill* 1576 both *Glyn*, cf. *the mill of Fontmel and Bedeshurst* 1317 Hutch[3], *Millway* (a coppice) 1618 *Map, the farms of . . . Funtmill and Funtmill mill* 1648 SC, *Mill Creates* 1837 *TA*, *v.* **myln, ēast, croft**; there were three mills in Fontmell M. in 1086 DB (VCHDo **3** 82), and four mills are mentioned in 15 *ShaftR* (Hutch[3] **3** 556), cf. also Woodbridge Mill *supra*, Piper's Mill and *Hurrelles Myll* both *infra*. HILL FM, possibly to be associated with *Alwine de*

Hill' n.d. (15) *ShaftR* (f. 62), a tenant in Fontmell, *v.* **hyll**, cf. Fontmell Hill Ho *supra*; for the form *atte Hulle* included here by Fägersten 24, *v.* under Compton A. par. *supra*; the nearby hill is called *Brandhurst Hill* 1826 Gre. HURDLE'S FM, cf. *Hurdles Md* 1837 *TA.* LITTLECOMBE BOTTOM, cf. *Littlecoomb Fd* 1837 *TA, v.* **lȳtel, cumb, botm.** MANOR FM (formerly MANOR HO), cf. *mansam domini* 1395 MiltC, *the farmes of . . . Funtmill and Funtmill mill* 1648 SC, and Robert *de Halle de Funtemel* 1327 *Glyn*, William *atte Halle* 1340 NI, John *atte Halle de Fontemel* 1359 *Glyn, v.* **h(e)all** 'hall, manor house'. MARSH CMN, cf. *la Marshe* 1310 Hutch³, *Estmerschvorlang, Westemersshforlang* 1395 *MiltC, Est-, Westmerssh'vorlang'* 1395 (e15) *MiltRoll, common of pasture in the Marsh* 1544 Hutch³, *F(o)unt(e)melles marshe* c.1560, *Fountmell' Marshe* 1576, *claus' voc' Marsh* 1700 all *Glyn, Marsh Cl & Md, Marshland* 1837 *TA, v.* **mersc, ēast, west, furlang**; for the tract of marshy land in question, cf. Guy's Marsh in Cann par. *supra* and Margaret Marsh par. *infra.* MAYO'S FM, cf. MAYO FM in Cann par. *supra.* MIDDLE FM. MILL POND (2 ×), cf. Higher Mill *supra*, Piper's Mill *infra.* MOORE'S FM, cf. *messuag' voc' Mores* c. 1560, *terr' voc' Moores* 1576 both *Glyn*, probably a surname, but cf. *prat' in la Moure* 1450 *ib, v.* **mōr** 'marshy ground'. PARSON'S COPSE. PIPER'S MILL (BRIDGE), *terr' voc' Pypers* 1576, *messuag' et molendin' vocat' Pypers Mill* 1701 both *Glyn, Piper's Mill or Great* [Bridge] 1791 Boswell, cf. *the mill of Fontmel and Bedeshurst* 1317 Hutch³, *Higher Mill supra*; from the surname *Piper, v.* **myln.** POUND, *The Pound* 1837 *TA.* ST ANDREW'S CHURCH, cf. *ecclesie de Funtemel* 1327 *Glyn*, William *atte Chirche* 1327 *SR, le Churche house* c. 1560 *Glyn.* ST ANDREW'S FM, cf. prec. SPEAR COPSE, -*Coppice* 1837 *TA.* SPRINGHEAD, at the source of Collyer Brook, probably to be identified with *Willeshed* 1505, *Wellhead* 1701 both *Glyn, v.* **spring, well(a), will(a), hēafod.** WELL HO. YEWTREE FM, cf. *Yew Tree Cl* 1837 *TA.*

FIELD-NAMES

The undated forms are 1837 *TA* 87, except for those marked † which are 1842 *ib* 66 (Compton A.). Spellings dated 932 (15) are *ShaftR* (S 419), 956

(14) are *ib* (S 630), 958 (15) are *ib* (S 656), 1280 are *Ass*, 1327¹ *SR*, 1332
SR, 1340 NI, 1395 *MiltC*, 1395 (e15) *MiltRoll*, 1618 *Map*, 1659, 1675,
1731 *Salkeld*, 1664 HTax, 1791 Boswell, 1829 *EnclA*, and the rest *Glyn*.

(*a*) Abbey Orchd and Gdn (no doubt an allusion to its earlier possession
by Shaftesbury Abbey); Acre Orchd; Alder Bed; Appletree Cl &
Coppice; Ash Cl; Ashen Grove; Bad Barn Cl (*bathe barne* 1576, *parocke
voc' Bottbarne* (sic) 1700, *claus' voc' Badbarne* 1701, *v.* bæð 'bathing place,
pool', **bere-ærn**); Bedchester Cmn (*v.* Bedchester *supra*); Little Bennys
(cf. *Will' Bennett* . . . *cotag'* 1699); Blich(')s Down(s), Blichs Md & Orchd
(*v.* Bleax Hill in E Orchard par. *infra*); Bottom Mead(s) & Orchd; Gt & Lt
Brach, Brack (sic) Md, Far & Near Brach Meads, Breach Cl (cf.
Buschebryche 1395, *in communi de Bussh'bryche* 1395 (e15), *Busshebreche*
1450, *Corn(e)bryche* 1395, 1395 (e15), *Cornebreche* 1450, *v.* **bræc** 'land
broken up for cultivation', the forms in -*a*- showing early shortening,
busc 'a bush, a shrub', **corn**¹ 'corn, grain'); Briers Grd; Broad Cl; Broad
Md (*Brademedesforlang'* 1376, *Brademede* 1450, *v.* **brād, mǣd**); Brook Cl,
Brookfurlong Cl (*Brokefurlond* (sic) 1576, cf. John *Attebrouke* 1327¹, -*atte
Broke* 1332, *v.* **brōc, furlang, atte** 'at the'); Brownshill (cf. Richard *Broun*
1327¹, 1332); Bunch Hay Cl; (Gt) Bushey Leaze(s); Chalk Grd & Md;
†Charles Down (*bynethe Cherlysdown'* 1395 (e15), from **ceorl** 'peasant' or
the OE pers.n. *Ceorl*, **beneoðan, dūn**); Cherry Orchd Coppice; Chestlens
Cl; Clay Land Orchd, Clay Lands; Close Cmn; Collier's [Bridge] 1791
(from Collyer Brook, *v.* RNs.); Comb Hays (*Combehaye, -hey* c. 1560,
-*haie* 1576, cf. Robert *de la Combe*, John *in la Combe* 1327¹, Robert *in la
Comb'* 1332, *ten' q' Rob' Combe tenet* 1450, *mes' et terre vocat' Combes* c.
1560, *prat' voc' Combesmo(u)re* 1450, 1505, *v.* **cumb** 'valley', **(ge)hæg**
'enclosure', **mōr** 'moor, marshland'); Common Cl ((*Lower*) *Common Close*
1698, 1701); Coppice (Cl); Crabhill Cl (*Crabb hill* 1576, cf. *grabtree ib, v.*
crabbe 'crab-apple', **crabbetre**); Crouches Md (cf. John *Crech* 1327¹,
-*Creich'*, Agnes *Creych'* 1332); Culverland Cl (*v.* **culfre** 'dove'); Dead
Acres (*v.* **dēad**, here in the sense 'infertile'); Gt & Lt Deweys; †(Lt)
Domonies; Down Hills; Hr Drove, Drove Rd; Dry Grd; 8 Acres (*2 mes'
voc' Eighte Acr' tenementes* c. 1560); Elm Cl; Farm Down; Felthams Pdk
(cf. Richard *Viltam* 1664); Fiferage (Cl); Flower Cl; Forward Lawn (*the
Forewode* 1395, 1395 (e15), (*prat'*) *atte Forthewode* 1395, *atte vorthwode*
1395 (e15), '(land) in front of the wood' or 'part of the wood that juts
forward', *v.* **fore, forð, wudu**); 4 Acres; French Grass (*v.* **french grass**);
French Md (perhaps a reference to the same crop as in prec.); Goggs Md
(*ten' nuper Johannis Gogge, ten' nuper Gogges* 1450, *mes' voc' Gogges* c.
1560, *terr' voc' Coggs* 1700, cf. Richard (*le*) *Gog(')* 1332, 1340); Goose Acre
(1702); Great Mdw & Orchd; Green Hay Cl (*v.* **(ge)hæg**); Grove Cl,
Coppice & Orchd (*Grove* 1701, *v.* **grāf(a)**); Ham (Corner, Md & Orchd)
(*v.* **hamm**); Hanging Grd & Md (*v.* **hangende**); Hartgrove Hill Cmn
(*Hargrove Hill, Hargraves hyll* 1576, named from Hartgrove in E Orchard
par. *infra*); Hawkham Cl & Coppice (*v.* Hawkcombe Lane in Compton A.
par. *supra*); Hen Md; Higher Mdw, Orchd & Pdk; High Grd; Highterrat
Cl (sic); Gt & Lt Hill, Hill Land & Orchd; How Md; Hoe Md; Gt & Lt

Holbrook, Holbrook Cl, Holbrooks (West Fd) (*(forlang' de) Holebro(u)k'* 1376, *Hollbrooke mead* 1701, to be identified with *(to) holebroke* 932 (15) in the Anglo-Saxon bounds of Fontmell, 'the hollow brook, the brook running in a hollow', *v.* **hol²**, **brōc**); Home Cl (*Homeclose* 1700); Home Grd, Md(w) & Orchd; Horsely Cl (*claus' voc' Horseleaze* 1702, *v.* **lǣs**); †Hossicks (probably to be associated with the family of William *Hushcock* 1564); Housland (*Howslond(e)* 1395, 1395 (e15), *v.* **land**; the first el. could be **hūs** 'house' or the possessive form of the ME surname *How*); Inner Lds; Jacob Md; Jedas Cl (*claus' voc' Judys* 1576, the pers.n. or surname *Judas*, often abbreviated *Jude*); Knapp Cl (*v.* **cnæpp**); Lake Hay Orchd (*Leakhay-* 1829, *v.* **lacu**, **(ge)hæg**); Lawdens Cl; Laywales Fd; Leg Md (*v.* **leg**); Little Coppice; Little Md(w); Long Grd; Long Md (Leg), Long Mdw (*Langemede* 1450, *v.* **lang¹**, **mǣd**); Long Orchd & Pdk; Lower Gdn, Orchd & Pdk; Luesome Clover Ld (first el. perhaps the plant-name **lucerne**); Marks Grd; Marl Pits; (Gt & Lt) Maurice (perhaps ME **mareis** 'marsh'); Mead Hays (*v.* **(ge)hæg**); Meadow; Middle Grd; Milking Barton Grove Cl; Milking Cl; Neck Cl; Netton Fd (perhaps 'cattle farm', from **nēat** and **tūn**, like Netton D, W); New Fd; North Hay(s Cl) (*v.* **(ge)hæg**); Odd Man Hay; Odd Md(w) (*Odemede* 1450, *v.* **ād** 'beacon, bonfire', **mǣd**); Orchard; Outer Lds; Oxendon (*-downe* 1450, *v.* **oxa** (gen.pl. *oxna*), **dūn**); Paddock (Orchd) (cf. *duo Parrokes* 1395 (e15), *v.* **pearroc**); Peaked Cl (*v.* **peked**); Pear Tree Cl; Penhill (Cl) (cf. *Penne Close* c.1560, named from Pen Hill in Sutton W. par. *supra*, *v.* also Sixpenny Fm *supra*); Penny's [Bridge] 1791; Late Perrys Gdn; Peters Plot Orchd; Pidgeon Cl; Piggs Pdk; Piles Grd & Md (*(pastur' voc')* *Pyles* c.1560, 1576, probably a surname); Pineywell Cl; Pit Cl; Plantation; Pond and Marsh, Pond Cl; Princes Cl & Gdn; Quarrendon Fd (perhaps from **cweorn** 'quern, hand-mill', and **dūn** 'hill', a common p.n., cf. Coringdon in Corscombe par. *infra*); Rakes (Mdw); Rickyard Cl (cf. *le Recke ham* c.1560, *v.* **ricke**, **hamm**); Ritham Mdw; Rit Hill; Roads (Grd) (cf. *(prat')* in the *Rode* 1395, *v.* **rod¹**, **rodu** 'a clearing'); Role Hays; Rowhays Cl; Rushey Cl; Rye Grass 1829; Ry(e)lands Cl & Grd (*Ryelond'* 1576, *v.* **ryge**, **land**); Sawdens; 7 Acres; Sharp Hays, Sharphays Md; Shortland Fd; 6 Acres; Skinners Cl; Smallbrook (Coppice) (*vnam acram . . . in Smalebrok'* 1327², *claus' voc' Smale Brooks* 1698, to be identified with *(to) smale broke* 956 (14) in the Anglo-Saxon bounds of Compton A., 'the narrow brook', with reference to Fontmell Brook near its source, *v.* **smæl** (wk.obl. *smalan*), **brōc**); Small Drinch; Small Hays (*v.* **(ge)hæg**); Smith Hays (cf. *tenement' voc' Smythes* c.1560, *Smith's Hole* [Bridge] 1791); Spawerland Cl; Spring Cl and Orchd; Square Cl; Stall Ho; Stills Grd (cf. James & Richard *Styll* 1664); Stone's [Bridge] 1791; Stubbles Md; Sturton Md; Summer Grd; Swallow Cl & Pce, Swallows; Sweatmans; Swelly Cl (possibly **(ge)swelg** 'pit', cf. Swilly D 241); Tapland (Cl & Orchd); Toothill or Sandy Cl, Toothill Fd (*Tutthill feild* 1702, *v.* **tōt-hyll** 'look-out hill'); Top Grds; Topps Mdw; Upp Fd (*Upfi(e)ld*, *-fy(e)ld(e)* 1576, *Up(p)feild* 1701, *v.* **upp** 'higher up', **feld**); Upp Lds (*Uplands* 1700, cf. prec.); Gt & Lt Wallence; Way Grd; Well Md; West Field Cl (*Westfyeld,*

West fild 1576, *v.* **west, feld**); Wheelers Cmn; White Cl; Whittles Md (cf. *close called (Little) Wheatehills* 1659, 1675, *v.* **hwǣte, hyll**); Winchard Cl ('gap fit for a wagon', *v.* **wægn, sceard**; the field lies beside the road from Bedchester where it crosses Fontmell Brook); Yonder Grd & Md; Young Orchd.

(b) *the Baycroft(e)* 1395, 1395 (e15) (*v.* **croft**, first el. perhaps ME **baie** 'berry' (1398 NED), cf. **beg**); *Bedhurst Lane* 1701 (*v.* Bedchester *supra*); *Berelond(')* 1395, 1395 (e15) (*v.* **bere** 'barley', **land**); *la Berton'* 1450 (*v.* **bere-tūn** 'corn farm, outlying grange'); *ten' nuper . . . Bolles* 1450 (a surname, cf. Bulls Wd in Compton A. par. *supra*); *the Brodecrofte* 1395, *the Brode Croft'* 1395 (e15) (*v.* **brād, croft**); *terre nuper Broukemannes* 1450; *to burch linken* 932 (15) ('ridges where birch-trees grow', *v.* **birce, byrce, hlinc** (-*en* probably representing dat.pl. -*um*)); *le Buttes* 1576 (*v.* **butte** 'short strip at right angles to others'); *terre voc' Carters* c.1560, *Carters Haym* 1576 (a surname with **hamm** 'enclosure'); *withinne da chealc seðas* 932 (15) ('chalk pits', *v.* **cealc, sēað**); *to cludesleghe, of þare lege* 932 (15) (probably to be identified with *to tudesleghe, of þere lege* 958 (15) in the bounds of Thorton (Grundy 5 98), *v.* **lēah** 'wood, clearing', first el. uncertain); *terr' voc' Cokemans* c.1560 (a surname); *Cotehey* c.1560 (*v.* **cot, (ge)hæg**); *Courteyate* 1576 (*v.* **court, geat**); *Cowperysclose, -parrok'* 1395 (e15) (the surname *Cowper* with **clos(e)** and **pearroc**); *ten' voc' Cryntes* 1450 (a surname); *on dollen berch* 932 (15) (corresponding to *oð dollen beorge* in the Compton A. charter, *v.* under Compton A. par. *supra*); *Est(e)filde, Estfield, -fyeld* 1576 (*v.* **ēast, feld**); *mes' voc' Fawkes* c.1560 (a surname); *Fernehill* c.1560 (*v.* **fearn, hyll**); *atte the Northerflotham i hamme, in the Sowtherflotham i hamme* 1395, *-vlotham-* 1395 (e15), *Floteham* 1450 (an earlier instance of a f.n. also found in Stinsford par. 1 372, probably from **flote** 'state of flowing', i.e. 'flooded', and **hamm** 'river-meadow' (note the appellative use 'one *hamme* at-/in-' in the 1395 forms), with **norðerra** 'more northerly', **sūðerra** 'more southerly'); *Foxhill* 1618 (*v.* **fox**); *Funtmill park* 1618 (*v.* **park**); *Garlandes* (a cottage) 1450 (a surname); *cotag' voc' Gas(se)way* c.1560, 1576 (*v.* **weg**; first el. probably the pers.n. or surname *Gace*, the Central French form of *Wace* (*v.* Reaney s.n.)); (*(cotag' voc')*) *Ger(r)ardes* c. 1560, 1576 (a surname); *on þa gereþrenc* 932 (15) (obscure, probably a corrupt form; Grundy 4 103 emends to *gereþrene* and takes it to be a late dat.pl. form of OE *gereþru* 'a bank of oars' (nautical), here used in a figurative topographical sense to describe minor ridges running off at right angles from the main ridge); *parocke voc' Gyddyes* 1700 (a surname, *v.* **pearroc**); *cotag' voc' Gillames* 1450, *Gylmannes* c. 1560 (a surname); *on done hagen* 932 (15) ('the hedge or enclosure', *v.* **haga¹**); *on halgan weies* (sic, probably for *welles*) *lake, þanen to þanen welle siluen* 932 (15) ('into the stream flowing from the holy spring, then to that same spring', *v.* **hālig** (wk.obl. *hālgan*), **well(a)**); *Harwood Gate* 1699; *Haybridge* 1699 (*v.* **hēg**); *one þe hegen, be weste hegen paðe, west anlang hegen* 932 (15) (this seems to be an actual instance of the postulated OE ***hægen** 'enclosure' (*v.* EPN s.v.), with **pæð** 'path'; other instances of *e* for *æ* in this charter include *on beteswirþe sled* discussed

under Bedchester *supra* and *on sandhellesled infra*); *on þa hege reawe* 932
(15) (*v.* **hege-rǣw** 'hedgerow'); *to heldmannes wrthe suthward* 932 (15)
(also a boundary point in three other Anglo-Saxon charters, *v. of eldmannes
wrthe* in E Orchard par. *infra*); *an to þan herepaþe, to þanen ealden herepaþe
þæt schet to blinchesfelde* 932 (15) ('the (old) military road or highway
(which runs to Blynfield)', *v.* **eald, here-pæð**, Blynfield (Fm) in Cann
par. *supra*); *the Heywode* 1395 (e15), *the Hyghwode* 1395, *Highwood(es
Mead)* 1659 (*v.* **hēah** 'high', **wudu**, cf. *Lowewode infra*); *to holencumbe, of
þanne cumbe* 932 (15) (*v.* Hawkcombe Lane in Compton A. par. *supra*); *to
holenwelle, of þan welle* 932 (15) (corresponding to *on holenwylle* in the
Compton A. charter, *v.* under Compton A. par. *supra*); *on holewei, of
holleweie* 932 (15) ('hollow way', *v.* **hol²**, **weg**); *Holl(e)mede* 1395, 1395
(e15), *Holmeade* 1576 (*v.* **hol²** 'hollow', **mǣd**); *mes' voc' Howpers* c. 1560 (a
surname); *on hriycsþeg* (sic), *þannen anlang hricg þeges* (sic), *of rig wei* 932
(15) (*v.* **hrycg-weg** 'ridgeway'); *Hurrelles Myll* c. 1560, *Hurrell's close*
1576 (a surname); *in la Hyle* 1327[1] (p) (*v.* **halh** (WSax dat.sg. *hēale*)
'nook'); *Inkepen'* 1450, *terr' voc' Inkepennis* 1505 (probably a surname from
Inkpen Brk 309); *Kedeham* 1395 (probably **kide** 'kid, young goat',
hamm); *Keybrooke gate* 1701 (named from Key Brook, *v.* RNs. *infra*);
(*mes' voc'*) *Knyghtes* c. 1560, 1576 (a surname); *one þat lake* 932 (15) (*v.*
lacu 'stream'); *Langleye* 1395, *the langley* 1395 (e15) (*v.* **lang¹**, **lēah**);
(*prat'*) *atte Leemede, (the) Leewode* 1395, 1395 (e15) (*v.* **lēah**, **mǣd**,
wudu); *terre nuper Leyndez* 1450, *mes' voc' Lynes* c. 1560 (a surname);
Longfordes (a coppice) 1618 (probably a surname); *Lowewode* 1395, *the
Lowe wode, lowewodemede* 1395 (e15) (*v.* **low, wudu,** cf. *the Heywode
supra*); *to ludmannes putte* 932 (15) ('Ludmann's pit', from an OE pers.n.
Ludmann and **pytt**, *v.* Forsberg 167); *the lytelland* 1395 (*v.* **lȳtel, land**);
Lyvettes (a cottage) 1450 (a surname); *Midfurlong* 1576 (*v.* **mid** or **midd,
furlang**); *Mishy gate, -Lane* 1699; *claus' voc' Monslade* 1700; *Muggle
paroc* 1702 (*v.* **pearroc**, first el. perhaps a form of S dial. **muckle** '(a heap
of) manure'); *Newlond'* 1450, 1505 (*v.* **nīwe, land**); *mes' voc' Newmans*
c.1560 (a surname); *Newshay* 1699 (cf. (*ten' nuper* . . .) *Nywes* 1450, a
surname with **(ge)hæg**; *prat' de Nithewode, prat' de la Nithe, -Nyth* 1450
(cf. the lost f.ns. *Nytheclose, La Nythe* in Cann par. *supra* where these
names are discussed); *ten' voc' Nypers* c. 1560 (a surname); *Okey* (a
coppice) 1618 ('oak-tree enclosure', cf. Richard *atte Houke* 1327[1], *-atte Ok'*
1332, *-at(te) Noke* 1450, *v.* **āc, (ge)hæg, atte(n)** 'at the'); *East Orchard
Lane* 1701 (leading to E Orchard par. *infra*); *ten' nuper* . . . *Plowmannes*
1450 (cf. Constance *Plowman* 1698); *Plyen'* 1450, *tenement voc' Pylen* c.
1560 (origin unclear); *mes' voc' Poukes* c. 1560 (a surname); *Proutesmoure*
1450 (the surname *Prout* with **mōr**); *Pushyll* 1395, *-hull'* 1395 (e15) (*v.*
peosu 'pease', **hyll**); *cotage called Raffehowse* 1539 (first el. possibly the
pers.n. *Radulf, Raulf,* but cf. lME *raff* 'rubbish, etc' (NED sb¹ from c.
1420), 'foreign timber, especially deal' (NED sb³ from c. 1440)); *on ða riþe*
932 (15) (*v.* **rīð** 'stream'); *Riveham* 1701 (probably 'reeve's enclosure', *v.*
(ge)rēfa, hamm); *Ruddo(c)kysbrygge* 1395, 1395 (e15) (the surname
Ruddock with **brycg** 'bridge'); *on sandhellesled* 932 (15) ('valley by the

sandy hill', *v.* **sand, hyll, slæd**, Tengstrand 272); *to scearpenhame* 932 (15) ('pointed enclosure', *v.* **scearp** (wk.obl. *-an*), **hamm**); *paroc voc' Selwood* 1701 (*v.* **sealh** 'a sallow'); *to þane shamelen* 932 (15) (corresponding to *to þan scamelen* in the E Orchard charter, *v.* under E Orchard par. *infra*); *Scheplond* 1376 (*v.* **scēap, land**); *Short(e)croft(e)* 1395, 1395 (e15) (*v.* **sc(e)ort, croft**); *Silly Orchard* 1700; *on sledwich* (sic), *of sledweie* 932 (15) ('valley way', *v.* **slæd, weg**, the first form showing confusion with **wīc** 'farm'); (*ten' nuper . . .*) *Sleyes* 1450, *Slyes* c. 1560 (a surname); *to snelles hamme weghe* 932 (15) ('way by or to Snell's enclosure', from the OE pers.n. *Snell*, with **hamm, weg**); *oð þas soces seað* 932 (15) ('drainage pit', or 'pit in the marsh', *v.* **soc, sēað**, Tengstrand 47–50, 67-8); *tenement voc' Soones* c. 1560 (a surname); *Square cops* 1618 (*v.* **copis**); *of dune to þare stigele* 932 (15) ('down to the stile', *v.* **stigel**); *Stoford'* 1450, *toftum voc' Stoffordes* c. 1560, *terr' voc' Stoffordes Roveles* 1576 (probably a surname from a p.n. Sto(w)ford (So, D, W, etc., 'stony ford', *v.* **stān, ford**); *Roveles* is eModE *roofless* (from 1610 NED), here used elliptically for 'roofless tenement'); *Stowey* 1450, *Standway cops* 1610 ('stony way', *v.* **stān, weg**); *Stumples Orchard* 1701 (a surname); *þurh sulangraf* 932 (15) (*v.* **grāf** 'grove'; the first el. is possibly a gen.sg. form of **syle¹, sylu** 'a bog, a miry place' with ME *-u-* for *y-*, cf. *Sulegraue* Gl **4** 177; an OE pers.n. *Sula* is not on record, but cf. the rare *Sola* and *Syla* (Redin 78, 79)); *Swinellesham* 1450 (*v.* **hamm**; first el. perhaps a p.n. 'swine hill' from **swīn¹** and **hyll**, or a surname derived from such a p.n.); *Theuerdenne, Deuerdenne, Tenerden(n)'* 1280 (a point in the 'in-bounds' of Cranborne Chase (*v.* **2** 193) and probably to be identified with *Tennerley ditch* 1610 (cf. 'Tennersditch' Hutch³ **3** 407); the second el. is clearly **denn** 'woodland pasture', though perhaps here with the sense 'den, lair' (*v.* EPN s.v.), the first may be **eofor** 'wild boar', in which case initial *Th-, D-, T-* are due to metanalysis of *at E-* (cf. Evershot par. *infra*) and *-n(n)-* is a scribal error which later influenced pronunciation); *three crosse* 1576 (probably a three road intersection, *v.* **þrēo, cross**); *Turnerysplace* 1395, *Thornerysplace* 1395 (e15), *Turners* c. 1560, 1576, *Torneres* 1576 (the surname *Turner*, *v.* **place**); *Turselway* (a coppice) 1618 (*v.* **weg**, first el. uncertain); *Uphill* c. 1560, *Uppehyll* 1576 ('(land) upon the hill', *v.* **uppan, hyll**, cf. Geoffrey *Uppehulle* 1327); *Upperclose* 1700; *Wal(l)dryggyshay* 1395, 1395 (e15) (*v.* **(ge)hæg**; first part of the name probably a surname from Waldridge Bk); *Webbes* 1618 (a surname); (*prat'*) *bynethe the Westwode* 1395, *-þe-, Westwode Abbatisse* 1395 (e15), *Westwood* 1731 (*v.* **west, wudu, beneoðan**; *Abbatisse* from its possession by Shaftesbury Abbey, *v.* **abbatissa** 'abbess'); *the mochewhetelond'* et . . . *the lytell'* 1395 (e15), *the Mochewhytelonde* 1395 (*v.* **land, mycel** 'big', **lȳtel** 'little'; the medial el. may be **hwǣte** 'wheat' or **hwīt** 'white'); *to-, fram Wigheardes stapele* 932 (15) (corresponding to *on þigerðes stapel* 958 (15) in the Thorton charter (*v.* under Marnhull par. *infra*), 'Wīgheard's boundary post', from the OE pers.n. *Wīgheard* and **stapol**); *Wyllames* 1450 (a surname); *to þe wines weie* 932 (15) (probably 'Wine's way', from the OE pers.n. *Wine* and **weg**, if the def.art. is excrescent (a scribal error?), *v.*

Tengstrand 50); *be Winteintune* 932 (15) (the form may be corrupt, but possibly 'farm called after Winta', from the OE pers.n. *Winta* and **-ingtūn**, cf. Wintney Ha (DEPN), Redin 112); *be wirtrune, be wyrttrune* 932 (15) (*v.* **wyrt-truma** 'root, root-stock', *-e* representing either dat.sg. *-an* or dat.pl. *-um*); *Witteridge* 1576 (origin unclear); *Wodefolde* 1395 (*v.* **wudu, fald**); *la Wodemede* 1395 (*v.* **mǣd**); *atte Yate* (p) 1332 ('at the gate', *v.* **atte, geat**); *Zwire* 1576 (*v.* **swīra** 'neck of land').

Sixpenny Handley

This par. is detached from the rest of the hundred to which it gives name.

SIXPENNY HANDLEY (ST 995173)

(*at*) *Hanlee* 871–7 (15) *ShaftR* (S 357 (1)), (*in*) *henlee* 871–7 (15) *ib* (S 357 (2)), (*at*) *heanlegen, Hanlee* (rubric) 956 (14) *ib* (S 630)

Hanlege 1086 DB, *-leige* 1166 RBE (p), *-le* 1230 Cl (p), 1325 FF (*-juxta Craneburn*), *-leg(h)*' 1244 *Ass, -legh* 1327 Pat, 1371 ib (-'by *Craneburn*'), 1440 ib, *-ley(e)* 1340 ib *et freq* to 1618 *Map, -leygh*(') 1371 *Salis et freq* to c. 1500 *Eg, -lee* 1425 Pat, 1441 Cl, *-leigh* 1454 Hutch[3], *Hanleigh-, -leyghe als. Hanley* 1575 *Ilch*

Henleȝe Hy 1 (15) *ShaftR, -le* 1182 P, 1265 Misc (p), 1268 *Ass* (p), 1280 FF, 1291 Tax, 1340 NI, 1428, 1431 FA, *-leg(h)(e)* 1212 Fees, 1249, 1268 FF, 1268, 1280 *Ass et freq* to 1428 FA, *-leye* 1270 Pat, 1288 *Ass, -lee* 1280 *Ass, -ly* 1303 FA, *-leigh* 1316 FA, *Hengh*' (sic) 1327 *SR*

Henelegh 1280 QW, *Hennele* 1331 *Cecil*

Hanghelegh 1327 Pat (p)

Handeleygh 1496 (1498) Pat, *Handly* 1664 HTax, *Handley* 1795 Boswell

Sexpennyhanley 1575 Saxton, *Sixpenny Handley* 1741 M.H.

'(Place at) the high wood or clearing', from **hēah** (wk.obl. *hēan*) and **lēah** (dat.sg. *lēage, lēa(e)*), a common p.n. The comparatively late addition *Sixpenny* is from the hundred name *q.v. supra*. In the N of the par. the ground rises to 500', and the whole par. is within the bounds of Cranborne Chase (**2** 193). However, Ekwall's supposition (DEPN) that

Handley is probably the old name of Cranborne Chase is unlikely, since he is mistaken in thinking that the form (*at*) *heanlegen* (cited above) occurs in the bdy of Compton Abbas. The bounds of Handley are given in 956 (14) *ShaftR* (S 630).

BUGDEN BOTTOM (ST 955168), *Est-, Westbokeden(e), Est-, Westbogheden', Westbogeden'* 1331, *Westbokeden(e)* 1349 *Cecil,* 1411 *MinAcct, Westbokynden'* 1382 *Cecil, Bu(c)kdean(e)* 1541 *Glyn, Est-, West Buck(e)den'* 1547 *Ct,* Buckden 1618 *Map,* Bugden *Md* 1841 *TA,* probably 'valley where beech-trees grow', from **bōc**[1] 'beech-tree', **bōcen** 'growing with beech-trees', and **denu,** with **ēast, west.** There are two other places with the name *Buckden* on the 1618 *Map* of Cranborne Chase, both in Wiltshire (cf. the f.n. Bugdens PN W 487).

DEAN (FM) (ST 977157), *la Dene, la Denn(e)* 1280 *Ass, la Denne* 1280 QW, *atte Dene* 1327 *SR* (p), *Dene* 1332 SR (p), 1340 NI (p), *Deane* c. 1500 *Eg,* 1618 *Map,* 'the valley', *v.* **denu, atte** 'at the'. On 1811 OS, Dean is *Updean,* Dean Fm is *Lowdean.*

FROGMORE FM (ST 999169), *Froggemer(e)* 1244 *Ass* (p), 1332 SR (p), 'pool frequented by frogs', *v.* **frogga, mere**[1]; for the later alteration to -*more,* cf. Ashmore par. **2** 201.

GUSSAGE ST ANDREW (ST 976143)
  Gissic 871–7 (15) *ShaftR* (S 357 (1)), *Gersicg* 871–7 (15) *ib* (S 357 (2))
  Gyssyh Hy 1 (15) *ShaftR, Gussich(e)* e13 *Wim et freq* to 1428 FA, *Gersiz* 1205 RC, *Gessich(')* 1242 Ch, 1244 *Ass, Gesriche* (sic) 1244 *ib, Gissiche* 1288 FF, *Gussych* 1431 FA, c. 1500 *Eg, Guss(h)ygge* 1432 Pat, *Gyssyg', Gussach* c. 1500 *Eg*
  Gissik St Andrews 1258 Ch, *Gyssich St Andrew* 1260 FF *et freq* with variant spellings *Gissich(e)-, Gyss(h)ych-* to 1409 Pat, *Gussich(e) Sancte Andr'* 1268 *Ass, -Sancti Andr(ee)* 1280 *ib,* 15 *ShaftR,* 1575 *Glyn, -St Andrew(s)* 1336 Fine *et freq* to 1374 Pat, *Giss-, Gysshych'-, Giss-, Gyssich Sancti Andr(ee)* 1280 *Ass,* QW, 1288

Ass, Guschich St Andrew 1337 Ipm, *Gussuch St Andrew's* 1356 ib, *Gussach Sancti Andree* c. 1500 *Eg, Gussage Sancti Andree* 1535 VE, *-St Andrewe(s)* 1618 *Map,* 1620 *Ilch Gussage St Andrew, Higher or Upper-Gussage* 1774 Hutch[1]

For etymology and for other early forms, *v.* Gussage All Snts par. **2** 276, cf. also M. Gelling, *Place-Names in the Landscape* (1984) 29, for the suggestion that the name may rather be from a word related to the postulated **gyse** with the noun-forming suffix **-ic.** *St Andrew* is from the dedication of the church, earlier a chapel. The late affix *Higher* or *Upper* is from its position relative to Gussage St Michael par. (*Middle*) and Gussage All Snts par. (*Lower*), cf. also foll. The forms *Gessich Gentil* 1236 FF, etc, placed under Gussage All Snts **2** 276 (following Fägersten 92), are identified with this Gussage by Drew, who also cites *Guschich Gentill* 1283, John *Gentyl* of *Gyssich St Andrew* 1291 Banco.

MINCHINGTON (FM) (ST 966147)
Munechingusseg, -gishegg 1291 Banco
Gussich(')   Munechenton 1302 Drew, 1348 Pat, *-Mu(n)chenton'* 1314 (15) *ShaftR, -Manecheton* 1323 Hutch[3], *-Menechenton* 1324 Inq aqd, *-Monechynton* 1340 FF, *Gyssich Mundecheneton* 1302 Drew, *Gyssych Munechenton* 1303 ib, *Gissych Monek Hampton* 1332 FF, *Gussichmincheueton* (for *-minchene-*) 1387 ib, *Guyssehich' Munchenton'* 1503 *Ilch Munecheneton* 1307 Pat, *Mynchyndon* 1499 Ipm, *Minchen-, Mynchynton* c. 1500 *Eg, Minching-, Mynchinton* 1575 *Ilch, Mynchenton* 1618 *ib*
(*Gissich*) *Myncheton als. Gissich St Andrew* 1440 Pat
Minchington, or Gussage-Minchington, or Manecheton 1774 Hutch[1]

'The farm of the nuns', from OE **myncen** (gen.pl. *myncena*) and **tūn**, alluding to its possession by the Benedictine nunnery of Shaftesbury. The earliest forms cited mean 'Gussage of the nuns', this place being only ½ mile NW of Gussage St Andrew *supra*.

MISTLEBERRY WD (ST 995195), *-Copse* 1811 OS, *Mistlebury* 1841 *TA*, named from the earthwork (an unfinished hill-fort, *v.* RCHM **5** 70) on the par. and county bdy referred to in the Anglo-Saxon bounds of Chalke hundred W as (*to*) *michelan byrg* 955 (14) BCS 917 (S 582), 'the big fortified place', from **micel** (wk.obl. *-an*) and **burh** (dat.sg. *byr(i)g*), this having given rise to the modern form, perhaps with some late influence from Misselfore 6″ (*-ford* 1808) in Bower Chalke par. W 205. The same earthwork seems to be referred to in the Anglo-Saxon bounds of Handley itself as *on mealeburg norþewarde* 956 (14) *ShaftR* (S 630), where the first el. is probably **mǣle** (wk.obl. *-an*) 'variegated, multicoloured', cf. Melbury Abbas par. *infra* (Ekwall DEPN mistakenly includes the form *mealeburg* under the latter place, but it is some 7 miles W of this point, as noted by Fägersten 27 fn.1). On 1618 *Map* the copse is called *Maplebery*, a form of the name showing confusion or alternation of the first el. with **mapel** 'maple-tree'.

WOODCUTTS (FM) (ST 972171), *Wodecote* 1244 *Ass* (p), Abbr (p), 1307 Pat, 1396 IpmR, 15 *ShaftR*, 1409 Cl, *c.* 1500 *Eg*, *-cot'* 1547 *Ct*, *Estwodecotes* 1387 FF, *Wodecotys* 1456 ib, *Woodcotes* 1575 Saxton, 1774 Hutch[1], *-or Woodcotts* 1869 Hutch[3], *Woodcotts* 1618 *Map*, *-cutts* 1811 OS, 'cottage(s) in a wood', *v.* **cot**, **wudu**, **ēast**, cf. Woodcutts Fm **2** 147. There is still a wooded area of Cranborne Chase to the N.

BARBER'S COPPICE, 1841 *TA, -Cl ib.* BARROW COPPICE, 1841 *TA*, near Church Barrow *infra* and another unnamed tumulus. BEEHIVE FM (Kelly). BRIDMORE RIDE, a track through woodland to Bridmore W 201, *v.* **ride** 'bridle-path', cf. Ridingway *infra*. BROCKWELL COPPICE, *Brock holes* 1618 *Map, Brockfells* 1841 *TA, v.* **brocc-hol** 'a badger hole, a sett'. BROOKES COPPICE, 1841 *ib, Brookes* 1618 *Map*, a surname. BUCK'S STILE, *Buck Stile* 1841 *TA*, cf. *Buck Md ib.* CALCOTS WD, *Chaldecott* 1618 *Map, Chalcotts Coppice* 1829 *EnclA, Chalkits* 1841 *TA,* cf. William *Chalcot* 1575 *Glyn, farm . . . called Brown's Tenement, otherwise Bingham's or Chaldecot's* 1869 Hutch[3], probably a p.n. 'cold cottage' from **ceald** and **cot,** but possibly a surname from such a p.n. CAPTAIN'S WD, -*Coppice* 1841 *TA.* CASHMOOR, 1869 Hutch[3], -*more* 1774 Hutch[1], *Cashmore Inn & Mill* 1811 OS, *Cashmere Fd* 1841 *TA,* probably 'pool where water-cress grows', from **cærse** and **mere**[1], with change to -*more* as in Frogmore *supra;* the place is on the small stream which gives name to the Gussages, *v.* Gussage St Andrew *supra* in this par. and cf. Cashbrook **2** 268. It is probable that the boundary point *on þannen mylen stede* 'to the mill site' in the Anglo-Saxon bounds of Handley (956 (14) *ShaftR* (S 630)) was at or near Cashmoor, cf. the mill here in 1811, *v.* **myln, stede.** CHAFFINGER'S COPPICE, cf. *Chaffinge* 1841 *TA.* CHAMPS FM. CHAPEL DOWN FM, named from a small chapel beside the farm-house. CHAPEL FM, named from St Andrew's Church *infra.* CHURCH BARROW. COMMON POND. THE CROSS, a cross-roads. CURRIER'S COPPICE, *Carriers-* 1829 *EnclA, Curriers'-* 1841 *TA,* a surname. DEANEND (BUSHES), *Dean End Bushes, Dean End Grove & Plot* 1841 *ib,* 'valley end', with reference to the valley which gives name to Dean *supra, v.* **denu, ende;** *Gains End* 1811 OS is possibly an error. DEAN LANE (DROVE) (6"), DEANLAND (1"), *Daine Lane* 1664 HTax, *Denland* 1811 OS, 1829 *EnclA,* (*Long*) *Dean Lane Grd* 1841 *TA, v.* **denu** 'valley', **lane**; a different valley to that at Dean (Fm) *supra.* DROW COPPICE, *Throake* 1618 *Map, Draw Coppice* 1841 *TA,* probably ModE (SW) dial. *throck, drock* 'a covered drain, a flat stone across a ditch', *v.* EPN *s.v.* **þroc** and PN W 339. ENDLESS PIT, 1841 *TA,* presumably so called from its extreme depth; this may be the feature referred to in the Anglo-Saxon bounds of Handley as (*at*) *mes delle* 956 (14) *ShaftR* (S 630), from **mēos** 'moss, lichen' or 'bog, swamp' and **dell** 'pit' (or 'valley' if *mes delle* refers to the valley in which Endless Pit is situated). FERNEY WAY. FIVE WAYS, now a meeting of *six* tracks. FOXBURY LOWER HEDGE (1841 *TA*), GREAT LOWER HEDGE (*Lawridge* 1618 *Map, Great*

Lower Ridge 1841 *TA*), adjacent coppices on the par. and county bdy to be identified with *Ruggecopyce* 1548 *Ct*, *v.* **hricg** 'ridge', **copis**; *Law-* (if a genuine form later rationalized to *Lower*) may represent OE **hlāw** 'mound, tumulus' or ME **lawe** 'law' (perhaps denoting the limit of some jurisdiction); *Foxbury* is 'fox's earth', *v.* **fox, burg**. GARSTON DOWN & WD, *La Garston'* 15 *ShaftR, Brode-, Longe Gaston'* 1575 *Glyn, Gatson* 1618 *Map, Graston Copse* 1811 OS, *Garston-, Gasson Grd, Long Gasson* 1829 *EnclA, (Coppice) Garston, Garston Fd* 1841 *TA*, *v.* **gærs-tūn** 'grass enclosure, paddock', **brād**, **lang**[1]. GREATSTONE COPPICE, LITTLESTONE COPPICE, *Stone Cops* 1618 *Map, Stone Grd* 1829 *EnclA, Gt & Lt Stone, Stone Fd* 1841 *TA*, *v.* **stān, copis**. GREEN LANE. HANDLEY CMN, 1811 OS, *Hanley Comon* 1618 *Map*. HANDLEY DOWN, *le downe, lez downes* 1575 *Glyn,* cf. John *atte Doune* 1327 *SR, Sheep Down* 1829 *EnclA, Down (Fd & Pce), The Down Cl* 1841 *TA*, *v.* **dūn** 'hill, down', **atte** 'at the'. HANDLEY HILL & HO. HILL COPPICE. HOE COPPICE, *Howe* 1575 *Glyn,* 1618 *Map, Hoe* 1841 *TA*, *v.* **hōh** (dat.sg. *hō(e)*) 'heel, spur of land'. HUMBY'S STOCK COPPICE, from the *Humby* family which owned lands in Handley in the 19th cent., *v.* Hutch[3] 3 545, cf. Stock Coppice *infra*. HUTCHINS COPPICE, *Hutchins* 1618 *Map,* 1841 *TA, Hutchens Coppice ib*, a surname. INWARD & OUTWARD LARDENHALL, *Lorden'-hallcopyce* 1547 *Ct, Lorden hall* 1618 *Map, Inner & Outer Lordenhall* 1841 *TA*, two coppices within a wooded area of Cranborne Chase, dissected by Oxford St *infra*, possibly a facetious name with the meaning 'lords' hall', if *-en* represents an analogical ME gen.pl. *-ene*, *v.* **-ena, hlāford, h(e)all, copis**. LITTLE BALL, 1841 *TA*, *v.* **b(e)all** 'rounded hill, hillock'. LITTLE DOWN CTGS, *litle downe iuxta Thorney Downe quondam voc' hoggen lease* 1575 *Glyn, v.* **lȳtel, dūn, hogg** 'young sheep' (with analogical ME gen.pl. *-ene*), **læs** 'pasture', Thorney Down Fm *infra*. LITTLESTONE COPPICE, *v.* Greatstone Coppice *supra*. LOWER FM. MAIDMENT'S CTGS, cf. *Maidments Fd* 1841 *TA*, a surname. MANOR FM. MILLER'S BARN & LANE. MINCHINGTON CROSS (a cross-roads) & DOWN (*Gt & Lt Minchington Down* 1841 *TA*), named from Minchington *supra.* MONKS' ARUNDELL COPPICE, *Little Arundell* (a copse) 1618 *Map, Monks Arundell* 1841 *TA,* cf. Arundell Coppice (6") just over the county bdy in Berwick St John par. W 202, all named from the *Arundell* family, lords of the manor of Berwick St John and (from the 16th cent.) of the hundred of Sixpenny Handley (Hutch[3] **3** 534), cf. Matthew *Arundel* 1575 ib **3** 542, William *Monck* 1664 HTax. NEW BARN. NEW TOWN. OAKLEY LANE, cf. *Oakley Fd* 1841 *TA*; the lane follows the Handley-Farnham par. bdy, crossing a hill at ST 961158 which is probably the '(field called) *Oak Hill*' mentioned by Hutch[3] **3** 547; the latter is thus almost certainly a survival of *on ac hylle* 956 (14) *ShaftR* (S 630) in the Handley charter, *v.* **āc, hyll**; Oakley may be a distinct name ('oak wood', from **āc** and **lēah**) or it may be an alternative development of *ac hylle*, with *-ley* from *-hill* as in Sandley in Gillingham par. *supra* (cf. EPN **1** 275), with some possible influence from Oakley Down & Fm **2** 266, a genuine **lēah** name some 3½ miles ENE at the other end of this large par. OLD CHALK PIT(s) (3 ×), cf. *Chalk Grd, Chalk Pit* 1841 *TA*. OLD MANOR HO (at Woodcutts *supra*). OXFORD ST., a woodland track that is long and straight, thus presumably a humorous transferred use of the London st.n., cf. Lardenhall *supra*. PLECKLEY, *Pleckey* (sic) 1841 *TA, v.* **plek** 'small plot of ground', **lēah** 'wood, clearing'. POLLARDS WD, *Pollards* 1841 *ib*, a surname, or a reference to pollarded trees, *v.* **pollard**. PRIBDEAN WD, *Priueden* 1618 *Map, Privdon* 1811 OS, *-den* 1841 *TA,* probably 'valley where privet grows', from **pryfet** and **denu**, cf. Prewley D 207. RIDINGWAY, *Riding waie* (a copse) 1618 *Map, Riding Way* (*Coppice*) 1841 *TA*, a copse dissected by Bridmore Ride *supra, v.* **riding, weg**. ST ANDREW'S CHURCH, cf. *Chapel Fd* 1841 *TA*, Gussage St Andrew *supra*. ST MARY'S CHURCH, cf. *ecclesie de Henlee* 1280 *Ass, ecclesia de Hanleygh'* 1407 *Weld*[1], 'the chantry of *Hanlegh*' 1440 Pat, *Church hill* 1829 *EnclA, Church Fd* 1841 *TA*. SCRUBBITY BARROWS (tumuli marked 6") & COPPICE, *Scrubbedy* 1841 *TA*. SESSIONS GATE, perhaps the surname *Sessions* (Reaney), unless this is the word *session* used in some special sense (the place is on the par. and county bdy, cf. Foxbury Lower Hedge

supra). GT & LT SHAFTESBURY COPPICE, *Shaftberies* 1618
Map, Gt & Lt Shaftesbury 1841 *TA*, cf. *Shaftesbury Fd ib*,
no doubt from its possession by the Earls of Shaftesbury,
cf. *Shaftsbury Copse* in Pentridge par. **2** 237. SHERMEL
GATE, *Shiremill gate* 1618 *Map*, cf. *Sheremill* (a copse) *ib*,
on the county bdy and in a marked valley though no
stream is shown 6″, *v.* **scīr**[1] 'shire', **myln** 'mill'. SHIRE
RACK, now the name of a stretch of the Do-Wiltshire
county bdy for some 2–3 miles (on 1″ it is marked 2 miles
further W than on 6″), thus suggesting that the second el.
might be ModE dial. **rack** 'a narrow path, a boundary' (*v.*
PN W 445), cf. *Shire way* 17 *CecilMap*; however it may
take its name from *Shire oke* 1618 *Map* (a copse just on
the Wiltshire side of the bdy), as suggested in PN W 205,
from **scīr**[1] and **āc** 'oak-tree'. STICKLEY'S BARN. STOCK
COPPICE, cf. *Stock Grd* 1829 *EnclA, Stock Fd* 1841 *TA*, *v.*
stocc 'tree-trunk, stump'. STRAIGHT LANE. TARRANT'S
BOTTOM & COPPICE, *Tarrants* 1618 *Map*, 1841 *TA*, a
surname from one of the Do places called Tarrant.
THORNEY DOWN FM, cf. *Thorny Down Inn* 1811 OS,
named from *pasturam . . . que vocatur la Thornedowne* 1503
Ilch, Thorneydowne 1575 *Glyn, Thornie Downe* 1629 *Ilch,
Thorny Down* 1811 OS, *Thorn(e)y Down Coppice & Fd*
1841 *TA*, *v.* **þorn** 'thorn-tree', **þornig** 'growing with
thorn-trees', **dūn** 'hill, down', cf. the f.n. Thorney Down
2 270. TOWN FM. UPWOOD, 1811 OS, -*Md* 1829 *EnclA*,
-*Fm* 1869 Hutch[3], *Vpwod*' 1575 *Glyn, v.* **upp** 'higher up',
wudu. VICARAGE, *the viccaridge house* 1664 HTax, cf. the
f.n. *Common vicarage* 1841 *TA*. WITHYWIND COPPICE,
Wythie Windes 1618 *Map, Withy wines* 1841 *TA*, ModE
dial. **with(y)wind** (from OE *wiþo-, wiþewinde*) 'bind-
weed', listed by Barnes as *withwind*. WOODCUTTS CMN,
Woodcut Cmn 1811 OS, *Woodcots Cmn* 1841 *TA*, from
Woodcutts *supra*. WOOD FM (lost), 1869 Hutch[3]. WOOD-
WARD'S WAY, in the woodland of Cranborne Chase, from
wudu-weard 'forester' or a surname of this origin.

FIELD NAMES

The undated forms are 1841 *TA* 190. Spellings dated 956 (14) are
ShaftR (S 630). Those dated 1291, 1302 are Banco (Drew), 1314 (15) and
15 are *ShaftR*, 1327 are *SR*, 1332 SR, 1346 FA, n.d. (1500), 1574, 1869
Hutch[3], 1547, 1548 *Ct*, 1575 *Glyn*, 1618 *Map*, 1620 *Ilch*, 1664 HTax, 1686
AddCh, and 1829 *EnclA* (DRO 21).

(*a*) Adams Cl; Avery's Grove (-*and Coppice* 1829, cf. Edward *Avery*
1664); Baker's Orchd; Barley Mdw (cf. *Barly Close* 1575); Barn Cl; Berry
Fd, Grd & Md (*claus' voc' Byryfyldes*, -*Byrye mede* 1575, probably from
ME *bury* (dat.sg. *byrig* of OE **burh**) in the sense 'manor house', with **feld,
mǣd**); Bingham's Coppice 1829 (cf. Calcots Wd *supra*); Blakes Fd and old
Lain (cf. Walter *le Blake* 1327, *v.* **leyne**); Border; Bottom Fd & Md;
Bourton (perhaps from **burh-tūn** 'fortified farmstead', cf. Bourton par.
supra; the field is near Minchington); Bowling Green Cl & Fd; Brack (*v.*
bræc[1] 'a brake, a thicket'); Bradley Bear Croft (cf. *Broadley* 1829, *v.*
brād[1], **lēah**, probably with **bǣr**[2] '(woodland) pasture'); Green Bratch,
Breach (cf. *the brache* 1575, *Brache, Breach* (*Fd*) 1829, *v.* **brǣc** 'land
broken up for cultivation'); Broad Fd; Browns Row (cf. Calcots Wd *supra*);
Burdens Wd (*Burdons-* 1829, cf. John *Bordon* 1332); Burr Mdw 1829;
Chantney (*Chantenay* 1829); Cherit(')s Fd; Clover Fd; Common Cl;
Constable's Pce; Cookmans Home Cl & 5 Acres 1829; Coppice (Cl); Court
Cl; Cowards' Bit; Cowleaze; Crowter(s) Cl (*Crowters* (a copse) 1618, cf.
John *Crowter* 1574 (bought estate at Minchington *supra*)); Dean Fd (cf.
Dean (Fm) *supra*); Doctors Grd; Down Fd & Pce (named from Week
Street Down **2** 144); Dunsiddle Grove; East Croat (Peak) 1829 (*croat* is
probably a variant of **croft**); Easterly Grd 1829, -Grove; 8 Acres (*the
eight acres* 1620); Farm Orchd (cf. *the Farme Feild of Hanley* 1686); 15, 5,
4, and 14 Acres; Four Cornered Fd; Godshill 1829; Goose Cl; Great Fd;
Green Hayes; Green Plot; Grove Coppice (cf. *The Grove* 1829, *v.* **grāf(a)**);
Groves Cl 1829 (*copic' vocat' Grovez* 1548, probably a surname); Half
Hide (named from Half Hide **2** 221); Ham 1829 (*v.* **hamm**); Handley Fd
1829 (*Hanley field* 1618); Hanging Grd (*v.* **hangende**); Harris Cl (cf.
Francis *Harris* 1664); (Gt & Lt) Head Fd (*v.* **hēafod**); Hedgerow(s) (freq);
Higher Cl, Fd & Md(w); Hill Coppice; Home Cl, Fd, Grd & Md(w);
Horne Pond (*Hornpond Cl* 1829); Horse Cl; Horse Leaze (-*Leys* 1829, *v.*
lǣs); Hundred Acres (an ironical name for a very small field); Hungry Hill
(*v.* **hungrig**); Ice Croft (possibly **ēast**, but cf. foll.); Icy Fd; Isaac's Home
Cl 1829; Jeffery's; Jerrard's Fd 1829; Jill Hill (*Gill-* 1829); Kemmon
(Hill) (*Kimming Hill Cl* 1829); Kings (Md) (cf. Ralph *le Kyng* 1327);
Lammas ('land reverting to pasture at Lammas (1 August)', *v.* **Lammas**);
Land; Lawn (*v.* **launde**); Little Fd, Mdw, Pdk & Plot; Loin's Gold (*Loins
Goal* 1829); Long Cl & Fd; Long Lds 1829; Long Md; Lower Cl, Grd &
Md(w); Lype (Coppice) ((land) *super lype* 1575, *v.* **hlīep** 'a leaping place');
Mackerell's Fm 1869; Middle Fd; Mount; Muston's Row; Nag Hill; New
Fd; New Leaze; Nippards Fd 1829 (cf. John *Nippard, -erd* 1664); North
Fd (*Northfeld* 1291, *v.* **feld**); Oakley Down (part of Oakley Down in

Wimborne St G **2** 266, cf. the quite distinct Oakley Lane *supra*); Old House Orchd 1829; The Paddock 1829; Parish Pound; (East & Lr) Park (possibly *greate Parke* 1620, *v.* **park**); Peaked Cl (*Picked-* 1829, *v.* **peked, pīcede** 'pointed'); Piece of Arable; Piece of Pasture; Pigs Coppice; Pike's Cl 1829; Pit Cl & Fd (*Pitt Hill Fd* 1829, cf. Helen- 1327, John *atte Putte* 1332, *v.* **pytt, atte** 'at the'); Pitcher's Grd; Play Cl; Pleasure Grds; Plot; Plovers Md; Pond Cl & Orchd; Ridge Fd (*v.* **hrycg**); Rookery; Ruddox (*terr' voc' Ruddockes* 1575, *Ruddex* 1829, the surname *Ruddock*); 7 Acres; (the) Shave (*Shave* 1829, cf. *Shawedowne* 1548, *v.* **sc(e)aga** 'a small wood, a copse', **dūn**); Sheep Drove 1829; Shetters Hill; Shrubbery, Shrubberies; 16 Acres; South Cl; South Fd (*in campo austral'* 1575); Stable Orchd; Sticklings Pce (cf. *Sticklands Home Cl* 1829, named from the *Stickland* family, *v.* Hutch³ **3** 545); Stinchley 1829; Stony Wood Fd; Stoutley; 10 Acres, Yonder 10 Acres or Bottom Parte; Three Cornered Fd; Timber Cl; Turnpike Ho; Higher Twelve; 12, 20 & 2 Acres; Upper Fd; Walter's Md (from the *Walter* family, *v.* Hutch³ **3** 545); Well Cl; West Fd 1829 (*campo occident'* 1575); Wheat Ridge or Witherds; Williams Fd (*-house* 1829, from the *Williams* family, *v.* Hutch³ **3** 545); Wind Mill Fd; Woman's Stubb (*v.* **stubb** 'tree stump'); Wood Fd; Yonder Fd; Young Orchd.

(b) *on pane an lipien þorn* 945 (14) ('the solitary thorn-tree', *v.* **anli(e)pig, þorn**); *on berendes beorh* 956 (14) (*v.* **beorg** 'hill, barrow'; the first el. is problematical and may be a corrupt form of a pers.n., but it could be a form with epenthetic *d* of OE **bere-ærn, beren** 'barn'); *Burch Hyll'* 1547 (*v.* **birce, byrce** 'birch-tree', **hyll**); *Dogetescroft* 1302 (the surname *Doget* with **croft**); *Donesplot* 15 (the surname *Don* with **plot**); *Erle of Shroseber'copyce* 1548 (from its possession by the Earl of Shrewsbury, *v.* **copis**); *Fountmyll'swod'* 1548 (from its possession by William *Skynner de Fountmyll'* ib, *v.* **wudu**, Fontmell Magna par. *supra*); *oð ða furuh, on land* (for *anlang*) *furuh* 956 (14) (*v.* **furh** 'furrow'); *una roda bosci qui vocat' La Gore* 15 (*v.* **gāra** 'point of land'); *atte Grnge* (sic) 15 (p) (*v.* **grange, atte**); *Greate Meade* 1575; *Haymed Close* 1575 (*v.* **hēg, mǣd**); *Hanley Coppices* 1686 (*v.* par. name *supra*); *Haynes close* 1618 (a surname); *on þane hege reawe* 956 (14) (*v.* **hege-rǣw** 'hedgerow'); *on þere herepað* 956 (14) (*v.* **here-pæð** 'highway'); *be þane on heueden* 956 (14) (*v.* **hēafod** 'hill, end of a ridge'; *þane on* may be a confused form of the def.art., cf. *on þannen mylen stede* (discussed under Cashmoor *supra*) in the same charter); *Hinok'* 1548 (*v.* **inhoke** 'land temporarily enclosed from fallow land for cultivation'); *hoggen lease* 1575 (*v.* Little Down Ctgs *supra*); *Kerlies* (3 separate copses) 1618 (a surname); *Langford* (a copse) 1618 (no stream or ford apparent, so probably a surname, cf. Henry *Langfford' de Wodeyat'* (= Woodyates **2** 271) 1547); *Lees* (a coppice) 1618 (probably **lǣs** 'pasture'); *La Leigh* 1314 (15), *La Legh'* 15 (*v.* **lēah** 'wood, clearing'); *Minchington field* 1618 (*v.* Minchington *supra*); *Morgans* 1618 (a surname); *no mans grounde* 1575 (a common p.n. type, usually land on a boundary); *on pegan beorh* 956 (14) ('Pǣga's hill or barrow', from the OE pers.n. *Pǣga* and **beorg**); *Quarnes* (a copse) 1618 (perhaps **cweorn** 'hand-mill', or a surname from this word); *Redcrafte* 1575 (*v.* **croft**); *on þat get at seuen diche suð ende, anlang diche*

956 (14) ('to the gate at the south end of "seven ditches", along the ditch',
v. **geat, seofon, dīc, sūð, ende**, probably with reference to the Dykes
(6") at ST 992145, just NW of the RB village on Gussage Down (**2** 145));
o þes sledes Northecge 956 (14) ('to the north edge of the valley', *v.* **slæd,
norð, ecg**); *Stanleys* (a copse) 1618 (cf. Thomas *de Stanlegh* 1346,
Christine *de Stanlegh* 15); *Steeles* 1618 (a surname); *on til luches lege* 956
(14) (this survives as Tinkley Down W 202 which is *(to) tilluces leage* 955
(14) BCS 917 in the bounds of Chalke hundred, cf. also Tinkley Bottom &
Coppice both 6" on the Wiltshire side of the county bdy, 'Tilluc's wood or
clearing', from an OE pers.n. *Tilluc*, a diminutive of *Tilli*, and **lēah**); *on
toten berg'* 956 (14) (possibly identical with *(to) tatanbeorge* in the bounds
of Tarrant Hinton **2** 122; *toten* may be an error for *taten*, but if *toten* is the
more correct form the first el. could be the OE pers.n. *Tota*, or **tōte**
(gen.sg. *-an*) 'a look-out', cf. Todber par. *supra*); *Wassockespitt'* 1548 (*v.*
pytt, with a surname); *adun to wege, andland* (for *andlang*) *weges* 956 (14)
(*v.* **weg** 'way, road'); *Westwode* n.d. (1500), c.1500 (*v.* **west, wudu**); *mes'
voc' Whytwoddes* 1575 (a surname, perhaps from Whitewood W 86);
Wrabbeshaw 1548 (*v.* **sc(e)aga** 'small wood', first el. probably on OE
pers.n. *Wrabba* proposed for Wrabness Ess 358)); *atte Wych(e)* 1327, 1332
(both (p), *v.* **atte** 'at the', **wice** 'wych-elm'); *Youngs, Yongs groue* 1618 (*v.*
grāf(a), cf. John *Young* 1664).

Iwerne Minster

IWERNE ['juːən] MINSTER (ST 868145)
  (*at*) *ywern* 871–7 (15) *ShaftR* (S 357 (1)), (*in*) *hywerna*
    871–7 (15) *ib* (S 357 (2)), (*at*) *Iwern* (3 ×) 956 (14) *ib* (S
    630)
  Evneminstre 1086 DB
  Ywern(e) Hy 1 (15) *ShaftR*, 1227 FF, 1268 *Ass et freq* to
    c.1500 *Eg, Iwern(e)* 1290 (15) *ShaftR*, 1316 FA *et freq* to
    1664 HTax, *Ewern'* 14 (16) *Salis, Iwarn(e)* 1392, 1415
    Pat (-*als. Iwerne Mynster*), *Iwerna, Ywernia* 15 *ShaftR,
    Euuern by Shaftesbury* 1448 Pat, *Ywarne* c.1500 *Eg,
    Iweren* 1664 HTax
  Iwern(e)-, Ywern(e)   Menstre,   -Munstre,   -Min(i)str(e)
    1280 *Ass*, QW, *Iwerne-, Ywerne Min(i)str(e), -Mynstre*
    1288 *Ass et freq* to 1428 FA, *Iwern(e)minster, -mynster*
    1291 Tax, 1461 Pat, *Iwarn' Minstr'* 15 *ShaftR, Yewen
    Mynster* 1569 *Comm, Vernemynster* 1575 Saxton,
    Ewern(e) Minster 1645 *SxAS*, 1869 Hutch[3]

Named from R. Iwerne which rises here and which also

gives name to Iwerne Courtney par. *supra* and Steepleton
Iwerne par. **2** 114, *v.* RNs. *infra*. The affix is OE **mynster**,
perhaps in the sense '(church of a) monastery', in allusion to
its possession by Shaftesbury abbey (from 956 if not earlier,
v. S 357 and 630), or simply '(large) church' if the church
here was particularly important even by the time of DB
(supported by the fact that later it had no fewer than five
chapelries, *v.* Hutch³ **3** 541 ff). In 1664 HTax the par. is
divided into two tithings, *Iwerne* and *Iweren West*. The
Anglo-Saxon bounds of the manor of Iwerne M. are given in
S 630.

HILL FM (PLANT.) (ST 886145)

> *Hille* 1086 DB, *Hill Parvo* (sic) 1346, *Hille Parva* 1428 FA
> *Hull(e)* 13 *Glyn* (p), 1270 (1372) *ChrP*, 1291 Hutch³ (p),
> 1303 FA, 1327 SR (p) *et freq* to 1412 FA, *-juxta
> Ywerneministre* 1336 FF, *-by Iwernemynster* 1461 Pat,
> *Hulla* n.d. (1372) *ChrP, Lytelhull* 1431 FA, *Hull or Hill*
> 1774 Hutch¹, 1869 Hutch³
> *Hulles, Hullys* n.d. (1372) *ChrP*

'(Place at) the hill', *v.* **hyll**; the farm stands at 619', the
highest part of Iwerne Hill *infra*. The affixes **lȳtel** 'little',
Lat **parva**, perhaps denoted the smaller part of a divided
manor. The DB identification follows Eyton, Fägersten,
DBGazetteer and VCH; DB *Hille* is tentatively identified
with Gold Hill in Ch. Okeford par. *supra* by C. & F. Thorn,
Domesday Book: Dorset, Phillimore, 1983.

PEGG'S FM (CTGS) (ST 852155), PEGGS MILL BRIDGE, *Pegges*
1346 Hutch³, 1390 FF, 1391 Hutch³, 1408 FF *et freq* to 1869
Hutch³, *curt'* . . . *q' Rob' Pegge nuper ten'* 1444 *MinAcct,
Pegges Farme* 1664 HTax, *Peggs* 1795 Boswell, cf. *Peggs
Hanging* (a coppice) 1618 *Map, Peggs Mill* 1811 OS (now
Corn Mill 6″), *Peggs Coppice & Marsh* 1841 *TA*, all named
from the family of John and Robert *le Peg* who had a
messuage, a mill and land here in 1317 FF, cf. also Michael
Peog 1327 *SR, -Peg* 1332 SR, 1340 NI, Robert *Pueg* 15
Hutch³.

PRESTON HILL (FM & PLANT.), PRESTON HO (ST 864139), *Preston(e)* Hy 1 (15) *ShaftR*, 1327 *SR*, 1332 SR, 1345 (*-juxta Shaftesbury*), 1354 ('-near *I(y)werne Court(e)ney, -ay'*), 1372 (*-juxta Sheftebury*), 1374 (*-juxta Shereueton*) all FF *et passim, Prestentun* n.d. (15) Hutch³, 'priest farm', from **prēost** and **tūn**, cf. Preston 1 230 which is identical in origin; it is ½ mile N of Iwerne Courtney or Shroton *supra*, 6 miles S of Shaftesbury *infra*. It was a tithing of Pimperne hundred in 1327 *SR*, 1332 SR, 1548 *Ct*, it is described as 'part in Blandford and part in Shaftesbury division' in 1645 Hutch³ 3 540, and a manorial or administrative connection with Steepleton Iwerne par. is suggested by the late affixed form *Steepleton Preston* used of that place, *v.* 2 114. On 1811 OS, Preston Ho is *Preston*, Preston Hill Fm is *Preston Barn*, and Preston Hill (1841 *TA*) is *Preston Down*.

BAREDEN DOWN (PLANT.), *Bearding Down & Fd* 1841 *TA*, adjacent to *Fredownes* 1574 SoDoNQ, *Iwerne free downe* 1618 *Map, -Free Down* 1811 OS, cf. *Le Shepe Downe* 1574 SoDoNQ, *Iwerne sheep Downe* 1618 *Map, New Down* 1829 *EnclA, Common Down* 1841 *TA, v.* **frēo, scēap, dūn**. HR & LR BARN PLANT. BEECH CLUMP. BROOKMAN'S FM & VALLEY, *lands called Brochmens* 1548 Hutch³, *Brookmans (Marsh)* 1841 *TA*, from a surname *Brookman* 'dweller by the brook', cf. Richard *attebroke* 1327 *SR, v.* **atte** 'at the', **brōc**. CHURCHILL'S COPPICE & FM, *Churchills Coppice* 1841 *TA*. CLAYESMORE SCHOOL (1″), named from Claysmore Mx 73, from where the school was moved to Iwerne in 1933. COMMON BUSHES. CORN MILL, earlier *Pegs Mill, v.* Pegg's Fm *supra*. THE COTTAGE. EAST PARK, part of Iwerne Minster Park *infra*. FARRINGTON BRIDGE, named from Farrington in Iwerne C. par. *supra*. FOLLY BARROW (local). (LR) FREAK'S COPPICE, *freakes* (a coppice) 1618 *Map, Hr & Lr Freakes* 1841 *TA*, cf. Thomas *Vreke* 1327 *SR* (Fontmell M.), Robert-, Thomas *Freke* 1578 Hutch³. FRY'S COPPICE, 1841 *TA, Row fries* (a coppice) 1618 *Map*, cf. Francis *Fry* who had a manor in Iwerne at the end of Elizabeth's reign (Hutch³ 3 540); *Row* may be 'rough', *v.* **rūh**. HR & LR FURZEY COPPICE, 1841 *TA, furzie* (a coppice) 1618 *Map, v.* **fyrs, -ig³**. GODMANS (lost, near Pegg's Fm *supra*), 1548,

1587, 1869 Hutch[3], (*Lt*) *Godmans, Godmans Orchd* 1841 *TA*, named from the family of John *Goudman* 1332 SR, 1340 NI, Roger *Godmon, -man* 15 *ShaftR*. HARBIN'S COPPICE, 1841 *TA, Harbins or Poynt* 1618 *Map*, cf. Harbin's Park in Tarrant G. **2** 247, Payne Coppice *infra*. HEATH COPPICE, *heathe* 1618 *Map, Heath, Heaths Coppices* 1841 *TA, v.* **hǣð**. HILL FLOWER COPPICE, *Hill Flower and Sargents Row* 1841 *TA*. IWERNE HILL, *montem de Ywerne* 1268 *Ass, Ewerne-, Iwerne Hill* 1814 *EnclA*, cf. Hill Fm *supra*. In 1869 Hutch[3] **3** 555 there is reference to 'the hill above *Ewerne*, called *Cheyne End*', this probably corresponding to *Chine Head* 1618 *Map, v.* **cinu** 'deep valley', **ende, hēafod**; the valley in question may have been Brookman's Valley *supra*, or *Romelles Deane infra*. IWERNE LODGE, cf. *Lodge Coppice* 1597 Hutch[3]. IWERNE MINSTER HO, *Iwerne Ho* 1811 OS. IWERNE MINSTER PARK, possibly *greate Parke* 1620 *Ilch*, cf. *Corn Park, First Park* 1841 *TA*, East Park *supra*. LAMBING YARD PLANT. LOWER FIELD STALL, *v.* **st(e)all**. MILL POND, near Oyle's Mill *infra*. THE NURSERY, *Nursery* 1841 *TA*. OYLE'S MILL, *Isles Mill* 1811 OS, cf. *Millheys* 1841 *TA*, Pegg's Mill Bridge *supra*; there were three mills in Iwerne M. in 1086 DB (VCHDo **3** 82). PARK HOUSE FM BLDGS, cf. *Park and Banky Lease* 1841 *TA, v.* **lǣs**. PAYNE COPPICE, *Harbins or Poynt* 1618 *Map, Poigns-* 1829 *EnclA, Poyne Coppice* 1841 *TA, v.* **point**, cf. Harbins Coppice *supra*. GT & LT PEAKEY COPPICE, *Gt & Lt Peakey* 1841 *TA*, corresponding to two coppices called respectively *Deeke* (probably for *Peeke*) and *Picked* on 1618 *Map*, cf. also *Piked* [Coppice] 1597 Hutch[3], *v.* **pēac** 'peak, point', **pīcede** 'pointed'. POND MEAD STALL, *Pond Md* 1841 *TA, v.* **st(e)all**. PRESTON WD, from Preston *supra*, cf. *Bosco de Ywerne* 1268, 1280 *Ass*. HR & LR ROGER HAYES, *-Hays* 1841 *TA, Rogerhays* 1597 Hutch[3], *Roger haie* 1618 *Map*, the pers.n. or surname *Roger* with **(ge)hæg** 'enclosure'. ROLF'S WD (1″). ST MARY'S CHURCH. SHILLINGSTONE LODGE, cf. Shillingstone par. **2** 238. SPINNEY PITS COPPICE. STUD FM. TALBOT INN, *Talbots Mead Inn* 1841 *TA*. TILLHAYS. TOWER HILL. VICARAGE, cf. *Parsonage Croft & Marsh* 1841 *TA*. WALES PLANT. WATERY LANE. WEST HILL, WESTHILL PLANT., *Westhill* 1811 OS, *West Hill Orchd* 1841 *TA*, W of the village. WEST LODGE, 1618 *Map*, 1811 OS, cf. *Lodg cops*

1618 *Map*, *v*. **log(g)e**, **copis**. WIGMORE COPPICES, *Wigmoor* (*Coppices*) 1841 *TA*, probably 'beetle marsh', *v*. **wigga, mōr**. WITHY BED, 1841 *TA*. WOODLYNCH PLANT., (*Green*) *Woodlinch* 1841 *TA*, *v*. **hlinc** 'ridge'.

FIELD-NAMES

The undated forms are 1841 *TA* 116. Spellings dated 956 (14) are *ShaftR* (S 630). Those dated 1270 (1372), n.d. (1372) are *ChrP*, 1327 *SR*, 1332 *SR*, 1340 NI, 1346 FA, 15 *ShaftR*, 1432 *Rent*, 1569 *Comm*, 1574 SoDoNQ (Vol 26), 1618 *Map*, 1645 *SxAS*, 1664 HTax, 1791 Boswell, 1829 *EnclA*, and the rest Hutch³.

(*a*) Alders Md (*Alder-* 1829, *v*. **alor**); Batcombe (*Buttcomb* 1829); Bay House Marsh; Biles Cl; Black Croft; The Bottoms, High Bottom (*East-* 1829, *v*. **botm**); Bower Batch, Bowers Grd (cf. Thomas- 1561, Henry *Bower* 1664, *v*. **batch**); Heath Boyne 1829 (cf. Boyne's Lane Pleck in Iwerne C. par. *supra*); Bramble Hay (*v*. **(ge)hæg**); Broad Md; Burnsey; Butchers Marsh; Butts (*v*. **butte**); Carters Cl; Catley ([-Bridge] 1791); Chalk Grd; Clay Stiles (cf. Walter *de Stigela* 15, *v*. **stigel**); Close; Collins Md; Common; Common Fd Rds; Coppice; Cowdrove; Cowleaze; Crooked Md; Culverly; Dagland Coppice (-*Row* 1829); Hr & Lr Damer; Damoneys Grd, Domeneys Cl; Drove Cl; 8, 18, & 11 Acres; Farm Fd; Filcox Md; 14 Acres Coppice & Furze; Framptons Md; Frogmoor [Bridge] 1791; Garstang or Gasson (*v*. **gærs-tūn** 'paddock'); Lt Goddens (cf. Nicholas *Go(u)dhyne* 1327, 1332); Goland (*Goolande* (*Mead*) 1597); Gouldens Cl (cf. Richard *Gowden* 1664); Hales Cl; Ham Orchd, Lt Ham (*v*. **hamm**); Hanging Fd, -Cl 1829; Hillum Fd, Marsh, Md & Orchd (on the par. bdy, no doubt named from Hellum Fm in Iwerne C. par. *supra*); Hogs Ditch; Home Cl & Grd; Horse Cl (*Basket Horse Cl* 1829); Humber ([-Bridge] 1791, probably to be identified with (land) *ad Hu'mere* . . . *terram inter lacam et regiam viam*, (land) *ad Hum'ere* n.d. 1372 *ChrP* ff. 122, 133, this being another example of the pre-English stream-name **Humber**, here referring to a small feeder of Fontmell Brook; the f.n. Humber Mdw in Iwerne C. par. *supra* refers to the same stream); Hutchings Pce (cf. Ann *Hutchins* 1664); Hutshay ([-Bridge] 1791); Gt Kings Cross, Kings Md (cf. John *Kyng* 1340); Lr Lake Cl (*v*. **lacu**); Lannens Md (cf. Richard *Lanning* 1550); Lawn Dog Kennells (*Lawne* 1618, *v*. **launde**); Gt & Lt Lease (*v*. **lǣs**); Leigh Croft (cf. Walter *de Legh* 1346 who held in Hill (Fm) *supra*); Limber; Little Md; Hr Long Cross; Lr Long Cl; Long Md (1574); Malthouse; Gt & Lt Marsh (cf. *fossatum de marisco* n.d. (1372), *le mareis* 15, *common called Le Marshe* 1574, *Marsh Lane* [Bridge] 1791, *v*. **mareis, mersc**); Middle Fd & Md; Miles's Fd, Miles Md; Hr Mills Fd; Monks Md; Moor Md; Muslins; New Breach; New Cl (*Newclose* 1645); New Fd & Grd; Newmans (Closes) (cf. Thomas *Newman* 1664); 9 Acres; Norn; North Hills; Nunneys Cl; Orchard (Leg); Gt & Lt Ovis; Oxen Croft; Picked Cl (*Peaked-* 1829, *v*. **pīcede, peked** 'pointed'); Pit Fd & Md; Plantation; Poley Fd; Press Marsh; Prince Md; Purchase; Rings Cross; Rocketts Cl; Rudmans Grd & Md (cf. Robert *Redman* 1664); Sargents Row; Scuffle Pce; Shayleys; Sheep Drove; Terry Shorts Grd (cf. John *Schort* 1432); Shroton Md (from Iwerne Courtney or Shroton par. *supra*); 6 Acres; Sixteens; Small Coppice; Spring Pits; Sproats; Summerleaze (*v.* **læs**); 13 Acres 1829; Town Fd; Turn Bridge 1791 (*v.* **trun**); Turnipwell (*-Wale* 1829); 12 & 20 Acres; Watts Marsh; West Fd (1574); Wood Lease (*-Leaze* 1829, *v.* **læs**).

(*b*) *Accherigge* 15 (possibly in this par., *v.* **hrycg**, first el. uncertain); *on agen þorn* 956 (14) (possibly for **hagen-þorn*, in which ***hagen** 'enclosure' has been substituted for **haga** in the usual compound **hagu-þorn** 'hawthorn', cf. the form *Hagenþorndun* 996 for Hatherton St (DEPN, and JEPN 1 22); however, if *agen* is for *acen* (cf. *g* for *c* in *on lippen stagen* in the bounds of Compton A. *supra* in the same charter), the first el. could be the OE pers.n. *Aca*); *Barewelles Coppice* 1574; *bryanescroft* 1270 (1372) (the pers.n. or surname *Brian*, *v.* **croft**); *on budencumbe hracan* 956 (14) (first el. possibly **byden** 'vessel, tub', thus 'throat of the tub-shaped valley', *v.* **cumb, hraca**); *on cing hille* 956 (14) (*v.* **hyll**; as it stands the first el. would seem to be **cyning** 'king' in an uninflected form (for which *v.* EPN 1 123)); *Cornefeyldes* 1574 (*v.* **corn**[1]); *on cranmere* 956 (14) (corresponding with *on cranemere, of cranemere* 958 (15) *ShaftR* (S 656) in the bounds of part of Iwerne C. par. *supra*, 'pool frequented by cranes or herons', *v.* **cran, mere**[1]); *on þare/þane crundel, on þere crundel northwarde* 956 (14) (*v.* **crundel** 'chalk-pit, quarry, gully'); *Deane* (a coppice, *v.* **denu**); *on þane ealden forð* 956 (14) ('the old ford', *v.* **eald, ford**); *on ears mores heaued* 956 (14) ('the end of arse moor', *v.* **ears** (probably used here of some topographical feature resembling a buttock or fundament), **mōr, hēafod**); *Erleshill* 1574 (*v.* **eorl**); *to fideriches dene uueward* 956 (14) ('(the upper part of) Friðuríc's valley', on the assumption that the spelling of this OE pers.n. is corrupt, *v,* **denu, ufanweard**); *on foxlee nortwarde* 956 (14) ('fox wood or clearing', *v.* **fox, lēah**, probably to be identified with the f.n. *Voxle* 1444 in Sutton W. par. *supra*); *pratum de Gillinghech'* 15 (possibly in this par., *v.* **hiche** 'enclosure of hurdles for penning sheep', first el. uncertain); *on þone grenwai* 956 (14) ('the green way', *v.* **grēne**[1], **weg**); *the Grove* 1645 (cf. Thomas *de la Grave* 1340, *v.* **grāf(a)**); *ii croftas scilicet haggestice* 15, *claus' voc' Howkestiche* 1569 (*v.* **sticce**[1] 'hurdle, place where hurdles are erected', first el. (if both forms denote the same place) doubtful); *on þa heren* (for *haran*) *apeldren* 956 (14) ('grey apple tree', *v.* **hār**[2], **apuldor**); *La Heuedlande* n.d. (1372) (*v.* **hēafod-land** 'headland, strip of land left for turning the plough'); *on hlinc reawe* 956 (14) (*v.* **hlinc-ræw** 'boundary line formed by a bank, line or row of banks', cf. Lynch Fm 1 15); *Hunfrayis-, Unfrayis-, Umfreies-, Umfreydescroft* n.d. (1372) (the pers.n. or surname *Humphrey* (OG *Hun-, Humfrid*) and **croft**); *Knappmeade* 1645 (*v.* **cnæpp** 'hill-top, hillock', **mǣd**); *on lacmere, þanen an lang streames* 956 (14) (corresponding with *to late* (for *lace*) *mere* 958 (15) *ShaftR* (S 656) in the bounds of part of Iwerne C. par. *supra*, 'pool in a stream', from **lacu** and **mere**[1] ; the stream in question is probably Fontmell Brook, *v.* Forsberg

3); *langelonde* n.d. (1372) (*v.* **lang**[1], **land**); *la Marledelonde* n.d. (1372) (*v.* **marlede** 'fertilized with marl', **land**); *at merewege uue* 956 (14) ('boundary way', *v.* **(ge)mǣre, weg**; *uue* is probably for *ufan* 'over, above', cf. *to fideriches dene supra*); North Field 1574; *Pinock Hill* 1618 (*v.* **pennuc** 'small pen'); *Queens* (a coppice) 1618 (probably a surname); *The Rails* 1634 ('a parcel of the chase . . . near West Lodge', *v.* **raile** 'fence'); *Roehull'* 1288, *Rukehulle* (perhaps for *Ruhe-*) 15 (*v.* **hyll**, first el. possibly **rūh** 'rough'); *Romelles Deane* 1574, *Rumbledeen or Retkersdeen* 1597, *Rumbles Deane* 1618 ('Rumbald's valley', from the OG pers.n. *Rumbald* (possibly here used as a surname) and **denu**); *sandford* 956 (14) ('sandy ford', *v.* **sand, ford**, probably identical with *funtemel forþ* in the Anglo-Saxon bounds of E Orchard *infra*); *on ne* (probably for *þe*) *smal þornes* 956 (14) (corresponding with *on ða smale þornes* 958 (15) *ShaftR* (S 656) in the bounds of part of Iwerne C. par. *supra*, 'the thin thorn-trees', *v.* **smæl, þorn**); *South Field* 1574; *Squibbes* (a coppice) 1618 (a surname); *Stone Deane Waye* 1574 (leading to Stony Bottom (earlier *Stonedeane*) in Ashmore par. 2 204); *on styb* 956 (14) (*v.* **stybb** 'stub, tree-stump'); *on swylles* 956 (14) (*v.* **swylle** 'sloppy mess, place where water flowed freely', probably applied as a stream-name to the small tributary of Fontmell Brook at ST 846150, cf. Swale Bank Sx 353, Swill Brook Gl 1 12; the original form was probably *swyllan* (obl.sg.), this being misunderstood as a wk.pl. by the ME scribe who then substituted an analogical strong inflection); *on terente dene* 956 (14) 2× ('Tarrant valley', with reference to Stubhampton Bottom in Tarrant Gunville par. 2 242, 248 where R. Tarrant rises, *v.* **denu**); *Varewaye* 1574 (probably **fær-weg** 'cartway'); *on waddene uuewarde* 956 (14) ('(the upper part of) woad valley', *v.* **wād, denu**); *at þare weie itwislen* 956 (14) ('the fork in the road', *v.* **weg, twisla**); *on wung wylle* 956 (14) (possibly to be associated with Hr & Lr Well Wood in Iwerne C. par. *supra*, *v.* **wyll(a)** 'spring or stream'; *wung* is probably a corrupt spelling and remains obscure).

Melbury Abbas

MELBURY ABBAS (ST 883201)

> *at Meleburge imare, on meleberig dune* 956 (14) *ShaftR* (S 630)
>
> *Meleberie* 1086 DB, *-beria* 15 *ShaftR; Melebur'* 1251 Cl, 1268, 1280 *Ass, -burne* (sic) 1268 *ib, -bury* 1290 (15) *ShaftR*, 1297 Pat, 1303 FA, 1304 (c.1407) *Shaft* (*-Abb'isse*), 1327 *SR*, 1332 SR, 1346 Pat (*-Abbatisse*), *-bure* 15 *ShaftR; Melebyr'* 1280 QW, *-bir'* 1288 *Ass*
>
> *Melleber'* 1280 *Ass,* QW, *-bury* 1280 ib, 15 *ShaftR*, 1428 FA (*-Abbatisse*), *-bir', byr'* 1280 *Ass*
>
> *Melbury Abb'isse* 1291 Tax, 15 *ShaftR*, 1564 *Glyn, Melbury* 1315 Pat, 1326 Banco (*-Abbesse*) *et passim,*

-beria 15 *ShaftR, -bery* 1618 *Map*
Molebury (sic) *Abbisse* 1332 (c.1407) *Shaft*

Probably 'multicoloured fortified place', from **mǣle** (wk.obl. *-an*) and **burh** (dat.sg. *byrig*); the form *on mealeburg norþewarde* in the bounds of Six. Handley (discussed under Mistleberry Wd in that par. *supra*) is etymologically identical, as is the Melbury group of names in the W of the county (Melbury Bubb, -Osmond and -Sampford), and there are three other probable examples of the name in Devon (PN D 105, 130, 496). Ekwall DEPN, comparing Millbarrow Down Ha which contains **beorg** 'hill', thinks it possible that the second el. of the Melbury names is also **beorg** with change of *eo* to *u*, but this seems an unnecessary assumption in spite of the existence, in the case of Melbury Abbas, of Melbury Hill (the *meleberig dune* of the charter cited, *v. infra*). The earthwork on Melbury Hill is an undated enclosure (RCHM 4 48).

This manor, like Compton Abbas par. *supra,* belonged to Shaftesbury Abbey from 956, hence the affix *Abbas*, a reduced form of Lat **abbatissa** (gen.sg. *-(a)e*) 'abbess'. The manor was divided into the two tithings of East and West Melbury *infra*, the latter occurring as an alternative to the par. name in 1795 Boswell.

ALLAN'S BROW & FM, *terr' voc' Alyns* 1564 *Glyn, Allens' Coppice & Plant.* 1839 *TA*, the pers.n. or surname *Alan, v.* **bru** 'brow of a hill'. BARFOOT FM. BREEZE HILL. BOWDENS HILL (lost, ST 897205), 1811 OS, *terr' voc'/quondam Bowdons* 1564 *Glyn*, cf. Alice *Bowden ib*, possibly the same surname as in foll. BUDDEN'S FM, cf. Robert *Buddon'* 1564 *Glyn, Buttons' Md & New Cl* 1839 *TA*, and prec.; the surname is perhaps to be connected with that of John *Boueto(u)n(')* 1327 *SR*, 1332 SR, 'above the village', *v.* **bufan, tūn.** CHURCH HOUSE FM, cf. *Church Md* 1839 *TA*, near St Thomas's Church *infra*. COAL PIT COPSE, *Cole Pit Coppice* 1839 *TA*, cf. *Colepit Md ib, v.* **col¹** (with reference either to 'coal' or 'charcoal'), **pytt**). CORNHILL CTG, cf. *Corn Hills* 1839 *TA*. CORN MILL, cf. *ter' et un' molendin' aquatic'* (in margin *nuper Kilpeckes*), *un' molendin' fullonicu' in West Melbury, prat' voc' Millehams in Weste Melbury* all 1564 *Glyn, Mill* (*Grd*) 1839 *TA, v.* **myln, hamm**, West Melbury *infra*; there were four mills in Melbury Abbas in 1086 DB (VCH Do **3** 82), and there is mention of three mills here in Hy 3 (15) Hutch³ **3** 561. DOWNSIDE. GARDINER FOREST (1"). GLYN ARMS (P.H.), from the *Glyn* family. GROVE FM, *v.* **grāf(a)**. HORDER'S FM, cf. William *le Horder'* 1332 SR, Robert *Horder* 1454 Hutch³. HOUSE'S FM, cf. *Houses Royal* 1839 *TA, v.* the f.n. Royal *infra*. INCOMBE (HEAD PLANT.), *Incombe Hr & Middle Md* 1839 *TA, v.* **cumb** 'valley', **hēafod** 'head of a valley', first el. probably **in** 'inner', denoting nearness to the principal residence of an estate. KEEPER'S LODGE. MANOR FM. MELBURY BEACON, on Melbury Hill, one of a series of fire-beacons in use at the time of the Armada, *v.* DoNHAS **81** 103–6, **(ge)bēacon**, but perhaps much older than that if *on þat ealde ad* in the Anglo-Saxon bounds of Compton A. is to be located here. MELBURY DOWN, 1811 OS, *Melbery Downe* 1618 *Map, v.* **dūn**. EAST MELBURY (FM), *Est Melebury juxta Shaftesbury* 1305 Banco, *Est Melbury* 1494 Ipm, *East(e) Melbury* 1564 *Glyn*, 1664 HTax, *v.* **ēast**, one of the two tithings into which the manor was divided, also referred to as *Estretuna* n.d. (15) *ShaftR*, 'more easterly farm or village', *v.* **ēasterra, tūn**, cf. West Melbury *infra*. MELBURY HILL, 1575 Saxton, 1811 OS, *on meleberig dune* 956 (14) *ShaftR* (S 630), *super montem de Melebur'* 1251 Cl, *super montes de West Melbury* 1564 *Glyn*, *v.* **dūn** 'hill', par. name *supra*. WEST MELBURY, 1664 HTax, *Westmel(e)bir'* 1288 *Ass, West(e)melbury* 1564 *Glyn, Westretun'* n.d. (15) *ShaftR, v.* **west, westerra** 'more westerly', **tūn**, cf. East Melbury *supra*. PARHAM'S FM, cf. *Parhams' Braad* (sic) *Cl* 1839 *TA*. PITT'S CTG, *terr' voc' le Pyttes* 1564 *Glyn*, *Pitts'* (*Coppice, Fd, Home Grd & Long Grd*), *Pitts Quarr* 1839 *TA, v.* **pytt** 'pit', **quarre** 'quarry'; a quarry is marked (6") just SW of Pitt's Ctg. PUG'S PARLOUR, a coppice; this is a term from servants' cant meaning 'room occupied by the upper servants in a large establishment' (NED s.v. *pug* sb.² I.4, quotation from 1860). RECTORY, *Parsonage Ho* 1839 *TA*. ST THOMAS'S CHURCH, cf. 'church of *Melebury*' 1297 Pat, *ecclesie de Melebury Abb'isse* 1304 (c.1407) *Shaft*. SWIRE

HILL (lost, part of Melbury Hill), 1826 Gre, v. **swēora** 'neck of land'. WHITE PIT CTG & LANE, no doubt with reference to a chalk pit, cf. *Chalkpit Pce* 1839 *TA*. WHITINGS FM, *terr' voc' Whytynges* 1564 *Glyn*, *Whitings* 1811 OS, cf. *Whiting's Lane Coppice* 1839 *TA*, the surname *Whiting*. WINTER FD, 1839 *TA*, *v.* **winter**[1]. WRITH FM & COPSE, *Long Writh, Writh Lane Coppice* 1839 *TA*, probably from **fyrhð** 'wood' as in Writh Ctg in Folke par. *infra*, cf. *Writham Gdn* 1839 *ib* which may have **hamm** 'enclosure' as second el. YOUNG COPSE, -*Coppice* 1839 *ib*. THE ZIGZAG, a twisting road up part of Melbury Down, *v.* **zigzag**.

FIELD NAMES

The undated forms in (*a*) are 1839 *TA* 144, in (*b*) 1564 *Glyn*. Spellings dated 1327 are *SR*, 1340 NI, 1564 *Glyn*, and 1664 HTax.

(*a*) Alder Bed, Alder Patches (*v.* **patche**); Alexander; Barn Cl & Grd; Batt Md (possibly ME **batte** 'stick, lump'); Bottom Md; Bramble Cl; Brinscombe; Broad Cl & Md; Broadhays'; Burbridge; Burnbakes (and Lanches), North Burnbake, Second Burnkake (sic) (*v.* **burnbake, lanch**); Bushey Md; Butts' (*v.* **butte**); Gt Chessel, Chessel Fd & Park, Chessel Old Way (*v.* **ceosol** 'gravel'); Cleve (*v.* **clif** (dat.sg. *clife*) 'cliff, bank'); Clover Hay (*v.* **(ge)hæg** 'enclosure', as freq. in this par.); Gt Coffin Plant.; Coppice; Corner Platt (*v.* **plat**[2]); Cow Grd; Cow Leaze (*v.* **læs**); Cow Stall (*v.* **stall**); Culver Ball (*v.* **culfre** 'dove', **ball** 'rounded hill'); Dinah Md (*terr' voc' Dyners* 1564, cf. William *le Dyuere* (for *Dynere*) 1327, John *Dyner* 1340); Dowlags'; Dry Grd & Md; Eldons' Ctg; Farm Fd; Hr & Lr Fens' (*terr' voc' Vennes* 1564, a surname from **fenn** 'fen'); Field Barn Grd ; 5 Acres; Flower Gdn; 4 Acres; French Wds (cf. French Mill in Cann par. *supra*); Gasson (*v.* **gærs-tūn** 'paddock'); Great Coppice, Grd & Md; Green Hays' (Orchd); Halfpence (cf. an identical f.n. in Compton A. par. *supra*); (N, S & W) Hanging (*v.* **hanging** 'steep slope'); Hanging Grd (*v.* **hangende**); Heath Cl and Coppice; Higher Orchd & Wd; Home Grd & Md; Homestead Fd; Hop Yard Orchd; Lanches (*v.* Burnbakes *supra*, Middle Fd, South Fd *infra*); Land; Leach Hay; Hr Leaker; Leg Md; Little Coppice, Grd & Md; Long Cl & Grd; Long Hay(s), Long Hay Hanging; Long Md; Gt & Lt Mainlane; Makem; Malthouse Grd; Mead; Middle Fd and Lanches (*v.* **lanch**); Middle Grd & Md; Mullens' Gdn (cf. Benjamin *Mullens* 1664); Nappy Cl (*v.* **cnæppig**); New Cl, Fd & Md; 9 Acres; North Cl & Fd(s); Gt & Lt North Hill(s'); Old Way Pce; Orchard (Gdn and Wd); Oysters'; Paddock; Park; Peaked Hay (*v.* **peked** 'pointed'); Plains; Plantation; Punch Hill; Quarr (Cl & Fd) (*v.* **quarre**); Quarry Grd; Gt Richmans', Richmans' Cl, Richmards' (sic) Md (*terre voc' Richemans* 1564, cf. Robert *Richeman* 1340); Rittle Fd; Rock Cl; Rose Hay; Royal Cl, Houses Royal, Longhouse royals (perhaps 'rye hill' from **ryge** and **hyll**, the spellings suggesting association with *royal*, cf. Rill Wt 172); Rye Cl; Shepherds' Cl; Shortlands'; Shorts Md Gdn; Shutts' Md; Sly Gate Grd; Small Ash Fd; Smithie Cl (*v.* **smiðõe**); South Cl; South Fd and Lanches (*v.* **lanch**); South Hill; Spraggs' Orchd (cf. Thomas *Sprague* 1664, *Sprag(g)s Mill* in Cann par. *supra*); Spring Cl; Storm Ld; Stubble Lane Coppice, Stubble Leaze and Wd (*v.* **stubbil**); Summers' (cf. John *Somer* 1332); 10 Acre Md; Turnpike Ctg; Small Underhill Pce; Water Cl & Md; Way Cl; Well Barn, Cl & Grd (possibly to be associated with John *atte Welle* 1327 SR, 1332 SR); West Brook; Willow Bed; Windhills'; Witchcraft (*v.* **wice, croft**); Woodfrys'; Yonder Md.

(*b*) *claus' voc' Bacons* (a surname); *Berefurlong* 1564 (*v.* **bere** 'barley', **furlang**); *terr' voc' Boyes* (a surname, cf. *Hoyes infra*); *le Breache* (*v.* **bræc** 'land broken up for cultivation'); *terr' voc' fawkes* (a surname); *terr' arr' de Bourdeland voc Gallez* (a surname, *v.* **bord-land**); *terr' voc' Gilbertes quondam Fewelles* (both surnames); *terr' voc' Gillockes* (a surname); *terr' voc' Gogges* (a surname); *terr' quondam Grenynges* (a surname); *terr' voc' Hoyes* (probably an error for *Boyes supra*); *terr' prius Syddenhams et quondam Parkers* (both surnames); *terr' prius Russelles* (held by *Franciscus dominus Russell Comes Bedford*); *terr' nuper Stackballes* (a surname); *terr' voc' Thrustelles* (a surname); *terr' voc' Warres* (cf. William *War'* 1340).

East and West Orchard

EAST ORCHARD (ST 834178), WEST ORCHARD (ST 824164)
>   (*ad-, at*) *Archet, to archet* 939 (15) *ShaftR* (S 445), (*at-, to*) *Archet* 963 (15) *ib* (S 710), *Archet* 1176 P (p), n.d. (15) *ShaftR*
>   *Orchet* 1317 Hutch[3] (*West-*), 1330 Cl (p), 1423 Pat, 1576 *Glyn* (*West-*), *Orchett* 1505 *ib* (*West-*), 1645 *SxAS* (*East-*)
>   *Orchard'* 1427 *Weld*[1] (*West-*), *Orcharda* 1535 VE (*West-*), *Est-, Westorchard* 1575 Saxton

As pointed out by Ekwall DEPN (cf. earlier discussion in *Anglia Beiblatt* **36** 149) and Jackson 327, this is a British name meaning '(place) beside the wood', from PrWelsh ***cēd*** 'wood' (Welsh *coed*) with ***ar*** 'beside, in front of, facing', identical with the Welsh p.n. *Argoed* (of which there are several examples, *v.* Melville Richards, *Welsh Administrative and Territorial Units*, Cardiff 1969, p. 7), cf. also *Argoedd* Ch **4** 29. From the 15th cent. the forms show association with *orchard*.

The division into East and West is early: the bounds of East Orchard are given in 963 (15) *ShaftR* (S 710), those of West Orchard (*þis sent þa land imare to archet þare westere fif hide*) in 939 (15) *ib* (S 445).

East Orchard

BLEAX HILL, named from *ten' nuper* . . . *Blikes* 1450 *Glyn* (in Fontmell M.), *mes' voc' Blykes* c.1560 *ib*, *Bleeks* 1846 *TA*, cf. Richard *le Blik* 1327 *SR*, John *Blyk(e)* 1332 SR, 1340 NI (both mentioned under Fontmell M.), *Blicksgate Lane* 1699 *Glyn*, *Bleaks Gate* 1811 OS, *Blich(')s Down(s)*, *Blichs Md & Orchd* 1837 *TA* (Fontmell M.); the hill is on the par. bdy.

HARTGROVE (FM) (ST 843183)
  Haregrave Hy 1 (15) *ShaftR*, 1254 FF, 1450, 1500, 1505
    Glyn, *-grove* 1450 *ib*, *Hargrave* c.1500 *Eg*, c.1560, 1576
    Glyn, *-grove* 1535 VE, 1576 *Glyn*, 1648 SC, 1699 *Glyn*,
    1869 Hutch[3], *-groue* 1618 *Map*, *-growe* 1664 HTax
  Harregraue 1268 *Ass*
  Hardgrove 1395 (e15) *MiltRoll*, *Hartgrove* 1698 *Glyn*, 1795
    Boswell, 1811 OS, 1846 *TA* (*-otherwise East Orchard*)

The second el. is **grāf(a)** 'grove, copse', the first may be **hara** (gen.sg. *haran*) 'hare' or **hār**[2] (wk.obl. *hāran*) 'hoar, grey' (perhaps used in a transferred sense 'boundary', the place being on the par. bdy with Fontmell M.). The former church or chapel here (recently rebuilt in 1869 Hutch[3], site marked 6″) is mentioned as 'the church of *Haregrave*' n.d. (15) *ShaftR* (Hutch[3] **3** 537), *East Orchard commonly called Hargrove chapel* 1650 Hutch[3], cf. *The Chapelry of East Orchard, or Hargrove East Orchard* 1869 *ib*, Church Lane *infra*. It will be noted that the intrusive dental consonant (*d, t*) only appears at a comparatively late date.

BOWLING GREEN FM. CHURCH LANE, probably named from the former church or chapel of Hartgrove *supra*, cf. *Chapel Grd & Md* 1846 *TA*. DROVE LANE, cf. *Drove* 1846 *ib, v*. **drāf**. FISHEY LANE, a lane running from R. Stirchel along the par. bdy, named from the adjoining fields called *Fishey*,

Fisshhay 1846 *TA* in this par. and *Wishey-* 1840 *TAMap*, *Wishing Cl* 1840 *TA* in W Orchard (where the form *Wysshis filde* 1576 *Glyn* also belongs); the first el. is probably **wisc** 'marshy meadow', perhaps with **īeg** 'island, dry ground in marsh' rather than **(ge)hæg** 'enclosure'; the first el. has been influenced by **fisc** 'fish' due to SW interchange of *f/v/w*, cf. PN D xxxv; the lane itself would seem to be identical with *higweg* in the Anglo-Saxon bounds of W Orchard discussed under Hay Bridge in that par. *infra*. GREAT HO. GULLIVER'S FM, cf. *Gulliver's* [Bridge] 1791 Boswell. HENBURY FM. LYCH GATE. MEAD'S HO. MILL BUSH, 1846 *TA*, near R. Stirchel, cf. *pasture . . . called Mullecombe* 1254 FF, *v.* **myln, cumb**. NEW TOWN. OAKLANDS. ORCHARD SCHOOL (lost), 1811 OS. ORCHARD WATER BRIDGE, probably on the site of *scealden forð*, *v.* W Orchard f.ns. *infra*. ST THOMAS'S CHURCH. SCOTT'S HO, cf. *Scotts Coppice & Md* 1846 *TA*. SIXPENNY COVERT, named from Sixpenny Fm in Fontmell M. par. *supra*. SWAINSCOMBE FM, *Swains Coomb Ho* 1846 *TA*, cf. the lost f.n. *Cumbe infra* which must have been near here. TRAPDOOR FM. WHITEGATE FM, cf. the two fields called *Wide Gate* 1846 *TA*, just SE of the farm, *v.* **wīd, geat**. WINCHELL'S FM, cf. *lands called Wincells* 1548 Hutch[3], probably a surname.

FIELD-NAMES

The undated forms in (*a*) are 1846 *TA* 100, in (*b*) 963 (15) *ShaftR* (S 710). Spellings dated 1254 are FF, 1395 (e15) *MiltRoll*, n.d. (15) *ShaftR*, 1645 *SxAS*, and 1791 Boswell.

(*a*) Acre (Coppice); Bain Cl (*Beane Close* 1645, *v.* **bēan**); Blackland; Bottom or Hickmans Md; Brack (*v.* **bræc**[1] 'a brake, thicket'); Brickhill; Broad Cl; Broadway; Burfurlong; Burnt Oak (*close called Burnedock* 1645, *v.* **berned, āc**); Leg Cleveland (Orchd), Scotts Cleveland (*Cleve-* may represent **clif** (dat.sg. *clife*) 'cliff, bank', *v.* **land, leg**, Scott's Ho *supra*); Clover Grd; Coal Pits (*v.* **col**[1]); Coppice Grd; Cow Leaze; Crate(s) (*v.* **croft**); East Hays (*v.* **(ge)hæg**); 8 Acres; Elm (Orchd); Emmets-, Emmits Hay (no doubt the surname *Emmet* rather than **æmette** 'ant' (Do dial. *emmet*)); Farm Grd; Fernhills (Md); (Gt & Lt) Fontmill Brook (fields by Fontmell Brook, *v.* RNs. *infra*); Four Elm Grds; Great Orchd; Green Hay Md (*v.* **(ge)hæg**); Hanging Md (*v.* **hangende**); Hatch Mdw, Hatch Rice (*v.* **hæc(c)** 'hatch, gate', **hrīs** 'shrubs, brushwood'); Hays (*v.* **hǣs** 'brushwood'); Hill Cl (Coppice) (*Hill Close* 1645); Hill Lawn (*v.* **launde**);

Home Fd, Grd & Md; Hoopers Lawn; House [Bridge] 1791; Jews Hay (*v.* **(ge)hæg**); Jubbers (Md); Keybrook [Bridge] 1791 (from Key Brook, *v.* RNs. *infra*); Gt & Lt Lench (*v.* **hlenc** 'hill-side'); Longfurlong; Long Md Orchd; Lough Md, Lower Md (*Lough* may be a spelling for *Low*); Moor Md; Mounthays; Mower (cf. Mower Lane in W Orchard par. *infra*); Mow Md (probably Do dial. **mow** 'a rick' (*v.* Barnes 83) from OE **mūga**); Neather Cl (*v.* **neoðerra** 'lower'); North Leaze (Orchd) (*v.* **lǣs**); Oatfurlong; Lt Oat Ld; One; Orchard Cl & Grd; Paddock Md & Orchd; Palmshay Orchd; Picked Cl (*v.* **pīcede** 'pointed'); Pitts; Plumpland (*v.* **plūme** 'plum-tree'); Pond Cl; Rail Cl; Rick Yd; Rive land (probably **(ge)rēfa** 'reeve'); Rolls (Hill); Rye Cl; Sod Hay; Gt & Lt Stockhay(s), Stockhays Orchd (probably **stocc** 'tree-trunk, stump', with **(ge)hæg**); Sutton Cl (named from Sutton W. par. *supra*); Tailors Grd; Thistle Hay; Three Horned Hay (*v.* **hornede**, used here in the sense 'having horn-shaped projections'); Wilderness (*v.* **wilderness**); Willow Bed; Wimbleham; Woodbridge Hay (from Woodbridge in Fontmell M. par. *supra*); Woodfurlong; Wood Hays.

(*b*) *bissopes imare* ('bishop's boundary', with reference to W Orchard which was held by the Bishop of Sherborne, *v.* **biscop, (ge)mǣre**); *croftam Bollahei* n.d. (15) (*v.* **(ge)hæg**, first el. uncertain); 'pasture . . . called *Cumbe*' 1254, *þe combe of Hardgrove* 1395 (e15), *Cumba* n.d. (15) (*v.* **cumb** 'valley', cf. Hartgrove, Swainscombe *supra*); *of eldmannes wrthe, on eldemanneswyrde* (this is the starting and finishing point of the Anglo-Saxon bounds of E Orchard, as well as of W Orchard (*of ealdmannes wyrde, to ealdmannes wyrþe* 939 (15) *ShaftR* (S 445)), and it also occurs in the bounds of Fontmell M. (*to heldmannes wrthe suthward* 932 (15) *ib* (S 419)) and of Thorton in Marnhull (*on ealdmannes þyerðe* (sic) 958 (15) *ib* (S 656)); 'Ealdmann's enclosure' from the OE pers.n. *Ealdmann* and **wyrð**); *oð funtemel forð, of þanne forð* ('Fontmell ford', i.e. 'ford on Fontmell Brook', probably identical with *sandford* in the Anglo-Saxon bounds of Iwerne M. *supra*, *v.* **ford**, RNs. *infra*); *anlang hina (-e) imares* ('boundary of the religious community', with reference to Fontmell M. which was held by Shaftesbury nunnery, *v.* **hīwan** (gen.pl. *hīna*), **(ge)mǣre**); *þurch ðene holt* (*v.* **holt** 'wood, thicket'); *oð kinghes imare, and* (for *andlang*) *gemare* ('king's boundary', with reference to Iwerne M. which was granted to Shaftesbury nunnery by King Edwy in 956, *v.* **cyning, (ge)mǣre**); *oð land scorforð, of þane forde* ('boundary ford', *v.* **land-scoru, ford**); *anlang leouen imare* ('Lēofa's or Lēofe's boundary', from the OE pers.n. *Lēofa* masc. or *Lēofe* fem. (*v.* Redin 51, 124, Feilitzen 310) and **(ge)mǣre**); *to þan lipgete, from þane gete* (*v.* **hlīep-geat** 'opening in a fence over which deer can leap'); *to þan scamelen, fram þanne scamelen* (corresponding to *to þane shamelen* in the Anglo-Saxon bounds of Fontmell M., *v.* **sc(e)amol** 'shelf of land, ledge'); *anlang streames, mid streame* ('with the flow or current, downstream'), *v.* **strēam**, with reference respectively to R. Stirchel and Fontmell Brook); *to sucgimade hauede, of þane hauede* (*v.* the f.n. Sow Md in W Orchard par. *infra*); *to Wlgares imaren, of þan imaren* ('Wulfgār's boundary', from the OE pers.n. *Wulfgār* and **(ge)mǣre**; this

Wulfgār was granted land in 958 at Thorton in Marnhull (which at this date included the present par. of Margaret Marsh)); *to anne wonàlre, of pane alre* (corresponding to *on pane alr* in the W Orchard charter, 'crooked alder', *v.* **wōh** (wk.obl. *wōn*), **alor**).

West Orchard

HAY BRIDGE (ST 825163), 1840 *TA, High-, Hygh bridge fild(e)* 1576 *Glyn, Haybridge* 1791 Boswell, cf. *anlang higweges þ' of higeweges ande* ('along hay way, then from the end of hay way') in the Anglo-Saxon bounds of W Orchard 939 (15) *ShaftR* (S 445); this *higweg* apparently describes the course of the present Fishey Lane in E Orchard par. *supra* which turns sharply to cross Manston Brook at Hay Bridge, *v.* **hī(e)g, weg, ende**; there are two instances of the same name in the Anglo-Saxon charters of Brk 715, 726, cf. also Highway W 269.

CHURCH (dedication unknown), cf. 'the chapel of *West Orchet*' 1317 Hutch[3]. MANOR FM. MANSFIELD'S FM. MOWER LANE, cf. the f.n. Mower in the adjacent par. of E Orchard, perhaps **mowere** 'one who mows', cf. Hay Bridge *supra* which lies ½ mile N. NAISH'S FM. WILLIS HO.

FIELD-NAMES

The undated forms in (*a*) are 1840 *TA* 160, in (*b*) 939 (15) *ShaftR* (S 445). Spellings dated c.1560, 1576, 1701 are *Glyn*, 1664 HTax, and 1795 *Salkeld*.

(*a*) Barnetts Md; Benny Cl; Broad hedge Cl; Broad Land(s) Cl & Md; Buggles Cl & Md; Cards Grd; Colesome Cl; Coppice Wd; Court Orchd; Field Grd (Cl); Field Md; 5 Acres; Fontmell (Brook) Cl & Md (named from Fontmell Brook which forms the S bdy of the par., *v.* RNs. *infra*, cf. *Fountemell Combe* 1576, *v.* **cumb**); 40 Acre Cl; 4 Acres; Gayson (Cl & Md) (perhaps **gærs-tūn** 'paddock'); Goosenap; Great Fd (1795); Great Ld & Orchd; Green Ash (Cl) (*Grene Ashe* 1576); Hassock (Cl) (*v.* **hassuc** 'clump of coarse grass'); Hatch Md (abutting Stirchel Brook, *v.* **hæc(c)** 'hatch, sluice, grating'); Hays Cl & Md; Holford Md (by Manston Brook, 'hollow or deep ford', *v.* **hol²**, **ford**); Home Md (1795); Keybrook Cl & Md (named from Key Brook, *v.* RNs. *infra*); Lake Brine; Little Coppice, Down, Ld, Md & Orchd; Lower Grd; Marsh Cl (*Marsh* 1795); Mead(ow); Milkinbarton (*v.* **milking**); Mouslade 1795; Neddy Style Cl 1795 (cf. *to stigel hege infra*); New Cl; Oorchard (sic), The orchard, Orchard Late

Groves, -late meatyards; Pecked Md (*v.* **pīcede** 'pointed'); Rifeham Md (*Reve hamme* c.1560, *Reve Mede alias Reveham* 1576, *v.* **(ge)rēfa** 'reeve', **hamm, mǣd**; the location of this **hamm** at least partly corresponds with that of the earlier *archet hamm infra*); Rossiter Orchd; Sellwood (Cl & Md) (*Cellwood* (*Cl & Md*) 1840 *TAMap*, *Syl Woode* 1576, to be associated with *on þa seales, of þan sealen* 958 (15) *ShaftR* (S 656) in the Anglo-Saxon bounds of Thorton in Marnhull par. *infra*, 'the willow trees', *v.* **sealh** (nom.pl. *sealas*, dat.pl. *sealum*); for the later combination with **wudu**, cf. Selwood So (DEPN)); Selly Cl & Orchd; 7 Acres; Sharp Hays Cl; Sowmead, (Lt) Sow Md (the situation of these fields not far from the par. bdy at about ST 829171 suggests a connection with the Anglo-Saxon bdy mark *to sugging made* in the bounds of W Orchard (939 (15) *ShaftR* (S 445)), corresponding to *to sucgimade hauede, of þane hauede* in those of E Orchard (963 (15) *ib* (S 710)). Perhaps the most likely explanation of the OE forms is that the first el. is a derivative in **-ing**[1] or **-ing**[2] of **sug(g)a** 'swamp, marsh, bog' (surviving as Do dial. *sog*), alternating with a denominative adjectival form ***sug(g)ig** 'swampy' (*v.* **-ig**[3], cf. ModE *soggy*), thus 'mead at **Sugging*' ('the swampy place') or 'swampy mead', *v.* **mǣd**, with **hēafod** 'head, upper end'. The later development of the name cannot be fully explained in the absence of intermediate spellings, but the *Sow* of the modern forms may be due to the substitution for the first el. of the near synonymous *sow* (also *sough*, derived from the obl. and nom. forms respectively of an OE ***sōg**, ***sōh** by Löfvenberg 194, *v.* **sogh** 'bog, swamp'), or due to confusion of **sug(g)a** with **sugu** 'sow, female pig' (cf. the interesting case of this confusion cited in EPN s.v. **sugga**, noting that the p.n. Southway So there adduced seems to be that to which the forms *Sogheweye, Soweye* discussed by Löfvenberg *loc.cit* may refer)); Speeds Orchd (cf. Edward *Speed* 1664); Gt & Lt Staves (*Stave* (*Close & Parrock*) 1795, *v.* **stæf**); 10 Acres; Wishing Cl (*Wishey Cl* on 1840 *TAMap*, cf. *Wysshis filde* 1576, discussed under Fishey Lane in E Orchard par. *supra*); Withy Bed; Woodhouse (Cl & Md).

(*b*) *on þane alr* (*v.* *wonalre* in E Orchard par. *supra*); *on archet hamm* (also *on arcetham* (2 ×), *of archethamme* 958 (15) *ShaftR* (S 656), the starting and finishing point of the Anglo-Saxon bounds of Thorton in Marnhull par. *infra*; 'the **hamm** ('enclosure', river-meadow') of Orchard', its location at least partly corresponding to that of the modern f.n. Rifeham Md *supra*); *terr' voc' Carpenters* c.1560 (a surname); *oþ eadelmes melne* ('Éadhelm's mill', from the OE pers.n. *Éadhelm* and **myln**; it was on Fontmell Brook); *of ealdmannes wyrde, to ealdmannes wyrþe* (*v.* *eldmannes wrthe* in E Orchard par. *supra*); *Eastover fild* 1576 (possibly **ōfer**[1] 'bank', **feld**); *to ginum hocum* (second el. is **hōc** 'hook, angle, bend'; if *ginum* is a poor spelling for *ginnum*, the first el. is OE *ginne* 'wide, spacious', a well recorded word but not noted in p.ns.; BTSuppl postulates a word ***gin** 'gaping' but its existence is doubtful, cf. the discussion of *to gynan bǣte* in PN Brk 714); *Home Haye* 1576 (*v.* **(ge)hæg**); *mes' voc' hortes* c.1560 (a surname); *to land share hegen þonne anlang heges* ('the hedge on, or forming, the boundary', *v.* **land-scearu, hege**); *at langhecgan* ('long hedge', *v.* **lang**[1], **hecge**); *mes' voc' le Overhouse* c.1560 (*v.* **uferra** 'higher, upper'); *beneþan scealdan forð* ('shallow ford', *v.* **sceald, ford**, probably the site of the present Orchard Water Bridge in E Orchard par. *supra*); *Somere Medes filde* 1576 (*v.* **sumor, mǣd**); *Southefyeld als. Mydlefyeld* 1576 (*v.* **sūð, middel**); *Southmeads Oake* 1701; *to stigel hege* ('hedge with a stile', *v.* **stigel, hege**, cf. the unlocated Neddy Style Cl *supra*); *to þrem land sharen* ('three boundaries', i.e. 'point where the boundaries of Thorton (in Marnhull), Manston and W Orchard meet', *v.* **þrēo, land-scearu**); *þry akeres* ('three acres', *v.* **þrēo, æcer**); *to þane twam þornen* ('the two thorn-trees', *v.* **twēgen, þorn**).

Shaftesbury

In 1894 large parts of the Shaftesbury parishes of St James and Holy Trinity were transferred to Cann for civil purposes, and at the same date parts of Cann were included in the borough of Shaftesbury, further parts of Cann being transferred to the borough in 1920, and parts of both Cann and Motcombe (Enmore Green) in 1933.

SHAFTESBURY (ST 862229)

Shafton(e) 833 (14) BCS 410, 860 (15) *ib* 499 (both rubrics, probably post-Conquest), 1258, 1262, 1272 Cl *et freq* to 1417 Fine, *Safton'* 1260 Cl, 1260 *Ass, Schafton(a)* 1268 *ib*, 1275 RH, 1280 QW, 1316 FF, 1380 Cl, *Scafton* 1277 Banco, *Shapton(')* (sic) 1288 *Ass*, 1313 Cl

(*in to, on, æt, at*) *Sceaftesburi* 871–7 (15) ShaftR (S 357 (1)), 956 (14) *ib* (S 630), *-byrig* c.950 (10) CottCh (S 1539, ASWills No 3), 971–83 (14) ASWills No 10, m11 ASC (C) s.a. 982, e12 FW, 12 ASC (E) s.a. 1036 [1035], *-beri* 958 (15) ShaftR (S 655), *-byri* 11 ASC (D) s.a. 1035, *-birig* c.1000 Saints, *Scea(f)(t)(e)* 979–1065, *Sceafi, Ceai* 1066 all *Coins, Sceafstesbyrig* 12 SD

Sheftesbury (rubric) 871–7 (15) ShaftR (S 357 (1)), 1089 (1371), 1447 Pat, *-byre* 1267, *-buri* 1269 Ch, *-byri* 1535–43 Leland, *Sceftesburg* 893 (e11) Asser, 12 SD, *-birio* 1001 (14) ShaftR, *-byrig* c.1000 Saints, m11 ASC (C) s.a. 1035, *-berie* 1086 DB, *-beria* Hy 1 (15) ShaftR, *-biry* 1155 RBE, *S(c)e(f)(t)(e)(s)(b)(r)(i)* 928–1134, *Ceft(esbi)* 985–1037, *Aeseftes(b), Eftes, Scect, Seftcs, Sceveti* 1017–62 all *Coins, Scheftesberia* Hy 2 (15) ShaftR, *-biry* 1275 Ext, *Shetesbury* (sic) Ed 1 (c.1407)

Shaft, Seftesbir' 1280 *AD, Sheftis-* 1430 Pat, *Sheftys-bury* 1431 FA

Schaftesbiry 932 (15) *ShaftR* (S 419), *-biri* 935 (15) *ib* (S 429) (*at-*), 1244 *Ass, -bury* 966 (15) *ShaftR* (S 744), 1302 Pat, 1356 *Sher, -buri* 983 (15) *ShaftR* (S 850), *-bir'* 1194–1230 P, 1244 *Ass, -beria* 1197 P, *-ber'* 1280 *Ass, -bery(e)* 1356 *Sher*, 1535–43 Leland, *-byri* 1535–43 ib, *Shaftesbury* 942 (15) *ShaftR* (S 485 (1)), 956 (14) *ib* (S 630) (rubric), 958 (15) *ib* (S 655) (rubric), Hy 1 (15) *ib*, 1242 Pat, 1243 Lib *et passim, -beria* 1155 PR, 1159 P, *-buri* John (15) *ShaftR, -biry* 1223, 1246 Pat, *-bir'* 1238–66 Cl, 1246 Lib, *-bur'* 1242, 1253 Cl, *-byr'* 1249 FF, *-biri* 1252 Ch, *-ber(')* 1252 FF, 1280 *Ass, -byry* 1258 Pat, 1535–43 Leland, *S(c)haftysbury(e)* 951–5 (14) BCS 913, 1417 *Marten*, 1437 Pat, 1547 *AD, -byrye* e15 LHyda (*Septoniam quæ est-*), (*at*) *Scaftesberi(a)* 958 (15) *ShaftR* (S 655), 1197–1212 P, *-bir'* 1195–1214 P, 1196 ChancR, *Saftesbur'* 1194 Cur, 1242 Cl, 1243 Lib, 1253 Cl, *-beri* 1201 Cur, *-bir(')* 1205 ChancR, 1239 FF, 1243 Lib, *-bury* 1253 Pat, *Saftisbur'* 1194 Cur, *Shaftisbyr'* 1280 FF, *-bry* 1325–50 GoughMap, *-bury* 1402–1506 Pat, 1548 *Weld*[1], *Shafesbury* (sic) 1291 Pat, *Schaftisbiri* e15 LHyda (*urbem Septoniæ, quod est-*); *Caft* 979–85, *Safti, Sa(f)(r), Sactt, Scaf, Saft(e)* 1074–1150 all *Coins*

(*to*) *Sceafnesbirig* 951–5 (14) BCS 912, *to sceaftenes byrig* 1015 (e11) StoweCh (S 1503 (1), ASWills No 20), *to Scæftenesbyrig* 1015 (e11) ASWills No 20 MS b (S 1503 (2)), *Ceften* 981–97, *Sceften(b)* c.997, 1009–17 *Coins*

monast' Septoniæ 951–5 (14) BCS 914 (probably post-Conquest), (*ad*) *Sceftoniam* e12 ASC (F) s.a. 980, 12 SD, *Scestoniæ* ib, *Seftonia* 1245 FF, *-ie* 1285 FA, *Sc(h)ephtonia, -ie* Ed 1 (c.1407) *Shaft, S(c)heftonia, -ie* ib, 1285, 1303 FA, 1433 *Salis*, 1474 *Wim, Septoniam quæ est Schaftysbyrye, urbem Septoniæ quod est Schaftisbiri* e15 LHyda

Scæftesbyrig c.1000 Saints, (*to*) *Scæftes byrig* 12 ASC (E) s.a. 980, *Scaef(t)* 991–7 *Coins*

(*to*) *soraflesbyring* (sic) c.1025 (c.1310) BurgHid

Septesberia Wm 1 (15) *ShaftR, Sceptesberie* 1086 DB,

Shaptesbur' Hy 3 (1371) Pat
Sancti Edwardi 1086 Exon, *uillata Sancti Ædwardi* 1194 P,
burgo/villa Sancti Edwardi 1199–1210 ib, 1204, 1214
Cur, 1244 *Ass, (libero) burgo de Sancto Edwardo* 1212
Fees, 1244 *Ass,* 15 *ShaftR, Sanctum Edwardum* 1218
Pat, *loco Sancti Edwardi* 1245 FF, *Edwardistowe* e15
LHyda
Sy(e)ftebury Hy 1 (15) *ShaftR, Siaftesberi* 1213 Cur,
Syeftebir' 1230 ChancR, *Scyaftesbir'* 1244 *Ass; Shiefi*
1074–7, *Sci(e)(f)(t)(i), Sieft(si), Siei, Scifiti, Siecf*
1077–86 all *Coins*
Schaftebir' 1200, 1205 P, 1230 ChancR, *-byr'* 1260, *-bury*
1377 Cl, *Scaftebir'* 1211 ChancR, *-biry* 1265 Pat,
Shafteburi 1216 Pat, *-bur'* 1216–72 (1371) Pat, 1242–55
Cl, 1268 *Ass, -bury* 1242 Cl *et freq* to c.1407 *Shaft,*
-biry 1243–80 Pat, 1280 Fine, *-bery* 1252 FF, *-bir'*
1254 ib, 1259–64 Cl, 1268, 1280 *Ass, -byry* 1255 Pat,
-byr' 1263 FF, 1268 *Ass, Saftebir* 1218 FF, *-bur'* 1253,
-b' 1260 Cl, *Schafftebir'* 1275 RH, *Shaftbirs* (sic) 1377,
-bury 1382 Cl
Scheftebir(e) 1220 *CottCh,* 1230 P, 1280 QW (p), *-byr(e)*
1268 *Ass, -byry* 1280 QW, *Scheftbyr'* 1268 *Ass,*
Sheftebury 1288 Pat (p), 1308 FF, 1338 Cl, *Shefte* (sic)
1373 ib
Shefton', Sephton', Sepfton' 1259 Cl, *S(c)hefton'* 1260 FF,
1261 Cl, 1268 *Ass et freq* to 1346 Ipm, *Sephton',*
Shepton' l13 (c.1407), *Sephon'* Ed 1 (c.1407) *Shaft,*
Scefton 1277 Banco, *Sefton* 1293 Ipm
S(c)haston(') 1260 Cl, 1275 RH, 1288 *Ass et freq* to 1650
ParlSurv
Scheston 1275 RH
(ad) Shaftoniam 1280 QW, *S(c)haftonie, -ia* 1303 FA,
1310 Pat, 1316, 1428 FA, c.1500 *Eg*
Shastbury 1391 Pat, *Shastesbury* 1432 *Wim, -burry* 1650
ParlSurv, Shasberrye e17 ShaftMR, *-bur(r)y* 1650
ParlSurv, 1651 *KCC*

Probably 'Sceaft's fortified place', from an OE pers.n.
Sceaft (cf. *Sceaftes hangra* 909 (12) BCS 629 (Ha)) and **burh**
(dat.sg. *byrig*). Some of the early spellings (*Sceaf(t)enes-,* etc)

suggest alternation of the pers.n. *Sceaft* either with a pers.n. **Sceaften* (< **Sceaftīn*), a hypocoristic form of *Sceaft*, as suggested by Ekwall (Studies[1] 12, DEPN), or with a reduced form of the pers.n. *Sceaftwine* (cf. *Sceftwine* 704 (?8) BCS 111), thought possible by Tengstrand (NoB **19** 168).

The possibility that the first el. of Shaftesbury is the word **sceaft** 'shaft, pole', used either of some actual pole or figuratively of the steepsided, prominent hill on which the town stands, looks less likely but cannot entirely be ruled out. For this view, found as early as 1774 Hutch[1] **2** 1, *v.* C.H. Mayo, DoNHAS **15** 37; Fägersten 32 cites Zachrisson's suggestion that **sceaft** may have had the meaning 'crag, protuberance' in English p.ns. evidenced for the cognate *skaft* in Scand p.ns. (EPP 8 n.3, cf. also Ekwall DEPN s.n. Shaftoe Nb) and that the alternative **sceaften* in this name may result from the addition of a noun suffix. For a similarly ambiguous name, cf. Shaftsey Brk 81 (*Sceaftesige* 911–19 (later copy)).

The Latinized forms *Sheftonia, Shaftonia* are probably of post-Conquest origin and arise from the addition of *-onia* to the first part of the English name, on the analogy of *Wintonia* for Winchester, etc, cf. R.E. Zachrisson, *Some Instances of Latin Influence on English Place-Nomenclature*, Lund 1910, 11, 13. It is probable that *Shafton', Shefton',* etc represent a reduction of these Latinizations rather than an English formation in **-tūn**, since no *Shaft(e)ston* forms occur (note that *-bury* forms without medial *-s-* do not occur until the 12th cent.). However the form *Shaston* (still in use locally) may have resulted from a reduction of the consonant cluster *-fts-* to *-s-*, although it may be partly due to the misreading of *f* as long *s*. The forms *Shast(es)bury*, etc are probably to be similarly explained. Early forms in *Shept-, Shapt-* are palaeographical errors due no doubt to the practice of writing *f* as *ph*.

The allusion in 'town/place of St Edward' is to Edward the Martyr, whose remains were transferred here from Wareham and buried in the abbey, *v.* Abbey Ho *infra*; *Edwardistowe* contains **stōw** '(holy) place'.

Shaftesbury is referred to by Geoffrey of Monmouth (c. 1138, *Historia Regum Britanniae*) as *oppidum (montis) Paladur quod nunc Sephtesberia/S(c)ephtonia dicitur*, this being echoed by later chroniclers such as Holinshed (*mount Paladour now called Shaftsburie*, 1577, *Holinshed's Chronicles*, **1** 446). It is fairly certain that Geoffrey's *oppidum Paladur* is simply a translation of the English name, based on his interpretation of it as 'fort of the shaft' (cf. Welsh *paladr* 'shaft'), and is thus an interesting example of early antiquarian etymologizing and invention, *v.* Hutch³ **3** 1–2, R.E. Zachrisson, *Romans, Kelts and Saxons in Ancient Britain*, Uppsala 1927, 55 fn. 1, J.S.P. Tatlock, *The Legendary History of Britain*, 1950, 43–4.

SHAFTESBURY PARISHES, CHURCHES AND CHAPELS

(*v.* Hutch³ **3** 3, Sydenham 75ff, K.J. Penn, *Historic Towns in Dorset*, 85, and RCHM **4** 57-67)

ABBEY and CONVENTUAL CHURCH OF ST MARY AND ST EDWARD (lost), *v.* Abbey Ho *infra*. ALL SAINTS (lost), *parochia Omnium Sanctorum* 1312 (c.1407) *Shaft*, 1340 NI, 1403 (c.1407) *Shaft, ecclesia Omnium Sanctorum* 1318 *Sher et freq* to c.1407 *Shaft*. CHRIST'S (lost), *parochia Christi ecclesie de Shafton* a1335 (c.1407) *Shaft* (not otherwise recorded). HOLY TRINITY, *parochia Sancte Trinitatis* 1293 (c.1407) *Shaft*, 1388 *HarlCh et passim*, *cimitarium Sancte Trinitatis* 1327 (c.1407) *Shaft*, 'church of the Holy Trinity' 1367 Pat, *ecclesie Sancte Trinitatis* 1428 FA, cf. *fraternitati Sancti Katerine ecclesie Sancte Trinitatis Shafton* 1372 (c.1407) *Shaft*. ST ANDREW (lost, cf. St Peter *infra*), *parochia Sancti Andree* 13 (c.1407) *Shaft et freq* to 1377 *Salis, capellam beati Andree* a1335 (c.1407) *Shaft*. ST EDWARD THE MARTYR (lost, on record pre-1299 according to Penn op.cit. 85), possibly to be distinguished from ST EDWARD'S CHAPEL (lost, *v.* Hutch³ **3** 38, 61), cf. *ecclesia Omnium Sanctorum et Edwardi Schaston'* 1318 *Sher*. ST JAMES, *capella sancti iacobi de coppehulla* c.1140 *AddCh*, *-Jacobi de Cepehulla* 1154–8 (1340) Ch, 'the church of St James' 1246 Pat, *Ecclesia Sancti Jacobi Scheston* 1291 Tax, *parochia Sancti Jacobi* 1297 *Salis et passim, the paryshe of Sayncte James* 1566 *Sher* (in the first form, *coppehulla* may be from OE **copp** 'summit', with **hyll**, cf. Coppice St. *infra*; *Cepe-* in the second form is probably an error for *Cop(p)e-*). ST JOHN (lost, site of church marked 6″, cf. foll., St John's Ctg & Hill *infra*), *Sancti Johannis Sefton'* e13 *Wim*, *parochia Sancti Johannis (Baptiste)* 1316 *Salis*, 1319 (c.1407) *Shaft et freq* to 1518 *HarlCh, parochia Sancti Johannis Bynetheclyft* c.1407 *Shaft* ('beneath the cliff', *v.* **beneoðan, clif**), *cimiterio Sancti Johannis* 1372 (c.1407) *Shaft, ecclesie Sancti Johannis* c.1407 *Shaft*, 1428 FA, *St Johns* 1615 Map, *St John's Burying Grd* 1799 ib, *St Johns Church Yd* 1840 TA. HOSPITAL OF ST JOHN THE BAPTIST (lost, *v.* Hutch³ **3** 38, VCHDo **2**

103–4), *Hospital' Sancti Johannis de Schyaftesbyr'* 1244 *Ass*, *-de Shaftebir'* 1268 *ib*, 'the hospital of St John on the Hill' 1381 *Pat*, '-on the Mount' 1381 VCHDo, *-super montem* 1395 ib. St LAWRENCE (lost, cf. Bell St. and Parsons Pool in st.ns. *infra*), *parochia Sancti/beati Laurencii* e13 *Wim*, 1283 *Salis et freq* to 1473 *Sher* (*-Laurencij Martiris*), 1562 Weld[1] (*-Laurentii*), 'the church of St Laurence' 1396 Pat, *Ecclesia Sancti Laurencii, -entii* 1428 FA, 1488 Hutch[3], *parish of S.Lawrence* 1585 BrEll. St MARTIN (lost, cf. the house called *St Martins* noted in JervoiseSh 3), *parochia Sancti Martini* 1294 *Wim et freq* to 1516 *HarlCh, ecclesia Sancti Martini* 1372 (c.1407) *Shaft et freq* to 1471 Hutch[3], *the parish of S. Martin* 1585 BrEll. St MARY (lost, cf. the st.n. Bimport *infra*), *cappellam beate Marie* 1347 (c.1407) *Shaft, ecclesie Sancte/Beate Marie* 1372 (c.1407) *ib et freq* to 1447 Hutch[3], *parochia Sancte/Beate Marie* 1372 (c.1407) *Shaft et freq* to 1417 *HarlCh, ecclesiam parochialem Sancte Marie* 1375 *HarlCh*, 'the parish of St Mary' 1455 Cl, *S. Marie's Chapell at the townes end . . . . now pullid downe* 1535–43 Leland. St MICHAEL'S CHAPEL (lost, *v.* Hutch[3] 3 38), *capell' Sancti Michaelis* 1460 Hutch[3]. St NICHOLAS'S CHAPEL (lost), 'the chapel of St Nicholas in the charnel in the cemetery of the church of St Edward' 1346 Pat, *capela Sancti Nicholai* c.1500 *Eg* (*v.* under Abbey Ho *infra*). St PETER, *capella*(m) *Sancti Petri* 1154–8 (1340) Ch, a1335 (c.1407) *Shaft, parochia Sancti/beati Petri* 1287 (c.1407) *ib et freq* to 1516 *HarlCh*, 'church of St Peter' 1297 Pat *et passim, parochia Sanctorum Petri et Andree* 1312 (c.1407) *Shaft, parochia beati Petir* (sic) 1318 *Sher, ecclesiam* (*parochialem*) *Sancti Petri* 1428 FA, 1482 *HarlCh, Peeters Parish* 1650 *ParlSurv, Shastone St Peters* 1692 *Salkeld*. St RUMBOLD (present church rebuilt on old site in 1840), *ecclesia*(m) *Sancti Rumbaldi* 1280 *Ass*, QW, *-Rombaldi* QW, *-Rowaldi* 1291 Tax, 1428 FA, 'the church of St Ronald' 1299 Pap, *parochia Sancti Rowaldi* 1340 NI, c.1500 *Eg*, 'the church of St Rowald' 1369 Cl, 1404 Pat, 'the church of St Rumbald' (*Rowaldo*) 1394 Pat, (*un' gardino juxta*) *Seynt Rowald* 1472 Hutch[3], 'the rectory of St Rumbald' 1546 ib, *the parish of St Rombols als. Romwalls* 1615 *Sher, St Rumbolds* 1615 Map, St Rumbalds 1618 *Map*, 1799 Map (*-or Cann Church*), *St Romball's church* 1620 Hutch[3] (cf. 1 349 for the same saint's name and *v.* Cann par. *supra*).

Note also 'fraternities of St Clement and of St Gregory' mentioned by Hutch[3] 3 39, and *Methodist Meeting, Presbyterian Meeting* and *Quaker's Meeting* all 1799 Map.

SHAFTESBURY STREETS AND BUILDINGS

ABBEY WALK, cf. Abbey Ho *infra*. ANGEL LANE, 1799 Map, formerly (*la*) *Hertlane* 1488 Hutch[3], *Hart(e)lane* 1562 Weld[1], 1669 *Waller, Hart or Angel lane* 1615 Map, named from *Angel* inn (marked and named 1615 ib) which according to JervoiseSh 3 was earlier called *Hert* inn (though there is no evidence for this). ANGEL SQUARE, 1840 *TA*, cf. prec. BARTON HILL, 1585 BrEll, 1799 Map, earlier *Barton street, -strete* 1446, 1471 Hutch[3], *Berton St.* 1456 ShaftMR, *Bertonestrete* 1473 *Sher, Barton Streete* 1673

Whil, named from the former manor of Barton for which *v.* Barton Hill
Fm & Ho *infra*; Barton Hill is called *High Street* 1615 Map but this is
probably an error according to JervoiseSh 8. THE BEECHES, earlier *Rayles*
1615 Map, 1693 Waller (*le-*), *v.* **raile**. BELL ST., 1799 Map, *Bell-Lane*
1774 Hutch[1], named from *Bell* inn *infra*, though the street was earlier *S[t]*
Lawrence S[treet] 1615 Map from the church and par. of St Lawrence
supra. BELMONT CLOSE, named from Belmont Ho *infra*. BIMPORT, 1615
Map, 1799 Map, *-portt* 1643 ShaftMR, *Binneport* c.1262 BrutC, *Bynneport*
n.d. (1372) ChrP, 1394 (c.1407) *Shaft*, 1401 *Salis*, *Bynport* 1461, *Byport*
1480, *Byndport* 1615 all Hutch[3], *Bymport, or Bynport-Street* 1774 Hutch[1],
'(place)' within the town', from **binnan** and **port**[2], cf. an analogous lost
st.n. in Malmesbury W 49; the W end of Bimport was formerly called
Seyntmarylane 1401 (c.1407) *Shaft*, *-mari-* 1406 (c.1407) ib, *Seyntmary*
Lane, venell' beate Marie 1509 Hutch[3], *St Mary* 1615 Map, cf. *Mary*
Green 1615 Hutch[3], *St Mary's Cross* 1774 Hutch[1] , from the church and
par. of St Mary *supra*. BLEKE ST., 1615 Map, 1840 *TA*, *-streete* 1548
Weld[1], *Blykysstrete* 1394 (c.1407) *Shaft*, *Blykestret(e)* 1401 *Salis*, 1407
Shaft, *Blyke-Street* 1774 Hutch[1], *Blake Street* 1615 Hutch[3], *Blyke St. or*
Ram St. 1799 Map, *Bleek-st, Ram-st* 1824 Pigot; the first el. is a surname
from the family of Walter *le Blyck* 1314 *Shaft* (then 'reeve' of the town)
and Margery *la Blikes* 1332 SR (taxed here), cf. also Bleax Hill in E
Orchard par. *supra* for the same surname; the alternative name *Ram St.* is
from the *Rame* inn *infra*. CHRISTY'S LANE, named from the *Christie* family
which owned Belmont Ho *infra* in the 19th cent. (JervoiseSh 1). CHURCH
LANE, 1774 Hutch[1], *Churchelane* 1477 *Russ*, *Churche Lane* 1585 BrEll,
named from Holy Trinity Church *supra*. THE COMMONS, now applied to
the junction of High St., Tout Hill and Bell St., cf. *closes-, gardens called*
the Comens Landes (3 ×), *-called Comen Landes* (2 ×) 1585 BrEll, *Commons*
1845 *TAMap*, *v.* **common**. COPPICE ST., 1840 *TA*, *Coppestrete* 1294
Wim, 1332 (c.1407) *Shaft*, 1388 ShaftMR, 1401 *Salis*, 1402 (c.1407) *Shaft*,
-streete 1585 BrEll, *Coppusstret* 1394 (c.1407) *Shaft*, *Copstreet Lane* 1615
Map, 1643 ShaftMR, *Copper Street* 1799 Map, 1845 *TAMap*, first el. OE
copp 'the top of a hill, a summit'; according to Sydenham 79 named from
Lone Coppice infra, but both date and spelling of the early forms forbid
derivation from ME **copis** 'coppice'. FRENCH MILL LANE, leading to
French Mill in Cann par. *supra*, cf. *Boywellane infra*. GOLD HILL, 1692
Salkeld (*messuage called-*), 1840 *TA*, *Chupyncliue* 1289 (c.1407) *Shaft*,
Chipingecliff als. Goldehill' 1507 Hutch[3], *Goldhull(e)* 1352 ShaftMR, 1407
Shaft, 1444, 1463 ShaftMR (*viam regiam pendentem vocat'-*), *Gold(e)hill*
1447, 1480, *-hylle* 1476 all Hutch[3], *Gouldehill* 1585 BrEll, *The long Hill*
(the road itself), *Gould hill* (the N end of the road at the top of the hill)
1615 Map, *Goldhill, Gold-cliff, or Chipping-Cliff, Goldhill-Cross* 1774
Hutch[1]; the earlier name means 'cliff or steep slope where markets are
held', *v.* **cī(e)ping, clif**, cf. *Gold Hill Market Tolls* 1840 *TA*; the name
Gold Hill is probably more likely to contain **gold** 'gold' (with whimsical
reference perhaps to the profitable trade carried on here?) than **golde**
'marigold', *v.* **hyll**. GREAT LANE, 1799 Map. GROSVENOR RD. HAIMES'

LANE, *Mille Lane* 1446, *Millane* 1452 ShaftMR, 1471, 1521 Hutch[3], *Mill lane* 1615 Map, *Mill-Lane* 1774 Hutch[1], *Haine(')s Lane* 1799 Map, 1840 *TA*, *Haimes Lane* 1845 *TAMap*, *Mill Lane or Haime's Lane* 1869 Hutch[3], named from the 'horse mill' here mentioned in 1475 and from John *Haymes*, miller, who had a tenement here in 1689 (JervoiseSh 9), cf. also Walter *Heym* 1280 FF, John *Haym* 1348 *Shaft*, John *Hayne* 1664 HTax, *v.* **myln.** HAWKSDEAN LANE, from Hawksdean Fm *infra.* HIGH ST., 1799 Map, called *Corn Hill or Corn Market* 1615 Map (the E-W section), cf. *Cornhull, le Carnhull* (sic) 1461 Hutch[3], *The Corne Markett Place* 1585 BrEll, *v.* **corn**[1] 'grain'; according to Hutch[1] **2** 5, *Alta-Strata* ('high street') occurs in 1488, although this may belong under Barton Hill *supra* which is *High Street* on 1615 Map. Other references to the market(s) in Shaftesbury include (*la Pillori-, la Pillory-, la Pyllory*) *in foro Shafton(ie)* Ed 1 (c.1407) *Shaft, ex oppositto Scabell' in foro in parochia Sancti Andr'* 1377 *Salis, Yarne Markett* 1553 JervoiseSh, *the Bochers Shambles, Chepmans Standinges, Les Tanners Standinge(s)* 1585 BrEll, *22 shopas carnificales Anglice voc' flesh shambles* 1590 ShaftMR, *v.* **pillory, sc(e)amol, standing**, cf. Gold Hill *supra.* KINGSMAN LANE, *Kinmans Lane* 1840 *TA, Kingmer L[ane]* 1615 Map, from the surname *Kingman* (cf. 'plot adjacent to *Kyngemans Wall'* 1572 JervoiseSh) and/or *Kin(g)mer* (cf. Richard *Cunemere* Ed 2 (c.1407), *-Kynemere* 1332 (c.1407) *Shaft*, John *Kynemere* 1427 *HarlCh); JervoiseSh* 13 calls it Kingmans Lane and says it was formerly the *Burgess-Lane anciently Mahounds Lane* mentioned in 1774 Hutch[1] **2** 5, cf. *le Style apud Mahoundeslane* 1476 Hutch[3] **3** 91, Lawrence *Burgeys* 1293 (c.1407) *Shaft, Burges Meade* 1671 *Waller.* LANGFORDS LANE, cf. John *de Langeford* 1334 (c.1407) *Shaft*, Alexander *Langforde* 1551 *AddCh.* LAYTON LANE, 1799 Map, *Leighton lane* 1476 Hutch[3], 1615 Map, *Leyton* [Lane] 1845 *TAMap, v.* Layton Ho *infra.* LION'S WALK, from *Red Lion* inn *infra.* LITTLE CONTENT LANE. LOVE LANE, cf. an earlier *Love Lane* now Parson's Pool *infra.* MAGDALENE LANE, *Maudlin lane* 1615 Map, 1840 *TA, Ma(w)dlen Lane* 1615 Hutch[3], *Magdalen Lane* 1799 Map, named from the poor-house called *Magdalen's* or *Maudlen's* (earlier *Belhous* or *Dolhous*) *infra.* MAWPITTS RD (6"), MAMPITTS LANE (TGuide), *v.* **malm** 'sand, soft stone', **pytt**, cf. **1** 151. MUSTON'S LANE, 1840 *TA, Collman Lane* 1546 ShaftMR, *Coulman Lane* 1615, *Coleman Lane als. Muston's Lane* 1629 Hutch[3], *Muston-Street* 1774 Hutch[1], *Multons Lane* (sic) 1799 Map, cf. Agnes *Coleman* 1332 SR (Melbury A. and Compton A.), Philip *Mustean* (sic) 1568, Albinus *Muston* 1629 Hutch[3]. OLD BOUNDARY RD, follows old boundary between Cann par. and Shaftesbury St James par. PARK LANE (1840 *TA*) & WALK, named from The Park *infra.* PARSON'S POOL, 1799 Map, named from *Parsons poole* 1615 Map, *the Parsons Poole* 1650 *ParlSurv*, 'a kind of reservoir for rain-water, used for washing houses, which is still known by the name of *Parsons Pool*' 1774 Hutch[1], from **pōl**[1] and either **persone** 'a parson' or a surname, cf. *ten' Johannis Parsons* 1372 (c.1407) *Shaft, Mrs Parsons* 1664 HTax; according to Hutch[1] **2** 30, this pool was earlier called *Fordmere* 1429 ShaftMR, *-mer* 1446 Hutch[3], 'pool at the ford', from **ford** and **mere**[1], cf. William *de la Forde* 1288 *Ass*, 1327 (c.1407) *Shaft*; the street now called Parson's Pool was earlier called *S*[*t*] *Laurence Lane* 1416 ShaftMR, *Lawrance Lane* 1615 Map, from the church and par. of St Lawrence *supra* (cf. Bell St. *supra*), or *Lovelane* 1446, *Love Lane* 1615 Hutch³, *v.* **lufu** (cf. Love Lane *supra*). RASPBERRY LANE. RATCLIFFES GDNS. ST GEORGES RD. ST JAMES'S ST., 1799 Map, 'the street of St James's parish' 1565 Hutch³, *St James* 1615 Map, *St James' Hill* 1643 ShaftMR, *Saint Jameses Street* 1782 *Eg*, from the church and par. of St James *supra*. ST JOHN'S HILL, *Seyn*(*t*)*johneshyll* 1461 Hutch³, *venel' vocat' S*ᵗ *Johanes* 1562 *Weld*¹, named from church and par. of St John *supra*, *v.* **hyll**; it is *Great Lane* 1799 Map, cf. another Great Lane *supra*. ST RUMBOLD'S RD, *v.* the church and par. of St Rumbold *supra*. SALISBURY ST, 1799 Map, *-or East Street* 1615 Map, *Estrete* 15 *Shaft*, *Est*(*e*)*strete* 1460, 1471 Hutch³, *Estret*(*e*) 1462, 1486 *Salis*, *Est*(*e*) *Stre*(*e*)*te* 1471 ShaftMR, 1585 BrEll, 'the road to Salisbury W', cf. *Salisbury square* 1824 Pigot, earlier 'east street', *v.* **ēast**. SHOOTER'S LANE, 1615 Hutch³, 1799 Map, *Shetewellane* 1447 Hutch³, 1453 *Midd*, 1488 JervoiseSh, *Shet*(*t*)*ewellane* 1460 Hutch³, *Shetewell lane* 1615 Map, 1774 Hutch¹, *Shetewell, als. Shootwell, als. Shooter's Lane* 1869 Hutch³, first el. probably **scēat** 'corner, angle, projection of land', with **well(a)** 'spring, stream'; the later form *Shooter's* is due to popular etymology. STONEY PATH, formerly *La*(*u*)*nder Lane* 1615 Hutch³, *Landry Lane* 1674 *Waller*, *Laundey Lane* 1799 Map, *Laundry or Lander Lane* 1869 Hutch³, from ME *la*(*u*)*nder* 'person who washes linen', eModE *laundry* 'washing of linen, establishment where linen is washed'; according to Hutch¹ **2** 5 (1774) 'Laundry-Lane runs down Park-Hill into St James's Parish. In a garden at the bottom is a well, called *Laundry-Well*, where the linen of the convent was probably washed.The Laundry-house is pulled down, but the well is still in use', cf. *the laundry-house, tholde laundry chamber next to the well* 1565 Hutch³, *the Lawndrye house* 1572 JervoiseSh, *Landry house* 1615 Map, *Laundry-Close* 1639 Hutch¹. TANYARD LANE, named from the tanyard here, referred to as *The Tanner* 1615 Map, *Tan Yard* (2 ×) 1799 Map, and *Tan Yard* (*Buildings*) 1840 *TA*. TOUT HILL, 1615 Map, 1840 *TA*, *Tothull*(*e*) 1298 GillCt, 15 *Shaft*, *Totehulle* Ed 2 (c.1407), *Tuthulle lane* 1325 (c.1407) *ib*, *Touthull*(*e*) 1388 HarlCh, 1407 *Shaft*, 1411 GillCt, 1418 HarlCh (*le*-), *-hill* 1693 *Waller* (*vie reg' ducen' a capite montis vel vie vocat'*-), *Toutehull'* 1441 GillCt, *Towtehill* 1446, *Towghthyll* 1521 Hutch³, *Toutehill* 1609 LRMB, *Toott Hill* 1643 ShaftMR, *Towt Hill* 1799 Map, cf. *Tot*(*e*)*hullesquarre* 1438 GillCt, from **tōt-hyll** 'look-out hill', with **lane** and **quarre** 'quarry'. UMBERS HILL, 1849 *TA*, probably a surname. VICTORIA ST, earlier *Godman lane* 1615 Map (cf. Philip *Godman* 1455 Hutch³, 1469 *Eton*), *Malthouse lane* 1840 *TA* (cf. *Malthouse Md ib*), *Brewhouse Lane* 1845 *TAMap*; renamed to commemorate the Diamond Jubilee of Queen Victoria. WATERY LANE, cf. *Boywellane infra* and cf. *via regia inter Holyrodmede et lez Graston est infunderat'* 1471 Hutch³ 90, *v.* Holy Rood Fm and the f.n. Gascoigns *infra*. WHITE HART LANE. WINCOMBE LANE, 1845 *TAMap*, leading to Wincombe in Donhead St Mary par. W, cf. *Wincombe Mdw* 1840 *TA*.

Lost st.ns. include *Anketilleslane* 1441 *Wim* (*v.* Anketil's Place in Cann par. *supra*); *Bisschupesstret* 1320 *Salis* (*v.* **biscop, strǣt**, but cf. Bishop's Fm in Cann par. *supra*); *Boywellane* 1476 Hutch[3], *Bowell Lane* 1650 *ParlSurv* (named from the spring (*fons*) called *Boywell* 1480 Hutch[3], which is probably to be identified with *of bogen wylle, on bokenwelle* 958 (15) *ShaftR* (S 655), the starting and finishing point in the Anglo-Saxon bounds of a small area in Shaftesbury; *Bowell Lane* is described in 1650 *ParlSurv* as 'leading from *Shaston* to French Mill' (*v.* Cann par. *supra*), so it was probably an earlier name for (part of) French Mill Lane or Watery Lane (both *supra*), and *Bo(y)well* itself may have been one of the two 'wells' shown on 1799 Map near Abbey Ponds (the other probably being *H(o)undeswell, v. H(o)undeswellane infra*); the OE forms suggest that the first el. is **boga** (gen.sg. -n) 'bow, arch', probably here in the extended sense 'curving hill-side', with **well(a)** 'well, spring' (or 'stream'), the 15th cent. *Boy*- forms being due to popular etymology; JervoiseSh 11 confuses the forms for this lane in the S of the town with those for the following lane in the N of the town); *Boreswelleslane* 1461, *Pereswelle Lane* 1471 both Hutch[3], *Pereswellane* 1471 ShaftMR (these discrepant forms probably belong together, though one or the other is clearly corrupt and the first el. cannot be established; in 1774 Hutch[1] (followed by 1869 Hutch[3]) this lane is said to have led from Bimport (*supra*) to Enmore Green (in Motcombe par. *supra*) 'where is a well still called *Bore-well*'); *Brewhouse Lane* (*v.* Victoria St. *supra*); *Burgess Lane* (*v.* Kingsman Lane *supra*); (*The*) *Butter Cross(e)* 1585 BrEll, 1615 Map (marked at junction now called The Commons *supra*; according to 1774 Hutch[1] (**2** 24) 'The Butter or Cheese Cross . . . seems to have been anciently called the *Pultry Cross*' and was taken down in 1727, cf. *le Pultrey Cross* 1509, *the Poultry Cross* 1533 both Hutch[3]; these names denote a market cross near which butter, cheese and poultry were sold); *viam regiam vocatum Benetheclyffe* c.1407 *Shaft* ('beneath the cliff', *v.* **beneoðan, clif**, cf. St John's parish *supra*); *Chipingecliff* (an earlier name for Gold Hill *supra*); *Collman Lane* (*v.* Muston's Lane *supra*); *Compton Gate* 1615 Hutch[3] (at end of Bell St.); *Corn Hill* (an earlier name for part of High St. *supra*); *Cropelane* 1475 Hutch[3] (identified with Coppice St. *supra* by Hutch[3] **3** 5 but almost certainly distinct, probably from OE **grōp(e)** 'a ditch, a drain' or from OE **grāpian** 'to grope', if the latter denoting a lane with a bad reputation, cf. **1** 155); *the Crown Alley* n.d. (1869) Hutch[3] (cf. the *Crown* inn *infra*); *Dark Lane* 1840 *TA*; *East Street* (now Salisbury St. *supra*); *Eld(e)portwey* 1352, 1380 *Sher* (*v.* **eald** 'old', **port-weg** 'road leading to a market town'); (*The*) *Fish(e) Cross(e)* 1585 BrEll, 1615 Map, *crucem piscariam* 1677 *Waller* (S of St Peter's Church, pulled down c.1780); *Godman lane* (*v.* Victoria St. *supra*); *Hatteslane* 1460 Hutch[3] (not to be identified with foll. as suggested by Hutch[1] **2** 5, cf. Thomas *Hatte* 1404 *Shaft*, 1418 *HarlCh*); (*la*) *Hertlane* (now Angel Lane *supra*); *street called Hockenbench* 1646 Hutch[3] (apparently 'oaken bench', or 'bank growing with oak-trees', from **ācen, benc**; possibly an alternative name for one of the main streets); *Holy Rood Lane* 1782 *Eg* (*v.* Holy Rood Fm *infra*); *Houndeswellestrate* Ed 1 (c.1407),

H(o)undeswellane 1312–1405 (c.1407), *venellam que vocat' Hundeswell* 1343 (c.1407), *Hundeswelle lane* 1345 (c.1407), *Hundeslane* 1415 all *Shaft* (named from *Hundeswelle* 1390 (c.1407) *Shaft, Houndeswell* 1480 Hutch³ (*fontes voc' Boywell et-*), cf. *ten' Nicholi de Houndeswelle* 1309 (c.1407) *Shaft,* probably 'well or spring of the hound' (i.e. 'frequented by dogs'), from **hund** and **well(a)**, although the first el. could alternatively be the OE pers.n. *Hund;* the 'well' was probably one of the two marked on 1799 Map near Abbey Ponds, cf. *Boywellane supra,* Hutch³ 3 44); *Le Hurlegogge* 1585 BrEll, *the Hurlegogg* 1631 ShaftMR (a form of *whirligig* 'roundabout', not of course strictly a st.n. but no doubt a lively feature of the street scene since it was situated 'between the churchyard of Holy Trinity and the inn called the *Starre*' 1585 ib); *La(u)nder Lane* (now Stoney Path *supra*); *Love Lane* (an earlier name for Parson's Pool *supra* although there is now a different Love Lane on the modern map); *Mahoundeslane* (*v.* Kingsman Lane *supra*); *Malthouse Lane* (*v.* Victoria St. *supra*); *Mill Lane* (an earlier name for Haimes' Lane *supra*); *N(h)ottelane* 1358 (c.1407), 1407 *Shaft* (probably the surname *Nott*); *Oatemell Row* 1684 ShaftMR (no doubt 'row where oatmeal was sold', from ME *otemel*); *Pallyngeslane* 1338 (c.1407), 1407 *Shaft,* 1351 ShaftMR (cf. John *Pallyng* 15 *Shaft*); *Pereswelle Lane* (*v. Boreswelleslane supra*); *Pokelane* 1317 *Salis, Pewke* (for *Powke*) *Lane* 1442 ShaftMR (from **pūca** 'goblin, puck', cf. Puck Lane O 259, 333); *le Pultrey Cross* (*v. Butter Cross supra*); *la Pylelane* 1386 *Salis* (*v.* **pīl** 'shaft, stake', cf. Piles Hill in Cann par. *supra*); *Rabbit Lane* 1845 *TAMap* (cf. *Rabbitts Fm infra*); *Ram St.* (*v.* Bleke St. *supra*); *crucem Sancti Johannis in Este-strete* 1471 Hutch³ ('so called from the chantry of St John within the monastery, which had an house belonging to it in East-Street' Hutch¹ 2 5, *v.* Salisbury St *supra*; this cross now stands on the site of the High Altar in the ruins of the Abbey, *v.* JervoiseSh 3); *St Lawrence Lane* (*v.* Parson's Pool *supra*); *St Lawrence Street* (*v.* Bell St *supra*); *Schollane* 1349 (c.1407), *Sco(u)lelane* 1374 (c.1407), 1394 (c.1407), *Scolane* 1407 all *Shaft* (*v.* **scole** 'school'); *Scotslane* 1380 ShaftMR (a surname); *Seyntmarylane* (the earlier name for the W end of Bimport *supra*); *Sleybrondesgate* 1280 *Ass,* QW, *Sleynbrende-, Sleynbrengegate* 1280 *Ass, Shey(n)bronde(s)gate* 1280 *Ass,* QW, *Sleborne gate* 1618 *Map, Sleybrongate* 1620 Hutch³ (a point in or near Shaftesbury mentioned in the 'out-bounds' of Cranborne Chase 2 193, *v.* **geat** 'gate, pass'; the first el. is probably a pers.n. or surname, though its form is difficult to establish in view of the discrepancy of the spellings); *Smale Lane* 1446 ShaftMR (*v.* **smæl** 'narrow'); *Snoteslane* Ed1 (c.1407) *Shaft* (cf. *curtillagium Walteri Snot'* 1294 (c.1407) *ib*); *Stigheleslane* 1349 (c.1407), *Stylyslane* 1394 (c.1407), *Stilane* 15, *Stileslane* 1407 all *Shaft* (cf. William *de la Stighele* 1268 *Ass, v.* **stigel** 'a stile'); *Strode Lane* c.1620 Hutch³ (*v.* **strōd** 'marshy land overgrown with brushwood'); *Swyneslane* 1359 (c.1407) *Shaft,* 1389 HarlCh, 1406 (c.1407) *Shaft, Swynyslane* 1401 (c.1407) *ib* (*v.* **swīn** 'a swine, a pig', perhaps here a surname); *Waggon road* 1740 *SRO; Wodehewereslane* 1415, 1452 ShaftMR (probably to be identified with *Woodman Lane* 1615 Hutch³, cf. 'tenement of the late

William *Wodehewere'* 1452 ShaftMR; *Wornould's Square* 1615 Hutch[3] (a surname).

Buildings include (*Old*) *Mens Alm(s)house* 1840 *TA*, 1845 *TAMap* (called *Spiller's Spittle* 1656 Hutch[3] after its founder Sir Henry *Spiller*, *v.* **spitel**, Hutch[3] 3 44, cf. foll.); *Almshouse* 1615 Map, *the A(l)mes Hous(e)* 1643, 1649 ShaftMR, *Chubb's almshouse* 1834 Hutch[3], *Old Womans Almshouse* 1840 *TA*, *Womens Alm House* 1845 *TAMap* (founded by Matthew *Chubb* 1611, *v.* Hutch[3] 3 43); *Bedbury* 1615, *-berie* c.1620 Hutch[1] (a house, probably named from its owner); *le Belhous* ('12 poor inmates of . . . ') 1386 Pat, (*la*) *Dolhous* 1429 ShaftMR, 1437 Hutch[3] ('the poor of-'), 1447 ib (*Pauperes de-*), 'the *Maudelyn* or *Belhous'* 1535 VE ('12 poor men in-'), 'a House called a *Magdalen*, once the home of 12 paupers' 1574 JervoiseSh, tenement called *Mawdelin* 1585 BrEll, *-the Magdalen* 1585 Hutch[3], *the ruinous house of Maudlins* 1586 ib, *Maudlin* 1615 Map, 1625 Hutch[3] (*messuage called the-*), *the Maudlyn* 1649 ShaftMR, *Magdalen's, Maudlen's, or Dolhouse* 1774 Hutch[1] (this poorhouse seems to have had three different names at various times. *Belhous* is **bell-hūs** 'a belfry'. *Dolhous* would seem to be 'dole house', with *dole* in the sense 'distribution of food and money for charity' (NED *dole* sb[1] sense 5), *v.* **dāl**. The later name, still found in Magdalene Lane *supra*, presumably reflects a change in the character of the inmates, *v.* eModE **magdalen** 'home for the refuge and reformation of prostitutes' (NED from 1603 in the alternative form *maudlen*)); *le Blyndehouse* 1476 Hutch[3], *the Blindhouse* 1631 ShaftMR (possibly **blind** in the sense 'windowless' (but cf. MED *blindhous* 'an asylum for the blind') and therefore a place of detention like the *Blindhowse* in Dorchester i 354, cf. *Grate infra*); *the church-house* 1585 Hutch[3]; *le Clemale House* 1590 ShaftMR; (*la*) *Dolhous* (*v.* (*le*) *Belhous supra*); *The Free-School* 1774 Hutch[1]; *Gas Works* 1845 *TAMap*; *Grate* (*the Blindhouse and-*) 1631 ShaftMR (eModE **grate** 'a prison or cage for human beings', *v.* le *Blyndehouse supra*); *The Guild Hall* 1496 ShaftMR, *the Newe Yeelde Hall, Oulde Ye(e)lde Hall* 1585 BrEll, *the Olde Guylde Hall* 1590 ShaftMR, *le New Guildhall* 1665 Hutch[3], *Town-Hall or New Guildhall* 1774 Hutch[1], *Town Hall* 1840 *TA*, *The present Guildhall* 1869 Hutch[3] (*v.* **gild-heall**; the 'new' guildhall was built c.1568, the present Guildhall/Town Hall was built in 1827); *Infant School* 1845 *TAMap; Laundry house* (*v.* Stoney Path *supra*); *Magdalen's* (*v.* (*le*) *Belhous supra*); *Market-house* 1855 Hutch[3] (for other references to markets in Shaftesbury, *v.* High St. *supra*); *National School* 1840 *TA*; *Le Ottlofte* 1585 BrEll, *the Ottloft, sometimes called the Alte lofte* 1631 ShaftMR (described as a tenement over the shambles, possibly **āte** 'oats', **lopt**); *la Outhouse* 1504 HarlCh; *Pembroke, -brook* c.1620 Hutch[3] (a house, probably named from William, Earl of *Pembroke* who was granted 'the Manor of the Abbess' in 1553 Hutch[3] 3 13); *Post Office* 1845 *TAMap; domum . . . voc' Puthus* Ed1 (c.1407) (*v.* **pytt, hūs**); *Sessions Hall* 1799 Map; *la Tolselde* 1356 Sher (probably 'toll-house', *v.* **toll, seld**); *Union Workhouse Yards* 1840 *TA; Well House* 1845 *TAMap*.

Inns include *Abbey Arms* 1840 *TA; Angel* 1615 Map; *the Anteloppe* (*tenement . . . called*) 1553 JervoiseSh; *le Bell'* 1480 Hutch[3], *Bell* 1824 Pigot, *Old Bell* 1840 *TA* (*v.* Bell St. *supra*); *Bird in Hand* 1824 Pigot; *Blue Boar* 1824 ib; *Bowles Arms* 1840 *TA; Crooked Billett* 1824 Pigot; *Cross Keys* 1824 ib; *the Crowne* 1600 Hutch[3], *Crown & Punchbowl* 1824 Pigot; *late 5 Bells* 1840 *TA; Flying Horse* 1824 Pigot; *Fox & Hounds* 1824 ib; *the George* 1615 Hutch[1], *George* 1824 Pigot; *Greyhound* 1840 *TA; Griffins Head* 1840 *ib; Grosvenor Arms* 1840 *ib; Half Moon* (on Salisbury St.) 1824 Pigot (called *New Inn* 1753 JervoiseSh); *Half Moon* (on Bleke St.) 1824 ib; *Hop Bag* 1824 ib; *King's Arms* 1824 ib; *the Kings Head* 1650 ParlSurv; *Knowles' Arms* 1840 *TA*; *the-* 1557 ShaftMR, *Le Lamb* (*the inn called-*) 1585 BrEll; *the Lion* c.1620 Hutch[3]; *Mitre* 1824 Pigot; *the New Inne* 1538 *AD* (cf. *Half Moon supra*); *Ox Inn* 1840 *TA; Platellesynne* c.1407 *Shaft* (*v. Platelplacet infra*); *La-* 1514 ShaftMR, *the Rame* 1585 BrEll; *Red Lion* 1799 Map; *the Rose and Crown* 1774 Hutch[1]; *Ship* 1824 Pigot; *lez Sterre, lez Starr* 1574 JervoiseSh, *the Starr* 1602 Eton, *Star* 1824 Pigot; *Sugar Loaf* 1824 ib; *Sun & Moon* 1824 ib; *le Swanne* (*ten' voc'*) 1460 Hutch[3], *the Swan* 1650 ParlSurv; *Two Brewers* 1824 Pigot; *White Lion* 1824 ib; *White Swan* 1824 ib.

ABBEY HO (ST 861228) (*-and Garden, Abbey Well Ho* 1840 *TA*) & PONDS (ST 864226) (*Abbey Gdn & Ponds* 1799 Map), cf. *campus Abbatisse Shafton* 1349 (c.1407) *Shaft, claus' Abbatisse Shafton'* 1426 *HarlCh, croftam Abbatisse* 1389 *ib, (magnum) pratum Abbatisse* 1315 (c.1407), 1415 *Shaft, the Abbey Park* 1585 BrEll, named from the former Abbey of Shaftesbury, a Benedictine nunnery founded in the late 9th cent., dedicated to the Blessed Virgin, later also (after 978) to St Edward (the Martyr), *v.* Hutch[3] **3** 21 ff, VCHDo **2** 73-9: *ecclesie de Sheftesbury, Sceptoniensis ecclesie* 871-7 (15) BCS 531 (rubric), 532, *monasterium iuxta orientalem portam Sceftesburg* 893 (e11) Asser, *monasterio civitatis que Schaftesbiry vocatur* 932 (15) *ShaftR, þa hiwan æt Sceaftesbyrig* c.950 (11) ASWills (*v.* **hīwan** 'religious community'), *Ecclesie de Shaftesbury* 956 (14) *ShaftR* (rubric), *to sce Eadwearde* 1015 (e11) ASWills, *ecclesie Sancte Marie et Sancti Edwardi de Septesberia* Wm 1 (15) *ShaftR*, 1089 (1371) Pat (*-Sheftesbury*), *Æcclesia Sceftesberie* 1086 DB, *monasterium iuxta orientalem portam civitatis quæ Sceftesburg appellatur* 12 SD, *for þare cherche of Shaftesbury, of þan munechene of Syftebury and of þan menstyre, ecclesie de Sceftesberia* Hy 1 (15) *ShaftR, abbatia/-e de Sancto Ædwardo* 1194 P, *ecclesie Sancti Edwardi de Shafteburi* 1216 Pat, *ecclesie Beate Marie et Sancti Edwardi de Shaftebur'* 1216-72 (1371) ib *et freq*, 'the *monastery of St Edward' 1217 Pap, abbacie/conventui (Sancti Eadwardi) de Shafte(s)bur(y)* 1242 Cl, *de loco Sancti Edwardi* 1246 FF, *cimitarium Sancti Edwardi* 1310 (c.1407) *Shaft, Abby* 1615 Map.

Among the chantries established in (or attached to) the conventual church were the following (*v.* further Hutch[3] **3** 35–6, 88, VCHDo **2** 75): *cantar' de Arne* c.1500 *Eg*, n.d. (1500) Hutch[3] (cf. *Arne* **1** 71); *cantar' de Blanforde* c.1500 *Eg*, n.d. (1500) Hutch[3] (cf. *Blandford* **2** 73, 87); *cantar' D'ne Dionisie Blont* c.1500 *Eg*, *-Dionysie Blunt* n.d. (1500) Hutch[3]; *cantar' D'ne Edithe Bonham* c.1500 *Eg*, n.d. (1500) Hutch[3]; *cantar' D'ne Cecilie Fovent* c.1500 *Eg*; *Cantar' de Gora* 1282 (15) *AddCh, Cantuarie de la Gore* 1358 *Salis, Cantarie Sancte Anne de La Gore* 1551 *AddCh*, cf. 'altar of St Anne' 1330 VCHDo (there was a chapel of St Anne at Gore (Fm) in Marg. Marsh par. *infra*); *cantar' S'ce Crucis* c.1500 *Eg*, cf. 'altar of Holy Cross' 1364 VCHDo, Holyrood Fm *infra*; *cantarie Sancti Johannis* 1472 Hutch[3], c.1500 *Eg*, 'chantry of St John the Baptist' 1547 VCHDo; *Abbesse Seynt John is Chauntrey* 1492 Pat, *cantar' Margarete Seynt John* 1509 Hutch[3]; *Seint Katerine Chauntrye* 1415 *Shaft, Cantar' St Katerine* c.1500 *Eg* (cf. the fraternity of St Katherine associated with Holy Trinity Church *supra*); *Cantar' Sancti Leonardi* c.1500 *Eg*; *cantar' in capella Sancti Nicholai* c.1500 *Eg*, cf. 'altar of St Nicholas' 1342 VCHDo, 'the chapel of St Nicholas in the charnel in the cemetery of the church of St Edward' 1346 Pat; *cantar' Walteri Schamell* c.1500 *Eg*; *cantarie Sancti Thome* n.d. (1500) Hutch[3], cf. 'altar of St Thomas the Apostle' 1334 VCHDo. There was also a chantry of St Mary (Hutch[3] **3** 36) and a chantry and chapel of St Edward (ib 35–6, 88, VCHDo **2** 75, cf. the distinct St Edward's chapel *supra* in St James's par.).

Various parts of the abbey are named in 1565 Hutch[3] **3** 37–8, including: *thalmery; the great backhouse; the base court; the bredhouse; the olde brewhouse; the brode chamber; the brode hall; the buttery; Carrents chamber; The cheker . . . and the Cheker chamber . . . where the court hath been allweys kept for the king; the dovehouse; the Fefosters chamber; the Fosters chamber; the frayter chamber; the fyer-house; the grene-chamber; the grynter-house; the hoopers house; Kechyn,* *the (covent) kitchyn; the kitchyn clerk's chamber; the larder house; tholde laundry chamber next to the well, the laundry-house (v.* Stoney Path *supra); the longe leden chamber; the Long Stable; the maltesmen's chamber; the malthouse; the myllhouse; the mynchen-chamber (v.* **myncen***); the Utter Nurcery; the pantrey; the pastryhouse; the lodging late called the Sextry* (cf. the f.n. Sexty Md in Cann par. *supra); the squiors' chambers; the starre-chamber; the vice otherwise called the stayers; the Steward's chamber; the wardrobe-chamber; the wollehouse; the wod-house; the (wyne) seller; the Yatehouse.*

ALCESTER (ST 856225), *Alcestre* 1433 *Salis*, 1494 *HarlCh* (*Hundrid' de-*), *Alyncestr'* 1453 *Midd* (*hund' de-*), 1518 *HarlCh* (*hundred' de-*), *Lybertye of Alynsester* 1566 *Sher*, hundred *de Alcetor* 1577 *AddCh*, *libertatem de Alcester als*. *Alincester* 1586 *Comm*, (*libertie of*) *Al(n)cester* 1585 *Sher et freq* to 1664 HTax, *Alcester als. Alincester* 1795 Boswell, a transferred name from Alcester Wa (PN Wa 193), from the possession of lands here by Alcester abbey from at least as early as the 13th cent., cf. *per diuisas inter dominum Regem et Abbatem de Alcestre* Hy 3 (14) Cerne (in a perambulation of the forest of Gillingham). For the extent of this small liberty, *v.* Hutch[3] **3** 54 and under Sixpenny Handley Hundred *supra*. Alcester formed a civil par. between 1894 and 1920.

BARTON HILL FM (ST 869231), HO & VILLA, *Berton(')* 1288 *Ass*, 1290 (15) *ShaftR*, 1364 *For et freq* to c. 1500 *Eg, La Berton(e)* 1293 *Ch*, 1447 Hutch[3], c. 1500 *Eg, la Breton* 1461 Hutch[3], *la Barton* 1471 ib, *bertona Shafton* c. 1500 *Eg, Barton* 1553 *AD, Barton Hill Gdn* & *Ho* 1840 *TA, v.* **bere-tūn** 'corn farm, outlying grange', cf. the st.n. Barton Hill *supra*.

BITTLESMORE (lost, near foll.), 1795 Boswell, *on bytelesmor, of bitelesmore* 958 (15) *ShaftR* (S 655), *parcum/clausum vocat' Myddelbeytell more* 1432, 1437 *Wim, la Bittelesmore* 1447 Hutch[3], *prat' triangulat' subtus Lytelbutellesmore* 1453 *Midd, Buttlesmore* 1460 Hutch[3], *Bytellesmore* 1461 Hutch[1], probably 'Byt(t)el's marshy ground', from an OE pers.n. *Byt(t)el* (suggested for Bittesby Lei by Ekwall DEPN and for Biddlesden Bk 42), *v.* **mōr, middel, lȳtel.**

HOLYROOD FM (ST 864224), *Holy-Rood Fm* 1841 *TAMap*, cf. (bequest) *to þære halgan rode* 1015 (e11) ASWills, *pratum Abbatisse vocat' holyrodemede* 1407 *Shaft*, 1441 *Wim*, *Holowroudemede* 1447 Hutch[3], *Hollie Rood Meade* 1641 ShaftMR, *Holy Rood Estate & Md* 1782 *Eg*, *Holy Rood Mdw* 1840 *TA*, 'the holy cross', *v.* **hālig**, **rōd**[2] with **mǣd**. Professor Whitelock notes: 'I have not found any other reference to the holy cross there [i.e. at the Abbey]. Possibly Shaftesbury received a portion of the wood of the true cross sent to Alfred (Asser chapter 71) or it may have possessed a famous crucifix like the Holy Cross of Waltham' (ASWills 58). Cf. also the chantry and altar of the Holy Cross noted under Abbey Ho *supra*.

LAYTON HO (ST 863227), 1824 Pigot, *Lecton* 1275 RH (p), (*la*) *Leig(h)ton* 1446, 1461, 1480, *Leyghton* 1460 all Hutch[3], cf. *Layton Cl* 1799 Map, *Layton* (*Ctg & Mdw*) 1840 *TA*, *Leyton Fds* 1845 *TAMap*, Layton Lane *supra*, *v.* **lēac-tūn** 'herb garden'.

BELLE VUE, 1840 *TA*, -*Ho* 1845 *TAMap*. BELMONT HO (1902), -*mount*- 1840 *TA*, later Royal Hotel, cf. the st.n. Belmont Close *supra*. BRIMSCOMBE FM, *Brinscombe* 1840 *TA* (a field now in Cann par. *supra*), perhaps transferred from, or analogous with, Brenscombe 1 9. BUTT'S KNAP, *Butts Knapp* 1845 *TAMap*, cf. *Butts' Md* 1840 *TA*, the surname *Butt* with **cnæpp** 'hill-top, hillock'. CANN HO, cf. *Cann-Ctg* 1840 *TA*, *Cann Rectory* 1845 *TAMap*, *v.* Cann par. *supra*. CASTLE HILL (1799 Map, *pasture land called Castell Hill* Eliz JervoiseSh), CASTLE HILL HO (1840 *TA*), cf. *Castle Hill Gate* 1585 BrEll, *v.* **castel(l)**; the earthwork probably represents 'a temporary fortification dating from the period of the 12th century civil war' (RCHM **4** 76). Cf. the bounds of Gillingham forest which proceed 'under the castle' in 1300 Hutch[3] **3** 620, and cf. Hutch[1] (**2** 23) who states: 'Though no mention is made of a castle, yet there seems to have been one on *Castle-Green*, a little W of St Mary's, by some called *Boltbury*; where the inhabitants have a tradition the old town or city stood'; the name *Boltbury* has not been noted elsewhere. COBBLERS PIT (local), a pit on Castle Hill.

COTTAGE GREEN. HAWKSDEAN FM, *Hawksdown Md, Broad, Hilly & Lt Hawksdown, Butlers' Hawksdown* 1840 *TA*, cf. *land called Haksen* 1655 *HBr* which may also belong here, *v.* **hafoc, dūn** or **denu**, cf. William *le Boteler* 1293 Sydenham, Henry *Botelere* 1403 *Shaft*. HIGHFIELD HO. IVY CROSS, *Ivy(e) Crosse* 1574 JervoiseSh, 1585 BrEll, *Ivy Cross Gdn* 1799 Map, *v.* **īfig, cros**. OLD RECTORY, *Rectory Ho* 1840 *TA*, cf. *Rectory Gdn & Lawn ib*. THE PARK, 1615 Map, 1840 *TA*, cf. *Park Garden(s)* 1565 Hutch[3], 1840 *TA, the Abbey Park* 1585 BrEll, *Park Hill* 1615 Map, 1869 Hutch[3], *The Park Wall* 1615 Map, *Under Park* 1840 *TA, the Out-Park* 1869 Hutch[3], Park Lane & Walk *supra, v.* **park**. ST DENIS (1927), *Cann Villa* (1902). ST JAMES, *v.* under parishes and churches *supra*. ST JOHN'S CTG, cf. *St John's mead* Eliz JervoiseSh, named from the church and par. of St John *supra*. SOUTHEAST CTGS. WILDERNESS, 1811 OS.

FIELD NAMES

The undated forms are 1840 *TA* 184 (*Shaston Holy Trinity, St Peter, St Martin* and *St Lawrence*), except for those marked † which are 1840 *TA* 186 (*Shaston St Rumbold alias Cann*) and those marked ‡ which are 1840 *TA* 185 (*Shaston St James*). Spellings dated 958 (15) are *ShaftR* (S 655), Hy1 (15) *ShaftR*, 1204 *Cur*, 1238, 1420 Cl, 1244, 1268 *Ass*, 1275 RH, 1297, 1320, 1321, 1339, 1341, 1385, 1386, 1394, 1401, 1416, 1426, 1433, 1439, 1486 *Salis*, 1300, 15, 1480, 1488, 1509, 1546, 1568, 1574, 1615, 1625[2], 1642, 1687, 1869 Hutch[3], 1327 *SR*, 1328, 1352, 1356, 1380, 1382, 1384, 1440, 1461, 1464, 1465, 1468, 1471, 1476, 1495, 1500, 1566, 1615[3], 1625 *Sher*, 1331, 1350, 1401[2], 1429, 1444, 1447, 1464 ShaftMR, 1332 SR, 1352[2] Pat, 1360, 1553 *AddCh*, 1388, 1408, 1410, 1479, 1493, 1516 *HarlCh*, 1411 *GillCt*, 1429[2] AD III, 1431 (15), 1432, 1441, 1474 *Wim*, 1450, 1564 *Glyn*, 1453 *Midd*, 1497 Ipm, c.1500, 1782 *Eg*, 1548, 1560, 1562, 1565, 1571, 1582 *Weld*[1], 1561 AD V, 1585 BrEll, 1586 *Comm*, 1615[2], 1799 Map, 1621 (17), 1628 (17) *Strode*, 1650[1] *ParlSurv*, 1650[2] *HBr*, 1664 HTax, 1670, 1671, 1693 *Waller*, 1740, 1766 *SRO*, 1845 *TAMap* (Holy Trinity), and the rest *Shaft* (c.1407). Some of the lost f.ns. in (*b*) may well have been in the area out of which the new par. of Cann was formed in 1894.

(*a*) Angel Cl & Gdn (cf. Angel Lane *supra*); †Bower(')s Md(w) (cf. Robert *Boghier'* 1332, *-Boure* 1516); Boys Md (cf. Robert *Boye* 1351 (c.1407)); Cables Gdn; †Chiswick Md ('cheese-making dairy farm' *v.* **cīese, wīc**); Cliffe Gdn (*clausis . . . vocat' les Clyues* 1356, 1382, *crofta pastur' vocat' les Clyves* 1440, *Cleve* 1461, *Cleue, Clyueclos* 1464, *Clyue(s)* 1465, 1468, *Clyves* 1476, *Clevys* 1495, *Cleves* 1500, *le Clyffe* 1548, *the Clyffe* 1566, *the Cliffe* 1625, *Cliff* 1799, *v.* **clif** (dat.sg. *clife*) 'cliff, bank');

Cockrams; ‡Cold Bath Gdn; ‡Coomb Hays; Copper Street Gdn (named from Coppice St. *supra*); Coppice Cl 1782; Crook Hays; ‡Culvers Cl (*Culver Close Gdn* 1782, *v.* **culfre** 'dove'); ‡Cuttings; Dry Cl 1782; Fountain Mdw; †4 Acres; ‡4 Acres or First Grd (1766, *First Md* 1740); †Garden Fd; ‡Garden Fd; Gascoigns ((*la*) *Garston* 1447, 1461, *le Graston* 1472, *v.* **gærs-tūn** 'grass enclosure'); George Yd (*v.* George Inn *supra*); Hilly Close Gdn (possibly to be identified with *the Hillis Cl* 1650[1]); †*Home Mdw* (-*Md* 1782); House Mdw; †Isaacs' Md; Ivy Close Gdn 1845; ‡Ivy House Fd, Jones Cl or Ivy House Grd; Kein Hill Fm 1869 (perhaps to be associated with *Keynesland* 1431 (15), cf. Hugh *Kene* 1342 (c.1407)); Lamb Gdn & Ho; ‡Lawn (*v.* **launde**); Ledge 1740; Leg Gdn 1782 (shaped like a leg, *v.* **leg**); Long Cl & Md; Lower Md & Plant.; Malthouse Md; Mathew Md Gdn *(Mathewes Meade* 1585, cf. Nicholas *Mathu* 1327); ‡9 Acres or Second Grd; Oathays 1869 (*Oteheys* 1433, cf. *ten' Johannis Oty* 1309 (c.1407)); ‡Orchard; Oxen Croft (*Oxenecroft* 1204, 'enclosure for oxen', *v.* **oxa** (gen.pl. *oxna*), **croft**); † ‡Paddock (*Paddocke* 1650[2], *v.* **pearroc**); Picked Paddock (*v.* **pīced** 'pointed'); †Picks' Md (cf. Peter *Pike* 1664); ‡Plantation; The Pound (cf. Richard *de la Punfaude* 1268 and *Pound* marked on 1615 Map at S end of Magdalene Lane, *v.* **pund-fald, pund**); Quarry (cf. *Quar Clos* 1740, *v.* **quarre**); Rabbitts Fm 1845 (cf. *Rabbit Lane ib*); late Rakes Ho and Gdn; ‡Ralcliffs; †Shaston Md; Shooters Lane Gdn (*v.* Shooter's Lane *supra*);‡ Snooks (cf. John *Snook* 1687); South Md 1782; ‡Speeds; ‡Spring Cl (1782); Stewards Craft 1782 (*v.* **croft**); Sweetmans (cf. Walter *Swetman* 1615); ‡10 Acres; † ‡3 Acres (1740, *croftam . . . q' vocat' proe Acrus* 1352, *Thre akres* 1380, *v.* **þrēo, æcer**); Vanners Md (1740, cf. *estate called Vanners ib,* William *Vanner* 1574); West Bridge 1845; Windmill Cl.

(b) *terram de la ashe, -le Assh'* 1493 (*v.* **æsc** 'ash-tree'); *Avoid's* 1615 (a surname); *Bartlet's* 1615 (cf. Robert *Bartilot* 1345 (c.1407)); *terram de la/le Bere* 1493 (*v.* **bær**[2] '(woodland) pasture' or **bearu** 'wood'); *Berndwode* 1453, *Brendewode* 1474 (*v.* **berned** 'burnt', **wudu**); *Blakehayes* 1562 (*v.* **blæc, (ge)hæg**); *le Blyndstile* c.1407, -*Style* 1415 (*v.* **blind** 'hidden', **stigel**); *atte Bothme* (p) 1314 (c.1407) (*v.* **atte** 'at the', **boðm** 'valley bottom'); *Bradford* 1553 ('broad ford', *v.* **brād, ford**); *on brandes hricg, andlang hrichtes* 958 (15) (*v.* **hrycg** 'ridge'; *brand* may be a late spelling for an OE pers.n. *Brant* found in many p.ns., *v.* Ekwall DEPN s.nn. Brandeston Sf, Branston Lei); *Brandyrescroft'* 1461 (a surname with **croft**); *Burges Meade* 1671 (*v.* **mǣd**, cf. Lawrence *Burgeys* 1293 (c.1407), Kingsman Lane *supra*); *pratum vocatum Canellake* 1358 (c.1407) (*v.* **canel** 'channel', **lacu**); *Canepwode* 1300 (*v.* **wudu**; for the first el. cf. Adam *Kanap', gardini Matillidis Canape* n.d. ?13 (c.1407), *domus Matillis Kanepe* 1297, *Knappes Hall infra*); *Churche Howse, -Lande* 1585; *claus' voc' Croppat* 1453, 1474 (etymology uncertain); *tenement' vocat' Crouchehouse, Walterus atte Crouche . . . ten' meum atte Crouchouse* 1323 (c.1407), (*la*) *Cro(u)ch(e)(h)ous(se)* 1385 (c.1407), 1401 *et freq* to c.1500 (*v.* **crūc**[3] 'cross', **hūs, atte** 'at the'); *ten't voc' Delacourt Dayes* 1670 (a surname); *la Dowre Oke* 1395 (c.1407) (*v.* **dowere** 'dowry', **āc**); *ten' voc' la Dunns Corner* 1394 (c.1407) (the surname *Dunn* with **corner**); *Dylemour* 1385, *Dylmoures* c.1407 (*v.* **dile** 'dill', **mōr**); *Elis-* 1339, 1416, *Elyslond* 1341 (*v.* **land**, cf. John *Elys* 1403 (c.1407)); *Estehegh* 1350, *Esthayes* (*close*) 1401² (*v.* **ēast, (ge)hæg**); *Esthamme* 1431 (15) (*v.* **hamm**); *Fooke's house* 1615 (cf. Richard *Fuk* ?13 (c.1407)); *Fordmere* 1429 (*v.* the st.n. Parson's Pool *supra*); *Foyles* 1615² (a house belonging to the *Foyle* family, *v.* Hutch³ 3 40); *Gappecroft* 1433 (*v.* **gappe** 'gap, breach', **croft**); *Gawen's Land* 1625² (cf. *mes' Joh'is Gowayne* c.1407); *Gerc'ehey* 1350 (*v.* **(ge)hæg**, first el. uncertain); *Goffe House* 1625² (a surname); *Goldesteclife* 1568 (a point in the bounds of Gillingham forest on the Motcombe-Shaftesbury boundary, *v.* **clif**; the first part of the name may represent **gold** or **golde** (cf. the st.n. Gold Hill *supra*) and **ēast** 'east', but the form may be corrupt); *de la Grave* (p) 1351 (c.1407) (*v.* **grāf(a)** 'grove'); *Grayes Barne* 1560, 1582 (cf. John *Graye* Ed 2 (c.1407)); *Gussyscorner* c.1407 (a surname with **corner**); *Halfepenny Land(e)s* 1548, 1560, 1693 (*v.* **halfpenny**, no doubt an allusion to a rent); *Litele-*, *Muchelhalhey* 1333 (c.1407) ('enclosure at a nook', *v.* **healh, (ge)hæg, lȳtel, mycel** 'big'); *tenement' voc' le Hall(e)* 1453, 1474 (cf. Richard *atte Halle* 1345 (c.1407), *v.* **heall, atte** 'at the'); *via regia versus Halywell* 1480 (*v.* **hālig, well(a)**, cf. Hutch¹ 2 6); *le Ham* 1360 (*v.* **hamm**); *claus' voc' Haywode* 1453, *-Heywode* 1474 (*v.* **(ge)hæg, wudu**); *Hintons Lands* 1693 (a surname from one of the Do Hintons); *Hoddyes* 1621 (17), *Huddys* 1628 (17) (cf. *tenement' Willelmi Hody* 1479); *Honihulle, -place* 1431 (15) (*v.* **hunig** 'honey', **hyll, place**); *croftam iuxta Horsmere* 1312 (c.1407), *Horsemer(es)croft(e)* 1319 (c.1407), c.1407 (*v.* **hors, mere¹** 'pool', **croft**); *le Horsse poole* 1548 (*v.* **hors, pōl¹**); *Huntemede* 1331 (*v.* **hunta** 'hunter', **mǣd**); *Joustyng croft* 1394 (c.1407), ioustyng- 1401, *Justingcroft* c.1407 ('croft where jousts were held', *v.* **justing, croft**); *Keate('s) barne* 1615 (a surname); *K(e)ymers* (*Rent*) 1546 (cf. Richard *Kynemere* 1332, Kingsman Lane *supra*); *Kilpekesplace* 1444 (cf. John *Kilpeke ib*, *v.* **place**); *Knappes Hall* 1464 (the surname *Knapp* with **heall**, cf. *Canepwode supra*); *Kowe lease* 1561 (*v.* **cū, lǣs**); *Ky(n)ggesheye* a1335 (c.1407) (cf. Robert *Kyng* 1327, *ten' Ricardi le Kyng* 1351 (c.1407), *v.* **(ge)hæg**); *Lakheigh* 1341, *Lakehey* 1394, *-hei* 1402 (c.1407), *-heys* 1433, *-haies* 1548, *-hayes* 1670 (*v.* **lacu, (ge)hæg**); *Lane's house* 1615; *Langelonde* 1432, *Longlonde* 1453 (*v.* **lang¹, land**); *Littlewood* 1509 (*v.* **lȳtel**); *Lone Coppice* 1546 (*v.* **lane**); *le Lynches* 1453, 1474 (*v.* **hlinc**); *Mad-* 1315 (c.1407), *Medhey* 1360 (*v.* **mǣd, (ge)hæg**); *Manstonys* (a tenement) 1429² (a surname from Manston par. *supra*); *la Marlyngput(t)e* 1394, 1395 (c.1407) (*v.* **marling, pytt**); *Mr Matthews's* (a house) 1615 (cf. *molendinum Johannis Mathies* Ed 1 (c.1407)); *Mawesmede* 1386 (the surname *Maw* with **mǣd**); *the Middle Close* 1650²; *Moggheye* a1335 (c.1407) (the surname or pers.n. *Mogg*, a pet-name for *Margaret*, with **(ge)hæg**); *Mouneks Parrock* 1642 (the surname *Mon(e)k*, with **pearroc**); *Mulehulle* (associated with *molendinum Johannis Mathies*) Ed 1 (c.1407), *Mulehulle* (associated with *Danyelesmulle*) 1328 (cf. the f.n. Daniels in Cann par. *supra*), (*le*) *Mul(l)ehulle* 1352, 1380, 1440, *Millehulle* 1465 ('mill hill', *v.* **myln, hyll**; for other (former) mills in Shaftesbury or Cann, cf. *molendinum Johannis*

Richeman 1312 (c.1407), *uno molendino equorum* a1335 (c.1407), *molendin' in venella voc' Hertlane* 1488 (*v.* Angel Lane *supra*), *molendino equino* 1497, *the Mill Howse* 1585, and *v.* Haimes' Lane in Shaftesbury *supra*, Cann Mill, French Mill and Gear's Mill all in Cann par. *supra*); *Myddel-* 1321, 1426, *Middelhegh'* 1341, *-hey* 1416 (*v.* **middel, (ge)hæg**); (*la*) *Neu(e)litton* 1352², 1394 (c.1407) (*v.* **nīwe** 'new', **līc-tūn** 'burial ground'); *Northey* (*v.* **norð, (ge)hæg**); *Northfeld* 1358 (c.1407) (*v.* **feld**); *Okhurst* 1358 (c.1407) (*v.* **āc, hyrst**); *Peryshers* 1447 (described as a spring, etymology uncertain but perhaps to be associated with the lost st.n. *Pereswelle Lane supra*); *fontem voc' Pilewelle* 1385 (*v.* **pīl** 'a stake', **well(a)**); *Pillowes* 1571 (a surname); *ten'* . . . *voc' Platelplacet* (sic) 1394 (c.1407), *Platellesynne* c.1407, *Platellysplace* c.1500 (cf. Thomas *Platel* 1327, *v.* **place, inn**); *de la Porte* (p) 1238 (*v.* **port²** 'town' or **port³** 'gate'); *Portmanneslond* c.1407 (*v.* **port-mann** 'townsman', **land**); *Putehey* 1360 (cf. *þan waterputte of Syeftebury* Hy1 (15), *v.* **wæter, pytt** 'pit', **(ge)hæg**); *Redeclyf* 1384 (*v.* **rēad** 'red', **clif**); *le(s)/la Redelond'* 1356, 1382, (*les*) *Redelondes* 1440, 1471, (*la*) *Red(e)landes* 1464 *et freq* to 1615³ (*v.* **rēad, land**); *Rodes* 1386 (cf. John *le Rode* 1320, 1327 who is probably identical with John *atte Rede* (sic) 1332, John *atte Rode* 1339; the surname may be from **rodu** 'clearing', *v.* Löfvenberg 167); *Rougheigh'* 1341, *Rowehey* 1394, *Roughey* 1401, *Rogh'hey* 1433 ('rough enclosure', *v.* **rūh, (ge)hæg**); *Ryhulle* 1453, *Ryhill* 1474 ('rye hill', *v.* **ryge, hyll**); *Sadelersplace* 1420 (a surname with **place**); *ten' voc' Siggeberne* 1320 (cf. *ten' quondam Roberti Sygge* 1289 (c.1407), *ten' quondam Nicholi Sigge* Ed 1 (c.1407), *v.* **bere-ærn**); *le Sondes* c.1407 (*v.* **sand**); *Sousters ten'* (a surname); *Stapenorescroftes* 1431 (15) (*v.* **croft**; the first part of the name may be a surname from a p.n. meaning 'steep bank', *v.* **stēap, ōra¹**); *Stillehey* 1433, *Stillhayes Meade* 1562, *Styll hayes* 1565, *Stilliehayes Meade* 1586, *Stilly Meade* 1671 (*v.* **(ge)hæg**, first el. perhaps **stiell** 'enclosure, place for catching fish'); *Strykelhey* 1453, *Styrkelheygh'* 1474 (*v.* **(ge)hæg**, R. Stirchel in RNs. *infra*); *Thorn Mead* 1625² (*v.* **þorn**); *le Thres(s)(h)fold(e)* 1439, 1486 ('enclosure where threshing was done', *v.* **þersc, fald**); *terram Ade atte Tone* 1323 (c.1407) (cf. Roger *atte Toneshende* 1332, *v.* **atte, tūn, ende**); *Treisborn* 1358 (c.1407) (*-born* perhaps for *-bern*, *v.* **bere-ærn** 'barn', cf. Walter *Tray* 1388); *Trustrum's* 1615 (a surname); *Tuyssh' Cornere* 1401, *Tusshescornere* c.1407 (*v.* **corner**, first el. no doubt a surname); *Vyellesmore* 1426, *Vill's* 1625² (the surname *Viel* with **mōr**); *ten' Galfridi de la Wadesynde* (sic, probably for *Wodes-*) 1293 (c.1407) (*v.* **wudu, ende**); *Wayt(e)hulle* c.1407 (*v.* **hyll**, possibly with **waite** 'watch, look-out'); *Weyleshey* 1464 (a surname with **(ge)hæg**); *West Close* 1650²; *Westmede* 1431 (15) (*v.* **mæd**); *la Wich' iuxta Touthull'* 1411 (*v.* **wīc** 'farm' or **wice** 'wych-elm', *v.* the st.n. Tout Hill *supra*); *Williames-* 1453, *Wyllyamsheyes* 1474 (a pers.n. or surname with **(ge)hæg**); *Wiltonesplace* 1372 (c.1407), *Wiltone place* 1388 (c.1407), *Wiltonys-* 1408, *Wyltonesplace* 1410 (*v.* **place**, cf. John *de Wylton* 1372 (c.1407); *atte Wowe* (p) 1351 (c.1407) ('at the crooked place', if this is a substantival use of **wōh** 'crooked', *v.* **atte**); *Wyghtlokeshei* c.1407 (the surname *Whitelock* and **(ge)hæg**); *crofta vocat' Wyȝtteney, Wyȝrtonehy* c.1500 (represented as

Wyrtteney, Wyrlonchy in Hutch[3] **3** 87; the forms are probably corrupt, and the etymology therefore is unclear); *on wyndrede dic, of þare diche* 958 (15) (*v.* **dīc** 'ditch'; the first part of the name is obscure); *Wytemore* 1268, 1317 (p) (*v.* **hwīt, mōr**); *Yong(e)wode* 1432, 1441 (*v.* **geong** 'young', **wudu**); *Yverehey* 1453, *Yveryhey* 1474 (probably the surname *Ivery* with **(ge)hæg**).

XXI. STURMINSTER NEWTON HINTON ST MARY

In c.1086 GeldR this hundred had a smaller extent than at present since at that date Okeford F. par. was in *Hunesberge* hundred **2** 86 (Anderson 134, VCHDo **3** 137, Eyton 124, 135). Bagber in Sturminster N. par. is a tithing in Cranborne hundred **2** 194 from 1327 *SR*, and Thorton in Marnhull par. is a tithing in Redlane hundred *supra* from the same date (it was earlier in the GeldR hundred of *Gelingeham*). Belchalwell in Okeford F. is a tithing in Cranborne hundred from 1664 HTax (**2** 95–6, 194). A tithing of *Redlane* is included in this hundred in 1664 HTax, but is not otherwise found, cf. Redlane hundred *supra*.

Newentone hundret c.1086 GeldR, *hdr' de Niwetona* 1130 PR, *Niwenton'* 1160, *Niweton' hdr'* 1168 both P, (*hundredum de*) *Niweton(')* 1177, 1188 both P, 1212 Fees, 1236 FF, 1265 Misc (*-and Boclande*), 15 ShaftR, *-tun(e)* (*Kastel*) 14 GlastC, *Newetonecastel, Nywetone Castel* 13 (m14) *Glast, New(e)ton'* 1244, 1268 *Ass*, 1280 *ib* (*-et Bokelaunde*), 1316 FA (*-et Bocland*), *Neu(e)ton'* 1244, 1268 *Ass*, *Nyweton* 1303 FA, 1340 NI, 1346, 1428 FA, *Nyeutone et Boclonde* 1327 *SR*, *Nywton' Bouclond'* 1332 SR, *Nuton Buckelon* 1539 LP, *Sturminster Newton Castle* 1664 HTax, 1795 Boswell. Named from Newton in Sturminster Newton par. *infra*. It belonged to Glastonbury Abbey, like Buckland Newton hundred *infra* with which it is often combined in early records (e.g. 1265 Misc, 1280 *Ass*, 1332 SR).

Hinton St Mary

HINTON ST MARY (ST 786162)

(*at, to*) *Hamtun(e)* 944 (15) ShaftR (S 502), 958 (15) *ib* (S 656)

Haintone 1086 DB, *-ton'* 1212 Fees

Henton' abbatisse Sancti Edwardi 1212 Fees, *Henton(e)* 1244 (p), 1268, 1288 all *Ass*, 1290 (15) ShaftR, 1291 Tax *et freq* to 1547 Ct, *Henton Mary* 1535 VE, 1584

Weld[1], *-Marie* 1581 *ib*
Heynton' 1327 *SR*
Hynton Mare (sic) Hy 8 *AOMB*, *-maries* 1575 Saxton,
Hinton Marye 1627 *SxAS*

'High farm, farm situated on high land', from **hēah**
(wk.obl. *hēan*) and **tūn**. Although this is a common name
(*v.* DEPN), the other Do Hintons have a different origin, *v.*
Hinton Martell par. 2 146. The village occupies a 300′ hill
overlooking R. Stour. The affix is from its possession by the
abbey of St Mary (and St Edward), Shaftesbury, as first
suggested by Hutch[1] 2 201, *v.* VCHDo 3 82, cf. the form
from 1212 Fees, and the boundary mark *on nunnen linc* in
f.ns. *infra*. The OE forms (from the 15th cent. Shaftesbury
Register) show confusion with the common el. **hām-tūn**.
The bounds of the Anglo-Saxon estate of *Hamtun(e)* are
given in 944 (15) *ShaftR* (S 502).

YEWSTOCK (ST 787155), *Hevedstokke, Hevedstokforlang'* e14
GlastE, la Hevedstocke 1338–40 Glast, m14 *Glast, la
Hendestok* (for *Heude-*) n.d. Fägersten 41, *la Handestock* (for
Haude-) n.d. Hutch[3], *Hewstock* 1811 OS, (*Lr*) *Yewstock* 1841
TA, v. **hēafod-stocc** 'a post on which the head of a
beheaded criminal was exposed', cf. Hewstock Fm in
Beaminster *infra* which has the same origin. The cottage of
this name stands on the par. bdy between Hinton and
Sturminster N., and most of the early forms occur as bdy
marks in medieval perambulations of Sturminster (*v.*
SoRecSoc 64 606, *Glast* f. 223, Hutch[3] 4 338).

BURT'S FM. CUT MILL (LANE), (*water greist mill called*)
Cut(te)myll(e), Cutmyl Close Eliz *LRMB, Cuttmill* [Bridge]
1791 Boswell, *Cut Mill* 1811 OS, from **cut** 'water-channel',
myln; there is mention of a mill at Hinton in 1086 DB
(VCHDo 3 82). HINTON LANE. JOYFE'S COPPICE, *Joyces-*
1841 TA, cf. the f.n. *Joices'* in Marnhull par. *infra*. LEIGH
LANE, cf. *Lye Close* Eliz *LRMB*, (*Long*) *Leigh* 1841 *TA,
v.* **lēah** 'wood, glade or clearing in a wood'. LOVELL'S
COPPICE, *Lovels-* 1841 *ib*, cf. Lovell's Court in Marnhull
par. *infra*. MANOR HO, cf. *the scyte or farme of Henton* Eliz

LRMB. Marriage Lane, cf. *Mar(r)edge (Close)* Eliz *ib,* *Marige* 1557 *Val,* 1627 *SxAS, Marudge* 1564 *Weld*[1], *Maryge* 1567 *Glouc, Marrage* 1841 *TA,* perhaps 'mare ridge' from **mere**[2] and **hrycg**, cf. Henstridge So which is 'stallion ridge' (DEPN). Meatyard's Coppice, cf. James *Metyard* 1664 HTax (Marg. Marsh). Park Coppice, 1841 *TA,* cf. *Parke Close, -Woode* Eliz *LRMB, Park Cl* 1841 *TA, v.* **park,** Cantor & Wilson **11** 173. Ridgeway Lane, cf. *Riggewaies* 1584 *Weld*[1], *(Hr & Lr) Ridgeway* 1841 *TA, v.* **hrycg-weg.** St Peter's Church, cf. John *atte Church'* 1332 SR, *Little Churchyard, Lyt'le Churche Yarde* Eliz *LRMB, The Church-acre* 1869 Hutch[3], *v.* **atte** 'at the', **cirice.** Steart Lane, cf. William *de la Sterte* 1316 *AD* (Marnhull), *(land called) Stertes* Eliz *LRMB, Steart* 1841 *TA, v.* **steort** 'tail of land'. (Hr) Twinwood Coppice, Twinwood Lane, *close called Twynwoode, -wodd* Eliz *LRMB, Twinwood Coppice* 1841 *TA,* probably '(land) between the woods', from **betwēonan** and **wudu,** *v.* Wood Lane *infra* which is nearby and cf. Tanwood Wo 238. Vicarage, cf. *Vicarage Gdn* 1841 *TA.* Wood Lane, cf. *Richard-* 1291 Hutch[3], William *Bithewode* 1327 *SR,* William *atte Wode* 1332 SR, *Wood Coppice, Fd, Md, Nursery & Orchd, (Lt) Wood(land), Hr, Lr & Middle Wood* 1841 *TA, v.* **bī** 'by', **atte** 'at the', **wudu,** cf. Twinwood *supra.*

FIELD NAMES

The undated forms are 1841 *TA* 109. Spellings dated 944 (15) are *ShaftR* (S 502), 968 (14) *Glast* (S 764), 1291 Hutch[3], e14 *GlastE,* 1327 *SR,* 1332 SR, 1338–40 Glast, m14 *Glast,* 1557 *Val,* Eliz *LRMB,* 1559 *DLCt,* 1564, 1581, 1584 *Weld*[1], 1567 *Glouc,* 1627 *SxAS,* and 1664 HTax.

(a) Ash Tree Grd (cf. *Aishcombe* 1584, *v.* **æsc, cumb**); Barbers Md (cf. Nicholas *le Barbour* e14 (Sturminster N.)); Barley Yard Orchd; Beerleigh (probably for *Been-*), Benleigh (*Bynley* Eliz, *Bindley* 1564, 'clearing where beans were grown', *v.* **bēan, lēah**); Blackland(s); Bothhill; Brake Flg (*v.* **bræc**[1] 'brushwood'); Broad Close (Orchd) (*Brodeclose* Eliz, *v.* **brād**); Broad Wall; Burlands Cl; Catsbrain (*v.* **cattes-brazen**); (Green) Chaffey, Chaffey Cmn, Lamberts Chaffey (*Chalfey Close, close called Chavey, Chawfhay, Lytell Chawf Hayes, Lytle Chawfhayes* Eliz, *Chaffehey* 1564, *Chaffey* 1584, 'calf enclosure', *v.* **cealf, (ge)hæg, lȳtel** cf. John *Lambert* Eliz, Chaffeymoor in Bourton par. *supra* which has a different origin, and the f.n. Chaff hay Cl **2** 98); Chiverick Md (*Cheveret, Cheverytt, Chyverett*

Eliz, *Cheverett* 1584, a name of Anglo-Saxon origin also preserved in the stream name Chivrick's Brook *q.v.* in RNs. *infra*); Corner Cl; Costly Md (*Cors(e)ley Meade* Eliz, Costel(e)y Meade 1557, 1627, possibly analogous with Corsley W 152 which is a hybrid name from Welsh **cors** 'marsh, bog' and **lēah** 'wood, clearing'; this field lies beside Chivrick's Brook); Crab Tree (Fd); Yonder and Hthr Crisplands; Dykes Hay (*Dyxey* Eliz, etymology uncertain); East End (*mead called Estende, East Ende* Eliz, *v.* **ēast, ende**[1]); 5 Acres; 40 Acres Orchd; 14 Acres; Foxen hills (perhaps a variant of the common f.n. Foxhill(s) (cf. PN Gl **4** 127, PN Brk 869) with an analogical wk.pl. in *-en*, *v.* **-ena**); Gardeners Md; Green Croft; Greenway (*Greneways* Eliz, *v.* **grēne**[1], **weg**); Hand Flg (*close called Hamfurlonge* Eliz, *v.* **hamm, furlang**); Harris Pce; Heart Lane Cl; Hempits (*mead called Impettes, Ympetts* Eliz, perhaps 'hemp pits' (cf. PN Ch **5** 207), *v.* **hænep, pytt**); Higher Grd; Hitsel (*Hedeswell Close* 1557, 1627, to be identified with the bdy point *of hefdeswelle, on efdeswelle* 944 (15) in the Anglo-Saxon bounds of Hinton St M, which corresponds with *to hedeswelle* 968 (14) in the Anglo-Saxon bounds of Sturminster N., and with *Hedeswell(e)* 1338–40, m14 in the 14th cent. bounds of Sturminster N., from **hēafod** 'head' (exact sense uncertain, possibly 'headland (in a field)' or 'end of a ridge', *v.* Forsberg 144) and **well(a)** 'spring'); Holly Acre (*Hollacre* Eliz, *Holleacres* 1557, *Hole Acre(s)* 1567, 1584, *Holey Acres* 1627, *v.* **hol**[2] 'hollow', **æcer**); Home Cl (*Whome Close* Eliz, *v.* **home**); Home Grd & Md; Hyle (probably to be identified with *close called Hill* Eliz although the forms are discrepant, the earlier pointing to **hyll** 'hill', the later probably to **healh** (dat.sg. *hēale*) 'a nook'); Lake (Fd & Orchd), Hthr & Yonder Lake (*Lak, Lak(e) Close* Eliz, (*Le*) *Lake* 1564, 1567, *the Lake* 1627, *Netherlake* 1559, *Yonder La(c)ke* 1564, 1584, *v.* **lacu** 'stream'); Landmoor; Long Ash; Long Cl; Long Croft (*Langcrofte* Eliz, *v.* **lang**[1], **croft**); (Higher or) Middle Fd(s); Middle Grd; Moor Cl & Md (*More close, Moremede* Eliz, *More* 1564, *v.* **mōr** 'marshy ground'); New Cl (*Newclose* Eliz, *v.* **nīwe**); Gt & Lt North Fd (*le North(e)feld(*' *)* 1557, 1567, *Northfe(i)lde* Eliz, *in campo Borial*' 1584, *the Northe Fyelde* 1627, *v.* **norð**); Orchard Grd; The Pound; Quar Fd (*v.* **quarre**); Rixey Moor (*Rixye More* Eliz, *v.* **riscig** 'rushy', **mōr**, cf. *Ryxbedd* ib 'rush bed', *v.* **risc, bedd**); Ryeland(s) (*Row-* 1557, *Raylandes* 1567, 1627; in spite of the first form which points to a first el. **rūh** 'rough', possibly **ēg-land**, **īeg-land** 'island' or **ēa-land** 'land by a river', with *R-* from ME *atter* 'at the', cf. Ryland C (EPN **1** 148), Nyland in Kington M. par. *supra*; the fields in question lie close to Chivrick's Brook); Sandmoor (Md); Sarge (Md & Orchd) (*meade in Sarge, Sergeclose, Serge Mede* Eliz, *Sergehais, -heis* 1564, *Seeghei(e)s* 1584; first el. uncertain, but perhaps a surname (*v.* Reaney *s.n.* Search) or ModE *serge* 'woollen fabric' used in some figurative sense, with **mǣd**, **(ge)hæg**); Sheepland (*Shepelandes* Eliz, *v.* **scēap**); Sheep Lease (*v.* **lǣs**); Short Cl & Hill; Small Coppice; Small Md (*Smal(le)me(a)de* Eliz, *v.* **smæl**); Soap Shop Orchd; Stockland (cf. *ij closes called Stockefurlonge* Eliz, *v.* **stocc** 'tree-trunk, stump'); Stony Hill & Ld (*Stonyland* Eliz, *v.* **stānig**); 3 Corner Moor; Town End; Whey and Curds (perhaps an allusion to soil-type); Wick pit (possibly **wīc** 'dwelling, dairy farm'); Wilds Wd; Winsel Fd; Withy Bed Md; Yeatmans Coppice (cf. *Elizabeth Yateman* 1664); Yonder Md; Youngs Wd (cf. Geoffrey *le Jeonge* 1291, *-le Yonge* 1327).

(*b*) *on adwines imare, up anlang imares* 944 (15) ('Ēadwine's boundary', from the pers.n. *Ēadwine* and **(ge)mǣre**); *be þane akere heueden* 944 (15) ('the ends of arable plots', *v.* **æcer, hēafod**); *le Backeside* 1557, *the backside* 1627 (*v.* **backside**); *Bookesfurlonge* Eliz (a surname); *Brode me(a)de* Eliz (*v.* **brād**); *cotag' voc' Chap(p)er cote* 1557, 1567, *Chapers* (*Cote*) Eliz, 1627 (*v.* **cot**, cf. John *Chaper* 1327 (Manston)); *on chelbrichtes dich* 944 (15) ('Cēolbeorht's ditch', from the OE pers.n. *Cēolbeorht* and **dīc**); *Colleshay* Eliz, *-Haye* 1584 (*v.* **(ge)hæg**, cf. Robert *Colle* 1327 (Stour P.)); *The Cop(p)ice* Eliz (*v.* **copis**); *Cow(e)ham* Eliz, 1584 (*v.* **cū, hamm**); *Culsham* 1557, 1627 (from **hamm** with a pers.n. or surname, cf. *Colleshay supra*); *Curshefurlonge* Eliz (*v.* **furlang**, first el. uncertain); *anlang diche, to dich þanen anlang dich* 944 (15) (*v.* **dīc** 'ditch'); *Egieclose* 1557, 1567, *Egiedye Close* 1627 (first el. uncertain); *Ferettes* Eliz (a surname); *atte Gore* (p) 1327, 1332 ('at the point of land', *v.* **atte, gāra**); *cottage called Hastylers* Eliz (the surname *Hastler*); *of* [for *on*] *þane hegen, of þane hegen* 944 (15) (*v.* **hege** 'hedge, fence'); *Hode Closse* Eliz (**hōd¹** 'hood' or **hōd²** 'shelter', *v.* **clos(e)**); *2 closes called Holcombes* Eliz (*v.* **hol², cumb**); *terr' voc' Huntes* 1581 (a surname); *Hurlesplecke* Eliz, *-Pleck* 1564 (a surname with **plek** 'small plot'); *on-*, *of litiges heuede* 944 (15) (corresponding with *on litegesheued* 968 (14) in the bounds of Sturminster N., *q.v. infra*); *Lytle Meades* Eliz; *Lytle Paroke* Eliz (*v.* **pearroc**); *parocke called Mantelles* Eliz (a surname); *on þane mapelder, of þane mapeldere* 944 (15) ('the maple-tree', *v.* **mapuldor**); *Myddelwaye* Eliz (*v.* **middel, weg**); *on nunnen linc, of nunnene linche* 944 (15) (corresponding with *on minnanlinche* (sic for *nunnan-*) 968 (14), *Mimuanlinch'* (sic) 1338–40 in the bounds of Sturminster N., 'ridge or bank of the nuns', from **nunne** (gen.pl. *nunnena*) and **hlinc**, in allusion to the nuns of Shaftesbury who possessed Hinton St Mary); *Odfurlonge, Odd Furlonge* Eliz (*v.* **odde** 'odd'); *at oxene bricge* 944 (15) ('river crossing used for oxen', *v.* **oxa** (gen.pl. *oxena*), **brycg**; on R. Stour); *the Pitts* Eliz (*v.* **pytt**); *Pleyclose* Eliz (*v.* **plega** 'play, sport'); *Rowham* Eliz (*v.* **rūh** 'rough', **hamm**); *atte Slade* (p) 1332 ('at the valley', *v.* **atte, slæd**); *le Southfeld* 1557, *the South Fyelde* 1627; *on þane stream, anlang streames* 944 (15) (*v.* **strēam** 'stream', with reference to Chivrick's Brook, *v.* RNs. *infra*); *at sudwde* 944 (15) ('south wood', *v.* **suð, wudu**); *Westfyeld, -feilde* Eliz; *Wires Close* Eliz (a surname).

Margaret Marsh

Formerly a chapelry of Iwerne Minster (Boswell, Hutch³ **3** 549)

MARGARET MARSH (ST 824187)

Margaretysmerschchurche 1395 *MiltC*, *-merssh'churche*

1395 (e15) *MiltRoll*
Margaret(t) Marsh(e) Eliz ChancP, 1575 *KCC et passim,*
Margret marshe 1575 Saxton
Margatt Mershe Eliz *LRMB, Margetsmarshe* 1581,
Marget(t) Marsh 1584 *Weld*[1]
St Margarets Marsh 1811 OS

From **mersc** 'marsh', with **cirice** 'church'. *Margaret* may
be from the dedication of the church as first suggested by
Hutch[1] **2** 202 (and accepted by Fägersten 41), but it is
probably more likely to have been the name of an early
owner of the ground itself, and, in view of its having
belonged to Shaftesbury abbey (Hutch[3] **3** 549), perhaps the
Margaret in question is one of the two 14th cent. abbesses so
named, *Margaret Auch(i)er* 1315–29 or *Margaret de Leucen-
ore* or *de Leukenore* 1350–62 (Hutch[3] **3** 27, VCHDo **2** 79).
The church dedication will then have followed at a later date,
as it did at Osmington **1** 211. The nearby Guy's Marsh in
Cann par. *supra* (with forms from 1401) may suggest that the
Marsh was originally a fairly extensive tract of marshy
ground, later divided and differentiated according to
ownership, cf. also the adjacent Marsh Cmn in Fontmell M.
par. *supra*. Indeed the following (mainly earlier) simplex
forms may (partly) belong here: *feodo quod vocat' Le Marays*
1244 *Ass* (ME **mareis** 'marsh'), *la Marshe* 1310 Hutch[3],
terra . . . Abbatisse in La Merssh' 1348 (15) *ShaftR* (with
reference of course to the abbess of Shaftesbury), *le Marsh*
1560 Hutch[3], cf. also *pastur' . . . voc Alfledemers* 1275 RH
(first el. the OE fem. pers.n. *Ælfflæd* or *Æðelflæd*), *Robert in
the Mersch* 1327 *SR, -in the Merssh'* 1332 SR (taxed in
Thorton and Todber).

Much of the present par. of Margaret Marsh seems to
have been included within the bounds of the Anglo-Saxon
estate of Thorton (in Marnhull par. *infra*) described in 958
(15) *ShaftR* (S 656).

GORE FM (ST 835205), *Gora* 1282 *AddCh,* 1282 (15) *ib*
(*Cantar' in monasterio Shafton vocat' Cantar' de*-), *la Gore*
1358 *Salis* (*Cantuarie de*-), 1358 (c.1407) *Shaft,* 1390 IpmR
(*-juxta Shaftesbury*), 1474 *Wim,* 1551 *AddCh* (*Cantarie*

Sancte Anne de-), *le Gore* 1360 *ib*, 1390 Hutch[3], 1774 Hutch[1], 1811 OS, *the Gore* (*by Shaftysbury*) 1390 Cl, *the Goore* 1395 (e15) *MiltRoll, Gore* 1431 FA (*cantarie de-*), cf. Adam-, Cristina *atte Gore* 1327 *SR*, John *atte Gore* 1332 SR (all taxed in Hinton St Mary), *Goore Wood* Eliz *LRMB, Gorestrete* 1576 *Glyn, Goore Coppice, -Grove* 1663, *Gore Close* 1689 *Whil.* 'The triangular plot of ground', *v.* **gāra**, still an accurate description of this NE end of Margaret Marsh, *v.* also **atte, strǣt**. For the former chapel and chantry of St Anne here (attached to Shaftesbury abbey), *v.* Hutch[3] 3 79, VCHDo 2 75.

CHURCH FM & LANE, cf. *Church Close* Eliz *LRMB*, 1843 *TA, -Orchd ib*, named from St Margaret's Church *infra.* HIGHER FM. JOPP'S FM, cf. *Joppysforde* 1395 *MiltC*, 1395 (e15) *MiltRoll, Joppes Grove, -Hill* Eliz *LRMB, Gope's* [Bridge] 1791 Boswell, named from the family of Geoffrey *Jop* 1291 Hutch[3], Juliana *Joppe* 1327 *SR*, 1332 SR (Hinton St M.), *v.* **ford, grāf(a), hyll.** The ford would have been by the farm where a road crosses Key Brook. The farm is *Jolston Fm* 1811 OS. LOWER FM. MARGARET MARSH FM, MARSH FM, *v.* par. name *supra.* ST MARGARET'S CHURCH, *Margaretysmerschchurche* 1395 *MiltC*, and *v.* par. name *supra.*

FIELD NAMES

The undated forms in (*a*) are 1843 *TA* 141, and those in (*b*) are Eliz *LRMB.* Spellings dated 1332 are SR, 16 *Glyn*, 1545, 1560, 1588 Hutch[3], and Eliz *LRMB.*

(*a*) Ash Md; Bottom Md (*v.* **botm**); Bushy Cl (cf. *Busshe Lees* Eliz, *v.* **busc, lǣs**); Clover Cl; Gt & Lt Coles (a surname); Corn Cl; Cranes Hay (*Craneshay* Eliz, cf. John-, Thomas *Cra*(*y*)*n* 1332 (Hinton St M.), *v.* **(ge)hæg**); Drove Lane; Forey Cl (the form may be corrupt if *Foxye Close* Eliz belongs here); 4 Acre Fd, 4 Acres, 4 Acre(s) Md; Gt Frickers, Frickers Md (a surname); Halter path lane; Hatch Md (*v.* **hæc(c)**); Heals (a surname); Higher Grd; Hills (cf. *close called Hill, Hill acre, Hillcloses* all Eliz, *v.* **hyll**); Home Grd, Md & Orchd (cf. *Whomeclose, -crofte* Eliz, *v.* **home**); Horse Cl; Lambs Md; Little Acre; Little Md (*Lytle Meade* Eliz, *v.* **mǣd**); Lodges Md; Long Grd; Long Md (*Longemeade* Eliz); Long Strap (*v.* **strap**); Lower or Home Md; Luffwood; Marnhull Md (*v.* Marnhull par. *infra*); Moor (*v.* **mōr**); 9 Acres; North Grd (Md); North Md; Lt, Old & Young Orchard; Pit Md (*v.* **pytt**); Priest Lds (*Prest*(*e*) *Land*(*s*) 1545, 1560, *Prestland*(*e*)(*s*) Eliz, 1588, 'priests' lands', *v.* **prēost** (gen.pl. *prēosta*), land); Second Cl; Sedge Md (v. **secg**[1]); Selt Md, Gt & Lt Sill Md, Silt Md (*Sikkemeade* (for *Silke-*) 16, *Sylke Me(a)de* Eliz, v. **sēoluc** 'gulley, small drain'); Shortlands (-*landes* Eliz, v. **sc(e)ort**); 6 Acre Fd; 16 Acres; Stall Md (v. **stall**); Summerfield, Summer Grd, Summerlease (v. **sumor, lǣs**); 2 Acre Md; Uplands (v. **upp**); West Leaze (*Westlees* Eliz, v. **lǣs**); Whettys Md (*Whetehayes* Eliz, v. **hwǣte** 'wheat', **(ge)hæg** 'enclosure'); Woodcock Mdw (v. **woodcock**).

(b) Barlye Close (v. **bærlic**); Beane close (v. **bēan**); Blackeland (v. **blæc**); Brache Meades (v. **brǣc** 'land broken up for cultivation', **mǣd**); Brode Close (v. **brād**); Chalcottes Meade (a surname); Chipman Close (a surname); Copped Close(s) (v. **coppede** 'peaked, pointed'); Foxye Close (v. **fox, (ge)hæg**, cf. Forey Cl *supra*); Great Close, Grete Meade (v. **grēat**); Grene Close, Grenehayes (v. **grēne**[1], **(ge)hæg**); the Grove, Grove Close, -Me(a)de (v. **grāf(a)**); Kynneshay (v. **(ge)hæg**, probably with a surname); Lagmeade (v. **lagge** 'marsh'); (Yandes) Longe Close (first el. probably a surname, though the third letter is doubtful); Myddell meade (v. **middel**); Northbroke (probably '(land) to the north of the brook', v. **norðan, brōc**); Northehaye(s) (v. **norð, (ge)hæg**); Oxen Lees (v. **oxa, lǣs**); the parock lye (v. **pearroc** 'small enclosure', **lēah** 'clearing in a wood'); Runnyng(e) Close, -Meade (v. **running**); (Brode) seven Acres (v. **brād**); Southeheyes (v. **sūð, (ge)hæg**); Uppenham (v. **uppan** 'higher up, upon', **hamm** 'enclosure'); West Closes, -Meade; Whe(a)t(e) Close (v. **hwǣte**); Woorthe, Woorthayes (v. **worð** 'enclosure', **(ge)hæg**).

Marnhull

MARNHULL (ST 782187) ['mɑːnəl]

Marnhull(e) 1267 (m14) Glast, e14 GlastE, 1303 Pat, 1316 FA, AD, 1330 Ch, 1332 SR, 1338–40 Glast, 1341–2 GlastF, 1343 Pat (p), 1347 Ipm, Cl, 1349 DCMDeed, 1362 Cl et passim, -hule 1338–40 Glast

Marenhull 1274 Pat, 1308 FF, Marenull(e) 1291 Tax, Maren Hull' 1327 SR

Marenil 1291 Tax

Marmhull 1340 NI, Marmehull 1369 Cl

Marnehull(') 1417 IpmR, 1443 KCC et freq to e17 Weld[1]

Marnell(e) 1426 IpmR, Hy 8 Rent, 1535–43 Leland

Marnehill 1428, 1431 FA, 1448 Pat

Marnhyll, -hill 1489 Ipm

v. **hyll** 'hill'. Ekwall DEPN supposes that the first el. here as well as in Marnham Nt (*Marneham* DB) and Marlcliff Wo, Wa (*Marnan clive, Mearnan clyfe* 9th cent. in 11th cent. copy) is an OE pers.n. **M(e)arna* (comparing OG

Marningum, v. Förstemann ON ii, 214), cf. PN Nt 190, PN Wo 314, PN Wa 202. On the other hand Kökeritz 122–3 favours a significant word **m(e)arn-*, perhaps to be connected with the OE adj. *mearu* 'tender, soft', which may have applied to 'some kind of stone or clay, for there are quarries both at Marlcliff Hill and at Marnhull'. As pointed out in PN Wa 202, however, the stone quarried at Marlcliff is marble-like whereas that at Marnhull is a Corallian limestone (RCHM 3 148, cf. Hutch³ 4 305), and there are no quarries at all at Marnham Nt.

In the absence of very early forms, there can be no certainty about the first el. of Marnhull. However, the frequency of *Maren-* (alternating with *Marn-*) among the earliest forms, and the relatively late appearance of forms with medial *e* (*Marme-, Marne-*), should be noted, and may suggest that the first el. here is different to that in the other two names. Unfortunately the OE adj. *mearu* (wk.obl. *mearwan*) itself, although perhaps topographically suitable if taken to refer to the limestone found here, is hardly likely in view of the total absence of *-w-* among the forms.

Two early forms *Meirnhylle* 12 and *Mereinhylle* 13, cited by F. Perks, *The Biography of the Dorset Village of Marnhull* (n.d.) from Salisbury diocesan archives, look unreliable in view of the run of spellings above and in any case do not help in identifying the first el.

BERE (lost), *maner'* . . . *de Bere* (*et More*) 1454 *HarlCh*, no doubt the home of Richard *de la Bere* 1285 FA, 1316 ib, *AD*, 1332 SR, 1339 *AddCh* (who held lands in Thorton *infra* and in the adjacent par. of Todber *supra*), cf. also Agnes *de la Bere* 1327 *SR*, 1332 SR, probably from **bær²** '(woodland) pasture', cf. Bere Marsh 2 239. *More* is Moor Court *infra*, so the place was probably near here or Thorton Fm in the E of the present par. In fact a more precise location is possible if the name is to be identified with the first el. of the f.n. *Berry Wood* 1838 *TA* (*boscus voc' Berewood* 16 *Glyn*, spelling slightly uncertain), which is SW of Thorton Fm at ST 800175.

BURTON ST.   (ST 775193)
   Buret(une), *Burton'* 13 GlastR, *Bureton(e)* 13 (m14) *Glast,*
      14 *GlastC*, 1338–40 Glast, *Burtun'* 1244 *Ass, Borton'*
      1268 *ib*, 1342 GlastF, *Burton(e)* 1288 *Ass*, e14 *GlastE,*
      1338 FF, 1347 Cl, 1350 Orig (*Asshe et-*) *et passim,*
      -*tona* 1338–40 Glast, *Boreton(e)* e14 *GlastE*, 14 *GlastC,*
      1338–40 Glast
   Asscheburton' e14 *GlastE, Naysshe Burton* 1477 IpmR,
      Asshburton 1517 Hutch[3] (-'otherwise called *Burton*
      Aysshe'), *Nashburton* 1590 *Hen*[2]
   Burtone Asshe 1347 Ipm, *Burton atte Nass(h)e* 1348 Misc,
      1362, 1372 Cl, *Bourton atte Nass(h)e* 1371 ib, Pat

   'Fortified farmstead', or 'farmstead near a fortification', *v.*
burh-tūn, cf. Bourton par. *supra*. *Assche, Naysshe, atte*
Nasshe, etc, refer to Nash Court *infra*. The name now
survives only as a st.n., mentioned as *Burton St.* 1870
Hutch[3], cf. *Bo'tons Lane* 1548 Ct.

EASTWELL LANE (ST 785178), from *Estwel'*, -*wulle* 13
GlastR, -*welle* e14 *GlastE, East Well, Eastwell* (*Md*) 1838
TA, 'eastern spring', *v.* **ēast, well(a)**; there is a spring
marked 6″ by the lane, which lies E of Walton *infra*.

KENTLESWORTH (lost, site unknown)
   Kenteleswrth(') 13 GlastR, 14 *GlastC*, -*wurth(')* 1236 FF,
      e14 *GlastE*, -*worth(e)* 1265 (m14) *Glast*, e14 *GlastE,*
      1313, 1333 FF, 1338–40 Glast, 1384 Cl, 1407 IpmR,
      1431 FA, 1451 IpmR, *Kentlesworth(')* 14 *GlastC*, 1342
      GlastF (-*qui modo dicitur Marnhulle*), *Kentelis-*
      1338–40 Glast, *Kentelysworth(')* 1394 *Russ*
   Kentelewor (sic) 1268 *Ass*
   Kenlesworth (sic) 1489 Ipm
   Kentisford or Kentisworth 1774 Hutch, 1870 Hutch[3],
      Kentisford 1795 Boswell

   'Centel's enclosure', from **worð** and an unrecorded OE
pers.n. *Centel* (which would be a derivative of *Cent-* in
Centwine, -*weald*, etc). According to Ekwall DEPN the
same pers.n. is evidenced in Kentisbeare D 564 (as well as in
two minor names in the same par.) and in Kentisbury D 49,

and Fägersten notes another lost *Kentelesworth* in So. It seems unnecessary to consider an appellative as first el., certainly in this name, cf. Kökeritz 123. The exact location of this place remains unknown, in spite of Taylor, DoNHAS **88** 208-9: any connection of the first el. of this name with the *Chetel* of DB (VCHDo **3** 73) is unlikely, this being a pers.n. of quite different origin, unless *Chetel* is taken to be a scribal error for *Chentel* due to the omission of the nasal stroke. The interesting alternation of the name with Marnhull in the form from 1342 GlastF should however be noted ('which is *now* called'): it suggests that Marnhull had probably by this date replaced *Kentelesworth* as the name of a larger unit, although at the same date both Knightstreet and Yardgrove *infra* were said to be *in Kentlesworth*.

KING'S MILL (BRIDGE) (ST 766171), *Kingesmulun* 13 GlastR (p), *-molne* 1268 *Ass* (p), *Kyngesmulle* e14 *GlastE* (p) (mention of *molendinum aquaticum*), *Kingsmill* [Bridge] 1791 Boswell, *Kines Mill* 1811 OS, *Kings Bridge* 1839 *TAMap*, *Kings* [Mill], *Kingsmill Bridge* 1870 Hutch[3], *v.* **cyning**, **myln** 'mill'. In 1086 DB some lands (and a mill) in Sturminster Newton, the entry for which probably included this part of Marnhull, were held of the king, *v.* VCHDo **3** 73.The property was a grant from the Crown in the reign of Eliz 1 (Roscoe 120).

KNIGHTSTREET (lost), 1774 Hutch[1], 1870 Hutch[3], *Knyghtestrete* e14 *GlastE*, 1342 GlastF (*-in Kentlesworth*), 1431 FA, *Kyngestret(e)* (sic) 1308 FF, 1327 *SR* (p), *Knightestrate* 1324 Inq aqd, *Knystret* 1340 NI (p), *Knyght-* 1379, *Knightstrete* 1396 FF, *Kingstete* (sic) 1479 IpmR, *Knygstrete* 1479 Hutch[3], *v.* **cniht** 'retainer, knight', **stræt** 'street', here perhaps in the sense 'hamlet'. According to Hutch[3] **4** 314, the large house called *Knightstreet*, situated 'about a mile from the church', was pulled down about the middle of the 18th century.

LYMBURGH'S FM (ST 812193), *Linberg'*, *Limbergh(e)* 1244 *Ass* (p), *Lymbergh(e)* 1268 *ib*, 1327 *SR*, 1332 SR, 1339

AddCh, 1345 FF all (p), *-borwe* 1404 *KCC, -bor(u)gh*(')
1431 FA, 1443 *KCC* all (p), *Lymbres* 1597, *Lymbergh House*
1614, *Lymborough* 1616 all Hutch[3], *Limburgh* 1774 Hutch[1],
1870 Hutch[3], *Lumbreys* 1811 OS. Either 'lime-tree hill' from
lind and **beorg**, cf. Limber L (DEPN), Lymbury D 575,
Limberrow Wo 215, or 'hill where flax is grown' if the first
el. is **līn** 'flax' (preferred by Fägersten 43), cf. Limbury Fm
in Netherbury par. *infra*.

MARNHULL HAM (ST 757194), *Ham* (*Yate*) 1838 *TA*,
probably to be identified with *Boretonyngehamme* e14 *GlastE*,
Burtilhame 16 *Glyn*, *Burtlingham* 1602 *Weld[1]*, 'river-meadow
of the people of Burton', *v.* **hamm, -ingas** (gen.pl. *-inga*),
Burton St. *supra*, **geat** 'gate'. This is a conspicuous example
of **hamm** in its more specific sense 'land in a river-bend',
since Marnhull Ham is enclosed by a marked loop in R.
Stour, *v.* Gelling, NoB **48** 140 ff. It is still marked with
strips on 1838 *TAMap*. Ham Lane *infra* is a continuation of
Burton St. leading to the Ham.

MOOR COURT FM, MOORSIDE (ST 798191), *Mora* 13 GlastR
(p), *la More* e14 *GlastE*, 1385 Hutch[3], *atte More* 1327 *SR*,
1332 SR, 1339 *AddCh*, 1345 FF, 1362 Cl, 1385 Hutch[3] all
(p), *le More* 1385 ib, *More* 1412 FA, 1452 Cl, 1454 *HarlCh*,
1543 *PlR*, *Moorecorte alias Mooreside* 1597 *ib*, *Mooreside
Common* 1653 *DCMSurv*, *Moorside als. Moore Court* 1672
SoDoNQ **10**, (*Lower*) *Moor Side* 1811 OS, *Moor Court* (f.n.)
1838 *TA*, *More or Moreside, Moreside Common, More Court*
1870 Hutch[3], *v.* **mōr** 'moor, marshy ground', **atte** 'at the',
court 'large house' (cf. Hutch[3] **4** 318 'a manor-house where
the courts were kept', probably an unwarranted assumption),
sīde 'side'.

NASH COURT (FM) (ST 782198), *Esse* 1303, 1346 FA, *Asshe*
1347 Cl, 1350 Orig, *Esshe* 1428 FA, *Aysshcourt* 1482
MinAcct, *man' de Asshecourte al' voc' Burton Asshe* 1497
Hen[2], *Naishe* 16 *Glyn*, *ferme of Nasshe* Hy 8 *Rent*, *Nasshe
Court(e)* 1564 *Hen[2]*, 1567 *Hen[1]*, *Nash-Court* 1774 Hutch[1],
Nash Ho 1811 OS, cf. John *Attenasshe* 1327 *SR* (Fifehead
M.), ('place at) the ash-tree', *v.* **æsc** (dat.sg. *æsce*), **court**

'large house'. For other early forms, *v.* Burton St. *supra.* The initial *N-* in the modern form is from metanalysis of ME **atten** 'at the', cf. Nash Fm in Marshwood par. *infra*, Nash Bk 71.

RAM'S HILL (FM) (ST 813170), *claus' voc' Rameshill* 16 *Glyn, Rams Hill* 1811 OS, *Long & Lr Ramshill* 1838 *TA*, possibly to be identified with *on Rumanhelle* 958 (15) *ShaftR* (S 656) in the Anglo-Saxon bounds of Thorton *infra*, apparently 'roomy or spacious hill', *v.* **rūm** (wk.obl. *-an*), **hyll**, cf. the f.n. Ramsom in the adjacent par. of Manston *supra.*

SHORTWOOD CMN (lost, at ST 767178), 1653 *DCMSurv*, 1870 Hutch[3], *Schortewude, S(c)hortwode* e14 *GlastE, comon called Shortwood* 1619 *Weld*[1], *Short Wood Cmn* 1811 OS, 'short wood', *v.* **sc(e)ort, wudu**.

THORTON FM (ST 805180)
    (*æt) þorntune, (at) þortune* 958 (15) *ShaftR* (S 656)
    Torentone 1086 DB, *Torynton* 1273 Banco, *Torintton'* 1280 *Ass*
    Torntone 1210–12 RBE (cf. Fägersten 44)
    Thornton(e) 1212 Fees, 1244, 1280 *Ass*, 1285 FA, 1288 *Ass*, 1316 AD (*-iuxta Marnhulle) et freq* to 1664 HTax, *Thornton or Thorton* 1870 Hutch[3]
    Thorenton(e) 1242 FF, e14 *GlastE, Thorin(t)ton(')* 1242 Ch, 1280 *Ass, Thorynton* 1273 Banco
    Thorneton(') 1244 *Ass*, 1266 FF, 1384 Cl *et freq* to 1547 *Ct Thorton* 1795 Boswell

'Thorn-tree farm' or 'thorn enclosure', *v.* **þorn, tūn.** Hutch[3] **4** 318 mentions a 'church' here, dedicated to St Martin and pulled down c.1800, cf. *capelle minores decimas villanorum domini de Thornton'* 1338–40 Glast, *capellam de Thornton* 1340 NI, *the chapel of Thorneton* 1504 Ipm. The farm is called *Thorley Farm* 1811 OS, but this is probably an error. The Anglo-Saxon bounds of Thorton (*þorntune*) are given in 958 (15) *ShaftR* (S 656), at which date the estate apparently included much of what is now Margaret Marsh par. as well as the SE corner of Marnhull.

WALTON ELM (ST 781180), WALTON ELM HILL & HO,
WALTON HO, *Walton'*, *Walton'* (p), *Valton'* (p) 13 GlastR,
Waltone, *Walton(e)* (p) e14 *GlastE*, *Walton(e)* 14 *GlastC*,
1327 *SR* (p), 1332 SR (p), 1548 *Ct*, *Walton (Elm)* 1811 OS,
Walton (f.n.) 1838 *TA*, *v.* **tūn** 'farmstead'. There can be no
certainty about the first el. The absence of medial *-e-*
(*Wale-* spellings) tells against the presence of **wealh**
'Briton, Welshman' in its gen.pl. form *weala*, though it
cannot entirely be ruled out (this Walton is not included in
the corpus of names containing **wealh** discussed by
Cameron, JEPN **12** 1–46). However, perhaps more likely
alternatives for the first el. are **weald** 'woodland' or **weall**
'wall'. The suggestion by Taylor, DoNHAS **88** 208–9, that
the first part of Walton preserves the name of the *Waleran*
who held 6 hides in Sturminster N. in 1086 DB (VCHDo **3**
73) is clearly unsupportable. *Elm* is apparently a fairly recent
addition, no doubt with reference to some conspicuous
elm-tree.

YARDGROVE FM (ST 775175)
   Erd'gue, *Boscus de Gerdeg've* 1258 *For*, *bosc' de Yerdgrave*
      1270 *ib*, *Yerdegrove* e14 *GlastE*, 1342 GlastF (*-in*
      Kentlesworth'), *Erdegrove* 1346, 1428, 1431 FA
   la Wrdegrove 13 GlastR
   Ygrove e14 *GlastE*
   Hierdegrave cum bosc' 1300 Hutch³, *Herdegrove* [*Erde-*
      grave] 1303 FA
   Yargrove e17 *Weld¹*, *Yeargrove* 1811 OS
   Yard Grove (Coppice & Corner) 1838 *TA*

Probably 'grove or copse where rods or spars are
obtained', from **gerd**, **gierd** and **grāf(a)**.

ANTELL'S FM, *Antills* 1811 OS, *Anthills Fm* 1838 *TA*, the
surname *Antell*, a later form of the surname present in
Anketil's Place in Cann par. *supra*, *v.* Reaney s.n. *Anketell*.
ASHLEY FM (*Ashley* 1811 OS) & PLANT., *Ashley* (f.n.) 1838
TA, near Nash Court *supra*, *v.* **æsc**, **lēah** '(clearing in) a
wood'. AVALON HO. BAT ALLEY, 1811 OS, *v.* **bat**, **aley**.
BLACKMOOR VALE INN. BODSMARSH LANE, (*Gt*) *Bods' Marsh*

1838 *TA*, cf. Edward *Bot* 1332 SR, *pasturam domini que vocatur Mersfrid* 13 GlastR, *la Mersh'dych', La Mersh'stiele* e14 *GlastE, claus' voc' la Merssh'* 1482 *MinAcct, v.* **mersc** 'marsh', **fyrhð** 'wood', **dīc** 'ditch', **stigel** 'stile'. BREACH FM 1811 OS, *claus' apud la Breche* 1482 *MinAcct, Breach* 1838 *TA*, cf. *claus' voc' thest Brach, the Southbrach, Northbrach* 16 *Glyn, v.* **brǣc** 'land broken up for cultivation', **ēast, sūð, norð**. BURGESS' CTGS, *Burgesses Cl, Burgess Orchd* 1838 *TA*, cf. Richard *Burge* 1664 HTax, and for the *Burges* family *v.* Hutch[3] 4 319. CARRAWAY LANE (lost, at ST 781182), 1811 OS, *Cara-* 1870 Hutch[3], from the *caraway* plant which must have been grown here, *v.* B. Kerr, DoNHAS **89** 254. CHIPPEL LANE, 1870 Hutch[3], to be associated with *Chippetts' (Pdk)* 1838 *TA* which may represent the correct form. CHURCH FM (1838 *TA*) & LANE, cf. *The Church house* 1653 *DCMSurv, (Gt) Church Fd* 1838 *TA*, from St Gregory's Church *infra*. CLOCK HO. COMMON LANE, named from *Shortwood Cmn supra*. COX HILL, COXHILL CTG, cf. *Cox Hill (Md & Orchd), Cox Hill Home Grd* 1838 *TA, Joh' Koc . . . mes'* e14 *GlastE*, John *Cok'* 1332 SR, *v.* **hyll**. CRIB HO, CRIB HO FM (1838 *TA*), *v.* **cribhouse**; on 1811 OS the name *Cribs Fm* apparently attached to Northwood Fm in Manston (c. ½ mile S) probably belongs to Crib Ho Fm. CROSSES FM, cf. George *Crosse* e17 *Weld*[1]. CROSS TREE FM, probably an allusion to a standing cross, *v.* **cros, trēow**, cf. PN Ch 4 307. CROWN P.H. FILLYMEAD, *Filly Md* 1838 *TA*, now a st.n., possibly **fileðe** 'hay', **lēah** 'clearing', cf. Filleigh D 42. FIRTREE CTG. FLANDERS, *Flanders' Orchd* 1838 *TA*, a surname. GANNETTS QUARRY, *Gannet-* 1870 Hutch[3], cf. *Gannetts' (Grd)* 1838 *TA*, named from Gannetts in Todber par. *supra*. GODDARDS, 1811 OS, a surname. GREAT DOWN BARN, LANE & QUARRY, *(Plat of) Gt Down* 1838 *TA*, cf. *Little Down ib, William in la Doune* 1327 *SR, v.* **dūn** 'hill, down', **plat**[2]. HAINS, cf. William *Hayne* 1664 HTax. HAM LANE, 1838 *TA*, leading to Marnhull Ham *supra*. HATCHER'S FM, cf. *Hatchers' Md* 1838 *TA*, John *Hatcher* 1664 HTax. HAYES CTGS & FM (1811 OS), *claus' apud Heis, claus' voc' Halle Hais, Halleis* 16 *Glyn, v.* **hǣs** 'brushwood', **heall** 'hall, manor house', cf. Hayes Coppice in Todber par. *supra*. HAYTER'S FM, cf. John-, William *Hayter* 1664 HTax.

HINGARSTON (a house-name in 1939 Kelly), from *Hind Gaston* 1838 *TA*, cf. *Long Gaston (Orchd) ib, Lopegarston'* e14 *GlastE, Northgaston* 1338–40 Glast, all from **gærs-tūn** 'grass enclosure', with **hindan** 'behind', **uppan** 'higher up' (with def.art. **le/la**). HISCOCK'S FM, cf. *Hiscocks Md* 1838 *TA*, a surname. HUSSEY'S COPSE , from the *Hussey* family, George *Hussey* having bought the manor in 1651, *v.* Hutch³ **4** 307. THE LODGE. LOVE LANE. LOVELL'S COURT, cf. Widow *Lovell* 1664 HTax. LUSH'S CTG & FM, cf. *Lush Cl, Lushes Marsh* 1838 *TA*, a surname; Lush's Fm was formerly *Maids-hole* 1811 OS, *Maidshole* [Fm] 1870 Hutch³ **4** 319, and was perhaps renamed through motives of delicacy, cf. *terra arabilis de Maydenecroft* 1338–40 Glast which must have been near here, *v.* **mægden** (gen.pl. *mægdena*), **hol¹** 'a hollow', **croft** 'a small enclosure'. MARNHULL ST. (lost), 1811 OS, perhaps identical with Burton St. *supra*. MOUNTERS, *Mounters' Orchd* 1838 *TA*, a surname. MUSBERRY LANE, cf. *claus' voc' Northe-, Southe Musbury* 16 Glyn, *Mussbury* 1838 *TA*, probably 'mouse burrow', *v.* **mūs, burg**, cf. Musbury La (DEPN). NASH LANE, leading to Nash Court *supra*. NEW INN & TROOPER (P.H.). NEW ST., 1811 OS. OLD MILL (LANE), cf. ·*(Old) Mill Orchd, Mill Md* 1838 *TA*, *Mylmeade* 16 Glyn, *Solverd's Mill* 1612 WRO, *Mill* [Bridge] 1791 Boswell, *Millbridge Md* 1839 *TA* (Fifehead M.), *v.* **myln, mæd**. ORCHARD VILLA, cf. *(Old) Orchard* 1838 *TA*. PHILIP'S HILL. PILLWELL, cf. Matthew *atte Pile* 1327 *SR*, William *atte Pyle* 1332 SR, *Pilestreet* 1518 Hutch³, *Pillcroft* e17 *Weld¹, Pill Acre* 1838 *TA, Pill Street* 1870 Hutch³, *v.* **pīl** 'stake', **well(a)** 'spring', **atte** 'at the', **strǣt, croft**. PLECK, 1811 OS, cf. *uno lez plekk siue parok* 16 Glyn, *Plock* 1838 *TA*, *v.* **plek** 'small plot of ground', **pearroc**. POND FM. POPE'S FM, 1870 Hutch³, cf. Mr *Pope* 1664 HTax, *Pope's Wd* 1838 *TA*; for the *Pope* family, *v.* Hutch³ **4** 319 . RECTORY, *The Parsonage* 1653 DCMSurv. SACKMORE LANE, no doubt analogous with *Sacmore* 1 169 which was thought to be 'marshy ground disputed about in a lawsuit', *v.* **sacu, mōr**; since this lane is near Burton St. *supra*, the 'moor' in question may be *la More in Borton'* 1342 GlastF, cf. also *prati Bistemora* 13 GlastR also in Burton, 'meadow to the east of the moor', *v.* **bī, ēastan**. ST GREGORY'S CHURCH, cf.

ecclesie de Marnhulle 1267 (m14) *Glast*, 'the church of St George, *Marnhull*' 1383 Pat; confusion between the names *Georgius* and *Gregorius* is not uncommon, and the church is 'dedicated to St George or St Gregory' according to Hutch[3] 4 320; for chantries in the church, *v.* under the f.n. Chantry *infra*. SALISBURY ST., 1870 Hutch[3], cf. the same name in Shaftesbury par. *supra*. SCHOOLHOUSE LANE. SODOM LANE, probably analogous with Soddon 1 150, Sodern 1 342; in 1974 there was an unsuccessful attempt by inhabitants of new housing in Marnhull to get this name changed (M.H.). STRANGWAYS, 1870 Hutch[3] (-*Fm*), *Strangeways-Fm* 1774 Hutch[1], cf. William *Strangweys* 1547 *Ct*. TAPSAYS, cf. *Tapsey Orchd* 1838 *TA*. TOOGOOD'S FM. WHITE WAY HILL & LANE, *Lane called White Way* 1705 *SxAS*, *v.* hwīt, weg. WOODLANDS FM. YEW HO.

FIELD NAMES

The undated forms are 1838 *TA* 142. Spellings dated 958 (15) are *ShaftR* (S 656), 13 are GlastR, 1244 *Ass*, 1300, 1442, 1606, 1870 Hutch[3], e14 *GlastE*, 1316 *AD*, 1327 *SR*, 1332 SR, 1338–40 Glast, 1340 NI, 1399, 1401 Pat, 1482 *MinAcct*, 16 *Glyn*, 1546, 1549 *PlR*, 1547, 1548 *Ct*, 1557 *Val*, 1567 *Glouc*, e17, 1602, 1619[2], *Weld*[1], 1619[1], 1627, 1705 *SxAS*, 1653 SoDoNQ, 1664 HTax, 1667 *Salkeld*, and 1791 Boswell.

(*a*) (Gt) Alderham, Alders' Md (*v.* alor 'alder', hamm, mǣd, cf. *pastur' vocat' le Alleret* 1482, from alret 'alder copse'); All Croft (first el. possibly heall 'hall', cf. *Halle Hais* cited under Hayes Ctgs & Fm *supra*); Andrews Gdn; Apple Tree Grd; Bait Leaze (Drove) (*Batelese* 1482, *the Inner-*, *lez utter Batelease* 16, *v.* lǣs 'pasture, meadow-land', innerra, ūterra; the first el. is no doubt bait 'pasture' suggested for Bait (Md) 2 259, cf. the NCy f.ns. explained as from ON beit 'pasture', e.g. PN YW 7 156, PN Ch 5 101); Bantis'; Barley Cl; Barnabys' (Orchd); Barn Cl & Grd; Barretts' Plot; Bay Flg (*Netherbawfurlonge* 1547; this field is near to Baywell *infra*, so the first el. may be bay[2] 'a dam', though the 16th cent. form suggests rather bēaw 'gadfly'); Bays' Hay (*v.* (ge)hæg); Baywell (cf. Bay Flg *supra*); Bean Cl & Grd; Berry Wd (*v.* the lost p.n. *Bere supra*); Blackland (Md); Blandfords' Cl (cf. John *Blandford*' 1548 (Sturminster N.)); Blind Pitt (*v.* blind 'hidden'); Nether Bones (cf. Richard *Bone* 1664); Bonny Cl; Bottom Grd; Bottoms' Cl (cf. *close called Bottome Lake* 1619[1], *v.* botm, lacu); Bowling Green; Boyne; Broad Cl (*Brodecloose* 16, *v.* brād, clos(e)); Broadhay, -Hay (*v.* (ge)hæg); Broad Md (*Broodemeade* 16, *v.* mǣd); Broad Moor (*Brodmoore* 1619[2], *v.* mōr); Brooks' Md (cf. Roger (*le*) *Brok*' 1316, 1332, John *le Brok*' 1332, Nicholas *Brooke* e17); Browns' Grd (cf. Elizabeth *Browne* e17); Bush Cl; Butley Moore; Butterwell (*v.*

butere); Butt's, Butts' End & Md (*v.* **butte**); Lt & Middle Cadenham (*pasturam bosci de Kadeham, mariscum de-, boscum ad Eadenham* (sic for *Caden-*) 13, *pastura de Cadenhammersche* e14, *copic' d'ne Regine vocat' Cadman* 1547, *Cadnam Wood* 1619², 'Cada's enclosure or river-meadow', from the OE pers.n. *Cada* and **hamm**, cf. Cadenham W 87, Cadnam Ha (DEPN); the fields in question are near to R. Stour); Calves' Cl (cf. *Chalvecrofte* e14, *v.* **cealf** (gen.pl. *-a*), **croft**); Camels' (cf. the lost *Corneles-, Covelesham infra*); Castlemans' Grd; Dry Causeway, Causeway Fd & Md (*v.* **cauce**); Lr & Upr Chantry, Chantry Orchd (cf. 'the chantry of (St Mary in the parish church of) *Marnhull'* 1399, 1401, *v.* Hutch³ 4 322 for this and other chantries); Claverall; Clay Hill; Clay Lands('); Cleales [Bridge] 1791; Coles' Hill; Comb Cl (*v.* **cumb**); Common Court; Coneygar (*v.* **coninger** 'rabbit-warren'); Coppice (Cl & Grd); Corn Grd; Corn Ham (*v.* **hamm**, cf. the lost *Cornelesham infra*); Gt Cowleaze, Cow Leaze Md (*Cowlease* 16, *v.* **cū, lǣs**); Cross Comb & Grd (*v.* **cross, cumb**); Cuddies' (cf. William *Crydye* 1332); Culver Cl, Culverhay (*Culuerhey* 16, cf. *Culverlane* 1549, *v.* **culfre** 'dove', **(ge)hæg**); Cutlers' Orchd; Darby's [Fm] 1870; Dibbens' Grd & Md; Dicks' Door (cf. *claus' voc' Dickes* 1546, Thomas *Dicke* 1664, *v.* **duru**); Dinhay; Dowdings' Grd (cf. Jeffrey *Dowdens* 1664); Drove (cf. John *atte Dreve* e14, *v.* **drāf, drǣf, atte**); Dunfords' (cf. John *Durneford* e17, Richard *Durnford* 1664); Dunny Moor (*Duninges Moore* 1602, a surname with **mōr**); East Cl; Edgy Lake; 8 Acres; Elkey Md (*Elkyn' Mede* 1547, a surname with **mǣd**, cf. Ilkins Ham *infra*); Elms' Cl; Fants'; Fee Grd; Field (cf. Gilbert *in tha Felda* 13, *Manell Fyldes* 1549, *Marnell(es) Fe(i)ld* 1557, 1567, *Marnell Fyelde* 1627, *v.* **feld** 'open country'); 5 Acres; Folly (*v.* **folie**); Footland(s'), Footland Orchd; 4 & 14 Acres; Francis Yarn; French Grass (from the crop); Furlong; Long Gibbs Pitt, Three Corner Gibbs' Pits (cf. Agnes *Gibbes atte Forde* e14 (Sturminster N.), *v.* **atte, ford**); Gilbert Hays' (Md); Gooseacre; Gores' (Halves) (cf. *Garslo(n)d', Garflond'* 13, *v.* **gāra, land, healf**); Graft Hays; Great Md; Green Hay(e)s'; (The) Grove, Grove Md (cf. *Groveclose* 1602, *Grove* [Bridge] 1791, *v.* **grāf(a)**); Gt & Lt Halves' (*v.* **healf**); Hanns' Grd (cf. Susanna *Hann* 1664 (Sturminster N.), *Hann's* [Fm] 1870); Hatch Md (*v.* **hæc(c)**); Hazelbrook, Hazle Coppice (*v.* **hæsel**); Hilly Cl; Hinton Gate (from Hinton St M. par. *supra*); Hixfords'; Hole Md (possibly to be associated with *Holepulemede* 13, *(H)ulpenemede* e14, 'meadow at the hollow pool' from **hol, pull** or **pōl, mǣd**, if the earliest form is reliable; the second form may have been influenced by Owlpen Gl 2 244); Holloways'; Home Cl, Grd & Md; Honeys' Croft & Orchd; Howes' Grd (cf. Ambrose *How* 1664); Hunts' Plott; Ice Cl; Ilkins Ham (Md) (*Ilkingsham* 16, *v.* **hamm**, with the same surname as in Elkey Md *supra*); Ivers' (Md), Hanhams' Ivers; Joices', Joices Crib Ho (cf. Nicholas *Joce* 1547, William *Joyce* 1664, Crib Ho (Fm) *supra*; on the *Joyce* family, *v.* Hutch³ 4 319); Jones's Cl; Gt & Lt Knaps'; Lady Leaze (*-Lease* 1870); Lamberts' Md; Land Croft (cf. *claus' voc' the Laund* 16, spelling not quite certain, probably **launde** 'woodland pasture'); Day & Hilly Lashmoor, Lt Lashmore, Lashmoor Md (*pastur' apud Lachemere* e14, 'pool near a boggy stream', from **læc(c)** and **mere**[1], cf. *Laishmead* [Bridge] 1791); Gt & Lt Lewisham; Lt Lights' Md; Limes (cf. John *Lyne* 1327, 1332); (Lt) Linch (v. **hlinc**); Little Grd & Md; Loins' (cf. the f.n. *Loynes* 1 236); Long Cl, Fd & Grd; Long Cross (possibly to be associated with *Longe Craft* 16, v. **croft**, cf. James Cross Lane 2 282); Longmans' Cl, Longman(s') Md (cf. John *Longeman'* 16); Lr Longston Md; Lower Md; Lye (cf. *terr' vocat' lez leyez* 1482, v. **lēah**); Maggot Hays' (cf. *Magattehayes* 2 70); Mare Md; Mathews' Md; May Thorn; Mead; Meadow Ld; (Gt) Middle Fd (*Middlefeild* 1619[2]); Middle Md; Middle Moor (*Middelmore* 1549, near Moor Court *supra*); Monks' Md (cf. John *Munck* 1664); Moon's Md; Moor Cl & Md (cf. *More Hedge* 1548); Mowed Wd (perhaps to be associated with *Mawdes House* 16, from the surname *Maud*); New Cl; New Grd Orchd; 9 Acres (Md); Nook Hays' (*Nokehay* 1546, possibly 'oak-tree enclosure', from **āc** and **(ge)hæg**, with *N-* from metanalysis of ME **atten** 'at the', cf. Oakey Cl *infra*, but the first el. may be ME **nok** 'a nook'); Notley; Nursery Orchd; Nut Hays'; Oakey Cl, Oakhay(')s (cf. Nook Hays' *supra*); Out Cl (cf. *Owtelese* 1482, *v.***ūte** 'outside, more distant', **læs**); Over Grd; (Lt) Paddock; Parkers' Md; Parting Mdw; Picket Cl; Pitt Cl; Plantation; Platt (v. **plat**[2]); Plotts'; Poins'; Post Cl; Poulter Cl (probably *claustur' parci de Pultone* e14, 'pool farm', from **pull** and **tūn**, cf. Robert *atte Pulle* 1327, v. **atte**, *the Park' infra*); Pound Md; Press Street (*Prestestret'* 13, *i forhurtham boveprestetrete*, *Prestret* e14, 'hamlet of the priests', from **prēost** (gen.pl. -a), **strǣt**, with **forierð** 'projecting piece of ploughland', **bufan** 'above', cf. Hutch[3] 4 306 ('a small field, part of it belonging to the glebe, called *Priest Street*, where are the remains of the foundations of many houses, most of which, in the memory of some very old people . . . were . . . inhabited by Roman Catholic priests . . . This, however, is probably no more than a vulgar tradition')); Quar Cl, Quarry Grd (v. **quarr(er)e**); Rakes' Grd (cf. *crofta que dicitur Rokescrof* 1338–40, Nicholas *Rake* e17, William *Rake, William Reeke(s house)* 1664, v. **croft**); Ram Cl; Ray Grass *(v.* **rye-grass**); Redbridge Md (*Redbridge* 1791); Redlands('); River Cl; Roddis Cl; Rodnell; Rose Orchd; Round Cl; (Inner) Round-Hills' (*clausum voc' Rowndehill'* 16, v. **round, hyll**); Rushmoor; Rutleys' Orchd; Sage Corner; Sagittary's [Fm] 1870; Salmons' Middle; Sand Hills' (Lane); Second Grd; 7 Acres; Shaw-, Strawbridge Md; Shelf (*Shelfe Close* 1705, *v.* **sc(i)elf**); Sheppards' Cl; Side Hills'; Silly (probably to be associated with John *atte Sele* 1332, which may be 'at the sallow grove' from **s(i)ele** with **atte**); Simmon(d)s' Md (cf. John *Symond(')* e14, 1332); 6 & 16 Acres; Slack Man; South Cl; South Fd (*-feild* 1619[2]); South Grove; South Hill (Md) (*Suthhull'* 13, *S(o)uth(h)ulle* e14, v. **sūð, hyll**); South Well (v. **well(a)**); Sperts' (perhaps from **spyrt** 'spirt (of water)'); Square Marsh; Staple Flg (v. **stapol** 'post'); Stibley (possibly 'tree-stump clearing', from **stybb** and **lēah**); Stone Cl; Stoney Lds; Summer Grd; Summer Leaze (v. **læs**); Hr & Lr Sweets'; 10 Acres; Tenneys' Cl (cf. Ambrose *Tenney* 1664); Thorn Hays' (cf. John *atte Thorne* 1332, v. **atte**, **þorn, (ge)hæg**); Thornton Down & Lane (1667, cf. *Thornton More* 1442, *Thornetons ˌMarshe* 16, v. **dūn, lane, mōr, mersc**, Thorton Fm *supra*);

Three Corner Cl; Tilley Md; Tinkers' Leaze; Tites' Md; Trill (v. Trill Bridge in Fifehead M. par. *supra*); Truss Fd (*Thrushefild'* 1547, v. **þrysce, feld**); Turnip Cl; 20 & 2 Acres; Valley Mdw 1870; Vounce Hill; Water Md (cf. *Wet'mede* 13, e14, v. **wēt, wǣt** 'wet', **mǣd**); Watership's [Fm] 1870; Way Cl; West Fd (Md); Wheat Cl (cf. *in campo frument'* 1547); White Fd; Whites' Orchd (cf. Edward *le White* e14, 1327); Wilds' Grd (cf. widow *Wild* 1664); Withey-bed, Withey Hedge (v. **wīðig** 'willow'); Witheys' (cf. Richard-, William *W(h)ither* e14 (Sturminster N.)); House, Lr, Middle & Upr Wood, Wood Cl (Md); Woolcroft; Yonder Grd.

(b) *Blackford orchard'* 16 (v. **blæc, ford, orceard**); *of breþling made* 958 (15) (v. **mǣd**; the spelling of the first part of the name is probably corrupt, but possibly represents an OE pers.n. *Be(o)rhtel* (Redin 139) with **-ing**[4]); *Buricrofta* 13 (p), atte *Buriecrofte* e14 (v. **atte, bury** 'manor house', **croft**); *Carmarantes Lane* 1653 (v. **cormorant**); *wood of Cornelesham, boscus de Covelesham* 1300 (second el. probably **hamm**, first el. uncertain; just possibly to be associated with one of the *TA* f.ns. Camels' or Corn Ham *supra*); atte *Dene* (p) 1332 (v. **atte, denu** 'valley'); *on ealdmannes þyerðe* (sic) 958 (15) (v. *eldmannes wrthe* in E. Orchard par. *supra*); *Estlease* 16 (v. **ēast, lǣs**); *Frelease* 16 (v. **frēo** 'free from service or charge'); *Grayshey* 16 (a surname with **(ge)hæg**); *Haydon* e14 ('hay hill', v. **hēg, dūn**); *Hewemoore* 16 (v. **mōr**, first el. uncertain); *Heyriscroft, -lond* 1338–40 (cf. *Joh' le Eyr' ten' in Thorneton'* 1244, v. **croft, land**, Thorton Fm *supra*); atte *Hile* (p) e14, 1327 (probably 'at the nook' from **atte** and dat.sg. *hēale* of **healh**); *Hupehulle* (p) 13 (v. **uppan, hyll**); *Langhemede* (probably for *Laughe-* 13, *La Laghemede* e14 (v. **mǣd**, first el. possibly ME **laghe** 'law'); *in la Lane* 1327, atte *Lane* 1332 both (p) (v. **lane**); *Marnhull Gate* 1619[1] (cf. Thomas atte *Ghet'* 1327, John atte *Yate* 1332, v. **atte, geat** 'gate, gap'); *Moorshey* 1619[2] (spelling of final letters uncertain); *Northfeild* 1619[2]; *Northmead* 1606; *Oxenlease* 16 (v. **oxa** (gen.pl. *oxena*), **lǣs**); *clausum voc' the Park'* 16 (v. **park**, cf. Poulter Cl *supra*); *Portbrigg(e)* 13, e14 ('town bridge', v. **port**[2], **brycg**; perhaps an early name for either King's Mill Bridge *supra* (in this par.) or Trill Bridge in Fifehead M. par. *supra*); *Salteheygh'* e14 (v. **(ge)hæg**, first el. perhaps **s(e)alt**[2] 'salty'); *le Stublefild'* 1547 (v. **stubbil, feld**); *to tudesleghe, of þere lege* 958 (15) (v. *cludesleghe* in Fontmell M. par. *supra*); *on þigerðes* (sic) *stapel* 958 (15) (v. *Wigheardes stapele* in Fontmell M. par. *supra*); atte *Wyke* e14, 1332, atte *Wych'* e14, atte *Wicke* 1340 all (p) (v. **atte, wīc** '(dairy) farm', cf. Henry *de Wich* 13, John *de Wike* 1316).

Okeford Fitzpaine

Part of this par. (Fiddleford, etc) was transferred from Child Okeford in 1884. Belchalwell, formerly a distinct par. in Cranborne hundred, is now within this par. except for a part in Fifehead N. par. **2** 95.

OKEFORD FITZPAINE (ST 807108)
    Acford 939–46 (1726) Finberg (S 1719), *Acford(e)* Hy 1

BM I, a1165 MontC, c.1185 Templar (-*ex dono Aluredi de Nicole*), 1236 FF, 1258 Pat (p) *et freq* to 1356 Cl, -*forda* John *AddCh*, *Hakeford'*, *Ackeford* 1244 *Ass* both (p), *Akeford* 1263 Ipm, 1264 (e15) *MiltRoll*, 1264 Cl, Ipm, *Okeford*(') 1264 (e15) *MiltRoll*, 1315 Ipm, *Hen*[1], *Hackeford'* 1268 *Ass*, *Ocford*(*e*) 1303, 1346, 1428 FA, *Okford*(*e*) 1315 *Hen*[1], 1337 *AddCh*, 1347 Cl
Adford (sic) 1086 DB
Acforde Aluredi de Lincoln 1155 MontC (Dugd 5, 167), *Hocford Aluredi de Lincoln* 1270 For, *Acford Alvredi* 1280 Ipm, -*Aurey* 1280 *Ass*, -*Auveray* 1287 Misc, -*Affray*, -*Alfray*, -*Aufrey*, -*Auuerey* 1288 *Ass*, -*Aufri* 1297 Pat, -*Alfred* 1323 FF, *Af*(*f*)*ord Aurey*, -*Auffrey* 1280 *Ass*, *Akford*-, *Okford Aufrey* 1288 *Ass*, *Atforde Alfredy* (sic) 1291 Tax, *Akforde Alfridi* 1340 NI, *Okeforde Alfredi* 1428 FA
Okeford Nichol 1282 Ch, -*Nic*(*h*)*ol*(*e*) 1288 *Ass*, *Acford Nicholas* 1337 Ch
Acford Fitz Paen 1316, -(*Fitz*) *Payn* 1317, -*Paen*, -*Fitzpayn* 1319 all Banco, *Ocford Fitz Payn* 1321 FF, 1412 FA, *Ok*(*e*)*ford*(*e*) *Fitz Payn* 1332 Pat, 1411 Cl, -*Fitzpayn* 1360 Ipm, -*Fytz Payn* 1431 FA, *Acford' filii Pagani* 1338–40 Glast, *Acfforde filtz Payn* 1366 *Hen*[2], *Hakford Fitzpayn* 1381 Cl, *Okforfiztpayn* 1412 FA, *Acford*(*e*) *Fitz Payn* 1417 *Hen*[2], 1420 Cl, -*fitzpayn* 1455 ib, *Ackeford*(*e*) *Fitzpayne* 1490 Ipm, -*Fytzpayn'* 1497 *Hen*[2], -*fitz payne* 1528 *AD*, *Ak*(*e*)*ford*(*e*) *Fitzpayne* 1535–43 Leland, 1541 *Hen*[2], *Acfurthfitzpayn'* c.1500 *Hen*[1], *Ockford*(*e*) *phitspaine* 1584 *Hen*[2], -*Fitzpayne* 1705 *Salkeld*
Fippeny aukford (sic) 1575 Saxton, *Foppen Okeford* 1618 *CH*

One of a group of pars. sharing the name Okeford, 'oak-tree ford' from **āc** and **ford**, cf. Shillingstone (*olim Okeford Shilling*) 2 238 and Child Okeford *supra* (*q.v.* for the possible site of the original ford). The distinguishing affixes are manorial. Four hides in Okeford Fitzpaine were part of the estate held of Glastonbury abbey by the wife of Hugh fitz Grip at the time of DB later held by *Alvred de Lincoln* and his heirs, probably as a result of his marriage to her, v. VCHDo 3 55–6, Hutch³ 4 327. The spellings *Auveray, Affray,* etc represent the OFr forms *Auverey, Auveré* of the OG pers.n. *Alverad. Nic(h)ol(e)* shows AN interchange of *n* and *l* in the name Lincoln, v. PN L 1 2–3, with further analogical rationalization in the form *Nicholas,* v. Zachrisson, ANInfl 130. The manor was held by the family of *Fitz Payn* (*filius Pagani*) from the second half of the 13th cent.; Robert *Fitz Payn* is named as one of the heirs of the last Alvred de Lincoln who died in 1264 (Ipm), and *Okeford Nichol* is said to be held by *Robert son of Payn* in 1282 Ch, etc, cf. Wootton Fitzpaine par. *infra.* The late colloquial forms *Fippeny* and *Foppen* for *Fitz Payn* are to be noted, the former perhaps showing some folk-etymological wordplay suggested by the affix of the neighbouring par. of Shillingstone (*Shillingauk-ford* 1575) 2 239.

STREET-NAMES: these include *Hyghstrete* 1497, *Hye Streate, -Street* 1584 *Hen²*; *Shillin(g)stone Lane* 1584 *ib* (to Shillingstone 2 238); *Weststrete* 1497, *-Streat* 1584 *ib; Whytstrete* 1497 *ib, Whitestreete* 1601 *Hen¹,* v. **hwīt**. Buildings include *le gildhall* 1564 *Hen²; officina* ('outbuilding') *sive le Shopp in occupacione Willelmi Howe* 1564 ib; *le Townehowse* 1584 *ib.*

BELCHALWELL (ST 793098)
    Chaldewell(e) 1109 Dugd, 1280, 1288 *Ass,* 1316 FA, 1398
        Cecil, 1412 FA, *-woll'* 1283 *Cecil, Cheldewell(e)* 1205
        Cur, 1270 Hutch³, *Calde-* 1207, *Chadewell'* 1223 Cur,
        Chalwell 1619 *CH*
    Bell' 1207 Cur, *Belle* 1223 ib, 1276 Hutch³, 1288 *Ass,*
        1291 Tax *et freq* to 1602 *AddCh, parochia de Bell* 1584
        Hen²
    '*Belle* and *Chaldwell'* 1286 Ch, *Belle et Chaldewell'* 1288
        Ass, Belchalwell 1575 Saxton, *Bell Chalwell* 1641 *Salkeld,*
        Bell Challwell Fifehead 1664 HTax

Originally two separate names. *Chalwell* is 'cold spring or stream', from **ceald** and **well(a)** (spring and stream marked 6" nearby). *Bell* is from **belle** 'a bell' here used in a transferred sense 'bell-shaped hill' with reference to Bell Hill, a steep hill-ridge (845') just SE of Belchalwell. In the 1664 form, *Fifehead* refers to Lower Fifehead or Fifehead St

Quintin (2 95), formerly in Belchalwell when the latter was a distinct par. in Cranborne hundred (2 194). References to a church here (the present one is undedicated) have been found from 1342 Cl.

DARKNOLL FM (ST 801118), *Derkenhull* 1286 Banco (Drew), *Darkenell* 1640 *DCMDeed*, *Darknell* 1811 OS, cf. *Gt & Lt Dartnells* 1840 *TA*, 'dark hill', from **deorc** (wk.obl. *-an*) and **hyll**. It gives name to Darknoll Brook, earlier called *Tril, v.* RNs. *infra.*

FIDDLEFORD (BRIDGE) (ST 805132), *Fitelford(e)* 1244 *Ass* (p), 1288 *ib*, 1315, 1345 FF, 1355 Ipm *et freq* to 1456 IpmR, *Fyt(t)elford(')* 1286 Banco (Drew), 1342 GlastF, 1350 Ipm, 1418 IpmR, 1504 *DLCt, Fitilford'* 1338–40 Glast, *Fytlefforde* 1497 *Hen²*, *Fytylforde* 1505 *DLCt, Phetylfforde* 1544 *PlR*, *Fittleford* 1575 Saxton, 1584 *Hen²*, 1870 Hutch³, *Fyttle-*, *Fyttelford* 1601 *Hen¹*, *Fitleford* 1646 SC, *Fiddleford or Fittleford* 1795 Boswell. 'Fitela's ford', from the OE pers.n. *Fitela* and **ford**. The same pers.n. is found in Fittleton W 330 and Fittleworth Sx 126. The Blandford F.—Sturminster N. road crosses Darknoll Brook here.

HILE COPPICE & FM (ST 792118), *Hele* 1244 *Ass* (p), *de la Hyla* 13 GlastR (p), *La Hele, atte Hile* (p) e14 *GlastE, close called Hile or Hiles* 1640 *DCMDeed,* cf. *Westhyla* 13 GlastR, *Westhile* e14 *GlastE, Helomede* (possibly for *Hele-*) 1307 (15) *ForReg*, from the WSax dat.sg. form *hēale* of **h(e)alh** 'a nook, a corner of land', with **west, mæd**. This name is probably to be identified with *bi merehale* 968 (14) *Glast* (S 764), *by Merehale* 1338–40 Glast, 'by the boundary nook', in the Anglo-Saxon bounds of Sturminster Newton, *v.* **(ge)mǣre**; there is a pronounced step in the par. bdy here near Hile Fm.

LOWBROOK FM (ST 789094)
> *Lollebrok(e)* 1263 Ipm, 1264 (e15) *MiltRoll*, 1303 FA, 1342
> GlastF (p), 1428 FA, 1602 *AddCh, -broc* 1264 FineR,
> *-brouk(e)* 1327 *SR*, 1332 SR both (p), 1346 FA, 1355
> Ipm (p), 1431 FA, *Lol(l)broke* 1535 VE, 1544 Hutch³,
> *Loolbroke* 1602 *AddCh*

Lullebrouk 1358 BM I, *-brok* 1383 FF
Lowbrok 1497, *-brooke* 1584 *Hen²*, *Lowbrooke or Lollbroke*
1795 Boswell, *Gt Low Brook* 1838 *TA*

'Lolla's or Lulla's brook', from an OE pers.n. *Lolla* or
Lulla and **brōc**. A pers.n. *Lolla* has been suggested for
Lowleth Sr 381, Lowden W 91 (and a strong form *Loll* for
Lolworth C 181). *Lulla* is well attested (Redin 100) and
occurs in Lulworth I 123. One or other of these pers.ns.
survives as the surname of Walter *Lolle* 1332 SR (Long
Bredy). For the vocalization of *l* in the later forms, cf.
Lowleth, Lowden *loc. cit.*, Lowfold Sx 133, etc.

STROUD FM (ST 792102), *Strode* 1497 *Hen²*, *(incl'm voc')* *(le)*
Strowde, West Strowde 1584 *ib, Stroude* 1600 *Hen¹, Stroud*
1705 *Salkeld*, 1811 OS, cf. *venellam ducent de Strowde*
(Elme), Strowde Lane, -Mede, Stroudwitch Lane, Strowd(e)-
witche Lane, -Pleck 1584 *Hen², Stroudes Tenement* 1721
Salkeld, Gt, Lt & Hilly Stroud, Stroud Md, Foreman's
Stroud, Stroud's Grd 1838 *TA*, from **strōd** 'marshy land
overgrown with brushwood', with **west, elm, lane, mǣd,**
wīc 'dwelling, (dairy) farm', and **plek** 'small plot'. The place
is no doubt to be associated with William *Strondman* (for
Stroudman) 1332 SR (taxed in Okeford F., 'man who lived at
the **strōd**', *v.* Fransson 207), and possibly with John *(de)*
Stro(u)de 1327 *SR*, 1332 SR (taxed in Manston).

SUGESTONE (lost, ST 782109), 1584 *Hen², Southgarston(')*
1315 *Hen¹*, Ipm, 1323 FF, *Suthgarson* 1316 Hutch³,
-garston 1321 FF, *Suggeston'* 1497 *Hen², Sugsons* 1601
Hen¹, Sugson (Md), Sa(n)gson (sic) 1838 *TA*, 'south grass
enclosure', from **sūð** and **gærs-tūn**. The grid reference can
be arrived at from the location of the *TA* fields.

ANGERS FM, 1811 OS, *Aungiers* 1601 Hutch³, *Andyers or*
Aungiers (a farm) 1774 Hutch¹, 1870 Hutch³, cf. *Gt & Lt*
Angers 1840 *TA*, no doubt to be associated with Baldewyn
Aunger 1315 FF, *Angerus capellanus de Childacford* n.d.
(1372) *ChrP*; for the Continental pers.n. *Anger*, either a
Norman form of ON *Ásgeirr* or Fr *Angier* from OG *Ansger,*
v. Reaney *s.n. Anger*, Feilitzen 166; the farm was in Child

Okeford par. until 1884. BANBURY HILL, *Banbury* (*Common*) 1773 Bayly, 1811 OS; probably to be identified with *boscum de Ban'ber'* 13 GlastR; there is an Iron Age univallate hill-fort here, *v.* RCHM 3 206, so the second el. is probably **burh** (dat.sg. *byrig*) 'fortified place', the first perhaps **bana** 'murderer', cf. Banbury O 412 explained as from **burh** with an OE pers.n. *Bana*. BELCHALWELL STREET, 1811 OS, probably from **strǣt** in the sense 'hamlet', but cf. *Bell Lane* 1584 *Hen²*, *v.* Belchalwell *supra*. BELLEAZE FM, *land called Belleys* 1590 *Hen²*, *Belleaze* 1811 OS, 'pasture belonging to *Bell'*, *v.* **lǣs**, Belchalwell *supra*. BELL HILL, 1811 OS, 1840 *TA*, cf. *Bell Knappe* 1584 *Hen²*, *Belchalwell Hill* 1840 *TA*, *v.* **hyll**, **cnæpp** 'hill-top', Belchalwell *supra*. CASTLE LANE, named from *incl'm voc'* le Castle 1584 *Hen²*, *claus' pastur' voc' Castell'* 1601 *Hen¹*, *Gt & Lt Castle, Castle Cl, Leg & Md* 1838 *TA*, *v.* **castel(l)**, **leg**; the two forms (*le*) *Castell* 1543, 1546 *PlR* cited under Shillingstone par. 2 240 probably also belong here, the 'castle' referred to perhaps being the earthworks near Bere Marsh Fm in that par. on which *v.* RCHM 3 241. COMMON GATE, 1811 OS, at the corner of Okeford Cmn *infra*. CONYGAR COPPICE, (*copic' voc'* le) *Coniger, Old Conyger* 1584, *woode called Conygere* 1590 *Hen²*, *Conygor Coppice* 1811 OS, *Gt & Middle Coneygaer, Con(e)ygar* (*Coppice & Leg*), *Coneygaer Md* 1838 *TA*, cf. *Coni-, Conyger Lane* 1584 *Hen²*, *v.* **coninger** 'a rabbit-warren'. COOKWELL BROOK, *v.* RNs. *infra*. THE CROSS, near *Cross Cl* 1840 *TA*, perhaps **cross** in the sense 'cross-roads', cf. *incl'm voc' Cowle Crosse, pictellum voc' Cold Crosse* 1584 *Hen²* which may have been named from an actual cross, *v.* **ceald** 'cold, exposed', **cros**. DIRTY GATE, on the par. bdy. EARL'S FM, perhaps an allusion to the Earls of Northumberland who owned the manor of Okeford F. at the end of the 15th century and until 1533 (Hutch³ 4 330). ETHERIDGE'S FM. FROG HOLE, *Frog Nole* 1840 *TA*, 'hollow frequented by frogs', from **frogga** (gen.sg. *-an*, gen.pl. *-ena*), **hol¹**. GARLAND'S FM, *terre voc' Garlandes* 1497 *Hen²*, *Garland* 1811 OS, *Garlands* [Fm] 1870 Hutch³, probably from the surname *Garland*. HIBBETT BOTTOM, COPPICE & LANE, *great hebbett woodd* 1578 *Hen¹*, *Hebed* (*Lane, -Woode*) 1584 *Hen²*, *Hibbett(s), Hibbett Coppice, Cross & Md, Hibbett*

4 *Acres* 1840 *TA*, second el. probably **bedd** 'plot of ground where plants are grown', first el. uncertain without earlier forms. KNACKERS HOLE, 1811 OS, *v.* **knacker, hol**[1], cf. 1 41. LITTLE LANE. MALTHOUSE CTGS. OKEFORD CMN, cf. *a Common* 1583 *SPDom*, Common Gate *supra*. OKEFORD HILL, 1811 OS, cf. *Ockford Downes, le Downe*(s) 1584 *Hen*[2], *v.* **dūn**. OKEFORD MILL, 1811 OS, cf. *mol' acquatic'* 1315 *Hen*[1], *Mylleyne* 1497 *Hen*[2], *molendinum granaticum, Mill Closse, Mill Mead, le Mill plecke, le Mill Way* 1584 *Hen*[2], *Mill Md* (*Mdw*), *Mill Plot & Ponds* 1838 *TA, v.* **myln, lane, clos(e), mǣd, plek, weg**; there is mention of a mill at Okeford F. in 1086 DB (VCHDo 3 73). THE PARSONAGE, *the parsonage howse* 1601 *Hen*[1]. POUND, POUND LANE, *le Pownde, Pounde-, Pownd Closse* 1584 *Hen*[2], *The Pound, Old Pound, Pound Cl* 1838 *TA, v.* **pund**. RECTORY, *Rectorie de Ockford* 1584 *ib.* ROOM FM, *messuage and tenement called Rome-house* 1544 Hutch[3], possibly from ME **rum-hous** 'a privy' (a jocularly ironical term, literally 'spacious house', found only in the 13th century poem O&N, *v.* OED s.v. *room* adj. sense 4, cf. MED where a different derivation is suggested); the farm is incorrectly called *Frome* on 1842 *TAMap*. ST ANDREW'S CHURCH, cf. *Acford church* 1336 Cl, *le Churche Litton, le Churche pathe, terre Rectorie voc'-, 3 incl'a voc' Church*(e) *Ways*(e) 1584 *Hen*[2], *Churchway* (*Md*) 1838 *TA, v.* **cirice, līc-tūn, pæð, weg**. SMITHY, (*cotagium voc'*) *Le Smithyes Forge* 1584 *Hen*[2], cf. *incl'm voc' Smithes* 1584 *ib, v.* **smiððe, forge**. SOUTHLEY FM, *Southley* 1497 *Hen*[2], 1601 *Hen*[1], *Southley*(e)s 1584 *ib*, 'south wood or clearing', from **sūð** and **lēah**. TELEGRAPH, 1811 OS. WHITMORE COPPICE, CROSS & DROVE, *incl'm voc Whit*(e)*mere, Whitmere Lane* 1584 *Hen*[2], *Whitmoor Cl, Whitmore Coppice* 1838 *TA*, 'white pool', *v.* **hwīt, mere**[1].

FIELD NAMES

The undated forms are 1838 *TA* 159 (Okeford Fitzpaine), but those marked † are 1840 *ib* 15 (Belchalwell, three of its original four parts) and those marked ‡ are 1839 *ib* 60 (Child Okeford). Spellings dated 1276 are Hutch[3], 1288 *Ass*, e14 *GlastE*, 1327 *SR*, 1332 SR, 1497, 1564, 1584, 1590 *Hen*[2], 1583 *SPDom*, 1601 *Hen*[1], 1664 HTax, and 1792 *Salkeld*.

(a) Acre Md; Back Lane Cl, (†) Back Md; Bakers Cl (cf. John *Pystor* ('baker') 1564, *communem pistrenam* ('bakehouse') 1584); Bankey Cl; Bark Hill (*4 claus' voc' Barkhill* 1584, *v.* **beorc** 'birch-tree', **hyll**); Barn Cl (*the-* 1792) & Grd; †Batten Acres; Bean Cl; †Bears; †Bell (Wd), (†) Bell Md (*v.* Belchalwell *supra*); Betty Hall(s Orchd) (probably to be associated with *incl'm voc' Bawt(y)e Hawe* 1584, from **haga**[1] 'hedge, enclosure', perhaps with a surname); Billets Grd (*pictello . . . voc' Billet* 1584, probably a surname); (†)Bottom Cl, †Bottom Grd; Bouches Md; Boughy, Bowey (*Bowaye* 1584, *Boweye hedge* 1590, *v.* **weg**, **hecg**, first el. uncertain); †Brake (*v.* **bræc**[1]); Hr, Lr, Middle & Yonder Breach (*La Breche* 1276, (*Great-, Upper*) *Brech(e)*, *Le great Briage* (sic), *Brech(e) Lane* 1584, *v.* **bræc** 'land broken up for cultivation'); Breeches Md; Broad Md (*Bradmeade, Broadmead* 1584, *v.* **brād**, **mæd**); †Gt Brooky Grd; Broom Cl (*the-* 1792, *v.* **brōm**); Bull (Ridge) (*Bullhedge* 1584, *v.* **bula**, **hecg**); †Bull Allies; †Bullings; Bunys Plot (spelling uncertain); †Gt & Lt Burables; †Butts; Cannass Hay (*Cannyshaye* 1584, from **(ge)hæg** 'enclosure', with a surname); Gt Chalkwell, Chalwell Mdw & Orchd (springs marked 6″ nearby, *v.* **well(a)**, first el. possibly **cealc** 'chalk, limestone'); †Chit Croft; Clackhay (spelling uncertain); Cobbs Md; Cocks Hays (*Cocke Hay* 1584, *v.* **(ge)hæg**, probably with a surname); †Cockrow Coppice; Commer-, Cummerwick (*Comerwick(e)* (*Lane*), *Comerwerk Lane* 1584, perhaps from the OE pers.n. *Cumbra* and **wīc**, but earlier spellings are needed); Cone Cross, Cone Grass (perhaps from **coninger**, cf. Conygar Coppice *supra*); Coombe Cl, †Co(o)mbe (*pictellum voc' le Combe* 1584, *v.* **cumb**); †Coppice, Coppice Cl, Copp(ice) Grd, †Copse Hay Cl (cf. *Coppes Woode* 1590, *v.* **copis**, **(ge)hæg**); Corner Grd; †Corn Fd, (†) Corn Grd; Corn Knap (*incl'm voc' Cornepp* 1584, *v.* **cnæpp** 'hill-top, hillock', first el. **corn**[1] 'corn' or **cweorn** 'hand-mill'); Cow Leaze; Crabtree Md; Crepham Md (perhaps to be associated with *Credohams* (*Lane*) 1584, cf. Henry *Crede* 1327); Cressy Ham Md, Cressy Ld (perhaps to be associated with *Crushland* 1584); Crib House Grd (*v.* **cribhouse**); Culverhay (1584, *v.* **culfre** 'dove', **(ge)hæg**, cf. *unius columbar'* ('a dove-cot') 1564); †Darbys Md; Dock Hill (*Dokhulle* 1327 (p), *Dockle* 1584, probably 'hill where dock grows', from **docce** and **hyll**); †Dock Yd (cf. prec.); †Dodford; Downs Cl & Md; Drove (Pdk); Dry Cl; †Corn East & Green East (elliptical for East Fd); 8 & 18 Acres; ‡ 11 Acres; Elm (*v.* **elm**); Fiddleford Md, Tiddeford Md (sic) (*Fittleford(e) Medow(e)* 1584, *v.* **mæd**, Fiddleford *supra*); (Melmoths) Field Grove (*Filgrove* 1584, *v.* **grāf(a)**, first el. uncertain, cf. William *Melemouth'* 1332 (Sturminster N.), Henry *Melmouth* 1664); 5 Acres; Fore Md (*v.* **fore**); (Bottom) 4 Acres, †4 & 6 Acres; 14 Acre Pce; †Freaks Md (cf. Mrs *Freke* 1664, Hutch[3] 3 373); Fursey Croft, Furzy Croft & Grd (*Furzey Crofte* 1584, *v.* **fyrsig**, **croft**); †Git Hay; Gluby Md; Bottom, Lt & Middle Gobson, ‡Gobson Cmn (*mes' . . . desuper Gopesdon'* e14, *Gobson Common* 1583, *Gobston, Gobson* 1584, second el. **dūn** 'hill', first el. perhaps a strong form *Gupp* of the OE pers.n. *Guppa* suggested for Guppy in Wootton F. par.; on the other hand *Gopes-* may represent a reduced form of the surname *Gopeheye* (from the p.n. Guppy) found in 1332 SR and probably surviving in this par. in that of Richard *Gobye* 1584; the connection could have been manorial, whereby someone from Guppy in Wootton may have been given land in Okeford by the Fitz Payns who held both manors in the 13th and early 14th centuries); †Goswell (*v.* **gōs, well(a)**); Goulds Grd (1792); Graces Plot; Great Grd & Md; Green Cl; Green Way; Gully Md (*v.* **gully**); †Half Crown Grd (probably named from its rent or cost, cf. Ch 2 283); (†) Ham Down (Coppice) (named from Hammoon par. 2 99-100); (†) Hanging Grd (*v.* **hangende**); Harbins Plot, †Herbans Plot (cf. Robert *Harbyn* 1664); Hard Clift (Haicliffe, Hartliffe 1584, *v.* **clif** 'cliff, bank', first el. uncertain); Hay Croft (*Haycroft* 1288 (p), 1327 (p), *Hay-, Heycrofte* 1584, *v.* **hēg** 'hay', **croft**); Head Pdk; High Bench (*Haybench(e)* 1584, *v.* **hēg, benc** 'shelf, bank'); Higher Grd & Md; †Hill Cl, †Hill Foot; Hill Grd; Hilly Cl; Hobbitt (probably a spelling for Hibbett *supra*); Hod Moor (*Hodmore* 1584, *v.* **hōd¹** 'hood' or **hōd²** 'shelter', **mōr**); Hollow Md & Moor; Home Cl (*Homeclose* 1601); Home Drove, († ‡) Home Grd, Home Md, ‡Home Orchd, Home Plot; Horse Fd; House B and Orchd (sic); Hunt's Grd & Md; In Md (*v.* **in** 'inner'); Jordan(s) (*incl'm voc' Jordaine* 1584, the surname *Jo(u)rdan* common in Do (e.g. 1327, 1332), or a transferred name from the River Jordan in the Middle East); †Lake Md (*v.* **lacu**); Landshard (*Lamsher, Langshere* 1584, referring to the same par. bdy, between this par. and Shillingstone, as gives name to Landchard Lane *q.v.* in Shillingstone 2 240; the TA fields are on this bdy); Langson (Mdw) (*Lang(e)stone* (*Way, -Wey*) 1584, *v.* **lang¹, stān, weg**); †Late Croft; Leaze Md (*v.* **lǣs**); Leg (*v.* **leg**); Leigh Md (*v.* **lēah**); Lillwood Mdw & Orchd (*claus pastur' voc' lilsworthe* 1601, from **worð** 'enclosure', probably with the OE pers.n. *Lill, v.* DEPN s.n. Lillesdon So, cf. the Do surname *Lil* 1327 *SR* (Bloxworth)); Little Cl & Md; Long Cl (Mdw & Orchd) (*Long Closse* 1584, *v.* **lang¹, clos(e)**); †Long Cl; Long Hill (Orchd & Md) (*Longhill* 1584, *v.* **hyll**); (‡) Long Md; Long Orchd; Long Wall (Orchd) (*Longwaile* (probably for *-walle*) 1584, *v.* **w(e)all**); Lower Md, Pdk & Pce; Malm Grd (*v.* **m(e)alm** 'sandy or chalky soil'); ‡Malthouse and Orchd; Marsh (cf. *le Mershes* 1584, *v.* **mersc**); Merry Gdn (*v.* **myrge** 'pleasant'); Middle Grd, Md & Pdk; Miller(')s Grd, Md, Orchd & Plot; (†) Moor Md; Naps; †Nashwell (first el. possibly **æsc** 'ash-tree' with *N-* from ME **atten** 'at the'); Nell, Nill (*Knill* (*Lane*), *Nellstede* 1584, *v.* **cnyll(e)** 'a knoll, a hillock', **stede**); (†) Netherway (Orchd) (*Nethe(r)way, Nethway* 1584, *v.* **neoðerra, weg**); New Cl (*New Closse* 1584, *v.* **clos(e)**); New Cross Plot (*New Crosse* 1584, *Newcrosse Lane* 1601, to be identified with New Cross Gate 2 240 on the boundary between this par. and Shillingstone); 9 Acres; No(r)ber (*incl'm voc' Narbor, Narbors-, Narburs Elmes, Narbors-, Narbures Lane* 1584, origin uncertain without earlier forms but possibly ME **erber** 'a garden, an arbour' with *N-* from ME **atten** 'at the', cf. also the form *Erver infra*, with **elm, lane**); Northfield (Coppice); Oakley Grd (*v.* **āc, lēah**); Okeford Hay & Md (*v.* **(ge)hæg**, par. name *supra*); Old Wood (Md) (*Oldwood* 1584, *v.* **eald, wudu**); (Old) Orchard (*pomarium* 1584); Overness (Mdw) (*Ovenest* 1584, possibly '(land) above the nest', *v.*

ufan, nest); †Overshut (*Overshott* 1584, second el. possibly **scēat** 'corner of land', with either **ofer³** 'above' or **uferra** 'higher'); ‡Oxenleaze (*v.* **oxa, lǣs**); ‡Patts; Peaked Grd (*v.* **peked** 'pointed'); Pear Cl & Md; Pedlars Plot; Penwell (Coppice & Md) (*incl'm voc' Pinwell, duo pictella voc' Pynwell* 1584, cf. *duo incl'a ex utraque riparum voc' Pinbrooke ib, v.* **well(a)** 'spring, stream', **brōc** 'brook'; the first el. of both names may be **pinn** 'a pin, a peg' or **pīn** 'a pine-tree'); Pess Md; †Pile; (†) Pit Cl (cf. *incl'm voc' Broadpitt* 1584, *v.* **brād, pytt**); Play Cross (*incl'm voc' Play Crosse* 1584, 'cross or crossroads where games were played', *v.* **plega, cros, cross**, cf. *Gren(e)hay(e) infra*); †Plot; Pond Cl & Orchd; Puxey Cl (cf. Puxey Lane in Shillingstone **2** 240, Puxey in Sturminster N. par. *infra*); Red Lake(s) (*incl'm voc' Redlake* 1584, *v.* **rēad, lacu**); †Richlings; Ridout's Md (cf. Robert *Ridout* 1664); †Corn & Green Riles; Rimple (Md) (*Remple (Lane)* 1584, perhaps lME **rymple** (ModE *rimple*) 'a wrinkle' in some figurative sense); (†) (Pit Cl or) Rodford (*Rodford Elmes, -Lane* 1584, 'reedy ford', from **hrēod** and **ford**, with **elm**, cf. Pit Cl *supra*); Roses Md & Orchd (cf. Richard *Rose* 1664); Rough Grd; Rush Knap (*Rushe Knappe, Rushe Knap(pe) Way* 1584, *v.* **risc, rysc, cnæpp, weg**); †Rushy Cl; Russell Md (cf. *Emma Russell . . . ten'* 1584); Long, Nether & Yonder Ryeland (*incl'm voc' Rayland, -lond, Reyland* 1584, possibly **ēg-land, īeg-land** 'island', or **ēa-land** 'land by a river', with *R-* from ME **atter** 'at the'); Sand Hill (*Sandhill* 1584, *v.* **sand, hyll**, cf. Old Sand Pit 6″); Sangson Md & Orchd (not identified with *Sugestone supra* and no doubt of different origin, possibly from **sand** and **gærs-tūn**); Scotts Grd (cf. Edward *Skott* 1584); Sedge Md (*v.* **secg¹**); †Sewells (Coppice), †Wood Serrell (sic, perhaps for *Sewell*) (a surname); 7 Acres; Shap Hay (*Shapehaye* 1584, 'sheep enclosure', *v.* **scēap, (ge)hæg**); Short Land (*Shortland* 1584); Shot Fd, Shotfield Barn (probably for *Stot-, v.* Stot field Md *infra*); †Shoulder of Mutton (so called from its shape); (†)6 Acres; †Smal-, Snailways; (Orchard) Smies; Spring Cl, ‡Spring Md; Square Cl; †Starvelings; †Stibles; Stoneyford (**2** *incl'a voc' Stonyford* 1584, *v.* **stānig, ford**); Stot field Md (*incl'm voc' Stotfold, Stot(t)fo(u)ld Drove* 1584, *v.* **stōd-fald** 'a stud-fold, a horse enclosure', **drāf**); Summer Cl, Grd & Leaze (*v.* **sumor, lǣs**); †Tansay (spelling uncertain); (†)10 Acres; 3 Cornered Pce; †Turnwell; 12 Acres; (†)2 Acres; Vessbury; Wall Md; Waters Cl; †Webbs (cf. Walter *Webb* 1664); †Westland Wd; West Wood (Orchd) (*Westwood(e), West(e)wood(e) Closse, -Lane* 1584, *v.* **west, wudu**); Williams Pdk (cf. Edward *Williams* 1584); †Wilsoms; †Wises; Wood Horn (*v.* **horn**); Woolbridge Norber (first el. perhaps **wiell(a)** 'spring, stream', cf. Wood **1** 188, *v.* Norber *supra*); Yonder Grd; Youngs Grd & Md (cf. William *le Yonge* 1332, Nicholas *Young* 1664).

(*b*) *Al(l)sett Hay* 1584 (*v.* **(ge)hæg**); *Artes* 1497, *Arthurs* 1584, *Arthur Hayes* 1590 (cf. John *Artur* 1327, *-Artour* 1332, *v.* **(ge)hæg**); *Bymber plecke* 1601 (perhaps **bēam** 'tree, beam of timber' and **bearu** 'grove', with **plek**); *Cheslane* 1584 (possibly **cis** 'gravel'); *copic' voc' le Cliff* 1584, *two coppes . . . called the Cliffes* 1590 (*v.* **clif**); *scitum manerii voc' Corte Closse* 1584 (*v.* **court, clos(e)**); *Cotiers-, Cotyars-, Cotyers Drove* 1584 (from

cotere 'a cottager' (or a surname) and **drāf**); *Emede* (*Lane*) 1584, *Ye Mede* 1601 (*v.* **mǣd**, first el. probably **ēa** 'stream'); *claus' voc' Erver* 1601 (perhaps for *Erber*, cf. No(r)ber *supra*); *Fesburye Knappe* 1584 (*v.* **cnæpp**); *incl'm voc' Fewlolars* 1584 (perhaps a poor spelling for the surname *Fowler*); *Fishers Closse* 1584; *atte Ford'* (p) 1332 (*v.* **atte, ford**); *Le Goore* 1584 (*v.* **gāra**); *Gren(e)hay(e)* (*als. Playing closse*) 1584 (*v.* **grēne**[1], **(ge)hæg, playing, clos(e)**, cf. Play Cross *supra*); *Horspo(o)le Pleck(e)* 1584 (*v.* **hors, pōl**[1], **plek**); *Loveland'* 1497 (perhaps a courting spot, *v.* **lufu**); *Mayre Land* 1584; *Mawredge, -rydge, Mayridge, -Rige* 1584 (*v.* **hrycg**, first el. uncertain); *at Porche* (p) 1601 (*v.* **porch**); *atte Poule* (p) 1327 (*v.* **atte, pōl**[1]); *Redland* 1584 (*v.* **rēad**); *South Closse* 1584; *incl'm voc' Whitpitt* 1584 (*v.* **hwīt, pytt**, cf. Chalk Pits 6"); *Bythewode* (p) 1584 ('by the wood', *v.* **wudu**); *3 incl'a voc' Worthe* 1584 (*v.* **worð** 'enclosure').

Sturminster Newton

STURMINSTER NEWTON (ST 786142)

> (*at*) *Stoure, Nywetone* (rubric) 968 (14) *Glast* (S 764)
> *Newetone Kastel* 1016 (1727) Finberg (p. 176), *Newentone* 1086 DB, *-ton* 1272 FF, *Neuton(e)* 1196 ChancR, 1210–12 RBE, *Niwetun, Niwatona* 13 GlastR, *Nyw(e)-, Niw(e)ton(e)* 13 ib, 1212 Fees, 1236 FF, 1288 *Ass et freq* to m14 *Glast, New(e)ton(')* 1268, 1288 *Ass et freq* to 1386 *Ilch, Nova Villa* 1286 Ch, *Nywthone* 1307 (15) *ForReg, Nieuton'* 1327 *SR, Neuwetone* m14 *Glast, Nuton* 1386 Fine, *Newton* 1795 Boswell; *Niwe-, Nyw(e)ton(e)-castel, -Castel* Ed 1 (m14) *Glast*, 1297 Ipm, 1330 Ch *et freq* to 1350 Ipm, *vill' de Chastell', Niueton' castel* 1280 *Ass, Nyw(t)hon' Castel* Ed 1 (15) *ForReg, Neuton Castell(e)* 1350 Ipm, 1425 Cl, *Newetoncastel* 1350 Ipm, *-Castell* 1427 Pat
> *Sturministr'* 13 GlastR, 1288 *Ass, -manstr'* 1275 RH, *-mynster* 1294 Banco (*-Abbatis Glaston'*) , *-men(i)stre* 1297 Ipm (*-by Niweton Castel*), e14 GlastE, 1342 GlastF (*-Abbatis*), *-minstre* 1301 (m14) *Glast* (*-Abbatis*), *-munstre* e14 GlastE, *-mynstre* (*Abbatis*) 1333 Pat *et freq* to 1444 Fine, *-mynstre Castel* 1355 Ipm, *-mestre* 1425 Cl (*-by Neuton Castelle*), *-myster* 1548 Ct, *Surminstre Abbatis* 13 (m14) *Glast, Stourminstr(e)* 1244 *Ass et freq* with variant spellings *Stoure-, -mynstre* to 1535–43 Leland, *Stormenstre* 1272 FF, *-mynstre Abbe* 1391 Pat, *Scyremestre* (sic) 1280 QW, *Sture(s)ministre* 1288 *Ass,*

Stir-, Styrmyst' Abb' c.1500 *Eg, Stourmister, Stoureton Minster* 1535–43 Leland, *Sto'myster* 1539 *AD Stur(e)m(n)inistr!(e)* *Nyweton(e)* 1291 Tax, *Sturmynstre Neuton* 1407 Pat, *-Newton* 1428 FA, *Stourmynstre and Neweton* 1411 Cl, *Stourmyster Newton'* e16 *Prideaux, Sturmister Newton* 1666 *Salkeld; Sturmynstre Neuton-castell* 1437 FF, *Sturmystre Newton' Castell* 1475 *DuCo, St(o)ur(e)mynster New(e)ton Castell* 1496 Pat, 1514 *PlR, Styrmyster Newton' Castell* 1533 *ib, Sturminster Newton Castle Towne* 1664 HTax, *Sturminster Newton Castle* 1870 Hutch[3]

The present name is a combination of the names of two originally separate places, Sturminster on the N side of R. Stour, Newton on the S side, the latter giving name to the hundred (now Sturminster Newton hundred *supra*). Sturminster is 'the church on R. Stour' and therefore identical in origin with Sturminster Marshall **2** 45, *v.* **mynster**, St Mary's Church, RNs. *infra*. The Lat affix *-Abbatis* 'of the abbot' refers to the possession of the manor by Glastonbury Abbey (from 968, cf. the Anglo-Saxon charter of 968 (14) *Glast* (S 764), which describes the bounds). Newton is 'new farm or estate', from **nīwe** (wk.obl. *-an*) and **tūn**; this is still the name of the part of the par. S of R. Stour. The affix *-Castle* refers to the earthworks (probably an Iron-Age promontory hill-fort, within which are the 14th cent. ruins of the medieval manor house of the Abbot of Glastonbury, *v.* Castle *infra*) just S of the Town Bridge, *v.* **castel(l)** 'castle, camp', RCHM **3** 282.

STREET-NAMES: GOUGH'S CLOSE, 1839 *TA*, cf. John *Goff* 1511 Hutch[3], Thomas *Goffe* 1664 HTax; MARKET PLACE, cf. *in loco mercat'* 1548 *Ct*; PENNY ST., cf. John-, William *Penny* 1664 HTax, unlikely to be connected with *Penstret', -strate* mentioned under Pentridge Fm *infra*; RICKETT'S LANE, from *Ricketts* 1839 *TA*, a surname. Inns include *Crown, Swan, White Hart* all 1824 Pigot; Bull, Jolly Brewer, Rose and Crown all 6″.

BAGBER (ST 754137)
   Bakeberge 1201 Cur (p), 1208 P (p), *-ber(e)* 1204 FF, 1208 ChancR, Cur, 1212 RBE (p), 1243 Fees, 1244 *Ass*, 1263

Ipm, 1268 *Ass* (p), 1280 *ib*, 1288 *ib et freq* to c.1500 *Eg,
-pere* (sic) 1316 FA (p), *Estbakebere* 1363 Pat, 1412 FA,
Westbakeber' 1398 *Cecil, Bakebeare* 1412 FA, 1436 Fine,
-bery 1445 ib, *easte Bakebeere* 1620 *CH*
Bakkeber(e) 13 (m14) *Glast* (p), 1342 GlastF, 1428 FA,
Backebere 1244 *Ass* (p), 1303 FA
Bakber' 13 GlastR
Baggeber(e) 1244 *Ass,* 1338–40 Glast, *-berg'* 1244 *Ass,
-ber'* [*Baggebur'*] 1303 FA
Bagbere 1475 IpmR, e16 *Prideaux,* 1515 Hutch[3] *et freq* to
1870 ib, *-bor(e)* 1575 Saxton, 1795 Boswell, *East &
West Bagber* 1583 *SPDom, Castle Bagber* 1619 *CH, East
Bagbeere* 1620 *ib, Bagbeare* 1680 *AddRoll*

Probably 'Bacca's wood or grove', from the OE pers.n.
Bacca (Redin 83) and **bearu** (some of the early spellings
showing influence from **beorg** 'hill, barrow'). Derivation of
the first el. from **bagga** 'bag-like feature, badger' as
suggested in EPN 1 23 is not supported by the majority of
early forms. The affixes *East* and *West* probably represent
the two parts of Bagber mentioned in Hutch[3] 4 339, one part
having belonged to the manor of (Sturminster) Newton
(hence perhaps alternatively *Castle-*), the other to the
hundred of Cranborne. The former chapel here is *capellam
de Bakebere* 1340 NI, *v.* Hutch[3] 4 340, cf. *Hr & Lr Chapel,
Chapel Cl* 1839 *TA.*

COLBER CRIB HO (ST 780147)
Colesberie 1086 DB, *-breia* Exon
Colbere 13 (m14) *Glast,* 1244 *Ass,* 1262 FF, 1268, 1288
Ass, 1327 *SR et freq* to 1870 Hutch[3], *-ber* 1308 Ipm,
1839 *TA, Colber(e) Lane* 1547 *Ct,* 1587 Hutch[3], *Colbury*
1605 ib
Couber 1244 *Ass, Cober* (*Grounds*) 1795 Boswell
Colebere 1281 Banco (Drew), 1288 *Ass,* e14 *GlastE*
Cowere 1342 GlastF
Coulbebere 1399 Cl
Colbeare Iryssh 1412 FA

Probably 'Cola's wood or grove', from the OE pers.n. *Cola* (Feilitzen 217) and **bearu**. The DB and Exon forms show alternation or confusion of the pers.n. with a strong form *Col* (adduced for Colesborne Gl 1 154) and of the second el. with **burh** (dat.sg. *byrig*) 'fortified place'. Disregarding these same forms, the first el. could formally be **col**[1] 'coal, charcoal' or **cōl**[2] 'cool'. The affix *Iryssh* in 1412 is no doubt manorial; no family of this name has been noted in connection with this place, but the surname is well evidenced in other parts of the county (e.g. *le Eyrisshe, Yreys* 1327 *SR, le Hirissh, (le) Yryss(c)h* 1332 SR). Crib is from **cribbe** 'crib, manger, oxstall', cf. f.ns. *infra*. A bridge here (*ponte de Colbere* 1288 *Ass, Cober* [Bridge] 1791 Boswell) may have been on the site of Blackwater Bridge *infra*.

COOMBS (ST 785132), 1870 Hutch[3] (*the rectorial house . . . called-*), *La Combe* (*boscus*), *the Combe* e14 *GlastE, clausum qui vocatur la Combe* 1338–40 Glast, *lands called Combes* 1562 Hutch[3], *Coombe Coppice & Plant.* 1839 *TA*, 'the valley', *v.* **cumb**. This name is to be associated with *on Conibrok'* of *þan brok'* 968 (14) *Glast* (S 764), *on Combrock'* 1338–40 Glast, *rivulum de Combesbrok'* 1338–40 ib, m14 *Glast*, in the Anglo-Saxon and medieval bounds of Sturminster Newton, 'valley brook', the **brōc** in question being that which rises just S of the par. bdy and flows N to join the R. Stour near Coombs. The form *Conibrok'* is no doubt simply an error for *Combrok'* (thus making unnecessary Wallenberg's speculation in PNK 415–16 that it may contain a unique early instance of ME **coni** 'rabbit').

KINGSDOWN (ST 799131), 1582 Hutch[3], 1811 OS, (*terre super*) *Kyngesdo(u)n(e)* e14 *GlastE, boscis . . . vocatis Kingesdon(e)* 1337 (m14) *Glast, Kyngges-, Kinggesdon'* 1338–40 Glast, (*Gt*) *King's Down* 1839 *TA*, probably 'the king's down', from **cyning** and **dūn**, with reference to old royal demesne, cf. the 4 hides in the manor of Sturminster N. held of the king by Goscelm the cook in 1086 DB (VCHDo 3 73). A surname as first el. is perhaps less likely, but cf. Alice *La Kynges* e14 *GlastE*. An earlier name for Kingsdown may have been (*on*) *Trildoune* 968 (14) *Glast* (S

764), 'the down by River *Tril*' (now Darknoll Brook, *v.* RNs. *infra*), mentioned in the Anglo-Saxon bounds of Sturminster N.

PEASE-, PEAZE LEAZE (lost, about ST 753138), 1839 *TA, la Southhurne de Pusleighesclos* m14 *Glast, la Southerne de Pisleysclos* 1338–40 Glast, *Pusleplace* 1398 *Cecil, Puselecroft* 1409 Hutch³, *Puseleyescrofte* 1411 Cl, 'the close, place and croft belonging to the (*de*) *Pusele*(*gh*) family', *v.* **clos(e)**, **place**, **croft**, cf. John *de Puselegh*' e14 *GlastE, -de Pusele* 1308 (15) *ForReg*, 1327 *SR*, Laurence *Pusele* 1332 SR, John *Pusele* 1355 Ipm; *Southhurne, -erne* is 'south corner', *v.* **sūð**, **hyrne**. The surname *Pusele*(*gh*) is from a p.n. (not necessarily local or even in this county) meaning 'clearing used for growing pease', *v.* **pisu, peosu, lēah**, such as *Peasley* Gl 2 16. It is clear that the modern form Pease Leaze is the result of popular etymology and rationalization of the possessive form *Pusleighes-*, cf. the interesting tradition reported by Hutch³ 4 342 that in this field Charles I 'was sumptuously regaled with green-pease for dinner, and that hence the field has ever since been called *Pease-lease*'.

PERRY FM (ST 752143), 1811 OS, *the manor called Perys House* 1511 Hutch³, *Per(r)y House* 1515, 1640 ib, *Perry-Court* 1774 Hutch¹, cf. William *de Piro* 13 GlastR, Edward *atte Purie . . . mes*' e14 *GlastE*, John *atte Purye* 1331 FF, Thomas *Pery* (conveyor of the manor) 1511 Hutch³, *v.* **pirige** 'pear-tree', **atte** 'at the'.

PIDDLES WOOD (ST 795129)
  Puttelesw(*u*)*rthe* (*boscum de-*) 13 GlastR, *-worth*(*e*) e14 GlastE, 1337 (m14) *Glast* (*boscis voc*'-), 1338–40 Glast, *Puteles-* e14 *GlastE, Puttellesworth*(*e*) 1307 (15) *ForReg, Puctelesworth*' (for *Putteles-*) 1342 GlastF
  Putteswurthe 13 GlastR (p)
  Puttekwurth' 1244 *Ass* (p)
  Pittelesworth' (*bosco de-*) 1338–40 Glast, *Pittelswo'the* 1548 Ct
  Puddlesworth or Puddlewood 1582 Hutch³
  Piddles Wood 1811 OS, *Piddle's Wd* 1839 TA

Probably 'Pyttel's enclosure', from the OE pers.n. *Pyttel* (Redin 143) and **worð**. The relatively late development of -*worth* to -*wood* (as in Wythwood Wo 359, etc) was obviously reinforced by the fact that this always was, and still is, a wood. Formally the first el. could equally well be the word **pyttel** 'a hawk, a mousehawk' which is the source of the pers.n. and which occurs in Do dial. as *dun-piddle* 'the kite or moor buzzard' (Barnes 62); in view of this possibility, the form *Puttekwurth*' 1244 is particularly interesting, since it seems to contain the related word **puttoc** 'a kite', or the equivalent pers.n. *Puttoc* (Redin 153). Pittleworth Ha 187 may be directly analogous, although it has some early forms without medial -*s*-, cf. also Pittsworthy D 207.

RIXON (ST 793144), HR & LR RIXTON ESTATE, *Ri-*, *Rygarston*' e14 GlastE, (*Bottom*) *Rixon, Rixon Cl & Elm, Rixon or Flewletts, -or* T Grd 1839 *TA*, 'enclosure for growing rye', from **ryge** and **gærs-tūn**; it was near to *Mauryesgarston*' e14 GlastE for which *v.* Fiddleford Mill *infra. Flewletts* may be an error, cf. Hewlett's Drove *infra* (1½ miles SW).

ALL SAINTS' CHURCH. BAGBER BRIDGE (1811 OS, *Bagbor-* 1791 Boswell), CMN (1811 OS) & WD, HR & LR BAGBER FM, *v.* Bagber *supra.* BEECH HO. BLACKWATER BRIDGE, over R. Divelish, suggesting that *Blackwater* may have been an alternative name for this part of the river where it joins R. Stour, *v.* RNs. *infra*; the site of the bridge may earlier have been that of *ponte de Colbere* 1288 *Ass, v.* Colber Crib Ho *supra.* BRIDGE, a hamlet named from Town Bridge *infra.* BROAD OAK (FM). BUTT'S POND, cf. Richard *Butt* 1664 HTax. CALF CLOSE LANE, cf. *Calves' Cl* 1839 *TA.* CASTLE (Remains of), cf. *a fair maner place of an hille made stepe rounde . . . caullid yn olde writinges Newton Castelle* 1535–43 Leland, Gilbert *de Castello* 1346 FA, *v.* par. name *supra.* DUCKS LANE, *Duck's Lane* Grd 1839 *TA*, probably a surname. DUNCH MOUTH, cf. *Dunch Flg* 1839 *TA*, possibly **dyncge** 'manured land', with **mūða** here referring to the mouth of R. Divelish where it joins R. Stour. FIDDLEFORD MILL, 1811 OS, *molendinum . . . de Fitilford*' 1338–40 Glast, cf. *Fiddleford Md* 1839 *TA,* named from Fiddleford in Okeford F. par. *supra*; the mill is probably identical with *molendinum Ricardi Mauri (pontem iuxta-)* m14 *Glast* mentioned in the bounds of Sturminster Newton, cf. *Mauryesgarston',* Alicia Maury . . . *mes'* e14 *GlastE,* Richard *Mauri* 1307 (15) *ForReg, -Maury* 1327 *SR, tenementi Ricardi Mauri* m14 *Glast, v.* **gærs-tūn** 'paddock'. GIRDLER'S COPPICE, *Girdler's, Girdles Coppice & Mead* 1839 *TA,* probably a surname. GLUE HILL. GOLDEN GATE (lost, about ST 768156), 1811 OS; somewhere near, and therefore probably to be associated with *bi targildenedich* m14 *Glast* in the bounds of Sturminster N., from **gylden** 'splendid' or 'gold-coloured' and **dīc** 'ditch', *tar-* perhaps representing OE *þære.* HAYDON CORNER, named from Haydon in Lydlinch par. *infra.* HEWLETT'S DROVE, cf. *Hewlett's Grd & Higher Cl* 1839 *TA,* Dinah *Hulett* 1664 HTax, *v.* **drāf.** HOLE HOUSE (FM), *Hole* 1811 OS, *Hole Grd, Hole-House Coppice & Grd* 1839 *TA,* cf. *Holemed* 1338–40 Glast, *v.* **hol¹** 'a hole, a hollow', **mǣd.** HONEYMEAD LANE, from *Hunimede* 13 GlastR, *Honymede* e14 *GlastE, Ho(r)ney Mead* 1839 *TA,* 'meadow where honey was produced', or 'sweet meadow', *v.* **hunig, mǣd.** HOSEY BRIDGE, acr' voc' *Hosebri(d)ge* 1557 *Val,* 1567 *Glouc,* 1627 *SxAS, Osier Bridge* 1839 *TA,* probably 'bridge by the shoots or tendrils', with reference to some kind of marsh plant, from **hos(s)** and **brycg,** cf. Ostbridge Gl 3 120, but alternatively from **hosa** 'stocking' applied to a stream or lane, cf. Hose Hill Brk 205. The site of this bridge is probably to be identified with either *pontem vocatum la Stone* or *Threbruggin* in the 14th cent. bounds of Sturminster N., *v.* lost names *infra.* THE LINDENS. MANOR FM, *Bagber* 1811 OS, *v.* Bagber *supra.* MILL (at Newton), cf. *stagnum molendini de Nywton', duo molendina aquatica,* Margaret *atte Mulle* e14 *GlastE, the Myll meade* 1578 *Salkeld, Fulling Mill, Mill Ham* 1839 *TA, v.* **myln, atte** 'at the', **mǣd, hamm;** there were three mills at *Newentone* in 1086 DB (VCHDo 3 73), cf. Fiddleford Mill *supra,* Rolls Mill *infra.* MULLINS' FM, cf. Thomas *Molyns* who held the manor of Bagber *supra* in 1537 (Hutch³ 4 339). NEWTON (FM), originally the name of a manor, still used for the part of the par. S of R. Stour, *v.* discussion of par. name *supra.* OAKS FM, cf. *Oak's Cl &*

Hill 1839 *TA*, John *Oake* 1664 HTax. PENTRIDGE FM (*Pentridge* 1811 OS) & LANE, no early forms, but probably to be identified with *Penstret'* 1332 SR (p), *firmam voc' Penstrate* 1619 *CH*, from **strǣt** with **penn²** 'a fold, a pen', or (if the name is older) **penn¹** 'hill' (Pentridge Fm is situated on the slopes of an elongated hill, so that a second el. **hrycg** might also not be out of the question; however, the later form may have been transferred from the par. name Pentridge **2** 235 which has a different origin but which like Bagber was in Cranborne hundred). THE PLANTATION, *Plantation* 1839 *TA*. PLEAK HOUSE FM, cf. *Pleck Willow Bed* 1839 *TA, v.* **plek** 'small plot of ground'. POPLAR FM. PUXEY (COPPICE, FM & LANE), *Pixey, Puxey Cmn* 1811 OS, *Puxey* (*Md*) 1839 *TA*, probably to be associated with John *Poke* 1327 *SR* (Bagber tithing), second el. perhaps **(ge)hæg** 'enclosure'. QUEEN'S COPPICE, 1839 *TA*, cf. *Will' Walton' tenent d'ni* (sic) *Regine in Bagbere* 1547 *Ct, v.* Bagber *supra*; the manor of Newton was granted to Queen Katharine in 1544 (Hutch³ **4** 337). RALPH DOWN (lost, ST 769133), 1811 OS, *Raffedune* 13 GlastR, (*croftam iuxta*) *Raffedoune* e14 GlastE, *Rafe-Down* 1605 Hutch³, *Raufe Down* (*Grd*) 1839 *TA, Ralph's Down* 1870 Hutch³, *v.* **dūn** 'hill, down'; the first el. is probably the pers.n. *Radulf, Raulf* (*Raffe* being a spelling found from the 13th cent., *v.* Reaney *s.n. Ralf*). RIVERS' CORNER, cf. Robert *Ryves* 1666 *Salkeld*. ROAD LANE FM, probably to be associated with Robert *de la Rode* 13 GlastR, William *atte Rode . . . mes'* e14 GlastE, William *atte Rod* 1323 (15) *ForReg*, from **rod¹, rodu** 'a clearing' with **atte** 'at the'. ROLLS MILL (*Mill* 1811 OS), ROLLS MILL BRIDGE (*Rolls Bridge* 1791 Boswell, 1811 OS, *Rolles or Rawles Bridge* 1870 Hutch³), cf. *Will' Rolf . . . mesuag'* e14 GlastE, *v.* Reaney *s.n. Rolf*. RUSHY CTGS, from *Hr & Lr Rushy* 1839 *TA*, probably from **risc, rysc** 'rush' and **(ge)hæg** 'enclosure'. ST MARY'S CHURCH, cf. *ecclesiam beate Mar' de Sturministr'* 1288 *Ass*. STALBRIDGE LANE, to Stalbridge par. *infra*. STOUR VIEW HO (1"). STURMINSTER CMN, 1811 OS, cf. *West Common* 1583 *SPDom*. TOWN BRIDGE, *pontem de Neuton Castel* 1300 Hutch³, *Stourmister bridge of stone* 1535–43 Leland (**1** 256), giving name to Bridge *supra*; Leland also describes it as *a very fair bridge of 6 arches at the towne*

ende (5 107). WHITE LANE, cf. *White Lane Ctg* 1824 Pigot.
WOODLANDS, 1870 Hutch³ (*an old house with lands called-*).

FIELD-NAMES

The undated forms are 1839 *TA* 212. Spellings dated 944 (15) are *ShaftR* (S 502), 968 (14) Glast (S 764), 13 *GlastR*, 13 (m14), Ed I (m14), 1274 (m14), 1307 (m14), 1337 (m14), m14 *Glast*, 1244 *Ass*, e14 *GlastE*, 1307 (15), 1308 (15), 1311 (15) *ForReg*, 1327 *SR*, 1332 SR, 1338–40 Glast, 1340 NI, 1346 FA, 1475, 1611 *DuCo*, 1482 *AD*, 1511, 1574, 1582, 1613, 1870 Hutch³, 1547, 1548 *Ct*, 1578, 1666, 1686, 1708, 1728, 1761 *Salkeld*, 1618, 1619, 1620 *CH*, c. 1620 *DCMSurv*, 1664 HTax, and 1795 Boswell.

(*a*) Allpits; Ash Cl (cf. John *atten Asche* 1327, -*atte Assh*' 1332, *v.* **æsc, atte(n)**); Bagber Cl (cf. *Bekebereshulle* 1338–40, *Bagber Lane* 1618, -*lease* 1620, all named from Bagber *supra, v.* **hyll, lane, lǣs**); (Gt) Baker's; Barn Cl & Md; Barretts' Grd (cf. William *Baret* e14, Henry *Baret* 1307 (15)); Barrow Cl & Md (cf. Adam *de la Bergh*' 13, *Walter atte Bergh*' . . . *mes*', *Berghforlang*' e14, *terram Walteri atte berwe* m14, *v.* **beorg** 'hill, barrow', **atte, furlang**); Bartlett's Cl; Bean Grd; Belbin's Cl (cf. Walter *Baillebyn* 1327, Richard *Balbyn* 1547, Robert *Belbyn* 1664); Benditch (or Summer-leaze) Md (*Bynedich*', -*dych*' e14, *Byndyche* 1548, *Benditch* 1728, probably '(land) within the ditch', from **binnan** and **dīc**, *v.* Summerleaze *infra*); Biles Cl & Grd (cf. Richard *Biles* 1664); Black Close (Md), Bla(c)kland (*v.* **blæc**); Blue Button; Bottom Grd; Boyte's Coppice & Md (cf. John *Boite* 1664 (Okeford F.)); Brach, Breach Coppice & Md(s) (*La Breche (de Suthlee)* e14, *v.* **brǣc** 'land broken up for cultivation', Southly Md *infra*); Braggs' Corner; Brayen Cl (probably **brægen** 'hill'); Gt & Lt Brickham, Gt Brick-Kilns, Brick-kiln Md, Brick Orchd, Bricks (*v.* **brick, brick-kiln**); Bridge Md; Brinsley (*v.* Maize Brinsley Md *infra*); Broad Cl; Broad Fd (Md) (*Broadfeilde* 1611); Broad Md (*Brademede* e14, *v.* **brād, mǣd**); Bucks (1611, a surname); Buffett's (North) Cl (cf. Thomas *Bussett* (sic) 1664); Bulland, Bullen Md, Bull Grd (cf. *Bolefordesweye* 1338–40, -*weie* m14, *v.* **bula** 'bull', **ford, weg, land**); Burnbake (*v.* **burnbake** 'land cleared by burning'); Burrough Md (cf. *Burgh'weye* e14, *v.* **burh** 'fortified place'); Honey Burt (perhaps to be associated with Adam *de la Burte* 13, *Bertham* e14, origin uncertain, *v.* **hamm**; for *Honey*, cf. Honeymead Lane *supra*; the field in question lies alongside R. Divelish); Hr & Lr Chapel, Chapel Cl (from the former chapel at Bagber *supra*); Chenoux; Churchill's Grd; Cleeve's Cl (cf. Reuben *Cleeues* 1664, probably named from foll.); Clift (Md) (*6 acr' in La clyve, La Clive* e14, *Le Clevys* 1548, *close called Cliffe* 1686, *v.* **clif** 'cliff, bank'); Clover Cl; Clutter's Plot; Bushy & Elbow Co(u)lbourne, Coulbourn(e)'s Coppice & Grd, Colbourne's New & Old Md (cf. Robert *Colborne* 1664, possibly from a local p.n. 'cool stream' from **cōl²** and **burna**; the fields in question lie between R. Stour and R. Divelish, *Elbow* describing the shape of one of the fields, *v.* **el(n)boga**); Cole Lane; Cole's Coppice; Common Altmt, Cl, Grd & Orchd; Cookman's

Cl (cf. *terr' Henrici Cookman'* 1547); Coppice (Grd), Coppice or Cole Lane Grd; Corn Grd; Cowl Acre; Cow Leaze; Crib Grd & Md, Crib House or Ham Plat, Cribhouse Grd (or Field Cl) (*v.* **cribbe, cribhouse,** *v.* Ham *infra*); (Hill's) Cribnear; Cuckoo Pdk; Cut Mill Md (named from Cut Mill in Hinton St M. par. *supra*); (Broad & Lt) Dalling, (Long) Dalling Grd & Md, Dallings (Grd) (probably *Dallond'* e14, from **dāl-land** 'land held in common', but cf. Richard *Dollyng* . . . *mes'* e14, William *Dollinges* 1307 (15)); Dandy; Day's Plot; Dean Md (cf. *Denelond'* 13, *v.* **denu** 'valley', **land**); Drove (Way) (*v.* **drāf**); Dry Close(s); Durrant (*Dirrant* 1578, *Darent* 1605, *Durrants* 1666, *Dirrants* als. *Durrants* 1761, possibly to be associated with *Durarde* e14); Dyke's Coppice; East Cl; 8 Acres; Ellfurlong (first el. probably **elle(r)n** 'elder-tree'); Elm Grd; Farr's Grd (for the *Farr* family, *v.* Hutch[3] 4 340); Ferry Ld; Fil(l)bridge Cl & Md (*Felbrige* 1548, *-bridge* 1728); 5 Acres; Flax Md; Short Fledge; Fore Cl; Forier; (Gt) 40 Acres, 40 Acres Md (*le Fortye acres* 1619); 4 Acres; (Yonder) Frenchgrass Grd (*v.* **french grass**); Froghole (*v.* **frogga, hol**[1]); Fryer's Moor (*Fryer More* 1548, *v.* **frere, mōr**); Furzy Grd; Gall Hill (perhaps **g(e)alla** 'wet place in a field'); Gaston (probably **gærs-tūn** 'paddock'); Gough's Cl (*v.* st.ns. *supra*); Gould's (North) Cl & Grd; Grammar's Grd; Grass Hays (*v.* **(ge)hæg**); Gravel Altmt; Great Cl, Grd, Md & Orchd; Green Cl & Md; Grotto Grd; (Hr & Lr) Ham, Ham Md & Pleck, Crib House or Ham Plat (*the Hamme* e14, *Hamme* 1327, 1346 both (p), *Hammede* 1338–40, *v.* **hamm, mǣd, plek, plat**[2]); Gt Hamesbury, Lt Shilling or Hemesbury) (cf. Peter *Haym* . . . *cotag'* e14, Hayne's Cl, Shillings *infra*); Hanging Grd (*v.* **hangende**); Harness; Hawkins; Hayne's Cl (cf. Thomas *Hayne* 1664); Higher Cl & Grd; Hillberry; Hill Cl (cf. *La Hulle* e14, Reginald *atte hille* 1307 (15), Richard *atthe hille* 1308 (15), *v.* **hyll, atte**); Hills' or Coombe Cl (cf. Coombs *supra*); Hilly Grd; Hither Grd or Wadmans; Home Cl, Fd, Grd, Md(w), Pdk & Plat (*v.* **plat**[2]); Hoopers' (cf. Richard *le Hopere* e14); Lr Horse Cl, Hr Horse Leaze; Hungerfoot; Hunt's Grd; Inclosed Common; Isle of Wight (a transferred name alluding to the shape of this field); King's Croft & Md (cf. Kingsdown *supra*); King's Mill Leaze & Md (named from Kings Mill in Marnhull par. *supra*); Kittle Cl; Landmoor Md; Lanning's Grd; Hr & Lr Leaze, Lees (*v.* **lǣs**); Leg (Md) (*v.* **leg**); Leigh (Md) (cf. *Litle Lygh* 1548, *v.* **lēah**); Liddon Cl (from R. Lydden, *v.* RNs. *infra*); Lilly's Cl & Md; Little Acre, Cl, Grd, Md & Orchd; Long Cl, Grd & Md; Lovel's (Lane & Md) (cf. John *Laffolle* 1327, *-Laffol* 1332); Lower Cl, Croft & Grd; Madden Bridge 1870 (*Mawdhambrige* 1548, *Maddam* [Bridge] 1791, *v.* **hamm, brycg**, first el. possibly the pers.n. or surname *Maud*); Magg's-. Mogg's Md; Maize Brinsley Md, Maize Brinzley (for the first el. cf. *Mays-, Mayhuswode* 1337 (m14), 1338–40, from the surname *May* or *Mayhew* (both alternative forms of *Matthew*) and **wudu**); Yonder Merryweathers; Middle Cl & Grd; Milk-House Md; Milking Barton; Hr & Lr Mount; Newman's Cl (cf. John *le Nywman* . . . *mesuag'* e14); New Md; Nob Crook Orchd (cf. *Crookehorne* 1611, *v.* **knob** 'knoll', **crōc** 'bend', **horn** 'horn-shaped piece of land'); North East Cl; North Fd (Md) (*campus borealis* 13, *le Northfeild* 1611, *v.* **norð, feld**);

Onions; Orchard (cf. Agnes-, John *atte Orchard'* e14, *v.* **orceard, atte**); Ox('s) Leaze (*v.* **lǽs**); Paddock (Orchd); Park; Parson's Md & Wd (*boscum persone, Personeswude, -wode* e14, *Persons Wodd'* 1548, *v.* **persone, wudu**, cf. *Agnes Parsons* 1664); Pasture (Grd); Patchell Md; Peaked Cl & Md (*v.* **peked** 'pointed'); Pear Orchd; Pelly's Cl (cf. John *Pilie* 1327, *-Pylye* 1332 (Marnhull)); Pindle (Orchd); Pit Cl (cf. *Puttes iuxta curiam,* Emma *atte Putte* e14, John *de la putte* 13 (m14), William *atte putte* 1307 (15), *v.* **pytt, atte**); Plot and Common; Plumber (Grd & Md) (named from Plumber in Lydlinch par. *infra*); Lt Plumpton, Plumpton's (cf. Christopher *Plimpton* 1664); Pond Cl; The Poor Altmts, Poor Md; the Pound, Pound Close(s) (*v.* **pund**); Press Md (*Prestemede* 13, 1338–40, m14, *v.* **prēost, mǣd**); Pudding Cl (*v.* **pudding**); Quag Mire Orchd (*v.* **quagmire**); Quarr(y) Cl (*v.* **quarre(re)**); Rackhay's (*v.* **rakke, (ge)hæg**); Rawlin's Grd; Ray Grass, Rye Grass; Red Acre; Red Lion Ho; Red Plush (cf. Plush in Buckland N. par. *infra*); Ricketts (*v.* st.ns. *supra*); Rick Hay (cf. *La Rekestede* e14, *v.* **ricke, (ge)hæg, stede**); Rideouts Md (cf. Thomas *Ridout* 1664); James Rose's Ho and Orchd (cf. Richard *Rose* 1664); Rough Grd; House in the Row; Sandmoor (Md), Oak Sandmoor Willow (*on sand mor, of þan more* 968 (14), *la Sandmora* 13, *Sandmor* 1338–40, *-more* 1548, 1611, *Sandmore Meade* 1728, 'sandy moor or marshy ground', from **sand** and **mōr**, a point in the Anglo-Saxon bounds of Sturminster N.); 7 Acres; Sharland; Sherrings Grd; Shillings (cf. Hamesbury *supra*); Short's Md (cf. Thomas *Short* 1664); (King's Croft or) Shoulder of Mutton (two separate fields, so called from their shape); Silver Md & Wd; 6 Acres; Slytrick(')s; Southly Md (*Suth(')lee, Litele-, Moresuth'lee, Southlegh'* e14, 'south wood or clearing', *v.* **sūð, lēah**, with **lȳtel** 'little' and (presumably) **māra** 'bigger'); Spanyard (probably to be identified with *terr'* in *La Spannette* e14, which seems to represent a derivative in **-et(t)(e)** of **spann**[1] 'strip of land' or the like); Spear Bed (*v.* **spear**); Spring Cl; Stall Grd (*v.* **stall**); Starve Ld (a derogatory name for poor ground); Steart Md(w) (*pratum de Stert* 13, *La Sterte, Storte* e14, *v.* **steort** 'tail or tongue of land'); Stone Ld; Stone's Grd (cf. Dunstan *Stone* 1547 (Marnhull)); Summer Grd, Summerleaze (Md) (*v.* **sumor, lǽs**); (Dockham's or) Sweet's Md; Sycamore, Boytes' or Sycamore Grd (*v.* **sycamore**, cf. Boyte's Coppice *supra*); 10 Acres; Thornhill Leaze; 3 Acres; 3 Corner Cl; Town Md; Turnpenny (a complimentary name for a profitable field); 12 Acres; Velstead; West Cl & Fd (*campus occidens* e14); Wet-Land; Whernal's Orchd; Willow Bed; Windall's Orchd; Wood Cl (cf. John *Bithewode* 1307 (15), Edith *atte Wode* 1332, *v.* **wudu, bī, atte**); Wood Croft (Md) (*Wodcrofte* 1548, *Woodcroft(s Meadow)* 1728, *v.* **wudu, croft**); Worthy (Md) (*v.* **worðig** 'enclosure'); Yard Fd; Yeatman's Grd (cf. Peter *Yateman* 1664); (Hr & Lr) Yewstock (named from Yewstock in Hinton St M. par. *supra*); Yonder Grd; Young's Gdn & Grd (cf. Rose *Young* 1574, Thomas *Young* 1664). (b) *Alcrofte* 1611 (*v.* **croft**); *Bernard's* 1582 (possibly a surname, or a later form of foll.); *pasturam que vocatur Bernut* 13, (*terre in*) *La Bernette* e14 (*v.* **bærnet** 'land cleared by burning'); *Bikenhurste* e14, m14, *Byken-* e14, 1338–40, *Bykan-* 1338–40, *Bikan-*

hurste m14 (*mora de-*) (*v.* **hyrst** 'copse or wooded hill', first el. **bic(a)** 'beak-like projection' or the pers.n. *Bica*); *Bluntt' Lane* 1548; *atte Bore* (p) e14 ('at the hill', *v.* **atte, bor¹**); *Bovetoun* (p) e14 ('above the town', *v.* **bufan, tūn**); *Broad acre* 1611; *Brockhold'* 1548 (*v.* **brocc-hol** 'a badger hole, a sett'); *Brodeyesmede* e14 (*v.* **mǣd**, cf. Agnes *Brodeye ib* (Marnhull)); *pastura de Bucheclive* 1274 (m14), 1307 (m14), *-clyve* 1338–40 (probably 'he-goat's cliff or bank', from **bucca** and **clif**); *crofta que vocatur Colfrot* 13 (perhaps to be identified with *meadow called Calroste* 1613); *Cardifis-* 1338–40, *Cardifizcroiz* m14 (*v.* **crois** 'cross', cf. Elias *Kerdif* 1327, *-Kerdyf'* 1332); *Chyggesdon'* 1311 (15) (*v.* **dūn**); *truthforlang* (probably for *cruch-*) Ed I (m14), *Cruhforlang* 1338–40 (*v.* **furlang**, first el. probably **crūc³** 'cross'); *on þer dich, be dich* (corresponding to *anlang diche* 944 (15) in the bounds of Hinton St M.), *on þar dich southward be dich* 968 (14) (*v.* **dīc**); *Disber'* 13; (*ten'*) *Dogget', la (h)esthurne de Doggeteslonde* 1338–40, m14, *Doggeteslestapele* 1338–40, *Doggeteses* (sic) *stapele* m14 (*v.* **ēast, hyrne** 'corner', **land, le, stapol** 'post' (no doubt marking the boundary since these names occur in the medieval bounds of Sturminster N.), cf. John-, Robert *Doget* 1327 (Beaminster)); *atte Doune* e14, 1327, 1332, *atte done* 1307 (15) all (p) ('at the hill or down', *v.* **atte, dūn**, cf. Henry *Bisuthedune* 13, John *Peny bi Sothedon'* e14, 'to the south of the down', *v.* **bī** , **sūðan**); *La Dryemore* e14 (*v.* **drȳge, mōr**); *Ernesberghe* e14 (*v.* **earn** 'eagle', **beorg** 'hill'); *Estacre* 1338–40 (*v.* **ēast, æcer**); *Estbury* 1619 (*v.* **burh**); *in campo orientali* e14 ('east field'); *atte Ewelle* (p) 1327 (*v.* **atte, ǣwell** 'spring, source of a stream'); *on filithleighe* 968 (14) ('clearing for making hay', from **fileðe** and **lēah**, cf. Haydon in Lydlinch par. *infra*); *de la forde* 1244, *atte Forde* e14, *atþefforde* 1308 (15) all (p) (*v.* **atte, ford**); *la Forsaken(e)gore* 1338–40, m14 (*v.* **forsacen** 'abandoned', **gāra** 'triangular plot'; in the medieval bounds of Sturminster N.); *Gavelerthe, Gaveleshurch'* (probably for *-hurth'*), *Gaveleshurgh'* e14 ('ploughed land subject to tax or rent', from **gafol²** and **erð**); *Godstiche* e14 (*v.* **gōd, sticce¹**); *la Grenedych'* e14 (*v.* **grēne¹, dīc**); *bi groue* 968 (14) (*v.* **grāf(a)** 'grove, copse'); *Hanecle* (probably for *Hauec-*) 1338–40, *Haveclee* m14 ('hawk wood or clearing', *v.* **hafoc, lēah**); *Haywardwyke* e14 (*v.* **hayward, wīc**, cf. *Wyke infra*); *Haywod* 1307 (15) ('enclosed wood', from **(ge)hæg** and **wudu**); *bi heuede* 968 (14) ('along the headland(s)', *v.* **hēafod**, Forsberg 144 fn.1); *atte Herch* (p) 1307 (15) (probably for *Herth, v.* **erð**, cf. *Gavelerthe supra*); *la Heyeweye* 1338–40, *la Heieweie* m14 (*v.* **hēg** 'hay', **weg**); *Hole(s)combesbrok'* 1338–40, m14 (*v.* **hol², cumb, brōc**); *Horsithe* e14 (probably 'dirt pit', *v.* **horu, sēað**, cf. *Horsyth* 2 210); 'ten' voc' *Hostry* 1475, *Hestroy(e Santymes)* 1611, c.1620, *Hestleer* 1613; *in the hurne* (p) e14 (*v.* **hyrne**); *Hydlonde* 1482 (*v.* **hīd, land**); *Is-, Ysbere* e14 (possibly from an OE pers.n. *Isa*, proposed for Isfield Sx 396, and **bearu** 'grove'; perhaps to be identified with *Insbury* 1728); *Kellawayes lande* 1620; *on landscher' ford ouer þane ford* 968 (14) (*v.* **land-sc(e)aru** 'boundary', **ford**); *in the Lane* e14 (*v.* **lane**); *Langh'sester* 13 (probably **lang¹** and **ceaster**); *Litelforlang'* e14 (*v.* **lȳtel, furlang**); *on litegesheued, of lutegesheued* 968 (14), *Litegesheved* 1338–40 (corresponding with *on-, of litiges heuede* 944

(15) in the bounds of Hinton St M. par. *supra*, 'Lytig's headland', from an OE pers.n. *Lytig* and **hēafod**, *v.* Forsberg 143-4); *Lithewortforlang*' e14 (*v.* **furlang**, first el. **liδ-wyrt** 'dwarf elder'); *la Lupyate* 1338-40, *-iate* m14 (*v.* **hlīep-geat** 'gate over which animals can leap'); *La Lyete* e14 (*v.* **hlīet** 'a share, a lot'); *bi merehale* 968 (14) (*v.* Hile Coppice & Fm in Okeford F. par. *supra*); *bi merehawe* 968 (14), *by Merehawe* 1338-40 ('boundary hedge', *v.* **(ge)mǣre, haga**[1]); *Midd(i)lforlang* Ed I (m14), 1338-40 (*v.* **middel, furlang**); *on minnanlinche* 968 (14) (corresponding with *on nunnen linc* in the bounds of Hinton St M. par. *supra q.v.*); *Monkedych* 1338-40, *-dich* m14 (*v.* **munuc, dīc**, with allusion to the monks of Glastonbury who possessed Sturminster N.); *Morforlang*', *Mormede* e14, *Morewod*(') 1308 (15), 1338-40 (*v.* **mōr** 'marshy ground', **furlang, mǣd, wudu**); *the Netherclose* 1578 (*v.* **neoδerra**); *Nethercote* 1338-40 (*v.* **cot**); *novum clausum* (*domini Abbatis*) e14 ('new close'); *Oldebury* e14 (*v.* **eald, burh**); *Oldelond* 1338-40 (*v.* **land**); *pontem vocatum la Overgange* 1338-40, m14 (*v.* **ofer, gang**, cf. an identical name in Lydlinch f.ns. *infra*); *Pateslane* 1338-40, m14 (probably the surname *Pate*); *la Pley-* 1338-40, *la pleiecrosse* m14 (*v.* **plega, cros**, cf. the f.n. Play Cross in Okeford F. par. *supra*); *atte Pole* (p) e14 (*v.* **atte, pol**[1] 'pool'); *Potescombe* e14, *Potecumb*' 1338-40, *-combe* m14 (*v.* **cumb**, first el. probably **potte** 'deep hole'); *Redelane* e14, *Redlane* 1547 (*v.* **rēad, lane**); *Reidplace* 1619 (*v.* **place**, cf. *ostium* ('door') *Walteri la Rede* 1338-40, *-la Ride* m14); *ouer sanddoune* 968 (14), *Sandonn*' 1338-40 ('sandy down or hill', *v.* **sand, dūn**; in the Anglo-Saxon bounds of Sturminster N. where it marches with Lydlinch, cf. the forms cited under Sandhill in Fifehead N. 2 98 which probably represent the same name); *Schepcrofte* e14 (*v.* **scēap, croft**); *Schorthurne* 1338-40, m14 (*v.* **sc(e)ort, hyrne**); *bi sixe acres north an heued* 968 (14) (probably 'north headland(s) of six acres', *v.* **siex, æcer, andhēafod**, cf. Forsberg 144); *la Stile de la Soutereshurne* 1338-40, m14 (*v.* **stigel, sūtere** 'shoe-maker' (probably as a surname), **hyrne** 'corner'); *on stanwey, of stanweie* 968 (14), *Stanwey(e)* 1338-40 (*v.* **stān, weg**); *Stath'acre* e14 (*v.* **stæδ** 'river-bank'); *Sterkforlang*' e14 (*v.* **stīrc** 'young bullock', **furlang**); *pontem vocatum la Stone* 1338-40, m14 (*v.* **stān** 'stone', perhaps elliptical for 'the stone bridge', i.e. 'the stone-built bridge'); *Strates* 1620; *terra arabil' seperalis bisuthesture, -binorthestoure* e14 ('to the south of-, to the north of R. Stour', *v.* **bī, sūδan, norδan**, RNs. *infra*); *on stut þare on vppe stut* 968 (14) (*v.* **stūt**[2] 'stumpy hillock'); *Sulaker* 13 (probably **sulh** 'plough'); *Suyle* 13 (*v.* **siele** 'willow copse' or **syle**[1] 'bog'); *targildenedich* m14 (*v.* Golden Gate *supra*); *on þare þorn rewe* 968 (14) ('row of thorn-trees', from **þorn** and **rǣw**); *Threbruggin* 1338-40, m14 ('three bridges', from **þrēo** and **brycg**, *-in* representing the analogical ME wk.pl. **-en**[5]); *Tragynes-* 1338-40, *Tragines Sevenacres* m14 (*v.* **seofon, æcer**, cf. John *Tregon* 1327, *-Tragyn*, Agnes *Trigyn* 1332); *on trildoune* 968 (14), *Trildonne* 1338-40 (*v.* Kingsdown *supra*); *on wadeleighe* 968 (14), *Wadlegh*' 1338-40 ('clearing where woad is grown', *v.* **wād, lēah**); (*iuxta*) *Wellam* 13 (m14), *Joh' atte Welle . . . mes*' e14, John *atte Welle* 1327, *-atte Woll*' 1332 (*v.* **well(a)** 'spring, stream', **atte**); *de la Were* 13, *atte Were* 1307 (15) both

(p) (*v.* **wer** 'a weir'); *fontem in la Westheye* 1338–40, m14 (*v.* **west, (ge)hæg**); *atte We(y)stelond(e)* e14, *atte Westlonde* 1327, 1340, *attewest lod* (sic) 1308 (15) (*v.* **atte, west, land**); *on þan olde wested'* 968 (14) (*v.* **stede** 'place', first el. probably **west** 'west', cf. Sandred 227); *Whit(e)ings* 1708, 1761 (a surname); *Wogh'mere* 13 (*v.* **wōh** 'crooked', **mere**[1] 'pool' or **(ge)mǣre** 'boundary'); *Woods Place* 1613; *Wrdegrove* 13 (*v.* **worð, graf(a)**)); *Wullys or Woolhouse* 1613 (*v.* **wull**); *Joh' Pinnoke atte Wyke . . . mes', terre apud Wykeyete* e14, William *atte Wyke* 1332 (*v.* **atte, wīc** '(dairy) farm', **geat**).

XXII. WHITEWAY HUNDRED

In c.1086 GeldR the hundred had the same extent as it now has (Anderson 116, VCHDo **3** 132).

Haltone hundret c.1086 GeldR
Hundr' de Wichteweia 1170, *-weie* 1171 P
Witeweihundredum 1188 P, *Witeweie* 1212 Fees, 1244 *Ass,*
    -weye 1265 Misc, 1285, 1346 FA, *Wytewaye* 1244 *Ass,*
    -weya 1252 Fees, *-wey(e)* 1268 *Ass,* 1275 RH *et freq*
    to 1428 FA
Whytewaye 1244 *Ass, -wey(e)* 1259 FF, 1270 Pat *et freq* to
    1316 FA, *Whitewey(e)* 1270 Pat, 1280 QW *et freq* to
    1431 FA
Wytteweye 1280 QW
Wet(ew)eye 1280 *Ass*
Whitwaye 1542 LP

The 11th cent. name is from Hilton par. *infra.* Whiteway means 'white road or way', from **hwīt** and **weg**, cf. Whiteway Fm **1** 90. According to Hutch[3] **4** 347, 'this hundred takes its name from the white or chalky road from Bingham's Melcombe to Hilton, where, near the top of the hill . . . is or was a bush or tree on Newton farm in the parish of Hilton, where the hundred-courts were formerly held'; however, it should be noted that there is another *Whiteway* in this hundred, with early forms, among the lost st.ns. of Milton Abbas par. *infra.* The 'hundred of *Iberton*' 1490 Pat no doubt refers to this hundred, *v.* Ibberton par. *infra.*

Cheselbourne

In 1882 a detached part of Milton Abbas (Lyscombe infra) was transferred to this par. (Kelly).

CHESELBOURNE (SY 763996)
> *be Chiselburne* 859 ?for 870 (15) ShaftR (S 334), ?870 (15) *ib* (S 342), *Chiselburne* 1242 Sarum, 1293 Ch, *-borne* 1412 FA, *Chisselbarne* (sic) 1268 *Ass* (p), *Chisilburn* 1275 Banco (p)
>
> *juxta Cheselburneam* (rubric) 859 ?for 870 (15) *ShaftR* (S 334), *ad Cheselburniam* (rubric) ?870 (15) *ib* (S 342), *at-, to Cheselburne* 942 (15) *ib* (S 485 (1)), *Cheselburne* 1019 (15) *ib* (S 955 (1)), Hy I (15) *ib*, 1212 Fees *et freq* to 1428 FA, *-burn* 1259 FF *et freq* to 1428 FA, *-born(e)* 1285 FA *et freq* to 1811 OS, *-bourn(e)* 1290 (15) *ShaftR et passim, Chesilburn* 1275 Banco (p), *-borne* 1540 *AD, Checelbourne* 15 *ShaftR, Chesselborne* 1795 Boswell
>
> *æt ceosol burnan* 965 (10) *Ilch* (S 736), *Ceosolburnan* 987 (13) KCD 656 (S 1217, Finberg 613)
>
> *Cheleburna* (rubric) 1019 (15) *ShaftR* (S 955 (1)), *Chelesborn'* 1280 *Ass*
>
> *Ceseburne* 1086 DB, *Ches(e)burn(e)* 1244 *Ass* (p), 1250 Fees (p) *et freq* to 15 ShaftR, *-bo(u)rn'* 1280 *Ass*
>
> *Chuselburne* 1166 RBE (p), *-bourn* 1338 FF
>
> *Longa Cheselburn(')* 1259 FF, 1269 Cl, *Langecheselburn(e)* 1269 Cl, 1371 *Ilch, Long(e) Chese(l)burn* 1288 *Ass*, 1297 Cl, *Long(e) Cheselbo(u)rn(e)* 1367 Cl *et freq* to 1575 *PlR, Lang(a) Cheselborn(e)* 1402 IpmR, 1431 FA, *Cheselborne Longa* 1456 IpmR, *Long Chesil-, -Chesylbo(u)rne* 1514, 1533 *PlR*
>
> *Chestelbourne* 1412 FA

'(Place by) the gravelly stream', from **cisel, ceosol** and **burna**. The stream itself is referred to in all five sets of bounds describing Anglo-Saxon estates here: *to chiselburne* 859 ?for 870 (15) *ShaftR* (S 334), *to cheselburne* ?870 (15) *ib* (S 342), *on cheselburne* (*stream*) 942 (15) *ib* (S 485 (1)), 1019 (15) *ib* (S 955 (1)), *on cyselburnan* 965 (10) *Ilch* (S 736). The affix *Long* (apparently with reference to the length of the village, *v.* **lang**[1]) distinguished this place from the lost *Little*

Cheselbourne in Puddletown par. 1 316. On the early forms *Chele-*, *C(h)es(e)–*, with AN loss of -*s*- and -*l*-, *v.* ANInfl 54, 146.

BRAMBLECOMBE FM (ST 775009) & LANE, *Bremelcumb'* 1268 *Ass*, *Bramblecombe Cl*, *Brimblecombe Lane* 1771 *DROMap*, *Bramble Combe Cmn* 1840 *TAMap*, 'valley where brambles grow', *v.* **brēmel**, **cumb**.

LYSCOMBE BOTTOM (ST 735020), FM & HILL
    (*at*) *Liscombe* 843 for 934 (eME) ASCharters, (*apud*)
        Liscombe 843 for 934 (17) BCS 739, *Liscome* 1086 DB,
        -*coma* Exon, *Liscumb'* 1200 CurR (p), 1212 Fees,
        -*combe* 1310 Inq aqd *et freq* to 1840 *TAMap* (-*Fm*),
        Lyscumb(*e*) 1288 *Ass*, 1317 *MiltC*, -*comb*(*e*) 1311 Pat *et*
        passim
    Lyssecomb(*e*) n.d. (1372) *ChrP*, 1546 Hutch[3]
    Luscombe 1351 Pat, *Luyscombe* 1535 VE
    (*in fundo de*) *Lussh'combe* n.d. (e15) *MiltRoll*, *Lyshcombe*
        Grove 1546 Hutch[3]
    Lescombe 1795 Boswell

'Valley where reeds grow', from **lisc** and **cumb**, *v.* Ekwall Studies[2] 109, Forsberg 141; the f.n. Liscomb 1 362 may be identical in origin. The stream here is referred to in the Anglo-Saxon bounds of Cheselbourne as (*of*) *lisebroke* 942 (15) *ShaftR* (S 485 (1)), (*on*) *liscbroc* 1019 (15) *ib* (S 955 (1)), from the same first el. with **brōc**. The *Grove* in the 1546 form is alternatively *Lussh'groue* n.d. (e15) *MiltRoll*, *v.* **grāf(a)** 'grove, copse'. The medieval bounds of Lyscombe are given in n.d. (e15) *MiltRoll* (m. 3r).

BOTTOM COPSE, from Lyscombe Bottom *supra*, *v.* **botm**. CALLWAY LANE, cf. *Calway-*, *Colway Flg* 1839 *TA*. CHESELBOURNE MILL, -*borne*- 1811 OS; there was a mill at Cheselbourne in 1086 DB (VCHDo 3 83). CHESELBOURNE WEST DOWN, -*borne*- 1811 OS, cf. *East & West Down* 1840 *TAMap*. COMMON BARN, cf. *Chesleborne Common* 1771 *DROMap*, *Common* [Bridge] 1791 Boswell, *Common* 1811 OS, *Common Md* 1839 *TA*. DRAKE'S LANE. EASTFIELD FM, cf. *Eastfield* 1839 *TA*. HYDE HILL (Kelly), *Hide*- 1811 OS, cf. *campo voc' la Hide* 1540 *AD, v.* **hīd**; the hill is probably that referred to as *Gretindune* in the 11th cent. bounds of Cheselbourne, *v. infra.* KINGCOMBE, *Kingcombe* (*Md*) 1839 *TA, v.* **cumb.** MANOR FM, CHESELBOURNE MANOR (1″). NEW BARN (2×, one being YETMAN'S BARN (Kelly), 1811 OS, cf. Thomas *Yateman* 1664 HTax). NINE CORNERED COPSE. NINETEEN ACRE HANGING, cf. *Nineteen Acres, Upr Nineteens* 1839 *TA, v.* **hanging** 'steep slope'. NORTHFIELD FM, cf. *North Fd* 1839 *TA.* RIVER ARMS INN. ROUGH COPSE, cf. *Rough Cl* 1839 *TA.* ROUND COPSE. ST MARTIN'S CHURCH, cf. *ecclesia omnium Sanctorum de Cheseborn'* 1280 *Ass, ecclesie de Long' Cheselbourne* 1367 *Ilch, Chircheset* 15 *ShaftR* (*v.* **(ge)set** 'dwelling, stable'), *Church* [Bridge] 1791 Boswell, *Church Hill* 1839 *TA.* STREETWAY LANE, , cf. *Furlong above Street Way* 1839 *TA, v.* **strǣt.** WATERSIDE FM, cf. (*Lr Living*) *Waterside Fd* 1839 *TA,* by the stream that gives name to Cheselbourne, *v.* **wæter.** WELL COPSE. WEST FM. YETMAN'S BARN (Kelly), *v.* New Barn *supra.*

FIELD-NAMES

The undated forms are 1839 *TA* 54. Spellings dated 859 ?for 870 (15) are *ShaftR* (S 334), ?870 (15) *ib* (S 342), 942 (15) *ib* (S 485 (1)), 965 (10) *Ilch* (S 736), 1019 (15) *ShaftR* (S 955 (1)), 1288 *Ass,* 1317 *MiltC,* 1332 SR, n.d. (e15) *MiltRoll,* 15 *ShaftR,* 1412 FA, 1540 *AD,* 1659 (1758) *DROMap,* 1664 HTax, and 1791 Boswell.

(*a*) Arnold's Cl (cf. John *Arnold* 1664); Bakers Cl (cf. *Bakers'* [Bridge] 1791, Andrew *Baker* 1664); Bank Flg (*v.* **bank(e)**); Bennetts Cl (cf. Margaret *Benet* 1664); Bottom Cl, Fd & Flg (*v.* **botm**); Bows Cl; Broad Md; Broadshard (*v.* **sceard** 'cleft, gap'); Brown Hill; Bryers Cl; Bulls Pound; Burts Cl; Captains B(r)ush Flg; Chalk Pit Flg; Chebert Flg (named from Chebbard Fm in Dewlish **1** 303); Close; Head of Close Flg; Cowards Cl (cf. William *Coward* 1664); Cowleaze; Culverlands (*v.* **culfre** 'dove'); Against-, By Dancing Cross Rd ('cross where dancing took place', cf. the f.n. Play Cross **2** 241); Davis Cl; (Cross) Docklands (*v.* **docce**); Dorchester (road) Flg; (Flg above) East Cl; East Md (Coppice); 8 Acres (cf. *Eghteacres* 1317, *v.* **eahta, æcer**); 11 Acres; Eweleaze; 15 Acres; 4 Acres; Frampton [Bridge] 1791; Frenchards Cl; Furze Altmt; Grays Barn, Cl & Orchd, Woo Greys Cl (cf. *Elizabeth Gray* 1664; *Woo* is probably **wōh** 'crooked'); Flg above Great Lanch (*v.* **lanch**); Halls Cl; Hayes Cl; Head Acre, Head Half, Head Yard (*v.* **hēafod** 'headland in a common field, **half, g(i)erd**); Hinton Corner (probably named from Henning Hill in Melcombe H. *infra*); Hog Down, Hoglands Cl (*v.* **hogg**); Holm B(r)ush

(Flg) (*v.* **holegn** 'holly'); Home Flg; Honeycombe (*v.* **hunig, cumb**); Horse saddle (referring to shape); The Hundred Acres (an ironical name for a tiny field); Kingsbury-, Kingbury's Cl (*Kingsbury's* [Bridge] 1791); Kitehill (*v.* **cȳta**); Lamps Flg; Links Flg; Little Fd & Md; Long Cl; Longlands (Fd) (cf. *Langlond* 1317, *v.* **lang**[1], **land**); Long Md (*Longemede* 1540, *v.* **mǣd**); Lower Flg & Orchd; Mays Cl (cf. Peter *May* 1664); Michel's [Bridge] 1791; Middle Fd, -Down (1840 *TAMap*); Middle Flg; Moors Cl; Mulletts Cl (cf. William *Mullett* 1664); New Md; 9 Acres; Orchard; Paddocks; Park Cl; Phelps Cl, Phelps Gate Flg; Picked Ash, Picked Cl (*v.* **pīcede** 'pointed'); The Piece; Pit Cl; Porters Brush (for *Bush* ?) Flg; Range (Fd) (*v.* **range**); Redlands; Red Pce; Rick Barton & Cl (*v.* **ricke**); Ricks Pdk (cf. *Ricks* [Bridge] 1791; Humphrey *Reekes* 1664); Rudge Flg, top of Rudge (*v.* **hrycg**); Scrags; Shepherds Cl (and Beer house), Shepherds Pdk; (The Hundred Goad in) Shortlands (cf. *Shortlond* 1317, *v.* **sc(e)ort, land**; **goad** is a measure of land); 6 & 16 Acres; Snatch Flg; Standly Flg (perhaps from **stān** and **lēah**); Stony Combe & Flg; Tadd Hill (*Taddehull'* n.d. (e15), *Tad hill(s)* 1659 (1758), *v.* **hyll**, first el. perhaps an OE pers.n. *Tāda* (suggested for Tadlow Ca 66) rather than **tadde, tāde** 'toad'); 10 & 3 Acres; Head 3 Yards (possibly to be associated with the grant of a small area of land in Cheselbourne in 965 (10) *Ilch* (S 736) which is endorsed: *þis is þara þreora gyrda land boc æt Ceosol burnan, v.* **þrēo, g(i)erd** 'a virgate of land', **hēafod**; the *TA* field is just E of Cheselbourne village); 20 Acres; Upper Flg; Vine's [Bridge] 1791; Waterlands Flg; Waterslud; Whitelands (Flg) (*le Whitelond'* 1288, *v.* **hwīt, land**); Withy Bed.

(*b*) *on þa-, of þare apeltreu* 1019 (15) (*v.* **æppel-trēow** 'apple-tree'); *been'vylyslond* n.d. (e15) (*v.* **land**; the first el. may be a surname from a p.n. *Benefeld*, cf. Benville in Corscombe par. *infra*); *to þe beorge, of þe berge* 942 (15), *on þane-, of þane berghe* (2 ×) 1019 (15), cf. *Berghlond* 1317 (*v.* **beorg** 'hill, barrow', **land**); *of-, on Bertes welle* 1019 (15) (*v.* **well(a)** 'spring, stream', first el. probably the OE pers.n. *Beorht*); *on þe blaken þornes northward of þane blake þornen* 942 (15) (*v.* **blæc-þorn** 'black-thorn, sloe'); *Blakthorn'hull* n.d. (e15) (*v.* **blæc-þorn, hyll**, not to be identified with prec.); *on bleomannes berge, of þa iberge* 859 ?for 870 (15), *on blieqz mannes beorg, of þa iberge* ?for 870 (15), corresponding with *on blacmanne bergh, of þanne berghe* 1019 (15) (*v.* **beorg**; the first el. is an OE pers.n., probably *Blæcmann* if the last spelling can be trusted); *on braden bergh, of brade berghe* 1019 (15) (**brād, beorg**); *La Breche* 1317 (*v.* **brǣc** 'land broken up for cultivation'); *Brodelond* 1317 (*v.* **brād, land**); *Brokacre* 1317, *Broke aker* 1540 (v. **brōc, æcer**); *to bur(n)stowe* 859 ?for 870 (15), *to burnstowe (þanen up anlang burnstowe)* ?870 (15), *on burestowe* 1019 (15) (*v.* **burn-stōw**, hitherto interpreted as 'place where people assembled at a stream, bathing place' or perhaps 'watering place for cattle', but R. Forsberg (*Studia Neophilologica* **56** 3–20) convincingly suggests a meaning 'the channel or bed of an intermittent stream'; these points in the Anglo-Saxon bounds are on the small stream flowing S from Lyscombe Fm *supra* and are to be associated with Bourne Fm in Piddlehinton 1 310);

Carterysacre n.d. (e15) (the surname *Carter* with **æcer**); *on anne castel . . .
of dy castele, to anne castel, of ði castele* 859 ?for 870 (15), *on anne castel . . .
of þe castele, to anne castel, of þo icastel* ?870 (15) (probably representing
ceastel 'heap of stones', cf. *stan castel infra*); *Ceernyslond'* n.d. (e15) (*v.*
land, cf. John *de Cerne* 1332 (Melcombe H.)); *on anne cnap* 859 ?for 870
(15), *on anne cinep* ?870 (15) (*v.* **cnæpp** 'hill-top, hillock'); *Cokerellyscombe*
n.d. (e15) (*v.* **cumb** 'valley', cf. John-, William *Cokerel* 1332 (Milton
A.)); *on anne crundel, wið anne crundeles, of þane/þi crundele* 859 ?for 870
(15), ?870 (15), *on þane/ðone crundel, of þane crundel(e)* 942 (15) (*v.*
crundel 'chalkpit, quarry'); *on þare diches hirne, of þere hirne* 1019 (15) (*v.*
dīc 'ditch, **hyrne** 'corner'); *Dokthorn'* n.d. (e15) (*v.* **þorn** 'thorn-tree', first
el. perhaps **dogga** 'dog', cf. *dog('s)-thorn* 'dog-rose' 1695 NED s.v. *dog*
sb. sense 18d, *Doggiþorn* Gl **4** 120, *Hownystuff*, *infra*); *Dowbell'putte* n.d.
(e15) ('double pit', *v.* **duble, pytt**; probably identical with *tweie pettes
infra*); *on þa ealde berig, of þane Bery* 1019 (15) (*v.* **eald** 'old', **burh** (dat.sg.
byrig) 'fortified place'); *on þare ealde diches heued, of þare dich* 1019 (15) (*v.*
eald, dīc 'ditch', **hēafod** 'head, upper end'); *on þane ealde þaþe, of þane
þaþe* 1019 (15) (*v.* **eald, pæð** 'path'); *on þat ealden reshbed, of þanne bedde*
1019 (15) (*v.* **eald, risc-bedd** 'rush bed'); *on þa ellen þirnen, of þare þirnen*
1019 (15) (apparently from **ellen** 'elder' and **þyrne** 'thorn-bush', no doubt
describing a variety of thorn); *on þane-, of þane fearngaren* 942 (15) (cf.
La Gore 1317, *v.* **fearn** 'fern', **gāra** 'gore, triangular plot'); *onne flescumbe*
942 (15), *on flexcumbes heuede* 1019 (15) (*v.* **fleax** 'flax', **cumb** 'valley',
hēafod 'head, upper end'); *to forda of ðam forda* 965 (10) (*v.* **ford** 'ford');
on þane forð erthe acre, of þane forerð akere 942 (15) (*v.* **forierð** 'projecting
piece of ploughland', **æcer** 'arable plot', probably to be associated with
Ierðlonde infra); *on anne furch* 859 ?for 870 (15), ?870 (15) (*v.* **furh**
'furrow'); *Gatefurlang* 1317 (*v.* **geat** 'gate', **furlang**); *on þane greate hlinc,
of þare linke* 1019 (15) ('stout ridge or bank', from **grēat** (wk.obl. -*an*) and
hlinc); *up on Gretindune* 1019 (15) (first el. probably **grēat** 'stout' (cf.
prec.), with **dūn** 'hill'; probably to be identified with Hyde Hill *supra*);
Grundalvesput 1317 (*v.* **pytt** 'pit', first el. uncertain, cf. discussion of
Watergrandelputtes, etc, **2** 14); *on ðone ham, of ðam hamme* 965 (10) (*v.*
hamm 'enclosure'); *on þare haren torre* 1019 (15) (*v.* **hār²** (wk.obl. -*an*)
'grey', **torr** 'rock'); *on þa iheafde, of þane theafde* (sic) 942 (15), *be anne
hefden* 1019 (*v.* **hēafod** 'head, end of a ridge'); *to þære hege ræwe* 965 (10)
(*v.* **hege-ræw** 'hedgerow'); *on þes heges hirne* 859 ?for 870 (15), *on des heges
hirnen* ? 870 (15) (*v.* **hege** 'hedge, fence', **hyrne** 'corner'); *Hegfurlang* 1317
(*v.* **hecg** 'hedge', **furlang**); *on anne herepaþ westward over herepaþ . . . est*
(sic for *eft*) *to herepaðe, of herepaðe* 859 ? for 870 (15), *on þere herepaþ
westward op ðe herepað . . . eft to herepað, of þe ereðe* (sic) ? 870 (15) (*v.*
here-pæð 'military road, highway'; this track runs NE and gives name to
Hartfoot Lane in Hilton par. *infra*); *to herpoðe of herpoðe . . . þonone to
herpoðe andlang herpoðes anfurlang* 965 (10) (*v.* **here-pæð**; *anfurlang* may
be a derivative of **furlang** 'furlong' with the prefix *and-* 'opposite' as in
andhēafod); *on hippe pad, of þane pade* 1019 (15) (*v.* **pæð** 'path', first el.
possibly an unrecorded OE pers.n. *Hippa*); *on hipiscbergh* (for *hiwisc-*), *of*

þane berghe 1019 (15) (cf. *Byhywyssch* 1317, *v.* **hīwisc** '(measure of land that would support) a family', **beorg** 'hill, barrow', **bī** '(place) near'); *on þane hlinc, of þat ihlinche* 859 ? for 870 (15), *on þanne hlinc, of þanne i hlinche* ? 870 (15) (*v.* **hlinc** 'ridge, bank'); *on anne hlinchesheaved, on anne linkesheaved* 859 ? for 870 (15), *on anne linkes haued, -heued* ? 870 (15) (*v.* **hlinc, hēafod**); *on hlinc reawe* 859 ? for 870 (15), *on þat hlinc reawe* ? 870 (15) (*v.* **hlinc, rǣw**, for the meaning *v.* Lynch Fm 1 15); *on holencumbe* 1019 (15) (*v.* **hol²** (wk.obl. *-an*) 'hollow, deep', **cumb** 'valley'); *Hollond* 1317 (*v.* **hol², land**); *on ða holu suthward* 942 (15) (*v.* **hol¹** 'a hole, a hollow'); *on þane hordþiuel, of þane þiuel* 1019 (15) (*v.* **þȳfel** 'bush, thicket', first el. apparently **hord** 'treasure' if the form is reliable, but cf. *þorþiuel infra* earlier in the same charter); *Hownystuff* n.d. (e15) (probably 'hound's tuft or cluster of trees', *v.* **hund, tuffe**, cf. *Dokthorn' supra* which was nearby); *anlang hricge weges* 942 (15) (*v.* **hrycg-weg** 'ridgeway'); *Nether-, Overhulle* 1317, *Hull'path* n.d. (e15) (*v.* **hyll** 'hill', **pæð, neoðerra, uferra**); *magnum huppyll'* n.d. (e15) (probably **hyppels** 'stepping stones'); *in (the) Hurn(e)* (p) 1317, 1332 (*v.* **hyrne** 'angle, corner'); *to hwitan wyllon, of hwitan willon* 965 (10), *on þone hwiten welle, of þane welle* 1019 (15) (identical in origin, but probably referring to two different boundary points, *v.* **hwīt** (wk.obl. *-an*) 'white', **well(a)** 'spring or stream'); *on anne Ierðlonde Northward* 859 ? for 870 (15), *on ðan zerðe* (sic) *nordewarde* ? 870 (15) (*v.* **ierð** 'ploughing, ploughed land', **land**; this boundary point was close to *forð erthe acre supra*); *on land scorhlinc, -scarlinc* 859 ? for 870 (15), *on landscar hlinc, on land scare hlinc* ? 870 (15) (*v.* **land-sc(e)aru, land-scoru** 'boundary', **hlinc** 'ridge, bank'); *Langacres* 1317 (*v.* **lang¹, æcer**); *on langhelee northward on langhelee* 942 (15) (*v.* **lang¹, lēah** 'wood, clearing in a wood'); *Lang(')lynch(e)* 1317, n.d. (e15) (*v.* **lang¹, hlinc**); *La Leye* 1317 (*v.* **lēah**); *in þane-, of þane miliere* 1019 (15) ('enclosure by a mill for catching fish', from **myln** and **gear**, cf. *mulen ger* Brk 645; this boundary point would have been on the stream flowing S from Lyscombe Fm *supra*); *uppen morhelle* 1019 (15) (*v.* **mōr, hyll**); *on neþan pol, of þane pol* 1019 (15) (*v.* **pōl¹** 'pool'; *neþan* may be for *neþran* from **neoðerra** 'lower'); *Pokershe* 1540 (*v.* **ersc** 'ploughed field', first el. perhaps **pūca** 'goblin'); *Pywysacre* n.d. (e15) (a surname with **æcer**); *Reynakre* 1317 (*v.* **æcer**, probably with **rygen** 'growing with rye'); *anlang ricges* 942 (15) (*v.* **hricg** 'ridge'); *on þane rugen bergh, of þane bergh* 1019 (15) ('rough barrow or hill', from **rūh** (wk.obl. *-an*) and **beorg**); *on sebergh, of seberghe* 1019 (15) (apparently 'sea barrow or hill', that is 'barrow or hill used as a sea-mark', from **sǣ** and **beorg**; this boundary point is at 500' and would be visible from parts of the coast 12 miles S; it probably gives name to *Seberdon(e)* in Milton Abbas *infra*); *Seveneakre* 1317 (*v.* **seofon, æcer**); *be suþe Scaftesbury* 859 ? for 870 (15), *be suðe ceatwanberge* ? 870 (15), *on shete bergh, of þane berghe* 1019 (15) (perhaps 'Ceatwa's hill or barrow', from an OE pers.n. *Ceatwa* and **beorg**, and probably to be associated with Chebbard Fm in Dewlish *q.v.* 2 303); *Shortakre* 1317 (*v.* **sc(e)ort, æcer**); *on þane snieren fyrsgaran, of þan garan* 1019 (15) (*v.* **fyrs** 'furze', **gāra** 'gore, triangular plot of land'; *snieren* is obscure and the form may be corrupt); *Sourlond* 1317 (*v.* **sūr** 'sour', damp', **land**); *By Southedich* 1317 '(place) to the south of the ditch', *v.* **bī, sūðan, dīc**); *Southemostefurlang* 1317 (*v.* **sūðmest, furlang**); *on anne stan castel, of þa icastele* 859 ? for 870 (15), *on anne stancastel, of þi castele* ? 870 (15), probably corresponding with *on þa stancysten . . . of þane stancyste* 1019 (15) ('heap of stones', from **stān** and **ceastel**, cf. *on anne castel supra*; the later forms, if the *-n* is an error, may represent the related **ci(e)stel** for which *v.* PNBrk 772); *on þa sticelen lane, of þare lane* 1019 (15) (*v.* **sticol** 'steep', **lane**, cf. Winterborne Stickland **2** 131); *on þane ston istel, of þan istelle* 942 (15) ('stone enclosure', *v.* **stān, st(i)ell**); *at swindune upward* 859 ? for 870 (15), *at swindone uueþearde* (for *-wearde*) ?870 (15) ('hill where swine are reared', *v.* **swīn, dūn**); *ten' acres* n.d. (e15) (*v.* **tēn, æcer**); *on þorndunes cnep, of þane sneppe* (sic) 1019 (15) ('top of thorn hill', *v.* **þorn, dūn, cnæpp**); *inne þa þornen, of þare þyrnen* 1019 (15) (*v.* **þyrne** 'thorn-bush'); *on þane þorn . . . of þan þorne* 1019 (15) (*v.* **þorn** 'thorn-tree'); *on anne þornstub, of þane stubbe* 1019 (15) (*v.* **þorn, stubb** 'stump'); *on þorþiuel, of horþiuele* 1019 (15) (probably 'thorn thicket', from **þorn** and **þȳfel**, cf. *hordþiuel supra*); *Tunforlang* 1317 (*v.* **tūn, furlang**); *on þa tweie þettes, of þone þetten* 1019 (15) ('two pits', *v.* **twēgen, pytt**; this boundary point probably describes the same feature as *Dowbell'putte supra*); *on þe twifelde dich, of þare dic* 942 (15) ('double ditch', *v.* **twīfeald, dīc**); *Verthilsakre* 1317 (*v.* **æcer**, first part of name uncertain); *Vifacres* 1317 (*v.* **fīf, æcer**); *Warland* 15 (*v.* **land**, perhaps with **wer, wær** 'weir'); *North-, Southwendlond* 1317, *Wenelond'* n.d. (e15) (*v.* **land**, first el. possibly **wende** 'bend'); *West(e)feld* 1540; *Wetherfurlang* 1317 (*v.* **weðer** 'castrated ram', **furlang**); *Wodefurlang'* n.d. (e15) (*v.* **wudu**, cf. Richard *Bythywood* (= 'by the wood') 1664).

Hilton

HILTON (ST 782030) ['hiltn]
 Eltone 1086 DB, *Heltona* Exon
 Haltone c. 1086 GeldR, *Halcton'* (possibly for *Haltton'*) 1210 P
 Helton(') 1212 Fees, 1213 Ch, 1227 FF, 1244 *Ass* (p), 1255 *Salis*, 1268 *Ass*, 1272 Ch, 1280 *Ass*, 1285 FA, 1288 *Ass*, 1291 Tax, 1303 FA *et passim* to 1774 Hutch[1], *-tun'* 1221 *Ilch* (p), *Heleton* 1321 Ipm (p)
 Hilton' 1280 *Ass*, 1795 Boswell

v. **tūn** 'farm, village'. There can be no certainty about the first el. Fägersten 189 tentatively suggests **h(e)alh** 'nook' or **hēla** 'heel' in some topographical sense, but **hēla** seems unlikely and **h(e)alh** does not account for the overwhelming preponderance of *e* spellings (though the early *Halc-* form now adds a little weight to the suggestion by supporting the hitherto isolated *a* spelling from GeldR, which occurs as the name of Whiteway hundred *q.v. supra*). Ekwall (DEPN) compares Hilton and Helton We and suggests either **helde, hielde** 'slope' or *helde* 'tansy' (the former el. is favoured by PN We 2 103, 200 for the two We names). For the Do Hilton, **h(i)elde** 'slope' would in fact be topographically suitable and, as Anderson 116 points out, is perhaps more likely than *helde* in spite of the absence of *u* spellings and the rarity of *i* spellings.

ALLER (FM) (ST 769029) ['alər], *Alre* 1332 SR (p), 1400 *Ilch, Aller* 1544 Hutch³, 1795 Boswell, *Allar* 1602 *AddCh,* '(place at) the alder-tree', *v.* **alor** (dat.sg. *alre*), cf. Arle Gl 2 104, Aller D (freq) and So (DEPN) which are identical in origin, and cf. the nearby Aldermore and the f.ns. Allers (Spring), Rotten Alders Md all *infra*.

ANSTY, HR (ST 768039) & LR (765032) ['aːnsti], *Anesty(e)* 1219, 1220 Cur, n.d. (e13) Osm, 1269 *Ilch* (p), 1288 *Ass, -sti* 1275 RH (p), *Auestye* (for *Ane-*) 1329 FF (p); *Ansty* 1244 *Ass* (p), 1355 Ipm (p), 1795 Boswell, *Anstey(')* 1399, 1400 *Ilch,* 1463 FF, 1544 Hutch³, *Anstie* 1602 *AddCh, Upper & Lower Ansty* 1870 Hutch³, cf. Pleck or Little Ansty *infra*. 'Path for one, narrow track', from **ānstiga**, identical with Anstey D 333, etc, cf. also a point in the OE bounds of Winterborne T. 2 82. M. Gelling, *Place-Names in the Landscape* (1984), examines the situation of this and other Anst(e)y place-names and suggests for **ānstiga** a meaning 'linking road, stretch of road linking at least four routes' (here with reference to the short length of road, forking at either end, near Ansty Cross).

HARTFOOT LANE (ST 763027) ['haːʀbət], *Harpers or Harefoot Lane* (a hamlet) 1774 Hutch¹, *Harpur's Lane* 1795 Boswell, *Harefoot Lane* 1811 OS, *Harpath, Harpers or Harefoot Lane* 1870 Hutch³ ('it is now sometimes spelt *Hartfoot* or *Hardput*'). Clearly subject to much recent popular etymology, but the form *Harpath* is the most historically correct, since this small hamlet is situated on the NE continuation of the **here-pæð** 'highway' of the OE bounds of Cheselbourne, *v. on anne herepað*, etc, in Cheselbourne f.ns. *supra*. Moreover, two miles further NE from the hamlet of Hartfoot Lane the same route is apparently *Harpydway* 1384 (e16) *Prideaux* in the bounds of Woolland par. *infra, v.* **weg**.

HATHERLY DAIRY & FM (ST 755054), *Hetherle* 1227 FF, *Hatherleghe* c.1325 *GlastE, Hederle* 1399, *He(y)derlegh'* 1400 *Ilch, Hatherl(e)y* (*Close*) 1544 Hutch³, 1602 *AddCh, Hatherleigh* (*Grounds*) 1795 Boswell, *Hatherly* 1811 OS, *Heatherly* 1842 *TA*. Probably 'hawthorn clearing', from **hagu-, hæg-þorn** and **lēah**, cf. Hatherley Gl 2 145, Hatherleigh D 142.

NEWTON FM (ST 775016), *New-, Neu-, Niwton'* 1400 *Ilch, Newton* 1544 Hutch³, Eliz ChancP, 1602 *AddCh*, 1811 OS, 1842 *TA* (*-Farmhouse*), 'new farm or estate', *v.* **nīwe, tūn**, cf. *Newton Hill* 1842 *TA*; there was a water mill here in 1400 *Ilch*.

PALBROKE or PARBROOK (lost, about ST 767052), 1870 Hutch³ (*-under Rawlsbury*), *Palbroc* 1258 *For, -brok(e)* 1317 *MiltC*, 1327 *SR* (p), 1552 Hutch³, 1602 *AddCh, -brouk(e)* 1332 *SR* (p), 1399, 1400 *Ilch, Pellbroke* 1544 Hutch³, *Pawlbroke* 1557 *Surv, Parbrooks, Parbrook Md* 1842 *TA, v.* **brōc** 'brook, stream', first el. probably **p(e)all** 'ledge'; this would be topographically suitable since the brook in question is that flowing beneath the steep slopes of Bulbarrow Hill (hence *under Rawlsbury*, which refers to Rawlsbury Camp *infra*) and beside Brooks Copse *infra* to which it may have given name.

RAWLSBURY CAMP (ST 767058), FM & WD, *Raulesbur(y)* 1399, 1400 *Ilch, Rowlesbury* 1557 *Surv, Ramesbury* (probably for *Raules-*) 1602 *AddCh, Rawlsbury* (*Fm*) 1811 OS, *Railsbury Rings, Ralsbury Copse & Md, Ralsbury Grove Mount* 1842 *TA*, from **burh** (dat.sg. *byrig*), here in the sense 'pre-English earthwork' since Rawlsbury Camp is an Iron Age hill-fort, *v.* also **hring**. The first el. seems to be the OG

pers.n. *Radulf* (Fr *Raoul*). The lost name *Rowleston* 1557
Surv has the same first el. with **tūn** 'manor'.

ALDERMORE, *Alder Moor* 1842 TA, *v.* **alor, mōr**, close to
Aller *supra*. ALL SAINTS' CHURCH, cf. *ecclesiam de Helton'*
1255 *Salis, Ecclesiam Omnium Sanctorum de Helton'* 1288
Ass. ANSTY CROSS (a crossroads, *v.* **cross**) & HOLLOW, HR
ANSTY FM, *v.* Ansty *supra.* BREACH WD, 1811 OS, *spinis in la
Brache* 1399, *la Breche* 1400 *Ilch, v.* **brēc, brǣc** 'land broken
up for cultivation'. BROADCLOSE, *Broad Cl* 1842 *TA.* BROOKS
COPSE, cf. *Brooks Cmn* 1842 *TA*, probably named from the
brook here which also gave name to *Palbroke supra*, but cf.
John *Brouke* 1400 *Ilch.* CASTLE LAKE SPRING, *Castle Lakes*
1842 *TA*; the 'castle' is probably the nearby Bingham's
Melcombe Ho in Melcombe H. par. *infra, v.* **lacu** 'stream'.
CHILMORE, 1842 *TA*, *Childemor(e)* 1399 *Ilch*, 'moor where
young people assembled', or 'moor belonging to younger
sons', *v.* **cild, mōr.** COOMBE BTM (1842 *TA*), HILL & WD,
cf. *Little Coombe* 1842 *TA, v.* **cumb** 'valley', **botm** 'valley
bottom'. CORN MILL, near Peck Mill *infra*; there was a mill
at Hilton in 1086 DB (VCHDo 3 80), and a water mill at
Newton *supra* in 1400 *Ilch.* COTHAYES DAIRY & DROVE,
Cotehay 1412 FA, *Cothays* 1795 Boswell, *Cothay(e)s Ho &
Md* 1842 *TA, v.* **cot, (ge)hæg.** CROCKERS FM, cf. *Crockers
Cmn* 1842 *TA*, a surname. CROWN INN. CUCKOO LANE (WD).
FERN WD, 1842 *TA*, cf. *Fernhill coppice* 1544 Hutch[3], *Fern
Cl* 1842 *TA, v.* **fearn.** HARTS (lost, ST 763044), 1811 OS, cf.
Jasper *Hart* 1664 HTax. HILL BARN, *Hill Barn Fd* 1842 *TA*,
near to Hilton Hill Bldgs *infra.* HILTON BOTTOM (BARN),
Hilton Bottom 1771 DROMap, cf. *Great Bottom* 1842 *TA, v.*
botm. HILTON HIGHER FM (DAIRY). HILTON HILL BLDGS, cf.
Hill Grd(s) 1842 *TA.* HILTON LOWER FM. HILTON WD, *silua
de Helton'* 1399, *Heltonswode* 1400 *Ilch, Hilton Wds* 1842 *TA,
v.* **wudu.** HOOPERS LANE (lost, ST 773048), cf. Richard
Hopere 1332 (Cheselbourne). ICE DROVE, possibly from **ēast**
'east', cf. East or Ice Hill **1** 369. LINKS PLANT., cf. *pastur' in
Westlincke* 1399 *Ilch*, *Links, Lynx Md* 1842 *TA, v.* **hlinc**
'ridge, bank'. LITTLE DOWN PLANT., *Little Down* 1842 *TA*,
cf. (*Plantation by*) *Great Down ib, Heltonysdown'* 1319 (e15)
MiltRoll, Helton' Downe 1573 Prideaux, *Hilton Down* 1811

OS, v. **dūn** 'hill, down'. LOWER GDNS. MASH WATER, *Marsh Water* [Bridge] 1791 Boswell, the name of a short stretch of Devil's Brook near Brewery (6"), probably from **mersc** 'marsh' but perhaps influenced by ModE *mash*, a brewing term meaning 'malt mixed with hot water to form wort'. MILL POND (2 ×), near Corn Mill *supra* and Peck Mill *infra*. MOOTS COPSE, (*Eynes*) *Moots Copse* 1842 *TA*. NORTH WD (lost, ST 756055), 1811 OS, *North-* 1399, *Nort(h)wode* 1400 *Ilch*, *Northwood* 1544 Hutch³, *-woode*, *-wodde* (*claus' voc'-*) 1602 *AddCh*, *Norwood Copse* 1842 *TA*, v. **norð, wudu.** PECK MILL, *Pick Mill* 1842 *TA*, from ModE **peck-mill** 'a pecker-mill', cf. PNCh 5 302. PLECK or LITTLE ANSTY (*Little Ansty* 1811 OS), PLECK FM & LANE, *Pleck* (*Lane*) [Bridge] 1791 Boswell, *Cutts and Pleck* 1842 *TA*, v. **plek** 'a small plot of ground', Ansty *supra*. RASPBERRY COPSE. SKINNERS BOTTOM, 1842 *TA*, cf. *Marger' le Schinnere* 1269 *Ilch*, v. **botm.** THOMAS'S HILL PLANT., *Thomas Hill, Thomas's* (*Md*) 1842 *TA*, cf. Christopher *Thomas* 1664 HTax.

FIELD-NAMES

The undated forms are 1842 *TA* 106. Spellings dated 1227 are FF, 1280 *Ass*, 1332 SR, 1340 NI, 1399, 1400 *Ilch*, 1544, 1552 Hutch³, 1557 *Surv*, 1602 *AddCh*, 1664 HTax, and 1791 Boswell.

(*a*) Abbot(t)s Fd & Mdw (possibly a reference to the abbot of Abbotsbury who held the manor from the time of DB, cf. *Abb' de Abbetesbyri tenet maneria de Hilton'* 1280, or to the abbot of Milton who also held lands here, cf. *clausum Abbatis de Middelton'* 1400, or to a surname, cf. Henry *Abbott* 1664); Allers (Spring) (*v.* Aller (Fm) *supra*); Ansty Down (*v.* Ansty *supra*); Aplin's Heath; Arleys Hill, Arleys 10 and 4 Acres; Arnolds Md (cf. Robert *Arnold* 1664); Ascombe (*v.* **æsc, cumb**); Bakers Md (cf. Richard *Baker* 1664); Balls Acre; Bar Hill; Basketts; Bennett Copse; Bickses Hole; Bombish Md; Bottom Md; Brandless Md; Brick Kiln Fd; Brights Md; Broad Md; Browns (cf. John *Broun* 1332, 1340); Bullocks Well (cf. *Bollecashe* 1399, *v.* **bulluc, æsc** 'ash-tree'); Burdles; Bushy Grd; Butts Md; Calve Hayes (*Caluehegh'* 1399, 1400, 'enclosure for calves', *v.* **c(e)alf, (ge)hæg**); Candys (cf. Alice *Candee* 1664); Chaldicotts (Hill) (cf. Rebecca *Chaldecott* 1664); Chalk Cl, Chalk Pit ((Old) Chalk Pits marked 6"); Chipps Fd (cf. widow *Chippe* 1664); Claver Lds (*v.* **clæfre** 'clover'); Common (Cl); (Raymonds) Conygree, Conigree Copse (*v.* **coninger** 'rabbit warren', cf. John *Reymond* 1552); Coopers Cl; Copse; Cowards Md (cf. Daniel *Coward* 1664); Cowleaze;

Crabb Tree (*v.* **crabbetre**); Davidge(')s Cmn, Md & Orchd, Davidges 9 & 13 Acres; Drakes(') (Fd), Drakes Hilton Wds (cf. Thomas *Drake* 1664, Hilton Wd *supra*); Dry Grd; (Lt) Dunning(s); 8 and 18 Acres; Fish Ponds and Copse; 5 Acres (and 4 Acres); Folly Plot (*v.* **folie**); Ford Cowleaze & Md (cf. *Ford Water* [Bridge] 1791, *v.* **ford**); Four Grounds; 14 Acres; Fox Church; Fox Inn; French Grass (*v.* **french grass**); Fripps Fd & Md; Furlong(s); Furzey-, Fuzzey Cl; Garden Hays (*v.* **(ge)hæg**); Gaston (*v.* **gærs-tūn**); Germans Mdw; Glydes Closes & Copse (cf. William *Glide* 1400); Goare (*v.* **gāra**); Green Md; Haggs (probably to be associated with *ten' nuper Rogeri Hake, herbag' in la hakehegge* 1400, *v.* **hecg**); Harts Md; Hass Copse & Drove, Skinners Hass (possibly (*les*) *Hawes* 1399, 1400, *v.* **haga**[1] 'enclosure', cf. Skinners Btm *supra*); Hawke; Hays (*v.* **hǣs** 'brushwood'); Higher Md; Hilly Grd; Hine Town; Hog Hill; Home Md; Honey Hills Md (*v.* **hunig**); Horse Cl; (Lt & Thomas') Ivis (cf. Thomas's Hill Plant. *supra*); Jefferys Fd & Launches (*v.* **lanch**); Kingwell, Kings Well (cf. John-, Thomas *King* 1332); Langers; Legg (*v.* **leg**); Lime Kiln; Little Grd; Little Mount; Loaders Cowleaze & Hill, Loaders 8 & 12 Acres, Loders Fd; Loins (cf. the f.n. *Loynes* 1 236); London Rd; Long Cl & Md; Long Meer (probably **mere**[1] 'pond'); Lousy Md (*v.* **lousi**, though perhaps from **hlōse** 'pig-sty'); Mattocks 3 Furlongs; Middle Fd; Milking Md; Miller's Md, Cock Millers (cf. *Will' Molendinario* 1332; *Cock* probably denotes 'chief', *v.* NED *s.v.* *cock* sb[1] sense 22); Milton Md (from Milton A. *infra*); Mitchells Md; Moses Ball (*v.* **ball** 'rounded hill'); Mount Md; Mount Pleasant; Mower; Mulletts Cmn; Musgrove; New Cl; Thomas' & Tripps Noddick (possibly a variant of **nattok**, cf. Thomas's Hill Plant. *supra*); North Grd; North Hay (*v.* **(ge)hæg**); Northmoor, North Moor Hill; Paddock; Park (Way); Parsonage Fd & Md (cf. Vicarage 6″); Pickett Cl, Picketts; Pile; Pinxy Md; Lt Pit Cl, Pit Grd (cf. Richard *atte Putte* 1400, *v.* **atte**, **pytt**); Plantation; Plot; Poplars; Potatoe Plot and Cmn; Prince Md; Rag Moor (*v.* **ragge**); Rectorial Barn and Barton; Gt & Lt Red Banks; Rotten Alders Md (cf. Aller, Aldermore *supra*); Row Borrow (**rūh** 'rough' with **burg** 'burrow'); Sage Mary Cmn & Md; Sandy Grd (cf. *Sandhill* 1557); Sandys Cl (cf. Ralph *Sandwey* 1340); Sellers Cmn & Md; 7 Acres; Shawford (probably **sc(e)aga** 'copse'); Shettles; South Down; South Moor; Starveall (a derogatory name for poor land); Stays Cmn; Stoys (Ho); Strap (*v.* **strap**); Swallows Pool; Swap Md; 10 & 30 Acres; Threecornered Grd; Town Md; Hr Town Well Head ('source of a stream', *v.* **well(a)**, **hēafod**); Trendle (*v.* **trendel**); Tuckers Orchd; Tuffins Cmn & Md (cf. John *Tussen* (for *Tuffen*) 1664); Tunnels; 12 Acres; Venice (Drove); Hr & Lr Vern (for possible meaning cf. Fern Down 2 225); Vines (cf. Hugh *Vine* 1664); Water Md(w); Water Slade (*v.* **slæd**); Watley; Wells Cmn; West Md; Wheat Grd; Widows Mdw; Willow Bed; Wills Leasehold; Wordells.

(*b*) *Bol(eh)egh'* 1399 (*v.* **bula**, **(ge)hæg**); *le Cleue* 1399 (*v.* **clif** 'cliff, bank'); *la Lake* 1399 (*v.* **lacu** 'stream'); *in the lane* 1332 (p) (*v.* **lane**); *la Mersshe* 1399 (cf. 'the marsh of *Helton*' 1227, *v.* **mersc**); *la Newdiche* 1400 (*v.* **nīwe**, **dīc**); *le Orchard'* 1400 (*v.* **orceard**); *Outhey's Close* 1544;

Ridelhegh' 1399 (*v.* **(ge)hæg** 'enclosure'; the first el. may be *hriddel* 'riddle, coarse-meshed sieve', or **ridel** 'rider' proposed for Riddlestreet Gl 2 235); *Shapehegh'* 1400 (*v.* **scēap** 'sheep', **(ge)hæg**); *cotag' voc' Shilford* 1602; 'all the closes of *Thorne'* 1227, (*le*) *Thurne* 1399, 1400 (*v.* **þorn** 'thorn-tree', **þyrne** 'thorn-bush', cf. foll.); *Thurnes-, Thurnyswode, la Thurnerswode* 1400 (probably 'wood at *Thurne'*, cf. prec., *v.* **wudu**, in spite of the last form which suggests confusion with a surname, cf. Henry *Turnour* 1340).

Ibberton

IBBERTON (ST 790076) ['ebəʀtn]
    Abristetone 1086 DB, *Abristentona* Exon
    Edbrich(c)testun' John, ? John *AddCh*
    Hedbredinton' 1212 Fees, *Edbrytyngton als. Edbrichton*
        1283 Ipm, *Ethbrichinton* 1285 FA, *Edbrightinton', -ynton',*
        -enton' 1288 *Ass, Ebryngton* 1462 Pat
    Edbrikton' 1244 *Ass* (p), *Edbrichton* 1245 Cl, *Eadbriston'*
        1258 *For, Edbrighton(')* 1284 Cl, 1288 *Ass, Edebrighton*
        1303 FA, *Edbryghton'* 1327 *SR, Edbriston'* 1332 SR
    Eb(b)richton 1245, 1294, 1299 all Ipm, *Ebrighton(e)* 1297
        Cl, 1240 Ipm *et freq* to 1461 Pat, *Ebriton* 1315 ib, 1329
        Cl, *Ebryg(h)ton* 1375 IpmR, 1377 Cl, *Ebrithton* 1391
        IpmR, *Ebyrton* 1424 Pat, *Eb(b)erton* 1442 IpmR, 1474
        Pat, 1479 IpmR
    Ebotestone 1258 *For*
    Ibrigton 1291 Tax, 1423 Pat, 1428 FA, *Ybruton* 1340 NI,
        Yberton(') 1384 (e16) *Prideaux*, 1431 FA, *Ibrygh'ton'*
        1385 (e15) *MiltRoll, Iberton* 1412 FA, 1485 Pat, 1501
        Ipm, *Iberghton* 1428 FA, *Ibberton* 1575 Saxton
    Iverton 1490 Pat   *Everton* 1563 Hutch[3]

'Farm called after Ēadbeorht', from the OE pers.n. **Ēadbeorht** and **-ingtūn**, cf. Abberton Wo 184, alternating with 'Ēadbeorht's farm', *v.* **-es²**, in three of the early forms. The 'hundred of *Iberton*' 1490 Pat no doubt refers to Whiteway hundred *supra*.

MARSH FM (ST 781084) & LANE, *in le Merche* 1327 SR (p), *atte Marsch* 1340 NI (p), *Marsh Tenement* 1672 *Salkeld, Marsh* 1811 OS, *Marsh Grd* 1839 *TA, v.* **mersc** 'marsh', **atte** 'at the'.

APLIN'S HEATH, 1811 OS, *Applins-* 1839 *TA*, cf. Roger
Aplin 1664. BAKER'S FOLLY, cf. George Harvey *Baker* 1870
Hutch[3]. BLACKLANDS LANE, cf. (*Hr & Lr*) *Blackland* 1839
TA, v. **blæc, land**. COOMBE BOTTOM, cf. *Lt & Long Coombe,
Bottom Grd* 1839 *TA, v.* **cumb, botm**. FARM DOWN BARN,
Farm Down 1839 *TA, v.* **dūn**. GALLOWS CORNER, on the par.
bdy, *v.* **g(e)alga**. IBBERTON HILL, cf. *Hill Cl & Md, Hill
Top, Little Hill (Cl)* 1839 *TA*. IBBERTON LONG DOWN, cf.
Lambdunesdich' John *AddCh* which may refer to Cross dyke
(1″) on the par. bdy at the NW end of Ibberton Long Down,
v. **lamb, dūn, dīc**. KITFORD ([-Bridge] 1791 Boswell, 1811
OS), -LANE, probably 'ford frequented by kites', from **cȳta**
and **ford**, cf. Kitford Bridge in Folke par. *infra*; a ford is
marked 6″. LAMBLANDS COPSE, *Lambsland (Coppice)* 1839
TA, cf. the early form cited under Ibberton Long Down
supra. LEIGH (1811 OS), LEIGH CROSS (1839 *TA*, a
crossroads, *v.* **cross**), LEIGH FM & LANE, cf. *Gt, Home & Lr
Leigh* 1839 *TA, v.* **lēah** 'wood, clearing in a wood'. MANOR
HO. MILL LANE, cf. *Mill Md & Orchd* 1839 *TA*, *Trunk Md*
in f.ns. *infra*. PARK WD, 1839 *TA, Parke-* 1547 Hutch[3], cf.
Lt Park Coppice, Park Md 1839 *TA*, *Ibberton Park* 1870
Hutch[3], *v.* **park**; for the existence of a medieval deer-park
here, *v.* Cantor & Wilson 7 176–7. RYALLS CROSS & LANE, cf.
Rile (Acre & Moor) 1839 *TA*, probably 'hill where rye is
grown', *v.* **ryge, hyll, cross** 'crossroads'. ST EUSTACE'S
CHURCH, cf. 'church of *Ibrigton*' 1423 Pat, *Church Cl* 1839
TA; according to Hutch[3] 4 361, near to the church there is 'a
spring called St Eustachius's well, to which saint the Church
was perhaps dedicated. It is vulgarly called Stachy's well, or
'the water-pound'; it might also be noted that a *Eustace*
(Latin *Eustachius*) was elected abbot of Milton in 1198
(VCHDo 2 62). ST QUINTIN'S FM, named from Lower
Fifehead or Fifehead St Quintin in Fifehead Neville par. 2
95. SOUTH DOWN, *Ebberton Down* 1839 *TAMap*. STIBLES
LANE, cf. *Stibles (Acre)* 1839 *TA*, probably a surname.

FIELD-NAMES

The undated forms are 1839 *TA* 114. Spellings dated 1288 are *Ass*, 1332
SR, 1384 (e16) *Prideaux*, 1385 (e15) *MiltRoll*, 1563 Hutch[3], 1664 HTax,
and 1791 Boswell.

(a) Acre; Alamber; Ash Acre; Barn Grd; Bartlett Plot and Barn (cf. Roger *Bertelot'* 1332 (Melcombe H.)); Bean Cl; Belfland and Ley (perhaps to be associated with the 'one acre for ringing the eight o'clock bell' (1774 Hutch[1] 2 422), cf. also 'the curfew bell is still rung occasionally in the year' (Kelly) and *v.* Curfew Grd *infra,* Udal 113; Belfland may represent **belle** with **furlang,** cf. Leigh *supra*); Berrywood; Broad Md; Bustles Plot; Butt (*v.* **butte**); Clenning (Orchd); Coppice; Corner Grd; Corn Grd; Cothays; Court Fd & Orchd; Cow Leaze; Cross Ld & Md; Curfew Grd (-*Grounds* 1563, from ModE **curfew,** *v.* Belfland *supra*); Cutler Cl; Dodlanch; Dry Grd & Md; 8 & 11 Acres; Elm Grd; Fidlers; 5 Acres; Foreland; 4 & 14 Acres; Gamblings; Gold Hill; Great Md; Green Cl; (Hr & Lr) Hay (*v.* **(ge)hæg**); Heath Brow, Heath Coppice & Grd; Higher Grd; Hither Flg & Grd; Home Cl (Little Hill), Home Md; Hundred Acres (an ironical name for a tiny field); Lady Md; Landshard (*v.* **lanchet**); Lark; Little Heath & Md; Long Grd, Ham (*v.* **hamm**) & Orchd; Lot Md(w) (*v.* **hlot**); Lower Grd; (Old & Way) Marnoll (perhaps analogous with Marnhull par. *supra*); Mead; Meathay; Middle Flg & Grd; 9 Acres; North Md; Oatland; Old Waters; Orchard (Plot); Parson's [Bridge] 1791; Partway (*v.* **port-weg**); Pauls Cl & Grd (cf. *Tremor* (sic) *Paull* 1664); Pit Cl; (Lt) Pupple; Roberts Md; Rot Furlong (Orchd); Rushy Corner & Md; Sadbroke; Selve Ld; Shavers Croft; Sharland; Sheeps Croft; 6 Acres; Starve Acre (a derogatory name for poor land); Stoneway; 10 & 3 Acres; Trunk Md (cf. *Milltrunck* [Bridge] 1791, *v.* **trunk**); Upper Grd; (Land) Waddon (probably from **wād** and **dūn**); Water Md; West Cl, Hill & Md; Woore, The Woores (cf. the f.n. Woor 1 287); Yonder Flg.

(b) Bat(t)escumb(e) 1288 (*v.* **cumb** 'valley', first el. probably an OE pers.n. *Bætti* suggested by Ekwall DEPN for Battisford Sf); *Roughdyche de Yberton'* 1384 (e16), *Rowgh'dych' de Ibrygh'ton'* 1385 (e15) (in the bounds of Woolland *infra, v.* **rūh, dīc**).

Melcombe Horsey

MELCOMBE HORSEY (ST 750024) ['milkəm 'haːʀsi]
   Malecomb, -cumb ?1151–7 France, *-combia* n.d. ib
   Melecum 1152–8 MontC, *-cumb(e)* 1198, 1199 Cur, 1205, 1206 P, 1206, 1207 Cur, 1212 Fees, 1228 Ch, 1236 Fees *et freq* to 1428 FA with affixes *Vp-, Up-* 1280, 1288 *Ass*, 1288, 1289 Pat, *West-* 1288 *Ass, Over-* 1296 Ipm; *Meleco(u)mb(e)* 1299 Ipm *et freq* to 1365 Cl with affix *Up-* 1315, 1344, 1350 Ipm, 1365 Cl
   Melcumba 1210–12 RBE, *-com(e)* 1265 Misc, *Upmelcumbe* 1320 FF, *Upmelcombe* 1332 Ch *et freq* to 1431 FA, *Melcomb(e)* 1346 FA, 1379 Cl (-'by *Middelton Abbatis'*) *et freq* to 1535–43 Leland, *Vp Melcombe* 1393

DCMDeed, NatT, Overmelcombe 1431 FA
Milecumb(e) 1229 Pat, 1268 *Ass*, *Milcombe* 1535–43 Leland
Mellecumbe 1244 *Ass*, 1303 FA
Turges Melcombe 1478 HarlCh, 1504 Ipm, 1506 Pat
Melcombe Horsey 1535 VE, 1583 *Digby*, *-comb-* 1811
OS, *Horsey Melcomb* 1601 Hutch[3]
Horses melcombe 1575 Saxton

Probably 'valley where milk was produced, fertile valley',
from **meoluc** and **cumb** (DEPN, EPN), thus identical
with Melcombe Regis 1 251. For DB spellings, *v*. Bingham's
Melcombe *infra*. The early affixes *Up-, Over-* and *West-*
are all in relation to Bingham's Melcombe, *v*. **upp** 'higher
up', **uferra** 'higher, upper', **west**, cf. HIGHER MELCOMBE
(1″, both for hamlet and house). The later affixes are
manorial. *Turges* is from Nicholas *Turges* 1384, Robert
Tourgeys 1430 Hutch[3], Richard- 1478 *HarlCh*, 1504 Ipm,
Robert *Turges* 1504 ib, 1506 Pat, cf. 'there is an olde maner
place of the Turgesis at Milcombe' 1535–43 Leland. *Horsey*
is from the family of this name which possessed the manor
from the 16th cent. (Hutch[3] 4 367, 376, 427), cf. one '*Adam
de Preston* of *Horsey*' (= Horsey So whence the family takes
its name) mentioned in connection with Melcombe as early
as 1374 Pat. Earlier names for the moiety of the manor later
called *Turges Melcombe* were, according to Hutch[3] 4 363,
367, *Up Melcomb Cerne* and *Melcomb(e) Bruning, -Bryning*,
from the families of Henry *de Cerne* 1224 Hutch[3], 1228 Ch,
and John *Brouning* 1367 Hutch[3] respectively.

BINGHAM'S MELCOMBE (Ho) (ST 772022)
Mel(e)come 1086 DB, *Melecoma* c.1086 GeldR, *Mele-
cumb(e)* 1206, 1207, 1208 Cur, 1291 Tax, *-combe* 1316
FA
Nether Melecumb' 1265 CottCh, *Nither-* 1268 *Ass*, 1297
Pat, *Nethermelecumb(e)* 1288 *Ass, Nethermel(e)combe*
1300, 1310 Cl *et freq* to 1433 ib, *Nythermellecombe* 1317
Ipm, *Nuthere Melcombe* 1318 Hutch[3]
Estmel(l)ecumbe 1280, 1288 *Ass*
Bynghammes Melcombe 1412 FA, *Melcombe Byngham* 1431
ib, 1433 Cl, *Bingeham melcombe* 1575 Saxton, *Freke and*

Binghams Melcombe Tithing 1664 HTax, *Melcomb Bingham* 1811 OS

Nether- from **neoðerra** 'lower', and **ēast** 'east', to distinguish it from Melcombe Horsey *supra*. The family of *de Byngham* held this manor from c. 1243 along with West Stafford *q.v.* 1 243, cf. also Robert *de Byngham* 1265 *CottCh*, 1303 Ipm, 1310 Cl, William *de Bingeham* 1274–81 Ipm, *cotag' Emme Bynghams* 1400 *Ilch* (Hilton), and Hutch³ 4 368. The name of the tithing in 1664 HTax is from Thomas *Freke*, mentioned alongside John *Bingham* in the same record.

HENNING HILL (ST 762017), 1811 OS, probably to be associated with *on heandene beorg* 859 ?for 870 (15) *ShaftR* (S 334), *on hendune beorch* ?870 (15) *ib* (S 342) in the Anglo-Saxon bounds of Cheselbourne *supra*, from **hēah** (wk.obl. *hēan*) 'high' and **dūn** 'down, hill' with **beorg** 'hill, barrow'; *-dene* in the first form is probably an error for *-dune*. The modern Henning probably represents the original *hēandūne*; an alternative modern form of the same name may survive in the *TA* f.n. Hinton Corner in Cheselbourne par. *supra*. It is interesting to note that another 600' hill just a mile or so to the W is called Highdon, a name identical in meaning with Henning though different in the form of the adjective and without early spellings.

ALDERMORE COPSE, *v.* **alor, mōr**. BOWDENS, *Browdon Hill* 1774 Hutch¹, 1870 Hutch³, the highest part of the par. (up to 855'), probably from **brū** 'brow, declivity, projecting edge' and **dūn** 'hill, down'. CHAPEL CLOSE, 1774 Hutch¹, cf. *Chapel Mead* 1577 Hutch³, *v.* **chapel(e)**; named from the chapel here mentioned in the 12th cent. (*v.* under St Andrew's Church *infra*) and in 1577 Hutch³, the ruins of which were still visible in 1774 (Hutch¹ 2 425). CONY-GAR COPSE, *v.* **coninger** 'rabbit-warren'. CROSS LANES, *v.* **cross**. DORSETSHIRE GAP, a gap in the hills where several tracks meet, *v.* **gappe**. DOWNS. GIANT'S GRAVE & STONES, *the Giant's grave* 1870 Hutch³; for the association of these names with a local tradition concerning 'two giants . . . contending for the mastery as to which of them would hurl the further', *v.* Udal 161–2. HIGHDON, 1811 OS, *v.* Henning Hill *supra*. HILL BARN (2 ×). HILL WD. HOG HILL, 1811 OS, *v.* **hogg** 'young sheep'. HUMBER WD, 1841 *TA* (Mappowder), probably an instance of the pre-English stream-name **Humber** with reference to the small stream (now unnamed) nearby. LITTLE WD. MELCOMBE COPSE. MELCOMBE HORSEY (6"), HIGHER MELCOMBE (1") (house), *v.* par. name *supra*. MELCOMBE PARK, -*Parke* 1583 SPDom, *the park* 1774 Hutch[1], *Melcomb Park* 1811 OS, *v.* **park**, Cantor & Wilson 3 145–8. MELCOMBE PARK DAIRY FM, *Melcomb Park* 1811 OS. NETTLECOMBE TOUT (PLANT.), *Nettlecomb Tout* 1774 Hutch[1], 1811 OS, *Nettlecombe Towt or Tuft* 1870 Hutch[3], named from the f.n. Nettlecombe in Buckland N. par. *infra, v.* **tōt(e)** 'look-out hill'. NEW BARN. NINE ACRE COPSE. NORDON HILL, *Nordon* 1811 OS, 'north down', from **norð** and **dūn**. NURSERY COPSE. ST ANDREW'S CHURCH, cf. 'the church of *Malecomb*, with the chapel of another *Malecumb*'?1151–7 France, *ecclesie de Melecumb*' 1205 P; for the chapel at Melcombe (Horsey) *v.* Chapel Cl *supra*. SANDY HOLE HANGING, *v.* **hanging**. SAW PIT. SUMMER HO PLANT.

FIELD-NAMES

There are no names in 1841 *TA* 148. All spellings are from Hutch[3].

(*a*) Town-hays 1870 (containing remains of former hamlet, *v.* **tūn**, **(ge)hæg**).

(*b*) *Comb* 1591 (*v.* **cumb**); *une pasture enclose appellé le Coysh* 1408 (probably **cosh** 'cottage, hut'; in 1869 'still called *Cosh*' according to Hutch[3] 3 727); *Hebbes Bottom* 1591 (a surname with **botm**); *Lady Mead* 1577 (*v.* **hlæfdige**).

Milton Abbas

In 1880 one detached part of this par. (Holworth) was transferred to Owermoigne par. 1 138, and in 1882 another detached part (Lyscombe) was transferred to Cheselbourne par. *supra*. In 1933 the part of Milton Abbas par. known as 'Whitchurch End' was added to Winterborne Whitchurch par. 2 82.

MILTON ABBAS (ST 806017)

(*in to*) *Middeltone* 843 for 934 (eME) ASCharters, 843 for

934 (17) BCS 739, *of-, to Middel tune* l1o ASC (A) s.a.
964, *Middeltun(e)* c. 1000 Saints
Mid(d)eltun(e) 1086 DB, *Miteltona* Exon, *Mid(d)elton(i)a*
12 SD, 1130 PR, 1156 RBE, *Mid(d)elton(e)* 1162, 1165
P, 1201 Cur, 1203 P *et freq* to 1558 *PlR, -tun(')* 1211
Cur, 1222 Pat, 1226 Cur, 1227 FF, 1247 Lib,
Mid(d)leton 1202 Abbr, 1280 Ch, 1291 Pat, 1338 Cl,
1575 Saxton, *Mid(d)ilton(')* 1261 Cl *et freq* to 1453 *Sher,*
Myddilton' 1268 *Ass, Myd(d)elton(')* 1268 FF, 1280 QW,
1291 Tax, 1428 FA, 1531 *AD, Mildeton'* (sic) 1271 Cl,
Mildelton' (sic) 1438 *Weld*[1], *Middeton'* (sic) 1440 *ib,*
'Middelton otherwise *Milton'* 1446 Cl
Med(d)elton(') 1262 (c. 1447) *Vaux,* 1341 Cl
Middelton' Abbatis 1268, 1288 *Ass et freq* to 1392 Pat,
-Abbas 1456 ib, *Middleton Abbatis* 1298 FF, *Myddelton*
Abbot's 1421 Pat
Milton(') 1268 *Ass,* 1275 Cl, 1305 Pat, 1318 Ch *et passim,*
-als. Middleton 1558–79 ChancP, 1582 *AD, Mylton*
1426 Cl, 1575 *PlR*
Melton 1392 Cl   *Multon'* 1412 *Weld*[1]
Milton Tregonwell c. 1566 Hutch[3]
the New Town of Milton l1i8 *SalisT*

'Middle farm or estate', from **middel** and **tūn**, 'middle'
possibly in relation to other neighbouring settlements but
perhaps more probably 'from its situation, which is as near
the centre of the county as its irregular form will permit'
(Hutch[3] **4** 382). The affix *Abbas* (Lat **abbas** 'an abbot',
gen.sg. *abbatis* 'of the abbot') refers to the former Abbey
here, which also possessed the manor in early times, *v.*
Milton Abbey *infra.* The manor was granted to John
Tregonwell in 1539 (Hutch[3] **4** 383). The 'New Town' refers
to the village rebuilt on its present site in 1786–7, the
original site of the village having been around the Abbey.
The bounds of the manor are described in 1385 (e15)
MiltRoll.

STREET-NAMES. Lost street-names, mainly from the 'Old Town' before its
removal, include: *Back Street* c.1660 Hutch[3], 18 *TPlan; Broad Street*
c.1660 Hutch[3], 18 *TPlan; Duck Street* c.1660 Hutch[3] (cf. foll.); *Fishway*
Hill c. 1660 Hutch[3], c.1771 *DROMap, Fishway* (or *Duck Street*) c.1771 *ib;*

Govers Lane 18 *TPlan*; (*Lr*) *Embury Walk* c.1660 Hutch[3], *Lr Henbury Lane* c. 1771 *DROMap* (no doubt to be identified with a 'foot-walk walled, called *Ambry Wall'* a1771 Hutch[3] **4** 393, where it is explained as from 'the almonry' (of the abbey); more probably however from **hēah** (wk.obl. *hēan*) 'high' and **beorg** 'hill, barrow'); *High Street* c.1660 Hutch[3], c.1771 *DROMap*; *Hollow's Way* (sic) c.1660 Hutch[3], *Hollow Way* c.1771 *DROMap*; *Rigg's Lane* c.1660 Hutch[3], *Johnsons or-* 18 *TPlan*; *Market Street* c. 1660 Hutch[3], c.1771 *DROMap* (cf. *foro de Middelton'* 1288 *Ass*); *Newport Street* c.1660 Hutch[3], c.1771 *DROMap* (*v.* **port**[2] 'market place'); *Pointers-* c.1660 Hutch[3], *Painters Lane* c.1771 *DROMap* (cf. William *Panter* 1392 *Winch*, John *Painter* 1664 *HTax*; *Water Lane* 18 *TPlan*; *Whiteway* c.1660 Hutch[3] (cf. Hugh *de Whiteweye*, John *atte Whiteweye* 1317 *MiltC*, 'white, i.e. chalky, road', *v.* **hwīt, weg**, and cf. hundred name *supra*). Inns include *The Crown Inn, The Kings Arms* c. 1771 *DROMap* (at Winterborne Whitchurch, cf. Milton Arms 6″), *the Portarlington Arms* 1852 SCat, Hambro Arms 6″.

BAGBER FM (SY 808992), WEST BAGBER BLDGS & COPSE, *Bakebere* 1249 FF, 1310 Inq aqd, 1311 Pat, *Bagber(e)* 1502 Ipm, 1544 *PlR*, 1635, 1639 *Ilch* (*-Downe*), 1659 (1758) (*-Farm, -House*), 1771 *DROMap* (*West-*), 1811 OS (*-Barn*), 1852 SCat (*-Farm, -Wood*), *Bagbore* (sic) 1795 Boswell. Apparently identical in origin with Bagber in Sturminster Newton par. *supra* where some of the early forms cited may actually belong.

CHESCOMBE FM & LANE (ST 829002), *Churchecombe* 1539 Hutch[3], *Chescom(be) Fm* 1659 (1758), 1771 *DROMap*, *Churchcomb vulgo Chescomb* 1774 Hutch[1], *Churchcombe or Chescombe* 1795 Boswell, *Chescombe Fm & Wd* 1852 SCat, 'church valley', *v.* **cirice, cumb**, with reference to St Mary's Church (Winterborne Whitchurch); for the development to *Ches-*, cf. *Chessen* 1675 for Churston D 510. Chescombe Lane is *Churchewey* 1385 (e15) *MiltRoll* in the bounds of Milton.

DELCOMBE BOTTOM (ST 790046), DELCOMBE DAIRY FM, DELCOMBE FM (1852 SCat, *Delcom Farm* 1659 (1758) *DROMap*, *Delcombe* 1811 OS, DELCOMBE MANOR 1″), DELCOMBE HEAD (1811 OS) & WD (1771 *DROMap*); probably to be identified with *Derecomb(e)shed(de)* 1384 (e16) *Prideaux, Dercombyshed(e)* 1385 (e15) *MiltRoll* (in the bounds of Woolland and Milton), *Deirelecombe, West*

Deirelecombyshyued n.d. (e15) *ib,* thus 'valley of the wood or clearing frequented by wild animals (perhaps specifically deer)', from **dēor, lēah** and **cumb,** with **hēafod** 'head, upper end'. Delcombe Head at 880′ on the par. bdy seems to be the feature referred to in the Anglo-Saxon bounds of Woolland as *on delesburg middenwearde* 833 (14) *ShaftR* (S 277); this form is probably corrupt, but may represent an original *dēorlēa(ge)sbeorg,* 'the hill of the *dēorlēah*', assuming also that **beorg** may have been confused with **burh** as in *on burg* in the same charter referring to Bul Barrow in Woolland par. *infra.* Delcombe Bottom (*v.* **botm**) is a long valley extending N from Deer Park *q.v. infra.*

HEWISH FM (ST 806002), HEWISH HILL BLDGS, *Hywysch', Hywyschcloos, -down* 1385 (e15) *MiltRoll, Huyshe* 1539 Hutch[3], *Hewish Sheep Downs* 1659 (1758), *Hewish Fm & Down* 1771 *DROMap, Huish* 1795 Boswell, *Hewish* 1811 OS, *Hewish Down Cl* 1852 SCat, *v.* **hīwisc** 'a measure of land that would support a family', **clos(e), dūn.** The form *æt Hiwis[ce]* 1001/2-1009/12 ASWrits (p. 484) may belong here or to Huish Fm in Sydling St Nicholas par. *infra.*

EAST & WEST LUCCOMBE FMS (ST 809012, 817012), LUCCOMBE DOWN &'HILL, *Louc(c)ome* 1317 *MiltC, Luckham Sheep Pasture* 1659 (1758), *Luccombe Fm & Hill* 1771 both *DROMap, Luccomb or Windmill Ashes* 1774 Hutch[1], *Luccombe* 1811 OS, probably 'valley with a shelter', or 'sheltered valley', *v.* **hlēo(w), hlēow, cumb,** cf. Luccombe in Netherbury par. *infra. Windmill Ashes* are described by Hutch[1] 2 441 as 'some trees on the top of the hill north of this farm, which are a sea mark', *v.* Windmill Clump *infra.*

MILTON ABBEY (ST 799024), *monasterium et abbathiam de Middeltone* 843 for 934 (17) BCS 739, *Abbatia de Middeltune* 1086 DB, *Middleton Abbey* 1331 Pat, *Monasterii beate Marie et S'cique Sampsonis de Mydelton* 1531 *AD,* a Benedictine abbey founded 933 by Athelstan (VCHDo 2 58–62), cf. also *Ecclesia Middeltunensis* 1086 DB, 'church of St Mary of Myddelton' 1268 FF, *ecclesiam S'ci Samps' de Middelton'* 1280 *Ass, Abby Church, The Abby Barn, Abby Gdn, Convent Gdn, Vicarage Ho* all c. 1771 *DROMap, v.* foll.

ABBEY CHURCH, THE ABBEY PARK, v. Milton Abbey *supra*.
ALMSHOUSES, removed from the 'old town' in 1779, formerly
The Alms House c. 1771 *DROMap* (in *Newport Street*).
AVENUE PLANT. BARNES'S HILL FM, *Barnes Hill* 1852 SCat,
cf. *Eva Bernes . . . ten' . . . mes' cum curtill'*, Nicholas *Bern*
1317 *MiltC*, John *Barnes* 1664 HTax. BLAGDON COPSE,
Blageden Down 1659 (1758), *Blagdon Gate* 1771 *DROMap*,
Blagdon 1852 SCat, 'dark-coloured hill', from **blæc** and **dūn**.
BROADFIELD, (*The*) *Broad Fd* 1659 (1758) *DROMap*, 1852
SCat. CAYLES DOWN COPSE, *Cayles Down(e)* 1659 (1758)
DROMap, 1852 SCat, a surname. COOMBE (PIT) PLANT., cf.
la Combe n.d. (e15) *MiltRoll*, *Combe* 1852 SCat, v. **cumb**
'valley'. CRINCOMBE BTM & CTGS, *Cumcombe Bottom* 1852
SCat, first el. uncertain, v. **cumb**, **botm**. DALE CTG. DEER
PARK, 1811 OS, *Derbarke* (sic) 1385 (e15) *MiltRoll*, *Dear
Park* 1852 SCat, v. **dēor**, **park**, cf. Delcombe Bottom *supra*,
Milton Park Fm & Wd *infra*. GALLOWS CORNER, *Gallows
Corner Fd* 1852 SCat, at a crossroads on the par. bdy, v.
g(e)alga. GREAT DOWN CLUMP, *Great Down* 1870 Hutch[3],
cf. *Down'dyche* 1385 (e15) *MiltRoll*, *Hr & Lr Down* 1771
DROMap, v. **dūn** 'hill, down', **dīc** 'ditch'. GREEN DOWN.
GREEN HILL (PLANT.), *Green Hill* 1659 (1758), 1771
DROMap. HAYDON PLANT., *Haden Down* 1659 (1758)
DROMap, *Haydon* 1852 SCat, probably from **hēg** 'hay' and
dūn 'hill'. HIGHER LODGE. HILL HO, cf. *Hill Croft* 1659
(1758) *DROMap* (2×), *Hill Cl* 1852 SCat. HOGGEN DOWN,
1659 (1758) (-*Farm*), 1771 *DROMap*, from **hogg** 'young
sheep' with a plural ending, v. **-ena**, cf. *Hogenhull'* n.d. (e15)
MiltRoll which has the same first el. with **hyll** 'hill'. HORSE
PARK PLANT., cf. *Horse Leaze* 1771 *DROMap*, v. **lǣs.** LADY
CAROLINE'S DRIVE, an allusion to Lady Caroline Damer, died
1775, cf. **2** 74. LONDONDERRY, *London Derry* 1771 *DROMap*,
no doubt a transferred name from the Irish place. LONG ASH
FM, 1852 SCat, *Long Ash* 1811 OS. LONG CLOSE FM, *Long
Close* 1771 *DROMap*, 1811 OS. LOWER LODGE (PLANT.).
MILTON MILL (CLUMP), *Milton Mill* 1811 OS, cf. Philip *atte
Mulle* 1327 SR, *Mill Mdw* 1659 (1758) *DROMap*, *Mill Grd
& Md* 1852 SCat, v. **atte** 'at the', **myln** 'mill'; there was a
mill at Milton A. in 1086 DB (VCHDo **3** 78). MILTON PARK
FM & WD, cf. *Milton Fm* 1852 SCat, *Milton Park* 1659

(1758), 1771 *DROMap*, probably *the Estpark'* 1385 (e15) *MiltRoll* in the bounds of Milton, *v.* **ēast, park**, Cantor & Wilson 7 173–6. MONMOUTH'S HILL, *Melmoth's Hill* 1852 SCat, cf. John *Mildemouth'* 1332 SR (Stoke Wake); it will be noted that the modern form of the name, with perhaps an implied association with the Duke of Monmouth (cf. Monmouth's Ash **2** 287), is only recent. NEW CLOSE (CTGS), *New Cl* 1659 (1758), 1771 *DROMap*. NEW LODGE. OXHOUSE CTGS, cf. *Oxhouse Pce* 1862 SCat. PIGEON HO PLANT. RUINS PLANT., cf. *Ruin's Bottom* 1862 SCat; 'Ruins' marked 6″. ST CATHERINE'S CHAPEL, cf. *Catherine Hill* 1659 (1758) *DROMap*. ST JAMES'S CHURCH. ST MARY'S CHURCH (at Winterborne Whitchurch). SHOP HO PLANT., *Shop House Md* 1659 (1758) *DROMap*, *v.* **scēap-hūs** 'sheep house'. SQUIBB'S KNOLL, *v.* **cnoll** 'hill top, hillock', cf. *Ric' Squibbe . . . ten'* . . . *i mes' cum curtill'* 1317 *MiltC*. STABLE BARROW, 1811 OS, *Stapyllbargh'* 1385 (e15) *MiltRoll* (in the bounds of Milton), 'barrow marked by a boundary post', *v.* **stapol, beorg**; tumulus marked 6″. WINDMILL CLUMP, 1852 SCat, *Windmill* 1659 (1758) *DROMap*, *Windmill-Ashes* 1752 Hutch[3], *Wind Mill Ash Plant.* 1771 *DROMap*, *v.* **wind-mulle, æsc**, Luccombe Fms *supra*. WOODSDOWN, *Arnolds Wood Down, Martin's Woods Down* 1771 *DROMap, Woods Down Gt, Hr & Lr Mead, Arnold's-, Moreton's Woods Down* 1852 SCat; the first el. may be **wudu** 'wood' or a surname, cf. Richard *Bythewode* 1332 SR, Robert *Arnold* 1613 Hutch[3].

FIELD-NAMES

The undated forms are 1852 SCat. Spellings dated 1298 are FF, 1317 *MiltC*, 1319 (e15), 1385 (e15), n.d. (e15) *MiltRoll*, 1327 *SR*, 1332 SR, 1372 or 1472 *Surv*, 1392 *Winch*, 1400 *Ilch*, 1664 HTax, 1659 (1758), 1771, c. 1771 *DROMap*, and 1870 Hutch[3].

(a) Andrews Md c.1771 (cf. John *Andreu* 1327); Apple Gate Md c. 1771; Ballowshake; Barn Cl (*Barne-* 1659 (1758)), Fd (1771), Grd, & Mdw (1659 (1758), c. 1771); Barrow Cl 1771; Barton Fd (*Barton Flg* 1659 (1758), *Barton Cl, Cow Barton* 1771); Bech-, Becklands (*Beckland Cow Lease* 1659 (1758), *Beckland(s)* 1771); Black Wall(s) (*Blackwell Fd(s)* 1659 (1758)); Bottom Md (1771); Bramble Croft & Hill (*Brimly Croft* 1659 (1758), *v.* **brēmel, -ig**[3]); Buddle Hill; Bushey Mdw (*Bushy Md* 1659

(1758), *Bushey Cl* 1771); Butler's Hill (cf. *Butlers Corner* c. 1771, John *Butler* 1664); Candy Grd; Chesleborne Lane 1771 (to Cheselbourne *supra*); Church Cl; Clump Grd; Cockroad (*v.* **cocc-rodu**); Cole Mill (*Coles Md, -Mill* 1659 (1758), *Cole Closes & Fd* 1771); Combs Ten't c. 1771; Condoch; Cow Cl (1659 (1758)), Cow Grass; (Old) Cowleaze (*South Cow Lease* 1659 (1758), *Gt-, Old Cow Leaze* 1771); Cowridge (*Cow Ridge* 1659 (1758)); Cross Lanes Cl; Cuckoo Lane 1771; Dead Hill (1659 (1758), *(Gt) Dead Hill* (*Closes*) 1771, *v.* **dēad**); Deep Coombe (*Deep Coom Fd* 1659 (1758)); Dods Corner; (Lt) Dollycoates; Drove; Dry Fd (*-Fd Mead* 1771); Dyett's Heath (1771, cf. Christopher *Diett* 1664); East and South Cl (*The East Close* 1659 (1758)); (The) 8 Acres (1771); (The) 18 Acres (1659 (1758), 1771); The 11 Acres (1771); Eweleaze (*The Yew Leaze* 1771, cf. *Ewe Lease Hill* 1659 (1758), *v.* **eowu, lǣs**); Fisherman's Grave 1870 (part of a boundary ditch, between Milton and Hilton, so called according to tradition from a fight between two fishermen in which one was killed, *v.* Hutch³ 4 409); 4 Acres (1659 (1758)); (The) 14 Acres (1659 (1758), 1771); Old French Grass (*v.* **french grass**); Furzey Grd; Great Cl; The Great Lawn 1771; Great Md; Green Cl (1771); Halsherds; Hanging Mdw & Pce (*v.* **hangende**); Hawcombe; Higher Fd (1771) & Md; Hills (cf. Richard *Hulle* 1400 (Hilton)); Holcombe (*Hollecombe* 1385 (e15), 'deep valley', *v.* **hol², cumb**); Home Fd (1771); The Hundred Acres c. 1771 (*Hundred Acres Fd* 1659 (1758)); Hunt's Wd (cf. *Hunts Coppice, -South Close* 1659 (1758), Robert *Hunt* 1664); Hut Grd; Jacob's Fd; Lady Well Orchd, Lads (sic) Well Md c. 1771; Leg Md; Lime Kiln Fd; Lodge Grd; Long Grd & Md(w) (*-Md* 1659 (1758), *-Mdw* 1771); Long Wd (1771, *Longwood Sheep Pasture* 1659 (1758), *Langwode* 1385 (e15), *v.* **lang¹, wudu**); Lower Gdn or Hams Orchd c. 1771; The Manor Pound; Meadow; Melborne Md (from Milborne St A. 1 306); Middle Hill (1771); Mount Pleasant c. 1771; New Grd (1771); 9 Acres (*The-* 1771); Noddick 1771 (cf. Hilton f.ns. *supra*); Oak Fd; Oakham (1771); Oak Tree Fd (1771); Oat Fd (1771); Osmonds Cl c. 1771; Ox Cl; Parson's Md; Payers Grd; Peak Fd (cf. *Lane to Peek Plot* c. 1771, *v.* **pēac** 'peak, knoll, point'); Pond Md (*-Mdw* c. 1771); Read's Hill (*-Fd* 1771); 7 Acres (*The-* 1771, *Westseven acres* 1385 (e15), *v.* **seofon, æcer**); The 17 Acres; Shepherd's Cl & Grd (cf. John *Shephurd'* 1332); Shoulder of Mutton Cl c. 1771 (with reference to shape); Stable Pce; 10 Acres; 30 Acres; Thistley Fd (1771, *Thistilie Field* 1659 (1758)); 3 Acres; (The) 12 Acres; (The) 20 Acres (1771); the 27 Acres (*Twenty Seaven Acres* 1659 (1758)); Vincents Cl c. 1771 (cf. William *Vincent* 1664); Water Mdw (cf. *Arnolds Water Mead, Whinnch Water Mead* 1659 (1758)); Well Grd; West Fd (1771); White Hill c. 1771; Young Plant.

Additional names recorded by WI include: Nomans Ld, Rifle Pce (used 1861 for shooting practice by Dorset volunteers) and Starve all (derogatory for poor land).

(b) *Alch'combe* 1385 (e15) (*v.* **cumb**); *Alvysch'thornys* 1319 (e15), *la Haluesch'thorne* n.d. (e15) (*v.* **þorn** 'thorn-tree', first el. ME **elvisch** 'pertaining to elves'); *Bagbers Lease* 1659 (1758) (*v.* **lǣs**, Bagber *supra*);

Bareleggudthorn' n.d. (e15) (ME **barelegged** (here in the sense 'having bare branches'?), with **þorn**); *Beerewey* 1385 (e15) (probably to Bere Regis 1 273, *v.* **weg**); *Blanefordyswey* 1385 (e15) (to Blandford F. 2 87); *crucem vocat' Bolecroys* 1385 (e15) (*v.* **crois** 'cross', first el. perhaps **bola** 'tree-trunk, log'); *Brags Corner* 1659 (1758) (a surname, *v.* **corner**); *Brokelond'* n.d. (e15) (*v.* **brōc, land**); *Buldown'* n.d. (e15) (*v.* **bula, dūn**); *Caryysdyche* (sic) 1385 (e15) (probably the ditch bounding Deverel Fm (earlier *Milborne Cary*) 1 307, *v.* **dīc**); *Canelyscroys* 1385 (e15) (a surname with **crois**); *Catts Clif Coppice* 1659 (1758) (*v.* **catt, clif**); *Cernyswey* 1385 (e15) (to Cerne A. *infra, v.* **weg**); *Chalfcombe* 1319 (e15), *la Sowthercheluecombyshyued'* n.d. (e15) ('valley for calves', *v.* **cealf** (gen.pl. -a), **cumb**, with **sūðerra** 'more southerly', **hēafod** 'head, top end'); *Chalmer(e)* 1319 (e15), 1385 (e15), *Chaluemere* n.d. (e15) ('pool for calves', *v.* **mere¹**, cf. prec.); *Chelkhull'* n.d. (e15) (*v.* **cealc** 'chalk', **hyll** 'hill'); *Chypmannyslond'* 1385 (e15) (*v.* **land**, first el. probably a surname, cf. Richard *Chipman* 1332, but cf. also *Chepman' Way* in Woolland par. infra); *Clenchestonyswey* 1385 (e15) (to Winterborne Clenston 2 79); *Colatyslond'* 1385 (e15) (a surname with **land**); *Comton Pitts Field* 1659 (1758) (first el. probably a surname); *The Coppice, Coppice Close* 1659 (1758); *Cow Pasture* 1659 (1758); *Damfretyswale . . . super aliud Wale* 1385 (e15), *Daumfretyslond'* n.d. (e15) (a surname with **walu** 'ridge' and **land**); *Dorchester-, Dochestreswey* 1385 (e15) (to Dorchester 1 346, *v.* **weg**); *Dry Close* 1659 (1758); *Elmer Coome* 1659 (1758); *Netherfennywey* 1385 (e15) (**neoðerra, fennig** 'marshy', **weg**); *Five Acres* 1659 (1758); *Fifteen Acres Field* 1659 (1758); *Gervaysgore, -lond'* 1385 (e15) (*v.* **gāra, land**, cf. John *Gerneys* (for *Gerueys*) 1298, *terram . . . Johannis Gervays* 1385 (e15)); *Westgorebargh'* 1385 (e15) (*v.* **gāra, beorg**); *Grymbargh'* 1385 (e15) ('barrow haunted by a spectre', *v.* **grīma, beorg**); *Grymyscombyshyued* n.d. (e15) ('Grímr's valley', from the ON pers.n. *Grímr* (cf. Grimstone 1 373), or a ME surname derived from it, and **cumb** with **hēafod** 'head, top end'); *aque vocat' Gygehorn'* 1385 (e15) (*v.* **horn** 'horn-shaped piece of land', first el. uncertain but cf. ME *gig(ge)* 'foolish young woman, boorish man'); *Westharpydwey* 1385 (e15) (*v.* **here-pæð** 'highway'); *la Heldevorugh'(ende)* n.d. (e15) (*v.* **furh** 'furrow, trench', **ende**, first el. probably **eald** 'old'); *Hell Close* 1659 (1758) (near to Dead Hill *supra, v.* **hell**); *Heltonyslake, -wey* 1385 (e15) (*v.* **lacu** 'stream', **weg** 'road', Hilton par. *supra*); *Heth'feldych'* n.d. (e15) (*v.* **hæð, feld, dīc**); *unum magnum Holme, una holme* 1385 (e15) (*v.* **holegn** 'holly'); *Hurnyston* 1319 (e15), *petram vocatum Hurn'ston'* 1385 (e15) ('corner stone', *v.* **hyrne, stān**); *petram vocat' Jaffraystoon'* 1385 (e15) (**stān** with the pers.n. or surname *Geffrey*); *Keats Cow Lease, Keats Mead* 1659 (1758); *Kyngton'clyf* 1385 (e15) (*v.* **cyning, tūn, clif**); *Lampeacre* n.d. (e15) (*v.* **lampe, æcer**); *the Lanhede* 1385 (e15) (perhaps 'lane end', *v.* **lane, hēafod**); (*petram vocat'*) *Lang(ge)ston'* 1319 (e15), 1385 (e15) (*v.* **lang¹, stān**); *Est-, Westladewynyspytte* 1385 (e15) (from **pytt** and a surname, cf. Adam *Ladewynd'* 1332 (Lydlinch)); *Latameryslond'* 1385 (e15) (cf. John *Latymer* 1332 (Dewlish)); *Lowysley, Weslowysleysclyff* 1385 (e15) (to be identified with the f.n. *Lous(e)l(e)ys* in Dewlish par. 1 305, *v.* **lēah** 'wood, clearing', **west, clif**; the first el. may be a pers.n. rather than **hlōse** 'pig-sty'); *Lytell Hull'* n.d. (e15) (*v.* **lӯtel, hyll**); *la Meedclose* n.d. (e15) (*v.* **mǣd, clos(e)**); *Melcombyspathe* 1385 (e15) (to Melcombe Horsey, *v.* **pæð**); *la Middelfeld'* 1392 (*in medio campo* 1317, *v.* **middel, feld**); *Middelmann(e)londe*, *Middelmannedon* 1372 or 1472 ('land and hill of the middlemen', *v.* **land, dūn**; the first el. is ME *middelman* 'a man in the midst' (c.1384 MED), but cf. the obscure ME occupational term **middelman**, thought by NED in the single ME example cited (from 1435) to mean 'a workman employed in the making of iron wire'); *Monketon'*, *Monketonyswey* 1385 (e15) ('farm of the monks', from **munuc** and **tūn**, with **weg**, probably with reference to La Lee Fm (in Winterborne Whitchurch 2 83) which belonged to Milton Abbey); *Mortons New Close* 1659 (1758); *Myddenhull'* n.d. (e15) (*v.* **hyll**, first el. perhaps **midding** 'a midden'); *the Netherlynche* 1385 (e15) (*v.* **neoðerra** 'lower', **hlinc** 'ridge'); *Northdon* 1372 or 1472 (*v.* **norð, dūn**); *North Field* 1659 (1758); *la Nywhegge* n.d. (e15) (*v.* **nīwe, hecg**); *atte Orcharde* (p) 1327 (*v.* **atte, orceard**); *Peaked Close* 1659 (1758) (*v.* **peked** 'pointed'); *Pykeacre* 1385 (e15) (*v.* **pīc¹** 'point', **æcer**); *Roe Close* 1659 (1758); *Rogeryswey* 1385 (e15) (the pers.n. or surname *Roger* with **weg**); *la Rowdyche* n.d. (e15) (*v.* **rūh** 'rough', **dīc**); *la Rygge* 1317 (*v.* **hrycg**); *Lange-, Lytelschure* n.d. (e15) (perhaps an OE **scӯr(e)** 'hut, shelter' proposed by Professor Löfvenberg for Skier's Hall YW 1 xi, *v.* **lang¹, lӯtel**); *Seberdon(e)* 1317, *Zeberdon'* 1385 (e15) (the later form occurs in the bounds of Milton and its location suggests identification of the first part of this name with (*on*) *sebergh* in the Anglo-Saxon bounds of Cheselbourne *q.v. supra*, with **dūn**); (*petram vocat'*) *Setelyston'* 1319 (e15), 1385 (e15) (*v.* **stān** 'stone', first el. probably **setl** 'seat, dwelling'); *Sheephouse mead* 1659 (1758) (cf. Shop House Plant. *supra*); *Sheep Pasture* 1659 (1758); *Shellbargh'* 1385 (e15) (perhaps identical in origin with *on schilleburghe* in Buckland N. par. *infra*); *Sheplond'* 1385 (e15) (*v.* **scēap, land**); *Shortcombe* 1385 (e15) (*v.* **sc(e)ort, cumb**); *Six Acres* 1659 (1758); *Skuttbargh'* 1385 (e15) (*v.* **beorg**, first el. possibly **scyte** 'steep slope'; for initial *sk*, cf. PN D xxv); *the Slubbe, the Lytellslubbe* 1385 (e15) (perhaps an early instance of ModE **slub** 'thick mud, mire', recorded from 1577–87 NED, cf. the f.n. *Slobs* 1 228, *v.* **lӯtel**); *Smokacre* n.d. (e15) (*v.* **smoke, æcer**); *Southamm* 1372 or 1472 (*v.* **sūð, hamm**); *montem vocat' the Southbach* 1385 (e15) (*v.* **sūð**, second el. apparently an early instance of ModE **batch** 'hillock'); *South Close* 1659 (1758); *South Field* 1659 (1758) (2 ×); *Sterthull'* 1385 (e15) (*v.* **steort** 'tail of land', **hyll**, cf. Sturthill in Shipton G. par. *infra*); *Stodefold'* 1385 (e15) (*v.* **stōd-fald** 'horse enclosure'); *paruam Stonschyly* n.d. (e15) (*v.* **stān-scilig** 'stony (ground)'); *Stonybrigg'* 1385 (e15) (*v.* **stānig, brycg**); *Stony Mead* 1659 (1758); *Stynkbargh'wyswey* 1385 (e15) (*v.* **beorg, weg**; the first el. is ME **stink** 'offensive smell', with reference no doubt to some plant or animal); *magnum holme vocat' threlanschore- bussh'*, *aceruum lapidum* ('heap of stones') *vocat' threlansshorys* 1385 (e15) ('(bush) where three boundaries meet', *v.* **þrēo, land-scoru, busc**, with **holegn** 'holly'); *T(h)remanlonde* 1372 or 1472 ('strip belonging to three

men', *v.* **þrēo, mann, land**); *la Thurleston'* n.d. (e15) ('stone with a hole
in it', *v.* **þyrel, stān**, cf. Durlston 1 57); *Towh'hylle* 1385 (e15) (*v.* **hyll**,
first el. uncertain); *Towkerwey*(*shyued'*) n.d. (e15) (*v.* **weg, hēafod** 'end',
cf. John *le Touker* 1317); *The Town Fields* 1659 (1758); *Wadbarough'* n.d.
(e15) (*v.* **wād** 'woad', **beorg**); *Welsteds Down* 1659 (1758) (cf. Elizabeth
Welsted ib); *Wen Close* 1659 (1758) (*v.* **wenn** 'wen, tumour', probably with
reference to a barrow); *West Close* 1659 (1758); *the Westekryppe* 1385 (e15)
(*v.* **west, crype** 'narrow passage, drain'); *atte Weye* (p) 1392 (*v.* **atte,
weg**); *Wynterbornysputte* 1385 (e15) (from Winterborne Clenston 2 79, *v.*
pytt).

Stoke Wake

STOKE WAKE (ST 764065)
> *Stoche* 1086 DB, *Stoga* Hy 1 (15) *ShaftR, Stok* 1212 Fees,
> 15 *ShaftR, Stoke* 1332 SR, 1375 Cl
> '*Stoke* in the forest of *Blakemore'* 1248 Pat, *Stok(e) in
> Blakemore* 1285 Hutch[3], 1290 Ch, 1304 Hutch[3] , *Stokes
> in Blakemore* 15 *ShaftR*
> *Stoke Wake* 1285 FA, 1288 *Ass*, 1348–50 Ipm, 1360 Cl *et
> passim*, -*Wak* 1316 FA, *Stok Wake* 1360 Ipm,
> *Stokewake* 1405 Cl, 1575 Saxton, *Stoke Wake als. Cofyn*
> (sic) 1428 FA
> *Stoke Cosin* 1288 FF, *Ass*, -*Cosyn* 1310 Banco (Drew),
> -*Cusyn in Blakemore* 15 *ShaftR, Stock Cosyn* 1291 Tax

'Outlying farm buildings, a secondary settlement', *v.* **stoc**,
Blackmoor Forest *infra*. The manorial affixes are from the
families of *Wake* (cf. Ralph *Wak(e)* 1285 FA, 1290 Ch, etc)
and *Cosin* (cf. William son of Thomas *Cosin* 1288 FF), *v.*
Hutch[3] 4 413–4, cf. East and West Stour pars. *supra*.

FOX ALLERS COPSE & DAIRY (ST 756058), *copicia . . . in le
Voxalres, Voxalrelese,* -*wode* 1416, *bosco . . . voc' Voxallers*
1418, *Voxallerlegh'* 1494, -*wode* 1497, *Foxallers, Foxaller
Coppice* c. 1750 all *Seymer, Foxalders Coppice* 1839 *TA, v.*
fox, alor 'alder', **lǣs** 'pasture', **wudu**. *Foxholes* (*Coppice*)
1640 *Seymer* probably refers to the same place, the
association with **fox-hol** 'a fox-hole, a fox's earth' being the
result of popular etymology.

WHITECOMBE (ST 756077), *claus' vocat' Whytecombe* 1494, *-Wydecombe* 1497, *Whitecomb(e)* c. 1750 all *Seymer*, *Whitcomb* 1811 OS, cf. *White Coom(e) Close*, *-Mead* 1640 *Seymer*, *Gt & Lt Whitcombe, Whitcombe Md* 1839 *TA*, *v.* **cumb** 'valley'; without earlier spellings it cannot be certain whether the first el. was originally **hwīt** 'white' (cf. White Hill *infra*) or **wīd** 'wide' (cf. Whitcombe 1 259).

ALDERMORE COPSE, LT ALDERMORE, *Gt & Lt Aldermoor* 1839 *TA*, cf. *The Aller Coppice, The Aller Mead* 1640 *Seymer*, *v.* **alor** 'alder', **mōr**, cf. Fox Allers Copse *supra*. ALL SAINTS' CHURCH. BALMERS COOMBE BARN, BTM & COPSE, *claus' pastur' vocat' Bamlettescombe* 1494 *Seymer*, *Balmerscombe Aldermoor* 1839 *TA*, a surname (cf. John *Bambflet'* 1332 SR (S. Caundle)) with **cumb** 'valley', cf. Aldermore Copse *supra*. KATE'S COPSE, cf. Mistress *Kete* (a tenant) 1640 *Seymer*. LAMPLANDS COPSE, *Langfurlang'* 1417, 1452, *Landfurlong Close, -Copice* 1640 all *Seymer, Long Furlong* 1839 *TA*, *v.* **lang¹**, **furlang**; popular etymology has contributed to the modern form. MANOR FM. MIDDLE COPSE, cf. *The Middle Copice in the Park* 1640 *Seymer*, cf. *Park Coppice infra*. POPES LEAZE ALDERMORE, *Popes leaz ouer the Hill* 1640 *Seymer, Popes Leaze* (*Aldermoor*) 1839 *TA*, cf. *Popes Copice ouer the Hill* 1640, *Mathew-, Thomas Pope* 1494, *Will' Pope . . . tenement'* 1559 all *Seymer*, *v.* **lǣs** 'pasture', Aldermore Copse *supra*. RECTORY, *Parsonage* c. 1750 *Seymer*. RIDOUTS FM, cf. Mr *Ridout* (a tenant) c. 1750 *Seymer*. SKINNERS FM, *Henry Skinners* (a holding) c. 1750 *Seymer*, *Skinners Ho and Orchd* 1839 *TA*, cf. Thomas *Skynner* 1664 HTax. STOKE CMN, 1811 OS, *le Comyn* (*de Stoke*) 1441 *Seymer*, *Stoke Wake Common* 1607 DROMap, *the Comon, The Inner-, The Vtter Comon* 1640 *Seymer*, *Inner Cmn* 1839 *TA*, *v.* **common**. STOKE MILL (lost), 1811 OS, *molend' domini* 1417 *Seymer, Stok Myll'* 1548 *Ct*, cf. Walter- 1332 SR, Robert *atte Mull(e)* 1340 NI, *Mullane, Mullelane* 1415, *Mille-, Myllelane* 1452, (*Little*) *Mill Mead, The Mill Orchard* 1640, *Mill(s) Mead* c. 1750 all *Seymer, Stoake Mill Lane* 1642 *Bundy, Mill-lane* [Bridge] 1791 Boswell, *v.* **myln, atte** 'at the', **lane**; there is mention of a mill at Stoke Wake in 1086 DB (VCHDo 3 83) and in 1288 FF. TWITCHINGS COPSE &

CTG, *Lower-, Upper Twichinges Close, Twichinges Copice* 1640 *Seymer, Gt & Lt Twitching, Twitchings Coppice* 1839 *TA*, probably from **twicen(e)** 'fork of a road, cross-roads, narrow lane'. WHITE HILL, 1811 OS, cf. *White hill Close* 1640 *Seymer, v.* **hwīt** 'white' (alluding to chalk, cf. nearby Chalk Pit 6″), **hyll**.

FIELD-NAMES

The undated forms are 1839 *TA* 203. Spellings dated 1248 are Pat, 1258 *For*, 1288 FF, 1327 *SR*, 1332 SR, 1340 NI, 1384 (e16) *Prideaux*, 1385 (e15) *MiltRoll*, 1400 *Ilch*, 1624 Hutch[3], 1664 HTax, 1791 Boswell, and the rest *Seymer*.

(*a*) Applin's Cmn, Hr & Middle Applins (cf. William *Applin* c. 1750); Barns's Md (cf. Percival *Barnes* 1640); Bean Cl; Gt & Lt Benscombe (*Benscoom Close* 1640); (Other) Biles's Cmn (*Byles('s) Common* 1750, c. 1750, cf. Adam *Byles* 1640); Rough Bishops (*Busshoppes-, Bysshopesclos, Busshopes-, Busshuppesyate* 1415, *Busshuppes-, Busshoppeslaneynde* 1418, *Bysshop ys drove* 1441, *claus' vocat' Bysshopys, Bysshop yslane* 1452, *Busshopp(e)s Drewe, -Meade* 1559, *Byshops* 1640, *Bishops feild* c. 1750, cf. Alice *Bisshoppes, -Bysshopes, -Busshop(p)es, -Busshuppes* 1415, *v.* **clos(e), geat, lane, ende, drāf, dræf, mæd**); Blacklands Md; Gt Breach 2 acres and Lt Breach, South Breach (*claus' voc' le Breche* 1415, 1452, 1494, (*The house and home mead at*) *Brach, South Brach Close, Brach* (*Close*) *Mead, the 4 Braches* 1640, *South Breach* c.1750, *v.* **brēc, brǣc** 'land broken up for cultivation'); Broad Md (c. 1750, *Brode-* 1640, *v.* **brād**); Butchers Fd (*Bouchersfeld'* 1495, *Boochers-* 1559, *Buchers Mead* 1640, *Three Butchers feilds* c. 1750, cf. John *Boucher* 1495, *v.* **feld, mæd**); Cave and park coppices, Caves Cmn (*Caves (Cmn)* 1750, c. 1750, cf. Thomas *Caue* 1640, Park Coppice *infra*); Colborns Md (*Ouer Colbornes Close Mead, Colbornes Mead* 1640, *Colbournes-* 1750, *Cobbins Mead* c. 1750, probably a surname); Common Plot (cf. *le Comen-, le Comyn-, le Comunewode* 1415, (*The*) *Comon Close (Mead)* 1640, *v.* **comun, wudu**); Cookneys Md; Corn Grd; Cote (cf. *The (great-, little) Cote Mead* 1640, *v.* **cot** 'cottage'); Cowleaze (*Three-, Two Cowleazes* c. 1750); Crib Cl & Grd (*v.* **cribbe**); Days Ho and Gdn, Days Lr Mead (*Dasie* (sic) *Mead* 1640, *Days Cottage* 1750, *Days Mead(ow)* c. 1750, cf. Richard *Day* 1640); Drove (Lane & Plot) (*The Drove* c.1750, *v.* **drāf**); 8 Acres; Field Cl (*Field close mead* 1640 (*freq*)); 5 Acres (c. 1750, *fiue acres mead* 1640); 4 Acres; 14 Acres (*14 acres mead* 1640); Galpins Md (c.1750, cf. Edmund *Gapin* 1640); Gores; Great Md & Orchd; Higher Cl (c. 1750); Home Md (*The-* 1640 (*freq*)); Home Plot; Horse Cl; Jenkins's Md (*Jenkins Meadow* c. 1750, cf. John *Jenkens* 1640); Kingmans (*Kingmans Close, -Mead* 1640, *Kingman* (sic) c. 1750, a surname); Leg (*Legge Mede* 1494, *Leggemeade* 1559, *The Long Leg Mead* 1640, *v.* **leg** 'long, narrow meadow', **mæd**); Little Cl (c. 1750); Marl Md (*Malles-* 1640, *Malls Mead* c.1750, from the pers.n.

Mall, a pet-form of *Mary*); Middle Coppice; Hr & Lr Middle Grd (*Middle Grounds* c. 1750); New Cl; North Md; Park Coppice, Gt Park, Horse Park ('the park' 1248, *Nether-, Ouerparke* 1415, *Parke Yete* 1452, *parco domini* 1494, *Stoke Parke* 1497, *The Lower-, The Middle Copice in the Park, The Ouer Park Close, Vpper Parke Close or Wester Close, Parke mead* 1640, v. **park, neoðerra, uferra, geat**; for the possibility of an early deer-park here, v. Wilson, DoNHAS 98 9-10); Plot (*Plott* c. 1750); Sand Cl (*Sand Close Mead* 1640, *Sandy Close* c.1750); 7 Acres (*Seaven acres mead* 1640); Sheep Down (cf. *Sheep Ground* c. 1750, *Stokedown(e)* 1384 (e16), 1385 (e15), v. **dūn**, par. name *supra*); Sidmans (*Sydenham* 1417, *Sidnams* 1640, 'large enclosure', v. **sīd** (wk.obl. *-an*), **hamm**); 6 Acres (*Six acres close ouer the Hill* 1640, *Six Acres* c. 1750); 16 Acres; Street Md (c. 1750, *Stretesmede* 1494, *The Street Mead* 1640, first el. **strǣt** 'street' or a surname); Surick's Lane [Bridge] 1791; Tan House Orchd, Home or Tanhouse Md (v. **tanhouse**); 10 Acres (c. 1750); 12 Acres (*Twelue acres ouer the Hill* 1640); 2 Acres (c. 1750); Water Md (*West Waters Mead* 1640); Gt & Lt West Md (*West Mead on ye east side of ye water, -on ye west side of ye water* 1640, (*Rough*) *West Mead* c. 1750); Wheat Cl (*The Wheat Close, Wheat Close Mead* 1640, *White Close* c. 1750, v. **hwǣte**); Willow Bed (cf. *Willoby Mead* 1640, *Withybed* c. 1750); Writh Md, Rough Writh (*le Fryth'* 1415, 1497, *le Frith(e)* 1416, 1418, 1423, *Frith Mead, Frithwood Close* 1640, v. **fyrhð** 'wood'; for the development to *w*, cf. PN D xxxv).

(b) *Blynneput* 1415, 1416 (v. **pytt** 'pit', first el. perhaps **blind** 'blind, hidden'); *Botitesyate* 1415 (v. **geat**, with a surname); *le Bruers* 1497, *Brewerne Mead* 1640, *Bruer* c.1750 (cf. Henry *Brewer'* 1332, Roger *le Brewer* 1340); *Churchill Mead* 1640; *Clanfield* 1640 (v. **clǣne** 'clean'); *Cleyepyttes* 1559 (v. **clǣg, pytt**); *The Copice on the top of the Hill, The Copices* 1640 (v. **copis**); *claus' pastur' vocat' Costell' et unum pratum vocat' Costelhampne* 1494 (v. **hamm**; *Costell'* may be from **cost**[1] 'trial', or 'tansy', and **hyll**); *Coward Close* 1640; *Densom Leaze, Great-, Little Densom Mead* 1640 (cf. Richard *Densham* 1497); *Estfeld'* 1418 (v. **ēast, feld**); *The Farme downe* 1640; *Fifteen Acres* (Glebe) c. 1750; *Fill* (possibly *Till*) *Close* c. 1750; *Fyshey* 1415 (v. **fisc, (ge)hæg**); *Green Hay* c.1750 (v. **(ge)hæg**); *Groue Close* 1640 (v. **grāf(a)**); *Gullimead* 1640 (v. **gully, mǣd**); *Guyes* 1640, *Guys Tenement* 1750 (cf. Richard *Guy* 1640); *Gyleworthy* 1495 (v. **worðig** 'enclosure', first el. possibly a pers.n. or surname of uncertain form); *Heyclyff* 1497 (v. **clif**, first el. doubtful); *Higher Mead* c. 1750; *Holemede* 1452 (v. **hol**[2] 'hollow'); *Home Close* 1640; *Home Ground* c. 1750; *John Howse's Cottage* 1750, *House Acre, -Cottage, Hows Cowleazes* c. 1750 (probably all from the surname *Howe*); *late Humber's* 1750 (a surname); *Hundred Acres* c. 1750 (a small field of one acre); *Hylle Close, Hil-, Hylmede* 1497, *the Hill, The Hether-, The Yonder Hill Close* 1640 (v. **hyll**); *Lansheriesyete, Lansheryet* 1417 (v. **land-sc(e)aru** 'boundary', **geat** 'gate, gap'); *The Little Mead* 1640; *The Little Wood Common* 1640; *Long (Close) Mead* 1640; *The Lower Close* 1640; *The Mead (ouer the Hill)* 1640 (cf. *Stoke me(e)de* 1384 (e16), 1385 (e15), v. **mǣd**); *le Merche* 1452 (v.

mersc 'marsh'); *The Middle Close* 1640; *Milettes-*, *Mylettes lese* 1494, *Mylettes* 1497 (cf. John Mullett c. 1750, *v.* **lǣs**); *The Moore Copice ouer the Hill* 1640 (*v.* **mōr**); *Moores* (cf. *Ric' Moore . . . aula* 1559); *pontem apud Nonemannes-* 1417, *Nomanneslond'* 1418 (*v.* **nān mann, land**); *The Northeast Close* 1640; *messuage called Old Barne* 1624; *le Orchard'* 1417 (*v.* **orceard**); *Pikes Mead* 1640, c. 1750 (a surname); *Rose Pleck Mead* 1640 (*v.* **plek** 'small plot', cf. *uno cotagio cum pratum q'd' Henr' Rose nuper tenuit* 1452); *Rough Ground* c. 1750; *Sannedrysshe* 1495 (perhaps 'sandy enclosure', from **sand** and **edisc**, if the *-r-* is excrescent); *bosco voc' Setylake* 1415 (*v.* **lacu** 'stream', for *Sety-* cf. the f.n. *Setty* in Stour P. par. *supra*); *Shit(t)ler('s) Cottage* 1750, c. 1750; *Lower-*, *Vper South Close* 1640; *The Southeast-*, *The Southwest Close* 1640; *Southerey(e)slane* 1415, 1417, 1418, 1452, 1497, *Sutherey(es)lane* 1415, *Southereylane* 1416, 1417, 1418, *Southerayeslane* 1423, *Suthere lane* 1441 (*v.* **lane**; *Southerey* may be a p.n. from **sūðerra** 'more southerly' and **īeg** 'island' or **(ge)hæg** 'enclosure', or a surname from such a p.n.); *ij cotagijs nuper denot' Stamford'* 1494 ('stony ford', *v.* **stān, ford**); *bosco de Stoccumb* 1258, *Stokecombe* 1384 (e16), 1385 (e15), *Stokyscombe* 1400 (*v.* **cumb**, par. name *supra*); *Stokeford'* 1452 (*v.* **ford**); *John Thomas Close* 1640; *Thorn Close* c. 1750, *Thorne Croft* 1494, 1559 (*v.* **þorn**); *Three Acres* c. 1750; *Turners (Common)* c. 1750 (cf. John *Turner* 1664); *The Vper Close* 1640; *The West Close next the Mead* 1640; *Westwode* 1288 (*v.* **west, wudu**); *Wetemour* 1415, *Whytemore* 1494 (*v.* **wēt** 'wet, damp', **mōr**); *Whites* c. 1750 (a surname); *Wilkokesclos* 1415 (*v.* **clos(e)**, cf. John *Wilcokkes* 1495); *Wodeyate* 1415 (cf. John *Bethewod* 1327 ('by the wood'), *v.* **wudu, geat** 'gate, gap').

Woolland

WOOLLAND (ST 776070)

    Wennland 833 (14) *ShaftR* (S 277)

    (*æt*) *Wonlonde* 843 for 934 (eME) ASCharters, 843 for 934 (17) BCS 739

    Winlande 1086 DB, *-landa* Exon, *Wineland* 1212 P, *Wynlond(')* 1288 *Ass*

    Wunlanda 1170, 1171 P, *-land(e)* 1231 FF

    Wuland' 1212 Fees, *Wullond(')* e16 *Prideaux*, 1535 VE, 1540 *Prideaux*

    Wollond(e) 1268, 1288 *Ass*, 1317 *MiltC*, 1384 (e16) *Prideaux*, 1385 (e15) *MiltRoll*, 1480 *DCM*, *Wolland(e)* 1531 *AD*, 1539 *Prideaux*, 1575 Saxton

    Wllonde 1280 *Winch*

    Woulond(e) 1285 FA, 1311 Pat, e16 *Prideaux*, *Woullond* 1535 VE

    Woodland (sic) 1664 HTax

'Meadow land, i.e. cultivated land consisting largely of meadow', from **winn**[1], **wynn** and **land**, as suggested by Kökeritz 131. The Anglo-Saxon bounds of Woolland are given in S 277 (*v.* C. Hart in DoNHAS **86** 158–9), and the bounds of Woolland are also described in 1385 (e15) *MiltRoll* (repeated in 1384 (e16) *Prideaux*) when it was included in the manor of Milton Abbas.

BROAD & LONG ALDERMORE (ST 777064), *Alder Moor(s)* 1839 *TA*, cf. *Brodnallers* 1539, *Brode Alders, Depalders* 1545, *Brode-, Deppe allers* 1550, *le Allers* 1569, *Shortallere yate* 1572 all *Prideaux, Broadalders* (*Green Lodge*), *Deep Alders* (*Orchd*) 1839 *TA, v.* **alor** 'alder', **mōr** 'marshy ground', **brād** 'broad', **dēop** 'deep', **sc(e)ort** 'short', **geat** 'gate'. Broad and Long Aldermore, together with Chitcombe Aldermoor and Swandhill Aldermore *infra*, lie along the upper courses of feeders of R. Divelish, which forms the par. bdy between Woolland and Ibberton and which is referred to in the Anglo-Saxon bounds of Woolland as *of alor riðe . . . to anne aler riðe* 833 (14) *ShaftR* (S 277), 'alder stream', *v.* **rīð**.

BUL BARROW (tumulus) (ST 776057) ['buːbəʀ], BULBARROW HILL, *Buleberwe* 1270 Roscoe (a point in the bounds of Blackmoor Forest, wrongly transcribed *Huleberwe* in Hutch[3] **4** 79), *Bulbarowe* 1545, *-baro* 1555, *-borowe* 1566, *-borough* 1569 all *Prideaux, Bull Barrow* 1771 *DROMap, Bulbarrow* 1811 OS, *v.* **beorg** 'barrow'; first el. apparently **bula** 'bull' (cf. Bulbury Camp **2** 33 where *Bul-* has a different origin), thought by Hutch[3] **4** 358 to be possibly applied in a transferred sense to imply 'hugeness', or an OE pers.n. *Bula*. Bul Barrow itself is referred to in the Anglo-Saxon bounds of Woolland as *on burg* 833 (14) *ShaftR* (S 277), where the form probably shows confusion of **beorg** with **burh** 'fortified place'.

CHITCOMBE FM (ST 785071), *Chidecome, Chudecumbe* (3 ×) 1317 *MiltC* all (p), *Chedecombe, Chidecombe* (2 ×) 1327 *SR* all (p), *Chydecombe* 1384 (e16) *Prideaux*, 1385 (e15) *MiltRoll*, *Chytcombe* 1540, *Chidcombe* 1557 *Prideaux*, 1811 OS, *Chitcombe* Eliz ChancP, 1795 Boswell (*-or Chidcombe*), 1839

TA (*-Fm*), *-comb* 1774 Hutch[3], probably 'Cydda's valley', from the OE pers.n. *Cydda* (Redin 91) and **cumb**.

CRATE WD (ST 768071), 1839 *TA*, *Croftewoodhegge* 1384 (e16) *Prideaux*, *Croftwodehegg'* 1385 (e15) *MiltRoll*, *Croft(e) Wood(e)* 1540, 1545, *Crafte Woode* 1545 all *Prideaux*, *Crat Wood* 1804 *Salkeld*, *v.* **croft** 'small enclosed field', **wudu**, with **hecg** 'hedge'.

ABLEY COPSE. CHITCOMBE ALDERMOOR, *v.* Broad & Long Aldermore *supra* and foll. CHITCOMBE DOWN, 1839 *TA*, cf. (*montem vocat'* . . .) *Chyd(e)combebache* 1384 (e16) *Prideaux*, *Chydecombysbache* 1385 (e15) *MiltRoll*, *Chitcombe Hill'* 1544, *Chytcom(b)e Hyll'* 1550, 1557, *Chidcombe Hill'* 1570 all *Prideaux*, *v.* Chitcombe Fm *supra*, **hyll**; *-bache* seems to represent another early instance of **batch** 'hillock', cf. *Southbach'* in Milton A. par. *supra*. FISH PONDS. HILL FM, cf. *Hyll' Close* 1548 *Prideaux*, *Hill Cl, Hill Pitts* 1839 *TA*, *v.* **hyll**. IVERS, *coppes callyd* . . . *Yeuers* 1545, *Yuers end* 1563, *Ivere coppice* 1568 all *Prideaux*, *Ives Wood* 1804 *Salkeld*, *Iveys Wood* 1839 *TA*, probably from **yfer** 'edge or brow of a hill', with **ende** 'end', **copis**; Ivers is applied to part of the high ridge of Woolland Hill *infra*. THE LAUNCH, not on a bdy, but possibly to be associated with *Lan(g)schor(e)forlang* 1317 *MiltC, Lanscherefurlong(e)*, *-lange* 1540, 1557, 1563 all *Prideaux*, from **land-sc(e)aru**, **land-scoru**, perhaps here in the sense 'share of land', with **furlang**. LAY WD, 1804 *Salkeld*, *Leywood'* 1545 *Prideaux*, cf. *Leyclose* 1543 *ib*, *v.* **lēah** 'wood, clearing in a wood'. LONG WD, 1839 *TA*. MANOR HO or THE PARSONAGE, cf. *the Ferme of the manor of Woullond'* 1545 *Prideaux*. SKINNERS FM, 1839 *TA*. SPRING HEAD. SWANDHILL ALDERMORE, cf. (*Hr & Lt*) *Sivandells* (*Mdw*) 1839 *TA* (no doubt from a surname), *v.* Broad & Long Aldermore *supra*. WOOLLAND DAIRY FM, *Dairy House* (*Fm*) 1811 OS, 1839 *TA*. WOOLLAND FIRS. WOOLLAND HILL, *Wullond' downe* 1384 (e16) *Prideaux*, *Wollondysdown'* 1385 (e15) *MiltRoll*, *v.* **dūn**, par. name *supra*. WOOLLAND HO.

FIELD-NAMES

The undated forms are 1839 *TA* 263. Spellings dated 833 (14) are *ShaftR* (S 277), 1317, 1321 *MiltC*, 1327 *SR*, 1332 SR, 1385 (e15) *MiltRoll*, 1664 HTax, 1804 *Salkeld*, and the rest *Prideaux*.

(a) Alleys; Ameys; Back Orchd; Barley Hill (*Estur-, Westerberlee* 1317, probably 'clearing used for barley', from **bere** and **lēah**, with **ēasterra**, **westerra**, but *-ber-* should perhaps be associated with *la Beere* 1317, from **bearu** 'grove'); Bean Cl (cf. *Nether-, Ouerbenfyld(e)* 1545, Benford Orchd *infra, v.* **bēan, feld, neoðerra, uferra**); Belbins Fm, Md & Orchd; Benford Orchd (probably *Bynworth* 1317, 'bean enclosure', from **bēan** and **worð**, cf. Bean Cl *supra*; **worð** is sometimes found with words for crops, e.g. Ryeworth Gl 2 98; for the development to *-ford*, cf. Dibberford in Broadwindsor par. *infra*); Bottom Fm (*v.* **botm**); Brick Kiln Fd; Brights Home Md & Orchd; Broad Fd (Legg) (*Brodefyld(es)* 1543, 1545, *Brodfyld yeat, porte de Brodefyld* 1544, *Brodefieldz* 1570, *Broad fields, Broadfield Md, Lt Broadfield* 1804, *v.* **brād, feld, leg, geat**; Broad Lees (probably *Bradelee* 1317, *-leygh'* 1385 (e15), *Bradley(close)* 1540, 1550, *Bradley* 1804, 'broad wood or clearing', from **brād** and **lēah**, with late confusion with **lǣs** 'pasture'); Castle ((*claus' voc'*) *Castel(l')* 1317, 1321, *Castell' dyche* 1546, *v.* **castel(l), dīc**); Chitcombe Cmn (from Chitcombe Fm *supra*); Clayfords (*Clayford Lane* 1542, *Cleyford* 1544, *-vord* 1550, *Claifordes lane* 1567, *v.* **clǣg, ford, lane**); Cocks Heart (1804, perhaps from **cocc-geset** 'place where woodcock are found'); Common (cf. *Woolland als. Prestholt Common* 1804, *v.* Presthill Md *infra*); Common Crofts (*Comes Crafte* e16, *Commaynnscroft* 1540, *Com(m)yns crofte* 1557, 1568, a surname (cf. John *Comyn* 1332 (Symondsbury)) with **croft**); First, Second Common Fd; Coppice Cl & Grd; Cothays; Cow Leaze; Dairy Cmn (1804, cf. Woolland Dairy Fm *supra*); Down (cf. Woolland Hill *supra, Sheep Down or Sheep Slight* 1804, *v.* **slǣget** 'sheep pasture'); Drove; Edwards Fd & Orchd; Eel Pits (*Eyle Pytte* 1569, *v.* **ǣl, pytt**); 8 Acres; Elverds Acre, Hr & Lr Elvirds; (The) 4 Acres (1804); Free yard, Fruits Hay (one or both of these two f.ns. are possibly to be associated with *Fuelles Haye* 1543, *Fywodeshey* 1566, *Fuardes heye* 1567, from a surname (or surnames) of uncertain form with **(ge)hæg**); Galpins (Closes & Grd (cf. *ten' Thome Galpyn'* 1542); (Lt) Garbrooks, Outer Garbrook (*aqua de Garbrok(e), Lytell Garbrok(e), West(e)garbrok(e) hegg(e)* 1384 (e16), 1385 (e15), *claus' voc' Gare Broke* 1539, *Garbro(o)kes* 1544, 1570, *Garbroke* 1566, *v.* **gāra** 'triangular plot, point of land', **brōc** 'brook', with **lȳtel, west**; the stream referred to is that at the W corner of the par. near Crate Wood); Green Cl (1804) & Ledge; Green Lodge; Abbey & Field Groan, Hr & Lr Fields Groan (perhaps from ME **grone, grane** 'a trap, a snare'); Grotten Cl (possibly to be associated with *la grutte* 1385 (e15) (rendered *a gulley* in 1384 (e16)), from **grytte** 'stony land', *v.* 1 237, but cf. **groten** 'gravelly'); Hanging Cl (cf. *Hangendelond* 1317, *v.* **hangende, land**); Hangsam (probably (*a hyll' callyd*) *Hangaryston'* 1384 (e16), 1385 (e15), first el. **hangra** 'wood on a steep hill-side', with **stān** or **tūn** (perhaps replacing earlier **dūn**)); Hasom

(*Haymesham, Haysam* 1317, *Hays(h)am* 1384 (e16), 1385 (e15), 1545, probably **hamm** 'enclosure' with a surname *Haym* or *Hay*; this p.n. gave rise to the surname found in foll.); Hasoms (*Haisams* 1568, *Haysoms* 1804, cf. Nicholas *Haysam* 1568, Robert *Haysome* 1664); Home Cl (*-closes* 1563) & Md; James Orchd (cf. Thomas *Janes*, William *Jane* 1664); Hr Johnsons and part of Salisbury Plain, Lr Johnsons Cmn (*Johnstons Common* 1804; Salisbury Plain must be a transferred name, *v.* PN W 17); Lt Kings Alders (*Kynges Allers* 1569, *v.* **alor**, cf. Broad & Long Aldermore *supra*; *Kyng* is probably a surname); Knap (*v.* **cnæpp** 'hill-top'); Legg Cl, Leggs (*v.* **leg** 'long narrow meadow'); Little Hams (*v.* **hamm**); Little Hill; Little Md(w); Long Croft (*Langcroft* 1317, *Langcroftes* 1567, *v.* **lang¹**, **croft**); Long Md (*Langemede* 1550, *Langmeyde* 1569, *v.* **lang¹**, **mǣd**); Mead by Marsh part of Ham (cf. *La Merch, Nuther-, Ouermerssch* 1317, *v.* **mersc**, **neoðerra**, **uferra**, **hamm**); Meagers Mdw; Meeting House Fd; Middle Fd; Mill Hams, Mill Ham Legg (*Mylhams* 1384 (e16), *-hamys* 1385 (e15), cf. (*le*) *Mill(e) Lane* 1541, 1543, *v.* **myln**, **hamm**, **leg**, **lane**; the mill and the 'ham' are mentioned in 1317 (*Phillipus Molendinar'* . . . *tenet* . . . *i molendinu' aquaticu' cum ij croftis et j haym*), cf. also *John Haysham held a myll'* e16; the stream on which the mill probably stood was R. Divelish, cf. *melenbroc* 833 (14), 'mill brook', in the Anglo-Saxon bounds of Woolland, *v.* **brōc**, which seems to refer to the small feeder of R. Divelish at the W corner of the par. near Crate Wood); Mushey Md (perhaps to be connected with *Moyshelles* 1543, *Moyscheus Marsche* 1556, *Ouermoysches*, from a surname with **mersc**, **uferra**); New Close(s); 9 Acres; North Cl; Oadhill(s), Oathill (*v.* **āte**); Oakleys; Park Md (*-Mdw* 1804); Parsons Wd; Pear Tree Orchd; Little Pest; (Second) Philliford; Pleasure Grd; Prestill Mead(s) (*Prest holte* 1321, *Prest(e)holte* 1384 (e16), *Prestholt(e)* 1385 (e15), 1539, 1540 (*co'ia de-*), 1542 (*-yeat*), 1545 (*Greate-, Lytell-*), 1566, *Prestholtes Mede* 1546, *Prestholde* 1555, 1563, *Prestoldes Mead* 1568, 'priests' wood', *v.* **prēost**, **holt**, with **geat**, **mǣd**); Ridge Cl (cf. *super unu' Rygge* 1384 (e16), *le Rugg', Ruge* 1544, *v.* **hrycg** 'ridge'); Rookward (*Rook Wood* 1804, *v.* **hrōc**); Rushy Vale; Sams Md; 7 Acres; 6 Acres; Stiert, Stierts Alders & Coppice, Stirts Cl (*Stert(e)* 1550, 1570, *v.* **steort** 'tail of land'); Stoke Drove; Strouds Grd; Sydenham(')s Down & Ho; Great T Hill (perhaps from its shape); 10 Acres; Tenants Down; Thorney Md (*Thorny(e) Mede* 1548, 1570, *-Meyd* 1567, *-Mead* 1568, *v.* **þornig**, **mǣd**); 3 Acres; Toots Ho; Turvill Ld (*Turnefurlonge* 1545, *Turvey land* 1804, *v.* **trun** 'round', **furlang**); Two Field Grd; Two Orchds; Upwards Fd; Up Wood; Home & Lt Warren (*2 closes called Warren* 1804, *v.* **wareine**); West Md(w) (*Westmeade* 1545, *v.* **mǣd**); Whitecrofts (*Whyte crafte* 1384 (e16), *-croft'* 1385 (e15), *White Crafte* e16, *-croft* 1563, *Whit-* 1542, *Whytcroft* 1544, *Northcroftes als. White croftes* 1557, *v.* **hwīt**, **croft**); Winsells; Wintermans Hay (*Winterbourn Hay* 1804, perhaps to be associated with *claus' voc' Wynterbury(e)s* 1557, 1570, *v.* **(ge)hæg**); Wormills Orchd.

(b) *puteum antiquum vocat' Boylondes Pyt* 1384 (e16), *Boylondysputte* 1385 (e15) (a surname (cf. John *Boilond* 1327 (Burton Bradstock)) and

pytt); *Brodclose yeat* 1542 (*v.* **brād, clos(e), geat**); *Brodemede* 1384 (e16), 1385 (e15), 1543, -*mead* 1570, *v.* **brād, mǣd**); *Brokfurlang* 1317, *Brokefurlond'* 1554, *v.* **brōc, furlang**); *on burg* 833 (14) (*v.* **burh**, possibly to be identified with Rawlsbury Camp in Hilton par. *supra*); *Chepman' Way* 1384 (e16), *Chypman(')wey* 1385 (e15) (probably 'road used by merchants', from **cēap-mann, cīep-mann** and **weg**, but cf. Robert *Chipman* 1556 (a surname derived from the same word); this road was on the bdy between Woolland and Milton A., cf. *Chypmannyslond'* in Milton A. par. *supra*); *Chyrdych(e)* 1384 (e16), 1385 (e15) (*v.* **dīc**, first el. perhaps **cierr** 'bend'); *le Court barn'* 1569 (*v.* **court**); *La Cumbe* 1317 (*v.* **cumb**); *to cylberge* 833 (14) (perhaps 'barrow marked by a pole', if the first el. is **ci(e)gel**, *v.* **beorg**); *on delesburg middenwearde* 833 (14) (probably to be associated with Delcombe Head in Milton A. par. *supra*); *on anne dich* 833 (14) (*v.* **dīc**); *Dud(e)hull(e)* 1384 (e16), 1385 (e15) (*v.* **hyll**, first el. perhaps an OE pers.n. *Dydda* found in Dedworth Brk 20, etc); *le Dunghyll'* 1557 (*v.* **dunghill**); *one pane ealdene hage, panen anlang ðies hagen* 833 (14) ('old hedge or enclosure', *v.* **eald, haga¹**); *Est Mede* 1550 (*v.* **ēast, mǣd**); (*monte de*) *Ewdon'* 1384 (e16), 1385 (e15) (*v.* **eowu** 'ewe', **dūn** 'down, hill'); *La Frythe, Wodefryth* 1317, (*the dyke of*) *Fryth'* 1384 (e16), 1385 (e15) (*v.* **fyrhð** 'wood', **wudu, dīc**); *Fydershaye* 1539, *Fethers Cote* 1540, 1566 (a surname with **(ge)hæg** and **cot**); *Fyldyate* 1572 (*v.* **feld, geat**); *Gollys Howse* 1543 (a surname); (*fontem vocat'*) *Gorewell(')* 1384 (e16), 1385 (e15), *Gorrewell'* 1564 (*v.* **gāra** 'point of land', **well(a)** 'spring'; not close to Garbrook(s) *supra*); *Gossehylles yeat* 1543, 1545, *Gossehyll'* 1544, *Gosehylles yate* 1556 (*v.* **gōs** 'goose', **hyll, geat**); *Grenelynch* 1317 (*v.* **grēne¹, hlinc**); *Gylysway* 1384 (e16), *Gyllyswey* 1385 (e15) (a surname with **weg**); *on hacggen hamme* 833 (14), *Hakeman'* (sic) 1384 (e16), *Hakenam* 1385 (e15) ('enclosure where haws grow', *v.* **hagga, hamm**, or the OE pers.n. *Hæcga*); *ten' voc' Hanby, Hanbyshold* 1542 (a surname with **hold** 'tenure'); (*the heygh way callyd*) *Harpydway* 1384 (e16), -*wey* 1385 (e15) (*v.* **here-pæð** 'highway', **weg**, probably the continuation of the road that gives name to Hartfoot Lane in Hilton par. *supra*); *Haynes Howse end* 1543; *on anne hege* 833 (14) (*v.* **hege** 'hedge'); *Holes* 1317 (*v.* **hol¹** 'hole, hollow', or a surname); *Holforlang* 1317 (*v.* **hol²** 'hollow', **furlang**); *Ho(o)rehegg(e)* 1384 (e16), 1385 (e15) (*v.* **hecg** 'hedge', first el. **hār** 'grey' (possibly with the sense 'boundary') or **horu** 'dirt'); *Kemeryscros(s)e* 1384 (e16), -*croys* 1385 (e15) (*v.* **cros, crois** 'cross', cf. *clausi Johannis Kemere* 1384 (e16)); *Landsherestone* 1384 (e16), *Landschoreston'* 1385 (e15) ('boundary stone', *v.* **land-sc(e)aru, land-scoru, stān**); *banke called Landshereborogh'* (probably for -*vorogh'*) 1384 (e16), *lyram vocat' Landschorevorgh'* 1385 (e15) (probably 'boundary furrow', *v.* **furh**, cf. prec.); *Langfurlang* 1317 (*v.* **lang¹, furlang**); *Lockettes yeat* 1542 (a surname with **geat**); *Atte Lupghete* (f.n.) 1317 ('(land) at the leap-gate', *v.* **atte, hlīep-geat**); *Marlyng' Pyttes* 1384 (e16), -*pyttys* 1385 (e15) (*v.* **marling, pytt**); *Mowles-, Mowlysmede* 1384 (e16), 1385 (e15) (*v.* **mǣd**, first el. **mūl** 'a mule' or a surname); *Newcroftes* 1557 (*v.* **nīwe, croft**); *on anne oc* 833 (14) (*v.* **āc** 'oak-tree'); *medow callyd Pentrydge* 1545 (perhaps analogous with Pentridge par. 2 235); *Perkyn(y)sdych(e)* 1384 (e16), 1385 (e15) (a surname with **dīc**); *þurh reowe* 833 (14) (probably **rǣw, rāw** 'row'); *Rough-* 1384 (e16), *Rowgh'stubbe* 1385 (e15) (v. **rūh, stubb**); *Sandhill'* 1570 (v. **sand, hyll**); *Sawe pyttes* 1563 (v. **saw-pit**); *cotag' vocat' Sewers* 1539 (a surname); *Shiplond* 1317 (v. **scī(e)p** 'sheep', **land**); *Shortecroft* 1317 (v. **sc(e)ort, croft**); *Shortlond* 1317 (v. **land**); *Smocaker* 1317 (v. **smoke, æcer**); *Innurestavorde, Utterstaneforde* 1317 ('stony ford', v. **stān, ford**, with **innerra, ūterra**); *on anne stapel* 833 (14) (v. **stapol** 'post'); *Stonybreche* 1317 (v. **stānig, brēc**); *(viam regiam voc')* le *Strete* 1542, 1549 (v. **strǣt**); *Tanners Crofte* 1543 (cf. Nicholas *Tannere* 1317, v. **croft**); *oð anne þorn, on anne þorn* 833 (14) (v. **þorn** 'thorn-tree'); *uppe on anne þoure* 833 (14) (apparently with reference to the ridge at the E corner of the par., but the form looks corrupt, possibly for **torr** 'rocky peak' with a spelling influenced by ME *tour* 'tower' (cf. a late 13th cent. spelling *Thour* for this noted by Löfvenberg 214, and cf. Towerhill Gl 3 21); however C. Hart (DoNHAS 86 158) suggests *þoure* should read *þonre*, for *þorne* 'thorn-tree'); *Thregores* 1317 (v. **þrēo, gāra**); *Tollerfyldes yeat* 1542 (a surname with **geat**); *Tonforlang* 1317 (v. **tūn, furlang**); *(curs' aque apud)* le *Trowe* 1542, 1551 (v. **trog** 'trough'); *La Twyste, Furthemuste-, Nethemuste-, Ovemisttwyste* 1317 (v. **twist** 'something twisted, a sharp turn or fork', with **furthermost, nethermost, overmost**); *Tynelake-hevede, Bytwynelake* 1317 ('(land) between the streams', from **betwēonan, lacu**, with **hēafod** 'head, end'); *Vote Way* 1384 (e16), *bowtwey* (sic) 1385 (e15) (v. **weg**, first el. **fōt** 'foot', or, if the second form is more reliable, **bōt** 'benefit'); *Vynynges (Sherde)* 1544, 1550, *Vynyns* 1555, *Vynescherde* 1563, *Vyninges hedges* 1568 (v. **sceard** 'gap', first el. **fīning** 'place where wood is heaped', or a surname); *on anne Walle dich* 833 (14) (v. **weall, dīc**); *the West hegge* 1384 (e16) (v. **hecg**); *Whiteforlang* 1317 (v. **hwīt, furlang**); *Whitelond* 1317 (v. **land**); *Wo(o)d(e)bryge* 1384 (e16), *Wodebrygg'* 1385 (e15), *Woodbridge lane* 1568, *copic' voc' le Wood'* 1550, *Woodmeade* 1545 (cf. Richard *Bythewode* 1317, v. **wudu, brycg, mǣd**); *Wydecroft* 1317 (v. **wīd**); *on wyrtruman* 833 (14) (v. **wyrt-truma** 'root, root-stock'); *Wyteweyaker* 1317, *Whiteway Shard'* 1570 (v. **hwīt, weg, sceard** 'gap'); *le Yeat* 1544 (v. **geat** 'gate').

XXIII. BUCKLAND NEWTON HUNDRED

In c. 1086 GeldR the hundred had the same extent as it now has (Anderson 113, VCHDo 3 146).

Bochelande hund' 1086 DB, *Bochene hundret* c. 1086 GeldR, *Bocheland' hdr'* 1160, *Bokelandhdr'* 1168 P, *Bokeland'* 1212 Fees, *-laund(e)* 1280 (*Neweton' et-*), 1288 *Ass* (*Neuton'-*), *-lond* 1428 FA, *Bok-, Boclaund(e)* 1244, 1280 (*Nyweton' et-*), 1288 *Ass* (*Newetone et-, -et Newe-, -Niweton'*), *-land(e)* 1265 Misc (*Niweton and-*), 1268, 1288 *Ass* (*Neweton'* *et-*), 1316 FA, *-londe* 1303 FA, 1327 *SR* (*Nyeutone et-*), *Bocklaund'* 1288 *Ass* (*Niweton et-*), *Bouclond(e)* 1332 SR (*Nywton'-*), 1340 NI, 1346, 1431 FA (*Neweton et-*), *Bucklond(')* 1539 LP, 1547 *Ct*. Named from Buckland Newton par. *infra*. It belonged to Glastonbury Abbey, like Sturminster Newton hundred *q.v. supra* with which it is often combined in early records (e.g. 1265 Misc, 1280 *Ass*, 1332 SR). This frequent combination of the two hundreds eventually resulted in the addition of *Newton* to the name Buckland, first in the hundred name, later in the par. name. The bounds of the hundred of Buckland Newton are given in c. 1325 *GlastE* (f. 520).

Buckland Newton

In 1933 Minterne Parva in this par. was transferred to Minterne Magna par., and at the same date the detached tithing of Plush was transferred to Piddletrenthide par.

BUCKLAND NEWTON (ST 687053)

> *Boklond toun* 854 (14) BCS 472, *Boclonde, -lande* 941 (14) *Glast* (S 474), ?*Bocland* 946–55 (1726) Finberg (S 1737), *Bok(e)londe* (rubric), *Bokelande* 966 (14) *Glast* (S 742(2))
> *Bochelande* 1086 DB
> *Bokeland(')* 1196 ChancR, 1212 Fees, 1387 Pat, *-lond(e)* m14 *Glast*, 1428 FA, 1429 *Wells*, 1450 Pat, *Bocland(e)* 1243 Fees, 1258 *For et freq* to 1316 FA, *-laund(e)* 1268 *Ass et freq* to 1338–40 Glast, *-lond(e)* 1268 *Ass et freq* to 1428 FA, *-lounde* l14 *GlastE*, *Boklond(e)* 1264 (e15) *MiltRoll*, 1338–40 Glast, *Bocklond'* 1548 *Ct*
> *Boukelond(')* 1264 (e15) *MiltRoll*, 1436 *Wells*, *Bouclond(e)* 1327 (m14) *Glast*, 1346 FA, *-laund'* 1332 SR
> *Buklonde* 1330 Ch, *Buclaunde* 1338–40 Glast, *Bukelond'* 1481 *DCMCt*, *Bucklond(')* 1547 *Ct*, 1553 *Weld*[1], *-land(e)* 1575 Saxton, 1593 *Weld*[1], 1625 *AddCh*
> *Boklonde Abbatis* 1336 Banco (Drew), *Bouclond Abbots* 1405 Pat, *Abbots Bokeland* 1423 Anderson, *Buklonde Abbatis* 1525 *Wells*
> *Newton Buckelond* 1533, *-Bucklande* 1575 PlR, *Buckland als. Newton Buckland* 1576, *Buckland Abbas otherwise Newton* 1703 Hutch[3]

'Land granted by charter', v. **bōc-land**, cf. Buckland Ripers **1** 239. In the earliest form *toun* is **tūn** 'estate'. The affix *Abbots* refers to the possession of this manor by Glastonbury Abbey, v. **abbat**, Lat **abbas** (gen.sg. *abbatis*). For the late addition *Newton* (from Sturminster Newton par. *supra*), v. discussion under hundred name *supra*. The Anglo-Saxon bounds of Buckland Newton are given in 941 (14) *Glast* (S 474).

ARMSWELL FM (ST 729038)
> *Ermingewell* 1225 FF
> *Hermingeswll'* 13 GlastR, *Hermyngeswell'* 1342 GlastF
> *Ermingeswell* 1258 *For, Ermyngyswell(e)* 1303 FA, 1428 *Weld*[1], *Ermyngeswell(')* 1309 FF, c. 1325 *GlastE*, 1417, 1421 *Weld*[1], 1431 FA, *-woll* 1346 ib, *Ermyngiswill* 1428 ib
> *Emmyngeswelle* e14 *GlastE*
> *Ermeswell* 1362 IpmR
> *Ermeneswell* 1366 *Ext*, IpmR, *-will* 1412 FA
> *Armyngswell* 1546 Hutch[3]
> *Armeswell* 1675 *Feth, Armswell* 1795 Boswell

v. **well(a)** 'spring, stream', referring to the small stream which rises near here (spring also marked 6″). The meaning of the first part of the name is uncertain without earlier forms. Fägersten's suggestion (205) that it contains the rare OE fem. pers.n. *Eormengȳþ* remains a possibility even though only the 1225 form is without medial *s*. If the first part of the name is indeed a pers.n., another possibility is that it is an **-ing**[3] derivative of an OE *Eorma* (a short form of names in OE *Eormen-*, postulated by Ekwall DEPN s.n. Irmingland Nf). On the other hand it is perhaps more likely that *Erming(e)* is an **-ing**[2] formation on such a pers.n., meaning 'Eorma's place' or the like, the whole name then meaning 'stream at *Erming(e)*' or even 'stream called *Erming(e)*'. It should also be noted that Zachrisson DTR 133 thinks the first part of the name may be identical with the river-name Erme in Devon, but this is itself of uncertain origin, v. discussion s.nn. Erme and Ermington in PN D 5, 272, Ekwall RN 150, DEPN.

BEAULIEU WOOD (ST 705063)
bosco de Bulog', -Bilog (sic, probably for -*leg*) 1258 *For
Beleye* 1288 *Ass, Beleygh (bosc' apud-), Beleyhg'* 1307 (15)
ForReg, Belee 1317 *MiltC* (p), *Belegh(')* 1332 SR (p),
1340 NI (p)
Belheie 1301 (m14) *Glast, Belheye, boscum . . . apud
Beleheyh(e)g'* 1338–40 Glast
Boelegh' (boscus in-) e14 *GlastE, Beolye wood* 1581 *Weld*[1]
Bewly Wood 16 *Shepherd*[2], *Bewli* e17 *Weld*[1], (*common
called) Bewl(e)ywood* 1648, 1676 *Feth, Bewley Wood
(Mill)* [Bridge] 1791 Boswell, *Bewley Wood Cowleaze*
1838 *TA, Bewly Wood or Beaulieu Wood* 1869 Hutch[3]

'Bee wood or clearing', i.e. where they often swarm, *v.*
bēo, lēah, cf. Beoley Wo 186, Beeleigh Ess 219. Some of
the 14th cent. forms suggest that the name has been
interpreted as containing **(ge)hæg** 'enclosure', in one form
with the further addition of **hecg** 'hedge'.

BOOKHAM (FM) (ST 707042), *Bubbecumb(')* 1244 *Ass* (p),
Bobbecombe e14 *GlastE, Bubbecume, -come* 1317 *MiltC* (p),
(*in culturis de . . .*) *Bovebob(e)comb(e)* 1327 (m14) *Glast,*
1338–40 Glast, (*feild called) Bowcombe* 1616 *Lane, Bocomb*
1795 Boswell, (*-Fm*) 1811 OS, *Buckham or Bowcomb* 1869
Hutch[3]; the one hide *æt Bubbancumbe* 1002–1012 ASWrits (S
1383) probably also belongs here rather than near Melbury
Bubb as suggested in ASWrits 484, Finberg 616, thus
'Bubba's valley', from the OE pers.n. *Bubba* and **cumb**;
Bove- is from **bufan**, used elliptically for 'land above'.

BROCKHAMPTON FM & GREEN (ST 715061), *Brochamtune,
-ton', Brechamtune* (sic) 13 GlastR, *Brochamton(')* 1224 FF,
1258 *For* (v.l. *Brocham*), e14 *GlastE*, 1342 GlastF, *Brok-
hampton(')* 1288 *Ass et freq* with variant spelling *Broc-* to
1547 *Ct, Brokehampton'* 1478 *Weld*[2], *Brockhampton(')* 1553
Weld[1] *et passim, Brockhampton Green* 1811 OS. 'Home farm
by the brook', *v.* **brōc, hām-tūn**, or possibly, if this name is
identical in origin with Brockington Fm 2 280, 'farm of the
dwellers by the brook', *v.* **hǣme** (gen.pl. *hǣma*), **tūn**, with
grēne[2] 'grassy spot, village green'. The brook in question is
a tributary of R. Lydden.

CHASTON FM (ST 718056) & LANE, *Chawson or Chalveston*
1795 Boswell, *Chawson* 1811 OS, a post-Conquest name in
tūn 'estate', the first el. probably being the surname *Chavel,*
Cha(u)uel; Richard and William *Chavel* held land here in c.
1343 GlastF (p.47), cf. also Robert *Chavel de Brocham* (sic),
Robert *de Chauuel de Brochamton* 1258 *For* (*v.* prec.),
Richard *Chaual* 1317 *MiltC*, Richard-, William *C(h)auel*
1327 *SR*, 1332 SR.

CLINGER FM (ST 668053), *Clehangr'* 1206 RC, *Cleha(n)ger*
13 GlastR (p), *Cleyhang(e)re* 1288 *Ass*, e14 *GlastE*, 1311 Pat,
Clayhangre 1305 *Winch, Cleyangre* 1317 *MiltC*, 1429 *Wells*,
1433 (e15) *MiltRoll, Coleanger* (sic) 1569 *Ct, Cleanger*
e17 *Weld*[1], *Bishopps-, Moudies Clinger* 1685 *DCMDeed,*
Clianger 1795 Boswell, 1869 Hutch[3], cf. *Cley(h)(e)ngerwell*
1544 *DCMDeed, Clengerwell* (*Wood*) 1545 Hutch[3], *Clinger-*
well 1869 ib. 'Clayey wooded slope', *v.* **clǣg, hangra**, cf.
Clingre Gl 2 216. *Clingerwell* no doubt refers to the small
stream here rising in Spring Head Coppice *infra, v.* **well(a)**
'spring, stream'. For the surnames *Bishopp* and *Moudi, v.* the
f.n. Bishop's Mdw and Modus Coppice (6″) *infra.*

COSMORE (CMN) (ST 675058), *Corsmor* e14 *GlastE, Cores-*
mor(') 1307 (15), 1308 (15) *ForReg, Corismor* 1334 *For,*
Cor(r)esmor(') 1338–40 Glast, *Kowysmore* (sic) 1433 (e15)
MiltRoll, Cosmore e16 Hutch[3] (*common called-*), e17 *Weld*[1],
1838 *TA* (*-Common*), *Casmore Common* 1811 OS, a hybrid
name from Welsh **cors** 'marsh, bog' and OE **mōr** 'marshy
ground'; Cosmore lies between two streams.

DUNTISH (ST 694064)
   on dounen tit 941 (14) *Glast* (S 474)
   Dunetes 13 Glast, *Dunethis* Hy 3 (14) Cerne, *Dunthete* 1248
      FF (Drew), *Dunhethis* 1249 FF, *Dunethys* 1258 *For,*
      Dunetisse 1264 Ipm, *Dunetys* 1270 *For,* 1280 Ch,
      Dunnetysh' 1288 *Ass*
   Dunedish(') 13 (m14) *Glast*, 1264 Cl, 1338–40 Glast,
      Dunedisse 1264 Ipm
   Doundish' 13 (m14) *Glast, Doundyssh* 1428 FA
   Donetisse 1258 *For, Donetys* 1268 *Ass, Donetys(s)h* 1288 *ib,*

1299 Ipm, -etis(s)h(e) 1289 Cl, 1314 FF, -etysse,
-etys(s)ch 1299 Ipm
Duntisse 1264 Ipm, *Duntys* 1270 *For*
Dundisse 1264 Cl, -dyssh' 1264 (e15) *MiltRoll*, -dys 1303,
-dissh 1346 FA
Dondyssh(e) 1264 (e15) *MiltRoll*
Donedis(s) 1268 *Ass*
Dontetis 1284 Pat
Duntish(') 1299 Ipm, 1314 Pat *et passim*, -tissh',
-tys(s)h(e) e14 *GlastE*, 1321 FF *et freq* to 1575 Saxton
Dountyssh 1299 Cl, -tysch 1366 Hastings, -tissh(') 1383
Ilch, 1428 FA, -tisch' 1404 *Ilch*
Duntich(e) 1315 Pat, 1316 FA, 1547 Ct
Dontyssh(e) 1332 SR, 1342 GlastF *et freq* to 1544 *PlR*,
-tissh 1334 *For*, 1342 GlastF, 1412 FA, 1462 Pat
Duntyge 1553 *PlR*
Dunch 1664 HTax

Probably 'pasture or plot on the hill', from **dūn** and an
unrecorded OE **etisc** (corresponding to Goth *atisk* 'corn-
field', OHG *ezzisch* 'piece of land'), as first proposed by
Ekwall Studies[1] 73. The spellings with *d* would then be due
to influence from **edisc** 'enclosed park' (a well recorded
word in fact favoured by Fägersten 204 as second el. in this
name). There was in any case an important park here,
referred to as 'the park of *Dunthete*' 1248 FF (Drew), 'the
park of *Alured* (de Lincoln) at *Dunhethis*' 1249 FF, *parci de
Dondyssh*' 1264 (e15) *MiltRoll*, park of *Dunetys* 1280 Ch,
Duntish(e) Parke 1583 SPDom, 1616 *Lane*, etc, *v.* **park**,
Cantor & Wilson **2** 147–9, cf. f.ns. *infra.*

HENLEY (FM) (ST 696042)
   Henele(e) 13 GlastR (p), 1244 *Ass* (p), *Henelegh(e)* 13
      (m14) *Glast*, 1338–40 *Glast*, 1342 GlastF (p)
   Hennelegh(e) 13 (m14) *Glast*, l14 *GlastE*
   Henlegh(') 13 (m14) *Glast* (p), e14 *GlastE*, 1311 Pat,
      1338–40 Glast (p), 1429 *Wells*, -leigh(e) 13 (m14) *Glast*
      (p), 1276 Banco, -le(e) 1244 *Ass* (p), 1272 Drew, e14
      GlastE (p), 1366 *Ext*, 3 acr' *Bovehenleg(h)* e14 *GlastE*,
      Henley e17 *Weld*[1] *et passim*

'Wood or clearing frequented by hens (of wild birds)', *v.*
henn (gen.pl. *henna*), **lēah**, cf. Encombe 1 12, Henley Sa
(DEPN). *Bove-* is from **bufan** '(land) above'.

KNOLL (ST 703047), 1568 *Ct*, 1811 OS, 1869 Hutch[3], *Cnolle*
13 GlastR, 1258 *For*, 1291 Tax, e14 *GlastE* (*hameletum de-*),
1332 SR, *Knolle* 1268, 1288 *Ass*, 1301 (m14) *Glast et freq* to
1616 *Lane, Knowle* 1795 Boswell, 1838 *TA*, cf. *Cnoldoune,
Cnolleyete, terre bisouthe Cnolle, tenacres bisuthenolle, terre
apud Forcnolle* all e14 *GlastE, v.* **cnoll** 'hill top, hillock', with
dūn, geat 'gate', **bī, sūðan, fore** 'in front of'. The rounded
hill here reaches 651'.

LANDSCOMBE LANE (ST 696047), named from (*capud de*)
Lem(m)aniscomb(e) 13 (m14) *Glast*, 1338–40 Glast,
Lem(m)anescomb(e) e14 *GlastE*, 1327 (m14) *Glast*, 1338–40
Glast, *rivuli fontis vocati Lemmanescombesheved* 1327 (m14)
Glast, 1338–40 Glast, (*capud de*) *Lem(m)anscomb(e)* 1338–40
ib, 1593 *Weld*[1], *Lambescomb'* 1429 *Wells, Lamynyscombe* 1548
Ct, Lanscombe (*Down Plant.*) 1838 *TA*, 'lover's or sweet-
heart's valley', from ME **leman** and **cumb**, no doubt a
popular courting place. The -*heved* in two of the 14th cent.
forms is **hēafod** 'head' in the sense 'river-spring', cf. Lat
capud, rivuli fontis; in the form *Bouelemmanescumbefonde* 1317
MiltC, -fonde may represent ME *font* (< Lat *fons, fontis*)
'fountain, well-spring', with **bufan** '(land) above'.

MINTERNE PARVA (FM) (ST 664035), 1315 Pat, 1669 *Batten*,
1795 Boswell, *parva minterne* 1296 (m12) *Glast, Myntern(n)e*
e14 *GlastE*, 1327 *SR*, 1332 SR, *Parva Myntern* 1431 FF,
Mynterne parva 1596 *Prideaux, Little Minterne or Minterne
Parva* 1869 Hutch[3], Lat **parva** 'small' to distinguish this
tithing of Buckland Newton hundred from the adjacent par.
of Minterne Magna to which it now (since 1933) belongs.

(Lt) MONKWOOD HILL FM (ST 734049), *Munkewod, -wdde*
13 GlastR both (p), -*wode* 1244 *Ass*, -*wude* e14 *GlastE*,
Monecwode, Monekewode (p) e14 ib, *Monekwode* 1327 *SR* (p),
Monkwode 1332 SR (p), (common called) *Monkewood Hill*
e16 Hutch[3], *Monegwood* e17 *Weld*[1], *Munchod Hill* 1649
Hutch[3], *Monkswood* (*Hill*) 1795 Boswell, *Monkwood Hill*

1811 OS, 1869 Hutch³, 'wood belonging to the monks', v.
munuc, wudu. The allusion may be either to Glastonbury
Abbey, to which most of Buckland Newton belonged, or to
Holme Priory, which held some land in Plush (cf. *Prior de
Holne tenet Plussche unam carucatem terr'* e14 *GlastE* f. 525,
v. Hutch³ 3 710, VCHDo 2 80).

PLUSH (ST 715022) [plɔʃ]
  Plyssch' (2×), *Plissh'*, *Plussh* (rubric) 891 (14) *Glast* (S
    347(2)), ad *Plussh'*, *Plyssh'* (rubric) 941 (14) *ib* (S 474)
  Plis m12 *Douce* (p), 13 GlastR (p), 1268 *Ass, Plys* c. 1165
    MontC, 1268 *Ass*, 1288 *ib* (p), *P'lis* 1201 FF (*v.*
    Fägersten 206 fn. 1), *Plis(s)ch'* 13 (m14) *Glast*, 1327 *SR,
    Plyhs* 1268 *Ass, Plysse, Plisse* 1288 *Ass, Plisses* 1291 Tax,
    Plyssh' 1332 SR, *Plys'* 1338–40 Glast
  Plus(s)h(e) e14, c. 1325 *GlastE*, 1338–40 Glast, 1340 NI,
    1342 GlastF, 1412 FA *et passim, Plussche* e14 *GlastE*
  Pluys(c)h' e14 *GlastE, Pluyssh* 1441 *Wells*, 1450 Pat,
    Plyusshe 1568 *Ct*

From an OE **plysc, plisc** 'pool', probably cognate with
plæsc which has a similar meaning and surviving as dial.
plish, as first suggested by Fägersten 206. The boundary of
the Anglo Saxon estate of *Plyssch'*, in 891 (14) *Glast* (S
347(2)), goes *west over Plissh'* where it crosses the deep valley
in which Plush is situated, and there is still a pool here c. ¾
mile S of the hamlet at ST 712009, cf. also *aque de Plys* 1268
Ass, Plusshebroke c. 1325 *GlastE* (*v.* **brōc**) and the TA f.n.
Wool Md *infra*.

POP MALLERS COPPICE (ST 689059), *Poplyngalres* e14
GlastE, Poplyngallers 1548 *Ct*, (common called) *Popling* e16
Hutch³, *Popmalters Coppice* (sic) 1838 *TA*, second el. **alor**
'alder'. The origin of *Poplyng* is uncertain, but it may be an
-ing¹ or **-ing²** derivative of **popel** 'a pebble', cf. however
the ME vb. *pople* 'to flow in a tumbling manner, etc.' (*v.*
NED s.v. *popple*); there is a small stream just N of the
coppice.

REVELS FM & HILL, REVELS INN FM (ST 675061), *Terra
Ryvel* 1264 Hutch³ (3 708), (*terra*) *Ryuell'* 1264 (e15)

MiltRoll, Dundisse Rivel 1264 FineR, *feod' Pet' Rivel* 1307
(15) *ForReg, Ryueslond* 1366 *Ext,* (*prat' voc'*) *Ryvell(*') 1510
MP, 1533 *PlR, Revels* 1795 Boswell, *Revels Fm, Hill & Inn*
1811 OS, *Revel's* (*Hill*) 1869 Hutch[3], named from the family
of Peter *Revel* 1299 Hutch[3] (a freehold tenant in Duntish),
Richard *Ryvel* 1325 Hutch[3], Robert *Ryuel* 1327 *SR*, etc, cf.
also *croft' Roberti Rivel in Henelegh'* 13 (m14) *Glast, v.*
Duntish, Henley *supra,* **land**.

SHARNHILL GREEN (ST 713055), *crofta . . . Abbatis de
Middiltone . . . appellatur Charnhulle* 1301 (m14) *Glast, crofta
de Charnhulle, Hidercharnhulle, Shernhulle* (p) 1317 *MiltC,
Charnhull*(*e*) 1327 (m14) *Glast,* 1338–40 Glast, *Sharnhull*
1795 Boswell, 1869 Hutch[3], *Charnell Green* 1811 OS,
Sharnals, Shernels, Sharnal Green 1838 *TA*, apparently a
hybrid name from PrWelsh **carn** 'cairn, rock, stones' and
OE **hyll**, with **hither**; it lies on the lower slopes of the hill
called Knoll *supra*.

STICKLEY COPPICE (ST 714013), *Stickley* (*Plant.*) 1838 *TA*,
to be identified with (*on an*) *Sticholnelinche* 891 (14) *Glast* (S
347(2)), *Sticholvelynch'* 891 (1338–40) Glast, in the
Anglo-Saxon bounds of Plush, 'steep ridge or bank', *v.*
sticol (wk.obl. *-an*), **hlinc**, cf. *Under-, Upestikeleclif* e14
GlastE which may refer to the same feature, *v.* **under**,
upp(e), **clif** 'cliff, bank'. OE **hlinc** survives in the nearby
f.n. *Linch* 1838 *TA*.

THORNCOMBE BARN (ST 723017), BOTTOM & EWELEAZE,
(*over*) *thorncombe* 891 (14) *Bodl* (S 347(2)) (in the bounds of
Plush), *Thorncombe* e14 *GlastE, Thorncombe Coppice, Eweleaze & Md* 1838 *TA*, 'thorn-tree valley', *v.* **þorn, cumb**.
The barn is *Whitcomb Barn* 1811 OS, cf. foll. although there
is another Whitcombe 1 mile S in Piddletrenthide par. *infra*.

WHITCOMBE BOTTOM (ST 676043), *Widecumbe* 13 GlastR,
-combe 1301 (m14) *Glast, Wydecomb*(*e*) e14 *GlastE,* 1338–40
Glast, 1429 *Wells, Wykombe* (sic), *Widecombefurlang', Wyde-
combesthrote* e14 *GlastE,* 'wide valley', *v.* **wīd** (wk.obl. *-an*),
cumb, with **furlang, þrote** 'throat, narrow place', cf.
Whitcombe par. **I** 259.

ALDERMORE (near Plush), *Allermoores* 1675 *Feth*, (*Stubbs's*) *Aldermoor* 1838 *TA*, *v*. **alor**, **mōr**, cf. *Stubbs* (pasture) 1675 *Feth*, from the surname *Stubb*. (LT & MODUS) ALDERMORE COPPICE , cf. *Gt, Home & Lt Aldermoor, Aldermoor Sleight* 1838 *TA*, *v*. prec., **slæget** 'sheep pasture', Modus Coppice *infra*. BALL BOTTOM COPSE, BALL COPSE & HILL, *Great & Little Ball* 1811 OS, *Ball Bottom* (*Copse*), *Ball hill* (*Eweleaze*), *Ball Wd* 1838 *TA*, *v*. **ball** 'rounded hill'; the hill here is the highest point in the par. (825'). BARNES'S LANE, cf. *Barns hay* 1838 *TA*, Thomas *Barnes* 1645 Hutch[3], *v*. **(ge)hæg**. BLADELEY HILL & HO, apparently changed from *Bradly* 1838 *TA*, 'broad wood or clearing', *v*. **brād, lēah**; not to be identified with the synonymous bdy point *on bradeleighe infra*, although *Brodelegh'* e14 *GlastE* may belong here. BOOKHAM DAIRY & LANE, cf. *Bookham Fd* 1838 *TA*, from Bookham *supra*. BRICKKILN COPPICE, cf. *Brick Kiln Park, Brick Yd* 1838 *TA*. BROCKHAMPTON BRIDGE (1791 Boswell), COPPICE (*Brockhampton or Bestland Copse* 1838 *TA*, cf. the f.n. Bestland's Cmn *infra*) & GATE, *v*. Brockhampton Fm & Green *supra*. BUCKLAND BOTTOM, cf. *Hr & Lr Bottom* 1838 *TA*, *v*. **botm**. CASTLE HILL (1773 Bayly, 1811 OS), cf. *bosco q' voc' Castelwode* 1270 *For*, (common called) *Castellwood* e16 Hutch[3], *Castle Gate & Wd* 1774 Hutch[1], 1869 Hutch[3], all referring to the nearby earthwork of Dungeon Hill in Minterne M. par. *infra*, *v*. **castel(l)**, **wudu**; *La Casteldych'* c. 1325 *GlastE* in the bounds of Buckland Newton hundred probably also belongs here, *v*. **dīc** 'ditch'; Castle Hill is a house built c. 1760 (Hutch[3]). CASTLE LANE, not very near prec., so perhaps referring to a different 'castle'. CHANDLER'S COPPICE. CHURCH FM, named from foll. CHURCH OF HOLY ROOD, cf. *the church of Boclaunde* 1275 FF, *church of Bokelond* 1450 Pat. CORN MILL (at Minterne Parva), cf. *Millwell* 1548 *Ct*, *v*. **myln, well(a)**. COURT FM, cf. *in Westmede iuxta Curiam* e14 *GlastE, Court-closes* 1838 *TA*. CROWTHORNE LANE, *Crowthorn* 1838 *TA*; the origin of this name may be the obvious one, but the first el. is possibly to be connected with the second el. of the boundary mark *on wibbancrowe infra*. DORCHESTER PLANT. DUNTISH COURT (site of, cf. *Curie . . . de Dunedish'* 13 (m14) *Glast*), CROSS (a crossroads, *v*. **cross**) &

(ELMS) FM, all named from Duntish *supra*. DUNTISH MILL (FM), *Duntishe Mill* 1811 OS, cf. *Mulmersche, -mersshe* e14 *GlastE, common called Myllemarshe* e16 Hutch[3], Thomas *atte Mull'* 1332 SR, *the Mill grounde in Duntish* 1597 *DCMDeed, one watermyll and watercourse with the Mylpounde, Milgroundes alias Vycars Lease* 1616 *Lane, Mill Grd, Millhams, Mill running, Millstream* 1838 *TA, Mill Gate* 1849 *TAMap, v.* Duntish *supra*, **myln, mersc, atte, pund, lǣs, hamm, running**. EAST PLANT. EIGHT ACRE COPPICE, *8 Acres* (*Copse*) 1838 *TA*. FIRLAND WD. FLINT PIT, cf. *Flinty Hill* 1838 *TA*. FOLLY, cf. *Folly Md* 1838 *TA, v.* **folie**. FORD DOWN LANE, named from *Fordoune* e14 *GlastE, Fore Down* 1838 *TA,* '(land) in front of the down', *v.* **fore, dūn**, cf. *la Doune* 13 (m14) *Glast,* e14 *GlastE,* 1338–40 *Glast,* 1429 Wells, *þe down'* 1433 (e15) *MiltRoll, Nethere-, Northere-, S(o)utheredoune* e14 *GlastE, v.* **neoðerra, norðerra, sūðerra**. FOWLEY'S CTGS, cf. *Fowley Mixen* 1838 *TA*, perhaps a surname with **mixen** 'dung-hill'. FURWAY PLANTATIONS. GALES HILL, cf. John *Gele* 1366 *Ext.* LITTLE GUNVILLE. HANOVER COPSE, *Hanover* (*Plant.*) 1838 *TA*, a transferred name, from the German province. HARVEY'S COPSE & FM, *Harvey's Bottom, Copse, Hill, Moor & Plot* 1838 *TA*, cf. widow *Harvey* 1664 HTax. HAYES FM, cf. *Hays Cowleaze & Md* 1838 *TA, v.* **hǣs** 'brushwood'. HIGHER HILL, 1838 *TA*, cf. *the Hill* 1675 *Feth, Lr Hill, Hill Thorn* 1838 *TA, v.* **hyll**. HILLING KNAP & LANE, cf. *Cranes Hillen* 1838 *TA, v.* **cnæpp** 'hillock'. HONEYPITS PLANT., *Honey Pitts* 1838 *TA, v.* **hunig**, with reference to sticky soil or to a place where honey was found. KENNEL DAIRY HO, cf. *Kennel Coppice* 1838 *TA*. KITHILL PLANT., *Ritehills* (sic) 1838 *TA*, first el. probably **cȳta** 'kite'. KNAPS HILL FM & PLANT., *the farme of Knapts hill* 1646 SC, *Knapshill* 1675 *Feth,* 1838 *TA* (*-Farm*), *Knapp's Hill* 1795 Boswell, *v.* **hyll**, cf. *Thom' Cnap . . . mes'* e14 *GlastE*, Gilbert *Nep* 1317 *MiltC, -Knap(p)* 1327 *SR,* 1332 SR. LAURENCE'S FM, cf. *Lawrences* 1811 OS (about a mile further W), Oliver *Laurence* 1688 Hutch[3]. LOCKETT'S LANE, cf. *Gt & Lt Locketts* 1838 *TA*, Giles *Lockett* 1664 HTax. LOVELACE'S COPSE, *Lovelace's Cmn* 1838 *TA*, cf. John *Lovelace* e17 *Weld*[1], widow *Louelasse* 1664 HTax. LOWER FM. THE MANOR. MANOR HO (at Plush), *Mansion Ho* 1838

TA. MILLERS FM, cf. *Miller's Lanscombe, Miller's Md* 1838 *TA,* Edward *Miller* e17 *Weld*[1], *v.* Landscombe Lane *supra.* MILL POND, near Corn Mill *supra.* MILL RACE, near Duntish Mill *supra.* LITTLE MINTERNE HILL, 1838 *TA,* cf. *Minterne Down* 1811 OS, *v.* Minterne Parva *supra.* MODUS COPPICE, *Mowdas Copse* 1838 *TA,* cf. *Will' Modi . . . mes'* e14 *GlastE, Modispleck* 1566 *Weld*[1], *Mowda's 15 & 11 Acres* 1838 *TA, v.* **plek** 'small plot'. HR & LT NARROW BRIDGE COPPICE. NEW BARN (PLANT.). NEW INN, 1838 *TA.* NOAKE FM, (*messuage called*) *Noake* 1658, 1665 *Feth, Noke* 1869 Hutch[3], cf. William *atte Oke* 1474 *Wells,* 'at the oak-tree', *v.* **atte(n), āc,** with initial *N-* from metanalysis of *atten oke,* cf. Nash Court in Marnhull par. *supra.* PIT PLANT., cf. *Putfurlang'* 1317 *MiltC, Pit Grd* 1838 *TA, v.* **pytt, furlang.** PLEASANT SPOT. PLUSH HILL, from Plush *supra.* POUND, cf. *Bull's Pound, Parish Pound* 1838 *TA, v.* **pund.** PROVIDENCE VILLA. REW (HEAD), *Rew* 1795 Boswell, *Rew Grd* 1838 *TA, v.* **rǣw** 'a row (of houses or trees)'. RIDGE HILL & WD (1838 *TA*), cf. *bosco super Rig'* 13 GlastR, *La Rigge, Rygdoune* e14 *GlastE, Buckland Ridge, Ridge Grd & Pasture* 1838 *TA, v.* **hrycg, dūn** 'down, hill', and the f.n. Rugwell *infra.* ROCK PIT, cf. *Rockpit Barn & Flg* 1838 *TA, v.* **rokke.** ROSE CTG. ROUSIBALL (LANE). ST JOHN'S CHURCH (at Plush); the former chapel was rebuilt on this site in 1848 (Hutch[3] **3** 710), cf. *Church Meade* 1675 *Feth, Plush Church* 1811 OS, *Church Md, Plush Chapel and Yard, Chapel Grd, Chapel 6 Acres* 1838 *TA*; the following reference may also belong here: *Nich' Loder habet dom' . . . in ruinos' in Les copell* 1568 *Ct,* where *copell* probably represents **capel**[1] 'chapel'. SHEEPLANDS COPSE, (*Hr*) *Sheeplands* 1838 *TA,* cf. *Sheephouse* (*Grd*) 1838 *ib.* SIX ACRE COPPICE, cf. *6 Acres* 1838 *TA.* SLOVEN'S CORNER COPPICE, *Sloven's Corner* 1838 *TA.* SPRING COPSE, -*Coppice* 1838 *TA,* cf. *Springs' Meade* 1675 *Feth, Spring Md* 1838 *TA, v.* **spring** 'well-spring'; a small stream rises nearby, possibly that referred to in the Anglo-Saxon bdy point *on an welle infra.* SPRING GROVE, SPRING HEAD (COPPICE), all near to springs (marked 6″), *v.* prec. TILEY KNAP, from Tiley in Minterne M. par. *infra, v.* **cnæpp** 'hillock'. WATTS HILL, *Watts's* (*Cowleaze*) 1838 *TA,* cf. Robert-, Thomas *Wattes* 1664 HTax. WEST HILL, 1838

TA. WHITE HO. WHITE WAY, cf. *Whiteweye* e14 *GlastE, v.* hwīt, weg, cf. the boundary mark *Wistonwey infra.* WILLOW BED, *Withey bed* 1838 *TA, v.* wīðig. WOODFALLS COPPICE, *Woodfalls* 1838 *TA, v.* (ge)f(e)all 'clearing'. WOOLFORD'S WATER, 1838 *TA,* perhaps to be identified with *Wodeleford* e14 *GlastE,* (*Brome*) *Wolfordgele* Eliz ChancP, cf. also John *atte Watere* 1315 Pat, Dyonisia *atte Watere* e14 *GlastE,* 'ford at the woodland clearing', *v.* wudu, lēah, ford, with brōm 'broom', wæter 'water'; -*gele* is probably manorial, cf. Gales Hill *supra.* A road crosses R. Lydden here.

FIELD-NAMES

The undated forms are 1838 *TA* 32. Spellings dated 891 (14) are *Glast* (S 347(2)), 891 (1338–40), 941 (1338–40), 1338–40 are Glast, 941 (14) are *Glast* (S 474). Those dated 13 are GlastR, 13 (m14), 1292 (m14), 1296 (m14), 1301 (m14), 1327 (m14) *Glast,* 1270 *For,* 1288 *Ass,* e14, c. 1325, l14 *GlastE,* 1307 (15), 1308 (15), 1311 (15), 1343 (15) *ForReg,* 1317 *MiltC,* 1327 *SR,* 1332 SR, 1350 Ipm, 1417, 1420, 1421, 1553, 1566, 1593, e17 *Weld*[1], 1428, 1429, 1436, 1474 *Wells,* 1433 (e15), n.d. (e15) *MiltRoll,* 1481 *DCMCt,* e16, 1545, 1578, 1674, 1703, 1804 Hutch[3], 1544, 1597, 1685 *DCMDeed,* 1547, 1548, 1569 *Ct,* 1572 *HarlCh,* 1616 *Lane,* 1658, 1665, 1675, 1679, 1689 *Feth,* 1664 HTax, 1791 Boswell, 1811 OS, and 1849 *TAMap.*

(a) Acre hay (*v.* (ge)hæg); (Gt & Lt) Alderbed (cf. foll.); Alders (Md); North Alders Copse (*Northallers* 1553, cf. *Schortenalres* 1327 (m14), *v.* alor 'alder', norð, sc(e)ort, cf. Aldermore (Coppice) *supra*); Andrews, Andrew's Bottom Grd & 8 Acres; Anthony's Md; Arberry (Cl) (*Erbury(e)* 1548, 1593, possibly eorð-burh 'earthwork'); (Lt) Arward; Ashey Cl; Ashley Cl (*terre atte Ayshleesfeyt* e14, cf. *firma molendini de Aysche* 1436, *Aysshemyll,* William *Atte Ayssh'* 1474, *v.* æsc 'ash-tree', lēah 'wood, clearing', myln 'mill', atte 'at the'; -*feyt* may represent the old dat.sg. fēt of fōt 'foot'); Bakers Pit (cf. Robert *Baker* 1428); Barley Cl; Barn Fd Pasture, New Barn Fd (cf. *Barne Meade* 1675, *v.* bere-ærn); Bartlett's Cl; Barton (Cl) (cf. *Hyder-, Westerb'ton* 1317, *Bertynhegge* 1481, *v.* bere-tūn 'outlying grange', hither, westerra, hecg 'hedge'); Batch (*la beche* 13 (m14), *Bache* 1597, *v.* bece[1], bæce 'stream, valley', batch 'small hill'); Batt's (cf. *la Batte* 1553, perhaps ME batte 'stick, lump'); Bean Cl (Copse) (cf. *Benford infra*); Beast Leaze horn (*v.* best(e), lǣs, horn 'projecting piece of land'); Gt & Lt Benford (probably *Beneworthe* 1566, cf. the analogous f.n. Benford Orchd in Woolland par. *supra*); Bestland's Cmn (cf. Henry *Bestland* 1674); Biles's Cl (cf. *in otherhalfacr' bilesmede* e14, from mǣd with a surname); Bishop's Mdw (cf. John-, William *Bisshopp* (tenants) 1544); Blackacres Md (*v.* blæc); Bloxford (Md); Botman(')s (Hill Cl); Bottom Md; Brackets End Gate 1849; Bradly (*v.*

Bladeley Hill *supra*); Bramble Hedge; Breach (cf. *Breaches* 1597, *v.* **brēc** 'land broken up for cultivation'); Breakhill; Brimly Flg (cf. *Brymelfurlonge* 1593, *v.* **brēmel** 'bramble', **furlang**; the modern form contains an adj. derivative, *v.* -**ig**³); Broad Down (*Brodedoune* e14 (*v.* **brād, dūn**); Broadleaze (*Broade Lease* 1685, *v.* **læs**); Broad Md (*Broade Meade* 1597, *v.* **mæd**); Broad Moor (*Brodemore* 1553, *v.* **mōr**); Brow (*v.* **brū**); Brown(')s Cl & Grd; Buckland Hill, Bucklands Cmn (*v.* par. name *supra*); Bucks Md (cf. John *Bucke* e17); Bullen's (*Bullens* 1675); Butlams; Butts (*v.* **butte**); Butty. Cl; Caines's Hill & Plot (cf. John *Kaines* 1664); Calfhay (*v.* **(ge)hæg**); Camel(')s (Aldermoor) (a surname, cf. Aldermore Coppice *supra*); Carrion Plant.; Cascliff; Catch Pond; Century; Chailham; Chason Cowleaze & Flg, Long Chason (from Chaston Fm *supra*); Clavell's Cowleaze & Md, Clavell's Knowle, Clavell's Lanscombe (cf. Roger *Clavell* 1545, *v.* Knoll and Landscombe Lane *supra*); Clay Pits; Clover Grd; Coblands; Cocks-, Coxthorns (*Cockes Thorne meadowe* 1597, *Coxthorne medowe* 1616, *v.* **þorn, mæd**; *Cock* is probably a surname); Hr, Lr & Lt Common; Common Cl & Md; Hr & Lr Coombe, Gt & Middle Coombs, Coombe's Hill (cf. *Cumba, Cumbforlang'* 1317, *La Combe de Mynterne* e14, *v.* **cumb** 'valley', **furlang**, Minterne Parva *supra*); Coppice, Copse Cl & Wd; Course Cl; Cousin(')s Hays (*v.* **(ge)hæg**); Coward's (Cmn, Copse, Hill & Md) (cf. Humphrey *Coward* e17); Cow Cl & Md; (Gt, Home & Lt) Cowleaze; Cox's Mdw; (Lesser & Lt) Crate, Crate End Flg (cf. *pastur' in la craft* 1548, *v.* **croft**); Crib Grd, Cribhouse. (Grd) (*v.* **cribbe, cribhouse**); Crocker(')s Cl & Orchd; Cross Plot; Cull's Home Md (cf. *domus Roberti Cule* 1288); Dominy(')s Orchd (cf. *Damynlyesmede* (sic) 1548, Edward *Dampney* e17, Reynold *Domptney* 1664); Down (on Hill) (cf. Ford Down Lane *supra*); Drove; Dry Grd; Duck's Nest; Dunnings, Dunneys Copse, Dunneys 5, 3 & 2 Acres (cf. Edmund *Downinge* 1572, William *Dunning* 1578, Dunning's Lane in Wootton G. par. *infra*); Duntish Cmn & Half Acre (*Duntishe Common* 1811, cf. *Duntish Oake* 1597, all named from Duntish *supra*); East Close(s); Hr & Lr East Fd (cf. *in campo orientali* 13 (m14), *La Estfelde* e14, *in campo orientali de Henelegh'* 1338–40, *v.* **ēast, feld**, Henley *supra*); East Md; 8 & 11 Acres; Elkins Md (cf. Agnes *Elkyns* 1548, Walter *Elkyns, -Ilkyns* 1616); Elvelands; Eweleaze; Farm Md; Fear (probably for *Far*) away; Fern(e)y Grd, Ferny Nap (*v.* **cnæpp** 'hillock', cf. *Verngore* 1317, *Frengrove* e14, *Ferngrove* 1327 (m14), 1338–40, *Vernam* 1474, *v.* **fearn** 'fern', **gāra, grāf(a), hamm**); Field Gate; 15 Acres; Fir Plant., Firs; (Home) 5 Acres; 5 Yard (*v.* **gierd**); Flashett (*v.* **flasshett** 'place characterised by swampy grassland'); Foot's Botmans, Foot's Palmer's Cl; Forest; (The) 4 Acres (*Foweracres* e14, *v.* **fēower, æcer**); Foxholes (cf. *La Langehegge Underfoxole* c. 1325, both from **fox-hol** 'fox's earth' although not referring to the same place, *v.* **lang¹, hecg, under**, cf. also *Foxburgh'* e14 from **fox** amd **burg** 'burrow'); The Fox Inn; French Grass Pce (*v.* **french grass**); Frendle's; (Hr & Lr) Furlong (cf. *La furlonge* 1553, *v.* **furlang**); Furzegold; Furzy Cl, Croft & Hill (cf. *Vursey Hedge* 1547, *v.* **fyrsig**); Gillam's; Glebe Altmt; Goosehams (*v.* **hamm**); Gt & Lt Gore (cf. *Goare Meade* 1675), Gore hay (cf. *unam*

acram vocatur la Gore 13 (m14), 1338–40, *v.* **gāra** 'triangular plot', **mǣd,
(ge)hæg**); Gould's Cl; Gray's (Cowleaze) (cf. Cristian *Graye* 1616); Great
Fd; Great Md (*the great Meade* 1597); Green Cl (*Greene Close* 1665);
Greenway ((*La*) *Greneweye* e14, *Greenewaye* 1593, *v.* **grēne**[1], **weg**);
Groves's Fd; Gulliver(')s Ctg, Fd & Orchd; Hagusson (to be identified
with *on hengersten* 941 (14), *Hongersten* 941 (1338–40), in the Anglo-Saxon
bounds of Buckland N., perhaps from **gærs-tūn** 'paddock' with either *hēan*
wk.obl. of **hēah**[1] 'high, chief' or **henn** 'hen'); Half Acre (cf. *Halfakre
Bytheweye, Halfakre in the Middelcomb, Halakre atte Helle* 1317, *v.*
h(e)alf, æcer, weg, and *Middelcomb, Helle infra*); Hanging Grd & Lawns
(*v.* **hangende**); Hant Md or Camel's (cf. *supra*); Harbour Cl; Hawcombe
Cl; Haybarton (cf. Barton (Cl) *supra*); Heave (9 Acres) (*v.* **heave** 'heap,
hillock'); Hen Acres Hill (*La Henacre* 1593, *v.* **henn, æcer**); Henley Fd, 4
Acres, Md & Rd (from Henley *supra*); High Grd; Highlands; Hill (Cl, Pce,
Thorn & Wd) (cf. *1½ acr' super La Hulle* e14, *la hill'* 1548, *Hill close,
-meades* 1597, *v.* **hyll**); Hilly Grds (cf. *Hillye Close* 1597); Holland's Grd;
The Home Cl (*Home Close* 1597, *the Home closes* 1616); Home Grd; Home
Mead (Grd), (The) Home Mdw (cf. *Home Meade* 1665); Homestead
Orchd; Horse Cl & Lds; Hountwell, Huntwell Moor (*terre . . .
Bovehontewelle* e14, *Huntewelle* 1317, *Huntwell Farm* 1703, 'hunter's spring
or stream', from **hunta** and **well(a)** with **bufan** 'above'); Hurdle Md (*v.*
hyrdel); Hyle (1593, from the dat.sg. *hēale* of **h(e)alh** 'nook, corner of
land'); Lt Inhams; Jackmen(t)s; Jollis's Pce (cf. Humphrey *Jolliffe* e17);
Kew Plot; Keyhole; King Fd; Kings Arms Inn; Knap Md (*v.* **cnæpp**
'hillock'); Maine Knowle, Young's Knowle (*v.* Knoll *supra*); Lambing
Grd; Lanchard Cl (*v.* **lanchet**); The Lane (cf. *les Lanes* 1568, *v.* **lane**
'lane' or **leyne** 'tract of arable land'); The Lawn; Leaze Md, The Leys (*v.*
lǣs 'pasture'); Legg's Half Acre; Lime Md; Little Md(w) (*Little-, Lyttle
Meade* 1597); Little Moor; Little Platt (*v.* **plat**[2]); Locks (cf. Hugh *Lock*
1548); Loke Acre (*Locacre* e14, *v.* **loc(a)** 'lock, fold', **æcer**); Long Acre
(*Langacre* e14, *v.* **lang**[1]); Long Cl; Long Down (Gdn & Md(w))
(*Longdowne* 1593, *v.* **dūn**); Long Fd; Longlawns (probably *Lang(e)lond(')*
1433 (e15), 1436, *Longe Landes* 1597, cf. *Langlondyshed', -putte* 1433
(e15), *v.* **lang**[1], **land, hēafod, pytt**); Long Md; Loscombe Bottom
(*Luscombe, North'loscombe* e14, *Loscum* 1317, 'pig-sty valley', *v.* **hlōse,
cumb**); Lower Fd & Md; Luckham's Md, Luckham's Ne(a)therway,
Luckham's 9 & 3 Acres; Lydgates, Lydiats (*Lydyate* 1553, *v.* **hlid-geat** 'a
swing-gate'); (Lt) Lye Md, Lye(')s (Md) (cf. *La Legh'* e14, William
Atteleigh 1474, *v.* **lēah** 'wood, clearing', **atte** 'at the'); Gt & Lt
Lymington; Majors Cmn (cf. Agnes-, Isaac *Maior* 1332); Marleys; Marsh
(head) Md; Meadow (cf. *Le Meade* 1593, *v.* **mǣd**); Meeches 5 & 4 Acres;
Messiter's 5 & 4 Acres; Middle Fd; Middle Flg (*Myddelfurlonge* 1593);
Middle Hill; Milking Barton; Moor, Moor Md(w) (cf. *La Moore* 1593, *the
Mormede, (prata) Atte Moreshevede, Bovemoreshevede* 1317, John *atte
Morheye* 1327, *v.* **mōr** 'marshy ground', **mǣd, atte, hēafod** 'end', **bufan**
'above', **(ge)hæg**); Mount Silver; Mowing Plot; Mowlam's Md; Mullett's
Codmoor, Mullett's 5 Acres, Mullett's Knowle (*v.* Knoll *supra*); Napp's

(cf. Knaps Hill Fm *supra*); Nappy Cl (Alderbed) (*v.* **cnæppig**); Nettlecombe Eweleaze (*Netlecombe* 1675, *v.* **netel(e), cumb**, giving name to Nettlecombe Tout in Melcombe H. par. *supra*); New Cl, Md (Alderbed) & Pce; North Fd (*campus borial'* e14, *Northfelde* 1553) & Hill; North Hows (Drove) (*v.* **howe**); Oakey Cl Orchard (Md); Overwood (*Overwode* 1436, *v.* **wudu**, probably with **uferra** 'higher'); Ox Cl; Paddock (Orchd) (cf. *the parocke* 1597, *v.* **pearroc**); Palmer's Cl (Mead); Paradise; Gt & Lt Park, Bottom Park (Md), Home Park, Park Md (cf. the medieval park at Duntish *supra*; there was also an early park near Plush, referred to as *claus' voc' la Parke* 1417, *v.* **park**); Parkers Md (cf. *Joh' le Parkere* . . . *mes'* e14, John-, William *Parker* 1332); Parsonage Plot (at Plush); Pasture Grd; Patchward (*Pachesworthe* 1317, *v.* **worð** 'enclosure'; *Paches-* could represent either the ME surname *Pache* (for which *v.* Reaney s.n. *Patch*) or an OE pers.n. *Pæcc* which would be a strong form of the *Pæcca* suggested for Patcham Sx, etc (DEPN)); Pease Acres (*Pus(e)acres* 1327 (m14), 1338–40, *Pusacre Crofte* l14, cf. *Binorth'pisacresthorne* e14, *v.* **pise, peosu** 'pease', **æcer, croft, bī, þorn**); Peter's Md; Piece; Pigpool; Pigs Louse (*v.* **hlōse** 'pig-sty'); Pig's Yoke; Pile Cl, Piles Bear (cf. Andrew *de la Pile* 1270, John atte *Pyle, Pylfurlang'* 1317, *venelle voc' Pylan'* 1481, *v.* **pīl** 'stake', **atte** 'at the', **furlang, lane**; *Bear* may represent **bearu** 'grove'); Pleek (*v.* **plek**); Plot; Polden's Plot; Pond Md; Poor Gdns (no doubt land given to the poor, *v.* Hutch³ 3 720); Potatoe Plot; Gt & Lt Pounts, Way Pounts; Pulham Cl (*Pulhams Close* 1616, cf. Pulham par. *infra*); Pye land; Quarry Cl (*Quarclose* 1597, *Quarr(e) Closes* 1665, 1689, *v.* **quarre**); Rayn Md; Redlands (possibly to be identified with *Re(a)dlane* (*Meade*) 1597, *v.* **rēad** 'red', **lane**); Red Lion Inn; Red Md; Rick Barton (cf. *Reykehay* 1436, *v.* **ricke** 'rick', **(ge)hæg**); Ricketson; Riles's Pce (cf. Thomas *Ryall'* 1548); Rocks; Ropers Lot & Md; Rough Md; Row Grd (*v.* **rūh** (wk.obl. *rūwan*) 'rough'); Rugwell (*fontem aque* . . . *surgentem in campo de parva minterne qui vocatur Ruggewell(e)* 1296 (m14), 1338–40, *Rigwelle* e14, *aquam de Ruggewelle* c. 1325 (in the bounds of Buckland N. hundred), *v.* **hrycg** 'ridge', **well(a)** 'spring, stream'; the 'ridge' probably refers to the southern extension of Ridge Hill *q.v. supra*, cf. also *on anne rig'* 941 (14) in the Anglo-Saxon bounds of Buckland N.; the stream may be the upper part of R. Cerne or a tributary of it); Russia Fds (no doubt a transferred name from the country); Ryehays (Mdw) (*Ryhey* 1317, *v.* **ryge** 'rye', **(ge)hæg**); Ryland (*Rielonde* 13 (m14), *Rylond'* 1338–40, *Righlond'* 1566, *v.* **ryge, land**); Sandal, Sandhill (*Sandhulle* e14, *v.* **sand, hyll**); 7 Acres; Sharn Md (*v.* **scearn** 'dung'); Sheepsleight, Sleight (*v.* **slæget** 'sheep pasture'); Sheppard(')s (12 Acres) (cf. *Ric' Bercari* . . . *mesuag'* 1317); Shitten Shard (cf. *the/la S(c)herde* 1433 (e15), *v.* **sceard** 'gap', **shitten** 'filthy'); Shortlands (*Schortelond* e14, *Shortlond atte Hareputte* 1317, *v.* **sc(e)ort, land, atte, hār², pytt**); Shrubbets (probably a derivative in *-et* of **scrubb**, denoting 'place characterised by shrubs or brushwood')); Sicketts Md; Silk Md (*v.* **sēoluc** 'gully'); Skillhays; 6 Acres (at Plush); Slade's Moor & Pce, Down Slades; Small Md & Orchd; Smetham's Cmn (*Smethams* 1804, from a family of this name, *v.* Hutch³ 3 694); South Cl; Spicer's Lawn; Spratt

Md; Stagmoor; Two Stanford Pces (*v.* **stān** 'stone'); Stockham (*Stockham* 1481, *v.* **stocc** 'tree-stump', **hamm**, cf. *Stockhay Little* [Bridge] 1791); Stoneyland(s) (cf. *Stone lond'* 1553, *v.* **stān, stānig, land**); Stooplands Btm & Nap (*v.* **cnæpp** 'hillside'; the first part of the name is perhaps to be associated with *Stoples infra*); Strap (*v.* **strap**); Stubb's Cowleaze; Sturmy's Md (Alderbed); Home Summer Leaze (*Somerlease* 1553, *v.* **sumor, lǣs**); Swede's Copse; Symes's Cmn & Orchd (cf. Richard *Simes* e17); Taylor's Md (cf. Richard *le Tayllur* 1307 (15), John *Taillur* 1332); Tee (probably descriptive of the shape of the two small fields so called); 10 Acres (*cultura (que) vocatur tenacre(s) in campo orientali* 13 (m14), 1338–40, *v.* **tēn, æcer**, East Fd *supra*); Thornhays (Mdw) (*Thornhayes* 1675, *v.* **þorn, (ge)hæg**); 3 Acres; 3 Yard (*v.* **gierd**); Timmiss-, Timmins Hill, Timmis's Md, Lt Timms's (*Tymmers hill* 1616, a surname); Tollerville's Acre & 5 Acres, Tollerville's Knowle (cf. John *Tollervile* . . . *un' tenement* 1569, William *Tollerfeild* 1664, Knoll *supra*); Trunk Cl (Orchd); Tuckley; Turnpike Ho; Twinley (*Twyneley* 1566, perhaps '(land) between woods or clearings', *v.* **betwēonan, lēah**); Twin Waters (for a possible first el., cf. prec.); Broad & Long Twist (*v.* **twist**, here referring to land in a curving valley); 2 Acres; Gt & Lt Tyn(n)ings (*v.* **tȳning** 'enclosure'); Under Hill; Upper Cl (*the-* 1679); Gt & Lt Vincents (cf. John *Vincent* 1664); Vines; Wall hays (*v.* **(ge)hæg**); Washing Pond Pce; Wash Md; Water (Md); Webbs leaze (*Lower Webbs Leaze, Upper Webbs Leaze or Upper Webbs Meade* 1675, cf. *gardin' voc' Web(be)hay* 1436, 1474, Thomas *le Webbe* 1327, *v.* **lǣs, (ge)hæg**); Well Cl; West Fd (*in campo occidentali* 13 (m14), 1338–40, 1548); West Side; Wheat Cl, Wheaty Cl (cf. *Wheate Close* 1675 (at Plush), *v.* **hwǣte**); Whetley Cowleaze; Whitelands (1675, *v.* **hwīt**); Whitmarsh (*Whitemershe* 1568, *v.* **hwīt, mersc**); Willow Bed (at Plush); Withey Bed (or Aldermoor) (cf. *Withie Meade* 1597, *v.* **wīðig** 'willow', cf. Aldermore Coppice *supra*); Woodlanes; Wood Md; Wool Md (probably to be associated with *terre apud Plush' iuxta La Welle, Wellefurlang'* e14, *v.* **well(a), wiell(a)** 'spring, stream', **furlang**); Writh (Cowleaze & Md) (probably *fyrhð* 'wood', cf. *La Frith infra*).

(b) *on alden doune* 891 (14), *Aldendonne* 891 (1338–40), *Eldoune* e14 (in the Anglo-Saxon bounds of Plush, 'old down or hill', *v.* **(e)ald** (wk.obl. -an), **dūn**); *Alwardescum* 1317, *Ailwardescomb(e)* 1327 (m14), 1338–40 (the OE pers.n. *Æðelweard* and **cumb** 'valley'); *on amesheal* 941 (14), *Annesheal* 941 (1338–40) (in the Anglo-Saxon bounds of Buckland N., *v.* **h(e)alh** 'nook, corner of land', first el. probably a pers.n. of uncertain form); *on apildore* 941 (14) (*v.* **apuldor** 'apple-tree'); *Aulis-* 13 (m14), 1338–40, *Aulescomb(e)* 1327 (m14), 1338–40 (perhaps identical in origin with Awliscombe D 608 the first el. of which may be **āwel** 'fork (of a river)', *v.* **cumb**); (*on*) *babbanmede* 941 (14), 941 (1338–40) (the OE pers.n. *Babba* and **mǣd**); *Baloneshey* 1474 (*v.* **(ge)hæg**, with a surname); *Bennetts Meade* 1675; *Bidlond'* 1547, *Bedlandes* 1616 (*v.* **land**, first el. probably **bydel** 'a beadle'); *on birninge* 941 (14), *Byrnynge* 941 (1338–40) (perhaps a derivative in **-ing²** of **bryne** 'burning' or **burna** 'spring, stream'); *in cultura Bitwenethecombe* e14 ('between the valleys', *v.* **betwēonan, cumb**);

La Blakealres c. 1325 (*v.* **blæc, alor**); (*on*) *bledhildewelle* 941 (14), 941 (1338–40) (an unrecorded OE fem. pers.n. *Blædhild* and **well(a)** 'spring, stream'); *bosco* . . . *super Blerek* 13 (perhaps to be associated with foll., but etymology uncertain); *Blerl(e)yfurlong(e)* 1548, 1593 (cf. prec., *v.* **furlang**); *Bochelneswode* e14, *La Boch'le* l14 (*v.* **wudu**, first el(s). uncertain); *la Bothett* 1593 (etymology uncertain); *on bournandign'* 941 (14), *Bournandgyn'* 941 (1338–40) (the first el. may be **burna** 'spring, stream' but the spellings seem corrupt); *on bradeleighe* 941 (14), *Bradelegh'* 941 (1338–40) (*v.* **brād, lēah**, cf. Bladeley Hill *supra*); *Brodefeld(e)* 1436, 1474 (*v.* **brād, feld**); *Brodelonde* e14, *Bradelond* 1436 (*v.* **land**); *de la Broke* (p) 1270 (*v.* **brōc**); *on-, of bromhulle* 891 (14), 891 (1338–40) (in the Anglo-Saxon bounds of Plush, 'broom-covered hill', *v.* **brōm, hyll**, cf. *Brumelforlang'* e14, *v.* **furlang**); *on brugh doune* 891 (14), *Brughdonne* 891 (1338–40), *borough'don'* n.d. (e15) (in the Anglo-Saxon bounds of Plush and the medieval bounds of Lyscombe in Cheselbourne par. *supra*, *v.* **burh** 'earthwork' (perhaps with reference to the Iron Age hill-fort on Nettlecombe Tout in Melcombe H. par. *supra*), **dūn**); *Bucklande Fealdes, -Feildes* 1597 (*v.* par. name *supra*); *on an burghen* 941 (14) (*v.* **byrgen** 'grave, burial place'); *Burialre* e14, *Buryallers* 1593 (*v.* **alor** 'alder', first el. ME *bury* (from dat.sg. *byrig* of OE **burh**) in the sense 'manor house'); *Busshyclose* 1616; *Byccheneburgh'* c. 1325 (in the bounds of Buckland N. hundred), *Buchonbargh* e17 ('earthwork or barrow frequented by bitches', from **bicce** (gen.pl. *biccena*) and **burh** or **beorg**; in the hundred bounds this place is next to *Hundyete infra*, cf. also *on doggeneford infra*); *Carswellesyate* 1317, *Cars(s)ewellesalr(e)s* 1338–40, 1343 (15) ('cress spring or stream', from **cærse** and **well(a)** with **geat** 'gate' and **alor** 'alder'); *Clarckes Clyffe* 1593 (a surname with **clif**); *Le Clif* 1317, *þe Clyff'* 1433 (e15) (*v.* **clif**); *on cliveleghe* 891 (14), *Clivelegh'* 891 (1338–40) ('wood or clearing at the cliffs or banks', *v.* **clif** (gen.pl. *clifa*), **lēah**, probably to be associated with *La Clyve* c. 1325 in the bounds of Buckland N. hundred); *Cloveneburgh'* c.1325 (in the hundred bounds, from **(ge)clofen** 'cloven, split' with either **burh** 'earthwork' or **beorg** 'barrow', cf. i 260); *Cnollisschefurlang'* e14 (*v.* **furlang**; the first el. is presumably a derivative with the suffix -*isc* of **cnoll** 'hillock' or the p.n. Knoll (from this el.) *supra*); *the corn close(s)* 1597 (*v.* **corn**[1]); *Craneforlong(')* 1327 (m14), 1338–40 (*v.* **cran** 'a crane', **furlang**); *on cristemeleighe* 941 (14), *Cristemelegh'* 941 (1338–40) ('clearing with a cross', *v.* **cristel-mǣl, lēah**); (land) *Atte Crouche, Felice Crouche* 1317 (*v.* **atte** 'at the', **crūc**[3] 'cross'; *Felice* is a surname, cf. Walter *Felyce* 1332); *on anne crundil* 891 (14) (*v.* **crundel** 'chalk-pit, quarry'); *Crympulforlonge* 1548 (*v.* **furlang**, first el. probably **crymel** 'small piece'); *Curnle* 1317, *Cronlesforlang* 1327 (m14), *Cornlesforlong* 1338–40 (the first el. may be **cweorn** 'hand-mill', with **lēah** 'clearing' and **furlang**); *Dame Alicemede* e14 ('Dame Alice's meadow', *v.* **mǣd**); *on ane dich, endlang dich* 941 (14) (*v.* **dīc** 'ditch'); *on doggeneford* 941 (14), *Doggenesford'* 941 (1338–40) ('ford frequented by dogs', *v.* **dogga** (gen.pl. *doggena*), **ford**; the next point in the Anglo-Saxon bounds of Buckland N. is *on doggeneberwe* which survives in Dogbury *q.v.* in

Minterne M. par. *infra*); (common called) *Dolyewood* e16; *Drythesclif'* c. 1325 (a surname with **clif**); *Dychehous* 1436 (*v.* **dīc, hūs**); *Dykers Meade* 1675 (a surname with **mǣd**); *the lower east grounde* 1658, *East grounds* 1665; *montem de Eiletzbergh(e)* 13 (m14), 1338–40 (from **beorg** 'barrow, hill' and an OE pers.n. *Æðelgēat*); *Eldehagh'*, *-hay* e14 ('old enclosure', *v.* **eald, haga¹, (ge)hæg**); *on þar elde lidyate* 941 (14) (*v.* **eald, hlid-geat** 'swing-gate'; not to be identified with the *TA* f.ns. Lydgates, Lydiats *supra*); *on þar Elde Waldich* 941 (14) (*v.* **eald, weall** 'wall', **dīc** 'ditch'); *Ellefurlang'* 1317 (*v.* **elle(r)n** 'elder-tree', **furlang**, cf. foll. and *Norther-, Sutherelemede* e14 which may also contain **elle(r)n** with **mǣd, norðerra, sūðerra**); *on ellene crundil* 891 (14), *Ellenecrundil* 891 (1338–40) (*v.* **elle(r)n, crundel** 'chalk-pit, quarry'); *Estere-, Estmostfurlang'* e14 (*v.* **ēasterra, ēastmest, furlang**); *Ewelme* e14, (land) *atte Ewelme(shevede)* 1317 (*v.* **ǣwelm** 'river-spring, source of a river', **hēafod** 'head', here probably also 'source of a river'); *on ane firesrewe* 941 (14), *Foresrewe* 941 (1338–40) (*v.* **rǣw** 'row of trees, hedgerow', first el. probably **fyrs** 'furze'); *La-, the Frith(')* de Brochamton' e14, *la Friht* 1338–40, *(the) Frith(')* 1429, 1568, *Friths Close alias Bushey Close* 1665 (*v.* **fyrhð** 'wood', Brockhampton, *Busshyclose supra*); *Froggegore* e14 (*v.* **frogga, gāra**); *Furbers tenemente* 1616 (held by Henry *Furber ib*, cf. Edward *Furber* 1547); *Fynslade* e14 (probably **fīn** 'heap (of wood)' with **slæd** 'valley'); *Fysschemere, Nythemostfys(sche)mere* 1436, *Nethemost Fysshemere, Nethemost Fysshemore al' Hammelond* 1474 ('pool where fish are caught', *v.* **fisc, mere¹, nethermost, hamm** 'enclosure, river-meadow', **land**, cf. *Visgherneheveede infra*); *atte Gate* (p) 1327 (*v.* **atte, geat**); *Gillond'* 1548 (*v.* **land**, perhaps to be associated with *Great-, Little Gyoll* 1665, possibly from **goyle** 'ravine'); *Godesgrave* l14 (from **grāf(a)** 'grove' with a surname); *Gold(e)crofte* e14 (*v.* **golde** 'marigold', **croft**); *Green Hayes, Green Haye Meade* 1597 (*v.* **grēne¹, (ge)hæg**); *Guldenelond* e14 (*v.* **gylden, land**); *on hagen* 891 (14), *on hawen endlang hawen* 941 (14) (*v.* **haga¹** 'hedge, enclosure'); *to hamme* 891 (14), *Hamme* 891 (1338–40) (*v.* **hamm** 'enclosure', cf. *lez hames* 1553, *Fysschemere supra*); *Hardyes Meade* 1675 (cf. Edward *Hardy* 1664); *les Hechynges* 1429 (*v.* **hēcing** 'the sown part of a field'); *Heldehegh'*, *cultura bithe Hulde* e14 (*v.* **hielde** 'slope', **(ge)hæg**); *Halakre atte Helle* 1317, *Helleclif* e14, *Helleclyvesupside* c. 1325 (*v.* **hell** 'hell' (used as a term of contempt), **atte** 'at the', **clif** 'cliff, bank', **upp, sīde**, cf. Half Acre *supra*); *Hemecrofte* e14 (probably 'enclosure belonging to the inhabitants', *v.* **hǣme, croft**); *on herebrittescombe* 941 (14), *Herebryttescomb'* 941 (1338–40) (the OE pers.n. *Herebeorht* and **cumb** 'valley'); *endlang herepathes* 891 (14), *on here path, on þar here path, endelang here pathes* 941 (14) (*v.* **here-pæð** 'highway'); *La Hethefelde* e14, *La Hethe* 1338–40, *Heyth Close* 1547 (*v.* **hǣð** 'heath', **feld**); *on anne heued* 941 (14) (*v.* **hēafod** 'head, headland'); *Heyhlegh* 1343 (15) (possibly 'enclosed wood', *v.* **(ge)hæg, lēah**, cf. foll.); *Heywod(')* 1311 (15), 1338–40 (*v.* **(ge)hæg, wudu**); *Hokedelond* 1317 (*v.* **hōcede** 'curved', **land**); *Holecomb(e)* 1327 (m14), 1338–40 Glast (*v.* **hol²** 'deep', **cumb**); *Hole Mede* 1436, 1474 (*v.* **hol¹** 'a hole' or **hol²** 'hollow', **mǣd**); *Hoopers Meade* 1665;

houndesete (sic) 941 (14), 941 (1338–40), *Hundesghete* 1317, *Hundyete*
c.1325 ('hound's gate', *v.* **hund**, **geat**, cf. *on doggeneford supra*, though the
first el. could alternatively be the OE pers.n. *Hund*); *Houshulle* c.1325 (*v.*
hyll, first el. probably **hūs** 'house'); *on an hul* 891 (14) (*v.* **hyll**); (*on*)
igland 941 (14), 941 (1338–40) (*v.* **īeg-land** 'island'); *Inmede* e14 (*v.* **in**
'inner', **mǣd**); *Instoncome* e14 (*v.* **in, stān** 'stone', **cumb**); *James Meade*
1597; *atte Lake* (p) 1436 (*v.* **lacu** 'stream', **atte**); *on langengroue* 941 (14),
-grove 941 (1338–40) (*v.* **lang¹, grāf(a)** 'grove'); *La Langehegge* c.1325 (*v.*
lang¹, hecg 'hedge'); *fro þe lanhed' by the lansshore* 1433 (e15) (*v.* **land,
hēafod**, 'headland', **land-scoru** 'boundary'); *legfurlang* 13 (m14), *Logforlong'* (sic) 1338–40 (*v.* **leg, furlang**); *on lillanwelle* 891 (14), *Lillanwell'* 891
(1338–40) (the OE pers.n. *Lilla* and **well(a)** 'spring, stream'); *la linche* 13
(m14) (*v.* **hlinc** 'ridge'); *Litelacr'* 1317 (*v.* **lȳtel, æcer**); *Lodewurthy*
(*pastur' voc'-*) 1436, *-worth* 1474 (*v.* **worðig, worð** 'enclosure', first el.
probably an OE pers.n. *Loda*, a strong form of which occurs in Lodsworth
Sx 26); *atte Londdeshende* (p) 1332 (*v.* **atte, land, ende¹**); *Medryde* 1436,
Mederedewode 1474 (*v.* **mǣd, rȳde, ryde** 'clearing', **wudu**); *Medyate*
1436, *Medeyede* 1474 (*v.* **mǣd, geat**); *Menewode* 1433 (e15) (*v.* **(ge)mǣne**
'common', **wudu**); *on þe merhawin endlang hawin, on þe mer(e)hawe
en(d)lang hawin* 941 (14) ('boundary hedge', *v.* **(ge)mǣre, haga¹**);
Mitchells Tenement 1675 (cf. Roger *Michell* e17); *the Middle Close* 1679;
Middelcombeforlang' e14, *Middelcomb(e)* 1317, 1429, 1548 (*v.* **middel,
cumb, furlang**); *Milwins meadow* 1597 (cf. *Walt' Milon . . . mesuag'* e14);
Murlese 1436, *Murle* (*claus' voc'-*) 1474 (first el. probably **mōr** 'moor'
(for the development to *Mur-*, cf. Murcot Gl 2 6), with **lǣs** 'pasture' or
lēah 'clearing'); *Netherbrooke* 1675 (*v.* **neoðerra** 'lower', **brōc**); *Nethercote*
1292 (m14) (*v.* **cot** 'cottage'); *Netherpece* 1317 (*v.* **pece**); *the New Howse*
1597; *Northe Mede* 1547; *Nywehay* e14 (*v.* **nīwe, (ge)hæg**); *Oldwode* 1474
(*v.* **eald, wudu**); *Othulle* 13, e14 (*v.* **āte** 'oats', **hyll** 'hill'); *the over Meade*
1597 (*v.* **uferra** 'higher', **mǣd**); *Les Pannes* 1568 (*v.* **panne**); *Podehegh'*
e14, *Podyhayes* 1553 (*v.* **pode** 'toad', **(ge)hæg**); *Porthegge* 1433 (e15) (*v.*
port² 'town', **hecg** 'hedge'); *Prycketherne* c.1325 (*v.* **pric(c)a** 'prickle',
þyrne 'thorn-bush'); *Pudecombe* 1436, *Pudcomb' mogacre* 1474 (*v.* **cumb**
'valley', first el. possibly the OE pers.n. *Puda*; *mogacre* may contain a form
of dial. **mag** 'magpie', *v.* **æcer**); *Alicia-, Will' atte Pulle . . . mesuag'* e14
(probably to be associated with *Pullesdon' ib, v.* **atte** 'at the', **pull** 'pool',
dūn 'hill', cf. foll.); *claustur' parci de Pulton'* e14 (*v.* **tūn**, cf. prec.); *Pyry-*
1436, *Purlond* 1474 (*v.* **pirige, pyrige** 'pear-tree', **land**, but the first el.
could be a surname, cf. *terre quondam Walteri Purye* 1436); (*on*) *radenwey*
891 (14), 891 (1338–40) (*v.* **rēad** (wk.obl. *-an*) 'red', **weg**); *riʒtwey* 941 (14)
(*v.* **riht²** 'straight', **weg**); *on þan rissbed* 941 (14) (*v.* **risc-bedd** 'rush-bed');
on risshdene 941 (14), *Ryshdene* 941 (1338–40) (*v.* **risc** 'rush', **denu**
'valley'); *la Rodehay* 1474 (*v.* **(ge)hæg** 'enclosure', first el. possibly **rōd²**
'cross'); *Rougheburghe* c.1325 (possibly identical in meaning with foll., but
a different location); *on Ruanberghe* (2 x) 891 (14), *Ru(w)anbergh'* 891
(1338–40) ('rough barrow or hill', *v.* **rūh** (wk.obl. *rūwan*), **beorg**); *on an
ruwe dich* 891 (14) (cf. *terr' . . . iuxta La Roghdych'* e14, *v.* **rūh, dīc**

'ditch'); *on Scheplegh'e* 941 (14), *Scheplegh'* 941 (1338–40) (*v.* **scēap** 'sheep', **lēah**); *on Scherdenberwe, on Scherdanbourgh* 941 (14), *Schordenberwe, Sche(r)danbourh* 941 (1338–40), *Sherdeburgh'* c.1325 ('mutilated hill or barrow', from **sceard** (wk.obl. *-an*) and **beorg**; *Shordon'* 1547 may also belong here); *on schilleburghe* 891 (14), *Schilleburgh'* 891 (1338–40) (in the Anglo-Saxon bounds of Plush, and to be identified with *on chellenberghe* 966 (15) *ShaftR* (S 744) in the Anglo-Saxon bounds of Piddletrenthide, possibly 'resounding barrow' (denoting perhaps a hollow barrow that produced an echo?) from an OE **sciell** or **scille** and **beorg**); *la Schilve* 13 (m14), 1338–40, *Shortshulve* 1317 (*v.* **scielf** 'ledge', **sc(e)ort** 'short'); *Schorte(n)alres* e14, 1338–40 (*v.* **sc(e)ort** (wk.obl. *-an*), **alor** 'alder'); *Schortedoune* e14 (*v.* **dūn**); *Sete-, Setylake* e14 (no doubt analogous with *Setylake* in Stoke W. par. *supra*); *on sic, of þan sice* 941 (14) (*v.* **sīc** 'small stream'); *Skochereshey* 1436, *Scochershey* 1474 (a surname with **(ge)hæg**); *Smythacre* 1301 (m14), *Smythesacr'* 1338–40 (cf. *Smyth'* hey 1436, *Smethey* 1474, *Joh' Faber* . . . *mesuag'* e14, *v.* **æcer, (ge)hæg**); *camp' australis* e14 ('south field'); *Splot* 1436, *Splottes* 1474 (*v.* **splot** 'plot of land'); (*on*) *stanbrok* 891 (14), 891 (1338–40) ('stony brook', *v.* **stān, brōc**); *on stanwey* 891 (14) (*v.* **stān, weg**); *La Sterte* 1350 (*v.* **steort** 'tongue of land'); *on stiþeleighe* 941 (14), *Stiyelegh'* (sic) 941 (1338–40) ('hard clearing', *v.* **stīð, lēah**); *Stohull* e17 (*v.* **stān, hyll**); *Stonesmede* e14 (probably a surname, with **mǣd**); *Stonardeslond(e)* 1436, 1474 (a surname with **land**); (land) *atte Stonyburgh'* c.1325 (probably 'stony barrow' from **stānig** and **beorg**); *Stoples* 1593 (probably to be associated with *Goldstonestople* e14, *Gelstonestople* 1317, from **stōpel** 'a stepping-stone' with a surname); *to-, on (þane) streme, end(e)lang stremes* 941 (14) (*v.* **strēam**); *La Stubbe vocat' La Landscharethorne* c.1325 (*v.* **stubb** 'stub', **land-sc(e)aru** 'boundary', **þorn** 'thorn-tree'); *Styl(e)hamwode* 1436, 1474 (*v.* **stigel** 'a stile', **hamm, wudu**); *Summill'* 1548; *Sunptun' Alres* 1308 (15), *Sunptonealres* 1338–40, *Sompton(')* Allers 1553, 1566 (*v.* **sumpt** 'marsh, swamp', **tūn** 'farm', **alor** 'alder'); *Suthmostfurlang'* e14 (*v.* **sūðmest, furlang**); *Swettinges Thorn* 1270 (a point in the bounds of Blackmoor Forest and possibly in this par., from **þorn** and a ME surname, cf. *John Swetyng* 1327 (Ibberton)); *Sweytacre* e14 (*v.* **swēte** 'sweet', **æcer**); *Syddeards* 1679 (probably a surname); *on an Wirnen* (probably for *þirnen*) 941 (14) (*v.* **þyrne** 'thorn-bush'); *on anne þorthn* (probably for *þorn*) 941 (14) (*v.* **þorn** 'thorn-tree'); *on þar thre landschere* 941 (14) ('the three boundaries', *v.* **þrēo, land-sc(e)aru**); *Tounforlang'* (2 x) e14 (*v.* **tūn, furlang**); *Twoburles* c1325 (for a possible meaning of *burle, v.* the f.n. Burlington 1 361); *the Upper Meade* 1597; *Uveraker* 1317 (*v.* **uferra** 'upper', **æcer**); *Uverpece* 1317 (*v.* **pece** 'piece'); *Visghernehevede* c.1325 (possibly 'spit of land used by fishermen', if the first el. is **fiscere** (with wk. ME gen.pl., *v.* -**ena**), with **hēafod**, cf. *Fysschemere supra*); *to þe vorouyshed'* 1433 (e15) ('head of the furrow', *v.* **furh, hēafod**); *Vycars lease* 1616 (*v.* **lǣs**); (*on*) *warrode* 891 (14), 891 (1338–40) (*v.* **warod** 'shore-meadow'; *fons voc' Waterdole* 1436, 1474 (*v.* **wæter, dāl** 'share (in the common field)'); *endlangweies* 941 (14) (*v.* **weg** 'way, road'); *on þar-, in on þe weilete* 891 (14) ('junction of

roads', v. **weg, (ge)lǽt**); *on an welle* 891 (14), *Anwille* 891 (1338–40) (v.
well(a), wiell(a) 'spring, stream', cf. *Spring Copse supra*); *Wenkelescrofte*
e14 (a surname with **croft**); *Westcombeshevede* c.1325 (v. **west, cumb,
hēafod**); *West(e)le(e)* 1420, 1421 (v. **lēah** 'wood, clearing'); *Westmede* e14
(v. **mǽd**); *La Whele* 1553 (from **hwēol** 'wheel' in one or other of its
senses); *on an White Wey* 891 (14) (v. **hwīt, weg**); *Wibbancrowe* 941
(1338–40), *Wybbecre* c.1325 (from the OE pers.n. *Wibba* (cf.
Redin 108), probably with **crōh²** 'nook, corner, narrow valley'; this name is possibly to
be associated with the first el. of Crowthorne Lane (6″) *supra*); *on þan
southerne Wistonwey* 941 (14) (thought by Grundy **1** 260 to be corrupt for
hwītan weg (cf. prec.), in which case this name is to be identified with
White Way (6″) *supra*); *(on) widdisgate* 891 (14), 891 (1338–40) (v. **geat**;
the first el. is probably an OE pers.n., cf. *Widi*, etc (Redin 159)); *on
windberghes* 891 (14), *Wyndberghs* 891 (1338–40) (in the Anglo-Saxon
bounds of Plush, corresponding to *La Wynburgh* c.1325 in the bounds of
Buckland N. hundred and to *Wynebarough*' n.d. (e15) in the bounds of
Lyscombe in Cheselbourne par. *supra, v.* **wind¹** 'wind', **beorg** 'barrow,
hill'; the next point to *La Wynburgh* in the hundred bounds is *La
Wyndyethorne* c.1325, *v.* **windig, þorn**); *bi wirtrone* 891 (14), *Wirtrove* 891
(1338–40) (v. **wyrt-truma** 'root, root-stock', *-e* representing either dat.sg.
-an or dat.pl. *-um*); *Withelescombe* e14 (v. **cumb**); *on an withi* 941 (14) (v.
wīðig 'willow'); *Wodelond* 1436, *the Wood* 1675 (v. **wudu, land**);
Wykmers(s)he e14, *Wykemersch'* heved l14, (common called) *Wykemarshe*
e16 (v. **wīc** '(dairy) farm', **mersc**); *cultura Upe Yerdbury* e14 (perhaps
from **eorð-burh** 'earthwork', cf. the forms for Yarborough, -burgh L
(DEPN), with **upp** 'upon'); *over yfre* 891 (14), *Ifre* 891 (1338–40) (v. **yfer**
'edge or brow of a hill').

Mappowder

MAPPOWDER (ST 735060)
Mapledre 1086 DB (3 ×), *Mapeldra* 1088–95 BrutC,
  1100–3 (1332) Ch, c.1155 BrutC, 1155–8 (1332) Ch, (*apud*)
  mapeldream 1121 AC, *Mapoldre* 1189 AD IV, *Mapeldre*
  1216 ClR, 1222 FF, *Mapheldre* 1231 ib (p), *Mapeldur'*
  1258 For
Mapaudre m12 Douce, *Mapodr(e)* 13 GlastR, 1236 Fees,
  1268 Ass, 1297 Ipm, 1332 SR, *Mapudr(e)* 1227 FF,
  1256 Hutch³, 1291 Tax, 1386 Pat, 1428 FA, *Mapedre*
  1244 Ass (p), 1281 Fine, *Mappodre* 1251 Pap, *Mapeudre*
  1346 Cl, *East-, West Mapoder* 1414 Hutch³
Mapwod' (sic) 1226 Cur
Maupodr(e) 1227 FF, 1268 Ass, 1305 Ipm, *Maupudre* 1249
  FF, 1260 Pat (p), 1270 For, 1280, 1288 Ass, 1303 FA,

1307 FF, 1311 (15) *ForReg*
Marpedereye (sic) 1280 *Ass*
Mapoudre 1280 *Ass* (p), 1303 FA, 1328 Ipm *et freq* to 1449
  BM I, *Mapowdre* 1438 Cl, 1442 *Ilch*, 1447 BM I,
  Mapowder 1446 Pat *et freq* to 1567 Hutch[3], *Mapouwdre*
  1450 Cl, *Mapouder* 1497 *Ilch, Estmapowder* 1504 Ipm
Maupoudr(e) 1274, 1330 Pat, 1338–40 Glast, 1399 Cl,
  Mawpowder 1547 *Ct, Maypowder* 1575 Saxton

'(Place at) the maple-tree', *v.* **mapuldor, ēast, west**, cf.
East Town(e) (*in Mapouder*) 1543, 1546 Hutch[3]. DB
Mapertune (f.75, Exon -*tona*) is also identified with
Mappowder by C. & F. Thorn, *Domesday Book: Dorset*,
Phillimore, 1983, cf. the comment s.n. Mapperton **2** 56; the
two names may have been confused, or the form with **tūn**
may represent a genuine alternative.

(OLD) BOYWOOD FM (ST 736093, 732079)
La Hulle 1274 Drew, *Hulle* 1290 Ch, c.1325 *GlastE*, 1360
  Cl, 1381 Fine, 1382, 1405 Cl, *Hille* 1301 Banco (Drew),
  Hull alias Candel Hull alias Boywood 1624 Hutch[3], *Hull
  or Boyswood* 1795 Boswell, *Hull, Candel Hull or
  Boywood* 1869 Hutch[3]
Boywode 1494, *Beywood* 1559 *Seymer, Boywood* 1642
  Bundy
Boyford 1811 OS (2 ×)

The earlier name is from **hyll** 'hill', probably referring to
the small hill just W of Boywood Fm. *Candel Hull* is
probably a spurious form, arising from a misunderstanding
of contexts such as that in 1382 Cl, where the *Wake* family
are recorded as holding the 'manors of *Caundelle* (= Caundle
Wake in Bps. Caundle par. *infra*), *Hulle* and *Stoke Wake* (=
Stoke W. par. *supra*)'. The later name *Boywood* may be from
the *Boys* family ('who seem to have had some concern in this
parish' Hutch[3] **3** 725), but it is perhaps more likely that the
first el. is **boi(a)** 'boy, servant' or the OE pers.n. *Boia, v.*
wudu.

THURNWOOD DAIRY (*Dairy* 1811 OS) & FM (*Turnwood Farm*
1811 OS) (ST 723049), *Thurnet* 1268 *Ass* (p), *Thurnet(t)*

1428 Hutch³, 1540, 1597, 1608 all *Bundy*, 1624 Hutch³ (*-als. Capon Hill*), 1795 Boswell, 1869 Hutch³ (*-or Thurnead*), *Thorn-, Thurnwodd*' 1567, *Thornet, Thornenett* 1604, *Thurnwood Comon*' 1632, *Thornewood* 1648, *Thurnehead* 1655, *Thurnett pownd* 1663 all *Bundy, v.* **þyrnet** 'a thorn copse', with **pund** 'pound', cf. *Capon Hill infra*; *-wood* is the result of folk etymology.

BAKER'S LANE. COCKROAD COPSE, *-Coppice* 1841 *TA, v.* **cocc-rodu** 'clearing where woodcocks were netted'. COW LEAZE STALL, cf. (*Common & Home*) *Cowleaze* 1841 *TA, v.* **cū, lǽs** 'pasture'. DAIRY HO, *Dairy* 1811 OS. DEVILS WOOD LANE, cf. (*the water in*) *Evills Wood* 1602, 1655 *Bundy, Evils Wood* 1811 OS, *Evils Wood Cowleaze* 1841 *TA*, probably from **ǣwiell** 'source of a stream', with reference to the small stream (no doubt the *water* of 1602) rising just W of the lane, cf. The Evils Brk 530. HAMMOND STREET FM, *Hamondes londes* 1536, *Hamond(es) Streete* 1602, 1663 all *Bundy, Hammond's* 1795 Boswell, *Hammond Street* 1811 OS, *Hammond's Lands* 1869 Hutch³, from the family of Walter *Hamond* 1297, 1321 ib, *-Hamund*' 1332 SR, *v.* **land, strǣt** (here probably in the sense 'hamlet'). NAG'S HEAD INN, *Nags Head* 1811 OS, *Nagshead Inn & Md* 1841 *TA*. PARSONAGE FM, *Parsonage* 1811 OS, cf. 'the rectory of *Mappodre*' 1251 Pap, *Parsonage Cowleaze* 1841 *TA*, Rectory *infra*. PLACE FM on site of MAPPOWDER COURT. ST PETER & ST PAUL'S CHURCH, cf. 'the church of *Mapudre*' 1282 Banco (Drew), 'the church' 1307 FF, *eccl*' *de Mapowdre* 1442 *Ilch, le Churchehouse* 1540, *cot*' *voc*' *Kytt Martyns Haies als Le Church(eh)owse* 1602, (*the well in the middle of the*) *Church Streete* 1655, 1663 all *Bundy, v.* **cirice, hūs**, *Kyttmartyns Hayes infra*. SAUNDERS DAIRY HO, *Saunders* 1811 OS, cf. *Saunders Great Md* 1841 *TA*, John *Saunders* 1519 Hutch³, Humphrey *Saunders* 1600 *Bundy*. SHORT WD, 1811 OS, *Shortwode* 1282 Banco (Drew), cf. *Shortwood Coppice, Short Wood Grd* 1841 *TA, v.* **sc(e)ort, wudu**. STILES FM, cf. *Mr George Stiles close called Linche* 1632 *Bundy, v.* the f.n. Lynch *infra*. STOKE LANE, from Stoke W. par. *supra*. TAYLOR'S LANE. TOWN'S KNAP, *v.* **cnæpp** 'hillock'. WEST-

FIELDS, *Westfyldes* 1536, *Westfild'*, *-fyld'* 1569, *-feild* 1648
all *Bundy, Gt & Middle West Fd* 1841 *TA, v.* **west, feld.**

FIELD-NAMES

The undated forms are 1841 *TA* 140. Spellings dated m12, 1373 are
Douce, 1189 AD IV, 1270 *For*, 1300, 1336 Banco (Drew), e14, 1309 Ass
(Drew), c.1325 *GlastE*, 1327 *SR*, 1332 SR, 1340 NI, 1536, 1537, 1540,
1547, 1567, 1569, 1595, 1597, 1600, 1602, 1604, 1605, 1632, 1633, 1642,
1648, 1653, 1655, 1663, 1698 *Bundy*, 1547[2], 1548 *Ct*, 1664 HTax, 1795
Boswell, and the rest Hutch[3].

(a) Abthorpe and Rawlins' 1795 (*Abthorp and Rawlins, or Hawkey's
Lands* 1869, cf. Edward *Abthorp* 1472, Richard *Bayly als.* Rawlins 1473,
Richard *Rawling* 1475, *Hawky's Lands* 1528, *Hawk(e)s Lands* 1598, 1624);
(Lt) Back Cl, Cokers Back Cl (*Mr Cokers Close called Back Close* 1632, cf.
Cokers' *infra*); Barnetts Grd; Barn Md; Berrys (perhaps to be associated
with (*la*) *Bere*, etc *infra*); Binghams Md (*Bingham's* (*Lands*) 1795, 1869, cf.
Robert *de Bingham* 1256, Robert *Byngham* 1343); Black Pits (*terr' voc'
Blackpittes* 1633, *v.* **blæc, pytt**); Bloosberry; Bottom Md; Brick Yd;
Broadends; Broadley Lains & Md (*Brodley, Brodly Meade* 1632, *v.* **brād,
lēah, leyne** 'tract of arable'); Broke 5 & 6 Acres (*v.* **brōc** 'brook'); Broom
Hills Pit; Browns Cl; Bryers Hills; Bully Moor (*Bullimore* 1648, *v.* **mōr,**
perhaps with **bula** and **(ge)hæg**); Chanters Md; Cokers' 1795 (cf. John
Coker 1490, *v.* Hutch[3] 3 722); Colehorn (*aquam* [*voc'*] *Colhourne Water als.
Colhourne bridge* 1595, *Colehorne gate* 1602, *v.* **horn** 'horn-shaped piece of
land', first el. perhaps **cōl[2]** 'cool' though other els. are possible); Colliers
Hill & Lake (*Colliers Hill* 1663); Common Drove; Gt, Hr, Lr & Middle
Common (*Great Common, the Little Common* 1698); Common Md;
Coombs Md; (Long) Corshals, Corshals Ham (*Costalle* 1309, *Costelham*
1548, cf. John *Costalle* 1327, *-Costal* 1332, probably
'site of cottages' from **cot** and **st(e)all**, cf. Costal Sr 77, with **hamm**);
Long Crates, Broad & Hr Crofts (*v.* **croft**); Cross Cmn (cf. John *atte
Crouche* 1336, *v.* **atte, crūc[3]** 'cross'); Culverlands (*v.* **culfre** 'dove');
Devon Hill; Drove Way; 8 Acres; 11 Acres; Fern Cl; 5 Acres; Forest; 4
Acres; Hr & Lr Furlong; Furze Brooks; Furzey Cmn; Gee Hay; Gill Hill
(Md) (*Gale Hill* 1632, 1648); Gilvershays; Glebe Md; Groves; Gulley Md;
Ham (*v.* **hamm** 'enclosure'); Hang Pce (*v.* **hang**); Hedge Row; High Grd;
Hilly Grd; Home Cmn, Md & Pce; Horse Langs (*Horselines* 1633, *v.*
leyne); House Cl, Lr House Grd; Humbers, Humber Wd 8 & 7 Acres (*v.*
Humber Wd in Melcombe H. par. *supra*); Hunts Md; Jack Thomas; (Lt)
Jones's (cf. Henry *Jones* 1540); Kiddles (cf. William *Cetel* Hy 8, *-Kittel*
1664); Kitchen Gdn; Laborers Ho and Gdn; Lime Kiln; Lines (*v.* **leyne**);
Littleton or Dacombe 1795, Littleton's or Dacomb's Manor 1869 (from
the family of Nicholas *Littleton* 1318, John *Daccomb* 1519); Loaders (cf.
widow *Lodder* 1664, Mill Md *infra*); Long hills; Long Md; Lynch (*Linche*
1632, *v.* **hlinc** 'ridge'); Madgore (Corn Grd); Malletts Orchd; Mareston;

Mayers Md (*Mayers Mead(e)* 1632, 1633, *-Meadowe* 1642, a surname); Middle Pce; Millers Md; Millhams, Gt & Lt Mill Md (*Milhames alias Swettershames* 1587, *Andrew Loders Millmeade* 1655, William *atte Mulle* 1327, 1332, *v.* **myln** 'mill', **hamm, mǣd, atte**, cf. Loaders *supra*; *Swetter* is no doubt a surname); Mitchells Md (cf. William *Michell* 1664); Nappy Grd (*v.* **cnæppig**); Newburgh's Lands 1869 (cf. John *Newburgh* 1432); New Cl; North Fds (*in campo boriali* 1537, *Northefyld', Northfild'* 1569); Notton Hays (*Northton* 1540, *-towne* 1567, 'north farm', *v.* **norð, tūn**, cf. Suttons *infra*); Nursery; Orchard (*le Orchardende* 1540, *v.* **orceard, ende**[1]); Parish Md & Pound (cf. Thurnwood *supra*); (Gt) Horse Pendalls, -Rendalls (one or other of the spellings is an error); Pigs Orchd (perhaps to be associated with *Pyckes Tenement* 1642); Pikey Cl; Pitmoor (5 Acres); Pond Md; Povert Pce (from Povert Bridge 2 103, earlier forms for which are *Polford(e)* 1256, c.1325, *Poulford'* e14, suggesting a first el. **pōl**[1] 'pool (in a river)'); Gt & Lt Quar Cl (*v.* **quarre**); Row Grd; Russel(l)'s (Lands) 1795, 1869 (cf. *domum Willelmi Russel* m12, Richard *Russel* 1207, Eustace *Rossel* 1270); 7 Acres; 17 Acres; Shepherds; Sidelings; Sinneyshays; 6 Acres; Smith Hams; Snipes Willows; Southhills; Lord Spencer's 1795 (cf. John *Spencer* 1745); Spray Md (cf. *Sprage* 1537, possibly **sprǣg** 'brushwood, twigs'); Spring Pce; Stony Lds (*Stoni(e)londe, -land* 1300, cf. *Stony Close* 1633, *v.* **stānig**); (Gt) Sturts (*Stert* 1653, *Stertland* 1663, *v.* **steort** 'tail of land'); Hr, Middle & Wet Suttons (*Suttons* 1537, 1648, possibly 'south farm', from **sūð** and **tūn**, cf. Notton Hays *supra*); Sweatmans; Syward's (Lands) 1795, 1869 (cf. John *Syward* 1395); 10, 30, 3 & 12 Acres; Walley's (Lands) 1795, 1869 (cf. Ingelram *de Walleys* 1310, Roger *le Walessch'* 1373); Warren; Way Grd; White Pits; Wolve Md (*v.* **wulf**); Woolands (*Wollondes Bridge, -gate, -yeate* 1597, probably a surname from Woolland par. *supra, v.* **brycg, geat**).

(b) 'place called *Attehalre'* 1300 (probably for *-nalre, v.* **atten, alor** 'alder'); *Barbers Hayes Well* 1655, *Barbors Well* 1663 (a surname with **(ge)hæg** and **well(a)**); (*pastur voc'*) (*la*) *Bere* 1256, *atte Bere* (p) 1327, 1332, 1340, *Berehyll'* 1536, *Barehill, Beryhill* (*gate*) 1540, *Beryhill yate* 1547[2], *Ber(e)hil(l) Lane* 1567, 1595, *Berhill' Yeat, Berie Hill'* 1595, *Berehill'* (*gate*), *Bery Hill' Comon'* 1597, *Bearehill* 1600, *Bere(hi)ll* 1605 (*v.* **bearu** 'wood, grove' or **bǣr**[2] '(woodland) pasture', **atte** 'at the', **hyll, geat, lane**; *Brode More gate* 1597 (*v.* **brād, mōr**); *Capon' Hill'* 1595, 1600 (*v.* **capon**); *atte chapele* (p) 1373 (*v.* **atte, chapel(e)**); *Cleylane* 1375, *Clay-, Clea-, Clee Lane* 1597, *Claielane* 1600 (*v.* **clǣg** 'clay', **lane**); *Coule Hayes* 1597, *Could' Hayes* 1604, *Coldhayes* 1605 (**hǣs** 'brushwood' or a pl. form of **(ge)hæg** 'enclosure'; for the first el. cf. Colehorn *supra*); *dicudemede* m12, *Dikedemede* 1189 ('meadow with a ditch', *v.* **dīc, -ede, mǣd**); *la Eldelond* 1256 (*v.* **eald, land**); *Feldyngfordesbrigge* c.1325 (probably 'bridge at the ford of the dwellers in open country', *v.* **filde**[2] (gen.pl. *fildena*), **ford, brycg**); *Flowerlandes* 1633 (cf. the analogous Flower Lds 1 343); *Hancokes lease* 1632 (*v.* **lǣs**); *Hatherly* 1422 (probably 'hawthorn clearing', *v.* **haguþorn, lēah**); *Inhams* 1597 (*v.* **innōm**); *jan'* ('gate') *apud By Kinges Barrowe* 1605 (from **cyning** and **beorg** with **bī** used elliptically in the sense '(place) near'); *Kyttmartyns Hayes* 1597, *Kytt Martyns Haies* als. *Le Church(eh)owse* 1602 ('Christopher Martyn's enclosures', *v.* **(ge)hæg**, St Peter & St Paul's Church *supra*); *le Lease grownd* 1632 (*v.* **læs**); *Oatehills* 1663 (*v.* **āte**); *Prior's Close* 1512 (belonged to the priory of Wilkswood 1 37); *Senehurd* 1329 (possibly for *Seue-* and thus perhaps 'seven yards of land', *v.* **seofon, gierd**); *John Stountes howse* 1663; *Sytenmede* 1431, 1439 (*v.* **mǣd**, first el. possibly **seten** 'plantation'); *Thornehay* 1632 (*v.* **þorn, (ge)hæg**, cf. foll. and Thurnwood *supra*); *Thornehyll'* 1536, *Thorn(e)hill, Thornill Comon'* 1540, *Thorne Hill* 1595, 1600, *Thornehull' Common'* 1597 (*v.* **hyll**, cf. prec.); *Towne Crosse* 1595, (*the streete called*) (*le*) *Towne Crosse gate* 1597, 1602 (*v.* **tūn, cros, geat**); *Westmore* 1569 (*v.* **mōr**); *Wunckett Hill* 1633, 1648.

Pulham

East Pulham in this par. was in Bindon Liberty (1 107–8)

PULHAM (ST 712085), EAST & WEST PULHAM
Poleham 1086 DB (2×), Exon, 1279 Ch, *Polham* 1234 (1279) Ch, 1251, 1260 Cl, 1270 *For*, 1297 Pat, 1331 Ipm, *Westpolham* 1332 SR
Puleham 1130 PR, 1213 PatR, 1291 Tax, 1428 FA, *Pullam* 1212 Fees, 1244 *Ass* (*West-*), 1440, 1466 Pat (*Est-, West-*), *Pulham* Hy 3 (14) Cerne, 1237 Cl, 1244 *Ass* (*West-*), 1258 *For* (*Est-*), 1268 *Ass et passim, Pulleham West* 1258 *For, Pullham* 1270 *For*, 1547 *Ct* (*Est-, West-*), *Est Pulhaump* 1412 FA, *Easte Pulham* 1567 *Glyn Westpoulham* 1394 Drew

'Homestead or enclosure by the pools', from **pōl** (gen.pl. -*a*) (with some influence from the synonymous **pull**) and **hām** or **hamm**, cf. Pulham Nf (DEPN); the R. Lydden flows through the SE of the par. and another stream forms the NW boundary. The two DB manors of *Poleham* (ff. 79, 81b) are probably to be identified with West Pulham and East Pulham respectively (DBGazetteer 120, 128, cf. VCHDo 3 93 and discussion under Haselbury B. par. 2 100), *v.* **ēast, west**, Cannings Court *infra*.

CANNINGS COURT (ST 718077), *mes' . . . q' Will' Canon . . . ten'* 1440 *Ct*, (land called) *le Court* 1544 Hutch[3], *venell' voc' Cannynge* 1548 *Ct*, 'manor and the site of it called *Canning's*

Court' 1566 Hutch[3], *Canning Court Farme* 1623 *DCMRent,
Canen Court, Farm called Canning Cort, Cannen Court Lane*
1784 *SalisT, Pulham W. or Canning's Court* 1795 Boswell,
The Manor of West Pulham or Canning's Court 1869 Hutch[3],
cf. *the Court Gates* 1784 *SalisT*, named from the family of
Thomas *Canon* 1327 *SR*, 1332 SR (in the earlier roll he is
the taxpayer with the highest assessment in West Pulham), *v.*
court 'a large house, a manor'. In an interesting footnote
Hutch[3] **3** 736 recognizes the correct original form of the
name, but explains *Canons* as alluding to the possession of
this manor by Cirencester Abbey (as in 1212 Fees).

GRANGE FM (ST 717090), named from a grange or granges
belonging to Bindon Abbey (**1** 189), referred to as (*usque ad*)
Grangias monachorum de Binnedune Hy 3 (14) Cerne (in the
bounds of Blackmoor Forest *infra*), *grangiam abbatis de
Bynendon de Pulham* 1237 Cl, *v.* **grange** 'an outlying farm
belonging to a religious house where crops were stored'.

CASTLE BARN. CROSS ROADS FM. DAIRY (lost), 1811 OS, cf.
Caning Court Dary House 1784 *SalisT*, *v.* Cannings Court
supra. EASTFIELD PLANT. FURZE HILL, 1811 OS. GRANGE
COPSE, *Grangewood* 1546 Hutch[3], from Grange Fm *supra*.
HALSEY ARMS (P.H.). HARTMOOR FM, *Hartmoor* 1811 OS, *v.*
heorot, mōr. HUMBER WD, 1811 OS, *Humbrewood* 1544
Hutch[3], another instance of the pre-English stream-name
Humber with reference to the small stream (now unnamed)
that skirts the wood. KINGSTAG BRIDGE, *Kingstake brydg* 16
Shepherd[2], *Kingstack Bridge* 1607 *DROMap, King's Stagge
Bridge* 1732 Coker, *King Stagg Bridge* 1869 Hutch[3], from
Kingstag in Lydlinch par. *infra*, *v.* **brycg.** LIPGATE FM,
perhaps to be associated with Adam *atte Lupehiate* 1270 *For*
(mentioned in connection with Blackmoor Forest), *v.*
hlīep-geat 'a leap-gate for deer and other animals'. MANOR
FM. NODDY WD. NORTH DAIRY HO. PARSON'S BRIDGE.
PELLWELL FM, near the source of a small stream, probably
from **pyll** 'pool, stream' and **well(a)** 'spring'. PICKETT'S
CTGS & FM. PULHAM COMMON, 1811 OS, cf. *Qeenes Commen*
1569–74 *Map* and lands in Pulham held of Queen Elizabeth I
in chief in 1593 Hutch[3] **3** 737. PULHAM GORSE & LAKE (*v.*

lacu 'stream'). EAST PULHAM FM. RANKSBOROUGH GORSE.
RECTORY, cf. *parsonage of Pulham* 1623 *DCMRent*. REDHILLS
PIT. ST THOMAS A BECKET'S CHURCH, cf. *ecclesiam de Pulham*
Hy 3 (14) Cerne, 'the church of *Pulham*' 1361 Pat, *the church
howse* 1623, *þe churchowse* 1625 *DCMRent*. TOWN'S END FM,
Towns End 1811 OS, on the par. boundary, *v*. **tūn, ende**[1].
WITHY BED.

FIELD-NAMES

The undated forms are 1784 *SalisT*. Spellings dated Hy 3 (14) are Cerne,
c.1325 are *GlastE*, 1327 *SR*, 1332 SR, 1340 NI, 1420 AD III, 1440, 1547
Ct, 1541, 1567, 1582 *Glyn*, 1546, 1645 Hutch[3], 1624 *DCMRent*, and 1648
Bundy.

(a) 8 Acres; 11 Acres of Meadow Grd; 5 Acres; 5 and 6 Acres of Glebe;
Maggses; the New Inclosures; Oxlain; 6 Acres; 10 Acres.

(b) *Le*(*z*)-, *the Beare* 1541, 1567, 1582 (*v*. **bearu** 'wood, grove' or **bǣr**[2]
'woodland pasture'); *Breach*(*e*) (*Meade*) 1541, 1582 (*v*. **brǣc** 'land broken
up for cultivation', **mǣd**); *Broade Mead* 1582 (*v*. **brād**); *atte Bro*(*u*)*k*(') (p)
1327, 1332 (*v*. **atte** 'at the', **brōc** 'brook'); *Buryfurlang* 1440 (*v*. **bury**
'manor house', **furlang**); *Chettecrofte* 1567, 1582 (*v*. **croft**, first el. possibly
a surname); *Cleylane* 1440 (*v*. **clǣg**); *Cotes* 1624 (*v*. **cot**); (*terr*' *voc*') *Farme
Landes* 1541, 1582, *Ferme landes* 1567 (*v*. **ferme**); *pastur*' *claus*' *voc*'
Ferthyng et Sciling 1440 (no doubt with reference to a rent, *v*. **fēorðung,
scilling**); *ten*' *voc*' *Frankelens* 1541, *Franklyns* 1582 (a surname); *ij closes . . .
called the Furlonges* 1567 (*v*. **furlang**); *Godesheye* 1440 (from **(ge)hæg**
'enclosure' with a surname); (*East Pulham*) *Grove* 1546 (*v*. **grāf(a)**, par.
name *supra*);*Halewfeld* 1440 (*v*. **feld**, first el. probably **h(e)alh** 'nook,
corner of land', cf. *Pulhammeshile infra*); *Hidemead* 1541, *Hyde Meade*
1567, 1582 (*v*. **hīd** 'a hide of land', **mǣd**); *claus*' *voc*' *Hilles* 1541, *Hylles*
1567, 1582 (probably from the *Hull* family who held the manor of East
Pulham in the 14th cent., *v*. Hutch[3] 3 736, cf. also Edward *Vppehull*(*e*)
1327, 1332, 'upon the hill', *v*. **uppan**); *Hokefurlang* 1440 (*v*. **hōc** 'angle,
bend'); *the Home Close* 1582; *Hurdle close* 1582 (*v*. **hyrdel**); *in the lane* (p)
1332 (*v*. **lane**); *Lathards Landes* 1541 (spelling -*ards* doubtful); (*the*)
Long(*e*) *close, Longele siue Longe close* 1582 (*v*. **lang**[1], **clos(e), lēah**);
Malenclose 1541, *Molyn-, Melyn*' *Close*(*s*) 1582 (the surname *Malin* or
Molin, cf. Thomas *Molyns* 1546); *Medehawes* 1440 (*v*. **mǣd, haga**[1]
'enclosure'); *Meregrauesyate* 1440 (*v*. **(ge)mǣre** 'boundary', **grāf(a)**
'grove', **geat** 'gate'); *Mulhammede Calfhey* 1420 (*v*. **myln, hamm, mǣd,
c(e)alf, (ge)hæg**); *Northehill*' 1541, *Northe Hyll*', *Northills* 1582 (*v*. **hyll**);
North(*e*)*meade* 1541, 1582, *Normead* 1645 (*v*. **mǣd**); *claus*' *voc*' *Orcherd*
1541, *Orchardes* 1567 (*v*. **orceard**); *Paynes* (*howse*) 1648; *Pit Close* 1582;
Pontem de Pulhammeshile, -hyle c.1325, *in la Hyle* (p) 1327, *Southhyle*
1420, *the Hyle* 1567, *Hele grounde* 1582 (probably from the WSax dat.sg.

form *hēale* of **h(e)alh** 'nook, corner of land', with par. name *supra*); *Redlane* 1541, 1582 (*v.* **rēad**); *terr'* . . . *voc' Rogers* 1541 (a surname); *hortum nuper Stevens* 1582 (cf. Walter *Stephens* 1541); *(aquam de) Taleford* Hy 3 (14) (*v.* **ford**, first el. possibly analogous with the r.n. *Tale* D 13); *domum Waremanni* Hy 3 (14) (cf. William *Warman* 1327); *Way Close* 1582 (*v.* **weg**); *Waterslade* 1547 (*v.* **wæter, slæd**); *atte Yate* (p) 1327, 1332, *in le Yete* (p) 1340 (*v.* **atte** 'at the', **geat** 'gate, gap').

Wootton Glanville

WOOTTON GLANVILLE (6"), GLANVILLES WOOTTON (1") (ST 680082)

Widetone 1086 DB
Wotton(') 1268 *Ass*, 1270 *For* (p), 1288 *Ass*, 1315 Pat *et freq* to 1547 *Ct, Wottun* 1270 *For*
Wotton' Clauyle (sic) 1280, *-Glaunuill'* 1288 *Ass, -Glannvill* (probably for *Glaun-*) 1317 FF, *-Glaunvyle* 1337 Ipm, *-Glamvyle* 1340 NI *et freq* with variant spellings *Glan-, Glame-, -vyll, -vile* to 1558 *PlR, Wottingglayvile* (sic) 1291 Tax, *Wotton Glaunvyle alias Wolverne Wotton* 1428 FA, *Wotton Glanf(f)yld(e)* 1543, 1545, 1546, *-feylde* 1597 *PlR, Wotton' Glandevile alias Gland(e)viles Wotton'* 1625 *AddCh*
Wolfrenewotton, Wolvernewotton 1303 FA, *Wolverene Wotton* 1311 Pat, *Wolvernewotte* (sic) 1317 *MiltC, Wolvern Wotton* 1346 FA
Woutton Glaunvylle 1344 Pat, *Wootton Glanvyll* 1533, 1553 *PlR, -Glandfeild* 1660 *Bent*
Glamvileswotton 1396 FF, *-uyles-, -vyles-* 1424 *Weld*[1], 1431 FA, *Glanvile-* 1428 ib, *Glanvyll' Wotton* 1431 *Weld*[1], *Glainveldes-* 1499 *CampbCh, Claundeveldis Wotton'* 1500 *AddCh, Glanfyld-, Glanfild Wotton* 1535 VE, *Glande feldes-* 1569–74 *Map, Glanfe(i)lde(s) Wotton* 1575 Saxton, 1606 (1770) *Lane*, 1617 *DuCo, Glandfeild' Wotten* 1664 HTax, *Glanvilles Wooton* 1811 OS

'Farm in or near a wood', *v.* **wudu, widu, tūn**, one of the three Do pars. so named; it is in Blackmoor Forest *infra*. The manorial affix is from the *Glanville* family, cf. Geoffrey *de Gla(u)nvile* 1258, 1270 *For*, Mabel *de Glamuill* 1268 *Ass*,

Henry *de Glaunvyle* 1303 FA, etc; the surname is from Glanville in Normandy (Tengvik 89–90). The alternative affix *Wolfrene-*, etc, apparently in use only in the first half of the 14th cent., probably represents the well-recorded OE fem. pers.n. *Wulfrūn* as suggested by Fägersten 208, although no one with this name has been noted in connection with this place, cf. DEPN s.nn. Wollerton Sa, Wolverhampton St.

BLACKMORE CTGS (ST 683097), named from the former manor of *Blakemor(e)* 1258 *For*, 1267 Pat, 1298 FF, 1344, 1349 Ipm *et freq* to 1445 *Weld*[1], FF, *Blakamore* 1396 IpmR, 1397 (1792) *DCMDeed*, 'dark-coloured moor or marshy ground', *v.* **blæc, mōr**; this gave its name to foll. as well as to Blackmoor Forest & Vale *infra, v.* also Newland and *Newton Montacute* both *infra*.

BLACKMORE FORD BRIDGE (ST 675096), *Blakemoresforde* c.1325 *GlastE* (in the bounds of Buckland Newton hundred), 1473 *Digby*, *(village of) Blackmores Forde* 1583 *SPDom*, *Black(e)more Ford* 1677 *Digby, Blackmore's Ford* [Bridge] 1791 Boswell, *v.* **ford** and prec.; the ford is across Caundle Brook.

BROAD ALDERS COPPICE (ST 686074), *Southbradenalles* 1423, *-alres* 1424, 1430, *-aller* 1442, *Northbradenallers* 1435, *Suthbradenalr'* 1444, *Southbrodenallars* 1445, 1450, *Southbrodnallers* 1451, *-allars* 1452 all *Weld*[1], *Broad Alders or Park Coppice* 1838 *TA*, cf. *les Shortealres* 1373 Hastings, *v.* **alor** 'alder', **sūð, norð, brād** (wk.obl. *-an*) 'large', **sc(e)ort** 'short'.

NEWLAND (ST 695085), OVER NEWLAND FM, NEWLAND LANE, *New Land* 1343, *Newland* ('manor of *Blakemore* called-') 1377 Hutch[3], *Blakamore maner' voc' Newelond* 1396 IpmR, 'the manor of *Blakemore* called *Neulonde*' 1409 Cl, *Newlond'* 1439, *Neulond'* 1452 *Weld*[1], *(vico de) Overnewland, Newland Strete* 1542, *Nether-, Overnewland* 1543 *Ct, Wootton Newland* (a tithing), *Newland or Newton Montacute* (a manor, tithing and farm) 1795 Boswell, *Newland* 1811 OS, *Newland alias Newton Montacute alias*

Blackmore Manor 1869 Hutch³. 'New land', from **nīwe** and **land**, no doubt with reference to land in Blackmoor Forest cleared for cultivation, with **uferra** 'higher', **neoðerra** 'lower', **strǣt**, *v.* Blackmore Ctgs *supra* and foll.

NEWTON MONTACUTE (lost, probably identical with or adjacent to prec.), 1554 Hutch³, 1795 Boswell (*Newland or-*), *Nyeutone Mountagu* 1344, *New-*, *Nyw-*, *Niweton' Mo(u)ntagu* 1345–47, *Niwe-* 1348, *New-* 1358, *Neuton* 1363 (*-Mountagu*), 1367, *Neu-*, *Newe-*, *Nyweton in Blakemore* 1367–76 all *Hastings, Newton Montague* 1428 Hutch³, *-Mountagu* 1430 Cl, *-Mowntagu* 1542, *-Mountegu(e)* 1543, 1544 *Ct.* 'New farm or estate', *v.* **nīwe**, **tūn**, cf. prec. and Blackmoor Forest *infra*. The affix is from the *Monteacute* family: Simon *Monteacute* had a grant from the king of 10 shillings rent in *Blakemore* in 1290, and William *Monteacute* had 'a certain waste in the Forest of *Blakemore*' in 1320 and held *New Land* at his death in 1343 (Hutch³ 3 292, 744). It is possible that *Westneweton* 1257 FF belongs here.

OSEHILL GREEN (ST 665088), *Oswaldeshille* m13 *Salis, -hulle* 1270 *For, Oswoldeshull(e)* 1314 Pat, 1365 *Hastings, Osweldeshulle* 1315 Pat, *Os(e)waldeshull* 1324, 1325 Banco, *Ouseleshull* 1405 Pat, *Osett(e)s Hill* 1546 *Lane, Surv,* oselles 1569–74 *Map, Osside hill* Jas 1 *TRMB, Offeild Hill* (sic) 1606 (1770) *Lane, Osydshill* 1612 *Bent, Osse(r)d(e)s Hill* 1617 *Add, DuCo, Osell* [Bridge] 1791, *Osehill* 1795 Boswell, *Ose Hill Green* 1800 *EnclA, Ossedshill or Osehill Green, Osehill, Odeeshill or Oakhill* 1869 Hutch³. 'Ōsweald's hill', from the OE pers.n. *Ōsweald* and **hyll**. There was a mill here, referred to as *Osewoldeshullemulle* c.1325 *GlastE* (in the bounds of Buckland Newton hundred), *Oushullesmulle* 1424 *Weld*¹, cf. *Walt' Muleward'* . . . *tenuit unu' molend'* 1363 *Hastings, cursu aque ad molend'* 1424, *Lytel-* 1423, *Litel-, Ouer Mulcroft, Milcroftesclos, -mede* 1424, (*Litil-, Litul-, Ouer)mullecrofte* 1430, *Milcroftmed(d)oo* 1445, *Milcroftdiche* 1446, *Milclos* 1447, *Milcroftes* (*alias dict' Dirlokkesmede*) 1451 all *Weld*¹, *Mill Close* 1614 *Bent, v.* **myln**, **lȳtel**, **uferra** 'upper', **croft**, **clos(e)**, **mǣd**, **dīc**, cf. William *Durlok'* 1424, *-Dirlok'* 1452 *Weld*¹.

ALDER MEAD, 1838 *TA*, cf. Broad Alders Coppice *supra*. BASKETT'S FM, cf. Thomas *Basket* Hy 8 Hutch[3]. BIRCH COPPICE. BUTTONS COPPICE, cf. *Buttons Two Fields* 1838 *TA*, William *Budden* 1664 HTax. CHURCH FM, cf. *Church Cl &* *Md* 1838 *TA*, named from St Mary's Church *infra*. COCKROAD, *Cockround* (sic) 1838 *TA*, *v.* **cocc-rodu** 'clearing where woodcocks were netted'. COMMON PLANT. COURT FM, 1811 OS. DARK'S BRIDGE, cf. *Lr Darks, Darts* (sic) 1838 *TA*. DUNNING'S LANE, cf. John *Dunnyng* 1327, Joan *Donnyng* 1332 (both taxed in Pulham par. *supra*), and the f.n. Dunnings in Buckland N. par. *supra*. FERNY KNAP COPPICE, cf. *Knapfurlong'* 1453 *Weld*[1], *v.* **cnæpp** 'hill-top, hillock', **furlang**. GOG & MAGOG (two trees), a Biblical allusion (Ezekiel chapters 38 and 39), cf. Gog Magog Hills Ca 35. GRANGE CTGS, named from Middlemarsh Grange in Minterne M. par. *infra*. GREEN WALL PLANT. HAMPER'S FM, 1811 OS. HARBIN'S FM, cf. *Harbins Md* 1838 *TA*, William *Harbyn* 1546 *Lane, Henricus Harbin . . . ten'* 1649 *Bent*. HAY WD, *Heywode* 1424, 1433, *Hay-* 1451, *Heywod* 1452 all *Weld*[1], *Haywodde* 1550 *PlR*, (*Lt*) *Haywood-, Hayward Coppice* 1838 *TA*, 'enclosed wood', *v.* **(ge)hæg, wudu**, cf. *Heyfurlang('*) 1424, 1444, John *in the Heye* 1434, *le Heye* 1444, 1445 all *Weld*[1], *Lt Hay Md, Lt & Green Hays, Hays Overclose* 1838 TA, all from **(ge)hæg** probably in the sense 'part of the forest (of Blackmoor) fenced off for hunting', with **furlang**. HOLMES'S CORNER. KENNELS LANE. LOADER'S HILL (FM), *Loders Hill* 1811 OS, *Leaders Hill* (sic) 1838 *TA*, from the *Loder* family which owned the manor of Osehill c.1700 (Hutch[3] 3 745). MANOR HO, cf. *Mansion House Lawns* 1838 *TA*. MEAD COPPICE, cf. *Mead* 1838 *TA*. MOATHILLS COPPICE, *Moot Hills, Moot Hill Coppice* 1838 *TA*. MOOR-LAND, cf. *le More* 1446, 1447, *Mouremede* 1423, 1428, *Mo(o)remede* 1426, 1427, *Mor(e)wey* 1423, 1424 all *Weld*[1], *v.* **mōr** 'marshy ground', **mǣd, weg**. MULLETT'S COPPICE, *Mulletts Coppice & Orchd* 1838 *TA*, cf. Ralph *Mulett* 1664 HTax. NEW COVERT. NEW INN. NURSERY LANE. PILLEY'S COPPICE, *Pelless's* 1838 *TA*. PITT'S FM, cf. the *Pitt* family which held part of the manor at some time after 1588 (Hutch[3] 3 744). PURE DROP INN. RABBITS' COPPICE, *Hr & Lr Rabbits, Rabbits Common Pce* 1838 *TA*, cf. John *Robert'*

1547 *Ct.* RANSOM COPPICE, 1838 *TA*, possibly *Remmescombe*, *Remscoombe* 1424 *Weld*[1], which may be analogous with Renscombe 1 65. ROUND CHIMNEYS DAIRY HO & FM, *Round Chimneys* 1811 OS, *Round Chimney Fm* 1838 *TA*, a 'mansion house [so] called from the form of the chimneys' (Hutch[3] 3 745). ST MARY'S CHURCH, *v.* Church Fm *supra.* SANDCLOSE ISLANDS, *Sand Cl* 1838 *TA.* SANDHILLS COPPICE, *Sandhull'*, *Litelsandehull'* 1424, *Sandehyll'* 1433 *Weld*[1], Hr & Lr *Sandhill, Sandhill Coppice* 1838 *TA, v.* l**ȳtel**, **sand**, **hyll**. SMITHY, cf. *Johannes Smyth qui ten' de domino unu' ten' voc' la Smyth* 1372 *Hastings, v.* **smiðõe** 'a smithy'. SOMERSET GATE CTG, on the par. bdy with Holwell which was a detached part of Somerset until 1844. SPLITMEAD COPPICE, *Split Md* 1838 *TA, v.* **split** 'an opening, a gap'. STOCK HILL (LANE), *Stoc-* 1441, *Stokhullane* 1442, *Stokhillane* 1445 all *Weld*[1], cf. *Stockehyll crosse* 1547 *PlR, Stockhill Cl* & *Orchd* 1838 *TA, v.* **hyll**, **lane**, **cros**, first el. probably **stocc** 'tree stump'. WHITE DOWN (COPPICE), *Whitedowne* 1424, *Whyte-do(u)n'* 1439, 1440, *le Whit(e)doun'* 1445, 1448 all *Weld*[1], *Whitdowne* 1553 *PlR*, (*Upr* & *Lr*) *White Down, White Down* (*or Parsons*) *Coppice* 1838 *TA, v.* **hwīt**, **dūn**, presumably a reference to chalky soil. WOOTTON GLANVILLE FM, cf. *messuage called Farm House* 1591 Hutch[3]. GT WOOTTON WD, 1838 *TA*, cf. *Lt Wootton* 1838 *ib, v.* par. name *supra.*

FIELD-NAMES

The undated forms are 1838 *TA* 92. Spellings dated Hy 3 (14) are Cerne, 1270 are *For*, 1317 *MiltC*, c.1325 *GlastE*, 1327 *SR*, 1332 SR, 1340 NI, 1347, 1348, 1352, 1353, 1358, 1359, 1361, 1366, 1368, 1369, 1372, 1376 *Hastings*, 1500 *AddCh*, 1542, 1543, 1548 *Ct*, 1545, 1546, 1547, 1550, 1553 *PlR*, 1554, 1806 Hutch[3], 1569–74 *Map*, 1664 HTax, 1791 Boswell, and the rest *Weld*[1].

(a) Abbs Crate (*v.* **croft**); Bakers Plat (*v.* **plat**[2], cf. John *Baker* 1664); Barn Cl & Md (cf. *Bernham* 1347, *v.* **bere-ærn**, **hamm**); Bottom Cl & Md; Brandy (*v.* Ryalls *infra*); Broad Leaze (*v.* **lǣs**); Broad Md; Brook Flg (*Brokefurlong'* 1450, *v.* **brōc**, **furlang**); Bulls (a farm) 1806; Burts Grd (cf. Henry *Burt* 1664); Caryfoot [Bridge] 1791; Causeway Cl (*v.* **cauce**); Caves Orchd, Caves 2 Acres and 3 Acres; Chantry Md (cf. *Chauntreclos* 1449, Richard *Chaunter* 1448, *v.* **chantry**, **clos(e)**); Charley Md; Coat's; Common Cl, Inclosure, Pce & Pleck (*v.* **plek**); (Orchard) Conygar (*Conyngar* 1446, *v.* **coninger** 'rabbit-warren'); Corn Grd; Cow Leaze (*v.*

lǣs); Cox's Plot (cf. John *Cocks*, William *Cox* 1664); Hr and Lr Croft; Darsells; Daws; Deep Fd (*Sutherdepfeld'* 1433, *Depefelde* 1435, -*fildes* 1452, -*Fylde* 1545, *v.* **dēop** 'deep', **feld, sūðerra** 'more southerly'); Dolly's Plott (*v.* **plot**); Double Cl; Downtons Lane (cf. John *Dounton* 1500); Dry Cl; 8 Acres; Ewe Leaze (*v.* **lǣs**); Fearn Cl (*v.* **fearn** 'fern'); Forbes or Willow Md (cf. *Forber-* 1545, *Verber lane* 1547); Fords (cf. *Wm' Foordes house* 1664); Fox holes and Plant. (*v.* **fox-hol**); Freehold Orchd; Frith (*Frythemede* 1546, cf. also *La Frythehurne, La Frythelake* c.1325 (in bounds of Buckland Newton hundred), *Nywefrith'* 1424, *Newfrythdyche* 1438, *le Neufrith'* 1447, -*freth'* 1448, *v.* **fyrhð** 'wood', **mǣd, hyrne, lacu, nīwe, dīc**); Frog Md; Furlong;Goulds and Straps, Goulds 2 Fds; John *Go(u)lde* 1424, 1437, *ye house of James Gould* 1664, *v.* **strap**); Great Md; Green Cl; Hr & Lr Haggard; Ham (*v.* **hamm**); Gt & Lt Hanging Grd (*v.* **hangende**); Hart's [Bridge] 1791; Hr Hawthorn; Hebditches; Higher Md; Middle & Yonder Hoares (cf. Thomas *Hore* 1542); Home Md; Honey Md; Kitchen Md; Knight Md; Lady Md (*Ladymede* 1424, 1450, *v.* **hlǣfdige, mǣd**, probably with reference to 'Our Lady', cf. St Mary's Church *supra*); (The) Lane; Leak Md; Little Md (*Litulmede* 1450, *v.* **lȳtel, mǣd**); Long Cl & Md; Long Orchd and Fd; Lovelass; Makenhays (*Malken hey* 1424, *Malkynhey* 1447, *v.* **(ge)hæg**, first el. either ME **malkin** 'wench' or the pers.n. *Malkin*, a diminutive of *Mall* (Mary), from which the word derives); Gt & Lt Marvills (*Merefeldde* 1317, (*cursu aque apud*) *Merefeld'* 1422–27, *Murefeld', Merefeldesdich'* 1424, *Meyr' feldesdyche* 1426, *Merefeldysdyche* 1427, *Myryfeld'* 1428, *Myrifeldis dyche* 1435, *Myryfeldys dych(e)* 1436, 1437, *Merfeld'* 1444, *Mirefeld'* 1445, -*fild'* 1448, *Mirifildes* 1450, *Marvylles* 1550, *v.* **feld**, first el. probably **mere** 'pool' (cf. Robert *Attemere de Wottun* 1270, Richard *atte Mere* 1327, 1332), later replaced by or confused with **myrge** 'pleasant'); Middle Cl & Grd; Monks [Bridge] 1791; Mowlands (*v.* **mow**); Nap Cl (**nǣp** 'turnip' or **cnæpp** 'hillock'); Newfoundland (possibly a transferred name, but cf. 1 314); 9 Acres; Oakhill or Cow Leaze, Lt Oakhill (cf. Robert *atte Ok'* 1359, *Okerode* 1450, *v.* **āc, atte, rod**[1], **rodu**); Oat Cl; Old's tenement 1774; Orchard; Paines Acre and Half, 5 Acres Paines, Lr Paines, Paines 2 Acres (*Pain's* [Bridge] 1791); Patty's Coppice, (Hr) Paty's, Two Patys; Hr Pigotts Fd; Pitt Md; Plantation; Platt (*v.* **plat**); Pleck by the Road (*Plick* [Bridge] 1791, *v.* **plek**); Pond Cl; Pound Cl; Pucketts Moor; Rags (*v.* **ragge**); Rough Grd; Rushy Md (*Ryssheymede* 1424, *Russhemede* 1424, 1447, *v.* **riscig, risc, rysc, mǣd**); Ryalls and Brandy (Ryalls may be a surname from a p.n. such as Ryall in Whitchurch C. par. *infra*; Brandy is *ten' voc' Bramdyr'* 1366, *terr' voc' la Brandyre* 1368, probably from ME **brandire(n)** 'a gridiron', used here in some figurative sense such as 'well-ridged field', cf. Brandier W 62); 7 Acres; 7 Yards (*v.* **gierd**); Shelves (*claus' voc' Shulves* 1453, *v.* **scielf, scylf**); Shorts Ctg and Orchd (cf. *Shortysclos* 1439, John *Short* 1424); 6 Acres; 16 Acres; Stall Grd (*v.* **stall**); Starve Orchd (probably denoting poor crops); Stoney Lands (Md) (*Stonylond'* 1424, *Stonilonde* 1434, *v.* **stānig, land**); Straps (*v.* **strap**); Stubby's; Summers' Orchd (cf. John *Somer* 1332); Sweets Md; 10 Acres; Thorne's [Bridge]

1791; 3 Acres; Torrwills; Tuff Md; 12 Acres; Virgins Platt (*v.* **plat**); Wall Orchd; Way Grd; West Cl; Willow Bed.

(*b*) *Bysshopbriggelane* 1436, *Bys(s)hop(p)ysbryggelane* 1437, 1439, *Byssypes lane* 1548 (*v.* **brycg, lane**, cf. John *Bysshopp'* 1442, William *Bysshope* 1548); *Brodemore* 1424, *-mour'* 1441 (*v.* **brād, mōr**); *Calfheys* 1450 (*v.* **calf, (ge)hæg**); *Chelles* 1553; *vetus Alnet'* ('old alder bed') *vocat' Cherchegot* c.1325 (*v.* **cirice**, second el. possibly **gotu, gote** 'stream', cf. Alder Md *supra*); *La Chese* 1376 (perhaps for *Chase, v.* **chace**); *lez Clyfes* 1453 (*v.* **clif**); *Condydeslane, (pastur' voc') Litel-, Muchelcondyd', Muchilcondyt* 1424, *Condyteslane* 1426, *Cundyteslane* 1441, 1446, *Brodecundytys* 1441, *Cunditeslane* 1448, *-mede* 1449, *Condytte lane* 1546 (*v.* **cundite** 'a conduit, a drain', **lane, lȳtel, micel, brād**); *Couches-* 1423–50, *Cowchesgore* 1452 (*v.* **gāra** 'triangular plot', cf. William *Couch* 1340; the form *Ouchesgore* (sic) 1369 doubtless also belongs here); *ten' voc' la Crouche* 1352 (*v.* **crūc**[3] 'a cross'); *Doggevellesheyeshurne* c.1325 (*v.* **(ge)hæg, hyrne**; the first part of the name is probably a surname from a p.n. such as Dogwell in Corscombe par. *infra*); *Feodary lands* 1554 (*v.* **feudary**); *La Forengore* c.1325 (*v.* **gāra**, first el. perhaps **forein** 'outside a boundary'; the name occurs in the bounds of Buckland Newton hundred); *Fronte* 1423 (*v.* **front**); *Goldehill'* 1447, *-hylle* 1547 (*v.* **hyll**, second el. probably **golde** 'marigold'); *Gosmede* 1447, *yosemede* (for *gose-*) 1550 (*v.* **gōs, mǣd**); *Greywythylane* 1435–37, *grey wethy lane* 1545 (*v.* **grǣg**[1], **wīðig** 'willow', **lane**); *Heryng(g)eshill'* 1447, *Heringes mede* 1546 (*v.* **hyll, mǣd**, cf. John-, Richard *Heryng'* 1424); *Hildebrondesheyeshurne* c.1325 (from **(ge)hæg** and **hyrne** with a surname *Hildebrand*); *Litelhorswill'* 1424, *Lytelhorswyll'* 1440 (*v.* **lȳtel, hors, well(a)**); *in la Hurne* (p) 1327 (*v.* **hyrne**); *atte Hyle* (p) 1347 (cf. *Kyngeshyle* c.1325, from the WSax dat.sg. form *hēale* of **halh** 'a nook, a corner of land', with **atte, cyning**); (*bosc' d'ni vocat'*) *le Iver, le Iuere* 1423, (*le*) *Yver(es)* 1424, 1428, *Iverwod(e)* 1442, 1447, *Yverdon'* 1444, *Shulve Iver* 1450, *Euerwod'* 1452, *Ivers hill* 1569–74 (*v.* **yfer** 'edge or brow of a hill', **wudu, dūn, scielf**, cf. the f.n. Shelves *supra*); *La Legh* 1347 (*v.* **lēah**); *Leverbeddes* 1450 (*v.* **lǣfer** 'rush, reed', **bedd**); *Ludecroft* 1424–38, *Luttecroft* 1447 (*v.* **croft**, first el. probably the surname (*de*) *Lude* (common in 1332 SR, etc)); *Menkes Tenement* 1353; (*le*) *Miremedoo* 1446, 1448, *Myremedoo* 1447, *Miri(e)mede* 1449, 1450 (*v.* **mǣd**, first el. probably ME **mire** 'a mire, a bog' but showing confusion with **myrge** 'pleasant', cf. the *TA* f.n. Marvills *supra*); (*Litel-, Muchel*) *Mo(u)rweyefe-, -yeve-, -yeuehay, -hey* 1424, *Mochellmorowhey* 1434, *Mochelmoreyevehey* 1440, *Morughhey* 1450 ('enclosure given by a man to his bride', *v.* **morgen-gifu, (ge)hæg**, with **lȳtel, micel**, cf. foll.); *Mour(we)lese* 1424, *Litelmorowlese* 1435 (*v.* **lǣs** 'pasture', **lȳtel**, first el. **morgen** 'morning' which may be a reduction of **morgen-gifu** as in prec.); *Myddelmede* 1543 (*v.* **middel, mǣd**); *Netelbed(d)e* Hy 3 (14), 1424, 1444, *Nettlebedde* 1427, *Netelysbedde* 1428, *Netulbed* 1445, *Nettlebed, Netylbedde Wodde* 1547 (*v.* **netel(e), bedd, wudu**); *le Northreclos* 1348 (*v.* **norðerra** 'more northerly'); *la Nyther-* 1361, *la Nutherclos* 1368 (*v.* **neoðerra** 'lower'); *bosc' voc' la Nywebreche* 1372 (*v.* **nīwe, brǣc**); *Nywehous* 1425 (*v.*

hūs); *La Ouer-* 1358, *la Overclos* 1361 (*v.* **uferra** 'higher'); *Overtebourneslake* c.1325 (*v.* **uferra, lacu** 'stream'; the middle part of the name is probably analogous with Tyburn Mx 6, 'boundary stream' from **tēo** and **burna**, appropriate since this is a point in the bounds of Buckland Newton hundred); *Pikede-* 1424, *Pykedmede* 1424, 1441 (*v.* **pīcede** 'pointed', **mǣd**); *Pypemedo* 1445, altered to *Pydemedo* 1446, *Pydmede* 1447 (*v.* **mǣd**, first el. **pīpe** 'pipe, conduit' (cf. *Condydeslane supra*) or **pide** 'marsh, fen'); *Reynaldeslare* c.1325 (probably for *-lane*, first el. the pers.n. or surname *Reynald*); *Southmanworth'*, (*Wester*) *Southmanneworth'*, *West Southamanneworth'* 1424, *Somerworthe* 1545 ('enclosure of the southern men', probably so called from its situation on the south side of the parish, *v.* **sūð, mann, worð**, cf. Westmancote Wo 103, Eastmanton Down Bk 489); *Stanput* 1423, *-pyt* 1428 (*v.* **stān, pytt**); *Stodeslonde* 1352 (*v.* **land**, cf. John *Stod* 1327 (Pulham)); *Stountes-* 1424, 1452, *Stountysclos*(*e*) 1428, *Stountysmede* 1444, *Stount Medoo* 1446 (*v.* **mǣd**, cf. Edward *Stount* 1424); *Terryeswater* 1441 (a surname with **wæter**); *Timberhurste* Hy 3 (14) (a point in the bounds of Blackmoor Forest, *v.* **timber, hyrst**, cf. *Tymerhustestensnement* (sic) 1352, Walter *Tymerhurste* 1327 (Pulham), *v.* **tenement**); *Totemede* (*v.* **mǣd**, first el. possibly **tōt(e)** 'a look-out'); *Trentlane ende* 1451 (*v.* **lane, ende**, cf. *pratum nuper Johannis Trent* 1425); *Trifulmede* 1424, 1433, 1447, *-medoo* 1446, *Trifelmede* 1424 (*v.* **mǣd**, first el. possibly ME **trufle, trifle** 'a trifle, a thing of little value' but cf. an OE **trifel** 'grinding' postulated for Trivel Mills Gl 3 95); *Vennyford'* 1433, *Fennyford* 1447 (*v.* **fennig** 'muddy', **ford**); *West Fylde* 1546 (*v.* **feld**); *le Worthe* 1450 (*v.* **worð**); *Wuttonys-* 1433, *Wottonyslane* 1434 (*v.* **lane**, par. name *supra*); *Wynard'* 1424, *Wynardes* 1450 (*v.* **wīn-geard** 'a vineyard'); *atte Yate* 1327, 1348, *atte Yete* 1348 (all (p), *v.* **atte** 'at the', **geat** 'gate').

BLACKMOOR FOREST & VALE

boscum de Blakemor(*e*) 1212 Fees, 1328 *Ct, foresta (regis) de Blakemor*(*e*) Hy 3 (14) Cerne, 1217 Pat, 1228, 1233, 1242 Cl, 1275 RH *et freq* to 1547 *Ct, foresta de Blakemar'* (sic), *-mora* 1232, *-mer'* 1240 Cl, *foresta de Blakamor*(*e*) 1239 Cl, 1288 (15) ForReg, *foresta de la Blakemor'* 1239 Cl, *Blakmor forest* 1273–83 Ipm, *pays de Blakemor* c.1338-40 Glast, *Blakemoure* 1340–45 Ipm, (*bosco de*) *Blakamore* 1397 (1792) DCMDeed, 1513 Ch, *Blakemore wood* 1409 Cl, (*king's forest of*) *Blakmore* 1469 Pat, 1544 *PlR, The Vaile of Whithart als. Blackemore* 1575 Saxton, *The Vale or Forest of Blakemore or White-Hart* 1774 Hutch[1], cf. *Blackmore Com*(*m*)*on* 1583 SPDom, 1615 *DuCo*, named from the former manor of *Blakemor*(*e*) for which *v.* Blackmore Ctgs in Wootton G. par. *supra*. The bounds of the Forest at various dates are described in Hy 3

(14) Cerne (also printed in Hutch³ **3** 662–3, Fägersten 35–6), 1270 *For* (No.11, m. 1r), Hutch³ **4** 79, Ed 1 (15) *ForReg* (f. 112), 1338–40 Glast (59, pp. 182–3), 1535–43 Leland (4. 106, quoting a charter of Hy 2), cf. also Hutch¹ **2** 492–4, Hutch³ **4** 516–9 and the full discussion of the extent of the Forest by C.D. Drew in Roscoe 33ff. The alternative name *White-Hart* derives from the story of Henry III and the white hart of Blackmoor, spared by him but killed by others, as related by Hutch¹ **2** 492 (and earlier by Camden and Coker), cf. Kingstag in Lydlinch par. *infra* which was also associated with the legend by popular tradition, and *v.* Udal 152–4.

XXIV. BROWNSALL HUNDRED

Caundle Wake (in Bishop's Caundle par. *infra*) and Stock Gaylard (in Lydlinch par. *infra*) are tithings in this hundred (1332 SR, 1664 HTax, Hutch³ **3** 664, etc). In c.1086 GeldR the hundred also contained Purse Caundle and the whole of Bishop's Caundle, both now parishes in Sherborne hundred *infra* (Anderson 135, VCHDo **3** 141–2). Holwell, a detached part of Somerset transferred to Dorset in 1844, is included in this hundred by Hutch³ **4** 520, Kelly 114.

> *Bruneselle hundret* c.1086 GeldR
> *Brumishill'hdr'* 1175 P, *Brimeshullehdr'* (for *Brunes-*) 1175 ChancR
> *Bruneshill(')* 1212, 1219 Fees, 1244 *Ass*, 1265 Misc, *-hull(e)* 1244 *Ass*, 1258 *For*, 1268 *Ass*, 1285 FA, 1288 *Ass*, 1310 Pat, *Brueshelle* 1270 *For*, *Brunnes-*, *Brummeshull'* 1288 *Ass*
> *Broneshille* 1244 *Ass*, *-hull(e)* 1268 ib, 1275 RH, 1303 Pat, 1327 *SR*, 1332 SR, 1346, 1428 FA, *Bronshill* 1431 ib
> *Bromeshill'* 1280 *Ass*, *-hulle* 1288 ib, *Bromshulle* 1280 *Ass*, 1335 AD I, *Bromhull'* 1280 *Ass*
> *Breoneshull* 1316 FA
> *Brown(e)shull* 1539, 1542 LP, *Brownshall* 1664 HTax

Originally the name of the hill about a mile E of Stourton Caundle on the bdy between that par. and Stalbridge, called *Browns Wheel* on 1811 OS. The name is also preserved in Brunsell's Fm and Brunsell's Knap both in Stourton Caundle par. *infra*. The second el. is **hyll** 'hill', the first is probably the OE pers.n. *Brūn*. However, the possibility that the first el. is the adj. **brūn** 'brown, dark' used substantively as a hill-name, *Brūn* 'the dark one', cannot be ruled out, *v.* Anderson 136, cf. Ekwall Studies[1] 63 where a hill-name *Brūne*, a derivative of **brūn**, is proposed for Brown So.

Stourton Caundle

STOURTON CAUNDLE (ST 714152) ['stɔːtən 'kɔːndl, 'stəːtən 'kændl]

 Candel (4 ×), *Candele* (2 ×), *Candelle* (2 ×) 1086 DB
 Candel Malherbe 1202 FF, *Kaundel Malerbe* 1243 CurR (Drew)
 Candel 1206 RC, 1208 P, 1212 Fees, 1235–6 Fees, 1236 FF, *Kaunvel* (sic) 1210–12 RBE, *Caundel* 1212 Fees, *Kandel* Hy 3 *HarlCh*
 Candel Hadden' 1270 *For, Kandel Haddon* 1271 CurR (Drew), *Caundelhaddon(e)* 1275 RH, 1288 *Ass*, 1291 Tax, 1330 FF, 1348 Pat, *Caundel Haddon(e)* 1276, 1280 FF, *CottCh*, 1308 FF, 1316 FA *et freq* to 1428 FA, *Kaundel Haddon', Candel(e) Haddon(e)* 1280 *Ass, Candel Haddon* 1285 FA, *Haddone(s) Caundel* 1310 Banco (Drew), *Caundel Hadden* 1340 NI, *Caundell Haddon* 1412 FA *et freq* to 1450 Cl, *Candelhaddon* 1433 *HarlRoll Sturton Candell* 1569–74 *Map,* -*caūdell* 1575 Saxton, -*Candle* 1664 HTax, *Stourton Caundell alias Caundell Haddon* 1588 DCMDeed, *Stourton Candel* 1709 *WRO, Caundle Stourton* 1795 Boswell, *Stourton Caundle* 1811 OS

The origin of Caundle is obscure. Ekwall (RN 72, DEPN) thinks it was probably an old British name for (one of) the chain of hills lying between this place and the other Caundles (*v.* Bishops Caundle, Caundle Marsh and Purse Caundle all *infra* in Sherborne Hd), and suggests a possible connection with the obscure British el. ***canto-** thought to be found in Camel and Quantock So as well as in the county-name Kent. Whatever its origin, the form may well have been associated at an early date with the common OE sb. *candel* 'a candle'. All the Caundles except Purse Caundle are on different arms

of Caundle Brook, which Ekwall takes to be named from the places.
The affixes are manorial. Robert *Malherbe* granted 2½ hides of land here to Henry *de Haddon* in 1202 FF, cf. also John *Mal(h)erbe* 1280 FF, *CottCh*, Henry *de Haddon* 1235–6 Fees, 1236, 1280 FF, etc, and *v.* Haddon Lodge *infra*. The Lords *Stourton* possessed the manor from the 15th century until 1727 (Hutch³ 3 666–7), cf. *The Lord Stourton hath a fair maner place* 1535–43 Leland.

Other references that may belong to this manor or part of it include *Candel Henrici Budde* 1178 P; *Candel Danielis de Brueria* 1202 P; *Candel Joce* 1256 FF ('the mill of-'), 1288 *Ass*; *Caundle Lydelinche* 1306 Ch (from Lydlinch par. 2 miles SE); *Caundel Pyle* 1335 FF, *HarlCh*, *-Pile* 1335 *ib* (probably from the family of William *de la Pile* 1244 *Ass*, etc, who are to be associated with Pile Lane (Coppice) in Stalbridge par. *infra* about 1 mile N of Stourton Caundle); and *Caundel Chidiok* 1483–5 *Harl* (cf. John *Chidiok* 1439 *HarlCh*).

BILCOMBE COPSE (ST 702154), *Bylecumbe, Balecoumbe* 1280 *Ass*, *Bylecomb(')* 1327 *SR*, 1332 SR all (p), *Belcom-*, *Belscomb Close, Bellcom medow* 1709 *WRO*, 'Bil(l)a's valley', from an OE pers.n. *Bil(l)a* (suggested for Bilborough Nt 140, Bilham YW 1 86, etc) and **cumb**. The variant spelling with -*a*- in 1280 (both forms refer to the same man) is no doubt an error.

BRUNSELL'S FM (ST 714152) & KNAP (ST 725148), *Brimeshull* (for *Brunes-*) 1201 Anderson, *Bruneshull(')* (p) 1244, 1268, 1280 *Ass*, 1284 Pat, *Broneshull(')* 1327 *SR*, 1334 *For*, 1340 NI all (p), 1348 *WRO*, *Bronehull'* (p), *Brunshull'* 1348 *ib*, *Brunsel Close, Bromsell Gate* 1709 *ib*, *Bronshall Knapp* 1839 *TA* (Stalbridge), named from the hill which also gave name to Brownsall hundred *q.v. supra*, *v.* **cnæpp** 'hillock'. In 1774 Hutch¹ 2 340 (followed by Hutch³ 4 137) the hamlet of *Brownsel Lane* is included in the neighbouring par. of Bps. Caundle (as also is the hamlet of *Brownshall* in 1795 Boswell).

COCKHILL COPPICE & FM (ST 703163), *Cokkul* 1327 *SR, Cokhull'* 1332 SR both (p), *Cockehill* 1588 *DCMDeed, Cockill, Cockhill (Close), Great Cock hill* 1709 *WRO, Cockhill* 1811 OS, probably from **cocc**[1] 'heap, hillock' with explanatory **hyll**, cf. Cock Hill W 134; it is perhaps less likely that the first el. is **cocc**[2] 'woodcock or other wild bird'. The farm lies on a 440' hill.

ROWDEN MILL COPSE, FM (ST 712135) & LANE, *Rowdonhill'* 1538, *Rowdenhill, Rowden yate* 1614 *Digby, Rowdon Hill* 1709 *WRO, Rawdon Mill* [Bridge] 1791 Boswell, *Rowton Mill Fm* 1811 OS, *Rowden(s) Hill* 1842 *TA* (Bps. Caundle), cf. *Mill Plot* 1839 *TA*, 'rough hill', from **rūh** (wk.obl. *rūwan*) and **dūn**, with **hyll**, **geat**. This may have been the site of 'the mill of *Candel Joce*' 1256 FF (*v.* par. name *supra*) and of the lost *Bradeford sub molendino de Candel* Hy 3 (14) Cerne (in the bounds of Blackmoor Forest, *v.* **brād, ford)**, cf. also the fourth part of a mill in *Caundel Haddon* 1280 FF, Simon *atte Mulle* 1327 *SR*, 1332 SR ('at the mill', *v.* **atte, myln**), and the mills at the two manors of *Candelle* in 1086 DB (VCHDo **3** 95).

WOODROW BUNGALOW & FM (ST 699156), HR WOODROW FM, LR WOODROW, *Woderewe* 1327 *SR*, 1332 SR, *Woodrowe* Hy 8 Hutch[3], *Wood Rowe* 1664 HTax, *Woodrow close* 1709 *WRO*, (*Lr*) *Woodrow* 1811 OS, 'the row of trees, the narrow wood', *v.* **wudu, rǣw**, cf. Woodrow Wo 239.

BARROW HILL FM, *Barrow Hill* 1709 *WRO*, 1839 *TA, v.* **beorg** 'hill, barrow'. CAT LANE, perhaps a reduced form of *Catherine Wheel Lane* 1706, so named from *the Katherine Wheel* 1770, now Trooper Inn *infra* (forms from G.W.L. Fernandes & A.E.G. Blades, *Stourton Caundle*, Dorchester 1974, pp. 51–2). CAUNDLE LANE. CHAPEL (remains of), cf. *Chaple Close* 1709 *WRO, v.* Hutch[3] **3** 666. CHURCH FM, near St Peter's Church *infra*. GARVEY HILL, *Gorforde hill, close called Gorverd* 1614 *Digby*, (*Great-, Litt*) *Gorvard* 1709 WRO, *Garved* [Bridge] 1791 Boswell, *Gorford* (*Md*) 1842 *TA* (Bps. Caundle), cf. *gorforde gate* 1569–74 *Map*, probably 'dirty ford', from **gor** and **ford**; Caundle Lane crosses an arm of Caundle Brook here. HADDON LODGE, probably a manorial name from the *Haddon* family, lords of the manor in the 13th cent., *v.* Hutch³ **3** 664 and par. name *supra*; however it is possible that *Haddon* 1202 FF (p), etc, was originally a local p.n., 'heather-covered hill' from **hǣð** and **dūn**, from which the family took its name; the lodge is on the same hill as Cockhill Fm *supra*. HOLT HILL (1811 OS), LANE & WDS, *holte woode* 1569–74 *Map, Holt* 1614 *Pitt, the Holt, Broad Hollt or Whittaker, Holt Close, -Coppes, -Wood* 1709 *WRO*, cf. *Knyghthold* 1315, *-holte* 1316 Banco (Drew), *v.* **holt** 'wood, thicket', **cniht**; *Whittaker* is from **æcer** with **hwǣte** 'wheat' or **hwīt** 'white'. JUBILEE OAK, planted in 1897 to commemorate the Diamond Jubilee of Queen Victoria. KNOLL COPSE, *v.* **cnoll**. MANOR FM. NEW LEAZE FM & WD, *New Leys Coppice* 1709 *WRO, v.* **lǣs** 'pasture'. ST PETER'S CHURCH, cf. 'the church of *Caundel Haddon*' 1348 Pat. TROOPER INN, *v.* Cat Lane *supra*. VEALE'S CTGS, cf. John-, William *Veale* 1664 HTax. VICARAGE, cf. *Parsnag Land* 1709 *WRO*. WOODCLOSE, *Wood Close* 1709 *WRO*.

FIELD-NAMES

The undated forms in (*a*) are 1709 *WRO* (383/319); there are very few names in 1839 *TA* 205. Spellings dated Hy 3 are *HarlCh*, 1280¹ *Ass*, 1280² FF, 1280³ *CottCh*, 1327 *SR*, 1332 SR, 1348, 1436 *WRO*, 1360 (15) *ShaftR*, 1664 HTax, and 1869 Hutch³.

(*a*) Alley Cl; Babhay Knowle (*v.* **cnoll**); Barly Cl & Hill; Bayty Hill; Bear Cl; Bench Hill (*v.* **benc**); Berry Cl; Blacklands; Blanford Rd (to Blandford F. **2** 87); Bottom Cl; Bramble Cl; Brands Land; Brook Hill; Bull Acres & Cl; Buloks Cl; Candle gate (*v.* par. name *supra*); Clootham Md; Codds Md; Coman-, Comon Cl; Court Mdw; Croo(c)k Cl & Md (*v.* **crōc** 'a bend'); Deep Mdw; Drove Cl & Lane; Flaxmead; Fukers Hill; Furlong Cl; Green Waye Cl; Haywood Coppice; Hill Cl; Home Cl, Grd & Md; Ice Cl; Inhams (*v.* **innōm**); Land Cl & Mdw; Loaders Md (cf. Andrew *Loder* 1664); Long Cl; Longhedge, Long Hedg; New Cl; Oat Cl; Park Cl (cf. *La Parrokke* 1436, *v.* **park, pearroc**); Hither Paradise 1869 (*v.* **paradis**); Quarry Cl; the Range; Rawls Leys (*v.* **lǣs**); Shappe Cl (*v.* **scēap** 'sheep'); Sharborn Waye Cl (by the road to Sherborne par. *infra*); Slaply More (second letter uncertain, *v.* **mōr**); Stanbrook, Stane Brook (*v.* **stān, brōc**); Gt & Lt Sucketh, Sucketh Cl; Town Cl; Towns End Cl; Twelve Acres Cl; Twichen-, Twiching Cl (*v.* **twicen(e)** 'fork of a road, cross-roads, narrow lane'); Uper Down (sic); Well Cl; West Cl; Weston Gate Cl (*v.*

Stalbridge Weston in Stalbridge par. *infra*); White Md; Willow Bed; Wood Flg.

(*b*) *Coppeland* Hy 3 (*v.* **copp, land**); Walter *ate Croft, -de Croft* 1280[1] (*v.* **atte, croft**); *Hundeslond* 1280[2], *H(o)undeslond* 1360 (15) (*v.* **land**, first el. either **hund** 'hound' or the pers.n. or surname *H(o)und*); *La Langbreche* 1436 (*v.* **lang**[1], **bræc**); *Ravenestorp* 1280[3] (from **þrop** 'outlying farm' with the OE pers.n. *Hræfn*); *atte Shute* (p) 1327, 1332 (*v.* **atte, scyte** 'slope').

Stalbridge

STALBRIDGE (ST 735178)

Stapulbrige 860–6 (14) *Cott* (MS Faustina A.ii, f.25, Finberg no. 571), *Stapulbreicge* 998 (12) *SherC* (S 895)

Staplebrige 1086 DB, *-bruge* 1125 (12) *SherC, -brig*(*g*)(*e*) 1297 Cl, Pat, 1382 Cl, *-bridg*(*e*) 1535–43 Leland

Stapelbrig(*g*)(*e*) 1145 (12) *SherC*, 1191 Sarum, 1212 P, 1214 FF, 1244 *Ass*, 1267 FF *et freq* to 1402 Pat, *-brug*(*g*)(*e*) 1244, 1249 FF, 1268 *Ass*, 1302 Ch, 1328 FF, 1338, 1344 Pat, *-bregg'* 1280 *Ass, -brygg*(*e*) 1291 Tax, 1303 Ipm, *Stappelbrigg'* 1214 Cur, *Stapellbrigg'* 1288 *Ass*

Stapilbrigge 1267 FF, 1428 FA, *-brig'* 1268 *Ass* (p)

Stalbrig(*g*)(*e*) 1327 SR (p), 1332 SR (p), 1385 Pat *et freq* to 1552 *Prideaux, -briggh* 1346 FA, *-brug*(*g*)(*e*) 1350 (18) *Add*, 1362 Pat *et freq* to 1463 AD III, *-brigg als.*

Stapelbrigg' 1415 IpmR, *-brygg* 1428 FA, *-bridge* 1535–43 Leland, *-brydge* 1551 *AddCh, Stalbridge als. Staplbridge als. Staple bridge* e17 *Cecil, Stallbridge* 1709 WRO

Stapulbrigg 1316 FA, *-brugge* 1383 Cl, *Stapolbrygg* 1340 NI, *Stabulbryge* (sic) c.1557 *Prideaux*

Stabrigge 1439 *HarlCh*

Stapleford(*e*) 1535–43 Leland (5.107)

Stawbridge 1644 Hutch[3] (3 671)

'Bridge built on posts or piles', *v.* **stapol, brycg**; K.J. Penn (*Historic Towns in Dorset*, 1980, p.100) thinks the name 'may refer to a bridge over the Stour or Bibbern Brook (and thus presumably some way from the present settlement)'. Leland's form *Stapleford*(*e*) (he also has *Staple-, Stalbridge*) is probably simply an error, influenced by the common p.n. Stapleford found in this and several other counties; *Stapleford* is listed by 1795 Boswell as a place in Stalbridge. *Stapel-, Stapilgraue* 1268 *Ass* (a tithing in Brownsall hundred) is probably also an error for Stalbridge, with the substitution of **grāf(a)** 'grove' for the second el.

INNS in 1824 Pigot: *Hind, Red Lion, Swan.*

ANTIOCH CTGS & FM (ST 731158), *Antioche* 1283 Banco (Drew), *Antioch* 1351 Hutch[3], 1795 Boswell, *Ontioche maner'* 1361 IpmR, *Aicnokes* (sic, spelling altered) 1414 *Weld*[2], *Antiokes* 1433 *HarlRoll*, 1439 *HarlCh, Antiockes* 1442 Hutch[3], *Antioches* 1450 Cl, *Anteo(u)x* 1577 *Comm*, a manorial name from the family of Roger *de Antioch(e)* 1244 *Ass*, John *de Antioch* 1267 FF, *Joh' fil' Henr' de Auntioch'* 1348 *WRO*, cf. also *Antioch Wood* 1535–43 Leland. According to Hutch[3] 3 676 the manor was also referred to as *Haddon Antioch* because held by the *Haddon* family for which *v.* Stourton Caundle par. *supra*. Antioch Ctgs and Fm appear to be *Smiths* 1811 OS, cf. *Smith's Cl* 1839 *TA*, Thomas *le Smyth(')* 1327 *SR*, 1332 SR.

BARROW HILL (FM) (ST 732177), *Barrow Hill* 1839 *TA*, possibly to be associated with *on beorhleage* 933 (12) *SherC* (S 423) in the Anglo-Saxon bounds of Stalbridge Weston, cf. also Phillip-, John *atte Bergh(')* 1327 *SR*, 1332 SR, *v.* **beorg** 'barrow, hill', **lēah** 'wood, clearing in a wood', **atte** 'at the'.

CHURCH HILL (HO) (Kelly), near St Mary's Church *infra*, possibly to be associated with *of-, on ciric hylle* 933 (12) *SherC* (S 423) in the Anglo-Saxon bounds of Stalbridge Weston, *v.* **cirice** 'church', **hyll** 'hill', cf. Ekwall Studies[1] 52.

FRITH FM, HO & WD (ST 706176), *la frithe* 1244 *Ass* (p), *bosco de Fryth* 1258 *For, atte Frith'* 1327 *SR, atte Frythe* 1332 SR both (p), *Frith woode alias Frith Coppice* e17 Cecil, *Frith* 1811 OS, *Frith Wd* 1839 *TA*, *v.* **fyrhð, (ge)fyrhðe** 'a wood, woodland', **atte**.

GUMMERSHAY FM (ST 759180), *Gumersheye* 1268 *Ass,*
Gummershaye 1276 Banco, *Gumbresheye* 1283 Drew, *Gom(m)-*
ereshey(e) 1315 FF, 1332 SR, 1350 (18) *Add, Gummeresheye*
1328 FF, *Gomershay(e)* 1327 *SR*, 1415 IpmR, 1664 HTax,
1811 OS, *Gummersey* 1765 Tayl, 1839 *TA* (*Gt-, Lr-,*
-Mdw), *Gomersey* 1869 Hutch[3]. From **(ge)hæg** 'enclosure'
with a pers.n. or surname *Gum(m)er* (cf. *Gummar* DB (Searle
270) related by Zachrisson DTR 135 to OG *Gummar*
(Förstemann 692), but Reaney s.n. *Gummer* derives a late
11th cent. form *Gumer* from an OE *Gūðmǣr*).

HARGROVE CTG, FM (ST 749155) & LANE, *Haregraue* 1258
For (p), 1268 *Ass*, 1332 SR (p), *-grove* 1258 *For* (p), *-groue*
1268, 1288 *Ass* both (p), *-grave* 1285 FA, 1288 *Ass* both (p),
Hargraue 1327 *SR* (p), *-grove* 1538, c.1557 *Prideaux*
(*mancione d'ni voc'-*), 1795 Boswell. Probably analogous
with Hartgrove in E Orchard par. *supra*; the present farm is
⅓ mile from the par. bdy (R. Lydden), but the grove that
gave the place its name may have been on the bdy.

MARSH FM (ST 758164), 1811 OS, *in la Mersch'* 1327 *SR*
(p), *Marsh* 1839 *TA*, cf. *Gt Marshmoor* (*Fd*), *Lt Marshmoor,*
Marshmoor Md 1839 *ib, v.* **mersc** 'marsh', **mōr** 'marshy
ground'.

NEWNHAM (lost, ST 759157), 1795 Boswell, 1869 Hutch[3],
Newenham 1244, 1288 *Ass* both (p), *Niw(e)nham* 1270 *For*
(p), *Nywenham* 1315, 1328 FF, 1431 FA, *Niweham* 1315
Drew, *Newnam* 1464 Hutch[3], cf. *Hr & Lr Great Newnham,*
Lt Newnhams, Newnham's Orchd 1839 *TA*, 'the new
enclosure or river-meadow', from **nīwe** (wk.obl. *-an*) and
hamm; its location, in a loop of R. Lydden, is suggested by
that of the *TA* f.ns., *v.* C. Taylor, DoNHAS **88** 207.

PILE LANE (COPPICE) (ST 718165), *de la Pile* 1244 *Ass* (p)
(under Brownsall Hd), *Pyle* 14 *Midd, de la Pyle* 1338 Pat (p),
cf. *Pile Cl* 1839 *TA*, from **pīl** 'a shaft or stake', cf. the
manorial *Caundel Pyle* discussed under Stourton Caundle
par. *supra*.

THORNHILL (ST 741149), *Thornhill(')* 1244 *Ass* (p), 1431 FA, 1795 Boswell, *-hull(e)* Hy 3 *HarlCh* (p), 1268 *Ass*, 1285 FA (p), 1280, 1288 *Ass* both (p) *et freq* to 1664 HTax, *Thorenhull'* 1288 *Ass* (p), *Thornehull* 1335 AD I (p), *-hul* 1535–43 Leland, *Thurnhulle* 1338–40 Glast (p), 'thorn-tree hill', *v.* þorn, hyll, cf. Thorn Hill Fm 2 152.

THORN HO (ST 712166), *Thornhouse Fm* 1811 OS, cf. *Thorn-house Md* 1839 *TA*, probably to be associated with Robert-, Thomas *atte Thorne* 1327 *SR*, *v.* atte, þorn, cf. prec.

CALLOW WESTON (lost), 1525 Hutch[3], 1795 Boswell, 1869 Hutch[3], *Calweston (in Nywenham)* 1431 FA. For Weston, *v.* foll.; the manorial affix is from the family of Ralph and John *le Calewe* who held lands in *Dunes Weston* a1277 and 1297 respectively (Hutch[3] 3 754), cf. also John *le Calewe* 1327 *SR*, 1332 SR (taxed under Stalbridge Weston) and SoDoNQ 3 81ff. The form *Westun Ralegh* (possibly for *Calegh*) 1270 *For* may also belong here. *Dunes Weston*, no doubt to be identified with *Callow Weston*, is perhaps to be associated with the family of John *le Doue* (possibly for *Done*) 1327 *SR* (also taxed under Stalbridge Weston). *Callow Weston* was probably E of Stalbridge Weston, in view of the 1431 form and the likely location of *Newnham supra*.

STALBRIDGE WESTON (ST 720166)
    (æt) Westtune, (apud) Westonam (title) 933 (12) *SherC* (S 423), *Westun* 998 (12) *ib* (S 895)
    Westone 1086 DB, 1327 *SR*, *Westona* 1125 (12), 1145 (12) *SherC*, *Weston(')* 1212 P, 1268 *Ass et passim, Westesun* (sic) 1535–43 Leland
    Weston' Abbatis 1280 *Ass*, *Weston Abbots* 1334 FF, *-Abbot* 1439 *HarlCh*
    Weston alias Stalbridge Weston e17 *Cecil, Stalbridge Weston* 1795 Boswell

'West farm or estate', *v.* west, tūn, referring to its situation in relation to Stalbridge. The earlier affixes

Abbatis (gen.sg. of Lat **abbas** 'an abbot') and *Abbot(s)* refer to its possession by Sherborne Abbey from the 10th cent. *North Weston* 1388 Hutch³ (3 675) may have been part of this manor or of *Callow Weston supra*. The Anglo-Saxon bounds of Stalbridge Weston are given in 933 (12) *SherC* (S 423), *v.* Grundy 7 60–65, Hart 159–160.

ANGLESEY CTGS. BASEL BRIDGE, 1811 OS, cf. *Bazles* 1839 *TA*, perhaps the surname *Basil, Bazell*. BIBBERN BRIDGE & FM, *Bibberne* [Bridge] 1791 Boswell, *Bibbern, Bibberns or Lane-end* 1839 *TA*, named from Bibbern Brook for which *v.* RNs. *infra*, cf. Beatrice *atte Brigge* 1327 *SR, v.* **atte, brycg**. BRICKYARD CTGS. BROOK HO, cf. *Brook Md* 1839 *TA*, Robert-, Thomas *atte Bro(u)ke* 1327 *SR*, 1332 SR, *v.* **brōc, atte**; Brook Ho is apparently *Holehouse Barn* 1811 OS, cf. *Hole House Cl, Little Hold* (sic) *Cl* 1839 *TA*, perhaps to be associated with Adam-, Edward *atte Hole* 1327 *SR*, 1332 SR, *v.* **atte, hol¹** 'hole, hollow'. BUNGAY'S FM, *Bungays* 1811 OS. CAUNDLE LANE, leading to Stourton Caundle par. *supra*, cf. (*Hr*) *Caundle Gate* 1839 *TA*. CHURCH CLOSE (1839 *TA*), COVERT & WALK, from St Mary's Church *infra*. COMMON PLANT., near Stalbridge Cmn *infra*. COOK'S FM, COOK'S LANE (WD), cf. Thomas *Cooke* 1664 HTax, *Cox's* [Bridge] 1791 Boswell. COPSE HOUSE FM, *Cops-* 1811 OS, cf. *Coppice* (*Cl, Grd & Md*) 1839 *TA*. CRIB HOUSE FM, *Cribhouse* 1839 *TA, v.* **cribhouse**. DEACONS, DEACON'S COPPICE. DRAKES MILL (lost, ST 737164), cf. *le Myll lane* 1599 Prideaux, *v.* West Mill *infra* for other references to mills in Stalbridge. DREW'S LANE, cf. *Drew's Grd or Milking Cl* 1839 *TA*. EASTOP LANE, *Eastip-* 1811 OS. ENRIS, *Ensis* (sic) 1839 *TA*. FUDGE'S COPSE, *Fridges* (sic) *Coppice* 1839 *TA*. FURGE PLANT. GIBBS MARSH FM, *Gibbs Marsh* 1811 OS, cf. *Gibbs and Marsh* [Bridge] 1791 Boswell. GRAY'S FM, *Grays* 1811 OS, *Grey(')s Grd* 1839 *TA*, cf. Roger *Grey* 1332 SR (Stourton Caundle). GROSVENOR RD. GROVE FM, *Grove* (*Grd*) 1839 *TA, v.* **grāf(a)**. HADDON LANE, cf. *Hadden or Langman's Md, Gt & Peaked Hadden* 1839 *TA*. HAM WOOD FM, cf. *Lr Hamwood* 1839 *TA*, named from Marnhull Ham in Marnhull par. *supra*. HARPITTS, *Harputts* 1811 OS, (*Lt*) *Harpits* 1839 *TA*, 'grey pits', from **hār²** and **pytt**, cf.

Harpitts Fm in Kington M. par. *supra*; 'Old Quarry' marked
6". HERRIDGE COPPICE. HEWISH PLANT., *Hewish* (*Plant.*) 1839
TA, v. **hīwisc** 'a measure of land that would support a
family'. HEWLATT'S FM, *Hewlets* 1811 OS, cf. Mary *Hulett*
1664 HTax. HIGHER WARREN, *The Warren, Hr & Lr Warren
Plant.* 1839 *TA, v.* **wareine**; within Thornhill Park *infra*.
HILL CTGS, cf. *Hill House Md* 1839 *TA*. HOLTHAM PLANT.
KING'S MILL LANE (CTGS), from King's Mill in Marnhull
par. *supra*. LANDSHIRE BRIDGE (1811 OS) & LANE, *Landshare*
(*Lane*) 1839 *TA, v.* **land-sc(e)aru** 'boundary'; the lane
forms the county boundary and crosses a small tributary of
R. Stour at the bridge. MANOR HO (site of). MARKET CROSS
(local), cf. *crucem iuxta domu' Will'i Chylde* 1557 *Prideaux*
and the f.n. Clark's Plot *infra*. NEW FM. NORTH LODGE, cf.
The Northern Lodge 1839 *TA*. OLD BARN. OXENLEAZE
PLANT., (-*Plant.*) 1839 *TA, v.* **oxa, lǣs**. OYSTER SHELLS,
(-*Plant.*) 1839 *TA*. PARK FM & WD, named from Stalbridge
Park *infra*. PHEASANTRY. POOLESTOWN, cf. *Poole's Plot* 1839
TA. POUND, *The-* 1839 *TA*. PRIOR'S DOWN, 1839 *TA,
Priorsdown* 1795 Boswell, according to Hutch³ 3 677 'a farm
. . . which seems anciently to have belonged to the prior of
Sherborne'. PUSEY (or PUXEY?) (lost), 1811 OS, cf. Puxey in
Sturminster N. par. *supra*. RIMPLES, *Rimpool(')s* (*Mdw*) 1839
TA, cf. Nicholas *de Rympel* 1268 *Ass* (202.32), William
Re(y)mpel 1327 *SR*, 1332 SR. THE RING, cf. *Ring Cl* 1839
TA, no doubt originally with reference to a circular
enclosure or other feature, *v.* **hring**. RUM COPPICE, cf. *Rum
Mdw, Runn Md* 1839 *TA*. RYALLS FM, *Ryal* 1811 OS, cf.
Robert *Ryall* 1664 HTax (Stourton Caundle). ST MARY'S
CHURCH, cf. *Ecclesiam de Stapelbrige* 1145 (12) *SherC*,
'church of *Stapelbrigg*' 1370 Pat. SHIPNEY LANE, cf.
Shippenhay, Shipney (*Mdw*) 1839 *TA, v.* **scypen** 'cow-shed',
(ge)hæg 'enclosure'. SOUTH LODGE. SPIRE HILL CTG, FM &
PLANT., *The Spire, Spire Hill* (*Fm House & Plant.*) 1839 *TA*,
perhaps figuratively with reference to the Obelisk (marked
6", also 1811 OS) on the hill, *v.* **spire**. SPRING PLANT.,
Spring Ponds Plant. 1839 *TA*. STALBRIDGE CMN, 1811 OS,
Stallbridg- 1709 *WRO*, cf. *le Est Comen'* 1552 *Prideaux*,
The Common, (*Long, Second & Square*) *Common, Common Cl*
1839 *TA, v.* **ēast, common**. STALBRIDGE PARK, 1811 OS, cf.

Hr Quarter, Lr Quarter in the Park, Deer Park, The New-, The Old Park, Weston Wd or Park Wd Coppice 1839 *TA, v.* **park**, Stalbridge Weston *supra*, Hutch³ 3 672–3. STANBROOK, *Standbrook* 1811 OS, *Stan(d)brook* (*Mdw*) 1839 *TA*, not to be identified with *stanbroc* 933 (12) *SherC* (S 423) in the Anglo-Saxon bounds of Stalbridge Weston as assumed by Fägersten 37–8, but analogous with it, *v.* **stān, brōc**. STURT COPPICE & FM, *Sturts* 1811 OS, *Stirt Coppice, Long Sturt, Sturt Flg* 1839 *TA, v.* **steort** 'tail or tongue of land'. SWAN'S POND, *Swan Ponds, Swan's Pond Willow Bed* 1839 *TA*, cf. *Swan's Mdw* 1839 *ib.* TEN ACRE PLANT, cf. *Ten Acres* 1839 *TA*. THORNHILL COPSE, FM (1811 OS) & PARK, cf. *comon called Fernehill alias Thornehill* e17 Cecil, *Thornhill* (*Layns*) 1839 *TA*, all named from Thornhill *supra, v.* **leyne** 'tract of arable'. TULKS, cf. *Tucks Coppice* 1839 *TA*, Richard *Podyngton alias Tucke* c.1557 *Prideaux*; *Tulks* 1811 OS is marked some 2 miles SW of the 6″ name. WARR BRIDGE, 1791 Boswell, 1811 OS. WATERLOO LANE, no doubt a transferred p.n. commemorating the battle of 1815; the lane forms the par. bdy. WEST COPPICE. WEST MILL (FM), *Stal Br Mill* 1811 OS, *Wester's Mill* 1839 *TAMap*, cf. Richard *atte Mulle* 1332 SR, *Mill Cl & Md* 1839 *TA, Drakes Mill supra, v.* **myln, atte**; there was a mill at Stalbridge in 1086 DB (VCHDo 3 71). WESTON CMN (lost), 1811 OS, from Stalbridge Weston *supra*. WEST WD, 1839 *TA*. WOOD CL, 1839 *TA*. WOOD LANE, 1811 OS, cf. *Woodlane Cl* 1839 *TA*.

FIELD-NAMES

The undated forms are 1839 *TA* 193. Spellings dated 933 (12) are *SherC* (S 423). Those dated 1244, 1268, 1288 are *Ass*, 1285 FA, 1317 Inq aqd, 1327 *SR*, 1332 SR, 1333, 1442, 1745, 1869 Hutch³, 1350 (18) *Add*, 1436, 1709 *WRO*, 1463 AD III, 1552, 1553, 1556, 1557, 1585, 1596, 1599 *Prideaux*, 1610 *AddRoll*, 1664 HTax, and 1791 Boswell.

(a) Ash Cl; Bagber Md (from Bagber in Sturminster N. par. *supra*); Bagnes (cf. Hugh *de Beygny de Stapelbrigg* 1270 *For*); Baker's Md (cf. Andrew *le Bakere* 1333, *backehowse close* 1552, *v.* **bæc-hūs** 'a bake house'); Balls; Barn Cl & Grd; Barretts Md (cf. John *Baret* (S. Caundle) 1436); Batt's Mdw; Bayley's Cl; Berry Croft; Bigmore, Biggmoor Md; Bill Croft; Bollands or Borelands; Bowers Gt & Lt Ground, Bower's (Gt) Mead; Brages (cf. Mrs *Bragg* 1664); Brake (*v.* **bræc¹**); Breach (*v.* **bræc**); Brent Ho 1869; Brimming-, Bruning Md (possibly to be identified with *on* *beorreding mæd* 933 (12) in the OE bounds of Stalbridge Weston, 'meadow associated with Beornrǣd', from the OE pers.n. *Beornrǣd*, **-ing-**[4], **mǣd**); Broad Cl & Fd; Broadhay and Poyne; Brooky Lain; Brown Cl; Browns or Summerleaze, Lt Browns (cf. George *Browne* 1664, Summerlease Md *infra*); Buck's Md (cf. George *Buck* 1664); Bulk; Burges Water Cl (cf. William *Burdge* 1664); Burgund Orchd; Burn (or Small) Md; Gt & Lt Bushay, Bushey Cl; Carter's and Andrew's (cf. John *Carter* 1664); Cave's Md (cf. James *Caue* 1664); Chaffey's Md (cf. Robert *Chaffie* 1664); Charity Md; Chivell's Md; Clark's Plot (cf. Nicholas *le Clerk* 1350 (18), *pratum . . . Thome Clarke* 1552, *Thomas Clarkes barres, le Barres Thome Clarke et Crucem ibidem* 1556, *v.* **barre**); Clover Grd; Cock Crow (perhaps from **cocc-rodu** 'clearing where woodcocks were netted'); Cockhill Md (named from Cockhill in S. Caundle par. *supra*, cf. foll.); Cockle's Hill (Mdw), Cockle's Hill or Furzy Grd, -or New Md (probably a surname from the p.n. Cockhill, *v.* prec.); Cole Cl & Mdw; Cole's Md; Coppernway; Corn Cl; Corner Cl; Betty Coward's Grd; Cross Cl (perhaps **cross** 'lying across', but cf. Market Cross and Clark's Plot *supra*); Crutching Md; Cuckoo Pound (for this f.n. type *v.* **1** 38, 335); Cumberland's Md; Cunage; Cunning Croft; Dewish; Doctor's Md; (Green) Doles, Dole's Md (*v.* **dāl** 'share of land'); Douches (cf. John *Douch* 1664); The Down, Lr Down, Down Bottom & Cl (*v.* **dūn**); The Drove; Dry Cl; Dulliver's Ham Hr & Middle Fd (*v.* **hamm**); Dunney Fd; East Fd; (Lt) Eastward; 8 Acres; Enocks (*v.* **inhoke**); Farm Md & Pdks; 5 (and 4) Acres; 40 Acres; 4 Acres; Foxley; Front Grd; Furz(e)y Grd; Gascoe Pound Mdw; Gaunts Md, Pound Gaunts, Rough Gaunts (*Ganutes* 1552, cf. Geoffrey *le Gaunt* 1327, 1332); Gill's Md; Glebe Md; Goosehams; Graze Cl; Great Fd, Grd, Md(w) & Wd; (Gt) Green Cl; Green Lain, -Lane; Guggleton; Hallett's Md; Harnham (Orchd); Hatch Md (*v.* **hæc(c)**); Haywoods; Gt & Lt Hedge Fd, Hedge Fd Mead; Higher (sic); Higher Cl, Fd, Grd & Pce; Close(s) by Hill(')s Bridge (*Hills* 1552, cf. Edward *Hull'* 1553, Hugh *Hill* 1610); Hilly Cl & Md(w); Himpits; Hind Fm; Hindley's Grd; Hinds; Hiscock's Hays (*v.* **(ge)hæg**); (The) Home Cl, Home Fd or Cl, Home Grd & Md(w), Old Home Orchd; Horse Cl; Hundred Acres (an ironical name, since this is a very small field); Hunger Hill (a common name for poor ground); Hurden; In and Out; (Anne's Stile or) Ives; Jarvis's Md; Jerrard's Md; King('s) Cl (cf. Walter *le Kyng* 1327, Benjamin *King* 1664); Lampton or Clover Grd; Lamplands (*v.* **lampe**); Lane Cl, Lane End; Larkwood; Lash Md; Lawns; Lemons Md (cf. John *Lemman* 1442); Lie (or Ives) (probably **lēah** 'wood, clearing'); Limekiln Cl and Orchd; Little Elms; Little Fd & Md(w); Liss Md; Long Cl; (Grass) Longman(')s; (Gerrards or) Long Md; Long Mdw; Louzard (and Potatoe Ho); Lower Cl, Fd, Flg & Grd; Mapland Cl & Mdw, Lt Mapland; Marwell; Meadow over the Bridge; Middle Cl, Fd, Flg, Grd & Pce; Milking Barton; Mitchell's Cl (cf. Edmund *Michell* 1664); New Cl (*New(e)-* 1557); New Md(w); 9 Acres; North Cl; (Gt) Orchard, Orchard Cl; Ozier Bed (*v.* **osier**); Paine's Hill (cf. Walter *Payn* 1350 (18)); Lr Parsonage Mdw; Pasture Pce under the wood; Gt & Lt Pease Leaze (probably identical in origin with *Pease Leaze* in Sturminster N. par. *supra*, cf. Christina-, Richard *de Puslegh* 1327, -*de Pusele* 1332); Phillips's Md (cf. Guy *Phylippe* 1442); Piece; (Brown's Md or) Pierces Hill; Pipe's Cl; Pleck (*v.* **plek** 'small plot'); Plum Cl; Pond Cl (cf. *Pond Ho* 1824 Pigot); Poor Grd; Prankerd's Orchd; Quair-, Quarr Cl (*v.* **quarre**, cf. Harpitts *supra*); Rag(g) (*v.* **ragge**); Redbrink)s); Redlands; Rices Md; Rick pits; Ricks Bed (Crib), Rix Bed Mdw (*v.* **risc** 'rush', **cribbe** 'manger'); Roger's Md, Roger's Pce or Back Cl; Rookery or Home Md; Rough Cl, Grd & Pce, The Rough Coppice; Roundhill Md; Row Cl (probably **rūh** 'rough', cf. foll.); Rowthorne; Rycrofts and Crowhouse, Rye Croft (*v.* **ryge, croft**); Sandhills; Scarrow Hill; Gt & Lt Scotts Banks (cf. John *Scot* 1327, *v.* **bank(e)**); Shepherds Cl (cf. John *Shephurde* 1327 (S. Caundle)); Ship Grd, Md & Orchd (*v.* **scī(e)p** 'sheep'); The Shop; Shortland; 6 Acres; Small Md by the River; Snook's (or Woodland) Cl, Snook's Mdw (cf. John-, Richard *Snooke* 1664); South Grd; Southwells; Springy Md; Square Md(w); Squibbs Ham (*v.* **hamm**); (Stale or) Stape Md; Stephen's Cl & Leaze Md, Stephens Great Grd (cf. Robert *Steevens* 1664); Stamford (probably 'stony ford', *v.* **stān, ford**); Stiching (*v.* **sticcen**); Stone(s) Grd, Stones Md or Rowthorne (cf. Thomas *Stone* 1664); Stoney Fd; Stubble Cl, Stubbles; Summerlease Md or Dry Cl, Summerley's Md Gt Ground or Summer Leaze (*v.* **sumor, lǣs**); Tadbrook, Tadbrooks (Md) (*Tadbrokes lake* 1552, 'brook frequented by toads', *v.* **tadde, brōc, lacu** 'watercourse'); Tellershell's Md; 13 Acres; Thomas's Grd; Thornwood; 3 Acres; Tucker's Cl or Larkwood; 20 Acres; 2 Acres; Vardy's; Wallbridge or Loader's Grd, -or Pit Cl, Guiters or Wallbridge Mdw, Wallbridge Summerleys (cf. John-, Mary *Loder* 1664, Summerlease Md *supra*); Walter's Md (cf. Peter *Walter* 1745); Ware's Hill; Watch Heath, Watch Yates or Rook(e)s Hedge (*v.* **geat**); Water Cl & Lake; West Cl & Fd; West Lodge Fd; Landshare or Weston, Weston Md (cf. *Weston gate* 1709, named from Stalbridge Weston *supra*, *v.* Landshire Bridge *supra*); Westward; (Joyner's Md or) Whitefield; (Beach) Whitemoor; Wigmoor (cf. Wigmore in Iwerne M. par. *supra*); Wilcox Md; (Gt) Wimsell Lain, Clover Wimsell Lane, Lt Wimsell Lane, Winsell Lains (*v.* **leyne** 'tract of arable land'; this is apparently the same name as the f.n. *Winshill* c.1759-73 DROMap (KL 21) in Purse Caundle par. *infra*, and is possibly to be associated with *on hean wifeles hylle* 933 (12) in the Anglo-Saxon bounds of Stalbridge Weston, cf. William *de Wyueleshill'* 1244, -*hull'* 1268, John *de Viveleshulle* 1285, -*de Wyneleshull* (sic) 1317, -(*de*) *Wyueleshull(e)* 1327, 1332, 'high Wifel's hill', from the OE pers.n. *Wifel* with **hēah**[1] (wk.obl. *hēan*) and **hyll**, although alternatively the first el. could be **wifel** 'a weevil, a beetle'; the early forms would normally have developed to *Wilshill*, but the change to *Winshill* may be due to dissimilation); Windsor Pleck (*v.* **plek**); Winterage; Woodlands (cf. John *atte Wodelond* 1350 (18), *v.* **atte, wudu, land**); Wood Md (cf. *Wodecrofte* 1288, *v.* **croft**); Woods End (*curs' aque apud le Woodes end'* 1596, *v.* **ende**); Yearage (on Hanging Grd), Weston Wd or Yearage Coppice; Yonder Grd; Close Late Youngs.

(*b*) *on æsc leage, of þam æsce* 933 (12) (*v.* **æsc, lēah**); *on bealtunes ersc* *nypeweardne* 933 (12) (probably 'Bealdhūn's ploughed or stubble field', from the OE pers.n. *Bealdhūn* (Searle 84) and **ersc**; the pers.n. (with *-lt-* for *-ld-* and omission of *-h-*, *v.* Feilitzen 97, 120) seems preferable to a lost p.n. *Bealtūn, a type apparently confined to eastern England and of controversial origin, cf. Ekwall Studies[2] 160–1, Smith EPN I 26); *on bilian wyrþe* 933 (12) (*v.* **wyrð** 'enclosure', first el. probably an OE pers.n. *Bil(l)a* for which *v.* Bilcombe Copse in the neighbouring par. of S. Caundle *supra*; the second *-i-* in *bilian* may be intrusive or an error for *-l-*); *a lane beyond Calpins dore* 1552; *claus' voc' Downe Affyldes* 1552 (perhaps '(place) lower down in the fields', *v.* **dūne, feld**, cf. *ut on feld infra*); *Dyrdauntes* 1463 (the surname *Durden*); *on þone ealdan hagan* 933 (12) ('the old hedge or enclosure', *v.* **eald, haga**[1]); *þone ealdan weg, andlang weges* 933 (12) ('the old road', *v.* **weg**); *ut on feld* 933 (12) (*v.* **feld** 'open country', cf. *Downe Affyldes supra* and foll.); *oþ fildena wylle* 933 (12) ('spring or stream of the dwellers in open country', *v.* **filde**[2] (gen.pl. *fildena*), **well(a)**); *la Gore* 1288 (*v.* **gāra**); *on þa greatan ac* 933 (12) ('the thick oak-tree', *v.* **grēat** (wk.obl. *-an*), **āc**); *on hagan* 933 (12) (*v.* **haga**[1] 'hedge or enclosure'); *atte Hile* (p) 1327, 1332 (from **h(e)alh** (WSax dat.sg. *hēale*) 'a nook, a corner of land', *v.* **atte**); *Hohgtesmulne, Huggescumbe* 1288 (apparently variant readings of the same name, second el. either **myln** 'mill' or **cumb** 'valley', first el. a pers.n. of uncertain form); *on horgan sloh* 933 (12) ('filthy slough', from **horig** (wk.obl. *-an*) and **slōh**); *Longcroftes* 1552 (*v.* **lang**[1], **croft**); *on anne mapulder* 933 (12) (*v.* **mapuldor** 'maple-tree'); *venella ducent a More yeat* 1552, *More yate, le Morelane* 1556, *Moore Yate* 1596, *Moorelane* 1599 (cf. Henry *Atte More* 1288, *v.* **mōr** 'marshy ground', **geat** 'gate', **lane, atte** 'at the'); *Sel(ke)croft(e)* 1463 (*v.* **sēoluc** 'a gully', **croft**); *Southamclos* 1463 (*v.* **sūð, hamm, clos(e)**); *Stagars* 1552 (a surname); *on anne stan* 933 (12) (*v.* **stān** '(boundary) stone'); *oþ stanbroc* 933 (12) ('stony brook', *v.* **stān, brōc**, cf. Stanbrook *supra* in this par. some 2 miles E of this bdy point); *Verne Hyll'* 1552, *Fernehill'* 1585 (*v.* **fearn, hyll**); *andlang weges* 933 (12) (*v.* **weg** 'road'); *atte Welle* (p) 1332 (*v.* **well(a)** 'spring, stream', **atte**); *on west mæd ufewearde* 933 (12) (*v.* **west, mæd** 'meadow'); *Whetclose* 1552 (*v.* **hwǣte** 'wheat').

XXV. SHERBORNE HUNDRED

In c.1086 GeldR the hundred was somewhat smaller than it is now, since at that date Bishop's Caundle, Purse Caundle and Stock Gaylard (in Lydlinch par.) lay in Brownsall hundred and Up Cerne probably lay in *Stane* hundred (Anderson 113, 135, VCHDo 3 131, 141, 145). Alton Pancras was in this hundred in 1285 FA, 1327 *SR*, 1332 SR. Lydlinch and Up Cerne are detached.

Sireburne hundret c.1086 GeldR, *Syreburna, -e* c.1160, 1238 Sarum, 1212 Fees, *Schire-, Schyreburn(e)* 1244 *Ass*, 1303 FA, *-bourne* 1280 Ass, 1327 SR, *Shire-, Shyreburn(e)* 1265

Misc, 1275 RH, Cl, 1288 *Ass, -bourn'* 1332 SR, *-born(e)*
1346 FA, 1500 *AddCh, Schirborn', -burn(e)* 1268, 1280 *Ass,*
-bourne 1402 *Sher, Shirburn* 1285, 1316 FA, *-bo(u)rn(e)*
1334 Ipm *et freq* to 1453 *Sher, Schyrborn* 1303 FA,
Shyrbourne 1493 *DCMDeed, Sherborne Out Hundred* 1664
HTax. Named from Sherborne par. *infra.*

Beer Hackett

BEER HACKETT (ST 599118)
 Bera 1175–86, 1194, 1195 P all (p), 1203 RC
 Bere 1244 *Ass* (p), 1270 FF, 1285 FA, 1290 Ch, 1299 Ipm
 et freq to 1431 FA
 Bere Plukenet 1346 *UD*
 Berehaket 1362 FF, 1454 *Sher,* Pat, 1483 *DCMDeed,*
 -hakat' 1495 *Sher, -ha(c)ket(t)* 1532, 1558 *Sher,* 1563
 Digby, *Bere Haket* 1368 *Sher,* 1383 Cl
 Beer(e) Haket(t) 1380, 1410, 1419 *Sher,* 1483 IpmR,
 -Hakatt' 1500 *Sher, -Hackitt* 1621 (17) *Strode,*
 -Hacket(t) 1667 *DCMDeed, Beer Hacket alias Hack-*
 wood 1795 Boswell
 Biere 1382 *Sher*
 Beare, Bear juxta Yatemynstre 1412 FA
 Beare hagard 1575 Saxton
 Berre Hackett 1621 (17) *Strode*

'(Woodland) pasture', *v.* **bǣr²**, or 'wood, grove', *v.* **bearu,**
cf. Bere Regis 1 273. The manor was held by *Haket de Bera*
in 1176 to 1186 P, cf. *Haket pater Hamonis de Bera* 1194 P,
William *Haket* 1203 RC, and the f.n. *Hakettysknoll* 1449
DCMDeed (*v.* **cnoll**); the pers.n. *Haket* is an AN diminutive
of ON, OSwed *Haki,* ODan *Hake* (Tengvik 212). Alan
Plukenet held a fee here in 1284–6 (Eliz) Kirkby, cf. also
Alan *de Plugenet* 1290 Ch. Bere Hackett is ½ mile N of
Yetminster.

KNIGHTON (ST 615115), *Knygteton* 1270 FF, *Knyteton* 1276
Banco, *Knythteton', Knycton'* 1288 *Ass, Knyghton(')* 1309
FF, 1411 *Sher,* 1412 FA (*-juxta Yatmynstre*), 1431 ib, 1500,
1585 *Sher, Knyghteton(')* 1310 Banco (*-juxta Shyreburn*),

1316 FF, 1352 *DCMDeed* (*-iuxta Yatemynstr'*), 1449 *ib*, *K(n)ynghton, Kyntghton* 1412 FA, *Knyghthton'* 1500 *Sher*, *Knighton'* 1582 *Digby*, 'farm of the thegns or knights', *v*. **cniht, tūn**, cf. W Knighton I 207, possibly with reference to the Knights Hospitallers who held land at *Sputel infra* from the early 13th century. Knighton is I mile NE of Yetminster and 3 miles SW of Sherborne.

SPUTEL (lost, probably about ST 602125), 1482 Hutch³, 1774 Hutch¹, 1870 Hutch³, *La Spitell', la Spytel'* 1244 *Ass* both (p), *Sput(t)ell(')* 1408 *Sher*, 1483 IpmR, *Spyt(t)ell(')* 1431 FA, 1582 *Digby, closes . . . called Spittle* 1621 (17) *Strode*, 'house of the Knights Hospitallers', *v*. **spitel**. Hutch³ 4 120 describes it as 'anciently a manor, which belonged to the Knights Hospitallers, now a farm', cf. the entry concerning Bere Hackett in 1203 RC and the reference to the manor of *Sputel* in 1482 Hutch³ 4 119. The site of *Sputel* is suggested by the location of the f.ns. (*Lt & Gt*) *Spitfield, Hr & Lr Spitfield, Five Acre Spitfield* 1839 *TA*.

TIBBLE'S COPSE & LANE (ST 609113), (*uno clauso . . . iuxta*) *Taddebolleslane* 1411, 1454, *Tedbolyslane* 1414 *Sher, Toppole Brygge, via apud Typpyllesbrygge* 1460, *Tedpollane* 1462 *Digby, Tibbles Coppice, Lt Tibbles* 1839 *TA, tenement . . . called Tibbles Water* 1853 *EnclA*. 'Bowl-shaped hollow frequented by toads', from **tadde** and **bolla**, with **lane**, **brycg**. The 1462 form probably shows influence from ME *taddepolle* 'a tadpole' (c.1475 NED). A ford and footbridge are marked 6″.

TRILL FM & HO (ST 590120)
æt *Tril* 1002–12 ASWrits (S 1383)
Trelle 1086 DB
Trulle l13 *Sher*
Tryll(e) 1316 FA, 1384 FF, 1421 Cl *et freq* to 1563 *Digby*,
Trill(e) 1412 FA, 1426 Cl *et freq* to 1563 *Digby*

Originally the name of the stream here (now unnamed), an affluent of R. Yeo, *v*. **tyrl** 'that which turns or rolls along', cf. Ekwall RN 409, 418, PN Gl I 13. There are six examples of this name in the SW besides this one, including an early name for Darknoll Brook, v. RNs. Cf. also *Trylford* 1563 Digby.

ALCROFT COPSE, *Alcroft* 1449 *DCMDeed, Alcraft(e)* 1614, 1623 *Weld*[1], 1675 *DCMDeed, Allcraft(e)s* 1614 *Weld*[1], 1793 Hutch[3], *Allcroft Cmn, Coppice Grd by Allcroft* 1839 *TA, v.* **croft** 'enclosure', first el. possibly **heall** 'hall, manor house' in spite of the absence of initial *H*-, cf. *le Hall Meade* 1614 *Weld*[1]. CLAYPITS FM & LANE, *Clay Pit* 1839 *TA,* cf. *Clay Hill ib.* HIGHER FM. KNIGHTON CMN (1839 *TA*), HILL (COPSE) (*Knighton hill* 1569–74 *Map, -or Coppice Grd* 1853 *EnclA*) & LANE. LOWER FM. LOWER WD, 1839 *TA.* REDSTALL COPSE, cf. *Spitfield and Stall* 1839 *TA* (small building marked on *TAMap*), *v.* **stall**, *Sputel supra*. ST MICHAEL'S CHURCH, cf. *Church Hill* 1839 *TA,* 'chapel of *Bere* by *Schireborn*' 1381 Pat.

FIELD-NAMES

The undated forms are 1839 *TA* 14. Spellings dated 1288 are *Ass,* 1316 FF, 1352, 1449, 1667, 1675 *DCMDeed,* 1394 *Shepherd*[1], 1454[2] Pat, 1464, 1516, 1531 *Digby,* 1569–74 *Map,* 1614, 1622, 1629 *Weld*[1], 1621 *DCMDeed,* 1621 (17) *Strode,* 1793 Hutch[3], 1853 *EnclA,* and the rest *Sher.*

(a) Anneshay; Backside Closes 1793, Backside Mdw or Lr Backside 1853 (*Backside end* 1614, *v.* **backside**); Barn Fd & Grd; Back Beer, Beer Hedge (1621 (17)), Lake (*Beere Lake* 1531, *v.* **lacu**) & Wd (*v.* par. name *supra*); Besants Backside & Orchd; Bess, Biss (Cl), Golden Biss (*cultura voc'-* 1411, *campo voc' Bisse* 1454, *Bys* 1414, *Bysse* 1614, *Bisse or Long Strap* 1853, perhaps ME *bis(s)(e)* 'fine linen', often used generally to denote things of fineness and value (a complimentary name is feasible since these are fertile fields), or ME *bis(se)* 'brownish or dark grey', with reference to soil colour, with **golden**, which may mean either 'productive, profitable', or 'gold-coloured' referring to crops or vegetation); Bishops Bridge Md (adjacent to the field called Bishops Bridge in Thornford par. *infra q.v.*); Bowl Bridge Md (*Bowedbrigge* 1410, 1419, 1454[1], -*brygge* 1410, *Bowebrigge* 1454[2], *Bovdebrigge* 1464, *Bode-* 1516, *Boudbryge* 1531, *bowe bridge* 1569–74, 'arched or curved bridge', *v.* **bowed, brycg**); Brimsome, Brinsome (Bottom), Great-, Longbrinsome (*Bromysham* 1449, *Brounsum, Brynescom'* (sic), *Brymsoms Hedge* 1614, from **hamm** 'enclosure', first el. probably the ME surname *Brom,* cf. *Bromeswood* 1614); Broad Acre (*Broade-* 1614); Broad Cl (Hill); Broad Croft (*Broade Crofte (corner)* 1614); Broflands (or School Lds 1853) (*Broffurlong* 1614, *v.* **furlang**, first el.

probably **brōc** 'brook'); Browns Lane; Calves Grd; Castway (perhaps **cast** 'a heap'); The Clerks North & South half Acre; Clickhay (cf. *Cleakewoode* 1614, first el. uncertain); Clotty Grd; Clover Grd; Coarse hill; (Gt & Lt) Common Cl (*Com(m)on close* 1621 (17), 1667); Common Md; Coppice (grd); Corn Croft (*Corne-* 1621, *v.* **corn**[1] 'corn, grain'); Cow Leaze; Cow Md; Crib House Grd; Crislain (*le Cresse Layne* 1614, *Creslain* 1793, *v.* **cærse** 'cress', **leyne** 'tract of arable land'); Dickers Md; Droves otherwise Brinsome (cf. Brimsome *supra*); Dry Grd; 8 Acres; Flax Lds; Gt & Lt Fleet (*v.* **flēot** 'stream'); 4 Acres; Foxes Backside; The Garden 1853 (cf. *Mich' en le Gardyn de Knythteton'* 1288, *v.* **gardin**, Knighton *supra*); Gilgers Gate (*le Gylgore* 1449, *Gyllgores gate* 1614, *v.* **gāra** 'triangular plot', first el. possibly the surname *Gille* found locally (e.g. John *Gille* 1332 SR (Oborne)) rather than **gyll** 'deep narrow valley'); Great Barton; Green hay (*Greenehay, Greenhayes end* 1614, *v.* **grēne**[1], (ge)**hæg**); Green Way (1621 (17)); (Lr) Hail, Hr Hail (or Stubbs) ((*claus voc'*) (*le*) *Hale* 1614, 1622, *Heall* 1621, *v.* **h(e)alh** 'nook of land', cf. Stubbs *infra*); (N & S) Half Acre; (Long) Ham, Ham Orchd (*le Ham* 1614, *the Hamms* 1621 (17), *Ham(m)* 1675, *v.* **hamm**); Hames Hill; (Gt & Lt) Hardwood; Harp (so called from its shape); Hawk Hill; Hill Md (*Hill meadow* 1675, cf. *Hillclose* 1622); Hipple Md (*Hypple-* 1614, *Hipple Close* 1629, probably **hyppels** 'stepping stones'; there is a ford at the corner of the field); Home Fd, Md, Orchd & Plot (cf. *le Home Close* 1614); Homestead; Hundred Acres (a very small field); Island; Jacks Md (*Jockes Meade* 1621); Jumead (sic for Inmead) 1793 (*Inmeade* 1614, *v.* **in** 'inner'); Knighton Wds 1793 (*in bosco de Knyghteton'* 1449, *Knighton wood* 1675, *v.* Knighton *supra*); (Coxs & Lt) Knowle, 8 Acre & 4 Acre Knowle (*Knolle* 1411, *Hakettysknoll* 1449, *le Knoll* 1614, *v.* **cnoll**, par. name *supra*); Lane; Lanes Md; Lawn; Little Md; Little Thorn; Lodford Md; Long Cl; Long Md (*-Meade* 1667); Long Strap (*v.* **strap**); Lower Backside, Barton & Md; Merry Thorne (*Mirey-* 1853); Metfellow, Lt Mitfellow (*the lower end-, the over end of Metfurlonge* 1614, *Metfellen* 1793, *v.* **furlang**, first el. possibly **mǣd** 'meadow', unless it is the el. suggested for *Met(e)lond* 1 184); Middle Fd; Milking Barton; Millers Md; Mill hill & Md (cf. *Beremull'* 1394, *v.* **myln**); Mower Leaze; New Cl; 9 Acres; Orchard Plot, Home & Long Orchard, Old & Young Orchard; The Paddock 1853 (*le Par(r)ock* 1614, 1622, *the Paddock* 1675, *v.* **pearroc**); Pattens Plot; Pennys Acre, Penny's Md; Petty Cl; Plantation Plough Grd; Pound Cl; Redicks Hay (*v.* (ge)**hæg**); Rickyard; Rosmore (*Rossmare* 1793); Round Ham (*Rownd-* 1614, *v.* **round**, **hamm**); 7 Acres; Shillands (possibly to be identified with *Shysforlang* 1449, from **furlang** and an uncertain first el.); Shortlands; 6 Acres; Snetherms Md; Square Grd; Stakeford (Angle) (*v.* **staca** 'boundary stake', **ford**, **angle** 'corner'; these fields are at the southern point of the par.); Stars Md; Strap (*v.* **strap**); Stub Acre (*Stubble acre* 1614, *v.* **stubbil**); Stubbs, Stubb(s) Lds, Stubbs Lane (*Stubbs (Knapp)*, Stubbs *Knyghton Woode* 1614, *Stubbs* 1675, the surname *Stubb, v.* Knighton Wds *supra*); Hr & Lr Subtrehays, Subtrehays Md (*Septrowe* 1368, *Shuptrowe* 1382, *Subtrow(e)* 1410 *et freq* to 1500, *Sol-, Sultrowe* 1426 *et freq* to 1437,

Sud(d)-, *Sod(d)trowe* 1439 *et freq* to 1452, *Suttrowe* 1532, 1558, apparently 'sheep trough', from WSax **scȳp** and **trog**, with the later addition of **(ge)hæg**); Summer hams (*v.* **hamm**); Symers Barton; Triangle Pce; Trill Lane & Md (*v.* Trill Fm *supra*); Up Fd (*Vpfeyll'* 1414, *Vpfeld'* 1454¹, *Upfe(i)ld(e)* 1614, *Upfeilds* 1622, *v.* **upp** 'higher up', **feld**); West Hay (*v.* **(ge)hæg**); Westover (bottom) (*Westouer(e)* 1411, 1454¹, *-ouir* 1414, *la Westover, Westovers Close* 1614, *Westover* 1675, situated west of a stream, *v.* **west**, **ōfer**¹ 'river-bank'); Wheatland; Willow Bed; Woolhay (*v.* **(ge)hæg**, first el. probably **wiell(a)** 'spring, stream').

(*b*) *Alyneshay* 1449 (a surname with **(ge)hæg**); *Beremede* 1413 (*v.* **mæd**, par. name *supra*); *le Breach* 1614 (*v.* **bræc**); *Chicunham mede* 1410, 1419, 1454¹, *Schycunham mede* 1410, 1411 (*v.* **cīcen** 'chicken', **hamm**, **mæd**); *Cossymour* 1411, *-more* 1414, 1454¹, *Cossemoore, Cos(s)more* 1614 (the later forms resemble Cosmore in Buckland N. par. *supra*, but in this name the first el. is perhaps an OE pers.n. *Cossa* suggested for Corsham W 96, with **mōr**); *Cothay* 1614 (*v.* **cot**, **(ge)hæg**); *common meadow called Cudman* 1675; *Depford'* 1368 (*v.* **dēop** 'deep', **ford**); *Donwodebrug'* 1368 (*v.* **wudu**, **brycg**, first el. probably **dūn** 'hill, down'); *in orientali campo* 1614 ('east field'); *Estforde pytt* 1614 (*v.* **ēast**, **ford**, **pytt**); *le Ferny Hill* 1614 (*v.* **fearnig**); *Knythton' Veyll'* 1414, *in campo de Knyghteton'* 1449 (*v.* **feld**, Knighton *supra*); *Ledgcote* 1614 (*v.* **cot**); *Lin(ing)ton gate* 1675 (perhaps for Lillington par. *infra*); *Lodgwood* 1675; *Longwoode* 1614; *Lopethorn'* 1413 (*v.* **lopped**, **þorn**); *Martynes Pooles end* 1614; *atte Mede* 1316, 1352, 1449 all (p) (*v.* **atte**, **mæd**); *Morleys* 1621 (17); *Nebb therne* 1614 (*v.* **þyrne** 'thorn-bush', first el. perhaps **nebb** 'point'); *Newnams* 1629; *le Porte ȝate* 1614 (*v.* **geat**, first el. perhaps **port**² 'town'); *Rockfurlongebridge* 1614 (*v.* **furlang**, **brycg**, first el. perhaps **hrōc** 'rook' rather than **rokke** 'rock'); *Rushe acre, -Furlonge* 1614 (*v.* **rysc**); (*le*) *South(e) Meade* 1614; *Uphull'* 1449 (*v.* **upp**, **hyll**); *le Vurse* 1614 (*v.* **fyrs** 'furze'); *Watcroft* 1449 (*v.* **croft**, with **wǣt** 'wet' or **hwǣte** 'wheat').

Bradford Abbas

BRADFORD ABBAS (ST 587143)

Bradford' 839–55 (14) *Cott* (MS Faustina A. ii, f.25, cf. Finberg p.164), (*apud*) *Bradeford* (rubric), *æt bradan forda* 933 (12) *SherC* (S 422), *bradanford* 998 (12) *ib* (S 895)

Bradeford(') 1086 DB, 1125 (12), 1145 (12) *SherC*, 1204, 1214 *Cur*, 1217, 1223 *FF*, 1224 *Cur*, 1268, 1280 *Ass*, 1285 *FA et freq* to 1460 *Digby*, *-forde* 1291 *Tax*, *Bradford* 1163 *Dugd*, '*Bradeford by Shirborn*' 1450 *Pat*, *Braddeforde* 1460 *Digby*, 1569–74 *Map*, *Bradfford'* 1462 *Digby*, '*Bradford by Yevell*' 1467 *Pat*, *Bradforde* 1546 *DCMDeed*

Braddeford Abbatis 1386 IpmR, *Bradforde Abbat* 1486
 Ipm
Glasen bradford 1575 Saxton, *Glasin-*, *Glazon-*,
 Glasen-, *Glazen Brodford*, *Glazen Bradford* 1648 SC

'Broad ford' (across R. Yeo), *v.* **brād, ford**, cf. Bradford
Peverell **1** 334, Sherborne par. *infra*; *Yevell'* is Yeovil So.
The affix *Abbas* (Lat *abbas* 'abbot', gen.sg. *abbatis*) is from
the possession of this manor by Sherborne Abbey. The
alternative affix *Glasen-*, *Glasin-*, etc is no doubt eModE
glassen (from OE *glæsen*) 'made of glass, fitted with glass',
presumably with reference to the glazing of the church
windows, *v.* St Mary's Church *infra*, cf. SoDoNQ **28** 42–3,
70. The bounds of the Anglo-Saxon estate of Bradford
(which included Wyke, now in Castleton par. *infra, v.*
Grundy **1** 250) are given in 933 (12) *SherC* (S 422).

BABYLON HILL (ST 583161), 1811 OS, *Balylondwey* 1531,
Bablynwaye, Bablinhill, Babline furlong 1563 Digby, *Gt & Lt
Babylon Hill, Barberlons* 1838 *TA* (Over Compton), *v.* **weg,
hyll, furlang**. The first el. may be a surname, but, especially
if the earliest form is an error for *Babylond-*, it is more likely
to be a biblical allusion to Babylon, *v.* Field 9. Since the hill
lies on the important road (now the A30) connecting Yeovil
and points further W with Sherborne, Salisbury and
eventually London, it may in turn have been a derogatory or
humorous reference to London or one of the other places en
route, *v.* NED s.v. *Babylon* for its application 'rhetorically to
any great and luxurious city' (from 1634).

COMBE (6"), COOMBE (1") (ST 588151), *Comb'* 1332 SR (p),
(*Hr & Lr*) *Coomb(e)*, *Coombditch Corner, Coomb Orchd* 1838
TA, v. **cumb** 'valley', **dīc**.

CROSS (ST 587143), the remains of a medieval cross, no
doubt referred to in the surname of John *atte Cruch'* 1332
SR, *-atte Crouche* 1350 (18) *Add*, 'at the cross', *v.* **atte,
crūc**[3]; it perhaps also gave name to 'an arched stone building
called the Cross' which stood at the centre of the village until
the beginning of the 19th cent. (Hutch[3] **4** 122), though this

may be **cross** in the sense 'cross-roads', cf. *viam ducent uersus Evyns Crosse, -Evins Crose* 1563 *Digby*, to be associated with Thomas *Ewyns, -Ewins ib.*

UNDERDOWN HOLLOW (ST 578157), *Undirdowne* 1486 Ipm, *Hundredowne, Hunderdownes meade* 1563, *Vnderdon* 1575, *Vnderdowne mead* 1583, *Under Downe* 1672 all *Digby, Underdown (Lane & Md(w))* 1838 *TA*, '(ground) under the down or hill', from **under** and **dūn**.

BACK LANE. BISHOP'S LANE, cf. John *Bishopp* 1664 HTax. BRADFORD ABBAS MILL, *Flax-Mill, Mill Mdw and Flax Ho* 1833 *TA*, cf. The Old Mill *infra*. BRADFORD HOLLOW. EAST FM. LEAZE LANE, named from *Bradford Leaze* 1838 *TA*, cf. *Newle(a)se* 1563, 1575, *Newe Leas* 1583 *Digby, v.* **nīwe, lǣs** 'pasture'. LITTLE COVERT. MANOR FM. NORTH FM. OLD LIMEKILN, cf. *Limekiln Cl, Limekiln Grd or three corner and Site of Lime-Kiln* 1838 *TA*. THE OLD MILL, *bradford myll* 1569–74 *Map, Bradford Mill* 1811 OS, *Water Grist Mill* 1838 *TA*, cf. *molend' aquatic'* 1473 *Digby, Estmill* 1540 Hutch[3], *Estemyllandes, Estmillandes* 1563 *Digby, Mill Md* 1838 *TA, v.* **ēast, myln, land**; there is mention of a mill at Bradford in 1086 DB (VCHDo **3** 71), and there were two mills here in 1870 Hutch[3] **4** 121, cf. Bradford Abbas Mill *supra*. OLD RECTORY, *the viccaridge of Glasin Brodford* 1648 SC, *Late Vicarage Ho* 1838 *TA*, cf. *Vycaredge hedge, Vikerich hedge* 1563 *Digby, v.* **vicarage, hecg**. POTTER'S LEAZE PLANT., *Poterdlease* 1563, *Poterlease* 1564, *Pottherdes-, Potterd' leas* 1583 all *Digby, Potter's Leaze, Potter's Leys (Grd)* 1838 *TA, v.* **lǣs** 'pasture'; the first el. is probably a surname, perhaps a later form of *Portherd* (Thuresson 55). QUARRY LANE, to Quarry (6″). ST MARY'S CHURCH, cf. *Ecclesiam de Bradeford* 1145 (12) *SherC*, Richard *atte Church'* 1332 SR, *v.* **atte, cirice**. SMITH'S BRIDGE, *Smiths* [Bridge] 1791 Boswell, cf. *Brad(e)ford Bridge* 1535–43 Leland. STEPPING STONES. TILLY'S HILL, 1838 *TA*. VICAR-AGE, built 1828, cf. Old Rectory *supra*. WELL HO, cf. *Lambridge Wells* 1838 *TA* (fields nearby) and John *atte Wolle* 1332 SR, *v.* **atte** 'at the', **well(a)** 'well, spring or stream'. YEOVIL BRIDGE, 1791 Boswell, named from Yeovil So.

FIELD-NAMES

The undated forms are 1838 *TA* 24. Spellings dated 933 (12) are *SherC* (S 422), 1332 are SR, 1664 HTax, and the rest *Digby*.

(*a*) Alderbed; Ambroses Cl, Above Ambroses; Gt & Lt Backland (*v*. **back**); Bakehouse Orchd; Baker's Pce; Balls pce or Blackmoor (*v*. *infra*); Banch; (orchard called) Barn Barton (*v*. **barton**); Beggar's Bush; Bides House Cl or Hemlet (cf. Henry *Byde* 1664, *v*. Hamlet *infra*); Gt Blackeymoor, Blackmoor Md (*v*. **blæc, mōr**); Bow Wd (*v*. Catling *infra*); Bristows Plot; Broad Oak (*v*. Wyke Fd *infra*); Broadshard (*v*. **sceard** 'gap'); Broadway; Bulsh Hill (*v*. Gaston *infra*); Butcher's Bars & Moor; Canny Coomb Corner; Castle Lake (*Caswell Lake* 1575, *Carswelles Lake* 1583, 'spring or stream where cress grows', *v*. **cærse, well(a)**, with **lacu** 'stream'); Catling (or Bow Wd); Chilve Acre(s) (possibly Do dial. *chilver* 'ewe-lamb', *v*. **cilfor**); Clay-Hill (*v*. **clæg**); Common Plot; Court Barton Md; Crabtree Cl; Croft (Orchd) (cf. *les pales iuxta Crafte Close* 1583, *v*. **croft**); Culverclay (near to Clay-Hill *supra*, *v*. **culfre** 'dove'); Cuttell Hill (*le Racke stare super le Cutted Hill'* 1575, *v*. **cutted** 'provided with a water-channel', **cutel** 'water-channel', **hyll, rakke** 'tenter-frame', **stæger**[1] 'stair, steps'; the hill is near Bradford Abbas Mill *q.v. supra*, as is Ring's Rack *infra*); Deborah's Park; Dilly or Denny Flg; Dole Orchd and Dole (*v*. **dāl**); Duck's Acre; East Hill (Orchd); 8 Acres; Encroachment; House . . . called the Five Bells; French's Cl (cf. William *French* 1664); Gaston or Bulsh Hill, Cold Ga(r)ston (or Underdown) (*Colgaston'* 1484, *v*. **gærs-tūn** 'paddock', cf. Underdown Hollow *supra*; *Col-* may represent **col**[1] 'charcoal' or the pers.n. *Col*, a pet-form of *Nicholas*); Goodford's Md; Gore (*v*. **gāra**); Gould's Orchd; Greenbowl, (Greenway or) Grumbowle, (Gt) Greenway; Gundry's Md; Ham (*v*. **hamm**); Hambreys; Hamlet, (Gt) Hemlet (presumably eModE **hamlet** 'hamlet'; the fields are near Combe *supra*); Hammershill, Lt Hammer's Hill; Harris's Furze; Hatchett Md (*v*. **hæcc-geat**; by R. Yeo); Hern, Hern's Hill, Hern(s)'s Moor (*Hurne* 1563, *v*. **hyrne** 'corner', here referring to land in a bend of R. Yeo); Holland; Home Cl; Hulkham Bottom (*Hulcu'*, *Hurcombe* 1563, second el. **cumb** 'valley', first uncertain); Hurst (*v*. **hyrst**); Jasper(')s (Cl); Kings Pit (cf. John *le Kyng'* 1332); Kitchen Md; Knights Furze; Leicester's Md; Little Md; Little Tree; Long Dick; Longhound; Longlands; Long Tree or Coombe Ditch Tree (*v*. Combe *supra*); Lower Fd; Lynch (*v*. **hlinc**); Midsummer Md (*v*. **mid-sumor**, cf. Field 137); Narrow Path; Nathaniels Cl or Denny Flg (cf. Dilly *supra*); New Cl; Normans Cl; Old Lane; Peachy; Plantation; Post and Post 4 Acres, Post Cl (cf. *les pales et les postes iuxta terr' Thom' Doune* 1583, *v*. **post**); The Pound, Site of Old Pound; Ring's Rack (cf. Cuttell Hill *supra*, first el. probably a surname); The Rose and Crown P.H.; Rough Md; 6 Acres; Middle Spear; The Strap (*v*. **strap**); Summer(s) Style; Thorne Style; Touching; Wanbind; (The) Warren, Warrens Coppice; Witches Trees; Withy Bed; Woolstrough; Worth (*v*. **worð**); Wyke Fd (or Broad Oak), Wyke Park (named from

Wyke in Castleton par. *infra*); Yeovil Bridge (pasture ground near Yeovil Bridge *supra*).
(*b*) *Anesmo(u)re* 1563, *Annes More* 1583 (*v.* **mōr**, first el. probably a surname; any connection with the Anglo-Saxon boundary mark *ennan pol infra* is perhaps unlikely); *le Backesyde* 1575 (*v.* **backside**); *Bachstocke* 1563 (second el. perhaps **stocc** 'tree-trunk, stump' rather than **stoc** 'secondary settlement'); *Blindlane* 1564 (*v.* **blind**); *oþ þa ealdan dic, þonne andlang dic* 933 (12) ('the old ditch', *v.* **eald, dīc**); *oþ ennan pol* 933 (12) (BCS 695 reads *ænnan*-) ('Enna's pool' (in R. Yeo), *v.* **pōl**; the OE pers.n. *Enna* is also found in *ennanbeorgum* Brk 727); *Framptons Yate* 1564 (*v.* **geat**); *Hillwale, Hyll' Wale* 1563 (*v.* **hyll, walu** 'ridge of earth or stone'); *andlang lace* 933 (12) (*v.* **lacu** 'stream'); *Meadedeath* 1575 (probably **mǣd** 'meadow', second el. obscure); *in the more* (p) 1332 (*v.* **mōr**); *to mylenburnan* 933 (12) (discussed under Bedmill in Castleton par. *infra*); *Narrow path* 1583; *Overlands* 1598; *Reckeham', Rekham* 1563 (*v.* **ricke** 'rick', **hamm**); *terr' apud le Shuttle* 1575 (probably eModE **shuttle** in the sense 'flood-gate' since this was near R. Yeo, *v.* **scyt(t)el**); *Sidberowe* 1564, *Sydborowgh'* 1583 ('large hill or barrow', *v.* **sīd, beorg**); *John Sters Corner* 1564.

Long Burton

LONG BURTON (6"), LONGBURTON (1") (ST 649128), *Burt(h)-on'* 1244, *Burton(')* 1280 *Ass*, 1332 SR, 1428 FA, 1462 *Digby*, 1552 *Shepherd*², *Borton(e)* 1280 *Ass*, 1406 *Digby*, 1415 IpmR, 1427, 1450 *Salis, Buryton(')* 1285 FA, 1288 *Ass, Bourton(')* 1316 FA, 1460, 1508 *Digby*, 1525 *Salis, Burtoun'* 1487 *Digby*; *Estboyton', -burton', -boryton'* 1288 *Ass, Esterborton'* 1460, *-bourton'* 1538, 1563 *Digby*; *magn' Burton'* 1450 *Salis*; *Langebourton'* 1460 *Digby, Longe Bourton'* 1542 *Shepherd*², *-Burton* 1569–74 *Map, Longburton* 1575 Saxton. 'Fortified farmstead' or 'farmstead near a fortification', *v.* **burh-tūn**, cf. East & West Burton 1 176, Bourton par. *supra*; **ēast** 'east', **ēasterra** 'more easterly', **magna** 'great', and **lang¹** 'long' (from the length of the village) distinguish it from Little Burton *infra*.

LITTLE BURTON (ST 642124), *parva Borton'* 1450 *Salis, West'· burton', Westburton'* 1484, *Westerburton'* 1487, 1531 *Digby, Westerbourton'* 1525 *Salis*, 1538, 1563 *Digby, West-burton'* 1555 *Shepherd*², *Litle Burton* 1569–74 *Map*, 1620 *CampbCh, Littleburton* 1599 *ib, West or Little Burton* 1774 *Hutch*¹, *v.* **parva** 'little', **west, westerra** 'more westerly',

lȳtel, par.name *supra*, cf. also *Westerbourtons poole* 16, *Westerbourton' bridge* 1563 Digby, *v.* **pōl**[1], **brycg**.

STREET LANE (ST 652116), (*viam voc'*) *Strete Lane* 1460 Digby, 1556 *Shepherd*[2], *Stret(e)lane* 1462, 1464, 1484, 1487, 1491, *Stretlande* 1531 all *Digby*; the continuation, S towards Dorchester, of *B(o)urton' Strete* 1555 *Shepherd*[2], 1563 Digby (cf. *in alta strat'* 1473 *ib*), *v.* **strǣt, lane**, par. name *supra*.

BLIND LANE. BRADFORD LANE, 'broad ford', *v.* **brād, ford** (its original location may have been at the NE end of the lane), cf. John-, Walter *atte Forde* 1332 SR. BURTON CMN, 1800 *EnclA*, 1844 *TA*. BURTON HO. LONG BURTON FM. DYKE HEAD (PLANT.), *Dickhead* 1844 *TA, v.* **dīc** 'ditch', **hēafod**. GLENWOOD. HIXON PLANT., *Hixons* 1844 *TA*, probably the surname *Hickson*. LEWESTON CTG & FM (*Lewston Fm* 1811 OS), from Leweston par. *infra*. LONGMEAD PLANT., *Long Mead* 1844 *TA, v.* **mǣd**. MANOR FM, *Lower Burton* 1811 OS. NEWCROSS CTGS, *Newcrosse* 1553, 1555 *Shepherd*[2], *New Cross* 1844 *TA*, at a T-junction, cf. *Burton crosse* 1569–74 *Map, v.* **cross**. OLD LIMEKILN, *Limekiln* 1826 Gre, cf. *Lime Kiln Grd* 1844 *TA*. ORCHARD CTG, cf. *Orchard* (*freq*) 1844 *TA*. QUARR SHRUB, cf. *Quarre Close* 1552, *le quarre* 1556 *Shepherd*[2], *Quarry* (*Grd*) 1844 *TA, v.* **quarre** 'quarry'. QUARRY LANE, cf. *Hr & Lr Quarry* 1844 *TA*, Quarry marked 6″. ST JAMES'S CHURCH, cf. 'the chapel of *Bourton*' 1405 Hutch[3]. SPRING HO. WATERY LANE. WEST HILL CTG, from West Hill in Castleton par. *infra*.

FIELD-NAMES

The undated forms are 1844 *TA* 130. Spellings dated 1270 are *For,* 1327 *SR*, 1332 SR, 1405 Hutch[3], 1525 *Salis*, 1542, 1552, 1553, 1554, 1555, 1558 *Shepherd*[2], 1569–74 *Map*, 1599, 1620 *CampbCh*, 1664 HTax, and the rest *Digby*.

(*a*) Acre Md; Banwell; Barn Grd; Batts (*v.* **batte**); Bread ('close called *Vicar's Breade*' 1405, *le Breede* 1464, *Vycaryesbrede* 1531, *vicaries bredde* 1569–74, *Vicarage bread* 1582, *v.* **brǣdu** 'a broad stretch of land', **vicare**, **vicarie, vicarage**); Bretts Ho (cf. John *le Brut'* 1332); Gt & Lt Brimley (no doubt to be associated with *Bremylcrafte* 1525, *Bremble lane, Brembles* 1555, *Bremble lake* 1582, *v.* **brēmel** 'bramble', **croft** 'enclosure', **lane, lacu** 'stream'); Broad Horn (*Brodhurne* 1563, *v.* **brād, hyrne** 'angle, corner'); Hthr & Yonder Broadway (*claus' voc' Brodewaye* 1553, *v.* **brād, weg**); Little Burton Md (cf. *pratum in Westburton'* 1555, *v.* Little Burton *supra*); Bushy Leaze (*v.* **lǣs**); But Hays ((ge)**hæg**, with either **butt**[2] or **butte**); Lr & Middle Cancer (*v.* Cancer Drove in Holnest par. *infra*); Cat Bridge (*Cadbryge* 1553, -*brige* 1558, *v.* **brycg**, first el. uncertain); Chillbatts (cf. Batts *supra*); Clay Cl, Clay Lands Md; Cow Leaze (cf. *Cowcrofte (lane)* 1487, 1552, *v.* **cū, lǣs, croft**); Hr Crazeys (*claus' voc' Squibtons nuper Crases* 1620, cf. Nicholas *Crase* 1552); Crib House Grd (*v.* **cribhouse**); Culverwell (*claus' voc' Coluerwell* 1555, 1558, *v.* **culfre** 'dove', **well(a)** 'spring, stream'); Dickers Md (cf. William *Deeker* 1664); Downs (*claus' voc' Downes* 1552, probably from a surname, but cf. *claus' voc' le Downe* 1558 which is from **dūn** 'hill'); 8 Acres; 18 Acres; Evely ((*Lyttell'*) *Eveley* 1552, *v.* **lȳtel, lēah**, first el. uncertain); 4 Acres; Gillwool (*Gylwulles* 1525, second el. possibly **well(a)** 'spring, stream'); Green Cl; Grist; Hackford (*Hawke forde* 1552, *Haukforde* 1558, *v.* **hafoc, ford**); Hr & Lr Hays Moor, Hay's Moor (*Hayshemore* 1525, *Hayes More* 1554, *Haysmore* 1558, cf. *Hayes lane* 1555, *v.* **hǣs** 'brushwood', **mōr** 'marshy ground'); Home Fd, Md & Plot; Hookey Ld; Horse Leaze (*v.* **lǣs**); Hungry Hill (*Hungerhyll'* 1563, a derogatory name for poor ground, *v.* **hungor, hyll**); Hutchings's Md; Kiddles Md (cf. Richard *Kettle* 1664); Knotleys Plot; Landers (cf. John *Lavender* 1599); Lipyeats (*claus' voc' Lyppe yates* 1552, *v.* **hlīep-geat** 'a leap-gate'); Little Md; Lower Md; Marsh; Nap Md (**nǣp** 'turnip' or **cnæpp** 'hillock'); 9 and 5 Acres; Nursery; Paddock; Parsley Bed; Plantation; Plot; Plumley (probably from **plūme** and **lēah**); Pound Cl (cf. *le Pownde* 1556, *pynfald' d'ni* 1558, *v.* **pund, pynd-fald**); Sand Croft (*v.* **croft**); Sand Nursery; 7 Acres; 6 Acres; Gt South Fd; Spry Md (*v.* **sprǣg** 'brushwood, twigs'); Lr Strap, Straps (*v.* **strap**); 10 Acres; Thornwood; 3 Acres; Three Cornered Md; Toogoods Md (cf. Geoffrey *Togood* 1552); Towns End; 12 Acres; 2 Acres; Well Cl (cf. John-, Richard *atte Welle* 1327, Alice-, Isabel *atte Wolle* 1332, *Welhayes* 1563, *v.* **well(a)** 'spring, stream', **atte** 'at the', **(ge)hæg** 'enclosure'); West Md (*Westmede* 1525, 1555, *v.* **west, mǣd**); Whistle Water (*Westhall' Water* 1555, from West Hall in Folke par. *infra, v.* **wæter** 'stream'); Wickams; Wilkins Plot; Willis's Grd; Woodhorne (probably **hyrne** 'angle, corner'); Yarn Barton Orchd (cf. Yarn Barton in Broadwindsor par. *infra*); Youngs Plot (cf. Richard-, Walter *le Yonge* 1332, *pratum nuper Laurencij Yong'* 1508).

(*b*) *le Backsyde* 1552 (*v.* **backside**); *Bradfeld'* (*v.* **brād, feld**); *claus' voc' Canelles* 1552 (probably a surname); *claus' voc' Crumbyll'* 1552 (*v.* **crymel** 'small piece (of land or water)'); *le Hemphay* 1554 (*v.* **hænep, (ge)hæg**); *pons voc' High'brigge, Hyebrygge* 1466 (*v.* **hēah, brycg**); *Lady hay* 1552 (*v.* **hlǣfdige, (ge)hæg**, probably land dedicated to the Virgin); *Longclose* 1525; *Lytelplace* 1538; *Mede Closse* 1554 (*v.* **mǣd, clos(e)**); *Moreleysyate* 1491 (perhaps to be associated with *Morlese* 1438, *v.* **mōr, lǣs, geat**); *Pylehede* 1460 (*v.* **pīl** 'pile, stake', **hēafod**); *Pyl(l)mede* 1552, *Pill' Me(a)de* 1554, 1582, *Pylle Mede closse* 1554 (*v.* **pyll** 'pool, stream', **mǣd, clos(e)**); *claus' voc' Shylbeth* 1552; *claus' voc' Skynges* 1552; *Sowthe Close* 1555;

claus' voc' Swypton' 1542, 1552, *Squybbe-* 1552, *Squypedowne* 1555, *claus' voc' Squibtons nuper Crases* 1620 (probably from **dūn** 'hill' with the ME surname *Squybbe, Squibbe* found in 1327 *SR* and 1332 SR, cf. *Skuyppeslane* 1491 in Holnest par. *infra* and Hr Crazeys *supra); Stancrofte* 1555, 1558 (*v.* **stān, croft**); *Stoke-* 1552, *Stocke furlonge* 1555 (*v.* **furlang**, first el. probably **stocc** 'tree-stump'); *Thornyrew* 1552 (*v.* **þornig, ræw**); *Westlondes* 1558; *Wodowne* 1508, *Oldowne* 1525 (probably 'old down', i.e. 'down formerly or long in use', from **eald** and **dūn**, with prosthetic *W-* in the first form, cf. the f.n. Downs *supra); la Wychole* 1270 (in the bounds of Blackmoor Forest and possibly in this par., perhaps from **wice** 'wych-elm' and **hol¹** 'hollow').

Castleton

This once small par. was considerably enlarged in 1895 by the addition of a large area previously in Sherborne, but part of the par. was transferred to the urban district and par. of Sherborne in 1928. The present par. of Castleton completely encircles Sherborne.

CASTLETON (ST 646165), *vill' de castello* 1268 *Ass, Libertas de Casteltone* 1327 *SR, Castelton(')* 1332 SR, 1426 *Sher (lib' de-)*, 1452 *Sher*, 1538 *Digby (-Burgus) et freq* to 1590 *ib (-manerium), la/le Castel(l)ton'* 1395 *Salis*, 1426, 1429, 1452 *Sher, -toun(e)* 1426, 1427 *Sher*, 1427 *Salis*, 1448, 1454 *Sher (lib' de-), -town(e)* 1439, 1465, 1471 *Sher, Casteltoun'* 1452, 1455 *Sher, -town(e)* 1484 *ib et freq* to 1617 *Pitt, Castletowne* 1569–74 *Map*, 1585 *Sher*, 1617 *Pitt*, 1639 *Digby, -ton* 1618 *ib*, 1626 *Sher*, 1811 OS, *Castle Towne* 1664 HTax, *Casselton* 1717 Hutch³, 'estate by the castle', *v.* **tūn**, with reference to Sherborne Castle *infra* (the 'old castle' built in the early 12th cent.). The market here is referred to as *Castelton mercat'* 1559 *Salis, the market(t) place* 1614, 1642, *Castleton Markett* 1614 all *Digby*.

BEDMILL (COPSE), BEDMILL FM (ST 609156), *Biddmyll* 1569–74 *Map, Bidmill* 1590 *Salis*, 1614 *Digby, Bedmill* 1677 *ib, Bed Mill* 1843 *TA*, probably identical in origin with *Bydemylne* in Wimborne M. 2 192, *v.* **myln**, first el. either **byden** 'a vessel, a hollow' or an OE pers.n. *Bida*. There was a mill at Bedmill (ST 606150) at an early date, since the former stream here (6″ but not 1″), an affluent of R. Yeo, is apparently referred to in the Anglo-Saxon bounds of Bradford A. as *mylenburnan* 933 (12) *SherC* (S 422) and in those of Thornford as *mylenburnna* 903 for 946–51 (12) *ib* (S 516), 'mill stream', *v.* **burna**, cf. Forsberg 6.

BLACKMARSH CTGS & FM (ST 650177), *Blakemersshe* 1531, 1538 *Digby, blackemershe* (*bridge*) 1569–74 *Map, Black(e)-marsh(e)* 1614, 1677 *Digby, Black Marsh* (*Mdw*) 1733 *DROMap,* 1845 *TA, v.* **blæc** 'black, dark-coloured', **mersc** 'marsh'.

COOMBE FM (ST 621184), *Combe* 1316 FA, 1324 Pat (p), *Combe* (*bottom*) 1600, 1614 *Digby, Coomb Field* 1733 *DROMap, Combe Fm* 1811 OS, *Coombe Bottom* 1843 *TA, v.* **cumb** 'valley', cf. Overcoombe *infra* and Nether Coombe in Sherborne par. *infra.* For *Coombe Bottom,* cf. *in vallo inter Ouerecumbe et Nythercumbe* 1349 *Sher, the buttome betwene Overcombe and Nethercombe* e17 *ib, v.* **botm** 'valley bottom',

HONEYCOMB CTG & WD (ST 633143), *in bosco domini de Honycomb'* 1427, *Honycombe* 1525 *Salis,* 1538 *Digby* (*-Wode*), 1542 *Shepherd*[2] (*-Wood'*), 1600 *Digby* (*-leases*), *honycome lease, honycombwoode* 1569–74 *Map, Honiecombe Closes, -Wood(es)* 1614 *Digby, Honeycombe Wood* 1811 OS, 'valley where honey is produced', *v.* **hunig, cumb**, with **wudu, læs.**

OVERCOOMBE (Kelly, about ST 617187), *Ouercomb(e)* 1327 *SR,* 1332 SR, 1406, 1538 *Digby, Ouerecumbe* 1349 *Sher, Overcomb(e)* 1427 *Salis et freq* to 1617 *Pitt, Ouyrcombe* 1473–1538 *Digby, Ouer Combe* 1531 *ib, Over Combe* 1664 HTax, *Overcoombe* 1795 Boswell, *Hither Combe* (sic) 1870 Hutch[3], 'higher or upper part of the valley', from **uferra** and **cumb**, thus distinguished from Nether Coombe in Sherborne par. *infra* which like Overcoombe was a tithing in Sherborne in-hundred. The same valley also gives name to Coombe Fm *supra.* For the former St Peter's Chapel in Overcoombe, *v.* the f.n. *Chapelhayes infra* and cf. *Saynt Peters lane* 1531 *Digby*; according to Fowler 10, the ground opposite the farmhouse at Overcoombe is still known as Chapel Hill.

PINFORD (LANE) (ST 665173)
Pinefort c.1160 Sarum, *-ford* 1280, 1288 *Ass*, *Pynefford*(')
1264 (e15) *MiltRoll*, 1331 Orig, *-ford(e)* 1275 Ipm, 1280
Ass, 1285 FA, 1299 Ipm, 1316 FA, 1332 SR, 1406
Digby, 1431 FA
Pinford 1263 Ipm, 1303 FA, 1621 *Pitt*, 1811 OS,
Pynford(') 1346 FA, 1380 *Sher* (p), 1428 FA, 1462 *Digby*
(*via que ducit uersus-*) *et freq* to 1563 *ib*, *-fforde* 1531 *ib*,
Pinforde (*Hill*) 1600 *ib*, *Pinford-*, *Pinferd farme* 1614
Pitt, *Pynforde Farme* 1614 *Digby*, *Pinfard farme* 1617
Pitt
Pynneford' 1487 *Digby*
Pimford 1870 Hutch[3]

v. **ford** 'ford'. The first el. is doubtful. OE **pīn** 'pine-tree'
as suggested by Fägersten 211 seems preferable to either
PrWelsh **penn**[1] 'hill' or OE **pynd** or **penn**[2] 'enclosure' as
suggested by Kökeritz 125. On the other hand, in spite of the
absence of *-nn-* spellings among the early forms, OE **pinn**
'pin, peg' or an OE pers.n. *Pinna* are perhaps also possible
here as in a number of other names like Pingwell Sx 414,
Pinley Wa 167, 219, Pinner Mx 63, cf. also the ME surname
Pyne which occurs in Do in 1327 *SR* (Kingston Lacy).

PRIMESLEY (lost about ST 660160)
Prumeleg' 1198, 1199 P, *Prummeslegh* 1252 FF, *Prumesley*
head 1598 *Digby*
Primeslee 1204 Cur, *-leg'* 1244 *Ass*, *-ley* 1583 *Digby*, 1870
Hutch[3], *Prymesley Hill* 16 *Digby*, *Prymysley* 1558
Shepherd[2], *Prymmesleighe* 1563 *Digby*, *Primsl(e)y* (*hedd*)
1569–74 *Map*, *Prymsley* 1575, *Prymesley* (*Mannor*) 1600,
1614, *Primsley Mannor*, *Prymsley Farme* 1677 all *Digby*
Pruneslegh (probably for *Primes-*) 1244 *Ass* (p)
Prinnesl[e] (probably for *Prumes-*) 1285 FA, *Prini(e)sley*
(probably for *Prim(e)s-*) 1614, 1617 *Pitt*
Bromesley (sic) 1288 *Ass* (p)
Promeslegh(') 1327 *SR* (p), 1332 SR (p), *-le* 15 *Digby*, *-ley*
1426 *Sher*, 1535 VE, 1552 *Shepherd*[2], *Prommesley* 1426
Sher, 1496 (*-Wodeyate*), *Promysleygh' ys curte* 1460,

Pro(u)mys-, Proumisleygh' 1462, *Promsleygh'* 1516,
Promysleyshedd 1531 all *Digby*

v. **lēah** 'wood, clearing in a wood', with **hyll, hēafod,
wudu, geat, court.** The first el. would seem to be an OE
pers.n. *Prym,* perhaps a variant of the *Prim* recorded as the
name of a moneyer in the time of Edgar (959–975, *v. England
before the Conquest,* Cambridge 1971, p. 203) and found in
Princelett Wt 171, cf. also Primethorpe Le (DEPN) and
Primley D 518. Primesley is said by Hutch[3] 4 298 to have
been 'about a mile south-east from Sherborne'.

SHERBORNE CASTLE (Remains of) (ST 648168), *Scireburnensis
castri ecclesie* 933 (12) *SherC* (S 423), *Ecclesiam Sancte Marie
Magdalene iuxta castellum* 1145 (12) *SherC, castelli de
S(c)hireburn'* 1193–1209 P, *castrum de Shyreburn* 1217 Pat *et
freq* (with various spellings for Sherborne) to 1253 Cl,
castrum regis de Shyreburn' 1258 Cl, *Castrum Shirbornie* 1454
Sher, The castelle of Shirburne 1535–43 Leland, *the Castle of
Sherborne* 1614 *Digby, Castle* 1811 OS, cf. *castle hill* 1569–74
Map, v. **castel(l).** This castle, built (on an earlier
foundation?) in the early 12th cent., gives name to Castleton
supra. For the church of St Mary Magdalen, and for a chapel
within the old castle dedicated to St Michael, *v.* under
Sherborne churches *infra.*

Various parts of the castle are recorded as follows: *turris de
Schireburn'* 1202 P, *turrim castri de Shireburn'* 1235 Cl, *4
great toures yn the castelle waulle, whereof one is the gate house*
1535–43 Leland; *la Arche in Orientali parte Castri* 1427 *Salis;
circa fossata Castri* 1427 *ib, a great dike . . . a false mure
without the dike* 1535–43 Leland, *the Castelldiches (close
called-)* 1579 *Russ, The Castleditches* 1614, *the Castlewall*
1677 *Digby, The Old Castle Ramparts* 1845 *TA; the castelle
court* 1535–43 Leland. Also named from the castle are: *The
Castlegroundes* 1614 *Digby, Castle grounds* 1617 *Pitt; la/le(s)
Castelmull'* 1427, 1450, *Castelmyll* 1525 all *Salis, duobus
molend' vocat' Castelmylles* 1538, *A water grist mill and a
Tucking mill called the Castle Mills* 1677 *Digby, Lodge or
Castle Mill now Scott's* 1802 Map, *Scott's (anciently called the
Castle) Mill* 1870 Hutch[3], *v.* **myln;** *the Old Castle Green*

1849 *EnclA*; and Castle Fm *infra*.

The present SHERBORNE CASTLE (also 6″) was built by Sir Walter Raleigh in 1594, on the site of a hunting lodge (cf. *the logge* 1535–43 Leland, *Lodge* 1569–74 *Map*), ¼ mile S of the old castle.

SHERBORNE PARK (ST 660163), 1811 OS, *in parco* 12 *SherC*, *in parco de S(c)ireburn(a)* 1162 P, 1200 Cur *et freq, Syreborn Park* 1261 DoNHAS **87** 227, *The parke of Shirburne* 1535–43 Leland, *Shurborne Parke* 1583 SPDom, *The Parke* 1600 Digby, cf. *Parkgate, la Westpark* 1375–88 Fowler, *(la) Park(e)mede* 1427 *Salis*, 1538 *Digby, pratum (iacent' iuxta palam) parci Ferarum* ('meadow situated near to the pale of the park for beasts of the chase') 1538, *la Parkyete* 15, *le Parke Yatte, Parkewey* 1531 all *Digby, Parkyate* 1601, *close by the parke* 1626 *Sher, Middle Park, New Park* 1733 DROMap, *v.* **park, mǣd, geat, weg**, cf. Deer Park and Old Park *infra*. For a detailed account of this medieval deer-park, *v.* Cantor & Wilson **5** 227–9.

SILVERLAKE CTGS & FM (ST 615154), *forlango iuxta Sewelake* 1454 *Sher, Sewellake* 1590 *Salis*, 1614 *Digby, Sevylake* 1605 Fowler, *Sevie Lake* 1733 DROMap, *Seven Acres Silver Lake* 1843 *TA, v.* **lacu** 'stream'; the first part of the name may represent 'seven springs' from **seofon** and **well(a)** (for this common combination *v.* EPN s.v. **seofon**). The late alteration to *Silver-* is due to folk etymology.

WYKE (FM) (ST 601145), *Wica(m)* 1125 (12), 1145 (12) *SherC*, 1163 Dugd, *Wyke* 1212 P, 1290 Ch, 1316 FA, 1319 FF *et passim, Wyk* 1355 Cl, *Wyke als. Wykam* 1415 IpmR, *Wike* 1535–43 Leland, *Weeke (ashe)* 1569–74 *Map, Wyke Farm* 1843 *TA, v.* **wīc** 'dwelling, farm, dairy-farm', **æsc** 'ash-tree'; *Wykam* is probably a Latinized form. For a former park here, *v.* Park Ctg *infra*, Cantor & Wilson **10** 208–9.

ALMSHOUSE WD, 1843 *TA*, belonged to the Almshouse in Sherborne *infra*. AMBROSE HILL, a Romano-British settlement site, so perhaps a recent name commemorating the Dark Age British general, Ambrosius Aurelianus, cf. J.

Morris, *The Age of Arthur* (1973) 100 . BEDFORD'S CAMP (Site of), (*Three Acre*) *Bedford Castle, Bedford Castle or Batemens Folly, -or Dampiers Hedge Lawn* 1843 *TA*, the camp now called *Bedford's Castle* 1870 Hutch[3] 4 269, named from the Earl of *Bedford*, leader of the Parliamentary forces which besieged Sherborne Castle in 1642, cf. John *Dampier* 1614, *Tenement Late Dampiers* 1677 Digby. BOWDEN HILL, *Bowdon' Hill'* 1566 Digby, 'curving hill', *v.* **boga, dūn**. BRICKKILN LANE. CASTLE FM, near Sherborne Castle. CHARLOCK HILL, *Charlotte Hill* [Bridge] 1791 Boswell, *Chorlock Hill* 1811 OS, *Charlick Hill* (*Plant.*) 1838 *TA* (Nthr Compton), possibly identical in origin with Charlock Nth 90, 'cold stream', from **ceald** and **lacu**, with reference to the stream rising on the W slope of the hill. (UPR) CLATCOMBE FM, CLATCOMBE HO & LANE, *Klatcombe* 1569–74 *Map*, *Clotcomb(e) Farme* 1614 Digby, 1617 Pitt, 1677 Digby, *the furzes in Clotcombe* 1614 *ib*, *Clatcoomb* 1733 *DROMap*, *Chatcomb* (sic) *Barn* 1811 OS, *Gt Clatcombe, Clatcombe Lane* 1843 *TA*, 'valley where burdock grows', *v.* **clāte**, **cumb**, cf. Do dial. *clote* 'the yellow water lily' (Barnes). COOMBE LANE, named from Coombe Fm *supra*. CRACKMORE WD, cf. Crackmore Lodge (6") and *Crackmacke hill* 1569–74 *Map*, *Crackments Hill* 1811 OS in Milborne Port par. (So). DANCING HILL, 1811 OS, *Daunsingehyll'* 1563, *Dawnesinghill* 1564 Digby, *dansing hill* 1569–74 *Map*, closes called *Daunc(e)-ing(e) Hill* 1614, 1677 Digby, 1733 *DROMap*, 'hill where dancing took place', *v.* **dauncing**; the hill lies just across the river (Yeo) from Sherborne. DARKHOLE FM, 1811 OS, *Darkhole Mill* 1849 *EnclA*, *v.* **deorc, hol**[1]. DEER PARK, part of Sherborne Park *infra*. DODGE CROSS, 1733 *DROMap*, *Dodcrosse* 1538, *Dodescrosse* 1614 Digby, cf. *Four Acres Dodge Close* 1843 *TA*, cf. William *Dodde* 1327 *SR*, 1332 SR, *v.* **cross**, probably in the sense 'cross-roads'. DYMOR, *close called-, sheepedowne at Dymer* 1614 Digby, *Dimor Boor & Bottom* 1733 *DROMap*, *Lawn in Dimor, Dimor Well Close* 1843 *TA*, second el. **mere** 'pool' (no water is marked 6" but the place lies in a pronounced valley) or **mōr** 'marshy ground', first el. possibly the OE pers.n. *Diga* (Redin 91) suggested for Dydon D 85; *Boor* may represent **bor**[1] 'hill', cf. the nearby f.n. Nettle Boor *infra*. GAINSBOROUGH DAIRY &

HILL (1811 OS), *Gauntesborewe* 1496, *Gaunsbury Hill* 16, *Gawnsebarowhill'*, *-hyll'*, *Gaunteshorooue* (*sic*, for *-borowe*) 1531 all *Digby*, *Gainsborowe Hyll* 1569–74 *Map*, *v.* **beorg** 'barrow, hill', **hyll**, cf. Henry *Gaunde* 1332 SR. GALLOWS PLOT, on the par. bdy, no doubt the site of a gallows (*v.* Fowler 147), cf. *via a lez Galowes vsq' Haukyniscrose* 1464 *Digby*, *v.* **galga**. GOOSELAND LANE, named from *Goos Lands* 1733 *DROMap*, *Gt Gooseland* 1843 *TA*, *v.* **gōs**; the northerly continuation of this lane is called *Thieveing Way* 1733 *DROMap*. HACK HILL. HALF MOON CLUMP, named from its shape. HARDING'S HOUSE LANE. HOME COVERT & FM. JERUSALEM, a hill in Sherborne Park. THE KENNELS. LENTHAY COPSE, DAIRY HO & LANE (1677 *Digby*, 1733 *DROMap*, 1843 *TA*), named from Lenthay Common in Sherborne par. *infra*; Lenthay Lane is *Drove Way* 1733 *DROMap*, cf. *the drovewaie, the driftewaie* 1600 *Digby*, *v.* **drāf**, **drift**. LIMEKILN CTGS & FM, cf. *Limekiln* 1733 *DROMap*, *Limekiln Pce* 1843 *TA*, possibly to be associated with *Limost'* 1464, *Lymyst* 1466, *Lymeston(e)* 1538, *Lymyster* 1563, *Lymster* 1614, *Lemster* 1677 all *Digby*, from **līm** 'lime', **āst** 'kiln', **stān** 'stone, stone quarry'. LONG PLANT. LOVER'S GROVE. LOW'S HILL LANE, *Lows Hill* 1733 *DROMap*, *Lows Hill* (*Lane*) 1843 *TA*, cf. Thomas *Lowys* 1249 FF, Edward *Lowe* 1617 *Pitt*. MIDDLE LODGE. OAKEY CLUMP. OLD PARK, 1733 *DROMap*, part of Sherborne Park *infra*. PARK CTG, named from *Wyke Park* 1540 Hutch[3] (4 298), 1838 *TA* (Nthr Compton), *Weekpark* 1838 *ib*, cf. Wyke Fm *infra*. PATSON HILL, *v.* Patson Hill Fm in Sandford O. par. *infra*. PIDGEON HO (lost), 1811 OS. PINFORD LANE, 1733 *DROMap*, leading to Pinford *supra*. REDHOLE LANE, 1843 *TA*, cf. *Red Hole* 1733 *DROMap*, *Lawn at Redhole* 1843 *TA*, *Seven Acre Pce at Redhole* 1849 *EnclA*, *v.* **rēad** 'red' or **hrēod** 'reed', **hol**[1] 'hollow'; the lane is called *Clatcoomb Path* 1733 *DROMap*, *v.* Clatcombe *supra*. ROUND HILL, 1843 *TA*. SANDFORD RD, *-Way* 1733 *DROMap*, to Sandford O. par. *infra*. SHERBORNE LAKE, cf. *There lyith at the ende of the castelle a mere* 1535–43 Leland, *Part of the Lake* (pasture), *Pleasure Ground adjoining Lake* 1845 *TA*, *v.* **mere**[1], **lake**. SIR WALTER RALEIGH'S SEAT, *v.* Sherborne Castle *supra*. THE SLOPES, earlier *Slepehyll'* 1566, *Sle(e)pehill* 1614 both *Digby*,

Sleep Hill 1733 *DROMap, Steep Hill* (sic) 1802 Map, *v.*
slæp 'slippery muddy place'. THE TERRACE. TITHE BARN
(near Wyke Fm *supra*). UNDERDOWN LANE, cf. *close called
Underdowne* 1614 *Digby, Under Down* 1733 *DROMap, Under
Down, Lawn-, Long Acre under Down* 1843 *TA*, '(land)
beneath the down', *v.* **under, dūn.** WATERY LANE, cf. *Water
lane* 1563, *Waterlaneende* 1614 *Digby, v.* **wæter, lane, ende.**
WEST HILL, 1733 *DROMap*, 1811 OS, cf. the f.n. *East Hill
infra.* WITHYBED PLANT. YETMAN'S COPSE.

FIELD-NAMES

Most of the undated forms in (*a*) are 1843 *TA* 187 (Sherborne) but those
marked † are 1845 *TA* 39 (Castleton). Spellings dated 933 (12) are *SherC*
(S 422), which describes the bounds of the Anglo-Saxon estate of Bradford
Abbas which included Wyke. Spellings dated 1145 (12) are *SherC* (f. 35v),
1294 FF, 14, 1375–88, 1525[2], 1594 Fowler, 1327 *SR*, 1332 SR, 1427,
1525, 1559 *Salis*, 1460, 1464[2], 1474, 1484, 1508, 1516, 1531, 1538, 1563,
1564, 1575, 1583, 1598, 1600, 1614, 1623[2], 1642 *Digby*, 1539, 1553, 1623
Hutch[3], 1542 *Shepherd*[2], 1569–74 *Map*, 1572, 1581 *DCMDeed*, 1601[2]
Russ, 1617 *Pitt*, 1664 HTax, 1733 *DROMap*, 1791 Boswell, 1849 *EnclA*,
and the rest *Sher*. For other lost f.ns. and minor names which may well
have been in the area out of which the new par. of Castleton was formed in
1895, *v.* under Sherborne par. *infra.*

(*a*) Almshouse Wd (belonging to The Almshouse in Sherborne par.
infra); Backside (*v.* **backside**); Bed Mill 7 Acres (*v.* Bedmill *supra*);
Black Ditch (Lane) (*Black Ditch* 1733); Broad Md; Lt Burnets, Burnets
Leaze; East Caines (*pastur' vocat Kaymez, -Esterkaymez, Cam(m)eslond*
1525, (*Weste*) *Kaymes, Westkeymes* 1542, cf. *Cotage . . . formerly Kaynes,
-late Kenneys* 1677, from a surname *Kaym*, etc, cf. Reaney s.n. *Cain,
Cam, Cane, v.* **land**); Chaffeys Lawn (cf. Thomas *Chaffe* 1664, Walter
Chaffy 1677, *v.* Lawn *infra*); Gt Clanfield ((*Lower*) *Clanfield* 1733, *v.*
clǣne, feld, cf. another instance of this f.n. in Sherborne st.ns. *infra*);
Compton Dean 1849 (1733, -*deane* 1569–74), Compton Knap (both named
from (Nether) Compton par. *infra, v.* **denu** 'valley', **cnæpp** 'hill-top,
hillock'); Core Pce 1849; Crockers Lawn; Deep Leaze (*Depelease* 1566,
Deep(e)lease 1614, *v.* **dēop, lǣs**); Denney Bridge 1802, †Denny Paddock
(*piscaria' de la Dunybrugge* 1427, (*clauso iuxta*) (*la*) *Denybrigge* 1452, 1461,
(*la*) *Dynebrygge, -brigge* 1464, 1465, 1469, (*la*) *Dynybrygge* 1476, 1488,
1500, (*molend' fulleretis apud*) *Dynnybryg(g)e, -brigg'* 1538, *Dyn(n)(e)y-
bridge* 1559, 1570, 1585 (*parock nere-*), 1601, 1626, *deny bridge* 1569–74, *le
parock iuxta Dymybridge* 1601, *Dinnie-, Dinnyebridge* 1614, *Dinny Bridge*
1677, *v.* **brycg, pearroc**; the first el. may be the obscure OE plant-name
dȳnige discussed under Dunmore Brk 237, cf. also William *Denyforde*
1474 recorded in connection with Sherborne, whose surname may contain

the same el. with **ford**. In PN Brk 237, 865 a possible side-form of this el.*, *dūni(g)e*, is postulated to explain Dunmore Brk 237 and the possibly analogous Dunny Sr 386 and Denny Ha, but in fact the recorded **dȳnige** would satisfactorily explain all the forms for these names: the early *u*-spelling for Dunmore may be due to the 13th cent. copyist (cf. *curspan-, cyrspan dic* in the same charter Brk 660), and *o* for OE *ȳ* can occur from the 13th cent. within the '*u*- area' (e.g. PN Gl **4** 71); it is possible that Duni and Denny Gl **3** 163, 202, two places ½ mile apart on R. Severn and whose forms may have been confused by their proximity to one another, should also be taken into account in considering this group of names); †Dry Grds; Dunfords (*A ten[ement] wherein the Durnfords long lived* 1677, cf. John *Durneford* 1664); †Home 8 Acres or Maudlins Cl (*close at Maud-, Mawdlynes* 1585, 1601, *Maudline* (*closes*) 1614, *Mawline alias Mawdeline close* 1623, *close at Mawdlyn* 1626, *Magdalen Close* 1677, *Magdalen or Maudlin's Close* 1849, named from the lost church or chapel of St Mary Magdalen, *v.* under Sherborne churches *infra*); Exlip (1733, *Exslip* 1849, perhaps 'muddy place used by oxen', from **oxa** (nom.pl. *exen*) and **slæp**); 4 Acre and 6 Acre Hill; 4 Acre Pce; Frog Dean (1733, *v.* **frogga, denu**); 15 Acres Gravel Pit; Harbour Fd (10 Acres), 3 Acres Harbour Fd (*campum de Haborogh'* 1474, *Hareborough* 1539, *Harbour Field, -Head* 1733, *v.* **here-beorg** 'shelter for travellers'; the field lies alongside Trent Path Lane for which *v.* under Sherborne street-names *infra*); Harts Hill (cf. Reginald *Harte* 1553, John *Hart* 1664); Lt Hassels Lawn (*Hassels* 1733, *Lt Hassell(s)* 1849); The Home Fd; Hundred Acres (a common ironical name for a very small field, this one having an area of 1 rood 13 perches); Jordans 1802 (*claus' voc' Jordans* 1563, *Jordens* 1614, a surname); Leigh Hill (perhaps **lēah** 'wood, clearing in a wood'); Linch (*v.* **hlinc** 'ridge, bank'); Long Grd; †Longman's Pdk 1849; Lords Bush (1733, *Lordesbusshe* 1614, *v.* **hlāford, busc**); Maudlins Cl (*v.* Home 8 Acres *supra*); Mill Orchd (probably to be associated with the lost *Hoddynottes myll, v.* under Sherborne Buildings *infra*); the Moor (Land in-, Lawn in-), Common Moor (*land in-, meadow in the Moore, the moores, the grounde moore, the upper moore* 1614, *the Moore* 1677, *Common Moor* 1733, cf. *Morehegge, Moremede* 1538, *More Yeate* 1539, *Mooregate* 1600, 1614, *-yate* 1614, *v.* **mōr** 'marshy ground', **hecg, mǣd, geat**); Nettle Boor 1849 (1733, *v.* **netel(e)**, perhaps with **bor**[1] 'hill'); Noakes Fd (cf. John *Noke* 1614); 3 Acres Oborne Water (cf. *Oborne Water* [Bridge] 1791), (3 Acres) Oborne Wd (from Oborne par. *infra*); (East Hills) Old Down (*la Oldedoune* 1427, *Oldowne* 1538, *Old Downe* 1600, *Oldedowne* 1614, *v.* **eald, dūn**); Paddock (freq); Partridge Hedge; Pease Flg (1733, *Pisforlong', -furlong, Pysfurlong'* 1454, *v.* **pise** 'pease', **furlang**); †Plantation; Poor Fd (1733); Rockley (1733); Gt Shorthound (*Longhounde* 1614, *Long Hound* 1733, *Gt Short Hound, Long Hound* 1849, probably from the plant-name **hūne** 'hoarhound'; the 16th cent. f.n. *Longehowne, -Hownde* in Holnest par. *infra* and the *TA* f.n. Longhound in Bradford A. par. *supra* are clearly analogous, though it is strange that the same qualifying adj. should appear thrice; it is unlikely that the 16th cent. forms belong to the Castleton f.n.);

6 Acres against Barn; Sopers Path (*Soper(s)lane* 1563, first el. probably a surname); Starve Acre (a derogatory name for unproductive land); Stockhill 1849 (*Stoke Hill* 1539, *Stock Hill* 1733, first el. probably **stocc** 'tree-stump'); Strap (*v.* **strap**); Symes Pce (cf. William *Symmes* 1476, *cottage* . . . *formerly Syms* 1677); 2 Acre Lawn in the 11½ Acre Fd adjoining Lenthay (*v.* Lawn *supra*, Lenthay in Sherborne par. *infra*); 2 Acre Pce; Vartnam Lane (Orchd), Vartmans Lane (3 Acres) (*via regia apud Verkenham* 1516, *Berkenham* (sic) 1539, *Vertnam(e)s bridge, -grounde* 1569–74, *close at Vertnam* 1614, *Vartnam* 1733 DROMap, *closes called Vartman* 1849, to be associated with VARTENHAM HILL (1″ and 6″) just over the par. bdy in Milborne Port So; second el. probably **hamm**, but earlier forms are needed for the first el.); Water Md (*Watermede* 1525, *v.* **wæter, mǣd**); Ways Mount 1849; Witleye Cowleaze; Woolf's Hill 1849 (cf. *Wolfes meade* 1575, 1677, *Wolfes Leases* 1677, Robert *le Wolf* 1327 (Sherborne)); (New) Wyke Hedge (*Wykeheggez* 1538, *Weekhedge* 1600, *Wikehedge* 1614, *Wyke Hedges* 1677, *Near Wyke Hedge* 1849, named from Wyke *supra*, *v.* **hecg**, cf. also *Wykegate Furlonge* 1600, *Wyke More* 1572, *v.* **geat, furlang, mōr**); Long Yealy (*Long-, Short Yealey* 1733).

(*b*) *to aettan dene middeweardre, andlang dene* 933 (12) (*v.* foll.); *of aettan* (BCS 695 reads *eastan*) *wylles heafde, to aettan wylle* 933 (12) (from an OE pers.n. *Ætta or fem. *Ætte*, cf. *Ættanpennes lacu* W discussed by Tengstrand 244, with **denu** 'valley', **well(a)** 'spring, stream', **hēafod** 'source'); *le Backwater* 1623[2] (*v.* **back**); *Batendean* 1733 (*v.* **denu** 'valley', first el. uncertain); *Belknappes* 1538; *Boke Close* 1525 (first el. probably **bōc**[1] 'beech-tree'); *the bridge, the bruge* 1642 (*v.* **brycg**); *domus/mes' vocat' le Cage* 1538 (*v.* **cage**); *the casway betwine the chapell and Richard Lodens house* 1642 (*v.* **cauce**, cf. foll.); *Chapelhayes* 1508, *Chaphaies Meade* 1598, *Chaple haies* 1614 (named from *S. Peters Chappell* 1569–74, at Overcoombe *supra*, *v.* **chapel(e)**, **(ge)hæg**; William *atte Churheye* (sic) 1327, taxed in Overcoombe, and *le Chirchehaye* m15, may also belong here, with **cirice** 'church' alternating as first el.); *Corton Path* 1733 (leading to Corton Denham par. in So); *Cross Crane* 1733; *Dallal'shedd* 1575; *Dawes Close* 1563, 1614 (a surname); *oþ þa dic, þon andlang dic* 933 (12) (*v.* **dīc**); *the downe* 1569–74 (*v.* **dūn**); *East Hill* 1733 (cf. West Hill *supra*); *on ecge, andlang ecge* 933 (12) (*v.* **ecg**); *oþ ecgulfes treow* 933 (12) (from the OE pers.n. Ecgwulf and **trēow** 'tree, post'); *cultura vocatur la Empnet* 1427 (*v.* **emnet** 'plain, level ground'); *Estbrygge* 1484 (*v.* **ēast, brycg**); *Floods* 1733 (a surname); *foxe hoales* 1569–74 (*v.* **fox-hol**); *Frydayshold'* 1538 (the surname *Friday* with **hold**); *Gildene-, Gyldenelond'* 1454, *Gilland(e)s* 1569–74, 1733, *Gillande* 1614 (cf. *ten' nuper Rogeri Guldene, ten' nuper Edmundi-, -Thome Gyldo(u)n* 1454, Henry *le Gildene* 1294, *v.* **land**); *Guckow hill* 1569–74, *Gogoehill* 1600, 1614, *Gogo Hill* 1733 (*v.* **cuccu** 'a cuckoo', cf. the Do dial. form *goocoo* in Barnes 66); *bosco de Hatherley* 1439, *Hatherl(e)y Hill* 1601[2], 1733 (probably 'hawthorn wood or clearing' from **hagu-þorn** and **lēah**, cf. Hatherley Gl 1 14, Hatherleigh D 142); *Haukyniscrose* 1464[2], *hawkins crosse* 1569–74 (*v.* **cros(s)**, cf. *ten' nuper Willelmi Hawkyns* 1454); *Heydon ball* 1569–74, *Haydon Ball* 1733 (a hill in

Sherborne Park named from Haydon par. *infra, v.* **ball** 'rounded hill'); *Hillclose* 1614; *ten' vocat' Hilnakes* 1427 (in Overcoombe *supra,* cf. Nicholas *(de) Hel(f)naked(e)* 1327, 1332, taxed in Overcoombe tithing); *Langemede* 1375–88, *Longmede* 1538, *Longe Meade* 1569–74, 1598 (*v.* **lang**[1], **mǣd**); *Lityl-, Lytelwod* 1538, *Lit(t)lewood* 1614, 1677 (*v.* **lȳtel**); *the Lodge Gate* 1677 (*v.* **log(g)e**, cf. Lodge 6″ in Sherborne Park); *Long Hill* 1569–74, 1733, *Longehill* 1600, 1614 (*v.* **lang**[1]); (*close called*) (*the*) *Mallards* 1594, 1677, *the Mallerdes* 1614 (probably a surname); *Manifordes close* 1614 (a surname); *Meers Wood* 1733 (cf. *Mr Henrie Meers Clo(a)se* 1600, *Ten'* . . . *formerly Meeres* 1677); *la murelese* 1427 (*v.* **lǣs**, first el. possibly **myrge** 'pleasant'); *Osmonds Garden* 1677; *Oxenlease* 1614 (*v.* **oxa, lǣs**); *Panters-* 1614, *Painters Hill* 1677, 1733 (cf. *ten' nuper Henrici Panter* 1448); *Pidgeon Down* 1733; *Pig Hill* 1733 (*v.* lost st.n. *Pighill Lane* in Sherborne *infra*); *porte yeate* 1583 ('town gate', *v.* **port**[2], **geat**); *le pounde* 1563 (*v.* **pund**); *Roghcroft* 1427, *Rowcroft(e)* 1614, 1677 (*v.* **rūh** 'rough', **croft**); *Saynt(e)barbes Farme* 1614, *St Barbes (farme)* 1614, 1677, *Simbarbs farme* 1617 (cf. Master *Symbarbe* 1525[2]); *shiluers hedge* 1569–74 (a surname); *A house called the Shipp* 1677; *ten' vocat' Snowkes* 1538 (cf. John *Snowke* 1531); *Stondene* 1427, 1538, *Stonedene* 1538, *-Dean* 1733 (*v.* **stān, denu**); *Swayne more* 1572 (*v.* **mōr**, first el. probably a surname); *Tabermeade* 1614, *-Meade* 1677 (a surname); *2 acres lienge at Twine Waies* 1600, *Twinways* 1733 ('(land) between the ways', *v.* **betwēonan, weg**; the field lay between Bradford Rd and Yeovil Rd); *la Vivere* 14, (*pastura in*) *la Fyner* (probably for *Fyuer*) 1427, *la Fever* 1455, 1476, (*prat' in*) (*la*) *Fyver* 1464 *et freq* to 1538, *Fyvermeade* 1563, *the feaver* 1569–74, *The longe Feaver, the* (*litle*) *Feaver me(a)de* 1600, *The feavers, Feavermeade(s)* 1614, *the Long-Feaver* 1677, *Fevors* 1733 (the forms correspond with those for OE *fefer,* ME *fever* 'fever', a loan-word from Lat *febris,* but the sense of its use as a f.n. is not apparent; alternatively perhaps an anglicization of Lat *vivarium* 'fishpond, game preserve'); *close called the Vyneyarde* 1614 (*v.* **vinȝerd**, cf. *de vinea* . . . *iuxta castellum* 1145 (12), *magnum vinarium* 1427); *Wasshyng' Place* 1538 (*v.* **washing**); *le Wayhowse* 1581, *one cotage called the Waiehouse with the issues and profites therof anie waie arisinge, and the profites of the Waightes there* 1614, *The Weighthouse and the Marketts* 1677; *Whityng ys Cros* 1460, *Whytynges Crosse* 1516, 1531, *Whiting(e)s Cros(s)e* 1564, 1614, 1677 (the surname *Whiting* with **cros(s)**, cf. *Whitynggestrete, Whytingeslane* in the adjacent par. of Haydon *infra*).

Bishop's Caundle

In 1886 detached parts of this par. were added to Caundle Marsh and Folke pars. both *infra*. Caundle Wake was a tithing in Brownsall hundred *supra*.

Bᴉsʜᴏᴘ's Cᴀᴜɴᴅʟᴇ (ST 696132)

    Candel 1224 Sarum, 1225 ClR, 1228 FF, *Caundele* 1294 Ch, *Caunnell* 1454 Pat

Kaunde(le) Episcopi 1268, 1280 *Ass, Candale Episcopi* 1270
For, Candel(l) Episcopi 1280 *Ass,* 1614, 1617 *Pitt,
Caundel(l) Episcopi* 1285 FA, 1288 *Ass,* 1291 Tax *et freq*
to 1617 *Pitt, Cawndell Episcopi* 1614 *Digby
Caundel Bishops* 1294, 1297 Pat, *-Byshopp* 1363 *Hastings,
Caundell Busshope* 1564 *Sher, Candell Bushopp* 1593
Batten, Cawndell Buisshoppe 1614 *Digby, Caundle
Bishopp* 1664 HTax
Busshopescaundell' 1497 *Ilch, Bisshops Caundel* 1535–43
Leland, *Bisshoppes Candle* 1569–74 *Map, Bishops
Ca(u)ndle* 1709 *WRO*

For the obscure name Caundle, *v.* Stourton Caundle par.
supra. The affix is from the possession of this manor by the
bishops of Salisbury, *v.* **episcopus, biscop.**

CAUNDLE WAKE (ST 700126)
Ca(u)ndel 1212, 1235–6 Fees (Drew), *Caundelle* 1382 Cl
Candelbeyvill (probably for *-beyvin*) 1276 Banco, *Kaundel
beyuyn, Ca(u)ndel Beyim, -Beyncin (sic)* 1280, *Candel
Beyuyn* 1288 *Ass, Kaundell Boyum* (probably for
-Boyuin) 1290 Ch, *Chaundelbeyuin, Caundele Boymyn*
1299, *Caundelbyuyn, Caundle Beyuyn, Caundelebeyuyn*
1300 Banco (Drew), *Candel-Beynin* (for *-Beyuin*) 1305
Hutch[3], *Ca(u)ndel Beym'* [rectius *Bevin*] 1316 FA
Caundelwak(e) 1288 *Ass,* 1348 Ipm, 1405 Cl, *Caundel
Wake* 1327 *SR,* 1332 SR, 1348 Ipm *et freq* to 1412 FA,
-Wak 1360 Cl, *Chaundelwake* 1381 Fine, *Caundell Wake*
1431 FA, *Candle Wake* 1664 HTax

Cf. the par. name *supra.* The affixes are manorial. William
Bevin occurs in connection with *Candel* in 1235–6 Fees (p.
426), cf. also Richard *Beyuyn* 1280 *Ass,* Agnes *Beuyn(g)*
1300, 1301 Banco (Drew). Ralph *Wake* was here in 1290 Ch,
cf. also John *(de) Wake* 1327 *SR,* 1332 SR, 1348 Ipm, 1405
Cl, and *v.* Wake Court *infra*; the same family gives its name
to Stoke Wake par. *supra.* Since there are no *alias* forms,
Caundel Beyvin may have been a separate holding within the
manor.

BERE LANE, cf. *La Bere* 1428 *Salis, close called Beare* 1614,

Beare (*mead*) 1630 *Digby, Bere* 1842 *TA*, probably **bǣr²** '(woodland) pasture'. BLIND LANE, *v.* **blind** 'leading nowhere'. BROWN'S ST., cf. John *Broun* 1332 SR, William *Brown* 1340 NI, *land at Streate ende* 1614 *Digby, Street End* 1842 *TA, v.* **strǣt, ende.** BISHOP'S CAUNDLE HO & WD, *Caundell' Woode* 1538 *Digby, v.* **wudu.** CHURCH (original dedication unknown, but now St Peter and St Paul), cf. *Churchweye* 1332, *Churche Wey* 1428 *Salis, Cottage . . . and a garden called Ye Church* 1677 *Digby, Church Cl* 1842 *TA, v.* **cirice, weg.** ELDERSFIELD HO. GILES'S LANE, probably to be associated with William *Gele* 1327 *SR*, 1332 SR. THE GORSE. HOLT LANE, *Holtway* 1709 *WRO*, leading to Holt Hill & Wds in Stourton Caundle par. *supra.* LAINES PLANTS., *close called Leyne* 1614 *Digby, Lains* (*Plant.*) 1842 *TA, v.* **leyne** 'tract of arable land'. LAUREL LODGE. OLD LIMEKILN, *Lime Kiln* 1842 *TA*. LIMETREE HO. MANOR FM, *messuage and Ferme of Caundell Buisshopp* 1614 *Digby*. MILBURN LANE, leading to Caundle Brook which is presumably the 'mill stream' referred to, cf. the mention of a watermill at *Caundelebeyuyn* 1301 Banco (Drew), William *atte Mulle* 1327 *SR, Muleweye* 1332 *Salis, unum molend' aquatic'* 1484, *a watergriestemill, Millclose* 1614 *Digby,* (*Old*) *Mill Grd, Mill Grd Mead, Mill Ho* 1842 *TA, v.* **myln, burna, atte** 'at the', **weg,** Caundle Wake *supra; Mill Ho* is situated just W of Milburn Lane. NORTH LANE. POUND LANE, named from *Old Pound* 1842 *TA*, cf. *Caundle Pound ib* (= Pound 6″), *v.* **pund.** RYALL'S FM & LANE, *Riall* 1630 *Digby, Ryal* 1842 *TA*, probably 'rye hill' from **ryge** and **hyll.** STONY LANE. WAKE COURT, 1677, -*Farme* 1630 *Digby*, cf. *Courtclose* 1614 *ib*, 'the ancient seat of the Wakes' (Hutch³ **4** 137), *v.* **court,** Caundle Wake *supra*, cf. *Wakes Land or Wakes Feldys* 1443 Hutch³, *Wake Woode* 1630 *Digby*. WHITE HART INN, -*Alehouse* 1842 *TA*, cf. *Inn Plot ib*.

FIELD-NAMES

The undated forms are 1842 *TA* 19. Some fields in Bishop's Caundle *TA* are now in Caundle Marsh or Folke par. *infra.* Spellings dated 1268 are *Ass*, 1327 *SR*, 1332¹, 1428 *Salis*, 1332² SR, 1340 NI, 1347 Pat, 1564 *Sher*, 1569–74 *Map*, 1664 HTax, 1791 Boswell, and the rest *Digby*.

(a) Ashpit (*close called Ashpitt* 1614, cf. *Ashbedmede* 1332[1], *Ayssheled* (sic) 1538, v. **æsc, pytt, bedd, mǣd**); Backside (*the backeside* 1614, v. **backside**); Baileys (*close called Bailie* 1614, cf. *William Bayly* 1664); Barley Cl; Berverlands (*Burforland* 1630, possibly **furlang** with either **būr**[1] 'cottage' or **(ge)būr** 'peasant'); Brewen and Plant. (*Bruere* 1332[1], *close called Brewerne* 1614, probably OFr **bruiere** 'heath' like Bruern O 337); (Gt) Bucknam(e) (*Bukkenam* 1428, *Bucknam* 1614, probably 'he-goats' enclosure', v. **bucca, hamm**); Bucksheaf (probably a form of the name Buckshaw in Holwell par. *infra*); Buddocks Md; Bunters Plot (cf. *John Bunter* 1614, *tenement and water grist mill formerly Bunters* 1677, cf. Milburn Lane *supra*); Carrot Cl; Chilveracres (Do dial. *chilver* 'ewe-lamb', v. **cilfor**); Copse Plot; Cote (cf. *Cothouse* 1630, v. **cot** 'cottage'); (Home) Cowleaze; Croft and Barton (v. **croft, barton**); Curtis's Cl (cf. *Walter Curteys* 1332[2] (Folke), *terr'* . . . *nuper Reginaldi Curtes* 1538, *ten* . . . *heretofore Curtis's* 1677); Custom Wd; Dolovers (cf. *Ten'* . . . *in Candle formerly Downtons and late Dalibers* 1677); Dry Md; Durrants Orchd; Englands (*close called Englandes* 1614, a surname); Fish Pond Grd & Orchd (cf. *piscaria* 1538, *Ten'* . . . *formerly Fishers* 1677); Furlong (*close called Furlande, -Furlonge* 1614, v. **furlang**); Furze (v. **fyrs**); Gorford (Md) (v. Garvey Hill in S. Caundle par. *supra*); Green Close (Md); (Lt) Grottons (Do dial. *grotten* 'a run or pasture for sheep' (Barnes 67), v. **grǣd-tūn**); Grove (v. **grāf(a)**); Hanging Grd (v. **hangende**); Harp (*close called Harpe* 1614, named from the shape of the field, v. **hearpe**); Hoe Md (*Howe meade* 1614, v. **hōh** 'heel, spur of land'); Holly Md (*Holmede* 1428, *-meade* 1614, v. **hol**[2] 'hollow', **mǣd**); Hollywell (near Spring 6″, perhaps from **hālig** 'holy', **well(a)**); Holwell Acre & Md (*Hollowell* 1614, *Holwell mead* 1630, v. **hol**[2] 'deep', **well(a)** 'spring, stream'); Home Grd & Md; Hulk (v. **hulc** 'a shed, a hut'); Hundred Acres (a common ironical name for a small field, this one having an area of only 36 perches); Hurdle Crafts (*Hureles-* 1332[1], *Hurlescrofte* 1614, the surname *Hurel* with **croft**); Kennells, Kernells; Lake Md (*Lakemeade* 1614, v. **lacu** 'stream'); Gt & Hr Leaze (*close called the Leaze* 1614, v. **lǣs** 'pasture'); Linch (*close called Linche, Lynche* 1614, v. **hlinc** 'ridge, bank'); Little Plot; Long Md (*Longmeade* 1614); Lower Md; Marl Pits; Marrow Md (Close) (*Marmeade* (*close*) 1630, first el. perhaps **marrow** used figuratively to denote rich meadowland, cf. Marley's Row 2 219); Murlains (*Morland* 1630, v. **mōr, land**); North Grd (*Northgroundes* 1614, v. **norð, grund**); Gt Oakhill, Oakhill Md (*Hokhull* 1332[1], *Ocehull'* 1428, *Okehill* 1538, 1630, *Okill* 1569–74, v. **āc, hyll**); Oathill (*Otehill* 1614, v. **āte, hyll**); Orchard (freq), Orchardwell; Paddock and Plot; Parsonage Ho; Partway (Md) (*Port(e)wey* 1566, 1569, *close called-* 1614, *cottage called Portway* 1677, v. **port-weg** 'road leading to a market town'; the fields lie beside the road to Sherborne); Peddi-craft Orchd; Piece (*Peece* 1630, v. **pece**); Pleeks (perhaps a form of **plek** 'small plot'); Plot; Punfield (perhaps **pund-fald** 'pinfold, pound', cf. Pound Lane *supra*); Quar Cl (*Quar(re)* close 1614, 1630, cf. *quarr'* in *tenur'* *Reginaldi Butte, -in tenur' Johanne Curtes* 1566, v. **quarre** 'quarry'); Routed Wd; Rowden(s) Hill (v. Rowden Mill Fm in

S. Caundle *supra*); Shoulder of Mutton (named from its shape); Shrubbitts (*close called Shrubbell* (perhaps for *-ett*) 1614, *v.* scrubb, -et); Smith (*close called Smithe, Smythe* 1614, probably smiðõe 'a smithy'); Sturt (*terr' voc' Sterttes* 1538, *close called Sterte* 1614, *v.* steort 'tail or tongue of land'); Surpett's [Bridge] 1791; 3 Acres (*close called Three-, iij acres* 1614); Townsend(s) (*close called Townesende* 1614, *v.* tūn, ende); Two Ways; Vanhers Orchd; West; West Md; Whitnam (*close called Whitenam* 1614, probably 'white enclosure', *v.* hwīt, hamm); Winterwell (*close called Winterwell* 1614, *Winterwellmeade* 1630, *v.* winter, well(a), mǣd); Winywick (*close called Whinnye Whitch* 1614, *Wynnyewich* 1630, probably from wice 'wych-elm'; the first el. may be a surname (*v.* Reaney s.n. *Whinney*) or a form of Do dial. *vinny* 'mouldy, mildewed' (Barnes and EDD)); Withy Md (*Withi(e)meade* 1614, cf. *Withibedd* ib, *v.* wīðig, mǣd, bedd); Woodbridge Md (1614, from Woodbridge in Holwell par. *infra*); Wood Cl; New Writh (*la Nywefryth'* 1332[1], *la Litilnywefrith'* 1428, *Newfrithe* 1614, *v.* nīwe 'new', fyrhð 'wood', cf. Writh Ctg in Folke par. *infra*).

(b) *abbey garden* 1630 (perhaps belonging to Sherborne abbey); *Bamfieldes tenement* 1614; *Barnehaies* 1614 (*v.* bere-ærn, (ge)hæg); *the Broad(e)comon* 1614; *Brokfurlong* 1428 (*v.* brōc, furlang); *Burnam* 1614; *Chethey* 1428 (*v.* (ge)hæg, first el. uncertain); *Chilton farme* 1630 (perhaps 'farm of the young noblemen', *v.* cild, tūn); *Cornhill* 1630; *Culvermeade* 1614 (*v.* culfre 'dove'); *Estfeld'* 1538 (*v.* ēast); *close called five acres* 1614; *Gatwey* 1428 (first el. probably gāt 'goat'); *tenement called Goodmans* 1677; *the greate comon* 1614; *Grenehaies* 1614 (*v.* grēne, (ge)hæg); *Halewey* 1538; *Hangleyate* 1428 (perhaps hangel 'slope', geat); *Harrisons Tenement* 1677; *Hebbedich* 1327 (p), 1428, *Hepedich'* 1332[1], *Hebdychelane* 1538 (from hēopa 'the dog rose, a bramble' or hēope 'the fruit of the wild rose, a hip', with dīc and lane); *close called Hichines* 1614; *land at Hilkes* (perhaps for *Hikkes*) 1614; *Hoc[k]emeade* 1614 (4th letter unclear); *Home Close* 1677; *crofta que vocatur Illonde* 1268 (*v.* īeg-land 'island'); *Kynggesmore* 1538, *Kingesmoore* 1614 (*v.* mōr, cf. William *Kyng* 1340); *Kitchineclose* 1614 (*v.* cycene, alluding to land where kitchen produce is grown); *Knulleweye* 1332[1], *Knyll' dych'* 1531 (*v.* cnyll 'a knoll, a hillock', weg, dīc); *closes called Maudlin Pittes* 1614 (*v.* pytt, first el. probably the surname *Maudlin* from the pers.n. *Magdalen*); *close called Moore, Mooreclose, the greate Moore, Litlemoore* 1614 (*v.* mōr 'marshy ground'); *Netherclose* 1614; *Neweclose* 1614; *North(e)close* 1614; *Northemeade* 1614; *Panhams* 1630; *claus' . . . vocat' le Parke* 1538 (*v.* park); *Pytthaies* 1614 (*v.* pytt, (ge)hæg); *Riecrofte* 1614 (*v.* ryge, croft); *Rixmede* 1428 (*v.* risc 'rush'); *Southfield* 1614; *la Southhull'* 1428 (*v.* hyll); *pastura in la Swelie* 1428 (probably (ge)swelg 'pit, whirlpool'); *Talpacr'* 1538 (*v.* æcer, first el. uncertain); *Thornerowe* 1614 (*v.* þorn, rāw); *upper woodd* 1564; *Westebrouke* 1332[1], *Westbrok alias Wollerston'* 1428 (probably '(land) west of the brook', from westan and brōc; the alternative name is obscure without earlier forms); (*close called*) *West(erne)crosse* 1614 (*v.* west, westerne, cros); *Wollies crosse* 1569-74; *Woodleaze* 1614 (*v.* wudu, lǣs); *Yates close* 1614 (cf. John *atte Yete* 1327, *-atte Yate* 1332[2], Oliver *atte Yate* 1347, 'at the gate or gap', *v.* **atte**, **geat**, cf. also *Hupeyatestret* 1332[1], *v.* **upp(e)** 'higher up', **strǣt).

Caundle Marsh

Detached parts of Bishop's Caundle par. *supra* were added to this par. in 1886.

CAUNDLE MARSH (ST 680130)
     Kaundel Mareys 1234 Drew, *-mareys* 1304 Banco (Drew),
     Candelemers 1245 FF, *Ca(u)ndelmar(e)ys* 1282 Banco
     (Drew), 1288 *Ass*, 1297 Pat, *-mareis* 1284 FF,
     Ca(u)ndel(l)mers(s)h(e) 1286 Banco (Drew), 1333 Pat,
     1334 FF *et freq* to 1450 Cl, *Caundel(l) Mareys* 1340
     Sher, 1362 AD *et freq* to 1454 *Sher*, Pat, *-Mareis* 1453
     Sher, Ca(u)ndel(l)(e) Mers(s)h(e) 1411 Cl *et freq* to 1491
     Ipm, *Caundelmarsh* 1575 Saxton, *Candle Marsh* 1605,
     1669 *SalisT*
     la Merse 1244 *Ass* (p), *La/Le Mers(s)h(e)* 1349 Ipm, 1361
     Sher, 1373 DCMDeed *(parochia de-)*, 1397 *Sher et freq*
     to 1563 Digby, *Mers(s)h(e)* 1428 FA, 1433 *Sher et freq* to
     1493 DCMDeed *(parochiam de-)*, 1500 *AddCh, Mersch*
     1529 *AddCh (the parische of-)*, *lez Mershe* 1531 *Digby,
     Marsh Parish* 1709 *WRO*
     Merssh Kaundel, Mersche Caundele 1311 Banco (Drew),
     Mershe Caundell' Episcopi 1515 DCMDeed, *Mers(h)ton
     Caundel* 1312, 1313 Banco (Drew)

For Caundle, *v.* Stourton Caundle par. *supra*. Marsh is OE **mersc** 'marsh', alternating in the early forms with the synonymous ME (< OFr **mareis**; two 14th cent forms contain **tūn** 'estate', cf. the *TA* f.n. Maston *infra*. Some of the simplex forms may denote the original area of marshland within the par. rather than the par. itself, cf. *la Mersshe in parochia de la Mersshe* 1373 DCMDeed. The earliest mention of this marsh is in the surname of John *de la Merse* who is associated with *Candel* in 1244 *Ass* (200.9). The marsh was probably the area of the present par. which until 1886 formed a detached part of Bps. Caundle par. *supra* (cf.

Mershe Caundell' Episcopi 1515) and which, together with another detached part of Bps. Caundle now in Folke, formed the tithing of *Down(e)* and *Marsh* 1664 HTax, 1795 Boswell, *v.* Bishop's Down in Folke par. *infra*.

ASHCOMBE FM (ST 679151) & WD, *Ascumbe* 1205, 1206, 1207 Cur, *Esscumbe* 1244, *Estcumbe* (sic) 1245 FF, *Assh'comb'* 1332 SR (p), *Ays(s)hecombe* (*lane*) 1496, 1516, 1531, 1563 all *Digby, Ashcomb* 1811 OS, 'valley where ash-trees grow', *v.* **æsc, cumb**, with **lane**. The form *Aysshcombeysyate* 1484 *Digby* may contain this p.n. or the surname formed from it, cf. *Ric' Ayshecombe pro terr' suis in Ayshecombe* 1516 *ib, v.* **geat** 'gate'.

POLL BRIDGE (FM) (ST 683125), *Poole bridge* 1569–74 *Map*, *Poll Bridge* 1811 OS, *Poolebridge Fm* 1939 Kelly, probably to be associated with *Deoulepole* Hy 3 (14) Cerne (2×, in the bounds of Blackmoor Forest), *Deuelepole* 1280 *Ass* (p), *Develpol* 1332, *Dellepol* 1428 *Salis, v.* **dēofol** 'devil', **pōl** 'pool', cf. also Alan *de la Pole* 1268 *Ass* (associated with *Caundel*). For somewhat analogous names, cf. Purbrook Ha (DEPN) and *Puckmere* Brk 898 (both containing **pūca** 'goblin') and *Nikerpoll* Sx 562, *Nykerpole* W 444 (from **nicor** 'water-sprite').

PRYTOWN FM (ST 679144), *Prydtoune* 1484, *firma terr'* *Johannis Pryde* 1538, *Pride Towne* 1677 all *Digby, Prytown* 1811 OS, *Pride Town* 1845 *EnclA*, cf. *Prydelane* 1484 *Digby*, 1493 *DCMDeed, Pryedmor(e)* 1493 *ib, Prudemore, -Moure* 1531 *Digby, Pride Moor* 1842 *TA*, Nicholas-, Richard *Pride* 1327 *SR*, 1332 SR (Folke), *v.* **toun** 'estate', **lane, mōr**.

BIRCH COPSE. CAUNDLE MARSH WD. HAWKINS'S FM, *Hawkins* 1811 OS, cf. Joan *Hawkines* 1614 *Digby* (Bps. Caundle), Giles *Hawkins* 1664 HTax (P. Caundle). HOLT CTGS, cf. *Holt* 1842 *TA*, named from Holt Hill & Wds in S. Caundle par. *supra*. MANOR FM. MARSH COURT, cf. *la Mersshe in parochia de la Mersshe* 1373 *DCMDeed, Mersshwelle* 1428 *Salis, Mersshefeld'* 1538 *Digby, Marsh Lane* 1709 *WRO, Marsh Common* 1842 *TA, v.* **court, well(a), feld**, par. name *supra*, and cf. also *in orientali parte Curie* 1428 *Salis*. NEW LANE.

PLECK CTGS, cf. Westhays Fm *infra, v.* **plek** 'small plot of ground'. ROWDITCH WD. SANDY VIEW. TUT HILL (COPSE & FM), *Tuthill* 1811 OS, *Toothill Fm* 1939 Kelly, *v.* **tōt-hyll** 'a look-out hill'. WESTHAYS FM, called *Pluck* 1811 OS, cf. Pleck Ctgs *supra.* YEW TREE FM.

FIELD-NAMES

There are no names in 1838 *TA* 42 (Caundle Marsh). The undated forms are 1842 *TA* 19 (Bishop's Caundle). Spellings dated 1332[1] are SR, 1332[2], 1428 *Salis,* 1333, 1454 Pat, 1348, 1709 *WRO,* 1349 Hutch[3], 1373, 1493 *DCMDeed,* 1499 *CampbCh,* 1500, 1529 *AddCh,* 1538, 1614, 1677 *Digby,* 1569–74 *Map,* 1605, 1669 *SalisT,* 1845 *EnclA,* and the rest *Sher.*

(a) Barn Cl; Barns Md; Inclosure called Batts 1845 (*v.* **batte,** or a surname); Breaches 1845 (*v.* **bræc**); Bretts (*tenement . . . heretofore Burts 1677, Birts meadow* 1709, cf. Ralph *le Bryt* 1332[1] (Folke), *-le Bret* 1349 (held lands in Caundle Marsh)); Bushy Leaze (*v.* **læs**); Bustles Md; 8 Acres; Eyedfields (*Edithfeld* 1428, *Ide feld* 1500, *Idvellgate* 1569–74, *Edefeilde* 1614, *v.* **feld,** first el. possibly the fem. pers.n. *Edith* (OE *Ēadgȳð*), cf. Ide Hill K 70); 4 Acres; Goose Acre (*Gooseacre* 1614, *v.* **gōs, æcer**); Harp 1845 (no doubt named from its shape); Hay(e)s Md (probably **hǣs** 'brushwood'); Hill Cl (*Hillclose* 1614); Home Grd; Hutchings; Lillys Cl (cf. Thomas *Lillie* 1614, *tenement . . . late Lillies* 1677); Little Md (*the litle meadowe* 1614); Long Cl (*Longclose* 1614); Maston (cf. par. name *supra*); Paradise (*close called Paradis* 1614, *v.* **paradis**); (The) Peak; Pennys Grd & Md (cf. William *Penny* 1677); Pit Cl (*Pyttclose* 1614, *v.* **pytt**); Rue Cowleaze & Orchd (cf. *Rue* (possibly misprinted *Rile*) 1811 OS, from **rǣw** 'row (of houses or trees)'); Slades (1614, probably a surname); Snooks (*firma Willelmi Snowke* 1538, cf. Richard *Snook* 1677); Spring Grd; Three Corner Grd; West Cl (*Westclose(s)* 1614).

(b) Aplins (*Close*) 1709; (*pratum vocat'*) *Attemede* 1340, 1344, 1402, 1453, 1454 (*v.* **mǣd,** first el. probably the OE pers.n. *Atta* rather than ME **atte** '(place) at the'); bales bridge 1569–74; *Candle Lane* 1709 (*v.* par. name *supra*); Carnabies, Carnebies 1709; *Cawndel-, Caundelmers(s)hmor(e)* 1440, 1448, *-mour(e)* 1488, *Mershmour(hegge)* 1485, *Moore mead* 1709 (*v.* **mōr, hecg,** par. name *supra*); *Chawneteryclos* 1493, *the Chaunterie grownde of Wareham* 1529 (*v.* **chantry, clos(e)**; these fields were probably part of the endowment of the two chapels in Wareham 1 154 held by Sherborne Abbey in the 12th cent.); *Chelhull'* 1332[2], 1428, *Chell Hille* 1500 (*v.* **hyll,** first el. possibly the OE pers.n. *Cēola,* or **ceole** 'throat, channel, gorge' (cf. Chilbridge 2 166), or the related **cille** '? spring' discussed PN Brk 857); (*meddowe . . . called*) *Chelling(s)* 1605, *Chellings* (*meadow*) 1669 (possibly a surname, or to be related to prec.); *Chitracke bridge* 1569–74 (origin uncertain); *Cope haies* 1500 (a surname with **(ge)hæg**); *the Glebe-, the gleeblands* 1605 (*v.* **glebe**); *Harri(e)s Close* 1605, 1669; *the Home Close* 1605; *Campus Borialis* ('north field') 1500; *Pile mede* 1500 (*v.* **pīl**); *Shetelese*

(*alias voc' Bussylese*), *Shetewod(e)* 1493, *claus' voc' la Shute* 1499, 1500,
Shute close 1529, cf. Bartholomew *apud la Shute* 1373 (**scyte** 'steep slope',
perhaps alternating with the synonymous **scēot**³, with **lǣs, wudu**; *Bussy*-
is probably ME **busshi** 'bushy'); *Campus Australis* ('south field') 1500;
Campus occidentalis ('west field') 1500; *Withye* 1333, *Wethyehey* 1432,
Wythy-, Withyhey(e)(s) 1433 *et freq* to 1442, *Wythy-, Wythehayes* 1476,
1478, *W(h)ythyhaye* 1488, 1495, (*la*) *Withyes*, (*la*) *With(i)es*, (*la*) *Wyth(y)es*
1462 *et freq* to 1500, 1569–74, *weethy-, withye acre, weethy-, withy ham*
1605 (cf. William *atte Whithie, -atte Whythie* 1348, *v.* **wīðig** 'willow',
atte, (ge)hæg, æcer, hamm).

Purse Caundle

PURSE CAUNDLE (ST 696176)
  Candel 1086 DB, Exon, 1091–1106 MontC, 1100–22
    (1270) Ch, 1203 AthelC (p), *Caundel* 1241 FF
  Pursca(u)ndel 1241, 1252 FF, 1273 AthelC, 1285 FA, 1288
    Ass et freq to 1341 Cl, *-ka(u)ndel* 1268, 1288 *Ass*, 1290
    Ipm, *Purs Caundel* (p), *Purscandel Episcopi* 1288 *Ass,*
    Purscaundell' 1425 Ilch, *Pursse Candle* 1569–74 *Map,*
    Purss Caundle 1709 *WRO, Purse Caundle* 1811 OS
  Purschondel 1252 FF
  Pruscandel 1275 RH
  Ca(u)ndel Purs 1270 *For,* 1280, 1288 *Ass,* 1291 Tax, 1332
    SR, 1340 NI, *Caundel(l)purs(s)(e)* 1428 FA, 1464, 1491
    Digby, *Caundell Purs(s)(e)* 1428 FA, 1436 *WRO et freq*
    to 1501 Pat, *Candelpurse* 1575 Saxton, *Candle Purse*
    1664 HTax, *Caundle Purse* 1795 Boswell
  Pres Caunde (sic) 1280 *Ass*
  Pors Caundel 1288 *Ass*
  Caundel Pours 1350 Ipm, *Caundell' Porc'* 1406, *-Pors'* 1460
    Digby
  Puscandel(le) 1535–43 Leland

For Caundle, *v.* Stourton Caundle par. *supra*. The affix is
manorial. Although no family of this name has been noted in
connection with this place, the name does occur elsewhere in
Do (e.g. Henry *Purs* 1327 *SR* (Corfe Castle), Henry *Purs*
1327 *SR*, 1332 SR (Puddletown)) as well as widely in other
counties (*v.* Fägersten 213 fn. 1 and Reaney s.n. *Purse*).
Ekwall's suggestion (DEPN) that Purse may represent OE

prēost (in allusion to the possession of the manor by Athelney Abbey) can hardly be correct.

Other forms that may belong to this manor or part of it are *Candell-* 1259 FF, *Caundel Columbers* 1268 *Ass* (cf. Robert *de Columbar(iis)* Hy 3 *HarlCh*, 1259 FF) and *Whetenecandel* 1252 FF, *Caundell Wethill* 1411 Pat ('wheaten, where wheat is grown', and 'wheat hill', *v.* **hwǣten, hwǣte, hyll**).

There is mention of a *taberna* ('tavern, inn') here in 1288 *Ass*.

RUSSON (ST 682161), 1811 OS, *Risseden'* 1244 *Ass, Russhedon'* 1327 *SR, Rissheden* 1332 SR all (p), 'valley where rushes grow', *v.* **risc, rysc, denu** (replaced by or confused with **dūn** 'hill' in the 1327 form).

BROADSILL COPSE. CAUNDLE BRAKE, *v.* **bræc**[1] 'thicket'. CHURCH FM, from St Peter's Church *infra.* CLAYHANGER, 1811 OS, *v.* **clǣg, hangra** 'wood on a steep hill-side', cf. Clinger Fm in Buckland N. par. *supra.* COURT FM, *Court Homestead* 1912 *TA* alt.app., cf. *Court Leasse* 1612 *SalisT, -Leaze* c.1759-73 *DROMap, v.* **court, lǣs**. CRENDLE, *v.* **crundel** 'pit, quarry', with reference to a quarry just S of the farm. DEADMAN'S COVERT & STILE, *v.* **covert**. DOLE'S COVERT, cf. *Lr & Upr Doles, Doles Orchd* c.1759-73 *DROMap, v.* **dāl**. FOLLY FM, *v.* **folie**. GOATHILL RD, from Goathill par. *infra.* HANOVER HILL, *Hen-* 1811 OS, probably 'high hill or ridge', from **hēah** (wk.obl. *hēan*) and **ofer**[2]. HOME FM, cf. *Homestead* 1912 *TA* alt.app. HUSSEN HANGING, presumably an error for *Russen-, v.* Russon *supra,* cf. *Hanging (Cops)* c.1759-73 *DROMap, v.* **hanging** 'steep slope'. MANOR FM & HO, cf. *the Mansion House* 1597 Hutch[3]. MUSE HILL, *Mews Hill* c.1759-73 *DROMap, Nurse Hill* (sic) 1912 *TA* alt.app. PLUMLEY WD, 1811 OS, *-Coppice* c.1759-73 *DROMap,* probably 'plum-tree wood or clearing', *v.* **plūme, lēah**. RUE FM (*Rue* 1811 OS) & LANE, *v.* **rǣw** 'row (of houses or trees)'. ST PETER'S CHURCH, cf. *Ecclesiam de Caundell'purs'* 1464 *Digby.* TRIP'S FM, 1811 OS, cf. Richard *Tripp'* 1332 SR. WOOD HO COVERT.

FIELD-NAMES

There are no names in 1840 *TA* 179. The undated forms are c.1759-73 *DROMap* (KL 21). Spellings dated 1288 are *Ass*, 1327 *SR*, 1332 SR, 1340 NI, 1545, 1559 Hutch³, 1612 *SalisT*, 1664 HTax, 1912 *TA* alt.app., and the rest *Digby*.

(*a*) Barn Cl; Beat Md, Middle & Upr Beats (*v.* **beat**); Belt 1912; Binegar Md (*v.* **bēan, hangra**); Black Cl; Calfs Cl; Cleverlands (*v.* **clæfre** 'clover'); Cops; Corn Cl & Grd; Home Cow Leaze; Cross Cl; Cutt Purse (presumably a derogatory name for an unproductive field, but also strangely echoic of the name of the par.); Dry Cl; 8 Acres; 4 Acres; Furzy Grd; Garden Cl; Great Fd & Orchd; Green Cl & Hill; Green Way; Grove; Hays Md, Upr Hays (*v.* **hǣs**); Higher Fd; Hr & Lr Holt, Holt Cops (cf. *Holt*(*e*) *lane* 1484, 1531, *v.* **holt** 'wood'); Home Cl, Md & Pce; Hoods Hill; Hop Md; Horse Cl; Horse Minty Grd; Hounds Gate; Knights Croft (Coppice & Md); Lake Cl; Laynes (Md) (*v.* **leyne**); Listers Md; Little Md; Long Cl & Md; Lower Fd & Md; Lye (*v.* **lēah** 'wood, clearing'); Marks Md; May's Pdk (cf. James *May* 1664); Mead; Middle Fd; Monkway (no doubt an allusion to the monks of Athelney Abbey, cf. *Abbotswood infra*); Moss Leaze (*v.* **lǣs**); New Md; 9 Acres; Over Cl; Ox Leaze; Paddock by the House; Park(s) Hill, New Park; (Rough) Pasture 1912; Pope's Md (cf. James *Pope* 1664); Quar Cl; The Rag (*v.* **ragge**); Ridgey Cl; Rough Craft (Cops) (*Roughcroft* 1545, *v.* **rūh, croft**); Rough Grd; Rush Moor Md; Russen Md (*v.* Russon *supra*); Share Md (*v.* **sc(e)aru**); Sheep Slait (*v.* **slǣget**); 6 Acres; 16 Acres; Slade Md (*v.* **slǣd**); Spinney 1912; Stock Wd (*v.* **stocc**); The Strip; Summer Leaze (*v.* **lǣs**); 10 Acres; Thistley Fd & Moore (*v.* **thistley, mōr**); 3 Acres; Toomer Hill 1912 (cf. Toomer Fm & Hill (1″) in Henstridge So); Upper Fd; White Fd; Winshill (*v.* Wimsell-, Winsell Lain(s) in the f.ns. of Stalbridge par. *supra*).

(*b*) *Abbotswood* 1545 (with reference to its possession by Athelney Abbey, *v.* **abbat**); *Berdlane* 1531 (cf. John *Brid* 1332); *atte Brigge* 1332, 1340, *atte Brugge* 1406 (all (p), 'at the bridge', *v.* **atte, brycg**); *de la Fenne* (p) 1288 (*v.* **fenn**); *the Gleabe Landes* 1612 (*v.* **glebe**); *Goggford'* 1464 (*v.* **gogge** 'a bog, a quagmire', **ford**); *Grenlane* 1531 (*v.* **grēne¹** 'green'); *tenement called Kendballs* 1559; *Parsons Lands* 1612; *Shenamyslane* 1466 (cf. John *Shyuenham* 1332); *Shetelane* 1460, 1473 (probably 'lane to *la Shute*, etc' in Caundle M. par. *supra*); *atte Welle* (p) 1327 (*v.* **atte, well(a)**); *atte Were* 1332, *atte War* 1340 both (p), *tenement called Warehouse* 1559 (*v.* **atte, wer, wær** 'weir, river-dam', **hūs**).

Up Cerne

UP CERNE (ST 658028), *æt Upcerl*[*e*] 1001-12 ASWrits (S 1383), *Obcerne* 1086 DB, *Upecerna* 1166 RBE, *Vp-, Upcerne* 1202 P, 1268 *Ass* (p), 1273 Banco, 1285 FA, 1288 *Ass et freq*

to 1586 *Batten, Uppecerne* 1218 FF, *Vpcherne* 1268 *Ass,*
Vp- 1280 *ib,* 1414 *Weld², Upserne* 1362 Pat, *Upcern* 1291
Tax, 1428 FA, *Upcerne, alibi in evidenciis vocata Upton* 1346
ib, *Vp Cerne* 1406 *Digby, Vpseron'* 1530 *Batten, Vp-,*
Upcearne 1589 *ib,* 1614, 1617 *Pitt, Upper Cerne* 1773 Bayly.
Like Cerne Abbas par. and Nether Cerne par. both *infra,*
taking its name from R. Cerne, *v.* RNs. *infra; Up* means
'upper, higher up', with reference to its situation on the
river, which rises here, *v.* **upp**. In the earliest spelling *-cerl*[*e*]
may be an error for *-cernel*; for this form *v.* Cerne Abbas par.
infra. The alternative name *Upton* in 1346 means simply
'upper estate', *v.* **tūn**. There is mention of a watermill at Up
Cerne in 1273 Banco, 1484 *Digby,* 1586 *Batten,* cf. the mill
here in 1086 DB (VCHDo 3 71).

BAZON BARN & HILL (ST 645037) ['bɑːsən], *Basens hedge*
1598, *Basen* 1601 (*the hedge att-*), 1607 (*lease called-*),
Balsdon hedg' 1602, *Balsen* 1610, *Balson* (*Laynes*) 1668, 1676
all *Batten, Bazon Fd* 1839 *TA,* probably from **dūn** 'hill,
down', first el. possibly an OE pers.n. *Bæll* or *Bælli*
proposed for Balsall Wa 54, Balscott O 409, Balsham C 114,
etc, with **hecg, leyne**.

CANK FM, HIGH CANK (700') (ST 657033), *Canckeclose* 1588,
The 3 Kanks c.1685 both *Batten, Hr, Lr & Middle Cank,*
Cank Md 1839 *TA, v.* **canc** 'a steep, rounded hill'; there is a
ring earthwork on High Cank (RCHM 1 87).

FERNYCOMBE COPPICE (ST 644034), 1839 *TA, Fernecombe*
1590, 1610, *Fern Comb* 1661, *Ferne Coomb* 1668 all *Batten,*
'valley where ferns grow', *v.* **fearn, cumb**.

WANCOMBE BOTTOM & HILL (ST 646022), *Wancombe* 1586
Batten, 1839 *TA, -comb* c.1685 *Batten,* from **cumb** 'valley'
and **wenn, wænn** 'a wen, a tumour' (with reference to the
tumulus situated on the hill above the valley).

BARN BOTTOM (COPPICE & PLANT.), *Barn Bottom Wd, Barn*
Pce 1839 *TA,* named from Whistle Barn *infra,* cf. *loco vocat*
le bottome 1661 *Batten, v.* **botm** 'valley bottom'. UP CERNE
WD, *Upcerne Wood* 1811 OS, cf. (*the*) *Comon Wood*(*e*) 1610,

1668, *Woodway* 1661, *Wodeway* 1668, *the great wood* c.1685 all *Batten, Common Wood, Great Wood* 1839 *TA*, v. **wudu**. CHURCH, cf. 'the church of *Upcerne*' 1361 Pat. EAST HILL, 1661 *Batten*, 1839 *TA*, *the-* 1610 *Batten*. GORE BARN & HILL, *Goore* c.1685 *Batten, Gore* 1839 *TA*, v. **gāra** 'triangular plot of ground'; situated in a corner of the par. GREAT DITCH. GREAT POND. HIGHER FM. LYNCH COPPICE, *Lynch* 1661, *Linch* 1663 *Batten, Hr & Hthr Linch* 1839 *TA*, v. **hlinc** 'ridge'. MANOR HO, cf. *the Farme house* 1664 HTax, *Up Cerne Farme* c.1685 *Batten*. THE PARK, cf. *Pigeon or Park Md* 1839 *TA*. POND CTG, named from Great Pond *supra*. RAMSHORN HILL. SELDON HILL, *Silden* c.1685 *Batten, Hr & Lr Sheldon* 1839 *TA*, probably from **dūn** 'hill', first el. uncertain. SHEEPHOUSE BOTTOM. TELEGRAPH HILL, named from *Telegraph* 1811 OS. THORN STUMP, on the par. bdy. WETHER HILL, near to Sheephouse Bottom, v. **weðer**. WHISTLE BARN, called *White Barn* 1811 OS but named from *the West Hill* 1676 *Batten*, so called in contrast to East Hill *supra*.

FIELD-NAMES

The undated forms are 1839 *TA* 235. Spellings dated 1340 are NI, 1664 HTax, and the rest *Batten*.

(a) Banton's Cl; Crotten Cl (*Gratton Close* c.1685, v. **grǣd-tūn** 'a stubble field'); The Down (*the Downe(s)* 1602, 1668, v. **dūn** 'hill, down'); East Fd (*in oriental' campo* 1586, *le Eastfeild'* 1676); Home & Washpond Eweleaze; Grove (*Pound Close alias ye Grove* c.1685, v. **pund, grāf(a)**); Hayward's Md (cf. Thomas *Hayword* (sic) 1340, Samuel *Hayward* 1664); Middle Cl; Nosters Md; Plantation; 6 Acres; 6 and 30 Acres; Spicers Fd; Sycamore Orchd; 30 Acres; 20 Acres; Vine Md; Withy Bed.

(b) *Allambrigge(s) Close* 1588, 1591, 1618 (probably a surname); (*the*) *Aller More, lez Allers More* 1586 (v. **alor** 'alder', **mōr**); *le Backsyde* 1586, *-side* 1661 (v. **backside**); *the Barred style* 1608 (v. **barred, stigel**); *Bartletts peice* 1661 (cf. *tenementum nuper in tenura Alexandri Bartlett ib*); *North-, South batch* 1661 (v. **batch**); *Ye Bowling greene* 1676; *Lez Breche* 1586, *le(z) breach* 1588, 1663 (v. **brǣc**); *Burnecombe* 1598 (v. **burna** 'stream', **cumb**); *Chalke Pytte* 1588; *Lacomb* c.1685, *Nother Comb* 1661, *Nether Coome* 1668 (v. **cumb, neoðerra** 'lower'); *Combes hedge* 1661, *Coomeshedge* 1668 (v. **hecg**, cf. Michael *Combe* 1668); *Courthay* 1668 (v. **court, (ge)hæg**); *the drove* 1588; *Drudon* 1610, 1668 (perhaps 'dry down', from **drȳge** and **dūn**); *East Close* 1668; *Eastcomb* 1676 (v. **cumb**); *claus'*

. . . *subter farthinge, farthinges ende* 1586 (*v.* **fēorðung**); *Frankcomb Wood* c.1685 (cf. Francombe Bottom in Cerne A. par. *infra*); *Grene Waie* 1608, *Gre(e)neway(e)* 1610, 1661 (*v.* **grēne**[1]); *the grene wall* 1602; *Hayes* 1586 (*v.* **hǣs** 'brushwood'); *Hedingsbarrow* 1608 (*v.* **beorg**); *le Highway* 1661; *Hilfeild corner* 1676 (*v.* Hillfield par. *infra*); *Home Close* 1663; *muru' apud Howked-, Hooked Walles* 1590, 1591 (*v.* **hōcede** 'curved', **weall**); *Huish* 1661, 1668 (*v.* **hīwisc** 'measure of land that would support a family'); *Layters Lane* 1596, *claus' prati vocatur Layters* 1661 (probably a surname); *Lyppehedge* 1588 ('hedge that can be leapt', *v.* **hlīep, hecg**); (*terr' voc'*) *Littell-, Lytle-, Littlebrooke* 1586, 1624, *ye pond called Little brooke* 1676, *Little Brock* c.1685 (*v.* **lȳtel, brōc**, cf. *the water Course wch runneth through the streete* 1661); *Longelondes* 1586, *Longlands* c.1685 (*v.* **lang**[1], **land**); *lez Middelfeld, le Myddell fylde* 1586, *lez Middlefylde* 1588, *le Middlefeild* 1676 (*v.* **middel**); *New(e) close* 1590, 1661; *in boriali campo* 1586, *the Northfielde* 1602, *le Northfeild* 1676; *parvis clausis vocat' Parockes* 1586 (*v.* **pearroc**); *tenement called Prestri(d)ges* 1661, 1663, *Prestrigs Barne* 1668 (cf. *prat' olim in tenura Susanne Prestridge* 1666); *Pucketts gate* 1661 (cf. *tenementum nunc in tenura Johannes Puckett ib*); *leaze called-* 1607, *the ground called Seate* 1668 (cf. Minterne Seat Coppice in the neighbouring par. of Minterne M. *infra*); *Shortlandes* 1661 (*v.* **sc(e)ort**); *Showtinge Crofte* 1588, 1590 (possibly **schoting** 'shooting, archery', *v.* **croft**); *in australi campo* 1586, *Ye South feild'* 1676; *le Souther' aker'* 1586 (*v.* **sūðerra** 'more southerly', **æcer**), *Southerco(o)mb(e) head(e)* 1608, 1668 (*v.* **sūðerra, cumb, hēafod**); *Sticklandes hedge end'* 1608 (*v.* **hecg, ende**, cf. Roger *Stickland ib*); *Stickle path* 1602 (*v.* **sticol** 'steep'); *Veales close* 1588; *in occidenta' Campo* ('west field') 1590; *Whyte acre* 1661 (*v.* **hwīt**).

Nether and Over Compton

Nether Compton (ST 598173), Over Compton (ST 595169)

Cuniton' (for *Cumton'*) 860–6 (14) *Cott* (MS Faustina A.ii, f.25, cf. Finberg p. 164 who reads *Cuncton*), *on-, to Cumtun bricgge* 903 for 946–51 (12) *SherC* (S 516), *Cumbtun* 998 (12) *SherC* (S 895), *Comtona . . . alia Comtona* 1125 (12) *ib*, *Cumtona et superior Cumtona . . . et parva Cumtona* 1145 (12) *ib*, *Comton(a)* 1160 Osm, *Comptonam et aliam Comptonam* 1163 Dugd, *Cumpton(e)* 1201 FF, 1212 P, 1236 FF, 1265 *CottCh*, 1280 *Ass*, 1285 FA, *Cum'ton* 1244 *ib*, *Compton'* 1280 *ib*, 1428 FA

Contone 1086 DB

Nethecumton' 1268, *Nethercumpton(')* 1288 *Ass*, *Nether(e) Compton* 1297 Pat, 1316 FA *et passim*, *Nythercompton(')*

1332 SR, 1396 FF (-*Abbatis*) *et freq* to 1516 *Digby,
Nethercompton*(') 1406 *Digby et freq* to 1575 Saxton,
Nethircompton 1428 FA, *Neither Compton* 1569–74 *Map
Ouerecumton*' 1268, *Ouer*(*e*)*cumpton*', *Ouer Cumpton*' 1288
Ass, Over Compton 1316 FA, 1340 NI *et passim, Ouer-,
Overcompton*(') 1332 SR *et freq* to 1473 *Digby,
Ouyrcompton* 1473 *ib, Ouer Compton* 1575 Saxton,
Compton Over, or *Hawey* 1795 Boswell
Cumpton' *Haweye* 1288 *Ass*, 1318 Banco (Drew), -*Hauwey*
1303 FA, -*Haweys* 1309 Banco (Drew), -*Harveye* 1318
FF, *Compton*(') *Hawey*(*e*) 1288 *Ass*, 1342 Misc *et freq* to
1542 Hutch[3] (-*alias Over Compton*), -*Howey* 1320 Cl,
-*Hawy* 1349 Pat, 1423 Pap (-*alias Over Compton*),
-*Hawe* 1391 Pat, 1408 Cl, 1431 Fine, *Coumbhaweye* (sic)
1325 Pat
Upcompton 1349 Pat

'Farm in the valley', *v.* **cumb, tūn**, the two pars.
distinguished by the affixes **neoðerra** 'lower' and **uferra**
'higher, upper' or **upp** 'higher up'.
    The alternative affix -*Hawey* for Over Compton is
manorial; John *de Hawey* held half a knight's fee in
Cumpton in 1285 FA, cf. also Hutch[3] 4 167. Both places
belonged to Sherborne Abbey, hence the addition -*Abbatis*
('of the abbot') in 1396. The form *Cumtun bricgge* occurs as a
boundary point in the Anglo-Saxon bounds of Thornford
par. *infra*. It is fairly certain that it refers to this place even
though the point in question is on R. Yeo about a mile from
(Nether) Compton itself, at ST 620149; the meaning must be
'river-crossing associated with Compton, i.e. on a route
leading to Compton', *v.* **brycg**.

Nether Compton

STALLEN (FM) (ST 605166), *Stawell*(') 1244 *Ass* (p), 1284–6
(Eliz) Kirkby, 1285 FA, 1332 SR (p), 1345 Hutch[3], 1535
VE, 1795 Boswell, *Stawil* 1284–6 Hutch[3], *Stauwell* (possibly
for *Stan-*) 1290 Ch, *Stovel* 1344 Hutch[3], *Stawel* 1544 *ib*,
1774 Hutch[1], *Stawelbusshe* 1563, *Stale bushe* 1575 *Digby,*

Stalen (F.) 1811 OS, *Stirling Farm Ho* 1838 *TA, Stawel alias Stallen, Stallen alias Stalling* 1870 Hutch[3], 'stony spring or stream', or 'stream with a stone-built channel', *v.* **stān, well(a), busc**, cf. the analogous Stowell Gl 1 183, W 326 which also show loss of *-n-* before a labial consonant as in Stoborough 1 73, W Stafford 1 243. A stream (one arm of Trent Brook) rises here. The relatively recent development to Stallen can hardly be a metathesised form of *Stanell* < *Stanwell*, since the *-n-* disappeared at a very early date (it is possibly present only in the form from 1290); it is perhaps more likely that Stallen either represents an eroded form of the name (cf. *Stale* 1575) with the addition of **ende** 'district of a village', or results from folk etymology, based on the similarity of the eroded form to the word *stall* 'cattle stall' and with the addition of the Do dial. pl. *-en*.

BUCKLER'S FM. THE CITY, cf. *City* [Bridge] 1791 Boswell, an ironical name for a small settlement, *v.* PN Brk 284, but cf. the f.n. Setty in Stour P. par. *supra.* THE COTTAGE. COURT ASH CTG, cf. *Court Ash* 1811 OS. GORE LANE, cf. *Gore* [Bridge] 1791 Boswell, *Gore (Orchd), Arnolds & Mildmay's Gore, Parsonage Gore* 1838 *TA, v.* **gāra** 'triangular plot of ground', cf. William *Arnold* 1664 HTax. GUINEAGORE LANE, named from (*Gt & Parsonage*) *Guinea Gore* 1838 *TA, v.* **gāra** (though not near prec.); *Guinea* may be a transferred name or allude to a rent or value, cf. Guinea Fd Ch 5 400, 403. HALFWAY HO, 1811 OS, *The Halfway House Inn* 1838 *TA*, so named from its situation roughly equidistant from Yeovil and Sherborne. HART'S LANE, cf. *Harts Close Orchd* 1838 *TA*, Nicholas *Harte* 1563 *Digby*, John *Hart(e)* 1623 Hutch[3]. HOME COPSE. KITTON LANE, cf. *Almshouse Kitton, Hr, Lt & Lr Kitton, Kitton Orchd* 1838 *TA*; for lands in this par. belonging to Sherborne Almshouse, *v.* Hutch[3] 4 160. LOWER FM. MUNDEN'S COPSE, *Mundens Coppice* 1838 *TA*. OATCROFT LANE, from *Oat Croft, Gt Oatcroft* 1838 *TA, v.* **āte, croft**. RATLEIGH LANE & WD, *Ratleigh (Young Plant.)* 1838 *TA*. ROUND HO, *Round Lodge Bathing House and Coppice* 1838 *TA*, cf. the 'cold bath of remarkable good water' in Nthr Compton noted by Hutch[3] 4 161. ST NICHOLAS'S CHURCH, cf. 'the church of *Nythercompton*' 1398

DorR, *ecclesie de Nethercompton'* 1458 *AddCh*. SMELLAND'S
LANE, cf. *Smellands* 1838 *TA*, probably 'narrow strips of
land', *v*. **smæl, land**. TUCKER'S CROSS, cf. Edward *le Touker*
1340 NI (Sherborne), William *Toukere* 1460 *Digby* (Bradford
A.), from **cross** in the sense 'cross-roads'.

FIELD-NAMES

The undated forms in (*a*) are 1838 *TA* 67. Two fields marked † are 1843
TA 187 (Sherborne). Spellings dated 933 (12) are *SherC* (S 422), 1268,
1280 are *Ass*, 1327 *SR*, 1332 SR, 1388, 1544, 1650 Hutch³, 1664 HTax,
1791 Boswell, 1849 *EnclA*, and the rest *Digby*.

(*a*) Alderbed; Backside (Orchd); Gt & Russells Barber (cf. Russells
Orchd *infra*); Barley Cl; Bartlett's Orchd (cf. Robert *Bartlett* 1664);
Beechlands Orchd; Bicknells and Malagan's Orchds (cf. Bicknells Pce in
Over Compton par. *infra*); Bottom Grd; †Bowl Dish Compton Bottom
(perhaps 'bull pasture' from **bula** and **edisc**, cf. Bowldish Pond 2 267, *v*.
botm, par. name *supra*); Brimpton Fd, Brympton Cl; Broad Cl; Butts (*v*.
butte); Caryhill Fd, Orchd & Plant.; (Gt & Lt) Caswell (*Caswell* (*Close*)
1650, 'spring or stream where cress grows', *v*. **cærse, well(a)**, Parish Grd
infra); Gt & Lt Checkham; (Lt) Chillons, Chillons Plant. (*Childonlond*
1388, *v*. **land**, first part of the name uncertain); (Gt & Lt) Clanfield (*v*.
clǣne 'clear of weeds'); Close Mdw & Orchd; Lt Cobis; Compton Lane
[Bridge] 1791; Co(o)mbe (Drang & Head), Lt Combe (*v*. **cumb** 'valley',
drong 'narrow drove for cattle', **hēafod**, cf. *Comes Leyne* 1563 which may
however contain a surname, with **leyne** 'tract of arable'); Coppice;
Corners Nap (*v*. **cnæpp**); Cowslake Lane [Bridge] 1791; Cross Brook
[Bridge] 1791; Cuthedge, Cutheridge; Cuckoohill Plant.; Culverhays (*v*.
culfre, (ge)hæg); (Gt) Dean, Three Corner Dean, Dean Orchd (cf.
Compton Dean in Castleton f.ns. *supra*, *v*. **denu** 'valley'); (Lr) Dives
(probably to be associated with *portam apud Diue yeate* 1583, from a
surname and **geat**); Downs; Draught; East Hill; Ellery's Cl (*Ellerays*-
1849, cf. Thomas *Hillary* 1650); Ellground; Elmshill; Firleaze Orchd;
Four Acres; Foxsholes (sic) (*v*. **fox-hol**); Foxmoor (Orchd), Almshouse
Foxmoor (*v*. **fox, mōr**; for lands belonging to Sherborne Almshouse, *v*.
Hutch³ 4 160); Garden Grd; Gaston (cf. *Gaston' lane* 1563, *v*. **gærs-tūn**
'paddock'); Goulds Orchd; (Broad) Gowell, Gowells Lane & Plant.;
Greengirdle; Haggetts; Hawkes (cf. *Hauckesbroke* 16, probably a surname
with **brōc**, and John *Haukyn'* 1484 (this surname is a derivative of *Hauk*
< **hafoc**)); Headstile Orchd; Hermits [Bridge] 1791; Highest Hill plain;
Hill's Orchd; (Lt) Hogs Leaze (*v*. **lǣs**, first el. probably **hogg** 'hog', but
possibly to be associated with *terr' int' backsid' Roberti Hodges* 16);
Hollyland(s); Home Cl; The Home Orchd; Hoopers Orchd; Horsepool;
Hurn Orchd and Ctg (cf. William *Hurneman* 1332, *v*. **hyrne** 'angle,
corner'); Ivy Cl; Jerry's Plot [Bridge] 1791; Kingslane [Bridge] 1791
(*Kines lane* 1583); Kithills Plant. (first el. probably **cȳta** 'kite'); The Lane;

Lanes Orchd; Langlands, †Lawn; Little Coppice & Gdn; Little Md & Plant.; Lodings Backside and Barn (*Loading's* [Bridge] 1791); Long Cl; Long Ford (cf. Humfrey *de La Forde de Cumpton* 1280, *v.* **ford**); Long Hills Orchd; (Tennys) Loscombe, Loscombe Orchd (and Webbery) (to be identified with *hloscumbes heafud* 933 (12) in the bounds of Bradford A. *supra* and also with *Hloscum* 1145 (12) *SherC* (f. 35v), *Loscumbe* 1163 Dugd, cf. also *Lossecumbe* 1268 (p), *Loscombecrosse* 1496, 'pig-sty valley', *v.* **hlōse, cumb**, with **hēafod** 'upper end, head' and **cross**); Malachia's [Bridge] 1791; (Gt) Maybrook; Mayo's [Bridge] 1791; The Mead; Wards or Gt Moor, Farm & Wards Mower, Lt Mower, Long Mower or Higher Grd, Mower Hearne (*v.* **mōr** 'marshy ground', **hyrne** 'angle, corner'); Mouseland(s); Mow Plot; New Cl; Newmans Gdn, Newmanshill (cf. John *Nieuman* 1327, John-, Richard *Niwman* 1332); Notleys Orchd; Nursery; The Old Road Plant.; Tom Paine's Hill; Parish Grd (in 1650 'several of the parishioners purchased . . . 2 acres of pasture land called *Caswell*, now called *Parish Ground* . . . in trust for the inhabitants of the . . . parish' (Hutch³ 4 160), *v.* Caswell *supra*); Parsonage Combe (in 1838 owned by Rev. Wyndham Goodden and 'occupied' by Isaac *Parsons, v.* Co(o)mbe *supra* and Rectory 6″, cf. foll.); Parsons Pce; Partway, Portway Plant. (*Portwaye* 1650, *v.* **port-weg** 'road to a market town', probably with reference to the Yeovil-Sherborne road; it is possible that *Pratstrote* (possibly for *Partstrete*) 1564 belongs here, *v.* **strǣt**); Pit Cl; Plainhill; Plantation; Plots; Pranchard(') Md & Orchd (for the *Prankard* family, *v.* Hutch³ 4 160); Quarr Cl, (Van Diemans Ld or) Foot of Quarr (*v.* **quarre** 'quarry'; Van Diemans Ld is a transferred name, probably for a remote piece of land, *v.* Field 243); Quissiners (cf. *Wyfiners* (for *Wysiners*) *Close* 1544); Red Leaze (with old Bucking house) (*Redlease Shard(e)* 1563, *Rydlease shearde* 1575, *v.* **rēad, lǣs, sceard**; *Bucking* means 'bleaching'); Ridgway Fd (*v.* **hrycg-weg**); Roundhill Combe (*v.* **cumb**); Rowes Orchd; Russells Orchd (cf. Robert *Russell* 1664); Rye Cl; Savages Cl (cf. widow *Savage* 1664); Shilliners; Shortlands; Shrubbery; Gt Snakewell; Stoney Fd; Strong Clay; Stubbs; Thompsons Orchd; Thorn's Orchd; Trask's Orchd; Uppingstock Fd; Van Diemans Ld (*v.* Quarr *supra*); West Fd (Orchd) (*West field* 1650); Willbarns; Wind Whistle (1849); Withey Bed, Withey-, Wetheyhill (*v.* **wīðig** 'willow'); Wormley; Wyke Park, Weekpark (*v.* Wyke Fm and Park Ctg in Castleton par. *supra*); Youngs Orchd (cf. *Young's* [Bridge] 1791).

(b) *Bulbury* 1563 (possibly from **bula** 'bull' and *byrig*, dat.sg. of **burh** 'fortified place'); *Slade* 1650 (*v.* **slæd** 'valley'); *Stranges* 1583 (a surname); *les Wales* 1583 (*v.* **walu** 'ridge').

Over Compton

Hᴿ Barton Ctg, *v.* **barton**. Chapel Plant., *Chapel* 1838 *TA*, probably the site of the chapel mentioned in 1291 and 1409 (Hutch³4 170), cf. also John *Chapeleyn'* 1460 *Digby*.

COMPTON HO, 1826 Gre. COMPTON PARK, cf. *New Parks*
1838 *TA*. OVER COMPTON MILL, *Mill* 1811 OS, *The Mill
House and Island* 1838 *TA*, cf. William *atte Mulle* 1332 SR,
unu' molend' aquatic' 1473 Digby, *Mill Cl, Mdw & Orchd*
1838 *TA*, *v*. **myln, atte**; there was a mill at Over Compton
in 1086 DB (VCHDo 3 71). HIGHER LODGE, cf. *Lodges* 1826
Gre. HOME FM, cf. *Home Orchd* 1838 *TA*. LOWER FM. MARL
LANE, cf. *Marlpits* 1838 *TA* and Hutch[3] 4 169 on the
'excellent marl' dug here. ST MICHAEL'S CHURCH, cf. 'the
church of *Cumpton Haweys'* 1309 Banco (Drew), 'the church
of *Compton Hawy*, -of *Upcompton'* 1349 Pat. WESTERN ST.

FIELD-NAMES

The undated forms in (*a*) are 1838 *TA* 68. Spellings dated 1327 are *SR*,
1332 SR, 1340 NI, and 1664 HTax.
(*a*) Alder Plot; Gt & Lt Asmore (first el. possibly **æsc** 'ash-tree', cf.
Henry *atte Naissh'* 1332, *v*. **atten** 'at the', **mōr**); Babylon Hill,
Barberlons (*v*. under Babylon Hill in Bradford A. par. *supra*); Barley Cl;
Bicknells Pce (cf. Andrew *Bicknell* 1664); Binghams Md & Orchd; Bottom
Breach (*v*. **brēc** 'land broken up'); Brachmelon; Chowell; Gt & Lt Coat
(*v*. **cot** 'cottage'); Common Cl; Cornlands; Cox's Orchd (cf. John *Cokes*
1332); Crib Ho Grd (*v*. **cribhouse**); Cross (Cl); Dives (cf. Nthr Compton
f.ns. *supra*); Durnford (*v*. **dyrne** 'hidden'); Hr & Lr Goar, Goar Orchd (*v*.
gāra 'triangular plot'); Green Cl & Lane; Ham Md (*v*. **hamm**
'enclosure'); Hands New Cl; Hanglands (*v*. **hang**); Beers Hearne, Gt &
Ploughed He(a)rne, Hearne Drang (*v*. **hyrne** 'angle, corner', **drong**
'narrow drove for cattle'); Higher Orchd; Hillarys Orchd (cf. Ellery's Cl in
Nthr Compton par. *supra*); Hollars Knap (*v*. **cnæpp**); Howell Wd; Island;
Jeans Bush; Jerrys Cl; Little Md; Lower Fd; Maidenwell (perhaps
alluding to a 'fertility' spring, *v*. **mægden, well(a)**); Mead over the
Water; Middle Grd; Mower Md; Oaker; Orchard; Pitts; Plantation; Quar
Breach (Coppice) (*v*. **quarre, brēc**); Rack Cl (*v*. **rakke**); Rough Grd;
Ruckless Bottom; Gt & Middle Ryalls, (Allotment Gdns or) Hr Ryalls, Lr
Ryall Fd (probably 'rye hill', from **ryge** and **hyll**); Short Batts (*v*. **batte**);
6 Acres; Sleight (*v*. **slæget** 'sheep pasture'); Slimmerslade; Summerleaze
(*v*. **sumor, lǣs**); Underhill Orchd, Gt Underhill; West Fd; Woodlands
(Orchd); Yearbury; Yeldon.
(*b*) *in the lane* (p) 1332, 1340 (*v*. **lane**); *atte Splotte* (p) 1332, 1340 (*v*.
atte, splott 'plot of land'); *atte Wych(e)* (p) 1327, 1332 (*v*. **wice**
'wych-elm' or **wīc** 'dairy farm'); *atte Yate* (p) 1340 (*v*. **geat** 'gate').

Folke

An area in the E of the par. (Bishop's Down) was until 1886 a detached part of Bishop's Caundle par. *supra.*

FOLKE (ST 660133) [fouk]

> *Fulk* 1166 LN (p) (Hutch[3] **4** 174), *Fulk[inges]* 1166 RBE (p)
> *Folk'* 1244 *Ass*, 1327 Pat, 1455 *DCMDeed, Folk* 1285 FA, 1291 Tax, 1303 FA, 1314 Pat *et freq* to 1431 FA, *Folke* 1337 Pat, 1340 NI, 1344 Ipm *et passim, Folcke* 1561 *NatT*
> *Falk(e)* 1283 Banco (Drew), 1393 *DCMDeed*
> *Foolke* 1453 *Sher*, 1454 Pat both (p), 1553 *NatT*
> *Foulk* 1558–79 ChancP, *Fowlke* 1563 *Digby*
> *Foke* Eliz ChancP, 1575 Saxton, *Fooke* 1569–74 *Map*

An unparalleled simplex use of OE **folc** 'folk, the people of a tribe or family, the common people', presumably denoting 'land held by the people', cf. Freefolk Ha (DEPN). The 12th cent. *u* spellings are probably AN, the second form perhaps suggesting confusion with Fulking Sx 284.

ALLWESTON (FM) (ST 666142)

> *Alveston(')* 1214 Cur, 1316, 1431 FA, 1516, 1531 *Digby,* 1553 *Prideaux,* 1661 Hutch[3], *Alueston(')* 1288 *Ass*, 1332 SR, 1377 FF, 1406, 1464, 1484 *Digby, Alveston, Alston* vulgo *Ason* 1870 Hutch[3]
> *Alfeston* 1214, 1390, 1436 FF, *Alfeeston* 1244 *Ass, Alpheston* 1268 FF
> *Alfletheston'* 1244 *Ass* (p)
> *Alueueston'* 1268 *Ass*
> *Alfresteston'* 1280 *Ass*
> *Bere Alueston'* 1288 *Ass*
> *Alueton'* 1484, 1491, *Alveton'* 1531 *Digby*
> *Avelstone* Eliz ChancP
> *Allweston* 1630 *Sher,* *All-Weston* 1664 HTax, *Alweston* 1811 OS

This is probably from an OE pers.n. in Ælf- such as *Ælfhēah* or *Ælfwīg* with **tūn** 'farm, estate', cf. Alvescot O

298, Alveston Gl 3 111. However the 13th cent. forms *Alfletheston'* and *Alueueston'* suggest the fem. OE pers.ns. *Ælfflæd* and *Ælfgifu*, and it is possible that Allweston is from one or other of these with **stān** 'stone'. The addition *Bere* in 1288 may be manorial, cf. Walter *le Bere* 1332 SR (Bishop's Caundle), or toponymic, cf. Robert *atte Bere* ib (N Wootton), from **bǣr**² '(woodland) pasture' or **bearu** 'grove'.

BISHOP'S DOWN (FM) (ST 673121), 1811 OS, *Dune, Denne* (probably for *Doune*) 1280 *Ass, Doune* 1332 SR, 1406, 1484 *Digby, La Doun', Bysshopesdoun'* 1332 *Salis, Down(e)* 1460 *Digby et freq* to 1677 *ib, Bysshopysdoune* 1468 FF, *Bysshops Downe* 1500 *AddCh, la Downe Episcopi* 1515 *DCMDeed, le-, la Downe* 1538 *Digby, Bu(i)sshop(p)s Downe* 1582 *ib,* 1583 *SPDom,* 1614 *Digby,* cf. *(Lower) Down, Down* Md 1842 *TA,* from **dūn** 'hill, down'; *Bishop's* because it belonged to the bishops of Salisbury, like Bishop's Caundle par. *supra* of which it was formerly a detached part, *v.* **biscop, episcopus.** In 1598, 1677 *Digby* there is a family of copyholders here called *B(u)is(s)hop(pe)*, but the affix clearly predates them. For the tithing of *Down(e) and Marsh* 1664 HTax, 1795 Boswell, *v.* Caundle Marsh par. *supra.*

BUTTERWICK DAIRY HO, (LR) BUTTERWICK FM (ST 667114, 674108), *Buterwik', -wyk', Buttewyk'* 1288 *Ass, Boterwyk(e)* 1328 FF, 1332 SR (p), 1431 FA, 1466 *Weld*¹, FF, 1493 *DCMDeed, Buterwyk* 1327 *SR* (p), *Butterwick* 1467 (16) *DCMDeed,* 1811 OS, *-wyke* 1489 (16) *DCMDeed,* 16 *Shepherd*² (*-moure*), 1561 *NatT, -we(e)ke* 1489 (16) *DCMDeed,* 1535 VE, *-wike* 1583, 1870 *Hutch*³, 'farm where butter is made', from **butere** and **wīc**, with **mōr** 'marshy ground'.

DENSHAM FM (ST 679118), *Denesham* 1332 SR (p), *Densham* 1516 *Digby* (p), 1550 *PlR,* 1811 OS, probably 'Dene's enclosure or river-meadow', from the OE pers.n. *Dene* (cf. Denstone St (DEPN), Redin 6) and **hamm.**

FONT LE ROI (ST 673136) ['fɒntlərɔi], *Fauntleroy(e)s Marshe* 1558–79 ChancP, *-mershe* 1569–74 *Map, Fantelaroymarsh* 1575 Saxton, *Fontleroy(s) Mersh(e)* 1582, 1598 *Digby,*

Fontleroy's Marsh 1795 Boswell, *Font le Roi Marsh* 1811 OS, named from the family of Roger *Le Enfaunt le roy* 1244 *Ass* (201.6), *-Fauntleray ib* (200.10), William *Fauntleroi* (*de Boterwyk*') 1332 SR, John *Fauntleroy de la Mersh* 1431 FA, etc, *v.* **mersc** 'marsh'; the place lies near the par. bdy with Caundle Marsh par. *supra.*

PIN BRIDGE (ST 676127), 1791 Boswell, *Pynkebrigge* 1332, *Pynkbrugge* 1428 *Salis*, *Pynkbrigge* 1464 *Digby*, *Pingebridge* 1569–74 *Map*, cf. *Pin Bridge Md & Plots* 1842 *TA, v.* **brycg**, first el. probably **pinc** 'a minnow'.

WEST HALL (FM) (ST 654129), *Westhall*(e) 1352 FF, 1362 Hutch[3], 1393 *DCMDeed et freq* to 1661 Hutch[3], *Westall*' 1353 *DCMCt*, *Westehall*(e) 1431 Hutch[3], 1563 *Digby*, *Westhall iuxta Shirborne* 1470 *NatT*, *West Halle* 1491 *Digby*, *West Hall* 1795 Boswell, cf. *Westhall Ld* 1841 *TA, v.* **west**, **heall** 'large residence, manor house'.

WIZARD BRIDGE (ST 656126), *Weseford*(') 1204 P, 1278 Pat, 1344 Cl, 1393 *DCMDeed, Wesard'*, *Weseford Lane, -Hill* 15 *NatT, Wes*(*e*)*ford*(*e*)*lane* 1464, 1473, 1484, *Wesefordbrygge* 1484, *Weysfordes lane, Weyswardbryge* 1516, *Wayesworthelane* 1563 all *Digby*, *Wesworthe bridge* 1569–74 *Map, v.* **ford**, **lane**, **brycg**. The first el. may be **wise** 'river, swamp', the *e-* spellings perhaps being due either to AN influence or to the lengthening of *i* in an open syllable, cf. Wisbech Ca 292 which has *e*(*y*)- spellings from 1342. For the late development of the second el. to -(*w*)*ard* and confusion with *worth*, cf. Hayward Bridge in Ch. Okeford par. *supra* and Dibberford in Broadwindsor par. *infra.*

BISHOP'S DOWN PLANT., cf. Bishop's Down (Fm) *supra.* BROKE LANE & WD (1836 *DCMMap*), cf. *Brokecorner* 1563 *Digby*, Richard *Yandbroke* 1455 *DCMDeed, v.* **brōc** 'brook', **corner**, **begeondan** 'beyond'; Broke Lane crosses two brooks. BURTON COPPICE, named from Long Burton par. *supra.* BUTTERWICK DROVE & WD (1836 *DCMMap*), *v.* Butterwick Fm *supra.* CAPHAYS DAIRY & DROVE, *Capheys* (*Mede*) 1557, 1559 *Prideaux, Caphays Knap* 1811 OS, *v.* **mǣd**, **cnæpp**; the first part of the name may be a surname, or from **cape** 'a look-out place' and **(ge)hæg** 'enclosure' or **hǣs** 'brushwood', cf. also *caplane* 1569–74 *Map*. CHAFFEY'S FM, *tenement . . . formerly Chaffeys* 1677 *Digby*, cf. Thomas *Chafe* 1664 Hutch³, John *Chaffe* 1664 HTax, Thomas *Chaffy* 1677 *Digby*. DOWN LANE, from Bishop's Down *supra*. FERNEY DOWN WD. FOLKE FM, 1826 Gre, *the Farme of Folke* 1634 *SalisT*. FOLKE LANE. THE FOLLY WD, *v.* **folie**. HUNTERS BRIDGE (COPPICE), *Huntyngford'* 1489 *DCMDeed*, *Huntingford brydge* 16 *Shepherd²*, *pons vocat' Huntyngfordys* 1516 *Digby*, *huntingforde bridge* 1569–74 *Map*, probably analogous with Huntingford in Gillingham par. *supra*, 'the ford used by hunters', from **hunta** (gen.pl. *huntena*) and **ford**. KING'S PLANT., cf. William *Kyng* 1340 NI (Bps. Caundle), Rev. John *King* 1770 Hutch³. KITFORD BRIDGE, 1791 Boswell, *Kytefordbrygge* 1484 *Digby*, *Kitfordebridge* 1569–74 *Map*, cf. *Kytefordelane* 1473 *Digby*, *Kitford* 1842 *TA*, 'ford frequented by kites', *v.* **cȳta, ford**, with **brycg, lane**. MUNDEN'S FM & LANE, cf. John *Munden* 1677 *Digby* (Bps. Caundle). PLECK CTGS, *v.* **plek** 'small plot'. RECTORY, cf. *Parsonage Ld* 1841 *TA*. RYALL'S FM. RYE CLOSE FM, 1836 *DCMMap*, probably to be associated with the nearby Rye Water Fm in Holnest par. *infra*. ST LAWRENCE'S CHURCH, cf. 'the church of *Folk(e)*' 1314, 1366 Pat. STAKES FORD & LANE, *Staklane* 1462, *Stakelane* 1473 *Digby*, *v.* **staca** 'stake, post', **lane**, cf. *Pilelane infra*. WENLOCK, *Winlock* 1811 OS, perhaps a transferred name from Wenlock Sa. WILLOW TREE FM. WRITH CTG, *le Frythe* 1563 *Digby*, *v.* **fyrhð** 'wood'.

FIELD-NAMES

The undated forms in (*a*) are 1842 *TA* 19 (Bps. Caundle). Spellings dated 1332¹, 1428, 1512 are *Salis*, 1332² SR, 1352 *Hastings*, 1353 *DCMCt*, 15 *NatT*, 1455 *DCMDeed*, 1500 *AddCh*, Eliz ChancP, 1569–74 *Map*, 1634 *SalisT*, 1664 HTax, 1791 Boswell, and the rest *Digby*.

(*a*) Barn and Plot, Inner & Outer Barn Cl; Bow Crafts (*v.* **croft**); Broad Cl (*Brodeclose* 1484, *v.* **brād, clos(e)**); Burn Beak Md (*v.* **burnbake**); Bushy Cl (*Busshieclose* 1614, *v.* **busshi**); Gt & Lt Bushy Downs; Coppice Grd; Cow Croft; Cuppers Plot (cf. Henry *Cooper* 1664); Dash Cl; Doatfields; Dole (*v.* **dāl**); Downs (*dwelling house . . . late Downes, tenement . . . formerly Downes* 1677); Dry Cl; Elverlands (*Elverlonges* 1614, *v.*

elle(r)n 'elder-tree', **furlang**); Goore (Md) (*Gore* 1332[1], 1614, *la Gore* 1428, *le Gore* 1455, *Gore mede* 1500, *-meade* 1614, *v.* **gāra** 'triangular plot', **mǣd**); Grove Md; Ha(y)dons (*Hayden* Eliz, *close called Haddon* 1614, probably identical in origin with Haydon par. *infra*, cf. Nicholas *de Haydon'* taxed under Folke in 1332[2]); Half Acre; (Lt) Ham ((*the*) *Hamme* 1614, *v.* **hamm**); Hilly Cl; Home Cl, Grd & Md; Hr, Lr & Middle Leaze (*v.* **lǣs**); Little Md; Long Cl & Md; Minty Grd; Monks Barn Cl (cf. *Tenement . . . late Muncks* 1677); Moor Md (*Moore mead* 1582, cf. *Langmore* 1563, *v.* **mōr, mǣd, lang**[1]); North Craft (*v.* **croft**); Orchard; Paddock; Pigshouse Md; Pit Cl; Pitlands; Ramslake (*remslake bridge* 1569–74, *close called Rimeslake* 1614, first el. uncertain, *v.* **lacu**); Ray Grass (*v.* **rye-grass**); Ridgey Cl; Rokers Wd; Rushy Cl; South Brook; Stony Lds; Three Corner Md; Three Corners; 12 Acres; Lt 2 Acres; Wells alias Rutford [Bridge] 1791; Hr Withy Cl (*v.* **wīðig**).

(*b*) *Balsyrecrosse* 1484, *Bellycrosse* 1487, *Belsys Cros(s)e* 1531 (*v.* **cros(s)**, probably with a surname); *Bayes lane* 1582 (possibly **bay**[2] 'barrier', or a surname); *Blakemor'* 1512, *Blakemore* 1575 (*v.* **blæc, mōr**); *Brandysecorner* 1464, *Brondeyce, Brondysecrose* 1531 (*v.* **corner, cros(s)**, with a surname); *Bryanscrosse* 1484; *Bryses* 1496 (cf. Henry *Bryse ib* (Holnest)); *cracketayle* 1569–74 (probably a manorial name, cf. *William Crake Craketaill'* (sic) 1332[2], John *Craktayl* 1352, both recorded in documents relating to the adjacent par. of Wootton Glanville *supra*); *Fursclose* 1473 (*v.* **fyrs**); *the Gleab Land of Folke* 1634; *Golbardysfrost* 1531 (the surname *Goldbard*, second el. uncertain); *Gosefurldych'* 1531 (*v.* **gōs, furlang, dīc**); *the Great Meadow* 1634; *Gunlane* 1531; *Harris Bridge* 1582; *Horselowe* 1531, *Horyslowe* 1563 ('filthy slough', *v.* **horig, slōh**); *Hyllett* 1531 (perhaps 'little hill', from **hyll** and the diminutive suffix **-ette**); *Newlond'* 1563 (*v.* **nīwe**); *atte Ok'* (p) 1332[2] (*v.* **atte, āc**); *Pilelane* 1464, *Pylane* 1484, *Polelane* 1496 (first el. probably **pīl** 'pile, stake', perhaps alternating with **pāl** 'pole, stake', cf. Stakes Ford & Lane *supra*); *Portebridge* 16 (*v.* **port** 'town', **brycg**); *litle close called Ragg* 1634 (*v.* **ragge**); *Rodenhurst* 1353, *Radenhurst* 15 (*v.* **rēad** (wk.obl. *-an*) 'red', **hyrst** 'wood, wooded hill'); *Russellane* 1496, *Russelles Yate* 1531 (the surname *Russell* with **lane** and **geat**); *Sampytdyche* 1496 (*v.* **sand, pytt, dīc**); *seven Ackers* 1634 (*v.* **æcer**); *Somerlese* 1455 (*v.* **sumor, lǣs**); *Southheyyscorner* 1484 (*v.* **sūð, (ge)hæg** 'enclosure', **corner**); *Stretelane* 1496 (*v.* **strǣt**); *taylors bridge* 1569-74; *ten Ackers* 1634 (*v.* **æcer**); *three Ackers* 1634; *atte Wolle* (p) 1332[2] (*v.* **atte, well(a)** 'spring, stream'); *Wyrwykelane* 1496 (*v.* **lane**, first el. a surname).

Haydon

Boys Hill now in Holnest par. *infra* was formerly a detached part of this par. (Hutch[3] 4 187)

HAYDON (ST 671158)
? (*æt*) *Hægdune* 1046 (12) KCD 1334 (S 1474)
Heydone, -a c.1163 Sarum, 1569–74 *Map*, *-don* 1253

Misc, 1278 Banco (Drew), 1284 Pat (p), 1288 *Ass*,
-*don*' 1473 Digby, *Heidon* 1202 FF, 1204 FineR
Hedon' 1204 Cur
Haydon(') 1258, 1268 *For*, 1280 *Ass*, 1285, 1316 FA *et
passim*, -*doun* 1385, 1412 Cl, *Haidon*(') 1406 Digby,
1412 FA, (-*juxta Shirburne*), 1614 Digby, *Haydon
Mannor* 1677 *ib*
Haddon 1303 FA
Hayden 1664 HTax

Probably 'hill or down where hay is made', from **hēg** and
dūn, but alternatively the first el. could be **hege** 'hedge' or
(ge)hæg 'enclosure', cf. Haydon So (DEPN), W 32, Heydon
Nf (DEPN). The identification of the 1046 form is doubtful;
it may belong to Haydon So (preferred by DEPN, though
ASCharters says 'Dorset or Somerset').

COACH HILL WD, possibly to be associated with *Tenement
. . . called Coxalls* 1677 Digby, cf. William *le Couk*' 1327 *SR*.
HAYDON DROVE, *Common called drove* 1697, *Drove Comon*
1698, cf. *Drene* (probably for *Dreue*) *Gate* 1696 all Digby, *v.*
drāf, drǣf. HAYDON FM, -*Farme* 1677 Digby. HAYDON
LODGE. HAYDON HILL WD, cf. *via desuper Hyll*' 1460, *Hill
Cloase* 1698 Digby, *bosco de Haydon*(*e*) 1258 For, 1280 *Ass,
Haydon woode* 1620 Pitt, *v.* **hyll**. HAYDON HOLLOW. HUISH
LANE, named from *Lt & Gt Hewish* 1857 *TA* alt.app., *v.*
hīwisc 'measure of land that would support a family'. ST.
CATHERINE'S CHURCH. WEST LANE. WYNMAN HILL COPSE.

FIELD-NAMES

The undated forms in (*a*) are 1857 *TA* 103 (alt.app.). Spellings dated 1327
are *SR*, 1332 SR, 1340 NI, 1569–74 *Map*, 1620 Pitt, 1664 HTax, and the
rest Digby.

(*a*) Burts Orchd; Gould's Orchd (cf. William *Gould*(*e*) 1332, 1340
(Folke)); Isaac's Grd; Lambert's Orchd (cf. Benjamin *Lambert* 1664);
Parsons Hill & Md; Lt Tommy; (Granger's) West Cl, West Cl Orchd
(*West Close* 1696, cf. Henry *Granger* 1664).

(*b*) *Coles Hill* 1677; *East Cloase* 1698 (*v.* **clos(e)**); atte *Felde* (p) 1340 (*v.*
atte, **feld**); *la Gretebussh*' 1460 (*v.* **grēat** 'thick', **busc**); *heydone yate*
1569–74 (*v.* **geat**); *home Cloase* 1698; *the home grounds* 1697; *William
Housneys Ragg* 1696 (cf. *Tenement . . . late Overs and formerly Holsneys*

1677, v. **ragge**); *Jurdons yate* 1531; *Leany mead* 1697; *atte Pile* (p) 1327, *atte Pyle* (p) 1332, 1340 (v. **atte, pīl** 'shaft, stake'); *Stokelane* 1531; *xx acres yate* 1569–74 (v. **æcer, geat**); *Whitynggestrete* 1460, *Whytynglane* 1487, *Whytinges lane* 1563 (cf. *Whityng ys Cros* in Castleton par. *supra, v.* **strǣt, lane**); *Whitly comon* 1620.

Holnest

Boys Hill was formerly a detached part of Haydon par. *supra* (Hutch[3] **4** 187).

HOLNEST (ST 656098) ['houlnest]
  Holeherst 1185–8, 1194, 1195 P, 1196 ChancR, *-hurst* 1288
    Ass
  Holenhurst(e) Hy 3 (14) Cerne, 1268 *Ass*, 1270 *For*, 1288
    Ass, Holnhust, Holnestre 1268 *ib, Holnehurste* 1279
    DEPN, *Holnhurst* 1375 *Hastings*
  Holnest(e) 1278 Banco (Drew), 1316 FA, 1327 *SR*, 1332
    SR, 1346 *UD et passim, Hollneste* 1569–74 *Map*

'Holly wood', from **holegn** and **hyrst**, cf. Holdenhurst Ha (DEPN) which is identical in origin, and cf. Holmbush Plant. in this par.

BOYS HILL (DROVE) (ST 673102), *Boynlane* (sic) 1464, *Boy(e)slane* 1474, 1491, 1531 all *Digby*, 1569–74 Map, *claus' voc' Boyes* 1552 *Shepherd²*, *boyes hill* 1569–74 *Map, Boies Hill'* 1582 *Digby, Boyshill* 1620 *Pitt*, 1698 *Digby, Boishill* 1677 *ib, Boy(e)s Hill* 1696 *ib et passim, Boys Hill Lane* 1845 *TA*, cf. *Boyscrose* 1464 *Digby*, named from the family of Adam-, William *Boye* 1314 Pat, William *de Boys* 1327 *SR*, Hugh-, William *le Boys* 1332 SR (taxed under Haydon), *v.* **lane, hyll, cros(s)**.

CANCER DROVE (ST 645108), 1845 *TA*, *Canschaue* 1394 *Shepherd¹*, *Canshaw-, Cannshavelane* 1464, *Canshauelane* 1474 *Digby, Canchers lane, Canshere Lawne* 16 *Shepherd²*, *Cansewlane* 1516 *Digby*, *claus' voc' Canshere, -Cansher(e)s* 1552 *Shepherd²*, *Cancer Drove & Grd* 1800 *EnclA*, cf. *Lr & Middle Cancer* 1844 *TA* (Long Burton), *v.* **sc(e)aga** 'small wood, copse', **lane**; the first el. may be **canne** 'hollow, deep valley', or an OE pers.n. *Cana* for which *v.* Canford **2 2**. The forms *Kaneschase* Hy 3 *CampbCh* and *Caushath'* (possibly for *Canshath'*) 1332 *SR* (p) are perhaps also to be associated with this place; if the spellings are reliable, the second el. in these forms shows alternation or confusion with **chace** 'chase' and **hǣð** 'heath'.

BACK DROVE COPSE. BELT PLANT., 1845 *TA, v.* **belt**. BERKELEY'S PLANT., perhaps to be associated with Agnes-, Richard *Berk(e)leford* 1327 *SR*. BINNIE'S COPPICE. BODDEL'S BRIDGE & PLANT., *claus' voc' Bud(d)elles* 1552, 1558 *Shepherd²*, *buddlebridge* 1569–74 *Map*, *Buttle* [Bridge] 1791 Boswell, *Boddel(l)s*, (*Upr*) *Boddells Grd* 1845 *TA*, from the surname *Buddell*; *Buddelane* 15 *Digby* may also belong here. BUNTER'S COPSE, cf. *Bunters* (*Arable & Long Grd*), *Bunters* 9 *Acres, 7 Acres & 12 Acres* 1845 *TA*, cf. Richard *Bunter* 1620 *Pitt*. BURN'S SHRUBBERY. BURTON HILL PLANT. & WD, *Burton Hill* 1845 *TA*, named from Long Burton par. *supra*. CHAFFEY'S COPSE, cf. *Chaffeys* (*Mdw, Pasture & Two Pieces*) 1845 *TA*, John *Chafie* 1718 Hutch³, Chaffey's Fm in Folke par. *supra*. CHURCH BRIDGE, 1791 Boswell, *Church'brigge* 1464 *Digby*, named from St Mary's Church *infra, v.* **cirice**, **brycg**. DAVIS'S PLANT., cf. Mark *Davis* who bought the manors of Holnest and Long Burton in e19 (Hutch³ 4 127). DUBBIN'S FM, *Dubbens* (*Fm & Md*), *Copse above Dubbins Down* 1845 *TA*, a surname. DUNN'S BRIDGE, COPSE & FM, *Dunns Coppice, Fm & Ho, Dunns Culverhayes* 1845 *TA*, a surname, *v.* **culfre, (ge)hæg**. DYER'S FM, *Dyers Fm & Orchd* 1845 *TA*, cf. *Jayleres* 1599, *Jaylers nuper Dyers* 1620 *CampbCh*, Adam *le Deghere* 1327 *SR* (Haydon), Margaret *Dyer* 1599 *CampbCh*; *Jayler* is probably also a surname, *v.* Reaney s.n. *Galer*; the farm was called *Holnest Fm* 1811 OS. ELM FM. ELSWORTH PIECE. GALLPITS GORSE, *Gore pytes* 16, *Gorepyttes, -pittes* 1523, 1541 (*claus' voc-*), 1553, *Goorepittes* 1523, *Westegorepittes* 1554 all *Shepherd²*, *Gall Pits* 1845 *TA*, cf. *le Gore* 1508 *Digby, claus' voc' Goore* 1541 *Shepherd², v.* **gāra** 'triangular plot of ground', **pytt, gorst**. GORDON'S GORSE, cf. William *Gordon* who possessed the Leweston estate until 1802 (Hutch³ 4 132). GRAVEL PIT PLANT., GRAVEL PITS WD, cf. (*claus' voc'*) *Gravle Pyttes* 1542, *Gravell pyttes, Grove Pyttes* 1552 all *Shepherd², v.* **gravele, pytt**.

GREAT COMMON. HIGHER COMMON (PLANT.), cf. *the estcomen* 16, *le Commen* 1542, *Holnest Commen* 1555 all *Shepherd*[2], *-Comon* 1650 *ParlSurv*, *-Common* 1800 *EnclA, the great comon* 1620 *Pitt, Gt, Hr & Lr Common* 1845 *TA, v.* **common**. HOLMBUSH PLANT., 1845 *TA, -Orchd ib*, named from The Holm Bushes in Lillington par. *infra*. HR HOLNEST. HOLNEST LODGE, 1845 *TA*. HOLNEST PARK. HOME COVERT. THE KENNELS. LONG PLANT. MACKEY'S COPSE, *claus' voc' Marchayes* 1541 *Shepherd*[2], *Machays Coppice, -Copse* 1845 *TA*, probably 'boundary enclosure' from **mearc** and **(ge)hæg**; it is on the par. boundary. NEW PLANT. OPENFOLD COPSE. OSMOND FM, cf. *Osmonds Plot* 1845 *TA*, John *Osmonde* 1474 *Digby*, William *Osmunde* 1542 *Shepherd*[2]. POUND DROVE COPSE, cf. *Powndclosse* 1541, *Pounde Close* 1552 *Shepherd*[2], *Poundfoldes* 1599, *Punfoldes* 1620 *CampbCh, Pound drove* 1845 *TA, v.* **pund, clos(e), pund-fald**; a Pound is marked 6″, cf. *Holnest pounde* 16 *Shepherd*[2], *Manor Pound* 1800 *EnclA*. RYE WATER FM, 1845 *TA, Dry Water* (sic) 1811 OS, probably to be associated with *Estrye, Westrye brydge* 16 *Shepherd*[2], *rie bridge* 1569–74 *Map*; Rye may be from **atter** '(place) at the' and **īeg** 'island, land partly surrounded by water, dry ground in marsh, well-watered land', with **ēast, west**; the farm lies in a bend of R. Cam, to which Rye Water no doubt refers, *v.* **wæter**, cf. also the nearby Rye Close Fm in Folke par. *supra*. ST MARY'S CHURCH, cf. 'the chapel of *Holneste*' 1405 Hutch[3], *le Churche Way* 1555 *Shepherd*[2], *Churchway Grd* 1845 *TA*, Church Bridge *supra*. SEVEN ASH CMN & FM, *Seven Ash Drove, The Seven Ash Cmn* 1800 *EnclA, Seven Ash Cmn & Pce* 1845 *TA*. SIX ACRE COPSE, cf. *The Six Acres, Rough Six Acres* 1845 *TA*. HR SWEETHILLS, cf. *Hr Sweets Grd and Brook* 1845 *TA*. WHITE HOUSE CMN (1845 *TA*), FM (*Whitehouse Fm* 1811 OS), LANE (*Whitehouse Lane* 1800 *EnclA*) & PLANT.

FIELD-NAMES

The undated forms in (*a*) are 1845 *TA* 111. Spellings dated 1327 are *SR*, 1332 SR, 1340 NI, 1375 *Hastings*, 1394 *Shepherd*[1], 16, 1523, 1541, 1542, 1546, 1551, 1552, 1553, 1554, 1555 *Shepherd*[2], 1525 *Salis*, 1569–74 *Map*,

1599, 1620 *CampbCh*, 1609 Hutch[3], 1620[2] *Pitt*, 1664 HTax, 1791 Boswell, 1800 *EnclA*, and the rest *Digby*.

(*a*) Acre Plot; Back Lane; Bakers Md & Orchd (cf. William *Baker* 1599, *Backehowmede* 1542, *Bakehowse mede* 1552, *v.* **bæc-hūs** 'bake house', **mǣd**); Barn Grd (cf. *le barne close* 1542, *Barnehaye* 1555, *v.* **bere-ærn, clos(e), (ge)hæg**); Barns Frith ((*prat' voc'*) *Barneffrith, -ffryth(e)* 1523, 1546, *Barn(e)frith* 1599, 1620, *v.* **fyrhð** 'wood', cf. prec.); Ctg and gdn now Barters Carters (*Farm house called Barters* 1800); Bears Hole 1800; Black Common; Black Lion Orchd & Pce; Bounds Md (cf. (land) *nuper Bondes* 1599); Bows Grd(s); Bretts Ctg (cf. Alexander *Bret* 1609); Bridge Md; Bridles 4 & 2 Acres, Bridles Md (cf. Thomas *Brydell* 1599, *-Bridle* 1664); Brook (East), West of the Brook (cf. Gunnilda *atte Brouke* 1327, *Estbroke* 1516, *v.* **atte, ēast, brōc**; these fields lie beside R. Cam); Browns Wd (cf. Robert *Browne* 1599); Butts Cl (*claus' voc' Buttes* 1546, *Buttclose* 1552, *v.* **butte**); Calves Grd; Cathams; Chalky Grd; Clay Pits (*claus' voc' Clepyttes* 1523, *greate-, Smale clepyttes* 1541, *v.* **clǣg, pytt, grēat, smæl**); Clouds (*Cloudes* 1552, cf. William *Clout* 1327); Coates; Gt & Lt Coblakes (*claus' voc' Cobla(c)kes* 1523, 1542, *Coblake* 1525, *v.* **lacu** 'stream', first el. **cobb(e)** 'round lump' or the common ME surname *Cobbe*); Collards Md (cf. Richard *Coulard* 1340 (Folke)); Common Cl (*le commen' Close* 1552, *v.* **comun**); Common Drove & Grd(s); Corner Grd (Plant.); (The) Cowleaze, Furzey & Home Cowleaze (cf. *le Cowhowsse* 1554, *v.* **cū, lǣs, hūs**); Cribhouse Grd & Md (*v.* **cribhouse**); Daws Ctg (cf. Robert *Dawe* 1332); Devenish's (Grd), Devenish's Mdw (cf. Henry *Debenissh, -Devenish* 1599); Double Ctg Drove; Downs (*claus' voc' (great) Downes* 1523, 1541, *Little Downes* 1542, *Greate Downe* 1546, *Lyttelldowne* 1552, *v.* **dūn** 'hill, down'); Drove (to the Barn); Gt & Lt Dry Cl (cf. *claus' voc' Dry(e)mede* 1541, 1552, *v.* **drȳge, mǣd**); Dunning Cmn; 8 Acres; Everetts Md; Farthing Gate Pce; (The) 5 Acres; Flamberts Long Md; Flax Pit Pce; 4 Acres; (Gt) Fowles (cf. *Foules-, Fowleslane* 1487, 1491, 1541, *Vowles lane* 1563, Joan *Fogles* 1327); Fox Covert; Furnace Md (*claus' voc' Furnis* 1542, *-Furnys* 1553, probably a surname); Furzey Grd, Furzey Pce Coppice (cf. *Fursyclose* 1541, *claus' voc' Fursey* 1546, *v.* **fyrsig**); The Glebe; Grangers Grd (cf. John *Gra(u)nger* 1599); Great Coppice, Md, Orchd & Plant.; Gundrys Md; The Ham (East of the Brook) (*v.* **hamm**); Hambleton's [Bridge] 1791; Hams Plot and Orchd; Hardys Plot; Hares Plot; Harris's(s) Ho & Md; Hay Croft (*v.* **hēg**); Haydon Rough Md (*Haydon Meade* 1677, probably named from Haydon par. *supra*); Higher Living (*v.* **living**); Hodders; Holnest Fd (*Holnestffylde* 1523, 1552, *Holnest(e)feld(e)* 1525, 1563, *-Filde* 1555, *v.* **feld**, par. name *supra*); Home Md (*Homemede* 1542, *v.* **home**); Gt & Lt Hoopers (*Hoperstyle* 1474, *claus' voc' Howperes* 1542, *Hopers* 1546, *cotag' voc' Houpes* (sic) 1555, cf. William *le Ho(u)pere* 1327, 1332, *v.* **stigel**); Horse Line(s) (*v.* **leyne**); Hutchings 4, 6 & 3 Acres (cf. Nicholas *Howchyn'* 1484); Librarys Orchd; Little Coppice & Grd; Little Md (*Lyttell Mede* 1552, *v.* **mǣd**); Little Plot; Loaders, Loders Drove & Mds; Long Cl (*Long(e)close* 1542, 1546); Long Grd Plant.; Long Orchd & Pce; (Second) Lower Grd; Lower Pce; Lowmans

(Md); Marle Pce; Gt & Lt Martins, Martins 5 Acres (cf. John *Marten* 1542, Thomas *Martyn* 1599); (Further, Hthr & Lr) Mead (*Holnestmede* 1496, *le Mede* 1542, *Nethermede* 1554, cf. *le Meteclosse* 1541, *Mede Close* 1542, *Medclosse* 1555, *v.* **mǣd, clos(e)**); Meadow; Middle Grd; Moulhams Lower Grd; Mow Barton (cf. *lez barton'* 1542, *v.* **mow** 'rick', **barton**); Lr & Upr Neales; Newinclosure; Newmans Cowleaze (cf. Richard *Neuman* 1327, *-Niwman* 1332 (Haydon), John *Newman* 1599); (The) 9 Acres; North Md; Old Gdn; Orchard (cf. *le Sowth orte yarde* 1554, *v.* **sūð, orceard**); The Pasture Fd; Pigs Hams (cf. *Pyggewyll'* 1508, *v.* **pigga, well(a), hamm**); Pit Grd (cf. *Pitte clos(s)e* 1542, *Pytt(e)clos(s)e* 1552, 1555, *v.* **pytt, clos(e)**); (Gt) Pithays, Pithays Md (*Pythay* 1525, *Pitheys* 1546, *Pythayes, v.* **pytt, (ge)hæg**); Plantation; Plott; Pollard Oak Pce (*v.* **pollard**); Pollards Grd; Pond Cl, Drove & Md; Popes Grd (cf. Henry *Pope* 1599); Potterne Row Fm (perhaps 'pottery' from **pott** and **ærn** like Potterne 2 257, cf. foll.); Potters Drove Coppice (*Potters Drove* 1800); Reves's; Ridouts Cowleaze & Md, Joe Ridouts Grd; (Gt) Rough Grd; 7 Acres; Shrubbery; Small Coppice & Orchd; Soapers Pool(s Coppice) (*Sopornepole* 1555, probably 'pool of the soap-makers', from **sāpere** (with analogical wk. ME gen.pl., *v.* **-ena**) and **pōl**, cf. foll.); Soaphouse Md; Stevens Md (cf. John *Stevens* 1599); Sticklands Hither Md (*Sticklandes* 1620, possibly from **sticol** 'steep' and **land**, or a surname); Stourton Leaze; Strap(s) (*v.* **strap**); Strip against the road; Swells Grd; Gt & Lt Tanners, Library Tanners (possibly to be read as Fanners, cf. Librarys Orchd *supra*); The 10 Acres; Third Grd; Late Thorns; (The) 3 Acres; Three Cornered Grd; Lt & Long Tippetts; (Second) Upper Grd; Upper Pce & Plot; With(e)y Bed (Copse) (cf. *le Wythybere* 1541, *Wythibere* 1542, *v.* **wīðig, bearu**); Woodcock's [Bridge] 1791; Wyke Street Green 1800 (*Wyke* 1525, *Weekestreete* 1569–74, *Weekstreet(e)* 1599, 1620, *v.* **wīc** 'dairy-farm', **strǣt**).

(b) *le Ba(c)ksyde* 1523, *Bakesyde Close* 1542 (*v.* **backside**); *Bakehey* 1541 (*v.* **(ge)hæg**, probably with the adj. **back**); *claus' voc' Belle* 1546 (*v.* **belle**); *Bigg-* 1462, *Bugputtlane* 1464 (*v.* **pytt**, first el. **big** 'big' or **bugge** 'hobgoblin'); *claus' voc' Blackeshet* 1542 (*v.* **blæc, scēat**); *Blackhouse* 1599, *-howse* 1620; *claus' voc' Botherreles* 1546 (a surname); *Brodecrafte* 1525, *-crofte* 1552 (*v.* **brād, croft**); *Brodehaye* 1554 (*v.* **(ge)hæg**); *Brod(e)mede* 1523, 1552 (*v.* **mǣd**); *Busshe-, Busshyclose* 1542, 1552 (*v.* **busc, -ig³**); *Byncrofte* 1552 (*v.* **bēan** 'bean'); *Byntis pyte* 16 (*v.* **pytt**, first el. probably a surname); *Chapulles* 1599, *Chappells* 1620 (a surname); *claus' voc' Chepmans* 1541, 1552 (cf. John *Chepman* 1620); *Cockbrygge* 1464 (*v.* **cocc¹** 'hillock' or **cocc²** 'cock'); *claus'-, cotag' voc' Collyers* 1546 (a surname); *Comes* (*cotag' voc'-*), *Combes lane* 1542 (probably a surname); *Cop(p)ham* 1516, 1531, *Cophambryge* 1516, *terris voc' Cophams nuper Denshams* 1599 (possibly from **copp** 'summit, mound' and **hamm** with **brycg**, cf. Densham Fm in Folke par. *supra*); *Corneclose* 1541, 1542, *Westcornehey* 1546 (**corn¹** 'corn' or **corn²** 'crane', with **clos(e), (ge)hæg**); *Coseberyate* 1484, *Cosbere* 1525, 1541, 1542, *Cosburyate* 1552, *aque apud Cosbroke yate* 1553, *Corsbere* 1555, *Cosbers* 1599 (possibly from **cors** 'marsh, bog' and **bearu** 'wood' or **bǣr** '(woodland) pasture' (once replaced by **brōc** 'brook'), with **geat**); *Cresheye* 1541, *Greshaye* 1546, *Cressehayes* 1555, *Cres(s)hay* 1599, 1620 (v. **cærse, (ge)hæg**); *Crofte* 1542 (v. **croft**); *claus' voc' Croke* 1541 (v. **crōc** 'bend'); *Estcropyhey* 1546; *Cuccowe ocke* 16, *quckowe oake* 1569–74 (v. **cuccu, āc**); *Der(r)e Holte* 1555 (v. **dēor** 'deer', **holt**); *diche uppon' castell'* 16 (v. **dīc, castel(l)**); *Dykemersshe* 1531 (v. **dīc, mersc**); *Estbrydge* 1542, *Estebreche* 1555 (probably the same name, v. **ēast, brycg** or **brǣc**); *Henry Millers estcloseyate* 16, *Estclos(s)e* 1541, 1542, 1553 (v. **ēast, clos(e), geat**; the form *Katerin'lestclos* 1375 may also belong here, from the pers.n. *Katerin*, with *-l-* possibly representing the Fr form of the def.art.); *Estlees* 1525 (v. **lǣs**); *Estlonde(s)* 1474, 1484, 1557, *-lande* 1531 (v. **land**); *Estmede* 1541, 1552 (v. **mǣd**); *le Estrete* 1487, *Est streete* 1569–74 (v. **strǣt**); *Flude yate* 1553 (v. **flod-yate**); *Foteslond'* 1552, *Votes landes* 1599 (a surname with **land**); *Cottage called Gast* 1677 (cf. John *Gast ib* who held lands in Lillington); *Genkynneshey* 1525 (a surname with **(ge)hæg**); *Gilles House* 16 (a surname); *Git(ti)sham* 1542, 1546 (v. **hamm**, probably with a surname); *Golymede* 1516, *Goldeme* (sic) 1531, *Go(w)ldmede* 1542, 1555 (v. **mǣd**, first el. possibly **golde** 'marigold' although the earliest form suggests **goulet** 'gully'); *happetes corner* 1569-74; *Heth(e)feldstret(e)* 1464, 1473, 1525, *Hethfeld'*, *-fild'* 1466, *Heth(e)fyldstrette* 1484, *Hettfilde strette* 1551, *Heathfeildstreet(e)* 1599, 1620 (v. **hǣð, feld, strǣt**); *le Hey* 1508 (v. **(ge)hæg**); *le Hill' Marsshe* 1555 (v. **hyll, mersc**); *Holnest Bridg* 16 (v. **brycg**); *Holneste Wo(o)de* 1538, 1569–74 (v. **wudu**); *Homecloses* 1555, *le Home haye* 1554 (v. **home**); *Honycombelane* 1473, 1491, 1531 (v. **hunig, cumb**); *Hyllemede* 1541 (v. **hyll, mǣd**); *claus' voc' Isn'brese* 1523, *In'bers* 1541 (origin uncertain); *Kitwayeshey* 1541 (v. **(ge)hæg**); *close . . . called Knollers* (sic), *ten' . . . formerly Knowles* 1677 (cf. John *Knolles* 1620[2]); *Lakehaye* 1546 (v. **lacu, (ge)hæg**); *Lansherdes busshe* 16 (v. **lanchet, busc**); *Lewestones Londe* 1394, *Lewston landes* 1569–74, *Lewestons Lawnes* 1599 (cf. John *Lewestone* 1394, v. **land**); *Lit(t)leclose* 1542, 1552 (v. **lȳtel**); *claus' voc' Londes* 1542 (probably a surname); *Long(e)crofte* 1546, 1552 (v. **lang**[1]); *claus' voc' Longehowne* 1541, *Longe Hownde* 1552 (cf. the analogous f.n. Gt Shorthound in Castleton par. *supra*); *Long(e)mede* 1541, 1546 (v. **mǣd**); *claus' voc' Lou'longe* 1546; *claus' super le lye* 1525, 1552, *-super Lee* 1546 (v. **lēah** 'wood, clearing'); *Lypeyatebrygge* 1460, *Lippyattes more* 16 (v. **hlīep-gēat, brycg, mōr**);*Manfeildes* 1620 (cf. Alice *Manfild* 1599); *(le) Midle Close* 1542 (v. **middel**); *Midle-* 1542, *Middelhaye* 1553 (v. **(ge)hæg**); *atte More* 1327 (p), *Morelonde(s)* 1523, 1552, *Litlemorelandes* 1554 (v. **atte, mōr, land**); *Myddle Fylde* 1546 (v. **middel, feld**); *atte Nasshe* (p) 1327, *atte Nasshe* (p) 1332 (v. **atten, æsc**); *Newclos(s)e* 1523, 1541 (v. **nīwe, clos(e)**); *Newlande(s)* 1554, 1555 (v. **land**); *Newmede* 1552, 1554 (v. **mǣd**); *Newpece* 1546 (v. **pece**); *Northecrofte* 1546 (v. **croft**); *claus' voc' Overheltes* 1523; *le Paroke* 1541 (v. **pearroc**); *Pedmanmede* 1516 (a surname with **mǣd**); *tenement . . . called Perrotts* 1677 (a surname); *Placehaye* 1542 (v. **(ge)hæg**, with **place** or a surname); *Plasshett* 1552 (v. **plaschiet** 'marshy pool'); *Poukes Hedyclose* 1541 (cf. Geoffrey *Pouke* 1332 (Nthr Compton), middle el. uncertain); *Qeenes grounde* 1569–74 (v. **cwēn**;

for a connection of Queen Elizabeth with Holnest, v. Hutch[3] **4** 127);
Row(e)close 1542, 1552 (probably **rūh** (wk.obl. *rūwan*) 'rough'); *Rune hurne*
16 (*v.* **hyrne** 'corner', first el. uncertain); *Sexten'acres* 1542 (*v.* **sextēne**);
lez Shadebusshez 1552 (*v.* **scēad** 'boundary' or **sceadu** 'shade', **busc**);
Shep(e)craftes 1523 (*v.* **scēap, croft**); *claus' voc' Sibles* 1541, *Sybelees* 1552
(the surname *Sibley*); *Skuyppeslane* 1491 (for the surname cf. the f.n.
Swypton' in Long Burton par. *supra*); *Somerles* 1523 (*v.* **sumor, lǣs**); *atte*
Stokke (p) 1327 (*v.* **atte, stocc** 'tree-stump'); *Stone Rige* 16, *Stonie ridge*
1569–74 (*v.* **stān, stānig, hrycg**); *Stowtlondes* 1546 (*v.* **stūt**[1] 'gnat' or **stūt**[2]
'stumpy hillock'); *le Thressyngplace* 1525 (*v.* **threshing**); *le Tollett* 1525;
Turdelhmes (sic), *Turdylham* 1552 (probably **hamm**, first el. uncertain);
Twelfeacres 1542, *grete-, Northtwelve acres* 1555 (*v.* **twelf**); *claus' voc'*
Verneys 1552 (probably a surname); *Wallis* 1620 (cf. *John Wallys* 1599);
Waterclosse 1554 (*v.* **wæter, clos(e)**); *Watermede* 1542 (*v.* **mǣd**);
Wecombelane 1508 (*v.* **cumb**, first el. uncertain); *Westbreche* 1508, 1542,
Weste Breache 1555 (*v.* **brǣc**); *claus' voc' West(e)bury(e)* 1542, 1552
(perhaps ME **bury** 'manor house'); *Westclos(s)e* 1542, 1552 (*v.* **clos(e)**);
Westfyldes 1552 (*v.* **feld**); *Westhey* 1541, (*Lyttell*) *Westhaye* 1552,
Westhayes 1554 (*v.* **(ge)hæg**); *West-* 1541, 1552, *Vestmede* 1541 (*v.*
mǣd); *Westwodde* 1541 (*v.* **wudu**); *Wexhayes* 1552 (*v.* **weax, (ge)hæg**);
Whitehyll 1552 (*v.* **hwīt, hyll**); *Whitmores* 1599 (probably a surname);
Wo(o)de- 1474, 1523, *Wodmede* 1523, 1552 (*v.* **wudu**); *Woodhurne* 16 (*v.*
hyrne); *Woodlondes* 1542 (*v.* **land**).

Leweston

Leweston (ST 636124)
  Luistuna 1145 (12) *SherC* (p)
  Leweston(') Hy 3 BM I, 1244 *Ass* (p), 1256 FF, 1275 Cl
    (p), 1285 FA, 1394 *Shepherd*[1], 1428 FA *et passim,*
    Lewestun' 1270 Roscoe, *Lewston'* 1422 *CampbCh*, 1458
    MP, 1811 OS
  Loueston 1242 Fees (p)
  Leuston(') 1244 *Ass*, 1327 SR (p), 1332 SR (p), 1340 NI,
    1346, 1431 FA, *Leueston'* 1244 *Ass* (p), 1346 *UD* (p)
  Lewiston' 1280 QW (p)
  Leuweston' 1288 *Ass* (p)
  Leuerston (rectius *Leuston*) 1303 FA
  Lauweston 1316 FA (p), *Lauston* 1346 *ib* (p)
  Loweston' 1380 *Sher* (p)

Probably 'Lēofwīg's farm or estate', from the OE pers.n.
Lēofwīg and **tūn**, as suggested in DEPN.

BOWLES'S WD. BRIERHILL WD. HIXON BRIDGE, cf. Hixon Plant. in Long Burton par. *supra*. HOLY TRINITY CHAPEL. LEWESTON (house), *Mr Lewstons howse* 1569–74 *Map*. LEWESTON PARK (*Lewston-* 1811 OS) & WD, cf. 'the wood of Henry *de Leyweston*' 1270 Hutch[3].

FIELD-NAMES

There is no *TA* for Leweston. Spellings dated 1394 are *Shepherd*[1], 1458 are *AddCh*.

(b) *Bernard' place* 1394; *Lagemede* 1458 (v. **mǣd**, first el. possibly **lagge** 'marsh'); *claus' voc' Lytelrobyns* 1458 (the pers.n. *Robin*); *le Northefelde* 1458 (v. **norð, feld**).

Lillington

LILLINGTON (ST 629128)
 Lilletone 1166 RBE, *Lillinton* 1180 P (p), 1232 Ch, *Lilliton'* 1180–85 P (p), *Lillington(')* 1244 *Ass*, 1285 FA, 1288 *Ass*, 1297, 1314 Pat (p), 1462 *Digby et passim*, *-tone* 1260 FF, *Vuerlillington* 1244 *Ass*, *Overelilengton* 1256 FF, *Lillingeton'* 1265 CottCh, *Lyllinton* 1285 FF, *Lyllington* 1285 ib (p) *et freq* with variant spelling *-yng-* to 1516 *Digby*, *Lilyngtone* 1327 SR, *Nich'* (for *Nith'* = *Nither*) *Lyllyngton* 1340 NI, *Nither-, Overlillyngton* 1356 FF, *Lillyngton'* 1406 *Digby*, 1411 *Sher* (p), *Lylyngton(')* 1484 *Digby*, 1569–74 (*Market of-*)
 Lullinton(') 1200 Cur, 1209 Abbr, 1268, 1288 *Ass*, *Lullington'* 1201 Cur, 1280, 1288 *Ass*, 1291 Banco (Drew), *Lullynton'* 1268, 1288 *Ass*, *Lulyngton'* 1380 *Sher* (p), *Lullyngtone, -done* 15 *Digby*
 Lollinton' 1268 *Ass*

'Farm called after Lylla', from an OE pers.n. *Lylla* (a side-form of the recorded *Lulla* and suggested by DEPN for Leybourne K and Lilstock So) and **-ingtūn**, with **neoðerra, niðerra** 'lower' and **uferra** 'higher, upper' (an early division of the manor perhaps reflected in the names Higher St., Lower St. and Upper Fm *infra*).

BAILEY RIDGE FM (ST 631098), *La Baillie* 1351 BM I, *Baillye juxta Yat(e)minster* 1387, 1419 IpmR, *-by Yatmynstre* 1388 Fine, *Le Bailly* 1412 FA, *Baylle* 1418 Hutch[3], *Baylyrygge* 1496, *Bayly Ryg(g)e* 1516, 1531, *Bayly* 1538 all *Digby*, *Baylierudge* Eliz ChancP, *Baylyridge* 1563, 1582, *-Ridge* 1677 all *Digby*, *Bailye* (*inclosed ground called-*) 1583 *SPDom*, *Baylie Rydge* 1605 *Batten*, *Bailie* 1614 *Digby*, cf. *Bailly-*, *Baylly Crofte* 1466 *ib*, *Bayly gate* 16 *Shepherd*[2], from **baillie** 'a bailliff's jurisdiction or district', with **hrycg** 'ridge' (cf. Walter *atte Rhygge* 1327 *SR*, William *atte Rygg*' 1332 SR, both taxed in the neighbouring par. of Holnest), **croft**, **geat**; this place was held by John *Stre(e)che* who in 1354 also held the bailiwick of eight Do hundreds and in 1391 the bailiwick of the whole county as well (Hutch[3] **4** 196), cf. Bailie Gate **2** 47. The farm lies about 2 miles ESE of Yetminster.

HR & LR STOCKBRIDGE FM (ST 638111), *Stokbrige, -brigg*' 1244 *Ass* (p), *-brigge* 1327 *SR* (p), *Stokebrugge* 1386 Pat, *-brygge* 1487 *Digby*, *Stokenebrigge* 1399 Cl, *Stockbrige* 1558 *Shepherd*[2], *-bridge* 1620 *CampbCh*, 1811 OS, cf. *Stokebrug3ate* 1441 *Sher*, *Stockbrygge-* 1460, *Stockbriggeyate* 1464 *Digby*, *Stokebryg(g)eyate* 1484 *ib*, 1487 Ipm, 1508, 1516 *Digby*, *Sto(c)kbrydge yate* 16, 1544 *Shepherd*[2], *Stock(e)bridge Gate* 16 *ib*, 1569–74 *Map*, 1599 *CampbCh*, 1800 *EnclA*, 'bridge made of logs', from **stocc**, **stoccen** and **brycg**, cf. Stockenbridge D 281, Stockbridge YW **4** 65, with **geat**; the bridge crossed the small stream just N of the farms.

WHITFIELD FM (ST 619109), *Wytfeld* 1270 Roscoe, *-folde* (sic) 1270 *For*, *Whitefeld(e) near Shireburne* 1309 Pat, *-iuxta Shireborn*' 1309 *Salis*, *Whytefeld(e)* 1395, 1525 *Salis*, 1538, 1566 *Digby*, *Whittefeld*' 1474 *ib*, *Whitefeild house* 16, *Whitffylde* 1523 *Shepherd*[2], *Whytefeld(e)* 1538, 1566 *Digby*, *Whytfyld* 1559 *Salis*, *Whitfelde* 1569–74 *Map*, *Whitefild* 1593 *Batten*, *Witfield* 1614 *Pitt*, *Whitfield* 1614 *Digby*, 1811 OS, *-feild* 1677 *Digby*, *Wo(o)tton(-)Whitfield* 1774 Hutch[1], 1795 Boswell, 1870 Hutch[3], 'white tract of open country', *v.* **hwīt**, **feld**. In the 18th and 19th cent. forms, *Wootton* may be manorial or an old name meaning 'farm in or near a wood', from **wudu** and **tūn**, cf. Wootton Glanville par. *supra* and Whitfield Woods *infra*. The form *Whyttfeldlane* 1464 *Digby* also belongs here, *v.* **lane**.

ALDER WD, cf. *Alder Bed Coppice* 1843 *TA, v.* **alor**. BAILEY RIDGE LANE (*Bayllylane* 1487 *Digby*) & WD (*-Coppice* 1843 *TA*), cf. Bailey Ridge Fm *supra*. BIG OAK STRIP. THE CLUMPS. EAST WD. GORDON'S LANE, perhaps to be associated with *claus' . . . vocat' Goddon'* 1438 *Shepherd*[1]. HIGHER ST. THE HOLM BUSHES, HOLM BUSHES FM, *Home Bushes* 1811 OS, *Home Bush Cmn* 1843 *TA, v.* **holegn** 'holly', cf. Do dial. *holm*. HONEYCOMB TOUT, cf. *Honycombeislane* 1464 *Digby*, named from Honeycomb in Castleton par. *supra, v.* **tōt(e)** 'look-out hill', **lane**. LILLINGTON COPSE. LILLINGTON HILL, 1811 OS, referred to in the boundary clause *up to hricgge, andlang hrigcges* in the Anglo-Saxon bounds of Thornford, *v.* the f.n. Ridge in that par. *infra*. LIMEKILN BEACON. LITTLE LANE. LOWER ST. MANOR FM. MIDDLE WD. ST MARTIN'S CHURCH, cf. *ecclesiam de Lullynton'* 1268 *Ass*. STOCKBRIDGE DROVE (cf. *Drove* 1843 *TA, v.* **drāf**), OAK & WD (cf. *Stockbridge Coppice* 1843 *TA*), named from Stockbridge Fms *supra*. UPPER FM. WEST WD, 1843 *TA*. WHITFIELD WDS, -*Wood* 1843 *TA*, 'wood of Bishop of Salisbury at *Wytfeld*' 1270 Roscoe, *Est Whittfelde Wood* 16 *Shepherd*[2], (*Est*) *Whytefeld(es) Wod*' 1538 *Digby*, *Whytfyld Wodd(e)* 1559 *Salis*, *Whitefielde Woodes* 1614 *Digby*, *Whitfeild Wood* 1646 SC, *v.* **wudu**, Whitfield Fm *supra*. WITHY BED.

FIELD-NAMES

The undated forms in (*a*) are 1843 *TA* 126. Spellings dated 1327 are *SR*, 1332 SR, 1340 NI, 1525 *Salis*, and the rest *Digby*.

(*a*) Babbeer; Back Door Grd; Barn Cl; Boarded House Grd; Bounds 11, 5, 4, 9, 7 & 6 Acres; (Lt) Bushes; Cancer Drove 9 Acres (*v.* Cancer Drove in Holnest par. *supra*); Causemoor (5 Acres); (Groves) Common Pce; Coppice; (Bailey) Cowleaze, Bottom Cowleaze, Knappy & Rushy Cowleaze (*v.* **cū,lǣs**, **cnæppig**, Bailey Ridge Fm *supra*); 8 & 11 Acres; Fern Cl; 15, 5, 4 & 14 Acres; Furzy Pce; Gold Hills; (Lt) Green Brook (*Grenebroke* 1525, 1538, *v.* **grēne**, **brōc**); Haw Plot (*v.* **haga**[2]); Hawest Cl; Hazel Md (*Haselmede* 1525, 1538, *v.* **hæsel**, **mǣd**); Home Grd & Md;

Lady Md; Little Grd; Longlands; The Mead (cf. William *atte Mede* 1327, 1332, *v.* **atte**, **mǣd**); Morey Md; 9 Acres; (Old) Orchard, Hr & Lr Orchard (cf. John *atte Orchard*(') 1327, 1332, 1340, *Orcherdlane* 1462, *v.* **atte**, **orceard**); Ox Md; Pit Cl & Grd; Plantation; Plot(s); Rag (*v.* **ragge**); Rye Cl; Rye Grass; 7 & 6 Acres; Squibs; Stake Ford Md, Lt Stake Ford (*v.* **staca**, **ford**); Stockbridge 20 Acres (cf. Stockbridge Fms *supra*); 10 Acres; Three Cornered Orchard; Totnell (from Totnell in the adjacent par. of Leigh *infra*); Turnip Plot Orchd; 20 Acres; Under Hill.

(*b*) *Berelane* 1484 (lane to Beer Hackett par. *supra*); *pastur' de Cleybagge* 1538 (*v.* **clæg** 'clay', with **bagga** 'bag', perhaps here used figuratively of a hill or other feature resembling a bag); *Indowne et Owtedowne* 1525, *Downecrafte alias Estlez, Indowne, Outedowne* 1538 (*v.* **dūn**, **croft**, **ēast**, **lǣs**, **in(n)**, **ūt(e)**)); *Fotebridge* 1563 (*v.* **fote-bridge**); *Hawkys* 1525, *Hawkes* 1538 (a surname); *Hokebrygge* 1496, *Hokeford'* 1464, 1487, *Hoke-* 1473, *Houke-* 1491, *Hookelane* 1531 (cf. Henry *atte Ouk* 1327, *-atte Houke* 1332, *v.* **hōc** 'angle, bend', **brycg**, **ford**, **lane**, **atte**); *Kingscroft* 1677 (*v.* **croft**, with a surname); *Longcroft* 1538; *Shepencrofte* 1538 (first el. **scypen** 'cow-shed' or **scēap** 'sheep' with ME *-en* pl., *v.* **-ena**); *atte Toneshende* (p) 1332 (*v.* **atte**, **toun**, **ende**); *atte Watere* (p) 1327 (*v.* **wæter**); *Wodecoklane* 1484 (from **wodecok**, or a surname).

Lydlinch

Stock Gaylard (formerly a separate par. but now in this par.) is a tithing in Brownsall hundred *supra*.

Lydlinch (ST 743134)

Litelinge 1166 RBE

Lidelinz 1182 P, 1206, 1207 Cur both (p), *-ling'* 1205 Cur (p), 1268 *Ass*, *-liz* 1205 Cur (p), *-lins* 1206 ib (p), *Liddeling* 1268 *Ass*, *Lydeling* 1279 Banco (Drew), *Lydelynch'* 1280 *Ass*, *-linch*, *Lidelinch*(*e*) 1285 FA *et freq* with variant spellings *-lynch*(*e*) to 1486 Ipm, *Lyddelynche* 1304 Banco (Drew), *Lydellynch'* 1414 *Weld²*, *Lydlynch*(*e*) 1491 Ipm *et freq* to 1575 Saxton, *-linche* 1533 *PlR*, *Lidlynche* 1514 *ib*, *Lidleing* 1709 *WRO*

Ledelinze 1244 *Ass* (p), *-lynch* 1316 FA

Ludeling' 1280 *Ass*, *-lynch*(') 1303 Ipm, 1406 *Digby*, 1462 IpmR, *Ludenlynche* 1428 FF, *Ludlinch'* 1462, *-lynch'* 1464 *Digby*

Lyndelinche 1318 FF

Lidlinch Beauboys Jas I Hutch³

Lydinch 1629–31 *Salkeld*

'Ridge by, or bank of, R. Lydden', *v.* **hlinc**, RNs *infra*; according to M. Gelling, *Place-Names in the Landscape* (1984) 164, this may be one of a number of names in which **hlinc** had the sense 'river terrace used as a road, terrace-way'. The estate of 12 hides granted to Sherborne Abbey *in Lydene* 740–56 (14) *Cott* (MS Faustina A.ii, f.25), Finberg (p.156), i.e. 'in the valley of R. Lydden', may refer to Lydlinch, cf. also VCHDo **2** 62. The affix *Beauboys* is manorial; Henry *de Beauboys* held half a knight's fee in Lydlinch in 1346 (Hutch³ **4** 188), cf. also John *Beauboys* 1318 FF and the former manor of Hydes *infra*.

BLAKELOND (lost), *le Blakelonde* 1380 *HarlCh*, *Blakelondes* 1412 FA, *Blakelond(e)* 1421 FF, 1431 FA, 1433, 1439 *HarlCh*, 1442 Hutch³, *Blaklond* 1439 FF, 'dark-coloured tract of land', *v.* **blæc**, **land**. Fägersten 34 places this in Holwell par. *infra*, but as Taylor, DoNHAS **88** 209, points out, it is more likely to have been in the old par. of Stock Gaylard, now part of Lydlinch. Taylor suggests a location about ST 729114, mainly on the assumption of a connection with *Blackfield Mead* 1844 *TA* alt.app. (Lydlinch), a field on the old bdy between Stock Gaylard and Lydlinch. However the f.n. *Inner & Outer Blacklands* 1840 *TA* (Lydlinch), near New House Fm at ST 745127 and within a mile of both parts of the former par. of Stock Gaylard, should perhaps also be reckoned with: in the 14th and 15th centuries there may well have been a further small detached area of Stock Gaylard par. within Lydlinch. Another f.n. *Blacklands* in the Lydlinch *TA* at ST 764115 is less likely to be relevant.

BLACKROW CMN & FM (ST 727120), *Blakerew(e)* 1421 FF, 1425 BM I, 1432 FF, 1433 *HarlCh*, *Blackrewe* 16 *Shepherd²*, *Blacke Rowe* 1646 SC, *Blackrow* 1811 OS, *Black Row Fm* 1840 *TA*, *Blackrow Cmn* 1844 *ib* alt.app., *v.* **blæc** 'dark-coloured', **rǣw** 'row (of trees or houses)', cf. Hydes *infra*.

HAYDON (FM) (ST 756121), *Heydon* 1279 Banco (Drew), 1648 SC, *Haydon(e)* 13 GlastR (*boscum de-*), e14 *GlastE*, 1308 (15) *ForReg*, 1324 Banco (Drew), 1338–40 Glast *et passim, Haidon'* e14 *GlastE,* cf. *Haydon Common* 1677 *Salkeld,* 1811 OS, probably identical in origin with Haydon par. *supra,* cf. *on filithleighe* 968 (14) *Glast,* in the Anglo-Saxon bounds of Sturminster Newton par. *supra,* probably to be located just NW of Haydon.

HOLEBROOK FM & GREEN, HOLEBROOK WATER (ST 749118), *on Holambrok',* of *þan brok'* 968 (14) *Glast* (S 764), *Holebrok(e)* e14 *GlastE,* 1338–40 Glast, m14 *Glast (hayam extra Rivulum de-),* 1412 FA, *-brouk'* 1307 (15) *ForReg* (p), 1332 SR (p), *Holbroke* 1545 *Salkeld,* 1603 *Weld²,* *-brooke* (*Tenement*) 1629, 1714 *Salkeld, Holebrooke* 1795 Boswell, 1811 OS (*-Green*), 'stream running in a deep hollow', *v.* **hol²** (wk.obl. *-an*), **brōc.** The stream is a tributary of R. Lydden and forms the par. bdy between Lydlinch and Sturminster Newton, the first spelling being from the Anglo-Saxon bounds of the latter. A ford is marked (6″) at Holebrook Water, cf. *pontem atte/de Henries de Holebrok'* m14 *Glast,* 1338–40 Glast, Henry *de Holebrouk'* 1332 SR.

HYDES (ST 733124)
> *la Hide, la Hyde* 1268 *Ass* (p), 1305 Cl (p), 1318 FF (p), 1335 AD I, *atte Hyde* 1332 SR (p), *Hide* 1436, 1870 Hutch³ (*-or Lidlinch Baret*), *Hyde* 1563 *Digby,* 1795 Boswell (*-or Lydlinch Baret*), 1811 OS
>
> *Hydes* 1431 FA, 1648 SC, 1714 *Salkeld (Great-), Hides otherwise Lydelynche Baret* 1438 Cl, *Lydelynch Baret alias Hydys maner'* 1450 IpmR, *Hides* 1646 Hutch³, 1779 *DROMap (-alias Blackrow), Hydes Fm* 1840 *TA*
>
> *Lidelynche Baret* 1375 Cl, *Lidelinch Baret* 1380 *HarlCh, Ludelynchebaret* 1384 Cl, *Lydel(l)ynch(e) Baret* 1414 *Weld²,* 1433 *HarlRoll, Lydlynch Baret* Hy 6 AD VI

'The hide of land, an amount of land for the support of one free family and its dependants', *v.* **hīd.** The form Hydes is manorial, from the family of Roger *de la Hide* 1268 *Ass,* Henry *de la Hyde* 1318 FF, John *atte Hyde* 1332 SR who in turn took their names from here. The affix *Baret* is also manorial; Henry *Baret* held land in Lydlynch in 1297 Misc, cf. also William *Baret* 1318 FF, Ivo *Baret* 1450 Cl. Hydes is near Blackrow Fm *supra.*

KINGSTAG, KINGS STAGG COPSE (ST 725106), *Kyngeslake* (for *-stake*) c.1325 *GlastE*, *Kingestake* 1337 DorR, 'king's boundary stake', *v.* **cyning**, **staca**. The first form is a point in the 14th cent. bounds of Buckland Newton Hundred; moreover, as pointed out by Fägersten 207, the par. boundaries of Lydlinch, Pulham and Haselbury Bryan meet at Kingstag Bridge here (in Pulham par. *q.v. supra*), and the boundary stake must be that referred to in the medieval bounds of Blackmoor Forest (Hy 3 (14) Cerne) as *ad truncum qui stat in tribus divisis*. For the association of this place, through folk etymology, with the legend of the white hart, *v.* Blackmoor Forest & Vale *supra*.

PLUMBER FM (ST 772118), -MANOR (1"), *Plumbere* 1086 DB, 13 *Salkeld* (p), 1242 Ch (p), 1268 *Ass* (p), 1288 *ib*, e14 *GlastE*, 1303 FA *et freq* to 1409 Cl, *-bera* (p), *le Plumber* 13 *Salkeld*, *-ber*(') 1242–3 Fees, 1280 *Ass*, 1285 FA (p) *et passim*, (*bosco de*) *Plumbar*(*e*) 1258 *For*, 1270 Ipm (p), *Plomber*(*e*) 1303 FA, 1350 Ipm, *Plumbeare* 1412 FA, *Plymber* 1429 IpmR, *Plumbers* 1535–43 Leland, *Plumber Ho* 1811 OS, 'wood or grove where plum-trees grow', from **plūme** and **bearu**, cf. *Plumbereslandschere* m14 *Glast* ('boundary of Plumber', *v.* **land-sc(e)aru**) in the bounds of Sturminster Newton par. *supra*.

RAMSBURY (lost, identified by Taylor, DoNHAS **88** 209, with Berry Fm *infra* at ST 737115)
> *Remmesber'* Hy 3 *HarlCh*, *-bir'* 1268 *Ass* (p), *-by* (sic) 1412 FA, *-burry* 1417 AD I, *-bere* 1419 Cl, 1421 FF, 1422 Cl *et freq* to 1442 IpmR, *-beare* 1435 IpmR, *-bury* 1455 Cl, *Remesbere* 1268 *Ass* (*bosco de-*), 1417 Inq aqd (*Parva-*), *-bury* 1285 FA (p), 1436 Fine, *-beare* 1436 ib, *Rem*(*m*)*ysbury* 1438 *Sher*
> *Ramesber'* (*bosco de-*) 1258 *For*, *Rammesbere* 1315 Ipm, *Hen*[1], 1336 Ch, 1433 *HarlRoll*, 1438 IpmR, *-bury* 1465 Pat, *Ram*(*e*)*sbury* 1544 Hutch[3], 1648 SC, 1840 *TA*, *Ramsbury alias Ridge* 1795 Boswell, *-and Ridge* 1870 Hutch[3]

Probably 'raven's wood or grove', *v.* **hremn**, **bearu**, or 'Hremn's wood or grove' from an OE pers.n. *Hremn*, cf.

Renscombe **1** 65, Ramsbury W 287. The second el. shows early alternation, or confusion, with **burh** (dat.sg. *byrig*) 'fortified place', by which it is eventually replaced, cf. Haselbury Bryan **2** 100. For *Ridge, v.* Ridge Fm *infra*. The field called *Ramsbury* in 1840 *TA* is just N of Berry Fm at ST 739118.

(LT) RODMORE FM & PLANT. (ST 723117), *Rodmor* 1318 FF, *-more* 1424 *Salkeld, (Lt) Rodmoor Fm, Rodmoor Md* 1840 *TA*, 'marshy ground where reeds grow', *v.* **hrēod, mōr**.

STOCK GAYLARD HO & PARK (ST 723130)
>   *Stoches* 1086 DB (f. 82), *Stok(e)* 1268 *Ass*, 1291 Tax, 1316
>   FA, 1338–40 Glast, 1428 FA, 1575 Saxton, *Stokke* 1327
>   *SR*, 1375 Fine, 1390 Pat, 1455 *Sher, Stocke* 1332 SR,
>   1439 *Sher*, 1527 Hutch[3] ('-otherwise called *Stoke
>   Colyard*'), 1569–74 *Map*, 1709 *WRO*
>   *Stok Coillerd* 1299 Banco (Drew), *Stock Coylard* 1302 ib,
>   *Stoke Coil(l)ard* 1304 Ipm, 1305 Cl *et freq* with variant
>   spellings *Stok(k)(e)-, -Coyl(l)ard* to 1431 FA, *Stocke
>   Kuylard* 1304 Ipm, *Stock Collyard* 1585 Hutch[3]
>   *Stoke Gaillard* 1316 Inq aqd, *-Goillard* 1340 NI,
>   *Stok(k)e-, Stock Gaylard* 1393, 1544, 1637 Hutch[3],
>   *Stocke- Gaylerd* 1629 *Salkeld, Stoke Galliard Hamlett,
>   -Galeard* 1664 HTax, *Stock-Galliard* 1779 *DROMap*
>   *Stokkeylore* 1412 FA, *Stockalliard* 1603 *Weld*[2]

'Outlying farm buildings, a secondary settlement', *v.* **stoc** (nom.pl. *stocu*, new ME pl. *stokes*). The affix is no doubt manorial, though no family of the name *Coilard* or *Gaylard* has been noted in connection with the place (the surnames of Nicholas *Callard'*, Richard *Coulard'* 1332 SR (taxed in Up Cerne and Folke respectively) and of William *Coulard* 1436 Hutch[3] (granted land in Stalbridge) are probably different in origin, cf. also Reaney s.nn. *Collard* and *Galliard*). The church here (dedication unknown) is mentioned as the 'church of *Stok Coilard'* 1410 Pat, cf. also Adam *atte Church* 1340 NI. The forms *Stoke Willams, Stok Willim* 1271 CurR (Drew), occurring in connection with the adjacent par. of Stourton Caundle, may also belong here, cf. the possession of the DB manor of *Stoches* by *William* de Eu in 1086 (VCHDo **3** 92).

STROUD FM (ST 727137), *Strode* (*Messuage called-*) 1621 (17) *Strode*, 1840 *TA* (*-Fm & Md*), 1870· Hutch³, *Stroud* 1811 OS, apparently named from the family of John (*de*) *Strode* e12 Hutch³, Alan *Stroude* 1340 NI, who probably took their name from Strode in Netherbury par. *infra, v.* Hutch³ **2** 131, **4** 191.

TWOFORDS BRIDGE (ST 751137), *Twyford*(') 1280 *CottCh*, 1288 *Ass* (p), *pons vocat' Twyford*(e) 1494 *Cecil*, 1496 *Digby*, *Twoford Bridge* 1811 OS, cf. *Tweyfordislane* 1462, *Tofordes lane* 1563 *Digby*, *Two fords lane* 1653 *SxAS*, *mersshe iuxta Twyford'* 1494 *Cecil*, 'double ford', *v.* **twī**, **ford**, with **brycg**, **lane**, **mersc**, cf. Twyford in Compton Abbas par. *supra*; the road here crosses R. Lydden and the tributary of R. Lydden which gives name to Holebrook Fm *supra*.

THE BELT, *v.* **belt**. BERRY FM, *Bury Fm* 1811 OS, *v. Ramsbury supra*. BISHOP'S BELT. BLACKMORE FM, cf. foll. BLACKMORE VALE DAIRY, named from Blackmoor Vale *supra*. BLACKROW LANE, *v.* Blackrow Fm *supra*. BRAKE PLANT., *Brake* 1779 *DROMap*, *Brake and Marl Fm* 1840 *TA*, *Break* 1844 *ib* alt.app., *v.* **bræc**¹. BRICKLES WD, *Brickells Copse* 1844 *TA* alt.app. BUFFET'S WD, *Buffets* 1779 *DROMap*, *Buffits* (*Md*) 1840 *TA*. CHURCH GROUND BELT, *Church Grd* 1840 *TA*, named from the church at Stock Gaylard *supra*. COOMBE FM, *v.* **cumb**. COX'S WATER (a ford), cf. *Coxs Bridge Cl, Coxs Home Md & Orchd* 1840 *TA*. DAIRY HO. FISH POND. GODDARD'S FM. GORSE TRIANGLE. GREEN COPSE. GREEN MAN (P.H.), *Greenman* 1811 OS. HAYDON LANE, cf. *Hayden Md, Haydon Md or Hills Cl* 1840 *TA*, named from Haydon *supra*. HOLLOW HILL PLANT., *Holly Hill* 1844 *TA* alt.app., cf. *Hollywell Md* 1840 *TA*. HOME FM & PLANT., cf. *Home Estate, Home Cl, Grd, Md, Orchd & Plot* 1840 *TA*. HYDES PLANT., cf. *Hides Barton* 1779 *DROMap*, *Gt & Lt Hides, Hides Md, Hydes Orchd* 1840 *TA*, named from Hydes *supra*. LITTLE MILL, *Little Mill* [Bridge] 1791 Boswell, *Little Mill Copse* 1840 *TA*, cf. Thomas *Attmyll'* 1464 *Digby*, *Milhams*

1840 *TA, v.* **myln, hamm**. LOWER PLANT. LYDLINCH CMN, 1840 *TA, Lidlinch Cmn* 1811 OS, cf. *Higher-* 1840 *TA, Broad Cmn* 1844 *TA* alt.app. MALTHOUSE CTGS. MANOR FM. MATRAVERS (lost, in the old par. of Stock Gaylard), 1870 Hutch[3] (**4** 686), *Matraverse* (a farm) 1795 Boswell, named from the family of this name, cf. John *Ma(u)travers* Hy 3, 1280 *HarlCh*, 1304 Hutch[3]. MIDDLE PLANT. NEW GORSE. NEW HOUSE FM, *New Ho* 1840 *TA*. PROWER'S FM. RICKETT'S WD, cf. *Ricketts Fm* 1840 *TA, Gt Rickets, Rickets Md* 1844 *ib* alt.app. RIDGE FM, named from Ridge (Drove) in Haselbury Bryan par. **2** 103. ROOKSMOOR COPSE. ST THOMAS À BECKET'S CHURCH, cf. 'the church of *Lyddelynche*' 1304 Banco (Drew), *ecclesiarum de Lydelynche* 1433 *HarlRoll*. SALKELD BRIDGE, named from the *Salkeld* family which held lands here from the 18th century. SAWPIT PLANT., cf. *Lr & Upr Saw Pits* 1844 *TA* alt.app. SHELLEYS. SHELVES PLANT., cf. *Gt Shelves* 1844 *ib, v.* **scelf**. STEPPING STONE BRIDGE. STOCK WD, cf. *Stock Fm* 1811 OS, named from Stock Gaylard *supra*. THREE BOARS HEADS INN, *-Bears Head-* 1840 *TA*. TREVISS COPSE. WITHYBED PLANT.

FIELD-NAMES

The undated forms in (*a*) are 1840 *TA* 133. Spellings dated 1280 are *Ass*, 1304, Hy 8, 1545[2] Hutch[3], 1313, 1319, 1345 Ipm, 1327 *SR*, 1332 SR, 1338–40 Glast, 1340 NI, m14 *Glast*, 1412 FA, 1496, 1531, 1563 *Digby*, 1510 *MP*, 1603 *Weld*[2], 1607, 1779 *DROMap*, 1653 *SxAS*, 1664 HTax, 1791 Boswell, 1844 *TA* alt.app., and the rest *Salkeld*.

(*a*) Ash Flg; Balsy(')s Coppice, Lower Md & 6 Acres; Barley Grd & Md; Barn Md 1844 (*-Mdw* 1779); Gt, Lt & Long Barrs; Barrels; Bartletts (Two Orchds); Battle Ray; Bencroft (*v.* **bēan**); Best Grd; Blackfield Md 1844, (Inner & Outer) Blacklands (*v. Blakelond supra*); Bottom Md; Brags (Md) (cf. John-, Stephen *Bragge* 1327); Bramble Cl 1844; Bridge Cl & Grd; Broad Cl; Broadlands; Brook Flg 1844 (*Brookfelland Mdw* 1779); Gt Browns (cf. Nicholas *Brown* Hy 8, John *Browne* 1664); Bucks; Burks Md; Gt Burts; Bushey Cl; Calving Cl; Calves Cl 1844; Carters 1844 (cf. James *Carter* 1664); Chapel Cl; Chicks Md 1844; Clarks Cl (cf. Rose *Clarke* 1664); Gt & Lt Coat (*v.* **cot** 'cottage'); Collins Fm Ho and Land; Common Cl, Md, Pce & Plot; Copse (*Gt & Lt Coppice* 1779); Corn Hills; Craffils (Md) 1844; (Course) Crawfords (Mdw) 1779; Crib Ho & Md; Gt & Lt Crooks Mdw 1779; Darby's (cf. John *Derby* 1327); Gt & Lt Days; Gt & Lt Doles (*v.* **dāl**); Downs; Drove; Dry Cl (1779); East Fds & Md; 8 Acres 1844; 11 Acres; Elveland and Hall,

Elveland Md; Eyres Md, Eyre's Summer Leaze (*Eyre's Tenement* 1714, cf. Samuel *Eyres* 1664); Fat Acre (*v.* **fat**); Fern Grd 1844; Fields; 15 Acres (1714); 5 Acres; Foots Grd; 4 Acres; Francis Md 1844; (Hr & Lr) Frosts 1844 (cf. Henry *Frost* 1664, *Frost Mill* 1762 (alternatively said to be in Lydlinch or Fifehead N., cf. under Fifehead Mill **2** 96-7); Frys Grd 1844 (cf. *Fry's* (*Cowleaze & Mdw* 1779); Lt Furzy Cl; Furzy Grd 1844; Hr & Lr Gales; Gallers Orchd 1844; Great Hills; Two Green Closes; Green Hills; Hatchards; Hatch Md; Hedge Croft; Hewletts; Hill Croft; Hips Marls 1844; Gt Hopses, Hopseys Plot (*Hopsey* 1779, cf. Joseph *Hopps* 1664); Horse Cl; House Grd 1844; Huds (cf. Nicholas *Hudde* 1327); Inhams; Jacobs Md 1844; Jenny Croft; Lake Md; Lamberts Md 1844 (cf. John *Lambert* 1664); Land; Larks Leaze 1844 (*v.* **lāwerce, lǣs**, cf. **2** 25); Leg (*v.* **leg**); Leigh Croft (Md), Lyecrofts Fm (*Lay Craft* 1779, *v.* **lǣge** or **lēah**, **croft**); Little Md (*-Mdw* 1779); Long Cl 1844 (1779); Long Coppice; Longlay (Copse); Long Md; Lower Leaze 1844; Lower Md & Pce; Mash Md; Middle Cl 1779; Middle Md; Gt & Lt Miles's 1844 (cf. Robert *Myles* 1664); Mitchells; Moggs Orchd 1844; (Pit) Morrals 1779; Mower (*v.* **mōr**); North Close (Md); Nipes Md; North Cl & Md; Oaks Cl; Old Man's Mdw 1779; Orchard (1779), Best & Old Orchard; Overgang (*Ouergangbridge* 1563, *v.* **gang** 'path, track', first el. probably **ofer** 'over, across', cf. ME *overgange(n)* 'to go over'; the *TA* field is beside R. Lydden at ST 748131); Ox Croft; Parkers; Peaches; Peak; Pit Cl; Pit Grd & Marls 1844; Pitlands 1779; Pitts; Plumber Copse & Md (*-meade* 1603, named from Plumber *supra*); Pond Cl 1844; Poor Downs; Pound Cl & Md; Pulpit Md; Puxey Cl 1844; Ragland (*v.* **ragge**); River; Roman Bridge Cl, Romans Md (cf. Nicholas *Romayne* 1545[1], 1629, Richard *Rummon*, William *Rumman* 1664); Rookson; Rudlands Copse; Rushy Grd; Ryles 4 Acres; Search; 7 Acres; Seymours; Sharplands; 6 Acres; Soapers Cl 1844; Sovels (Crib) Md, Ambuses Sovels, Coat Sovels (cf. Coat *supra*), Hollowtree Sovels 1844; Spring Cl 1844; Stags (Md) 1844; Starveland(s) (a derogatory name for unproductive land); Stock Grd, Stock Md & Orchd 1844 (named from Stock Gaylard *supra*); Stot Fd (*v.* **stott**); Stubble; Styles (cf. John *Stylle* 1332); Tail end; Tapper's [Bridge] 1791; 3 Acres (1779); Three Crofts; Top Md; Trims Md 1844 (cf. Leonard *Trim* 1664); Turn (Orchd); 2 Acres; Upper Leaze 1844; Vitlands 1844; Walbridge Fd & Md (*Walbryggelane* 1496, *v.* **brycg**, **lane**, first el. uncertain); Wallace (cf. Ingelram *le Waleys* 1304 (held Stock Gaylard at his death), John *le Walysche* 1327); Water Mdw 1844; Webb Cl 1844; Weeping Ash; White Croft 1844; Gt Whittings 1844 (*Gt & Lt Whitings, Whitings Md* 1779); Wicket Orchd; Wiltshire(')s (Orchd); Woolhams 1844; Worthy (*v.* **worðig**).

(*b*) *Barnes Tenement* 1714; *Bay yardes et Bayyardes lease* 1545[1], *Baynard's lease, Boyard's or Boyard's Lease* 1545[2], *lands called Bayards alias Beres* 1706; *Edmondesthorp* 1412 (possibly in or near Lydlinch, from **þrop** 'hamlet, outlying farm' and the OE pers.n. *Ēadmund*); *la Forge* (p) 1280 (*v.* **forge**); *Hauckins House* 1607; *Kylbelles Lake* 1531; *in La Lane* (p) 1340 (*v.* **lane**); *Lyden(e)holte in Blakemore* 1313, 1319, 1510, *Lyndeholte in*

Blackemoure 1345 (possibly in or near Lydlinch, first el. probably R̥.
Lydden (cf. par. name *supra*) with **holt** 'wood', *v*. Blackmoor Forest &
Vale *supra*); *parrocke called Perryhay* 1653 (*v*. **(ge)hæg**, first el. probably
pirige 'pear-tree').

Oborne

OBORNE (ST 655185)
>   (*æt*) *womburnan,* (*apud*) *Woburnam* (rubric) 970–75 (12)
>   *SherC* (S 813), *Waburnham* 970–75 (14) *Cott* (MS
>   Faustina A.ii, f.25), (*in*) *Wonburna* 998 (12) *SherC* (S
>   895)
>   *Wocburne* 1086 DB, *Wogburne* n.d. (12) *SherC*
>   *Woborna* 1125, *-born*(*e*) 1145 (12) *SherC*, 1163 Dugd, 1291
>   Tax, 1332 SR *et freq* to 1585 *Sher, -burna*(*m*) 1145 (12)
>   *SherC*, c.1160 Sarum, *-burn*(*e*) 1212 P, 1249 FF, 1271
>   FineR, 1285 FA *et freq* to 1626 *Sher, -bourn*(*e*) 1280
>   *Ass*, 1350 (18) *Add*, 1406 Digby, 1473 *Sher*
>   *Wuburn* 1227 FF, *-born* 1268 FF (p), *Wouburn*(*e*) 1268 *Ass*,
>   1316 FA, 1317 FF, *Wooburne* 1442 Hutch[3]
>   *Wodebourne* (sic) 1428 FA
>   *Oburne* 1479 Cl, 1535 VE, 1569–74 *Map*, 1575 Saxton,
>   *Obourne* 1535 VE, 1774 Hutch[1], *Oboorne* 1567 Hutch[3]

'Crooked stream', from **wōh** (wk.obl. *wōgan, wōn*) and
burna, here applied to the winding course of R. Yeo. This is
a common name, cf. Woburn Bd 143, Ekwall RN 468–9; for
the loss of initial *W-*, cf. Old Nth 128, Ullington Gl **1** 253,
etc.

HR & LR BOYSTON LANE, cf. (*Hr*) *Boysom, Burts & Noaks
Boysom* 1839 *TA*, possibly from **hamm** 'enclosure' with the
ME surname *Boye* or *Boys* found in Boys Hill in Holnest
par. *supra*, cf. also f.ns. *infra*. THE GRANGE, GRANGE FM.
LOWER FM. OBORNE HILL. OBORNE WOOD, 1839 *TA*,
Woborn(*e*)*wode* 1454 *Sher*, Pat, 1461–1500 *Sher, Woborne
Wod'* 1538 Digby, *Oburne Woode* 1569–74 *Map, Woburne
wood* 1614 Digby, *v*. **wudu**. RECTORY, cf. *Parsonage Cl &
Grd, Vicarage Pce* 1839 *TA*. ST CUTHBERT'S CHURCH
(remains of), *Oborne old church* 1870 Hutch[3], cf. *capellas de
Woborn* 1145 (12) *SherC, Church Grd* 1839 *TA* (owned by

'Church wardens for repairs of the Church'). ST CUTHBERT'S
CHURCH (built 1862 on new site). WHITEPOST GATE, *White
Post Gate* 1811 OS.

FIELD-NAMES

The undated forms in (*a*) are 1839 *TA* 158. Spellings dated 1332 are SR,
1484 *Digby*, 1664 HTax, 1791 Boswell, and 1870 Hutch[3].

(*a*) The Acre; Bishops Hill (the manor of Oborne anciently belonged to
the Bishop of Salisbury, as in DB, VCHDo **3** 71); Blind Hall Corner,
Blind Well (*v.* **blind**); Bottoms; Bragge's Well 1870 (a chalybeate spring,
perhaps named from Charles *Bragge*, vicar here 1589-1639); Brines Barn,
Gdn & Hill; Broad Md; Burts Hill & Orchd, Burts Little Md, Burts 7 & 3
Acres; Chance Orchd; Court Ham (*v.* **hamm**); Crates Hill; Critch Hill
(perhaps, like Creech Hill **2** 268, analogous with Crichel **2** 274, *v.* ***crūg**);
Daisy Hill; Easeham's Ld; East Grd; 8, 18, 11, 5 & 4 Acres; Hackman
Bars; Bishops Hacksom, Hthr & Lt Hacksom (cf. Bishops Hill *supra*);
Hatchet Grd (*v.* **hæcc-geat**); Hazels, Huzels; Hill Cl; Hooperby Lane,
Hooperty Lane; Horse Cl; Hoys Orchd; Hulls Orchd, Hulls 3, 2 & 4 Acres
(cf. Peter *Hull* 1664); Jupsey; Kit Md; Lime Kiln Grd; Little Fd; Little
Md (Orchd); Masterford; Middle Cl, Hill & Pce; Mill Lane & Md (cf.
High Mill [Bridge] 1791, *mill near Oborne old church* 1870); New Cl; 9
Acres; Noaks Orchd & 7 Acres; Old Quarry; Orchard; Ory Hill;
Pointingdon Path (from Poyntington par. *infra*); Poplar; Purse Hill Lane;
Round Hill; Rye Pce; Sandy Pce; 7 Acres or Middle Whole (v.l. Old)
Slade (*v.* **slæd**); Jenny Simms' Grd, Molly Simms' Orchd; (Lt) Slithy-,
Slitly Banks; Stoney Flg; Stubland; Swan Cl; 10 Acres; Thoms Hill; 3
Acres; Three Corner Grd; 12 & 20 Acres; Lt 2 Acres; Vartelham Grd (to
be associated with Vartnam Lane in Castleton par. *supra*); Whole Slade (cf.
7 Acres *supra*); Wick Lane (from Milborne Wick in Milborne Port par.
So); Gt & Lt Wine Pits; Withy Bed; Wood side.

(*b*) *Wobornelane* 1484 (*v.* par. name *supra*); *atte Wolle* (p) 1332 ('at the
spring or stream', *v.* **atte**, **well(a)**, cf. Spring marked 6").

Sherborne

A large part of Sherborne was added to the reconstructed par. of Castleton
in 1895, although a small part of Castleton was transferred to Sherborne in
1928.

SHERBORNE (ST 635169) ['ʃɔːrbən]

Scireburnan (*to þaere halgan stowe aet-*) 864 (12) *SherC* (S
333), (*æt*) *Scire burnan* l9 ASC (A) s.a. 860, 867 [866],
e10 ib (A) s.a. 910 [909], 11 ib (D) s.a. 910, m11 ib (C)
s.a. 978, (*in, æt*) *Scir(e)burna(n)* 893 (e11) Asser, 970–5

(12) *SherC* (S 813), 998 (12) *ib* (S 895), 1012 (12) *ib* (S 1422), 1014 (12) *ib* (S 933), 1046 (12) *ib*, 12 ASC (E) s.a. 860, 867 [866], 1145 (12) *SherC, Sciraburn'* 1065 CartAnt, (*on, æt*) *Scirburnan* e12 ASC (F) s.a. 861

Scireburne 1086 DB, 1205 FF, 1206, 1209 P, -*burn'* 1199–1214 P, 1244 *Ass*, 1275 *AD, in vicus Scireburnie* 1145 (12) *SherC, Scyr(e)b(ur)n(e)* 1244 *Ass*, FF, *Scirrborne* 1393 *NatT*

Sireburne 1123 CartAnt, 1212 Fees, 1284 FF (p), -*burn('*) 1195 P, 1196 ChancR *et freq* to 1265 Pat, *Syreburn(e)* 1202 FF, 1212 Fees *et freq* to 1285 FA, *Sireborn* 1218, 1219 FF, *Sirburn* 1244 FF, *Sirebur'* 1258 Cl

Schireburn(e) 1193–1214 P, 1223 Cur, FF *et freq* with variant spellings *Schyre-, -bo(u)rn(e)* to 1349 Ipm, *Schirburn* 1227 FF *et freq* with variant spellings *Schyr-, -bo(u)rn(e)* to 1428 FA, *Schyirburn* 1249 FF

Shireburn(') 1208 Memo (p), 1217 FF, 1219 Cur *et freq* with variant spellings *Shyre-, -bo(u)rne, -burne* to 1558 *Sher, Shirburn* 1236 FF, 1285 FA *et freq* with variant spellings *Shyr-, -bo(u)rn(e), -burn(e)* to 1566 *Sher, Shirboure, -borme* (sic) 1454 Pat

Chireburn' (sic) 1268 Cl

Shereburn 1288 Pat, Fine, *Sherbourn* 1333 Cl, -*born(e)* 1415 IpmR *et passim*, -*burne* 1579 *Sher*

Schirborn Abbatis 1291 Tax, *Shirburn Abbatis* 1428 FA

Schireburn-, Schirborn Camel 1303 FA

Shirneburn (sic) 1333 Fine

Shurbourne 1545–1551 *Sher*, -*borne* 1551 *ib*, 1593 *Batten*

'(Place at) the bright or clear stream', *v.* **scīr²** (wk.obl. *scīran*), **burna**, perhaps originally with reference to the upper course of R. Yeo (although Fowler 12 believes that the stream referred to may have been the small tributary of R. Yeo flowing S on a limestone bed from Coombe (in Castleton par. *supra*) past the Abbey). The name is found in several other counties, *v.* Ekwall DEPN, RN 362, cf. Leland (**1** 296): 'John Myer abbate of Shirburne said that he had redde in Latine bookes of his house that Shirburne was caullid Clarus fons'. In the form from 864, *to þaere halgan stowe aet-* ('to the holy place at-', *v.* **hālig, stōw**) refers to the religious foundation here, *v.* Sherborne Abbey *infra* for other (and earlier) references. The Latin affix *Abbatis* means 'of the abbot'. The single instance of the manorial affix *Camel* in 1303 is presumably from the family of John *Cammel* 1332 SR (taxed in Houndstreet tithing) and Robert *Camel* 1375 Hutch³ 4 214 (who held half a knight's fee here).

SHERBORNE (including Castleton) CHURCHES & CHAPELS (*v.* Hutch³ 4 228ff, RCHM 1 200ff)

ALL HALLOWS (lost), *Ecclesiam Omnium Sanctorum de Shireburn'* 1288 *Ass, the parisshe Churche of all Hawlows* 1529 *Sher, the chapelle of Al-Halowes, Al-Halowes chirch, Al-Hawlois* 1535–43 Leland. ST ANDREW (lost), *Ecclesiam Sancti Andree in Scireburna* 1145 (12) *SherC,* cf. *the Brid(e)well, St Andrew's Mill infra.* ST EMERENCIANA (lost, *v.* Fowler 208), a church only referred to as once having existed by Leland: *Ther was a paroche chirch of S. Emerentiana in the north part of the toune, wher now is a playn close* 1535–43 Leland (1 295). ST JOHN (lost), *Capella Sancte Johanis in villa de Shireburne* 1288 *Ass,* cf. *S. John Heremitage by the mylle now down* 1535–43 Leland, and *v.* the f.n. Saint Jones's *infra.* ST MARY MAGDALEN (lost, site marked 6″ NE of the old Sherborne Castle), *Scireburnensis castri ecclesie* 933 (12) *SherC* (S 423), *ecclesiam Sancte Marie Magdalene que in insula est ubi castellum situm esse conspicitur* 12 *SherC, Ecclesiam Sancte Marie Magdalene iuxta castellum* 1145 (12) *SherC, ecclesia beate Marie (Magdalene) de Shirebourn'* 1280 *Ass, Capella Marie Magdelene* 1464 *Digby, capellam/-e beate Marie Magdalene* 1499 *Sher,* 1525 *Salis,* 1538 *Digby, Mawdline Chappell* 1614 *ib,* cf. foll. and the f.n. Home 8 Acres or Maudlins Cl in Castleton par. *supra.* ST MARY MAGDALEN (the present church in Castleton, built 1714), *Castleton Church* 1802 *Map.* ST MICHAEL (lost, within Sherborne Castle in Castleton par. *supra*), *capellis sancti Michaelis et sancti Probi* 1163 Dugd (i. 339), 'the king's chapel (of St Michael) within the castle of *Shireburn(e)*' 1267, 1315 Pat, *S. Michel Chapelle now doune* 1535–43 Leland, cf. St Probus *infra.* ST PETER'S CHAPEL (lost, in Castleton), *v.* Overcoombe in Castleton par. *supra.* ST PROBUS (lost, near

Sherborne Castle), *Propeschirche* 1145 Dugd (i. 339), *-churche* 1145 (12) *SherC* (f. 35v), *capellis sancti Michaelis et sancti Probi* 1163 Dugd (i. 339), *capellis Sancti Mathei* (sic) *et Sancti Probi* 1303 (1648) *Bodl* (f. 91v); this former church or chapel is almost certainly to be identified with the form *Lanprobi* 643–72 (14) *Cott* (MS Faustina A.ii, f. 25, Finberg p. 155, cf. Sawyer 228), occurring in a list of estates belonging to the church at Sherborne as a grant by King Cenwalh of Wessex of '100 hides at *Lanprobi*' (*Lanprobi de C hyd*'). This form is particularly interesting because, if genuine, it suggests the continued existence of a British church at the time of the West Saxon expansion into Dorset during the 7th century; it is from PrWelsh ***lann** 'an enclosure, especially a churchyard', hence 'a church', and the later Cornish saint's name *Probus* found in only one other dedication, the p.n. Probus in Cornwall (on which *v.* B.L. Olson & O. Padel, *Cambridge Medieval Celtic Studies* **12** (1986) 51–2.). It has been argued by K. Barker, on insufficient evidence, that *Lanprobi* lies beneath the higher part of the medieval town of Sherborne (*Antiquity* **54** (1980), 229–31), but L. Keen has shown convincingly that the identification of *Lanprobi* with *Propeschirche*, etc (associated in the sources with the church of St Mary Magdalen and the chapel of St Michael *supra*) is reasonable, and that the location of *Lanprobi* is likely to have been the site of the old castle itself (*Anglo-Saxon Towns in Southern England*, ed. J. Haslam, 1984, pp. 208–12). The spelling *-probi* in the Celtic name-phrase *Lanprobi* is curious; it would appear to be a Latin gen.sg. form, although the correct vernacular form of the pers.n. would have been *-probus*, cf. *Propes-* in the 12th cent. spellings, which may have been thought of as an English gen.sg. form. St Thomas (lost, *v.* VCHDo **2** 105, Fowler 129 ff), *capellam Sancti Thome* 12 *SherC* (f. 38v), 1228 (1330) *Sher*, 'St Thomas's chapel' 1228 (1381) Pat, *Capellam beati Thome Martiris* 1337 DorR, 'the (free) chapel of St Thomas *up(pe) Grene*' 1349, 1380, '*-on the Grene*' 1395 all Pat, *cimiterium capelle Sancti Thome* 1427 *Salis*, 'free chapel of *Grene*' 1450 Pat, *Thomas Bekkettes chapelle by the new Yn* 1535–43 Leland, *v.* The Green, New Inn *infra*. Sherborne Abbey (founded as a house for secular canons c.705, reconstructed as a monastery for Benedictine monks in 998, given the status of an abbey in 1122, v. VCHDo 2 62–70), *Scireburnensi(s) ecclesie* 671 (12) *SherC* (S 228, spurious), 774 (12) *ib* (S 263), 844 (12) *ib* (S 294, 295), 903 for 946–51 (12) *ib* (S 516), 998 (12) *ib* (S 895), 1035 (12) *ib* (S 975), *ecclesie Scireburn'* 844 (12) *ib* (S 294), *to þaere halgan stowe aet Scireburnan* 864 (12) *ib* (S 333), *Scireburnensis monasterii* 933 (12) *ib* (S 422), *Sancta Maria . . . aet Scireburnan* 970–75 (12) *ib* (S 813), *Sancte Marie Scireburnie* 998 (12) *ib* (S 1382), *monasterium . . . Scireburnan* 1014 (12) *ib* (S 933), *to þam halgan mynstre to Scireburnan* 1046 (12) *ib, monachi Scireburnenses, terra Sireburnensium monachorum* c.1086 GeldR, *monasterii Sancte Marie in Scireburnea* 1125 (12), *-Sancte Marie Scireburnie* 1145 (12) *SherC, Abbatie de Schireburn'* 1212 P, 'church of St Mary' 1217 FF, 1344 Pat, *Shirborne abbey* 1360 ib, *the abbay chirch dedicate to our Lady, S Marye chirch* 1535–43 Leland, *v.* **hālig, stōw**; also associated with the Abbey are *abbay yate* 1460 Digby, *the churche Stile* 1529 Sher, *the Frayter* 1535 Fowler ('the refectory'), *the chapelle of our Lady of Bow on the south side of the old Lady Chapel, A new chapelle in S. Mary Chirch yard on the south side, the chapitre house* 1535–43 Leland, *Abbey courte* 16 Digby, *the abbey lytten* 1554 Hutch³, *the Churchyard* 1579, *the Abbie Litton or church yarde* 1630 Sher, *Abbey Litten* 1802 Map (*v.* **litten** 'burial ground'), *le Pryory* 1583 Digby, *The Priory, destroyed since 1735* 1802 Map, *the Ancret house* 1639 Fowler, *The Abbey Brewhouse, the Easter part of the Abbey House, the Abbey Mill* 1677 Digby, *Abbey Mill, The Abbey House, Abbey Gardens, Abbot's Fish Ponds, The Refectory, now Mr Gouger's Silk Works* 1802 Map, *v.* also Abbey Rd, Abbey Grange and Abbot's Fee all *infra*.

SHERBORNE STREETS & BUILDINGS

ABBEY RD, *venellam que ducit versus Abbathiam* 1424, 1453, *Abboteslane* 1426, (*le/la*) *Abbeylane* 1427–1627 all *Sher,* 1454 Pat, *venell' abbatis* 1464, *la Abbaylane* 1468 Sher, *Abbey Lane* 1601 Russ, 1802 Map, *Abbylane* 1605 Sher, 1733 DROMap, named from Sherborne Abbey *supra*. ACREMAN ST., *Acremanstret* 1531 Digby, *agremanns streete* 1569–74 Map,

Acreman Street 1677 *Digby, Acremen Street* 1733 *DROMap, Ackerman Street* 1802 Map, *v.* **æcer-mann** 'farmer, husbandman, ploughman', cf. PN Hrt 179. BACK LANE, 1824 Pigot, *Backelane* 1575 *Digby, v.* **back**, cf. Hospital Rd *infra*. BLACKBERRY LANE. BRADFORD RD, 1733 *DROMap, Bradford Waie* 1614 *Digby,* cf. *Fifteen Acres Bradford Road* 1843 *TA,* the road to Bradford Abbas *supra.* BRISTOL RD, 1733 *DROMap,* 1843 *TA,* the road to Bristol. CASTLETON RD, CASTLE TOWN WAY (TPlan), *Castelton Waie* 1600 *Digby,* both named from Castleton *supra.* CHEAP ST., 1802 Map, *Chep(e)strete* 1342–1570 *Sher,* 1427 *Salis, Shepstrete* (sic) 1484, *Chepstrete iuxta le Shamles* 1488, *Chepstrette* 1495, *Chip(e)stre(a)te* 1585, 1601, 1626, *Chepstreat(e)* 1622, 1628, *Che(a)pestreete* 1630, 1657 all *Sher, v.* **cēap** 'market', cf. *Market-st, le Marketplace, Shambles infra.* CHRYSANTHEMUM Row (TPlan). CLANFIELD (TPlan), from a f.n. *forlango de Clanneveile, -veyle* 1454 *Sher, Clameveyle* 1454 Pat, *Clanfield* 1614 *Digby, v.* **clǣne** 'clean, clear of weeds', **feld**. COLD HARBOUR, 1733 *DROMap,* 1802 Map, cf. *A cottage . . . in Coldharbo(u)r, five closes . . . called Coldharbour Grounds* 1677 *Digby,* originally a p.n., 'cold shelter' from **c(e)ald** and **here-beorg**, later applied to the street (alternatively called *The Higher Road to Shaftsbury & London* on 1802 Map). COOMBE RD, to Nether Coombe *infra.* CORNHILL (TPlan), cf. an identical st.n. in Dorchester **I** 350. EAST MILL LANE, cf. *the mill lane* 1642 *Digby, the East Mill* 1870 Hutch[3]. FACTORY LANE (6″), so called because leading to Westbury Silk Mills, *v.* Ottery Lane *infra.* GEORGE ST., named from *George Inn infra.* GREEN HILL, 1802 Map, *Green's-hill* 1824 Pigot, named from foll. THE GREEN, 1733 *DROMap, loco qui dicitur Grene* 12 SherC (f. 38v), *Will' Smyth' uppe greyne* ('upon the green') 1332 SR, *supra Greyne* 1337 DorR, 'the (free) chapel of St Thomas up(pe) Grene'* 1349, 1380, *-on the Grene* 1395 all Pat, *(la/le) Grene* 1438–1551 *Sher, (the streate called) the Gre(e)ne* 1585–1626 *ib, v.* **grēne**[2] 'grassy spot, village green', **uppan** 'upon', *St Thomas* supra. HALF ACRES (TPlan), cf. *Half Acre Lawn in Common Md* 1843 *TA.* HALF MOON ST., *Lodborne* 1733 *DROMap, Half Moon Street anciently Lodborne* 1802 Map, named from *a cottage . . . called the halfe Moone* 1677 *Digby, Halfmoon* [Inn] 1802

Map, cf. also *Half Moon Close* 1802 Map, a field to the S of the street on a bend of R. Yeo; for the earlier name *Lodborne*, *v.* Ludbourne Rd *infra*. HORSE CASTLES, *Horsecastle lane ende* 1600 *Digby*, *Horse Castle Lane* 1802 Map, named from *(lez) Horscastell'* 1484, 1563 *Digby*, *(pastur' in) Horsecastell'* 1538 *ib*, 1590 *Salis*, *horse castell'* 1574 *Sher*, *The Litle-*, *The Midle Horsecastle*, *The Lower Horsecastell* 1600 *Digby*, *Five closes called The Horse Castles* 1677 *ib*, *Horse Castle Close(s)* 1802 Map, *Horsecastle Fd* 1849 *EnclA*, cf. *Horscastell' Well'* 16 *Digby*, *Horsecastlewell* 1614, 1677 *ib*, apparently self-explanatory with reference to a place where horses were kept, from **hors** and **castel(l)** with **well(a)** 'spring, stream', though it is not clear to what structure or earthwork the second el. originally referred, *v.* Horsecastles Fm *infra*. HORSECASTLES LANE, named from prec. HOSPITAL RD (6″), -LANE (TPlan), *Back Lane* 1733 *DROMap*, 1802 Map. HOUND ST. (formerly also a tithing), *Hundestret(e)* 1288 *Ass*, 1327 *SR*, 1332 SR, 1443–1473 *Sher*, 1460 *Digby*, *Hundesstrete* 1288 *Ass*, *(decenna de) Houndestrete* 1406 *Digby*, 1419–1500 *Sher*, 1427 *Salis et freq* to 1525 *ib*, *la Houndestrete* 1485, 1488 *Sher*, *Houndstret(e)* 1450 *Salis et freq* to 1566 *Sher*, *Hound(e)strett(e)* 1484 *Digby*, 1495 *Sher*, *(la) Hounstrete* 1484, 1551 *ib*, *Howndestret(t)e* 1485, 1500 *ib*, *Houndstrete Fee* 1529 *ib*, *Hund-* 1531 *Digby*, *Hunstrete* 1551 *Sher*, *Hound(e)-streat(e)* 1585 *ib et freq* to 1627 *ib*, *Hown(de)streat(e)* 1612 *ib*, 1614 *Digby*, *Hounstreet* 1614, 1617 *Pitt*, *Hound Street Tithing* 1664 *HTax*, 'street frequented by dogs or where they were kept', *v.* **hund** (gen.pl. *hunda*), **strǣt**, cf. an identical st.n. in Wallingford Brk 536. KITT HILL, 1733 *DROMap*, 1802 Map, cf. *Kitehill Farme* 1614 *Digby*, *v.* **cȳta** 'a kite'. LENTHAY CLOSE & RD, *Lenthaieclose, Lenthay(e) Close* 1600, 1614, 1677 *Digby*, named from Lenthay Common *infra*, *v.* **clos(e)**, cf. Lenthay Lane in Castleton par. *supra*. LONG ST., *Langstret* 1397 *Sher*, *(la/le) Lang(e)stret(t)(e)* 1426–1478 *Sher*, 1454 *Pat*, *Long(e)stret(e)* 1416 *Sher et freq* to 1601 *ib*, *Longestrette* 1500 *ib*, *Long(e)streat(e)* 1566–1626 *Sher*, 1614 *Digby*, *Longstreet* 1677 *ib*, *v.* **lang**[1] 'long', **strǣt**. LUDBOURNE RD, preserves the name *Lorteborn(e)* 1439–1500 *Sher*, 1464 *Digby*, *-b(o)urne* 1448, 1476 *Sher*, *Lurteborn'* 1440, 1446 *ib*, *(vico vocat') Lortbo(u)rn(e)* 1453–88 *ib*, 1454 *Pat*, *Lotborn(e)*

1454, 1558–1626 *Sher, the streate called Lotborne* 1617 *ib,* *Lodborne* 1551 *ib*, 'dirty stream', *v.* **lort(e)**, **burna**, perhaps originally applied to part of the brook which flows from Coombe (in Castleton par. *supra*) and Newell (*q.v. infra*) into R. Yeo; this brook flowed past the Abbey and must have carried much of the town's sewage. On 1802 Map, *Lodborne* and *Lodborne Lane* are said to be earlier names for Half Moon St. *supra* and South St. *infra* respectively, so that the application of the name to the present Ludbourne Rd seems to be relatively recent. MARSTON RD, 1733 *DROMap,* *Marston Waie* 1600 *Digby*, cf. the f.n. *Marston Road 8 Acres* 1843 *TA*, from Marston Magna (So.). MILL LANE, leading to West Mill *infra*. NETHERCOMBE LANE (TPlan), from Nether Coombe *infra*. NEWELL, *ten' apud le Newell'* 1446, (*-apud*) *Nywell'* 1452, 1476 *Sher*, 1525 *Salis*, 1531 *Digby*, (*mesuag' iuxta*) *la Nywelme* 1461, 1464, *Nywyll'* 1500 *Sher, Newell(')* 1563, 1677 *Digby, New Well Hill* 1733 *DROMap*, 1802 Map, 'the new spring or stream', from **nīwe** and **well(a)** (in two 15th cent. forms apparently alternating with the near-synonymous **welm** 'spring, source of a stream'), cf. *Newelle, a litle burne rising in the ·west part cummith by the west part of the abbay, The hedde of this water . . . is caullid New Welle* 1535–43 Leland, *the Conduite headd in Wellclose* 1630 *Sher, New Well* (*Water*), *The Conduit Head* 1802 Map, *v.* Fowler 327; for the possibility of a different origin for Newell, *v. atte Ewelme* in f.ns. (b) *infra*. NEWLAND (formerly also a tithing), *in vico de la Niwe-, la Nywelande* 1288 *Ass*, (*Libertas de*) (*la*) *Nyw(e)lond(e)* 1306 *Sher*, 1327 *SR*, 1332 *SR· et freq* to 1500 *Sher*, (*lib' de*) (*la*) *New(e)lond(')* 1402 *Sher et freq* to 1577 *ib, Neulond* 1417 *Fine, la Neuland* 1427 *Salis, la Ni(e)welond'* 1440, 1448, *la Nyewlond'* 1440 *Sher, Nuelond'* 1538 *Digby, in burgo de Newlond* 1559 *Salis, Newland(e)* 1566 *Digby et passim, Newlande manerium* 1590 *Salis, -Burgus, -Mannor* 1614 *Digby, Newland streete* 1569–74 *Map, -streate* 1601, *the streat(e) called Newland'* 1614, 1651 *Sher, Borough of Newland and Castle Towne* 1664 HTax, 'land newly cleared for cultivation', *v.* **nīwe**, **land**; the western end of the street now called Newland is marked *St Swithins Street* on 1802 Map, cf. *Newlands formerly called St Swithin's Street* 1870 Hutch[3] **4** 282, St Swithin's Rd *infra*; the eastern end of the street is marked *The Borough of Newland* 1802 Map. OBORNE RD, *Wobornelane* 1487 *Digby*, leading to Oborne par. *supra*. OTTERY LANE (TPlan), called Factory Lane (6"), *Oteris-, Oteryslane* 1454, 1459 *Sher*, 1454 Pat, 1462, 1464 *Digby, Otereslane* 1454 Pat, *Otur-* 1466, *Otyr-* 1484, *Oterlane* 1508, *Otters lane* 1531, 1598 all *Digby, Oterslane* 1548 *Sher, Ottar lane* 1569–74 *Map*, named from a family from Ottery D, cf. the quitclaim from Robert Font' to Robert *de Otery* of right and claim in *tenemento quod fuit Johannis de Oteri* 1324 *Sher*, and cf. William *de Ottery* 1289 Fowler, Bartholomew *(de) Otery* 1294, 1309 FF, John *Otterey* 1516 *Digby*. PRIESTLANDS, 1843 *TA* (f.n.), *Priests Lands* 1802 Map, possibly to be associated with the glebe land which Bishop Joselin gave to provide a priest for St Thomas's chapel in 1177 (Fowler 134). QUARR LANE, cf. *Quar* 1733 *DROMap, Quar Pce, Top Quar* 1843 *TA*, named from the quarry (6") near Clatcombe Fm in Castleton par. *supra, v.* **quarre**. ST ALDHELM'S RD (TPlan), from St Aldhelm's School, *v.* Vernalls Lane *infra*. ST SWITHIN'S RD, cf. Newland *supra*. SHEEP LANDS LANE, *Sheplande Waie* 1600 *Digby*, named from the f.n. *Sheplandes* 1614 *ib, Sheep Lands* 1733 *DROMap, Sheepland* 1843 *TA, v.* **scēap, land**. SOUTH ST., *Duck Street anciently Lodborne Lane* 1802 Map, *Duck-st* 1824 Pigot; for *Lodborne Lane, v.* Ludbourne Rd *supra*. TINNEYS LANE, *Twiney Lane* 1802 Map, named from the family of Henry *Teny* 1476, John *Tynney* 1558 both *Sher*, Elizabeth *Tynnye, -Tynney* 1614 *Digby*. TRENDLE ST., 1824 Pigot, *via regia apud Trendelles* 1531 *Digby*, cf. (*tenemento in*) *le/la Trendell'* 1465–1499, *la Trendyll'* 1484, *la trentell'* 1500, *le Trendale* 1566, *the Trendle* 1585, 1626 all *Sher, v.* **trendel** 'a circle, a ring'; it is not now clear to what circular feature this originally referred, but it might be noted that the area bounded by Trendle St., Westbury and Acreman St. is markedly curved on its S and E sides. TRENT PATH LANE, cf. *Trent Path* (*late Downs*), *Lawn in Trent Path* 1843 *TA, Trent Path Fd* 1849 *EnclA*, leading to Trent par. *infra*; the lane is *Sheep Lane* 1733 *DROMap*. VERNALLS LANE & RD; the former is St Aldhelm's Rd (TPlan). WESTBURY (formerly also a tithing), *decena de Westeber'* 1280, *Westbur'* 1288 both *Ass, Westbury* 1327 *SR*, 1406 *Digby*, 1427 *Salis* (*decenam de-*),

1433, *1454 Sher* (*vico vocato-*) *et passim*, *Westtebury* 1332 SR, *vico de Westbyry* 15 *Sher*, *Westbery* 1487, *Weystbury* 1531 *Digby*, *Westburie* 1590 *Salis*, *the streate and Tythinge called West*(*e*)*bury*, -*burie* 1612, 1625 *Sher*, *West Bury* 1802 Map, probably from ME **bury** (from dat.sg. *byrig* of OE **burh**) in the sense 'manor' or 'urban area outside the main part of the town', 'west' to distinguish it from Eastbury (also a former tithing) *infra*, *v.* **west**. THE WILDERNESS. WYNNES CLOSE & RISE, cf. Nicholas *Winnisse* 1614 *Digby*. YEOVIL RD, 1733 *DROMap*, 1849 *EnclA*, *Euell Waye* 1569–74 *Map*, *Yevell Waie* 1600 *Digby*, leading to Yeovil So.

Lost st.ns. include *la Blyndlane versus abbay yate* 1460 *Digby* (*v.* **blind**); *Bollane* 1474 *Digby*, 1488 *Sher*, 1531, 1563, *Dollane* (sic) 1516, *Boll lane* 1614 *Digby* (first el. probably **bolla** 'bowl, bowl-shaped hollow' rather than **bula** 'bull'); *Bowlane* 16 *Digby* (named from the building called *the Bow infra*); *Chese Crosse* 1538 *Digby* ('cross where cheese is sold', *v.* **cīese**; on 1802 Map the locations are marked of three former crosses, two of them being *The Lower Cross* and *The Upper Cross*, cf. also *la/le Mere iuxta Crucem* 1468–88 *Sher* (in Newland), *Braggyscrosse* 1516 *Digby* (the surname *Bragg*), *crucem politarie* ('cross where poultry is sold') 1531 Fowler); *Church-lane* 1824 Pigot; *East Bury* 1802 Map (given as the name for the E end of Long St., taken from the former tithing of Eastbury *infra*); *fryglane* 1531 *Digby* (first el. obscure); *Market-st* 1824 Pigot, cf. *mercato de Schyreburn'* 1244 Ass, *ij shoppar' in loco mercati* 1452, *in vico fori* 1454, *le Marketplace* 1499 all *Sher*, *in loco forali* 1525 *Salis*, *in mercato de Shirbourne* 1538 *Digby*, *the market*(*t*)(*e*) *place* 1585 *Sher et freq* to 1677 *Digby*, *le Cornemarkett* 1598 *ib* (*v.* **market**, cf. Cheap St *supra*, *Shambles*, *The Markett House infra*); *Parade* 1824 Pigot; *Pighill Lane* 1849 *EnclA*, cf. *Pig*(*g*)*hill* 1614, 1677 *Digby*, *Pig Hill* 1733 *DROMap* (*v.* **pigge**; it is probable that *Swyneshill'* 1563 *Digby* also belongs here, *v.* **swīn**); *Prydelane* 1563 *Digby* (cf. William *Pryde* 1458 *AddCh*); *Sewes-*, *Sewyslane* 1538 *Digby* (probably a surname); *altam viam regiam ducent' versus Thorneford'* 1473, *Thornefordlane* 1484, (*lez barres versus*) *Thorneford Way* 1582 all *Digby*, *Thornford Lane* 1733 *DROMap*, cf. *Thornfordeslaneend'* 1459 *Sher* (leading to Thornford par. *infra*, *v.*

barre); *Town's-end* 1824 Pigot.

Buildings include ACREMAN HO (named from Acreman St. *supra*); THE ALMSHOUSE, *le/la Almeshous* 1430–1464 *Sher*, *domus Elemosinar' Sanctorum Johannis Baptiste et Johannis Euangeliste de Shirbourn'* 1438 *ib*, *the Almeshous of Seynt John' Baptiest and Seynt John' Euang'liste* 1518, *the Almyshouse* 1579, *thalmeshouse* 1585, *Sherborne Almeshouse* 1626 all *Sher*, *St John's Hospital or Alms House* 1802 Map (*v.* **ælmesse, hūs**; the almshouse was founded in 1437, *v.* VCHDo **2** 104-5); *cotagium voc' Babcaries, -caryes* 1590 *Salis*, *Babcaries* 1677 *Digby* (a surname from Babcary So); *placea . . . in veteri manerio vocat' la Baillifeschaumbre* 1427 *Salis* (*v.* **baillie, chambre**); *le/la Baley iuxta Cumtarium* 1453, 1454 *Sher* (*v.* **baille** 'palisade, wall of a castle courtyard, prison', cf. *Contehowse infra*); Robert *sub la Blyndbowe* 1460 *Digby*, (*la/le*) *Blyndebowe* 1461–1500 *Sher*, *Blynbowe* 1495 *ib*, *una domo vocat' le Blyndbowe* 1538 *Digby* (*v.* **blind**, probably in the sense 'windowless', **boga** 'arch', cf. foll.); *le/la Bowe* 1400–1476, *ten' Abbatis de Shirbourne iuxta la Bowe* 1454 *Sher*, *duobus shopis subt' le Bowe* 1538 *Digby*, *the Bow(e)* 1647 *Sher*, 1677 *Digby*, cf. Adam *atte Bowe* 1406 *ib* (cf. prec. and an identical name in Dorchester **1** 349); *the Bridwell* 1677 *Digby*, *A building late the County Bridewell, supposed the Site of St Andrew's Church* 1802 Map (cf. *Brydewel(l)myll' infra*, *v.* **bridewell** 'a gaol', cf. Hutch[3] **4** 284); *le Charterhous* 1440 *Sher* (*v.* **chartrouse** 'a house for Carthusian monks'); (*tenemento voc'*) *Chep(e)manrewe* (*in Westbury*) 1476–1500 *Sher* ('row (of houses) belonging to the merchants', *v.* **cēap-mann, rǣw**, cf. Westbury *supra*); *the churche hows(e)* (*the Kyngges Stere in-*) 1513, 1531 Fowler, *le churchhowse* 1551, *the Churc(he)house* 1585, 1626 all *Sher*, *the Church House* 1802 Map (*v.* **cirice, hūs, stǣger**[1]); (*mes' . . . in*) *angulo iuxta venellam que ducit versus Abbathiam* 1424, 1454, *angulare mesuag'm . . . ad orient'm finem de Abbeylane* 1535, (*the*) *Cornerhouse* (*by Abby Lane*) 17, 1627 all *Sher* (*v.* **corner, hūs**, Abbey Rd *supra*); *the house of Correction* 1614 *Digby*; *cumtarium* 1453, 1454 *Sher*, *Contehowse* 1531 *Digby* (ME *counte-hous* 'counting-house'); *Courthouse* 1576 *Digby* (*v.* **court**); DIGBY SCHOOL (founded by the 5th Lord *Digby* in 1743, since 1931 occupying Sherborne House *infra*);

Durnfords (*An Ancient Building called-*) 1802 Map; *the Easterne Cottage* 1677 *Digby*; FIRTREE HO; FOSTER'S SCHOOL (founded and endowed in 1640 by Richard *Foster, v.* Hutch³ 4 299, cf. *House in which Forster's School is held* 1802 Map and the f.n. *Fosters Close infra*); *cotagium voc' le greatehouse* 1590 *Salis, the Great House* 1677 *Digby*; HARPER HO; *dom' voc' Hulettesplace* 1452 *Sher* (a surname with **place**); *Cottage called Jog(g)ans* 1614, 1677 *Digby* (a surname); (*Richard*) *Lodens House* 1642, 1677 *Digby*; LYON HO, cf. *A cottage . . . called the Lyon* 1677 *Digby*; *cotag' vocat' le Lytton* 1538 *Digby* (*v.* **litten** 'burial ground'); *The Markett House* 1677 *Digby, Market House* 1802 Map (cf. *Market-st supra*); (*la*) *Oldehall'* 1464–68 *Sher* (*v.* **(e)ald, hall**); *the plumbe-house* 1554 Hutch³, *the Plumbhouse . . . and . . . the Plumbehouse garden* 1630 *Sher* ('store-house for lead' according to Fowler 334, from ME *plum*(*b*) 'lead'); *ten'/mes' iuxta la Pyl(l)er* 1441, 1453, *-la/le Peler, -o(u)r* 1442–1464, *le/la Pilour* 1464, 1468, *le Pylour* 1476–1500 all *Sher, una vacua placea iuxta le Pylour* 1538 *Digby, mes' iuxta le pyllory* 1551 *Sher* (*v.* **piler** 'a pillar'); (*The Old*) *Presbyterian Meeting House* 1802 Map; *The Quakers Meeting House* 1802 Map; *Grangeam Willelmi Romayn'* 1464, *a barne called Romans* 1614 *Digby*; *the Ropers Standinges uppon the Churche Walle* 1612 *Sher*; RYDAL TOWER; *dom' apud le Shamell'* 1452, (*ij shopis apud*) *lez Shamelles* 1461, 1476, *lez/les Shamels* 1448–1464, *dom' apud' le Shamell'* 1452, (*ij shopis apud*) *lez Shamelles* 1461, 1476, *le(z) Shamles* 1484–1500 all *Sher, fower shamells in the market place* 1614 *Digby, Shambles* 1802 Map (marked at the S end of Cheap St., *v.* **sc(e)amol** 'a market stall'); SHERBORNE HO, 1802 Map (*-late Mr Seymour's*); SHERBORNE SCHOOL, *the free grammer schole* 1614 *Digby, Edward VIth's Grammar School* 1802 Map, cf. *the schole-house* 1554 Hutch³, *the Scho(o)le-house, -howse, the Schoole barton* 1630 *Sher*; *cottage called the Stockehouse* 1614 *Digby*; *The Town Hall* 1802 Map; *The Vicar's House* 1802 Map; WESTCOTT HO; *le Whitehaull* 1590 *Salis* (*v.* **hwīt, hall**); *dom' voc' Wodehous* 1459 *Sher* (*v.* **wudu**); *The Parish Work House* 1802 Map; *la Yeldehalle* 1377 Fowler, *ten' vocat' la Yeldehall', cotag' vocat' la Yeldehous* 1427 *Salis* (*v.* **gild-hall** 'guild-hall', **gild-hūs**).

Inns include *Cottage . . . called the Angell* 1677 *Digby,*

Angel 1824 Pigot; *cotagij . . . vocat' le Bell'* 1538 *Digby, Bell* 1824 Pigot; *Black Horse* 1824 Pigot; *Castle* 1824 Pigot; *Crown* 1824 Pigot; *Cross Keys* 1824 Pigot; *Inne called the Feathers* 1677 *Digby* (in Castleton), cf. *Plume of Feathers* 1824 Pigot; *ten' Rectoris de la Grene de Shirbourne . . . vocat' le Georges Inne* 1454 *Sher, le George hostill'* 1460 *Digby, le Georgesyn'* 1461, *hospicio voc' (le) George In(ne)* 1476, 1488, *the George* 1585, 1626 all *Sher, George* 1824 Pigot (*v.* The Green *supra*); *Greyhound* 1824 Pigot; *cottage . . . called the halfe Moone* 1677 *Digby, Halfmoon* 1802 Map (*v.* Half Moon St. *supra*); *hospic'm de la/le Hert* 1476, 1477 *Sher*; *dwelling house called the Horshedd* 1614 *Digby*, cf. *Cottage . . . called the Nags-Head* 1677 *ib*; *hospic' vocat' Juliannys Inne* 1446, *la Juliane* 1448, *le Julyans Inne* 1454, *Julian is In* 1471, *tenement called the Julyan* 1651 all *Sher*; *Cottage . . . called the Mermaide* 1677 *Digby, Mermaid* 1824 Pigot; *the new Yn* 1535–43 Leland, *Nueyn'* 1538 *Digby, the New Inn* 1802 Map; *dwelling house . . . called the Rose and Crowne* 1677 *Digby*; *Sun* 1824 Pigot; *Wellington* 1824 Pigot; *White Hart* 1824 Pigot (cf. *la/le Hert supra*); *dwelling house . . . called the White Horse* 1677 *Digby*. Cf. also *taberna de Schyrebourn'* 1280 *Ass* (204.43d).

Mills include *the Abbey Mill* (on the stream from Newell *supra, v.* under Sherborne Abbey *supra*); *Brydewel(l)myll'* 1531, 1538 *Digby* (*v.* **myln**, named from *the Brid(e)well supra*); *Castle or Scott's Mill* (on R. Yeo, *v.* under Sherborne Castle in Castleton par. *supra*); *Castleton Mill* 1802 Map, 1870 Hutch[3] (on R. Yeo W of Castleton Church, cf. *mill bayes* 1642 *Digby, v.* **bay**[2] 'embankment to form a dam'); *molend' de Dollerford', Dol(l)erford(e)mylle* 1484, *molend' voc' Dolerforde* 1487 *Digby*, cf. *Dellerford* 1427 *Salis* (SW of Sherborne in Westbury tithing, possibly on R. Yeo, *v.* **ford**, first part of the name perhaps a surname (cf. Reaney s.nn. *Deller, Dollar*) or to be compared with Dullar **2** 29); *the East Mill* 1870 Hutch[3] (**4** 209) (giving name to East Mill Lane *supra*); *Forrester's Mill* 1802 Map (on the stream from Newell *supra*, cf. Abraham *Forrester*, Margery *Forster* 1664 HTax); *Hart's Mill* (*v.* Riverside Works *infra*); *Hoddynottes myll* 1569–74 *Map* (on R. Yeo S of Lenthay Common *infra*, cf. *Hoddinottes Myllwaie* 1600, *Cottage . . . late Hoddinotts*

1677 *Digby*, and the f.n. Mill Orchd in Castleton par. *supra*);
Okes myll' 1548, 1574 *Sher, Oakes myll* 1569–74 *Map, -mill*
1824 Pigot, cf. *duob' molend' aquatic' in Westbury prius in
tenur' Johannis Oke* 1538, *Plott of ground formerly Oakes* 1677
Digby, Oke's Mill [Bridge] 1791 Boswell (a mill on R. Yeo,
marked on the 16th cent. map near to the present
Westbridge Fm, although Pigot, perhaps confusing it with *St
Andrew's Mill*, places it in *Duck-st*, now South St. *supra*;
Bedmill in Castleton par. *supra* was also at one time held by
members of a family called *O(a)ke*); *Pyd(de)mylle* 1474, 1487
Digby, Pedemyll' 1525 *Salis (Pudemylle* 1380 *Sher* (p) may
also belong here; the first el. may be an OE pers.n. *Pyda*
suggested for Pidley Hu 211, Piddington Nth 150 (cf. also
the Do surnames *Pide* 1327 *SR, Pede* 1332 SR), or **pide,
pidu** 'marsh, fen'; this mill was in Hound St. tithing);
molendinum iuxta eccl' Sancti Andree 1145 (12) *SherC,
Molendinum . . . juxta capellam sancti Andreæ* 1163 Dugd,
molendinum quod vulgaritur Seynt Andrees mulle nuncupatur
1309, *molendinum Sancti Andree* 1427 *Salis*, 1516, 1531, 1538
Digby, Seynt Andrewys Myll' 1516 *ib*, *S. Andrews myll*
1569–74 *Map*, (*two watergri(e)st(e)mill(e)s called) St
Andrew(e) Mills* 1601 *Russ*, 1677 *Digby, St Androwes Mylles*
1614 *ib*, *St Andrew's now Melmoth's Mill* 1802 Map (on R.
Yeo at the end of the present South St., named from the
former church or chapel of St Andrew, *v*. Sherborne
Churches & Chapels *supra*, cf. *Milmouthes infra*); *la
Weremull'* 1427, *Weremyll'* 1525 *Salis, duob' molend' vocat'
Weremylles* 1538, *water Grist mill called the Weare Mill* 1677
Digby (to the E of Sherborne near *Castle Mill supra*, named
from *the Great Weare of Sherborne* Eliz ChancP, *meadow
named Longwear* 1594 Fowler, *The Weares*, (*The) Broad-
weare(s), Litleweare, (the) Long(e) Weare, The Wearegroundes*
1614 *Digby*, cf. *Horsewere* 1538 *ib*, *v*. **wer** 'a weir, a
river-dam', cf. the two weirs still marked 6″ near Sherborne
Castle); WEST MILL, *v. infra*. Other Sherborne mills are
mentioned in 1288 FF, 1473 (*molend' aquatic'*), 16 (*molend'
Ricardi Cupper*), 1538 (*molend' aquatic' prius Thome Corn-
ysshe, molend' fulleretis quondam Ricardi Towker*), 1566
(*molendino brasino*), 1614 (*a watermill* held by Katherine
Cupper) all *Digby*.

ABBOT'S FEE (lost), 1664 HTax (-*Tithing*), 1870 Hutch[3], *Tething Abbatis* 1288 *Ass*, *Feodum Abbatis* 1332 SR, 1406, 1460 *Digby*, 1557 *Sher*, *decennam de Abbotisfe(e)* 1453, 1454, -*ys*- 1454 *Sher*, *Abbottes fee* 16 *Digby*, 1518, 1551 *Sher*, *Abbott's Fee* 1795 Boswell, 'the abbot's estate', *v.* **abbat, fee**, cf. also *ten' Abbatis de Shirbourne* 1454 *Sher*; the tithing of Abbot's Fee is described in Hutch[3] **4** 297 as 'including principally the estate anciently belonging to, and lying in, the neighbourhood of the abbey'.

BARTON FM (ST 632168), *Richard de la Berton' de Shireburne* 1288 *Ass*, *Bertona d'ni* 1460 *Digby*, *Barton Farm(e)* 1600 *ib*, 1614 *Pitt et passim*, *man' de Sherborne Barton* 1601 *Russ*, *Barton* 1614 *Pitt*, *Barton Mannor* 1614 *Digby*, cf. *via . . . apud Barton' Crosse* 1531 *ib*, *Barton Barne* 1569–74 *Map*, 1600, 1677 *Digby*, *Barton land* 1617 *Pitt*, *Barton Cl* 1802 *Map*, *v.* **bere-tūn** 'a corn farm, an outlying grange, a demesne farm', cf. Abbey Grange *infra*.

CULVERHAYES (TPlan) (ST 641164), 1849 *EnclA*, (*the*) *Culverhey(e)* 1461, 1566, (*la*) *Culuerhay* 1464, -*hey* 1561 (17) all *Sher*, *one close called Culverhaie alias Butclose . . . and a Douecot in the same close* 1614 *Digby*, *Culuerhaie* 1626 *Sher*, *Culverhaies* 1677 *Digby*, *Culver Hays* 1802 Map, cf. *the Culverhouse* 1542 (17), *a Coluerhowse* 1548, (*the*) *Dovehouse* 1566, 1626, *the Doffehouse* 1585 all *Sher*, *Culverhouse Close*, *Culverhouse alias Buthey* 1677 *Digby*, 'dove enclosure(s)', *v.* **culfre, (ge)hæg**, with **dovecot, culverhouse, dovehouse**; *But-* in *Butclose*, -*hey* may be from **butt**[2] 'archery butt'.

EASTBURY (lost as a p.n., but surviving in Eastbury Hotel in Long St.; formerly a tithing), *Estbur'* 1288 *Ass*, -*bury* 1327 SR, 1406 *Digby* (*dec' de-*), 1427 *Salis et freq* to 1566 *Sher*, -*bery* 1487, 1496 *Digby*, -*burie* 1577 *Sher*, -*burye* 1590 *Salis*, 1614 *Digby*, *Esttebury* 1332 SR, *Estebury* 1508, 1531 *Digby*, -*burie* 1590 *Salis*, *Eastburey* 1579 *Russ*, -*burie* 1590 *Salis*, -*bury(e)* 1614 *Pitt et passim*, *v.* **ēast, bury**, cf. Westbury (now a st.n.) *supra*; *East Bury* 1802 Map is given as the name for the E end of Long St. (about ST 643167).

HYLE FM ('TPlan') (ST 634158, = Westbridge Fm 6"), John *de la Hele* 1242 Pat, Henry *de la Hele* 1249 FF, (*firma de-, ten' voc'*) *la/le Hele* 1426–1471 *Sher*; *La Hyle by Shirbourne* 1334 Ipm, *Hile near Shirbourne* 1334 Cl, (*ten' voc'*) *la/le Hyle* 1397–1601, *Hyle* 1425, *la Hile* 1448, (*Ferme called*) *the Hyle* 1566, 1585 all *Sher*, (*Farme of*) *Hile* 1614 *Digby*, 1626 *Sher, Hyle Farm, Hyle House Grd* 1843 *TA*; *ten' voc' la Hyll in Shyrborn'* 1484–8 *Sher*; *Hail* 1811 OS. '(Place at) the nook or corner of land', from the dat.sg. *hēale* of WSax **healh**, *v.* Gt & Lt Hyle in f.ns. *infra* and cf. Hile Fm in Okeford F. par. *supra*.

LENTHAY CMN (ST 620152), 1733 *DROMap*, 1811 OS, *pastura in/voc'* (*la*) *Lenthey* 1427 *Salis*, 1461–1566 *Sher*, 1538 *Digby, Lent(e)hay(e)* 1454 Pat, 1454–1500 *Sher*, 1569–74 *Map, Lentehey* 1561 (17) *ib, Lenthayes* 1590 *Salis, Lent(e)haie* 1600, 1614 *Digby*, 'the enclosure used in Spring', *v.* **lencten, (ge)hæg**.

NETHER COOMBE (6"), NETHERCOMBE (Kelly) (ST 634171), (*vill' de*) *Nethercumb'* 1288 *Ass*, *-comb(e)* 1332 SR, 1406 *Digby* (*dec' de-*), 1427 *Salis et passim, -coombe* 1795 Boswell, *-Combe* 1802 Map, *Nuthercombe* 1327 *SR, Nythercumbe* 1349 *Sher, -combe* 1516 *Digby*, 1525 *Salis*, 1538 *Digby, Nithercombe* 1460 *ib*, 'lower part of the valley', from **neoðerra, niðerra** and **cumb**, thus distinguished from Overcoombe in Castleton par. *supra* which like Nether Coombe was a tithing in Sherborne hundred, cf. *Nether and Hither Combe* 1870 Hutch[3] **4** 297.

STOCKLAND (lost, about ST 655172), *Stocland* (*centum agelli in loco qui dicitur-*) 998 (12) *SherC* (S 895), 1145 (12) *SherC* (f. 35v), *Stoc-, Stokland* 1377 SoDoNQ, *Stok-* 1427, *Stockelond* 1525 *Salis*, 1538, (*Stope*)*stoclond, Stopestokelond* 1538, *Stock(e)lande Meade* 1600, 1614, (*Coopes*) *Stocklande* 1614 all *Digby, Stocklane* 1617 Pitt, *Closes . . . called Stockland* 1677 *Digby*, *Stock Land* 1733 *DROMap*, probably 'estate or tract of land belonging to a religious foundation', *v.* **stoc, land**. The name is discussed by Ekwall, Studies[2] 32, along with Stockland D and Stockland Bristol So which are

analogous (in spite of PN D 647). The *stoc* here probably
refers to the monastery at Sherborne, which in 998 was
reconstructed as a Benedictine house, *v.* Sherborne Abbey
supra; the earliest mention of *Stocland* occurs in the
foundation charter of the reformed monastery, *v.* further L.
Keen, *Anglo-Saxon Towns in Southern England*, ed. J.
Haslam, 1984, pp. 211–2. *Stope(s)-* 1538 and *Coopes-* 1614
are no doubt surnames.

WESTBRIDGE FM (6″) (ST 634158, = Hyle Fm on TPlan),
named from (*le*) *Westbrug(e)* 15, 1531 *Digby*, (*la*) *West(e)-
bryg(g)e* 1464 *Sher, Digby*, 1491, 1516 *ib, la Westbrigge* 1465
Sher, West(e)bridge 1563, 1614, 1677, *Westbrudge* 1563 all
Digby, Lawn in West Bridge, Two Acre West Bridge 1843 *TA*,
'the west bridge', *v.* **west, brycg**, where the main road from
the S crosses R. Yeo.

ABBEY GRANGE, *Abbey barton'* 1583 *Digby, Abbey Barn &
Bartons* 1802 Map, cf. 'the barton of the Abbey' 1249 FF,
Barton Close alias Abbey Lane Close 1677 *Digby, v.* **bere-tūn**,
cf. Abbey Rd, Barton Fm *supra*. BARTON GDNS, named from
Barton Fm *supra*. DURRANT'S CLOSE (TPlan). HORSECASTLES
FM (6″), now called OLD FM (TPlan), *v.* the st.n.
Horsecastles *supra*. MULBERRY GDNS (TPlan). NETHERTON.
NEWELL GRANGE & HO, *v.* Newell in st.ns. *supra*.
NORTHGATE. PAGEANT GDNS, named from the Sherborne
pageant of 1905 which commemorated the twelve hundredth
anniversary of the founding of the Abbey. RIVERSIDE WORKS,
on the site of *Hart's Mill now Willmott's Silkwork* 1802 Map
and near foll. WESTBURY SILK MILLS, named from Westbury
supra. WEST MILL, 1826 Pigot, *Mill* 1811 OS, giving name to
Mill Lane *supra* and possibly to be identified with *Mr
Couthes myll* 1569–74 *Map*, cf. Matilda *Couch* 1327 SR. For
other (lost) mills in Sherborne, *v.* under Buildings *supra*.

FIELD-NAMES

The undated forms are 1843 *TA* 187; fields in this *TA* but now in
Castleton are included under that par. *supra*. Some of the lost f.ns. in (*b*)
may well have been in the area out of which the new par. of Castleton was
formed in 1895. Spellings dated 1227, 1228 are FF, 1309, 1375, 1395,

1427, 1525, 1590 *Salis*, 1324, 1344 Pat, 1327 *SR*, 1332 SR, 1340 NI, 1347 *AddCh*, 1375–88 Fowler, 15², 1460, 1464², 1466², 1474, 1484², 1487², 1491, 1496, 16, 1508, 1516, 1531, 1538, 1563, 1566², 1569, 1598, 1600, 1614, 1623, 1677 *Digby*, 1410 Fine, 1436, 1539, 1553, 1641, 1746, 1870 Hutch³, 1466 *Weld*¹, 1487³ Ipm, 1569–74 *Map*, 1601² *Russ*, 1617 *Pitt*, 1629 *Ct*, 1664 HTax, 1733 *DROMap*, 1791 Boswell, 1802 Map, 1811 OS, 1845 *TA* 39 (Castleton), 1849 *EnclA*, and the rest *Sher*.

(a) Almshouse Lawn (belonging to The Almshouse *supra*); Arnold's Md 1802; Ashleys Elm (Home Fd or-) (*A*(*i*)*shleys* (*Tenement*) 1677, *Ashley's Elm* 1802, cf. John *Aysheley* 1436); Bailey's-, Barley's Croft 1849 (*Bailie Crofte, Ballye crafte* 1600 (*v.* **croft**, first el. **baillie** 'a bailiff' or a surname); Bridport's 19 ((*firma de*) *Brydportysplace, Bridportesplace* 1443, *Brideportes-* 1452, *Bridportisplace* 1464, *Bridportislandes* 1453, *Bridportestenement* 1455, *Britporttes*(*ten't*), *Britportespplace* 1459, *Byrtportes-* 1476, 1500, *Byrtpordesplace* 1488, *Byrtportes* 1484², *Burtporte* 16, *Byr-* 1548, *Birportes* 1551, *Burport*(*t*)*es* 1585, 1626, *v.* **place**, cf. the acre of arable land granted to Robert *de Brudeport* (i.e. from Bridport) *in campo de Shirbourn'* in 1349; Bridport's was in Westbury *supra*); Burt Hill 1849; Butchers Steps (*v.* **stæpe**, cf. Walter *le Bochere* 1332, Cary *Boucher* 1677); Chafie's Nursery 1802 (cf. the f.n. Chaffeys Lawn in Castleton par. *supra*); Close; Common Md (1733, *the comon meadowe* 1614, *the Comon' Meade* 1677, *v.* **mæd**); Conduit Fd (cf. *The Conduit Head* 1802 (near Newell *supra*), and The *Conduit* 1802 (at the S end of Cheap St. *supra*) which is also *le Condyte* 1538, *the Conduit* 1677, cf. *the lawe gutter'* 16, *v.* **cundite**, **gotere**, **lawe** 'law' (denoting the limit of some jurisdiction, cf. *le Lawegutter* Gl 1 63)); Cow Lease Gate 19 (*Cowleaze* 1375–88, *v.* **cū**, **lǣs**); Dag Md 1849 (*Dagmede* 1375–88, 1427, 1525, 1538, -*meade* 1614, 1677, *Dagmede yete* 16, *Daggemede* 1538, *v.* **mæd**, first el. possibly the surname *Dag*(*g*) but cf. ME *dag*(*ge*) 'ornamental point or incision on edge of garment, a shred or strip', Do dial. *dag* 'a small stump of a branch' (Barnes 59)); Dollens 1802 (*terr' voc' Dollynges* 1538, cf. William *de Dolling* of *Shireburn* 1228); Dry Cl 1849; Edwards Grd (cf. William *Edwardes* 1664); Englands or Meeting House Grd (cf. *Cottage . . . heretofore Englands* 1677, *Meeting House Cl* 1802); Fair Fd (*v.* **fæger**, but cf. Fair Fd in Dorchester 1 359); Farmers Hole; Field Walls (1733, *Fieldwalls* 1614, cf. Watts *infra*); Four Pits 1849 (*close . . . at Foure Pyttes* 1561 (17), 1566, *Forpittes* 1600, *Four-, Fowerpites, -pittes* 1614, *Fourpitts* (*close called-*) 1677, *v.* **fēower**, **pytt**); Golden Ball (*v.* **golden**, **ball** 'rounded hill'); Hick Park 1849 (*Hickeparke Corner* 16, *Hickeparke, Hickparkeyate* 1614, *Hick Parke Gate* 1677, *v.* **park**, **corner**, **geat**, first el. probably the pers.n./surname *Hick*, a pet-form of *Ric*(*h*)*ard*, cf. John *Hickes* 1332, taxed in the tithing of Westbury *supra*); Home Cl (*The-* 1614, 1677); Home Fd (*v.* Ashleys Elm *supra*); Home Grd & Pdk; Gt & Lt Hyle, Hyle Cow Leaze & 6 Acres (*pratum vocat' la Hilelandis* 1462, (*la*) *Hile-, Hylelandes* 1464–1500, *pratum voc' la Hele* 1471, *terr' voc' le Hyle* 1551, *Hyleham', Hylemeade* 1566, cf. *the hile Barne* 1559, *la Hilecomyns, la Hylecomen* 1462, *Hyleplace* 1499, (*la*) *Hylewode* 1426–1500, (*la*) *Helewode* 1426–1459, *Hyllewode* 1439,

1487, *la Hilewode* 1464, 1468, *Hylwode* 1485, *v.* Hyle Fm *supra*, **land, hamm, mǣd, common, place, wudu**); Loaders 2 Acres 1849; Long Acre 1802; Lucas's or Horsecastles 1849 (*v.* the st.n. Horse Castles *supra*); the Morass or the Marsh 1845 (*le Morrice* 1623, *A close . . . called the Marsh* 1677, *Marsh* 1746, *The Marsh* 1802, *v.* **mersc, morass** (first recorded 1655 NED)); Miller's Cl 1802; Napperty Hall or Abbotty Hall 1802 (cf. Edith *atte Knappedehalle* 1327, probably 'hall provided with a roof ornament', from **knappede** and **hall** with **atte** 'at the', cf. an identical name in Winfrith N 1 184); Newmans Culver Hayes (cf. Elizabeth *Newman* 1614, *Tenement heretofore Newmans* 1677, *v.* Culverhayes *supra*); Nursery; (The) Orchard ((*pastur' vocat'*) *le(z) Orchard(')* 1477, 1538, 1563, *le Orchard' hegge* 1508, *the Orchard or Fosters Close* 1677, *v.* **orceard**, *Fosters Close infra*); (Small) Paddock (*the paddocke* 1626, *the Parocke* 1677, *v.* **pearroc**); Parsley Bed (*clous-, close called Parsley bedd* 1614, *v.* **bedd**); Parson's Cl 1802; Pidgeon House Cl (cf. *the pigeonhouse* 1614, cf. Culverhayes *supra*); The Pound 1802; N & S Purley, Purley N & S of River (*prat' voc' Purlee* 1309, (*le*) *Purley* 1460, 1496, *Purleyyate* 1487[2], *Purlieu* [Bridge] 1791, 'wood or clearing frequented by the bittern or snipe', *v.* **pūr, lēah, geat**, cf. Purbeck 1 2 and the analogous Purley Brk 215, Purleigh Ess 222); Rack Cl (1677, 1802 (2 ×), *v.* **rakke** 'rack, framework of bars'); Raw Mds 1849 (probably to be identified with *Rammede* 1375–88, 1427, *Rayme(a)de* 1525, 1614, *v.* **mǣd**, first el. possibly **ramm** 'a ram'); Ridge Way (*forlango de Rigge-, Rygeway* 1454, *Rudge Waie* 1600, *Middle Ridg Way* 1733, *v.* **hrycg-weg** 'ridgeway', perhaps originally with reference to Bradford Rd *supra*); Quar Cl 1802 (near the Abbey, cf. *quarr' de Shirborn'* 1441, *terre . . . iuxta Oldequarre* 1454, *Quarre* (*Close*) 1539, 1677, *v.* **quarre** 'quarry', cf. Quarr Lane *supra*); Plantation called Saint Jones's 1849 (*St Jonesclose* 1563, *claus' voc' Seynte Johns* 1566, *close called Sainte Jones, St Johns* (*hill*) 1614, *2 closes called St Jones's, St Joanes late Stephens* 1677, *Saint Jones* 1733, *a field belonging to the Alms-House, called St Johns, said to be the Site of a Chapel* 1802, probably named from the lost chapel or hermitage of St John, *v.* Sherborne Churches and Chapels *supra*; the fields lay S of R. Yeo at about ST 645164); Stile Cl (1614, 1677, 1802, cf. Walter *atte Style* 1459, 1461, *Stile acre* 1614, *v.* **stigel** 'a stile', **atte** 'at the'); Stokeham 1870 (*Slocombe* (*bottom*) (sic) 1614, *Stocoomb* 1733, *v.* **cumb**, first el. probably **stocc** 'tree-trunk', cf. *forlango vocat' Stok* 1454 (perhaps a Latinization of *Stokfurlong*) which may be from the same el. rather than **stoc** 'place')); Thorne's Orchd 1849 (cf. Thomas *Thorne* 1614); Troy Town 1802 (on Westbury street at ST 637163, *v.* **troy town** 'a maze'); Vicar's Gdn 1802; Vowells (4 Acres) 1849 (cf. Richard *Fowell* 1436, William *Vowel* 1553); Watts or Field Walls 1849 (*Wats* 1733, cf. Thomas *Watts* 1664, *v.* Field Walls *supra*); Westbury Cl 1849 (from Westbury *supra*); tenement called Wests 1849 (cf. Walter *West* 1327 (Castleton)); Withey-, Withye Bed (cf. *claus' voc' Withehey* 1448, *Wytheheye* 15, *le Wethibere* 1461, *v.* **wīðig** 'willow', **(ge)hæg, bearu**).

(b) the backeside 1614 (v. **backside**); Barnenplace 1531; Bartons Tenement 1677 (a surname); Bedwell', Bedwelmede 1538 (v. **well(a)**, **mǣd**, first el. probably **byden** 'a vessel'); Bemynstretenement in la Nywlond' 1464 (cf. mes' qua' Thomas Bemynstr' nup' tenuit 1464, v. **tenement**, Newland supra); Blakelond 1427, Blackelond 1538, (The farther) Black(e)land(e)(s) 1600, 1614, 1677 (v. **blæc, land**); close called Board Land alias Overland 1677 (v. **bord-land, uferra**); Bold(e)mede 1454 (first el. possibly a surname, v. **mǣd**); prat' voc' les Borgh's 1427, prat' voc' Barowys 1538 (probably referring to the same meadow, from either **burg** 'a burrow' or **beorg** 'a barrow'); Botmede 1375–88 (possibly **bōt** 'help, advantage'); Boulemede 1525 (first el. perhaps **bula** 'bull'); Bowland(e) 1590, 1614 (v. **boga** 'arch', cf. the building called la Bowe supra); Boxhyll' 1499 (v. **box, hyll**); Bradfyld 1525 (v. **brād**); Brerdesfold 1427 (v. **fald**, first el. possibly **brerd** 'border, hill-side'); Brodemede 1538 (v. **brād**); la/le Brodeston(e) 1427, 1487², 1601 (fontem voc'-), Brod(e)stone 16 (cursum aque subtus-), 1531, 1538 (v. **brād, stān**; Brodingeston 1227 and Brodsen 1375–88 may also belong here); Bydelhill' 1459 (v. **bydel** 'a beadle', or a surname); (crofto voc') Cadenham 1427, 1454, 1461 (brode-), 1464 (Litil-, Mochill'-), 1471, Cadenhamesmede 1454, claus' voc' Cadenhampmes 1461, -hammes 1464, Cadnam' 1548, 1574 ('Cada's enclosure or river-meadow', from the OE pers.n. Cada and **hamm**, with **mǣd, brād, lȳtel, mycel**, cf. Cadenham W 87, Cadnam Ha (DEPN), and foll.; bosco de Cadoham 1258 For may also belong here); (closes called) Cadwell 1614, 1677 (v. **well(a)**, probably with the same first el. as prec., cf. Cadwell O 121); Caples Land (a surname); Cheselyngfurlong 1427 (v. **furlang**, first el. possibly **cisel** 'gravel' with -**en²** or -**ing²** suffix); Claypyttes 1531, (land called) Cleypitt(e)s 1614, 1677 (v. **clæg, pytt**); Cloudes 1525; Cootehous' 1464², Coate Acre 1677 (probably from **cot** 'cottage', but cf. ten' nuper' Alicie Cote 1454); Cosbere 1525; Courtham 1531 (v. **court, hamm**); Crundle- 1600, Crundell Bottom 1614, Crundle 1733 (v. **crundel** 'pit, quarry'); forlango vocat' Decombe 1454 (v. **cumb**); Derewell' 1538 (v. **dēor, well(a)**); Dolemeade 1614 (v. **dāl**); Dotleng 1228; Downe Crafte 1525 (v. **dūn, croft**); le Dungehill' 1460 (v. **dunghill**); (the) E(a)st(e)field(e) 1600, 1614, the East feild 1677 (v. **ēast, lǣs**); Estlondes 1525 (v. **land**); atte Ewelme (p) 1327, atte Ewolme (p) 1332 ('at the river-spring', v. **atte, ǣwelm, ǣwielm**; this local surname is perhaps to be associated with the st.n. Newell supra, since ME atten ewelme may have produced a form Newelme, later rationalized as containing **nīwe** 'new', through metanalysis, cf. Newell KPN 84); Fitonsplace 1487³ (a surname); Fookes Close 1677 (cf. Two cottages . . . formerly Fookes 1677); (the Orchard or) Fosters Close 1677 (cf. 2 cottages . . . heretofore Fosters 1677, Richard Foster 1614, Foster's School supra); (la) Frythe 1476, 1477 (v. **fyrhð** 'wood'); Furlongs 1733; Furs(e)hill' 1566², 1569 (v. **fyrs, hyll**); Gavel- 1427, Gaulemede 1538 (v. **gafol²** 'tax, rent', **mǣd**); (cultura voc') la Gore 1427 (v. **gāra**); Graffardesmor' 1427, Graffordmore 1538, Graffers Moore 1600, 1614 (from the surname Graffard (v. Reaney s.n. Graff) and **mōr**); Greberdes Busshe 1590 (a surname with **busc**); Greneclose 1614;

Halewell' 1427, *Holi(e)well* (*Gate*) 1600, *Hol(l)owell* 1614 ('holy spring or stream', *v.* **hālig, well(a)**, cf. Holwell 1 240); *prat' voc' les Hampmes* 1427, *le Hamps* 1538, *Hammes* 1614 (*v.* **hamm** 'enclosure, river-meadow'); *Ham(p)don'* 1440, 1441, 1455 (*v.* **dūn** 'hill, down', first el. possibly wk.obl. case *hēan* of **hēah** 'high'); *Hamondys* 1539, *Hamondes wood* 1614 (a surname); *the harpe like peace lienge under Yevell Waie* 1600 (*v.* **hearpe**, Yeovil Rd *supra*); *Heincomb Woods* 1641; *la Hemphey* 1427 (*v.* **hænep, (ge)hæg**); *Henyman' a Preny* 1508, *terr' vocat' Honymanmy Prenny* 1538, *tenement(e) called Hynny Mynnye Prynnye* 1614, *Hinny-minny-prinny* 1677 (perhaps a manorial name, from *Henyman* (a diminutive of the pet-form *Hen* < *Henry* + *man*) or *Honeyman ap* (Welsh 'son of') *Rennie* (a pet-form of *Reynold*), with subsequent modification through rhyming, cf. Reaney s.nn. **Henn, Honeyman, Rennie,** and Robert *Honyman* 1327 (Oborne), John *Prany* 1327 (Yetminster));*Hides* 1677 (probably a surname); *Hind(e)s* 1677 (cf. *ten' Willelmi Hyne* 1459); *close of pasture or Sheep Sleight called Hogshill* 1677 (*v.* **slæget, hogg** 'young sheep'); *Hokemede* 1525 (*v.* **hōc** 'angle, bend', **mæd**); *la Humber'* 1484 (apparently the pre-English stream-name *Humber*); *Iver Mead, -Wood* 1539 (*v.* **yfer** 'the edge or brow of a hill'); *Kyngesmore* 1563 (*v.* **mōr**, cf. *Cottage . . . late Mr Kings* 1677); *in la Lane* (p) 1327, 1340, *in the lane* (p) 1332 (*v.* **lane**); *Langcrofte* 1525 (*v.* **lang**[1], **croft**); *Lang(e)don(e)* 1375, 1395, 1538 (*v.* **dūn**); *Lygheplace* 1538 (first el. probably a surname from one of the places called Leigh); *Lynes, Lynys* 1455, *lez laynez* 1525 (*v.* **leyne** 'tract of arable land'); *Mabell Closes* 1677 (a pers.n. or surname); *the Meade* 1600, 1677, *Meadclose* 1614, *Meadestile* 1600 (*v.* **mæd, stigel**); *la/le Mere* (*iuxta Crucem*) 1468–88, *Meermede* 1525 (*v.* **mere**[1] '.pool'); *ten' voc Milmouthes, -is* 1455, *Melmouthes(ten't)* 1459, 1476, 1488, *mes' voc' (le) Mildemouthes, -is* 1461, 1464, 1465, *Meldemouthis* 1464 (cf. *tenement nuper Johannis Melmouthe in Longestrete* 1477, *v.* Long St. *supra*); *Mirr(e)-, Myrr(e)meade* 1614, 1677 (first el. possibly **mire** 'mire, bog');.*Molewudcombe* 1538 (*v.* **wudu, cumb**, first el. possibly **mole** 'a mole'); *Mouse-* 1538, *Mowshill* 1614 (*v.* **mūs**); *atte Nasshe* (p) 15[2] ('at the ash-tree', *v.* **atten, æsc**); *(the) New(e)close* 1600, 1614; *Northcumb(e)* 1288 *Ass* (*v.* **norð, cumb**); *campo boriali* 1454, *the North(e)field(e)* 1600, 1614; *Oldelond* 1454 (*v.* **(e)ald, land**); *la Paskarie* 1427 (perhaps for **piscary** 'a fishery'); *(cursus aque apud) Popwellake* 1525, 1563, 1614 (*v.* **lacu**, first el. probably **popel** 'pebble'); *Pyglonddes* 1538 (*v.* **pigga, land**); *de la Pyle* (p) 1324, *atte Pyle* (p) 1327, 1344 (*v.* **atte, pīl** 'a pile, a stake'); *two plottes called the Pyne being used for a waie* 1614, *the Pine* 1677 (probably **pīn** 'pine-tree'); *Pynteldirne, -dyrne* 1454 (the first el. is **pintel** 'penis', perhaps used in some figurative topographical sense, cf. *le Pyntyll'* L (EPNS **58** 186); the second el. is **dierne** 'hidden', here used substantively of a hidden place); *Pyryhille* 1466, *Peryhylle* 1491 (cf. Richard- 1327, William *atte Purye* 1410, *v.* **pirige, pyrige** 'a pear-tree', **hyll, atte**); *Pytbroke* 1563 (*v.* **pytt, brōc**); *Radwell* 1629 (*v.* **rēad** 'red', **well(a)**)); *Redlake* 1538, *Redd' Lake* 1598 (*v.* **lacu**, first el. **rēad** 'red' or **hrēod** 'reed')); *Roufold* 1614 (*v.* **rūh** 'rough', **fald**); *Sergers Meade* 1614, 1677 (a surname); *Sextens Mede* 1516, 1525, *Sextons Meade* 1601[2], 1677 (*v.*

secrestein 'a sexton', or a surname); *prat' voc' Sherlehamps* 1525, *Charles Hammes* 1569–74, 1614, -*Hams* 1677 (*v.* **hamm**; *Charles* seems to be a rationalization of an earlier form which may be a p.n. 'bright wood or clearing' from **scīr** and **lēah**); *Sherbourn Commen* 1569–74; *campo de Shirbourn(e)* 1349, 1464; *Shittles* 1614, 1677 (possibly **scyt(t)el(s)** 'a gate which bolts shut', or a surname); *Shorthey* 1538 (*v.* **sc(e)ort, (ge)hæg**); *Sourehams, Sowrehamps* 1538 (*v.* **sūr** 'sour', **hamm**); *Sparke Meade* 1677 (*v.* **spearca** 'brushwood'); *Spurles meade* 1617 (a surname); *Squybbes* 1538 (a surname); *Standemorefurlong* 1454 (*v.* **stān, mōr, furlang**); *Stanlynche* 1474 (*v.* **stān, hlinc**); *atte Stone* (p) 1327 (*v.* **atte, stān**); *la Thornylese* 1427 (*v.* **þornig, lǣs**); *a three cornerde close* 1600; *the great-, the litle trenches* 1600, *(meadow in) (the) Trenches* 1614 (*v.* **trenche**); *Tristrams* 1614 (a surname); *Welplace* 1538, *Wellplaces* 1614, 1677, *Wellclose* 1630 (cf. *Walter atte Welle* 1347, *v.* **well(a), atte**, cf. the st.n. *Newell supra*); *Welsh-* 1600, 1677, *Walchwood* 1614 (probably the surname *Welsh* or *Walsh*); *Welteswurthe* 1538 (*v.* **worð** 'enclosure', first el. probably a pers.n., cf. EPN s.v. **w(e)alt**); *in campo occidentali* 1427, *the West(e)field(e)* 1600, 1614, *the West Feild* 1677; *Westgardon'* 1531 (*v.* **gardin**); *West(e)more* 1454, 1525, 1538 (*v.* **mōr**); *Whynnysmyll'* (probably for -*wyll'*) 1466[2], *Wynneswell'* 1477, *Whynnes Well'* 16, *Wines-* 1614, *Wyneswell* 1677 (*v.* **well(a)** 'spring, stream', first el. probably the surname *Wynn(e)*); *atte Wode* (p) 1332 (*v.* **atte, wudu**); *the/le Woodbarton* 1593, 1601, 1627 (*v.* **barton**); *furlango vocat' la North-, la Southwrendell'* 1427 (origin uncertain); *Wygrymesplace* m15 (cf. *mes' . . . nuper Willelmi Wygrym* 1453).

Thornford

THORNFORD (ST 603133) ['ðɑːʀnvərd]
> *ðornford, Torneford* (rubric) 903 for 946–51 (12) *SherC* (S 516), *þorford* 998 (12) *ib* (S 895)
> *Torneford* 1086 DB, 1212 P, 1125 (12), 1145 (12) *SherC*
> *Thorneford(e)* 1163 Dugd, 1249 FF, 1288 *Ass*, 1316 FA *et freq* to c.1500 *Eg*, -*fford* 1531 *Digby*, *Thornford(')* 1249 FF, 1268, 1280 *Ass*, 1285 FA, 1288 *Ass*, 1290 Ch *et passim*
> *Thurneford'* 1420 *Weld*[1]

'Ford where thorn-trees grow', *v.* **þorn, ford**; the *Thurne-* spelling represents the related **þyrne** 'thorn-bush'. The site of the original ford may have been where Bembury Lane crosses R. Yeo, N of the present village. The bounds of the

Anglo-Saxon estate of Thornford, dated 903 for 946–51 (12), are given in *SherC* (S 516).

BEMBURY LANE. BLACKSMITH'S LANE, cf. the f.n. Ridgeway *infra*. BOOT LANE, named from *The Boot Inn* 1849 *TA*. CALF'S HORN LANE, alongside fields called *Calves Horn* (*or Hr Horn*), *Slope Horn or Soap Ho* 1849 *TA*; named from the sharp bend in the lane, or from the bend in the stream alongside the fields, *v.* **horn**. COURT HO DAIRY, *-Fm* 1811 OS, *cotagiu' vocat' Cowtehouse, -howse* 1563, *tenement' vocat' Courte howse* 1575, *Cote howse* 1583 all *Digby*, first el. apparently **cot** 'cottage' later replaced by **court** 'large house' (for this substitution cf. PN Brk 860), *v.* **hūs**. GAUL HILL, (*Lt*) *Gall Hill* 1849 *TA*, *v.* **g(e)alla** 'wet or barren spot in a field'; two small streams meet here. GLEBE CTG. GREEN LANE. HORSEPOOL LANE, *Horspole lane* 1563 *Digby*, named from *claus' vocat' Horsepole*, (*Wodcrofte alias*) *Horspole* 1563 *ib*, *Gt Horse Pool* 1849 *TA*, *v.* **hors**, **pōl**, **wudu**, **croft**; in the last-named field there are still traces of the pool (B.K.), this being the feature referred to in the Anglo-Saxon bounds of Thornford as *on merc* 903 for 946–51 (12) *SherC* (S 516) (corrected to *on mere* in BCS 894), 'to the pool', *v.* **mere**[1]. KING'S RD, cf. *terr' Thome Kyng* 1563 *Digby*. LAKE COPSE & FM (1811 OS), cf. *claus' apud-, claus' vocat' Lake* 1563 *Digby*, and nearby fields called (*Gt & Lt*) *Lake* 1849 *TA*, *v.* **lacu** 'stream', with reference to an affluent of R. Yeo; in spite of Fägersten 221, this name is not to be connected with either of the *andlang lace* boundary marks of the Bradford A. charter, *v.* Forsberg 6. LONGFORD BRIDGE, 1791 Boswell. MANOR FM. MIDDLE FM. PITMAN'S LEAZE, cf. *Pitmans Orchd* 1849 *TA*, Thomas *Pytman* 1563 *Digby* (Nthr Compton), *v.* **lǣs** 'pasture'. PYT HO. RATCOMBE BARN & WD, cf. *Ratcombe or Lye Hill* (*Md*), *Lt Ratcombe, Ratcombe Coppice, Md & Plant.* 1849 *TA*, *v.* **cumb**; first el. may be **ræt** 'rat', but perhaps **rōt** 'cheerful' if the form *ffotcombe* (*ff* written over some other letter, possibly *R-*) 1583 *Digby* belongs here, cf. the nearby fields called Heaven and Mount Pleasant; for these and Lye Hill (Md), *v.* f.ns. *infra*. RECTORY, cf. *Parsonage Hill & Md(w)* 1849 *TA*. ST MARY MAGDALENE'S CHURCH, cf. *Thorneford cum capella* 1163 Dugd. THORNFORD

HILL PLANT. THORNFORD HO. WAVERLAWNS, a house named from *Weyfurlong'* 1563 *Digby*, *Weave(r)lands* 1843, 1849 *TA*, *v.* **weg, furlang**; the *TA* field lies beside the road to Sherborne. WHITE HILL WD.

FIELD-NAMES

The undated forms in (*a*) are 1849 *TA* 225. Spellings dated 903 for 946–51 (12) are *SherC* (S 516). Those dated 1317 are FF, 1327 *SR*, 1544 Hutch³, 1569–74 *Map*, 1664 HTax, 1843 *TA*, and the rest are *Digby*.

(*a*) Amery 1843, Amory (*Amerey close, -landes, -Wood'* 1563, perhaps from the surname *Amery* (recorded as *Ammory* in 1332 SR though not from this Hundred), but a p.n. from **amore** 'a bird, perhaps the yellow hammer' and **īeg** 'island, well-watered land' is also possible; it is in any case of interest that this field is listed as *Yellow Hammer* in 1974 WI; it is a level field by R. Yeo subject to waterlogging (B.K.)); Backside Mdw & Orchd (*claus'-, curtill' vocat' le Backeside, -syde* 1563, *v.* **backside**); Balshams; Barn Md; Bayland (freq), Gt & Parsonage Bayland, Bayland Md, Baylands, Hibberts Ballands 1843 (first el. uncertain, but possibly ME **baie** 'berry' or ModE **bay²** 'embankment to form a dam'; the fields lie beside a small stream, an affluent of R. Yeo); Bencroft (*v.* **bēan, croft**); (Lt) Benjays Md; Bindells 1843, Bindles; Bishops Bridge (*pons voc' Bysshopysbrygge* 1460, *Bysshoppys-* 1516, *Busshopesbryge* 1531, (*claus' vocat*) *Buysshop(p)es Bridge* 1563 (*v.* **brycg**, first el. **biscop** 'bishop' or perhaps a surname, cf. John *Bysshoppe* 1460; the bridge is where the road to Yetminster crosses a small affluent of R. Yeo); Black Pool Culture (*v.* Culter *infra*); Bottom (*v.* **botm**); Bristland (possibly **(ge)byrst¹, -brist** 'a crack in the soil, a landslip'); Broadhams (Orchd) (cf. *Thorneford' Ham'* 1563, *v.* **hamm**); Bub Hills (*Bobehill* 1564, *v.* **hyll**, first el. possibly the OE pers.n. *Bob(b)a* for which *v.* Redin 85); Butts (Mdw) (*claus' terr' iuxta le Buttes* 1563, *v.* **butt²** or **butte**); Calves Plot; Coppice; Cow leaze; Cribhouse Fd (*v.* cribhouse); Croft (*v.* **croft**); Crooked Mdw; Culter 1843, (Lt & Gt) Culture, Culture Md & Orchd (*claus' vocat' Culter* 1563, hardly so called from a fancied resemblance to a coulter (*v.* **culter**), perhaps rather ME **culture**, an anglicized form of MedLat *cultura* 'piece of cultivated land, furlong', *v.* B. Kerr, DoNHAS **89** 236); Custards Croft 1843; Dales 1843; Dodge Grd; Dolls Md; Dools; Drove; Dry Grd 1843; 8 Acres (or Longlands); 11 Acres; 5 Acres; 4 Acres (Md); Fox Wd; Fudges Lease (*v.* **lǣs**); Gauze- 1843, Gause Hill; Gores; Great Md; Lt, Middle & Hr Hale, Hale Coppice (probably from **healh**, here with the meaning 'nook of land in the corner of a parish'; for the form *Hale* rather than *Hyle*, unusual in Do, cf. **2** 250 and PN D 47, 640; the name is recorded as *Hell* in 1974 WI, perhaps a popular etymology on the analogy of Heaven *infra*); Hannams Md; Haycroft, Elm Hay Croft (*Haycrafte, -crofte* 1563, *v.* **hēg, croft**; recorded as *Haycrat* in 1974 WI); Heaven (no doubt a complimentary name for productive land or a pleasant spot, cf. PN Brk

283; it is perhaps worth noting that the fields so named, like Mount Pleasant *infra*, lie close to Ratcombe *supra*); Hodges Leaze; Hollow Drove; Holly's Md; Home Fd, Grd & Hill (cf. *Homecloses* 1563); Honeycombe (from Honeycomb in Castleton par. *supra*); Honey Cl; Ivey- 1843, Ivy Md(w); Ivy Wd; Jacobs; Gt & Long Lains, Lr Lains (or Lains four Closes) (*claus' pastur' vocat' le leyne* 1563, *Laine* 1583, *v.* **leyne** 'tract of arable land'); Lambrooks Md (alongside a stream); Gt Levedges 1843, Gt Learges; Lever Beds (*v.* **lǣfer** 'rush'); Ley (freq), Lye 1843 ((*claus' vocat'*) *Lye* 1563, 1575, *Lygh'* 1583, *Estelighe-, Westlygheclose* 1563, cf. Henry *de Legh* 1317, *v.* **lēah** 'wood, glade or clearing in a wood'); (Gt) Ley Hill, Long Leigh Hill, Lye Hill (Md) (*Lyhyll', le(y) Hyll'* 1563, *le Hilles* 1583, *v.* **lēah** (cf. prec.), **hyll**); Little Bay (near to Millditch, etc *infra*, possibly from **bay**[2] 'embankment to form a dam'); Little Gdn, Grd, Md & Orchd; (Lt) Long Down (*claus' vocat' Langdowne* 1563, *v.* **lang**[1], **dūn**); Longlands; Long Md; Long Whale (*claus' apud Langwale* 1563, *v.* **walu** 'ridge'); Lower Croft; Meadow; Mendip; Middle Croft; Millditch (Mdw), Millers Md (Hill), Millers Hills, Mill Hills (a group of fields near where Bembury Lane crosses R. Yeo at ST 603138, cf. also Little Bay *supra*; there is mention of a mill at Thornford in 1086 DB (VCHDo **3** 71), cf. also *unum molendinum aquaticum* 1473, 1563; the present fields suggest the possibility of a diversion of R. Yeo to provide a mill stream (B.K.)); Morston (Orchd), Moxton Orchd 1845 *EnclA* (*Mor(e)ston', Mor(e)stons lane* 1563); Mount Pleasant (a complimentary name, cf. Ratcombe and the f.n. Heaven *supra*); (Gt & Lt) Mythe (where the stream that gives name to Trill in Beer H. par. *supra* meets R. Yeo, *v.* **(ge)mȳðe** 'a confluence of rivers'); New Cl (*New(e)close* 1563); New Croft; Night Pool (a field alongside the meandering R. Yeo, probably from a ME *atten yte* 'at the small island', *v.* **atten, īegeð**); 9 Acres; Orchard; Paddock; (Gt) Park, Park Laine, Park Lains or Lains Md, Park Md (*claus' vocat' Parkeridge* 1563, *fossat' inter' Parkeleyne et le Parke* 1564, *v.* **park**, cf. Lains *supra* and Ridge *infra*; on the possibility of an early deer-park here, *v.* Wilson, DoNHAS **98** 10); Plantation; Plot; Potkins Md (*terr' Radulfi Potkyn'* 1563); Quakers Hill; (Three Corner) Ridge, Rudge 1843 (*claus' vocat' Rydge* 1563, *Thornforde ridge* 1569–74, *Ridge* 1575, to be identified with *up to hricgge, andlang hrigcges* 903 for 946–51 (12) in the Anglo-Saxon bounds of Thornford, where **hrycg** 'ridge, long narrow hill' refers to Lillington Hill (in Lillington par. *supra*) which forms the SE boundary of the par.); Ridgeway (Orchd), Inner & Outer Ridgeway 1849 *EnclA* (probably named from the lane, now called Blacksmith's Lane, leading from Ridge *supra* to the village); (Lt) Round Hill; (Hedge or) 7 Acres; Hr & Lr Sharland Head or Millditch (Mdw) (*v.* Millditch *supra*); Side Hill; 6 Acres; Snardshill 1843, Stewards Hill (called *Stuarts Hill* 1974 WI, which suggests the 1843 form is an error); Spring Cl (Hill); Stockland(s) (cf. *Stock(e)furlong* 1563, *v.* **stocc** 'tree stump'); Stone Hill; Sweetnaps; Three Corners; Tucks Ley & Orchd (cf. *terr' Tristrami Tucke* 1563, George *Tuck* 1664); Uphill (Orchd), Uphills 1843; Well Cl; Winshard (Mdw) (*claus' vocat' W(e)yneshard(e)* 1563, 'gap fit for a wagon', *v.* **wægn, sceard**; the field is in a dip crossed by the road to Sherborne); Woolfarms (a group of fields where a stream rises, no doubt from **wiell(a)** 'spring, stream' as in Wool par. 1 188); Woollands (*Wollands* 1575, also beside a stream, cf. prec.); Yonder Acres & Croft.

(b) *claus' vocat' Barefurlong, -land* 1563 (probably **bær**[1] 'bare, without vegetation', with **furlang, land**); *claus' voc' Bradon', (Lytell') Brodon'* 1563, *Brodden'* 1575 (v. **brād, dūn**); *claus' vocat' Brecheland'* 1563 (v. **bræc** 'land broken up for cultivation'); *Cleypittes, -pyttes* 1563 (v. **clæg, pytt**); *be ecge* 903 for 946–51 (12) (v. **ecg** 'edge, escarpment'); *Fornends lanes* 1575; *Goswells lane* 1575 (v. **gōs** 'goose'); *þone eastemestan holan weg* 903 for 946–51 (12) ('the eastmost hollow way', v. **ēastmest, hol**[2], **weg**); *ð lace* 903 for 946–51 (12) (v. **lacu** 'stream', referring to a tributary of R. Yeo about ½ mile NE of the stream which gives name to Lake Fm *supra*); *on lyngaerstun easte werdne* 903 for 946–51 (12) ('flax enclosure', v. **līn, gærs-tūn**); *mylenburnna* 903 for 946–51 (12) (discussed under Bedmill in Castleton par. *supra*); *Morecrafte, -crofte* 1563 (v. **mōr, croft**); *le Out howse* 1583 (v. **ūt(e)**); *Poundfoldes Hamme* 1563 (v. **hamm**, cf. *Joh' Poundfold' de Thornford'* 1516); *Pudley Hill'* 1563; *oð-, of ran wylle* 903 for 946–51 (12) ('spring or stream by a boundary strip', v. **rān, wiell(a)**); *Raynoldes Crofte* 1563; *le Strowhouse* 1563 (v. **strēaw** 'straw'); *on slaep* 903 for 946–51 (12) (cf. *fossat' uersus Shlapewell'* 1563, probably **slæp** 'mud, mire, marsh' (v. Löfvenberg 189) rather than **slæp** 'slippery muddy place', with **well(a)** 'spring, stream'; the boundary point is incorrectly transcribed *on slæw* in BCS 894); *atte Touneseynde* 1327 (p) (v. **atte, toun, ende**); *West Lease land* 1544 (v. **læs** 'pasture'); *Westmore* 1531 (v. **mōr**).

North Wootton

NORTH WOOTTON (ST 655148)

> *Wotton(')* c.1180 Sarum, 1285 FA, 1288 *Ass*, 1294 Ch *et freq* to 1617 *Pitt*, *Wuttun'* 1226 Cur, *W(o)tton(e)*, *W(o)ttune* 1228 Sarum, *Wottoune* 1491 Digby, *Wutton'* 1516, 1538, 1563 *ib*, 1590 *Salis*, *Wotten* 1593 *Batten*, *Wootton* 1614, 1617 *Pitt*
>
> *Wotton Episcopi* 1316 FA, 1383 FF, 1412 FA, *Wotton Bishops* 1393 FF
>
> *North(e) Wotton* 1569–74 *Map*, 1575 Saxton, *North Wotten* 1664 HTax, *North Wooton* 1811 OS

'Farm in or near a wood', v. **wudu, tūn**, one of the three Do pars. so named. The earlier affix is from the possession of this manor by the bishops of Salisbury, v. **episcopus, biscop**. *North* is in relation to Wootton Glanville par. *supra*.

CLOTFURLONG LANE, cf. *Clotfurlongyate* 1484, *portam apud Clotfurlong* 1531 Digby, *Clatfurlongate* 1569–74 *Map, Clodvill Land* 1811 OS, *v.* **furlang, geat**; the first el. is possibly **clott** 'lump of earth, clod', but alternatively it may be a shortened form of the surname of William *Cloter* 1484 *Digby*, who occurs in the same document as the first form.

GREEN LANE (COPPICE). ST MARY MAGDALENE'S CHURCH. SNAGHARBOUR WD, perhaps from **here-beorg** 'shelter' with **snag** 'tree stump' or Do dial. **snag** 'sloe'. THREE ELMS INN, cf. *iiij*ᵒʳ *Elmys* 1531 *Digby, iiij elme crosse* 1569–74 *Map, v.* **elm, cross**. NORTH WOOTTON COPSE, cf. *Wootton Wd* 1844 *TA*. NORTH WOOTTON FM, *the Farme of Wotton* 1614, *Wotton Farme* 1677 *Digby*. NORTH WOOTTON LODGE.

FIELD-NAMES

The undated forms in (*a*) are 1844 *TA* 264. Spellings dated 1569–74 are *Map*, 1870 Hutch³, the rest are *Digby*.

(*a*) Folke Stile (named from Folke par. *supra, v.* **stigel**); Haydon Cl (named from Haydon par. *supra*); Hole Ditch (*Holditch* 1614, *v.* **hol²** 'hollow', **dīc**); the Hot Spring 1870 (cf. *Watersheete infra*); Moor ((*the*) *Moore* 1614, *v.* **mōr**); Quar Cl (*Quarreclose* 1614, *v.* **quarre**); Rocketts; Yonder Fd.

(*b*) *Beaneclose* 1614 (*v.* **bēan**); *Beshypw* . . . 1484 (*v.* **biscop**; final part of name illegible, probably *-wode, v.* **wudu**); (*West*)*braylondes* 1538, 1558, *Brai-, Braylandes* 1614 (the first el. is probably the ME surname *Bray* (freq in the Do Subsidy Rolls of 1327 and 1332, though not in this hundred), cf. Braylands Brk 295 (not explained) and Bray ib 43 (explained as from OFr **bray(e)** 'mud')); *Bullockeley* 1614 (*v.* **bulluc, lēah**); *Buttclose*, ½ *acre at Buttes* 1614 (*v.* **butt²** or **butte**); *Castelwey* 1487 (probably leading to Sherborne Castle in Castleton par. *supra, v.* **castel(l)**); *Cleyhill* 1614 (*v.* **clæg**); *Combes doore* 1614 (*v.* **duru**, cf. John *Combe* 1614); *Corneclose* 1614 (*v.* **corn¹**); *Dokle* 15, *Dokley(s)yate* 1473, 1484, *Dockleysehegge* 1531, (*greate-, litle*) *Dockley* 1614 (probably from **docce** 'dock', with **lēah** and **gēat**); *Elstopyate* 1558, *Estubb yate, Eastubbfurlonge* 1614 (probably 'elder stump', from **elle(r)n** and **stubb** with **geat, furlang**); *E(a)stfield* 1614; *Estfurlonge* 1614 (*v.* **ēast**); *close called Floteshorte* 1614 (the first el. may be the el. **flote** suggested for *Floteham* 1 372, the second could be a substantival use of **sc(e)ort** 'short', although the derivative **scyrte** 'short piece of land' (according to EPN 2 108 found only in K) is also possible); *Gorley* 1614 (*v.* **lēah**; first el. **gor** 'dirt' or **gāra** 'triangular plot'); *Half Acre* 1614; *Hallclose, -meade, -peece* 1614 (*v.* **hall**); *bosco de Ha'me* 1258 *For, Hamme* 1614 (*v.* **hamm**);

Haukeford' 1491, *Haukesford Bryge, Hauckfordlane* 1531, *Hakefordebridge* 1569–74, *Hawkeforde* 1614 (first el. probably **hafoc** 'hawk', with **ford, brycg, lane**); *Hill'* 1558 (*v.* **hyll**); *the Homeclose* 1614; *Kesford furlonge* 1614; *Longley* 1614 (*v.* **lēah**); Maberhill 1614; *Moresplace* 1558 (a surname, with **place**); *Myllmeade* 1614 (*v.* **myln**); *Neweclose, -meade (ende)* 1614; *Upper Papels* 1614 (reading doubtful); *Parkfeilde, the Parkefield, Parkewall* 1614 (probably named with reference to Sherborne Park in Castleton par. *supra*, cf. also *clausum Johannis Parker* 1516); *Pesehull'* 1538 (*v.* **pise** 'pease', **hyll**); *Plasshet(t) Meade* 1614 (*v.* **plaschiet** 'marshy pool'); *Prinscott* 1614 (*v.* **cot**); *Priors Hedlande* 1614 (*v.* **hēafod-land**); *Pucksey* 1614 (perhaps analogous with Puxy 1 203); *Pyttes* 1614 (a surname or **pytt** 'pit'); *close called Quyntine* 1614 (perhaps from **quintaine** 'a post set up to be tilted at', cf. Quince Hill 1 39); *the South-, the Sowthfield* 1614; *Speryngges* 1538 (a surname); *Stonielande* 1614 (*v.* **stānig**); *Stro(w)de* 1614 (*v.* **strōd** 'marshy land overgrown with brushwood'); *Townesende* 1614 (*v.* **toun, ende**); *Uppfurlong* 1614 (*v.* **upp**); *Watersheete* 1614 (probably 'place where water shoots forth, i.e. a river-spring', and therefore analogous with Watershute D 104 which Löfvenberg 187 derives from **wæter** and **scyte**); *(Ouer)weaverland(e)* 1614 (probably analogous with Waverlawns in Thornford par. *supra, v.* **uferra**); *(the) Westfield(e), Westfieldmeade* 1614; *Werber (meade)* 1614; *Westhey* 1538, *Westhaies* 1614 (*v.* **(ge)hæg**); *Whitlande* 1614 (*v.* **hwīt**); *Whorewaie* 1614 (*v.* **weg**, first el. probably **hār²** in the sense 'boundary'); *Withipittes* 1614 (*v.* **wīðig, pytt**); *Woodway* 1614; *Wotton Hill* 1569-74; *Wutton' Feld'* 1563; *Yonderhaie* 1614 (*v.* **(ge)hæg**).

PARISHES FORMERLY IN SOMERSET

Holwell, formerly a detached part of Somerset in Horethorne Hundred, was transferred to Dorset in 1844 (see note under Brownsall Hundred *supra*). Four other Somerset parishes formerly in Horethorne Hundred, Goathill, Poyntington, Sandford Orcas and Trent, were transferred to Dorset in 1896. Although these five parishes have been included here for the sake of completeness and convenience, the material so far available is inevitably not very full; it is to be expected that a more extensive treatment of the names will be possible when the survey of Somerset is complete. A sixth par. transferred from Somerset to Dorset, Seaborough, will be dealt with in the next Part of the Dorset survey.

Goathill

GOATHILL (ST 676172)
  Gatelme 1086 DB, *Ingatelma* Exon
  Gathulla 1176 P
  Cotehull (sic) 1234 Pat, *Cochull* (sic) 1254 Cl
  Gothull(e) 1254–6 DEPN, 1283 Banco (Drew), 1290 Ch,

1316 FA, 1320 Ipm, -*hill* 1284 Banco (Drew)
Gotehull 1487 Ipm, -*hill* 1495 ib, 1535 VE, 1575 Saxton
Gotylle 1569–74 *Map*

Probably self-explanatory, 'hill where goats are pastured', from **gāt** and **hyll** (so Fägersten 301 and DEPN). The DB form may be simply erratic (the Exon form in addition wrongly incorporating the preposition *in*), but it could suggest that the second el. was originally **helm** 'helmet', used in a figurative sense such as 'summit of a hill'.

GOATHILL FM. GOATHILL MILL, *gottyllsmyll* 1569–74 *Map*, *v.* **myln**. GOATHILL WD. ST PETER'S CHURCH.

FIELD-NAMES

The forms are taken from 1839 *TA* 30/202.
(*a*) Barn Mdw; Heamoors Bridge (cf. HIGHMORE'S HILL in the neighbouring par. of Milborne Port); Plot.

Holwell

HOLWELL (ST 699119) ['houlwel]
    Holewala 1188 P, -*wal*(*e*) 1194, 1195 P, 1196 ChancR, 1197, 1200, 1201 P, 1201 ChancR, 1207 PatR (-*in Blakemor*), 1210 P, 1210–12 RBE, 1212 Fees, 1216 ClR, Hy 3 (14) Cerne, 1225 FF, 1230 P, 1251 Misc (-*in Blakemore*), 1282–4 Ipm, 1288 *Ass*, 1291 Tax, 1305 FF, 1323, 1329 Pat, 1336 Ch, 1340 NI, 1368 *Hastings*, 1399 Pat, 1412 FA, 1425 *Weld*[1] (p), 1428, 1431 FA, *Holwayle* 1557 *Val*
    Holewella 1194, -*well*(') 1206, 1208–14 all P, 1239 FineR, 1242–3 Fees, 1268, 1280 (p) *Ass*, 1335 Pat, -*wil* 1258 For, *Holwell*(*e*) 1378 Cl, 1709 *WRO*
    Holewall(*e*) 1198, 1202–5 P, 1208 PatR (-*in Blakamor*), 1212 P (-*Roberti de Bikel*'), 1244, 1268 *Ass*, 1316 FA, *Hollwalle* 1569–74 *Map*, *Holwall* 1623 *DCMRent*
    Holeweia (sic) 1207 P

'Ridge or bank (of earth or stone) in a hollow', from **hol**[2] (wk.obl. *holan*) and **walu**; Ekwall DEPN suggests 'sunk hedge, ha-ha', pointing out that **walu** may also have been used of a fence or enclosure. There are several instances of the el. **walu** in medieval Do f.ns., note particularly the analogous 13th cent. f.n. *Holewal* in Motcombe par. *supra*. The spellings for the second el. show confusion with **w(i)ell(a)** 'spring, stream', **w(e)all** 'wall' and (probably a palaeographical error) **weg** 'road'. The 13th century forms *Blake-, Blakamor(e)* refer to Blackmoor Forest *supra*. The family of *de Bikele(i)a* held lands here between 1194 and 1230 P, e.g. William *de Bikelea* 1194, Huard *de Bikeleia* 1208 P.

BUCKSHAW HO (ST 688114), (HR) BUCKSHAW FM, LR BUCKSHAW

> *boscho de Buggechage* 1194, *bosco de Bug(g)ehag'* 1195 P, 1196 ChancR, 1197 P, *Bugge-, Bog(g)eshawe (Wod)* 1258 *For, Bogeshagh', Bogessbagh'* (for *-hagh'*), *Buggeshagh(e), -hathe* 1327 *SR* all (p), *Boggeshath', Boughessch'* 1332 SR both (p), *Bu(r)gheschawe* 1334 Cl, Ipm, *Bugeshagh'* 1342, *Buggeshathe* 1390 *Sher* both (p)
>
> *Buckshaw* 1335, 1465 Hutch[3], *Bukshawe* 1420, 1421, 1426 Cl, *Buckshawes* 1569–74 *Map, Buckshave* 1630 *Digby, Hr & Lr Buckshaw* 1811 OS, *Buckshaw Ho* 1839 *TA*

The second el. is **sc(e)aga** 'small wood, copse', the first is probably the OE fem. pers.n. *Bucge* although ME **bugge** 'boggart, hobgoblin' is also possible, cf. Bugley in Gillingham par. *supra*. Ekwall's view in DEPN, that in spite of the early *g*-spellings the first el. is probably **bucc** 'buck, male deer', looks less likely.

CORNFORD BRIDGE (ST 693121), CORNFORD HILL (FM), *Querneford* Hy 3 (14) Cerne, *corneforde bridge, -myll* 1569–74 *Map, Cornhill* [Bridge] 1791 Boswell, *Corn Ford* 1839 *TA*, 'ford by the mill', *v.* **cweorn, ford**, no doubt with reference to an early mill on the site of the 16th cent. mill documented above, cf. John *atte Forde* of *Holwelle* 1378 Cl. Quarnford St (DEPN) and *Cornford* Gl 1 35 are identical in origin. The form *Querneford* occurs in the bounds of Blackmoor Forest *supra*.

SANDHILLS (FM) (ST 687103), (*Boscum de*) *Sandhulle* Hy 3 (14) Cerne, *Sandhills* 1811 OS, cf. *Sandhill Cmn & Drove* 1839 *TA*, 'sandy hill', *v.* **sand**, **hyll**, cf. Sandley in Gillingham par. *supra*. The early form occurs in the bounds of Blackmoor Forest *supra*.

WOODBRIDGE (FM) (ST 712123), HR & LR WOOD BRIDGE, *Wudebrige* 1194 P, *la Wdebrigge* Hy 3 (14) Cerne, *la Wudebrug'* 1251 Cl, 1268 *Ass* both (p), (*la*) *Wodebrigg*(') 1256 FF (p), 1268 *Ass, ib* (p), (*atte*) *Wodebrugg'* 1258 *For* (p), (*la*) *Wudebrigg'* 1268 *Ass, ib* (p), *Woodebridge* 1569–74 *Map*, *Wood Bridge* (*Fm*) 1811 OS, probably 'the wooden bridge' rather than 'the bridge in or by a wood', *v.* **wudu**, **brycg**, cf. Woodbridge in Fontmell M. par. *supra*. The Sherborne-Sturminster N. road crosses Caundle Brook here.

BARNES CROSS, (*Lt*) *Barns Cross, Barn's Cross Fd* 1839 *TA*, cf. *Barns Md ib*, at a prominent cross-roads, from **cross** probably with a surname; the form *Baudewynes crosse* 1368 *Hastings* (first letter doubtful, but if correct, from the pers.n. or surname *Baldwin*) may belong here. THE BELT, *v.* **belt**. THE BOROUGH, near the village, cf. Hutch[3] **4** 520: 'the village itself is very small . . . but, for some reason or other, it has been immemorially dignified with the name of "Borough", or "Borough of Holwell"'. BUCKSHAW BRAKE, cf. *Buckshaw Cmn & Hill, Brake Md* 1839 *TA*, *v.* **bræc**[1], Buckshaw Ho *supra*. BULHAMS, *Bull Hams* 1839 *TA*, *v.* **bula**, **hamm**. COOMBE VILLA. COUNCIL COPSE. CROUCH HILL (FM), CROUCH LANE, *Crouch Hill* 1811 OS, *-Hill Close* 1839 *TA*, at the highest part of the par. (300'), probably from PrWelsh **crüg* 'hill'. DOLIVER'S FM, *Dollivers* (*3 acres*) 1839 *TA*, a surname. ELM TREE FM, cf. *Elm Grd* 1839 *TA*. FOX INN. GUNVILLE. THE HAZELS. HILL ST., 1811 OS, named from Crouch Hill *supra*, with **stræt** in the sense 'hamlet'. HOLWELL DROVE & (HILL) GORSE, *Holwell Drove, Drove Cl, Md & Plot* 1839 *TA*. LADYSMITH (a copse), no doubt commemorating the relief of Ladysmith (1900) in the Boer War. MANOR FM & PLANT. MANOR HO (*Holwell Ho* 1811 OS). NAISH FM, *Nash* 1811 OS, from ME *atten ashe* 'at the ash', *v.* **atten**, **æsc**, cf. *Ashmoor Fds* 1839 *TA*. NOWHERE, on the par. bdy, so called from its remoteness or because claimed by the neighbouring par. of Pulham. PACKERS BRIDGE (-*Bridge Cmn* 1839 *TA*) & HILL (1811 OS, -*Hill Corner* 1839 *TA*), a surname. PARADISE (a copse), 1839 *TA*, probably a complimentary name for a pleasant spot, *v.* **paradis**. PEACEFUL LANE, *Piercefield Lane & Mdw* 1839 *TA*, first el. probably the surname *Pierce*; an interesting example of popular etymology. PENNY'S FM, cf. *Pennys Grd* 1839 *TA*. LOWER & MIDDLE PICCADILLY, no doubt transferred from the London st.n. for which *v.* PN Mx 170. PLECK (GREEN), *Pleck Green* 1839 *TA, v.* **plek** 'small plot of ground'. POOLS CORNER, cf. *Pooles Cmn* 1839 *TA*. PROCTOR'S CTG. RECTORY, cf. *parsonage of Holwall* 1623 *DCMRent, Parsonage Ho* 1839 *TA*. ST LAWRENCE'S CHURCH, cf. *church of Holewale* 1399 Pat, *Church Croft & Md* 1839 *TA*. STONY LANE. THE STRIP, a narrow plantation, *v.* **strip**. WARRY'S PLANT. WATKINS'S FM, cf. Humphrey *Watkins* who held the manor of Holwell in the 18th cent. (Hutch[3] **4** 521). WESTROW CTGS & HO, *Westrow* 1811 OS, *v.* **rāw** 'row (of houses)'. WINDMILL HILL, 1811 OS. THE WITHIES, WITHY BED, cf. *Withy Bed* (*Little Md*), *Withy Md* 1839 *TA, v.* **wīðig** 'willow'. WOODBRIDGE COPSE, cf. *Woodbridge Md* 1839 *TA*, named from Woodbridge *supra*.

FIELD-NAMES

The undated forms in (*a*) are 1839 *TA* 30/223.

(*a*) Acre; Alders (*v.* **alor**); Antells Cmn; Ashes; Barn Md & Orchd; Bartons; Bean Cl & Fd; Black Bears; Beers Plot; Bennett Hill (perhaps **beonet** 'bent grass'); Beyond the Stream; Bind Leaze; Birds Fd; Blacksmiths Shop Grd; Bowling Green; Brandies; Brick Hill & Yd; Broad Md; Broad Oak Cmn; Brock Hill (probably **brocc** 'badger'); Brook Fd (cf. William *attebroc* 1258 *For, v.* **atte, brōc**); Brook Verland (probably **furlang**); Buckford (cf. Buckshaw *supra*); Burnt Ho Orchd; Burts Grd; Butlers Grd; Cadies Plot; Chapel Orchd (named from Wesleyan Chapel ib); Clever-, Clover Lds, Clover Md (*v.* **clǣfre** 'clover'); Coal Pits; Hthr & Yonder Coat (*v.* **cot** 'cottage'); Cock Road (*v.* **cocc-rodu**); (Bottom, Hr & Lr) Common; Common Cl & Pce, Common (Drove) Plot; Coombs Common (Cl) & Plot; Coppice (Cl); Corn Grd; Cowards Cmn; Cowleaze; Crib Md; Crockers Ham (*v.* **hamm**); Daisy Grd; Dogs Kennel; Dool; Downs; Downton's Cmn; Drakes Orchd; Dry Cl; Durents Plot; East Fd; 8 & 18 Acres; Ellford Md; Hr Ellsworth; Englishes Closes; Ewe Leaze; Farm Acre; 15 Acres; Fisherland; 5 Acres; Flaishet (*v.* **flasshett** 'place

characterised by swampy grassland'); Flat Pce; Flint Cl; 4 & 14 Acres;.
Frog Md; Front Md; Furze (Cmn); Furzy Grd; George; Gillingham Fd
and Ho; Grahams Cmn & Plot; Green Cl; (Furzy) Green Fd; Green Md;
Green Ways; Hammonds Hr & Lr Common; Hams Grd; Hardy's Md;
Hay Grass (probably **eegrass** 'aftermath'); Haywards Cmn & Md; Hibs
Croft (Md); Higher Md; Hill Cl; Hilly Grd; Holmes Plot (Cmn); Holwell
Ctg, Fd & Plant. (*v.* par. name *supra*); Home Cl, Grd & Md; Horse Cl
(Md) & Grd; (Clover) Inhams (*v.* **innōm** 'piece of land taken in or
enclosed'); Jemsys Plot; John's Croft; Jolly Boy; Kings Cmn; Kitchen Md;
Lake Md or Lr Bear Lawns; Landed Cl; Lane Barton and Waste;
Langhorns Cmn; Lawn; Little Md; Long Cl, Croft, Grd, Lds, Md &
Wood; Lot Md; Lower Md; Lydlinch Cl (named from Lydlinch par.
supra); Map Md; Marsh Md; Miles Lr Cmn; Millers Md; Moor Lane 6
Acres; Moor Md; Nap Grd; New Md; 9 Acres; (Furzy) North Fd, Lt
North Fd (Md); (Home) Orchard; Outer Md; Overs Fd; Paddock (Orchd);
Middle Panters; Peakhead Cl; Peddimore (5 & 7 Acres); Penhams Md;
Perrisses Plot; Pickets Closes; Pit Cl & Md; Poolhouse Md, Pool Ho
Orchd; Pound Cl; Quar Cl and Lime Kiln; Rape (probably with reference
to the crop); Raptey Md; Redlands; Road Cl; Rodmins; Rowden Mill Md
(named from Rowden Mill in S. Caundle par. *supra*); Rushy Md; Sawpit
Md (*v.* **saw-pit**); 7 Acres; Shortland(s); Shrubbery; 6 Acres; Smith Croft;
Sodom; South Fd & Flg; Spencers Md; Spicers Md; Standish's Plot;
Stounts; Strap (*v.* **strap**); Summer Leaze; Thick Thorn(e)s; Thornes
(Orchd); 3 Acres; 3 Corner Cl; Tizards; Trims Grd; Tulks Orchd & Plot;
12 Acres; Vetch Hams (*v.* **vetch, hamm**); Wall Croft; West Cl & Fd;
(Downtons) Whitelands (*v.* **hwīt**); Witches (*v.* **wice** 'wych-elm'); Wood
Cl & Md; Downtons, Morgans & Thornes Worthies (possibly **worðig**
'enclosure'); Wrenches Plot; Young Orchd & Plant.; Youngs 5, 4, 9 & 3
Acres.

(*b*) *de la Hele* (p) 1270 *For* (*v.* **h(e)alh**, WSax dat.sg. *hēale*);
Horstedesyete c.1325 *GlastE* (in the bounds of Buckland Newton Hd, from
geat 'gate' and a surname derived from Horste(a)d Nf, Sx, Kt); *le Whytok*
1323 Hutch[3] (*v.* **hwīt, āc**).

Poyntington

POYNTINGTON (ST 650199)
>   *Ponditone* 1086 DB, *-tona* Exon, *Pondintun(e)*, *-tone*
>   1091–1106, 1107–22, 1152–8 MontC
>   *Pundinton(e)* 1100–18 MontC, 1199 FF, 1254 Cl
>   *Puntintun(a)* 1100–22 (1270) Ch, 1135–7 MontC, *-ton(')*
>   1206 P, 1249 FF, *Puntington* 1258 ib, 1316 FA
>   *Puthintone* 1152–8 MontC
>   *Poncintone* (for *Pont-*) 1166 RBE (p), *Pontington* 1250 FF,
>   1265 DEPN, *Pontynton* 1285, *Pontindon* 1331 Ipm

Pudynton 1258 Ch, *Pudington* 1285 FA
Poininton 14 Mansel (p), *Poyntington* 1326 Ipm *et passim,*
-yng- 1431 *DCMDeed, Pointyngton*(') 1440 *Sher* (p),
-ing- 1575 Saxton

Probably 'farm called after Punt', from the OE pers.n.
Punt and *-ingtūn*. For the pers.n., cf. Pointers Sr 89,
Pounsley Sx 393, Powtenstone W 216.

ALL SAINTS' CHURCH. CHURCH FM. FLAXLAND LANE,
Flaxlands 1840 *TA, v.* **fleax**. FURLONG, 1840 *TA, v.*
furlang. HOLWAY HILL, 1811 OS, *v.* **hol²** 'hollow, sunken',
weg. MANOR HO. POINTINGTON HO. POYNTINGTON DOWN,
Point- 1811 OS, cf. *Four Downes* 1747 *Salkeld, Fore down*
1840 *TA, v.* **fore** '(land) in front of', **dūn**. RED POST, 1840
TA. THE RIDGE, cf. (*Grass & Long*) *Ridge* 1840 *TA, v.*
hrycg. SOUTHERN HILL, 1811 OS, *Southerne-* 1747 *Salkeld,*
v. **sūðerne**.

FIELD-NAMES

The undated forms in (*a*) are 1840 *TA* 30/339. Spellings dated 1744 and
1747 are *Salkeld*.

(*a*) Badcary (perhaps named from Babcary So); Beckfords Strap (*v.*
strap); Boyston; Brabant Md; Buddens Orchd; Calves; Catherine bench;
Chants Hill; Chippets; Long Chisel (*v.* **cisel** 'gravel'); Club Cl; Common
hill; Coombe bottom (*v.* **cumb**); Court Orchd; Croft or Crate (*v.* **croft**);
Damsels Md; Farm Cl, Md(w) & Orchd; Gt & Lt Farncomb(s) (*v.* **fearn**
'fern', **cumb**); Fooks cl; Foots Orchd; Foresters Orchd; Frys Cl; Furze Cl;
Games Md; Garden; Gaslands Mdw (*close called Gaslands* 1744); Giffords
Quar (*Guiffords Quarr* 1747, *v.* **quarre** 'quarry'); Girdle; Great Cl; Greys
well; Gutter Lds; Ham (*v.* **hamm**); Hanglands (*v.* **hang**); Hare Castle
(Mdw) (perhaps a fanciful name for a place frequented by hares, cf. foll.,
v. **castel**); Hare Lds; Hawcomb down; Hunts Orchd; Kittle hill; Limster;
Long barrow; Long Hedge; Long Md (acre); Middle Fd; Mill acre, Bank,
bottom, hanging, Md & Orchd (cf. *Mill* 1811 OS at ST 655196, *v.*
hanging); Millers Orchd; Moor cl; New Cl (Orchd); New Gate; Noakes
Orchd; Oborne hole (from the adjacent par. of Oborne *supra, v.* **hol¹** 'a
hollow'); Orchard; Paddock; Paradise (a complimentary name for good
ground); Parsonage Md; Penny Lands (Md) (probably referring to a rent,
v. **pening**); Perkins barrow; Pig acre; Pitmans Md; Plantation; Proles
Orchd; Quar (cl) (*Quarr Close* 1744, *v.* **quarre**); Quoiting Place (an
allusion to the game of quoits); Ragmantle; Ridgway (*Short Ridgeway*
1747, *v.* **hrycg-weg**); Common Sheep slait (*v.* **slæget**); Shortlands; 6

Acres; Smokeham (*v.* **smoke, hamm**); South close orchd (*-Meadow* 1747); Spars Md, Spears Md(w) (*Spiers Meadow* 1747); Square cl (1747); Strap (*v.* **strap**); Stub cl (*v.* **stubb**); Swanpit Gdns; Short Swans; 10 Acres; The Tenants Cow down; Townsend barn and barton (*v.* **toun, ende**); Turnip cl; Twinways (*v.* **betwēonan** '(land) between'); (Lt) Warren; Washing pool cl; West side cl, Yonder West side; Wheel Goar & Grove (*v.* **hwēol** 'a wheel' (here used figuratively of a curving hill and road), **gāra**); White door; Willow Bed, Withye Bed (*v.* **wīðig**); Young Orchd.

(*b*) *East Mead Acre* 1744; *Little Mead* 1744.

Sandford Orcas

SANDFORD ORCAS (ST 622210)

> *Sanford* 1086 DB, *-forda* Exon, *-ford*(') 1199 Cur (p), 1210 P, 1365 *Digby*, 1373 *DCMDeed, -fford'* 1367 *Digby, Sandford*(') 1243 Fees, DEPN, 1303 FA, 1360 *Digby, Saun(d)ford* 1276 RH, 1285 FA, *Saumford* 1316 FA, *Sandeford* 1400 BM I, *Sampford* 1431 FA, *Samford*(*e*) 1535–43 Leland, 1569–74 *Map*
>
> *Sandford Orescure* 1309, *-Oscuth* 1313, *-Orescois* 1315 Banco (Drew), *-Orskuys* 1348 DEPN, *-Horscoys* 1372 *Digby, -Orskoys* 1428 IpmR, *-Or(e)skeys* 1428, 1429 *Digby, -Escures* 1431 *DCMDeed, Saunford Oskeyth, -Oskeych, -Oscuch* 1312 Banco (Drew), *-Crescoys* (for *Ores-*) 1353 Cl, *-Crestois* (for *-Orescois*) 1353 Ipm, *San-, Samford' Orskeys* 1423, 1464 *Digby, Samford Orescoys* 1427 Pat, *Saundeford' Orskeys* 1439 *Digby, San(d)forde Orskoys* 1454 Cl, *Sampford Orkas* 1535 VE, *Samfordorcas* 1575 Saxton

'Sandy ford', *v.* **sand, ford**; the ford was where the road from Sherborne crosses the stream now called Mill Stream. The affix is manorial, from the family which held the manor from the 12th cent. (Helye *Oriescuilz* 1177, Richard *Dorescuilz* 1195, *-Orescuilz* 1210 all P), cf. Stourpaine 2 116 and Reaney OES 291.

HAIL (ST 625205), (*terre apud*) *Hayle* 1360, 1376, 1380, 1429, *la Hayle* 1378, *campo voc' Hayll'* 1465 all *Digby*, *Hail* (*Acre & Close*) 1838 *TA*, probably 'hay clearing' from **hēg** and **lēah** with eventual loss of the weakly stressed final syllable, cf. Hailey O 321 which has identical medieval forms in -*le*.

PATSON HILL FM & LANE (ST 617191), *Padesdon'* 1378 *Digby, Patson Hill* (*Plant.*), *Patson Md* 1838 *TA, v.* **dūn** 'down, hill', first el. probably a pers.n. or surname the exact form of which cannot be determined, but perhaps to be associated with the surname in the f.n. Patts *infra*.

PENMORE RD (ST 613200), *Lytelpeynemer'* 1378 *Digby*, (*Gt, Lt & Yonder*) *Penmore, Penmore Md & Orchd* 1838 *TA*, second el. probably **mere**[1] 'pool' with later replacement by **mōr** 'marshy ground' as in Ashmore **2** 201; the first el. is uncertain without earlier spellings, but it may be the gen.pl. *pēona* of **pēo, pīe** 'gnat or other insect'.

HIGHER SANDFORD (ST 627200), 1811 OS, *Ouersandford'* 1369, *Ouer' Sandford'* 1430, *Ouersaundeford'* 1439 all *Digby*, 'the higher part of Sandford', *v.* **uferra** 'higher, upper'.

WEATHERGROVE (FM) (ST 620219)
> (*on*) *wederangrafe scagan* 938 (12) BCS 730, (*oþ*) *wederan grafes suð ende* 956 (12) ib 931
> *Weregrave* 1086 DB, *Weregraua, Werregraue* Exon
> *Wedergrove* 1276 RH, 1310 Cl, -*grave* 1303 FA, -*graue* 1378 *Digby, Wedegrave* 1278 Misc
> *Wethirgrave* 1454 Cl, *Wethergrave* 1471 IpmR
> *Weathergrove, Weather Grove Md* 1838 *TA*

Possibly 'Wedera's grove', from **grāf(a)** and an OE pers.n. *Wedera* which would be a weak form of a pers.n. recorded once as *Uuedr* (probably from OE *weder* 'weather', *v.* Redin 24) in 704 (14) BCS 108 (S 245; this Wessex charter may be spurious, but its witness list is considered authentic), cf. Wetheringsett Sf (DEPN) which may contain the same pers.n. *Weder(a)*.

BENCHY HILL, 1838 *TA*, cf. (*Lt*) *Benchy ib*, perhaps from **benc** 'shelf, bank' and **(ge)hæg** 'enclosure'. CONEYGORE HILL, 1811 OS, *v.* **coninger** 'rabbit-warren'. CULVER HOLE (a well), cf. *Culverhays* 1838 *TA, v.* **culfre** 'dove', **hol**[1] 'hole,

hollow', **(ge)hæg** 'enclosure'. DARK LANE. GORE GATE, cf.
Gt & Lt Gore 1838 *TA, Harpydegor'* 1361 *Digby, v.* **gāra**
'triangular plot of ground'; *Harpyde-* may represent
here-pæð 'highway'. GREAT PIT LANE. HATCH. HIGHER FM
(lost), 1811 OS. JERRARDS, cf. *ten'* . . . *q'd Johannes Gerard'*
tenet 1464 *Digby.* MANOR FM & HO, cf. John *at(t)e Halle*
1368, 1375, 'at the hall', *v.* **atte, h(e)all.** MIDDLE FIELD
LANE, cf. (*Lt*) *Middle Fd* 1838 *TA.* MILL STREAM, named
from Sandford Corn Mill *infra.* MOORWAY LANE, *Moorway*
(*Orchd*) 1838 *TA*, cf. *la Mourhous* 1380, pratum vocat'
Morys 1430 *Digby, Moor Md* 1838 TA, *v.* **mōr** 'marshy
ground', **weg, hūs, mǣd.** PINK KNOLL HOLLOW, perhaps to
be associated with *Pinkwell* 1838 *TA*, first el. possibly **pinc**
'a minnow' with **well(a)** 'spring, stream'. RECTORY, 1838
TA. ST NICHOLAS'S CHURCH, 'church of *Saunford Oskeyth'*
1312 Banco (Drew), *ecclesie de Sanford'* 1373 *DCMDeed*, cf.
Site of old Chapel 1838 *TA.* SANDFORD CORN MILL,
molendinum aquatic' 1430, 1464 *Digby, Flour Mill* 1838 *TA,*
cf. *Mullebrigge* 1377 *Digby, Plat or Mill Mead Orchd* 1838
TA, v. **myln, brycg, plat².** SHILLER'S LANE. WINDMILL
HILL, cf. *Knoll and Windmill* 1838 *TA, v.* **cnoll.**

FIELD-NAMES

The undated forms in (*a*) are 1838 *TA* 30/368. All 14th and 15th cent.
forms in (*a*) and (*b*) are *Digby.*

(*a*) Akeham Orchd; Back Orchd; Barn Orchd; Batgell Orchd (*Batkyll'*
1423, *Backylle* 1423, 1425, origin uncertain); Biscomb; (Long) Bowden;
Broad Leaze (*v.* **lǣs**); Broad Lons (*v.* **land**); Broad Md, Broadmead Shord
(*v.* **sceard** 'a gap'); Broom Cl & Fd; Bruscotts; Bull Path; Cooks Orchd
(cf. *Cokkeslose* (*sic*, for *Cokkesclose*) 1372); Cratts or Croft(s) (*les Croftes*
1380, *v.* **croft**); Cuckoo Hill Plant.; Cullivers Leaze (*v.* **lǣs**); Dalcomb
(*-comb'* 1378, *v.* **cumb** 'valley'; the first el. is probably **dæl¹** 'pit, hollow,
valley', in spite of the compound appearing to be somewhat tautological);
Days Md; Deppard; Dowdles Grd; Gt & Lt Down (*v.* **dūn**); East Fd; Gt
Emlems, Lt Emlens; Farm Fd & Orchd; Flax Cl (*claus' voc' la Flexey*
1373, *v.* **fleax** 'flax', **(ge)hæg** 'enclosure'); The 4 acres; Fridays Md (*ten'*
quod Thomas Fryday nuper tenuit 1446); Gapple (*Gapewell'* 1464, *v.*
well(a), first el. uncertain); Gason (Md) (*la Gaston'* 1378, *v.* **gærs-tūn**
'paddock'); Great Md (cf. *Lytelmede* 1464, *v.* **lȳtel, mǣd**); Gully; Hacket
Stile; Hicks Cl; Hill Close (Orchd) (cf. *Hullecroft'* 1364, *v.* **hyll, croft**);
Hollow Cl; Home Fd & Orchd; Hop Yard; Hornes Orchd; House Crofts;
Hundred Acres; Kettles Grd; Gt Knoll (*v.* **cnoll**); Lane End (Orchd);

Little Head; Long Hedge; Longmans Whale (cf. (*claus' apud*) (*le*) *Walys* 1364, 1372, *Walesende* 1366, 1370, *claus' voc' Brodewalys* 1464, *v.* **walu** 'ridge of earth or stone', **ende, brād**); Marlpitts; The Mead, Mead Below (cf. *Medehey* 1423, *v.* **mǣd, (ge)hæg**); Mellams Md; Middle Hills; Mow Barton (Do dial. **mow** 'rick', **barton**); New Cl; New Ditch; The 9 Acres; North Fd; (Bottom & Long) Orchard; Palmers Barn (cf. *ten' nuper Johannis Palmer'* 1464, *feod' voc' Palmerys* 1465); Patricks Ham (*Petres-* 1364, *Petrokesham* 1372, the pers.n. or surname *Petrock* (*v.* Reaney s.n. *Petherick*), with **hamm** 'enclosure'); Patts (*Pattysclose* 1464, *Pattysheye, Pattisheis* 1465, from a surname *Patt* with **clos(e), (ge)hæg**, cf. Patson Hill Fm *supra*); Petty Cl; Picked Cl (*v.* **pīcede** 'pointed'); Pidgeon House Orchd; Plantation; Polson Orchd; Pond Cl; Poor Ground (Orchd); Popes Md; Raiments Grd; Ricksbeds (*v.* **risc-bedd** 'a rush bed'); Rickslade (*la Ryeslade* 1375, 'valley where rye was grown', *v.* **ryge, slæd**, the first el. showing confusion with **risc, rix** 'a rush' in the later form); Ridge (Md) (*v.* **hrycg**); Ridouts Grd; Samuel's Orchd'; The 7 Acres; Shrewsley; Shud ((*1 acr' super*) *Shud(de)* 1378, 1380, *Shudhegge* 1464, *v.* **scydd** 'shed, pig-sty', **hecg**); The 6 Acres; (Gt & Lt) Sleight (*v.* **slæget** 'sheep pasture'); Small Orchd; Starve Acre (a derogatory name for poor ground); Summer Wells (*Litelsomerwell'* 1370, *Somerwell'* 1378, 1464, -*woll'* 1380, 'spring or stream flowing in, or used in, summer', *v.* **sumor, well(a), lȳtel**); Tan Yard Orchd (named from Old Tan Yard *ib*); Tenzel; Thorn(e)y Lake (Orchd); White Fd Lawn; (Long) Whore (probably **ōra**[1] 'bank, edge'); Willow Bed; Winterhead (*Wynterhurde* 1378, probably 'store-house used in winter', from **winter** and **hord** 'hoard, store'); Withy Bed (Orchd) (*v.* **wīðig**); Wood and New Cl (cf. *claus' circa bosc' d'ni* 1369); Woolcomb (*Wolcombe* 1425, 1428, *v.* **well(a), wyll(a)** 'spring, stream', **cumb**); Young Orchd Hewletts.

(*b*) *Alderford', Alfordmede* 1464, *Alfordismede* 1465 (*v.* **alor** 'alder', **ford, mǣd**); *le barrys* 1361 (*v.* **barre**); *Brasyesclose* 1465; *Brokefurlonge* 1464 (*v.* **brōc, furlang**); *Churchutt'* 1373, *Chursshete* 1375 (perhaps 'steep slope by the church', from **cirice** and **scyte**); *Clyfforlang'* 1366, 1380 (*v.* **clif** 'cliff, bank', **furlang**); *pratum vocat' Combes* 1430 (cf. John *Combe ib*); *Dumbelledaresclos* 1423, 1425, *terr' voc' Dum'uldar'* 1430 (a surname with **clos(e)**)); *Dychforlang'* 1380 (*v.* **dīc**); *prat' apud Gretestone* 1370 (*v.* **grēat** 'large', **stān**, cf. Stone 6″ near St Nicholas's Church); *Grotehill'* 1464 (*v.* **hyll**, first el. perhaps **groten** 'sandy'); *Gyllond'* 1464 (*v.* **land**, first el. probably the surname *Gill*); *Hesdhelfacre* 1378 (*v.* **æcer**); *atte Hethe* (p) 1367 (*v.* **atte, hǣð**); *curtill' voc' Hodierue* 1364; *claus' voc' Holmys* 1464 (probably a surname); *Horthorn'* 1376 (*v.* **hār**[2] 'grey', **þorn**); *claus' voc' Joyes* 1430 (cf. *duobus clausis pasture que Thomas Joy prius tenuit* 1423); *1 acr' super Kuttyng'* 1380 (*v.* **cutting** 'a piece of land cut off'); *la Lake* 1380 (*v.* **lacu** 'stream'); *Westlongmedesherde* 1465 (*v.* **lang**[1], **mǣd, sceard** 'a gap'); *Louelesmerssh'* 1375, *Louelysmerch'* 1376 (the surname *Lovel* with **mersc**); *atte Lynch* (p) 1360 ('at the ridge or bank', *v.* **atte, hlinc**); *Lytelparrok'* 1464 (*v.* **lȳtel, pearroc** 'a paddock'); *terre apud Mapul(l')* 1425, 1428 (*v.* **mapel** 'maple-tree'); *la Mersh'* 1378 (*v.* **mersc**);

Pondefald', *punfald'* 1366 (*v.* **pund-fald** 'a pound'); *Pynnesorchard'* 1464 (cf. *ten' nuper Johannis Pynne* 1465); *Shabenam* 1375, *Scheppenham* 1376 (*v.* **hamm** 'enclosure', first el. perhaps the OE pers.n. *Sceobba* postulated for Shabbington Bk 128, Shebdon St (DEPN), or **scypen** 'a cow-shed'); *Shortbrokforlang* 1380 (*v.* **sc(e)ort**, **brōc**, **furlang**); *Southbury* 1370 (*v.* **sūð**, **bury** 'manor-house'); *Sterte* 1372 (*v.* **steort** 'tail of land'); *Walyshlane, via in Walysh'* 1379, *Walysshelane* 1423, 1425, *Waldyche(s)lane* 1428, 1431, *Walkedichelane* 1439 (if the earlier spellings are correct, probably from the surname *Walsh* and **lane**, the later spellings perhaps showing influence from Walditch in Bothenhampton par. *infra*); *feod' voc' Wodys* 1465 (cf. *pratum quod Joh' atte Wode prius tenuit* 1425); (*le*) *Worth'* 1464, 1465 (*v.* **worð** 'enclosure'); *feod' voc'* . . . *Wydecomb' al' Joh'is Parke* 1465 (cf. Simon *Wydecomb'* 1375).

Trent

TRENT (ST 589185), *Trente* 1086 DB, 1225 DEPN, 1234 Pat, 1249 FF, 1265 Misc, 1275 Ipm, 1285 FA *et freq* to 1409 Cl, *Trenta* 1086 Exon, 1163 P, *Trent* 1575 Saxton. Originally the name of the stream here, a tributary of the R. Yeo now called Trent Brook, *v.* RNs. *infra*. For this British r.n., identical with Tarrant, *v.* Ekwall RN 415 ff., Jackson 257, 503.

ADBER (FM) (ST 599204)
  Eátan beares (gen.) 956 (12) BCS 931 (S 571)
  Ateberie, Ettebere, Etesberie 1086 DB, *Ateberia, Eattebera, (In)etesberia* Exon
  Attebare 1091–1106 MontC, 1303 FA (p), *-bere* 1280 MontC, 1409 Cl, 1498 Pat (*Nether-, Over-*), *Over Attebar* 1303 FA, *Attebeare* 1325 Ipm, 1402 Cl (*Nether-, Over-*), 1415 Cl (*Nyther-, Over-*), *Nuther-atteber'* 1353 Digby, *Nytherattebere otherwise Nyther-attebare, Ouerattebere otherwise Overattebare* 1446 Cl
  Athebare 1100–18, 1152–8 MontC
  Atebere 1221–3 MontC (p), 1303 FA, *Ate(le)ber'* 1276 RH, *Parva Atebar(e)* 1303, 1346 FA, *Atebear* 1321 Ipm, *Over Ateber* 1346 FA
  Overateberg 1274 Ipm
  Atbare 1428 FA
  Adebere 1429 IpmR, *Nethir-, Over Adbere* 1496 Ipm, *Adber* 1575 Saxton, *Adbeer* 1811 OS

'Ēata's grove', from the OE pers.n. *Ēata* (Redin 64) and **bearu**, with **neoðerra** 'lower', **uferra** 'upper', Lat **parva** 'little'. Nether Adber is marked (6″) in the neighbouring par. of Marston Magna (So).

HUMMER (FM) (ST 589198), 1811 OS, *Humbre* 1091–1106 MontC, *Homere* 1311 FF, 1346 FA (p), 1402–1446 Cl, 1498 Pat, *Hemere* (sic) 1415 Cl, the common pre-English r.n. *Humber*, originally with reference to the small tributary of R. Yeo flowing to the S of the settlement, cf. the f.n. (*Lt*) *Hummer Lake* 1839 *TA, v.* **lacu** 'stream'.

ADBER CROSS, a cross-roads near Adber *supra*. ANCHOR FM, cf. *Little Anchor* 1839 *TA*. BARROWS LANE, cf. *Gt & Lt Barrows, Lt Barrow* 1839 *TA*. HR BARTON. BIRCH HILL (GULLY & STILE), *Birchills* 1839 *TA*. CHURCH FM, named from St Andrew's Church *infra*. DOWN FM & LANE, cf. *Down Orchd, Lt & Long Down* 1839 *TA*. FLAMBERTS, from Daniel *Flambert* c.1778 Sandison. GLEBE FM. GORE, *Gore* (*Orchd*) 1839 *TA, v.* **gāra**. GREENWAY (lost, ST 587190), 1811 OS. HAM LANE, 1740 Sandison, *Hams Lane Grd* 1839 *TA*, cf. *Ham* (*Md*) *ib, v.* **hamm**. HOLYWELL (Spring marked), *Hol(l)y Well, Lt Holy Wells* 1839 *TA, v.* **hālig, wella**. HUMMER BRIDGE & PLANT., cf. *Hummer Cl, Hummer Lane Plot* 1839 *TA*, named from Hummer *supra*. LADY CHAPEL, cf. *Chapel Grd* 1839 *TA*. LADY'S LANE. LOWSOME LANE, named from *Lowsome Common Fd* 1740, *Lousham, Louson* (or *Cop's Hill, -or Cox's Fd*), *Lowsam,* (*Gt & Lt*) *Lowsome* 1839 *TA*, possibly a name containing **hamm** 'enclosure', with either **lūs** 'louse' or **hlōse** 'pig-sty'. MALTHOUSE LANE. MANOR HO. MILL LANE, leading to Trent Mill *infra*. MOUNT HUNGER, probably denoting poor or infertile ground (*v.* Field 111–2). PARKS PLANT., cf. *Parks* 1839 *TA*. PLOT (LANE). RIGG LANE, *v.* **hrycg**. RIMPTON HILL, from Rimpton par. (So). ROWBARROW, 1811 OS, -HILL 1839 *TA*, cf. *Rowbarrow Common* 1740 Sandison, *v.* **rūh, beorg**. RYLAND PLANT., *Rye Lands* 1839 *TA, v.* **ryge, land**. ST ANDREW'S CHURCH. TRENT BARROW, 1811 OS, -BRIDGE, -MILL, 1650 Hutch[3] (**4** 166), 1811 OS, cf. *Mill Banks & Cl* 1839 *TA*, TRENT WD, *v.* par. name *supra*.

FIELD-NAMES

The undated forms in (*a*) are 1839 *TA* 30/428. Spellings dated 1740 are. Sandison.

(*a*) Ashments (*Ashman's* 1740); (Lt) Bewhy (*Bewey* 1740); Bishops Md; Gt Blackmoor, Lt Blackmore; Bowards; Bowdage Orchd; Breeches Pce; Brideham Hill (*Briteham* 1740); Brimhills (*Broomhills* 1740); Brimton; Brines Orchd; Broad Cl; Brown's Md; Burbers Leaze (*Burford's Leaze* 1740); Burnhouse Orchd; Churchills (*Church Hills* 1740); Cleavers Leaze; Coddy (*Cotty Md* 1740, *v.* **cot, (ge)hæg**); Coneygar (*Cunnigear* 1740, *v.* **coninger**); Coppice Grd; Counsellor's Orchd; Cow Leaze; Crab Orchd; Crib Ho Grd; Croft; Cross Orchd; Daniels Wd; Dead Man ('field where a body was found', *v.* Field 60); Dewdneys Grd; Dicketts; Dive; Dog Hill; Dogs Kennell; Drain Grd; Drove; Dry Cl, Lt Drye; 8 Acres; 11 Acre Md; England; Fairy Cross (probably a spot thought to be haunted by fairies, *v.* Field 74); Fish Pool; 5 Acres; 4 Acres; 14 Acre Md; Furze Grd; Garstone (*Gaston* 1740, *v.* **gærs-tūn** 'paddock'); Germans Cl; Glover's Grd (*-Md* 1740); Goose Acre; Gorse Orchd; Great Orchd; Green Cl; Grove; Gwyers Grd; Hannams Grd; Harbins Hill; Hatch Plot (*v.* **hæc(c)**); High Hayes, Hind-, Hine Hayes (probably **hǣs** 'brushwood' with **hindan** 'behind, at the back'); Hazel Walls; Head Grd, Upon Head (*v.* **hēafod**); Hempland Corner; High Hills; Highway Grd; Hill; Home Grd & Orchd; Hound (possibly **hūne** 'hoarhound', cf. the f.n. Gt Shorthound in Castleton par. *supra*); Huxors Grd; Judghills; Lain (*v.* **leyne**); Lake Grd (*v.* **lacu**); Langland (*v.* **lang**[1] 'long'); Lark Hill; Leaze (*v.* **lǣs**); Lies Leaze; Little Fds, Grd, Mdw & Orchd; Long Bridge Grd; (Lt) Long Cl, Behind Long Cl; Long Orchd; Lotland (*Lotfelland* 1740, *v.* **hlot, furlang**); Low Hills; Mansims (*Mansoms* 1740); Marl Grd & Lds (*Moorlands* 1740); Maul Leaze (*Moorleaze* 1740); (Lt) May Brook; Mead; Meads Plot and Orchd; Merryhill Fd (*v.* **myrge**); Mow Barton; Lt New Cl; New Ditch & Grd; New Ho; 9 Acres; North Fd; Nursery; Old Road; Orchard; Oxen Leaze; Paddock; Passcroft (*Parish Croft* 1740); Peas Ditch (*v.* **pise**); Perry Hayes (1740, *v.* **pirige** 'pear-tree'); Pigeon Ho Orchd; Piggs Barn; Pilevy Orchd; Pits; Plantation; Pond; Pool Md (*Pulmead* 1740); Poor Grd; Pound; Quar Grd (*v.* **quarre**); Queenbury Fd; Queenthorn; Quintly Md (*Quently* 1740); Reynolds Grd; Samson's Orchd; 7 Acres; Sharlands; Sharpland (*v.* **scearp**); Shilners Hill; Barn Shipton Orchd (*Barren Shepton* 1740, 'sheep farm', *v.* **scēap, scī(e)p, tūn**); Short Cross; Shortlands (1740); Long & Short Slade (*v.* **slæd** 'valley'); 6 Acres; Slab Fd; Sloughs (*Slow* 1740, *v.* **slōh**); Staggs Doors (*Stagg Door* 1740); Stockey; 10 Acres; Lt Thicketts (*v.* **þiccett**); Tom Hodge; Tow Ditch; Trent Bar Cl, Trent Fd (*v.* par. name *supra*); Trues Orchd; Twelve Acres; Veinham (*Farnham* 1740, *v.* **fearn, hamm**); Water Slade (*v.* **slæd**); White(')s Grd & Orchd; Withey Beds (*v.* **wīðig**); Woodhern (*v.* **hyrne** 'corner, angle'); Wood Leaze.

(*b*) *Huntley's Md* 1740; *Twinbarrow Common Fd* 1740 (*v.* **betwēonan** 'between').

LIST OF DORSET PARISHES

Parishes followed by **1, 2** or **3** and page number are dealt with in Part I, II or III respectively; the rest will appear in Part IV. Abbreviated forms of affixes, if used in the text, are given in brackets.